THE 1991 GUIDE TO FRANCE

Contents

This 1991 edition published by Ebury Press
an imprint of Random Century Group
20 Vauxhall Bridge Road, London SW1V 2SA

ISBN 0 85223 974 2

Editor: Mandy Morton-Smith
Illustrations: Gary Brazier

Typeset by Flair Plan Phototypesetting Limited, Ware
Printed and bound in Great Britain at The Bath Press, Avon

FOREWORD

Welcome to the Routiers Guide to France, the ideal travelling companion for all those who wish to experience the real flavour of France, but on a reasonable budget.

You will find The Routiers Guide a reliable source of reference when looking for real French food, an authentic atmosphere and good value. Routiers exists to point the traveller in the direction of places where they can eat and stay at real value for money. All 'Relais Routiers' are regularly inspected to ensure that standards are maintained. Our philosophy is that value for money can be found in a variety of establishments – from family restaurants to local bars and brasseries; as long as they provide a warm welcome, serve good quality food, offer at least one fixed price menu, and observe rules of hygiene in kitchens, bedrooms and bathrooms. We are sure you will agree that travelling can be a far more enjoyable and relaxed experience if you know of a reliable place to eat and rest.

French cuisine is celebrated throughout Europe and most areas of France will have their own versions of traditional French dishes but remember to look out for regional specialities for which each area is justly proud.

Visit Champagne, easily accessible for the Channel ports, with its obvious attraction of that most famous of sparkling wines. Local specialities include 'andouillettes' from Troyes, fresh water fish and the 'boudin blanc' of Brienne. Alternatively, Normandy is the place for cheese lovers. There is even a 'Route de Fromage' in Normandy which will take you through the countryside which produces Camembert, Pont-l'Eveque and Livarot. Don't forget the Normandy cider and Calvados either.

Wherever you are in France, whether you wish to sample regional dishes or one of the traditional alternatives, the Routiers Guide is your guarantee of finding authentic French cuisine at good value for money. The following pages will explain how to get the best from your Guide. There are many different flavours to France and Routiers will help you to explore them.

Bon voyage and bon appetit.

WHAT MAKES A RELAIS ROUTIERS

Relais Routiers have been carefully selected since 1934. With the increase in the number of travellers through France, the Routiers establishments have adapted themselves to cater more readily for families and tourists but the philosophy of Routiers remains unchanged – all Relais Routiers are inspected regularly to ensure they provide a warm and friendly welcome, good food and value for money.

Relais Routiers come in all shapes and sizes, from roadside cafe to locals' bar, pretty country hotel to lively town brasserie – but whatever the style of the establishment, quality and value are served with a generous helping of authentic French cuisine and atmosphere.

The hallmark of the French Relais Routiers is the fixed price menu. To display the red and blue Les Routiers sign, this menu must be available and be displayed on the door of the establishment. The menu will normally be for a 3 course meal and may or may not include drinks. An a la carte menu may also be offered, but this will be more expensive.

HOW TO FIND A RELAIS ROUTIERS

1. You want to know whether there is a Relais Routiers in a certain locality.

Look for the name of the town in question in the alphabetical list of entries. If the name is not there, then there is no Relais Routiers there. Each establishment entry is followed by the department and number (the French equivalent of the county and postcode), the main road reference for the town and the map reference.

eg. **Abbeville 80100 Somme RN1 Map 5–A3** This means that Abbeville is in the Somme Department on Route Nationale 1 and can be found on map 5 grid reference A3.

2. You are following an itinerary, and you want to know where to find a Relais Routiers.

Turn to our List of Maps of France, where you will find 25 maps covering the whole of the country. The main roads are shown on all these maps: it is easy to turn to the regional maps which are numbered when you have noted which regions the roads traverse. All the places where there are Relais are marked thereon. After that, all you have to do is turn to the alphabetical list of places, as you did before.

3. You wish to find a hotel.

Although the majority of Relais Routiers are restaurants, many of them also have accommodation. These are denoted in the guide by the hotel symbol followed by the number of rooms. However, as the standards in these may vary considerably, we have cited the official classification awarded by the French Tourist Board. On pages 52 to 60 you will find a list of Relais Routiers approved by the French Tourist Board by department. A map showing their location is on pages 50 and 51.

4. What is a Casserole Relais?

You will find a 'Casserole' symbol beside certain guide entries. This symbol distinguishes those Relais Routiers where particular care is taken to offer above-average meals with perhaps a special menu or specialities of the region. The 'Casserole' is the Les Routiers mark of excellence. A map showing their location can be found on pages 44 and 45 and a list of all 'Casseroles' on pages 46 to 49.

SYMBOLS USED IN THIS GUIDE

⊗   BAR, CAFE, SNACKS

♀   RESTAURANT

⌂   HOTEL – bed and breakfast available

🍲   CASSEROLE – the Les Routiers mark of excellence
      awarded annually to those Relais Routiers where
      particular care is taken to offer above average meals.

☆   OFFICIAL CLASSIFICATION OF THE FRENCH
      TOURIST BOARD – the number of stars (1–4) indicates
      the degree of comfort.

☎   TELEPHONE NUMBER

NB. Each Routiers has a reference number eg. (No RR AVR
1804). Please use it on all correspondence concerning
specific Relais Routiers.

WHEN IN FRANCE..

1.   Take your Guide with you into restaurants and hotels – it
will let the owners know that you have chosen their
establishment by using the Guide and that you expect a high
standard of food and service.

2.   There are two types of meal available – 'repas complet'
and 'casse croute'. 'Repas complet' is a full meal and is served
at set meal times. 'Casse croute' is a snack meal, can be
served at any time and usually consists of something simple,
such as an omelette, sandwhich or plate of cold meats.

3.   Following a change in the laws in 1987, the service
charge must be included in the price of a meal. Tips are
rarely expected and are usually given by rounding up the
bill.

4. The price quoted for accommodation will be for the room and not per person but a small supplement will be charged if more than 2 people are sharing a room. This is usually minimal and a great help for families travelling on a budget. The price of the room is usually shown on a card on the back of the door, along with the price of breakfast.

5. French hotels are officially classified on a star system. The stars provide a rating of 1–4 (NN) and luxe, and are usually shown on a plaque by the main entrance. These are the 'Hotels de Tourisme' but there are many unclassified hotels in addition where the standards are perfectly acceptable.

6. It is normal practice to see the room offered before deciding to take it. You will therefore be able to check on the degree of cleanliness and comfort. However, if you wish to make an advance booking at a hotel before you arrive, we strongly advise you to make your selection from the approved Relais Routiers 'Tourist Hotels'.

7. If you have booked a hotel room, try to arrive before 6 pm unless you have advised the hotel of your time of arrival. If you have been delayed, do try to contact the hotel. If you do not have a reservation, the chances of finding a room are far better if you arrive before 6 pm.

8. Many small hotels will lock their doors quite early at night so, if you wish to go out, remember to advise the proprietors of this and they will probably make arrangements for you.

9. Many French people take their holiday between 14th July and 15th August and you may find some hotels and restaurants closed during this period. It is advisable to book accommodation well in advance if you wish to travel at this time.

The British Embassy
Ambassade de Grande-Bretagne
16 rue d'Anjou
Paris 8
France
TEL: 42 66 38 10 (prefix 010 33 1 if dialling from the UK).

A L'HOTEL...

Monsieur,

Votre hôtel m'a été recommandé par Les Routiers. Je vous prie de vouloir bien me retenir une chambre à un lit/pour deux personnes avec/sans salle de bain/douche pour la nuit du.../du... jusqu'au...

Soyez assez aimable de nous confirmer cette location et de nous dire si'l vous faut une caution.

Avec nos remerciements anticipés,

Veuillez agréer, Monsieur, nos sentiments les plus distinguées.

Dear Sir,

Your hotel has been recommended to me by Les Routiers. I would be grateful if you would reserve me a single/double room with/without bathroom/shower on the... for one night/ from... to..

Please could you confirm this and let me know if a deposit is required.

Thanking you in advance.

Yours faithfully

Single room – une chambre à un lit
Double room – une chambre pour deux personnes avec un grand lit
Twin room – une chambre avec deux lits
Bathroom – salle de bain
Shower – douche

Breakfast – le petit déjeuner
Half board – demi-pension
Full board – pension complète

I'd like to book/reserve...	– Je voudrais retenir/réserver...
How much does the room cost?	– Combien coûte/vaut la chambre?

AU RESTAURANT...

Choosing a restaurant and deciding what to eat can be one of the most enjoyable parts of your stay in France. One of the delights of eating in Relais Routiers lies in the discovery of authentic French cuisine and atmosphere. Providing the season is right, you can experiment with regional dishes and taste the true flavours of France. Here are a few useful points:

1.   Note the difference between the 'set menu' and 'à la carte'. The set menu is a complete 3 or 4 course meal and may or may not include drinks. Many restaurants will offer more than one set menu and the lunchtime menus will often cost less than those of the evening. Please note, you are not entitled to a reduction of the cost of the set menu if you do not eat all courses.
The a la carte offers a full choice of dishes. The price of each dish is marked separately. A menu selected 'à la carte' is always more expensive, even if it comprises the same dishes as the set menu. Every Relais Routiers must state if drinks are not included in the menu price. In these cases a 25 cl of wine will be about 6,00 Frs.

2.   Soft, drinks are much more expensive in France than in the UK. 'Sirops', which are mixed with water like a cordial or squash, are a cheaper alternative to coke and lemonade.

3.   Prices in cafés must be clearly shown. Drinks are more expensive if you sit down than if you stand at the bar.

4.   Tap water must be provided free by law. If you are unwilling to drink the tap water ask for 'l'eau mineral' but you will be charged for this.

5.   Vin compris – ordinary or house wine is included in the price; Boisson compris - check which drinks are included. This could be a pichet (jug) of wine, a beer, or a bottle of mineral water.

BON APPETIT

EN ROUTE...

Traffic rules in France are very similar to Britain with the obvious exception that in France you drive on the right. When leaving a restaurant after a relaxing lunch, setting off from your hotel early in the morning or after using a one-way street, beware momentarily forgetting – many experienced British drivers in France will have stories to tell about the times they have forgotten and happily set off on the left hand side of the road.

Here are a few extra points:

1. Speed limits:
    60 km (approx 37 miles) per hour – in built up areas.
    90 km (approx 56 miles) per hour – main roads
    110 km (approx 68 miles) per hour – dual carriageways
    130 km (approx 80 miles) per hour – motorways

NB: Some motorways may also have a **minimum** speed limit.

2. Motorways:
France has over 3,000 miles of motorways and tolls (peages) are charged on most of these. Usually a ticket is issued and a toll paid when you leave the motorway or at intermediate points during the motorway journey. Some motorway stretches have automatic collection where you throw the change into a basket (like the Dartford Tunnel). If you do not have the correct change, use the marked, separate lane. Travellers cheques are NOT accepted but Visa card can be used as an alternative.

To escape the motorway tolls and the most congested routes, follow the Green Arrow routes (Itineraires Bis) marked by green arrows. Traffic should be less and the routes are designed to provide the holiday maker with a more attractive alternative.

3. Insurance:
Minimum age for driving an imported car or motorbike in France is 18 and you are not permitted to drive on a provisional licence. Insurance is compulsory and a green card advisable as it will give you better cover than the minimum otherwise applying in France. Europ Assistance do special schemes for motorists and passengers and discounts

10

can be obtained through membership of Les Routiers' Club Bon Viveur.

4. Lights:
Headlights must not dazzle oncoming drivers and should be adjusted for right hand drive. Headlamps should have a removable yellow plastic paint added to the lenses or deflectors with yellow lenses to ensure that a yellow beam is emitted.

5. Breakdown:
A warning triangle and hazard warning lights are compulsory for all vehicles in the event of accident or breakdown. Free emergency telephones are available every 2 km on motorways and 24 hour services can be found on motorways at regular intervals of about 40 kilometres.

6. Petrol: – **L'ESSENCE:**
NB. **Petrole** – crude oil or parafin

| Super | – **de super** | ordinary | – **d'ordinaire** |
| lead-free | – **sans plomb** | diesel | – **gazole** |

Unleaded petrol is widely available in France.

During August the motorways South are very busy with French families heading to the coast for their summer holidays, but most of the time French roads are relatively empty. Equip yourself with a good map and driving in France can be an enjoyable part of your holiday.

BON ROUTE/BON CONTINUATION/BON RETOUR

DISCOUNT LES ROUTIERS

Knowing the impossiblity of putting a real Relais Routiers on a motorway, we asked motorway companies to do something about it. On production of the current edition of the Guide, or your Club Bon Viveur membership card, you are entitled to a price concession at many motorway restaurant chains.

NB. To obtain this price concession, you must show your Guide or card to the personnel concerned before ordering your meal. If they show ignorance of this concession, ask for the manager.

JOIN CLUB BON VIVEUR

You've bought the Guide – now join Club Bon Viveur and receive 15 months membership for the price of 12.

The Club promotes quality and value in travel, food and wine in both Great Britain and in France. Membership benefits include:

- Your Club Bon Viveur membership card which entitles you to special concessions at selected Routiers.
- Regular newletters.
- A privileged price of £6.99 (including postage and packaging) when you buy additional copies of either Routiers guide.
- A special pre-publication offer on the 1992 Routiers Guides to Britain and France.
- The Routiers Motoring Service – with discounts off Europ Assistance's overseas motoring services, personal travel insurance and UK motoring services.
- Discounts off all holidays in the Paris and France 1991 brochures through the French Travel Service.
- Many regular promotions.

To join Club Bon Viveur, simply complete the questionnaire on the following page and return it to us with the annual subscription fee of £9.50.

CLUB BON VIVEUR QUESTIONNAIRE

ABOUT LES ROUTIERS

In order to improve the package we offer you please complete the following:–

1. Have you bought a Routiers Guide Before?   [YES/NO]
If YES, in what year did you buy your last Routiers Guide?

_____

2. Was your last Routiers Guide?

The British Guide   ☐   (Please tick as applicable)

The French Guide   ☐

Both   ☐

3. How did you first find out about Les Routiers?

_____

4. Where did you buy this Guide from?

_____

5. How many times do you eat at a British Routiers each year?

_____

6. How many nights do you stay in a British Routiers each year?

_____

7. How often do you refer to this guide?

_____

8. How many people, apart from yourself, refer to this Guide?

_____

9. What other guides do you use? (Please specify)

_____

10. What does the Les Routiers sign mean to you?

_____

ABOUT YOURSELF

We would like to get to know a little bit more about our members so that we can tailor the Club to cater for your specific needs:

1. Are you: Single ☐ Married ☐ (please tick as applicable)

2. Are you: Male ☐ Female ☐ (please tick as applicable)

3. Are you: 16–24 ☐ 25–34 ☐ 35–44 ☐ 45–54 ☐ 55+ ☐
   (tick as applicable)

4. What is your occupation?

_____

5. What type of car do you drive? What year?

_____

6. What Sunday newspaper do you read?

_____

7. How often do you visit France?

_____

8. How many times do you travel on a continental ferry? (e.g. once every three years.)

_____

NAME _____

ADDRESS _____

_____

_____ POSTCODE _____

To receive your 15 months Club membership send your questionnaire and cheque for £9.50 to:

Routiers Limited, 354 Fulham Road, London SW10 9UH

Please allow at least 30 days for delivery of your registration pack.

LIST OF MAPS

15

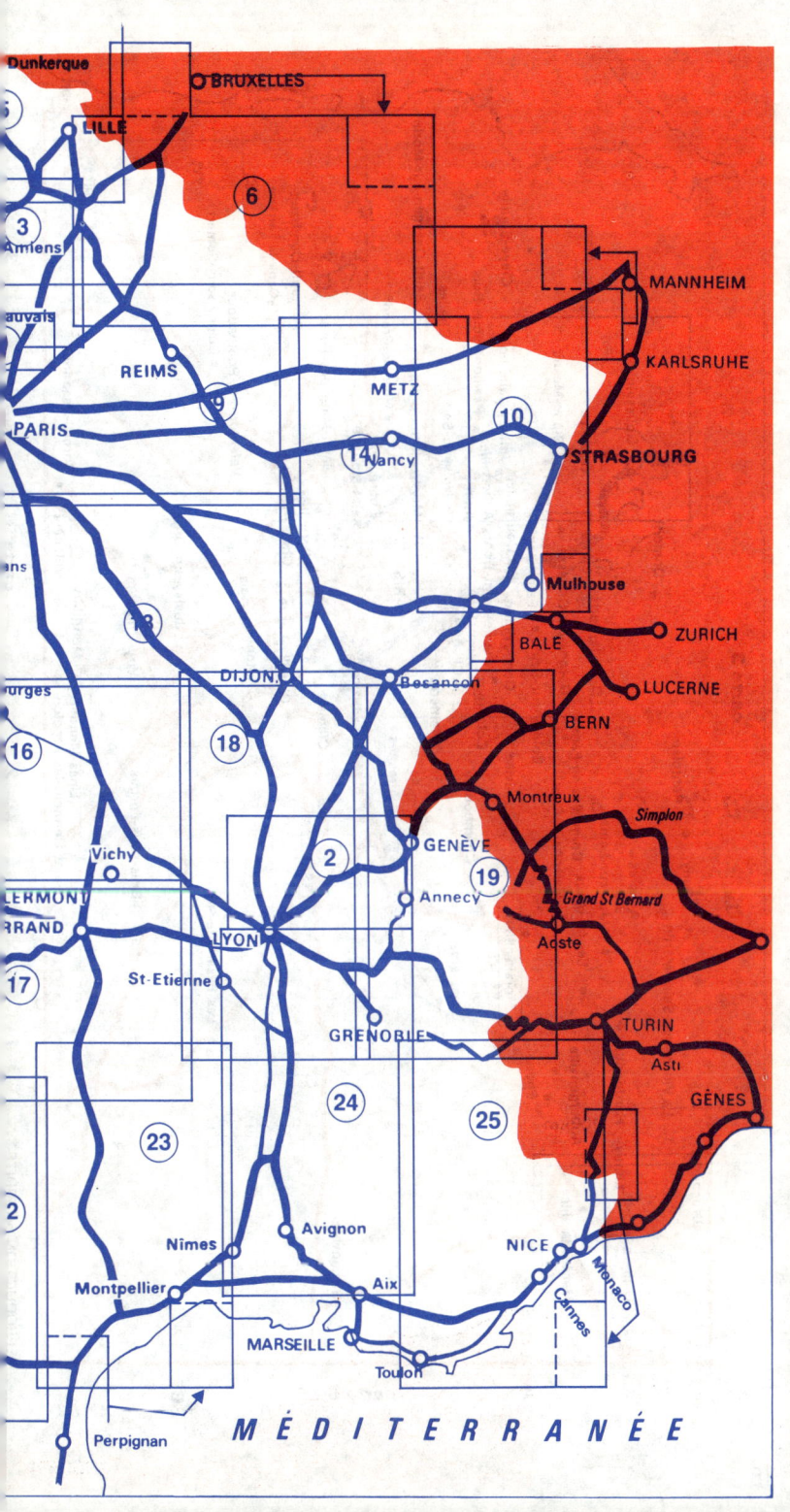

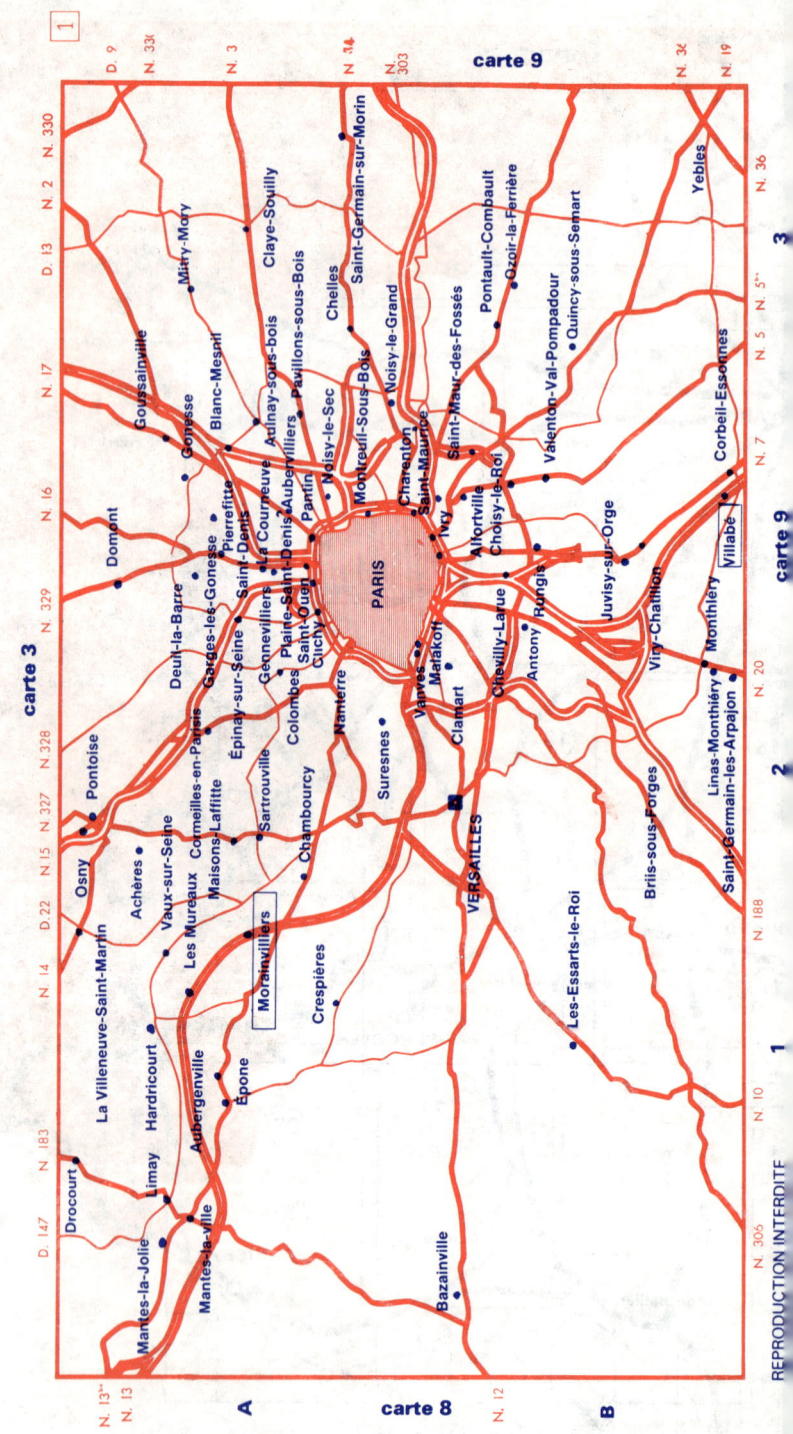

carte 9

carte 3

carte 9

carte 8

PARIS

VERSAILLES

N. 9
N. 33∦
N. 3
N. 34
N. 303
N. 3∦
N. 19
N. 330
N. 2
D. 13
N. 36
N. 17
N. 5∦∦
N. 5
N. 16
N. 7
N. 329
N. 328
N. 327
N. 20
N. 15
D. 22
N. 188
N. 14
N. 1
N. 10
N. 183
N. 306
D. 147
N. 13∦∦
N. 13
N. 12

Claye-Souilly
Misy-Mory
Saint-Germain-sur-Morin
Pontault-Combault
Ozoir-la-Ferrière
Quincy-sous-Semart
Yebles
Goussainville
Blanc-Mesnil
Aulnay-sous-bois
Pavillons-sous-Bois
Chelles
Noisy-le-Grand
Saint-Maur-des-Fossés
Valenton-Val-Pompadour
Corbeil-Essonnes
Domont
Pierrefitte
Gonesse
La Courneuve
Pantin
Montreuil-Sous-Bois
Charenton
Saint-Maurice
Ivry
Alfortville
Choisy-le-Roi
Juvisy-sur-Orge
Villabé
Deuil-la-Barre
Saint-Denis
Garges-lès-Gonesse
Plaine-Saint-Denis-Aubervilliers
Noisy-le-Sec
Saint-Ouen
Clichy
Vitry-Châtillon
Montlhéry
Genevilliers
Epinay-sur-Seine
Colombes
Nanterre
Vanves
Malakoff
Clamart
Chevilly-Larue
Antony Rungis
Linas-Monthléry
Saint-Germain-lès-Arpajon
Pontoise
Sartrouville
Suresnes
Osny
Chambourcy
Briis-sous-Forges
Achères
Vaux-sur-Seine
Cormeilles-en-Parisis
Maisons-Laffitte
Les Mureaux
Morainvilliers
Crespières
Les-Essarts-le-Roi
La Villeneuve-Saint-Martin
Hardricourt
Aubergenville
Epone
Limay
Drocourt
Mantes-la-Jolie
Mantes-la-ville
Bazainville

REPRODUCTION INTERDITE

18

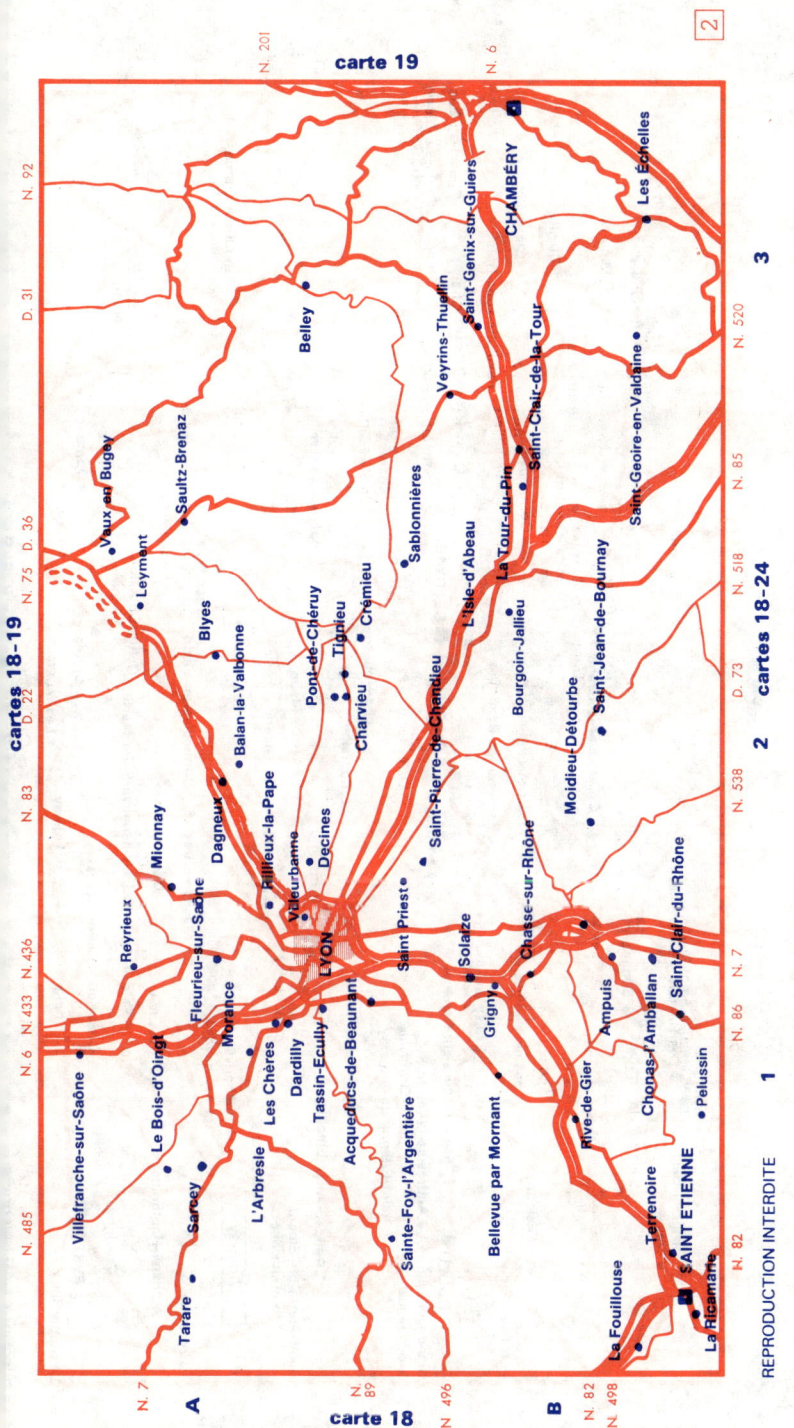

2

cartes 18-19

cartes 18-24

carte 18

N. 201

N. 6

N. 92

D. 31

D. 36

D. 22

N. 75

N. 83

N. 433

N. 436

N. 6

N. 485

N. 7

N. 89

N. 496

N. 82

N. 498

N. 82

N. 520

N. 85

N. 518

N. 538

N. 7

N. 86

A

B

1

2

3

CHAMBÉRY

Les Échelles

Saint-Genix-sur-Guiers

Veyrins-Thuellin

Belley

Saultz-Brenaz

Vaux-en-Bugey

Leyment

Saint-Clair-de-la-Tour

Saint-Geoire-en-Valdaine

La Tour-du-Pin

L'Isle-d'Abeau

Sablonnières

Saint-Jean-de-Bournay

Bourgoin-Jallieu

Moidieu-Détourbe

Blyes

Pont-de-Chéruy

Tignieu

Crémieu

Charvieu

Saint-Pierre-de-Chandieu

Balan-la-Valbonne

Dagneux

Mionnay

Rillieux-la-Pape

Décines

Villeurbanne

Vieurbanne

LYON

Saint Priest

Solaize

Chasse-sur-Rhône

Reyrieux

Fleurieu-sur-Saône

Morance

Les Chères

Dardilly

Tassin-Écully

Acqueducs-de-Beaunan

Grigny

Ampuis

Saint-Clair-du-Rhône

Chonas-l'Amballan

Pélussin

Rive-de-Gier

Le Bois-d'Oingt

Villefranche-sur-Saône

Tarare

Sarcey

L'Arbresle

Sainte-Foy-l'Argentière

Bellevue par Mornant

Terrenoire

SAINT ÉTIENNE

La Ricamarie

La Fouillouse

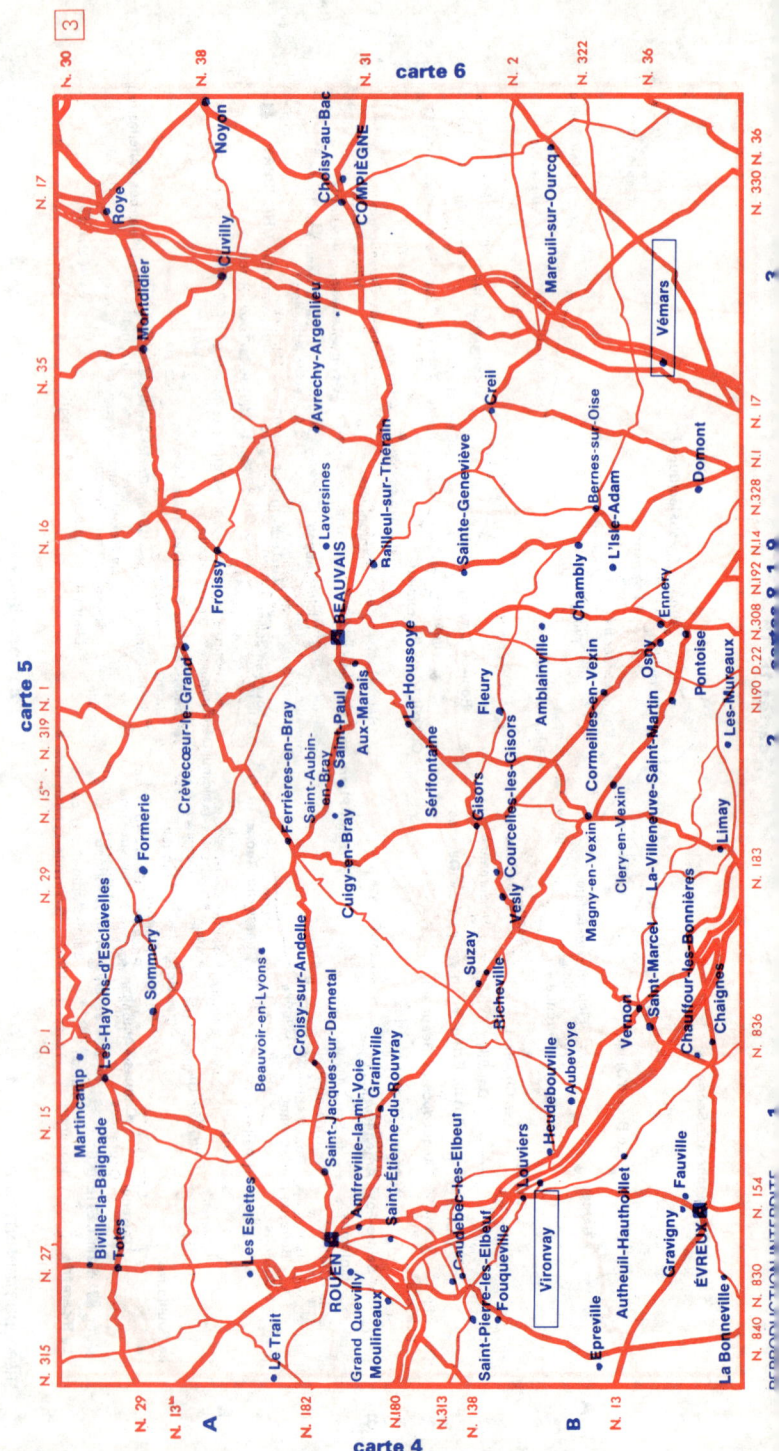

carte 5

carte 6

carte 4

3

20

N. 30 N. 38 N. 31 N. 2 N. 322 N. 36

N. 17

N. 35

N. 16

N. 15ᵇⁱˢ · N. 319 N. 1

N. 29

D. 1

N. 15

N. 27

N. 315

N. 330 N. 36

N. 17

N. 1

N. 328

N.192 N.14

N190 D.22 N.308

N. 183

N. 836

N. 154

N. 840 N. 830

N. 13

N. 29

N. 13ᵇⁱˢ

N. 182

NJ80

N.313

N. 138

A

B

Noyon
Choisy-au-Bac
Roye
COMPIÈGNE
Cuvilly
Montdidier
Avrechy-Argenlieu
Mareuil-sur-Ourcq
Vémars
Creil
Laversines
Bernes-sur-Oise
Domont
Ranheul-sur-Thérain
Sainte-Geneviève
L'Isle-Adam
BEAUVAIS
Froissy
Chambly
Crèvecœur-le-Grand
La-Houssoye
Amblainville
Cormeilles-en-Vexin
Osny
Ennery
Ferrières-en-Bray
Saint-Aubin-en-Bray
Saint-Paul
Aux-Marais
Fleury
Pontoise
Formerie
Sérifontaine
Gisors
Vesly Courcelles-les-Gisors
Magny-en-Vexin
La-Villeneuve-Saint-Martin
Les-Mureaux
Sommery
Cuigy-en-Bray
Clery-en-Vexin
Limay
Beauvoir-en-Lyons
Croisy-sur-Andelle
Suzay
Saint-Marcel
Bicheville
Chaignes
Les-Hayons-d'Esclavelles
Saint-Jacques-sur-Darnetal
Grainville
Bacqueville
Chauffour-les-Bonnières
Martincamp
Amfreville-la-mi-Voie
Saint-Étienne-du-Rouvray
Vernon
Heudebouville
Aubevoye
Biville-la-Baignade
Tôtes
Les Eslettes
ROUEN
Grand Quevilly
Moulineaux
Caudebec-les-Elbeuf
Louviers
Vironvay
Saint-Pierre-les-Elbeuf
Fouqueville
Epreville
Autheuil-Hauthouillet
Gravigny
Fauville
La Bonneville
ÉVREUX
Le Trait

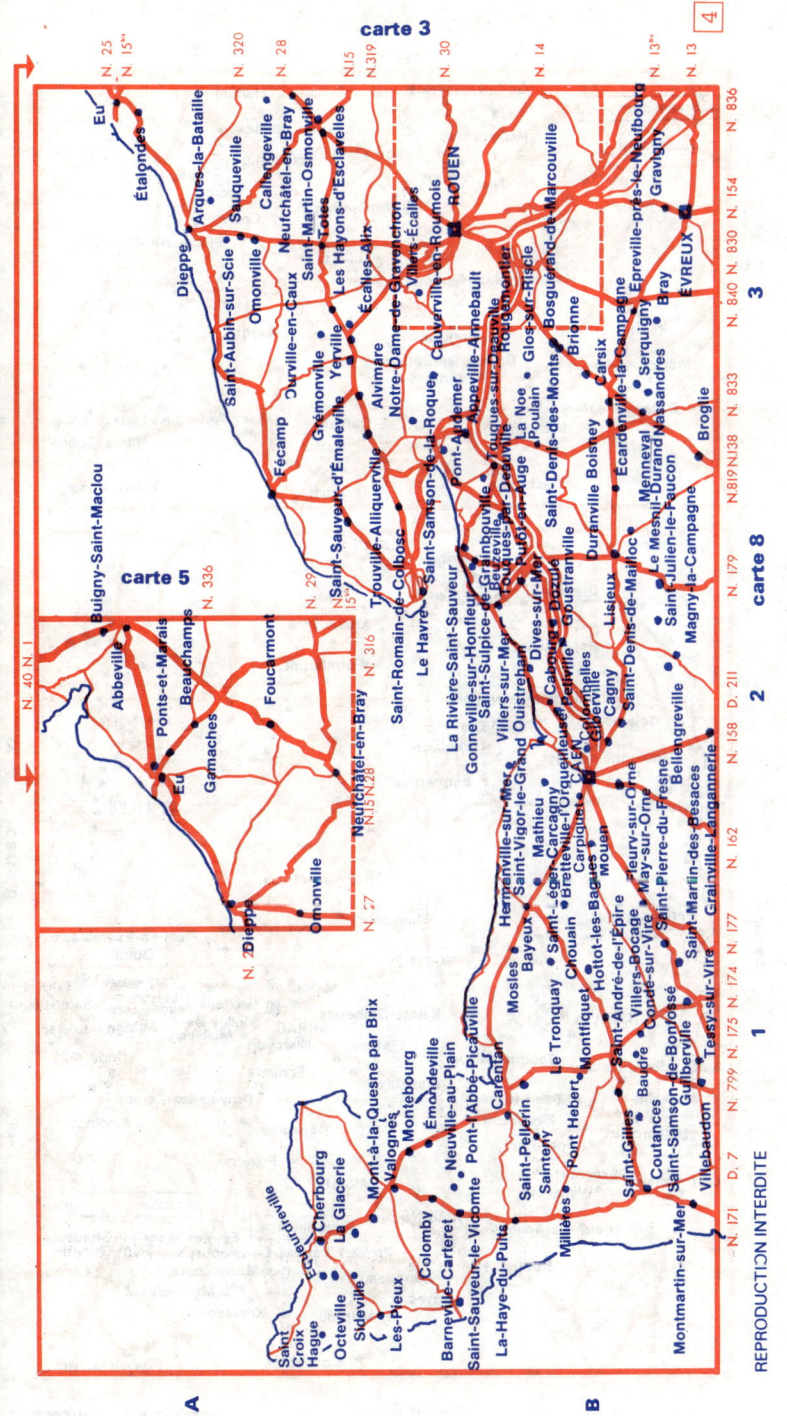

carte 3

carte 5

carte 8

N. 40 N. I

REPRODUCTION INTERDITE

A

B

1

2

3

4

21

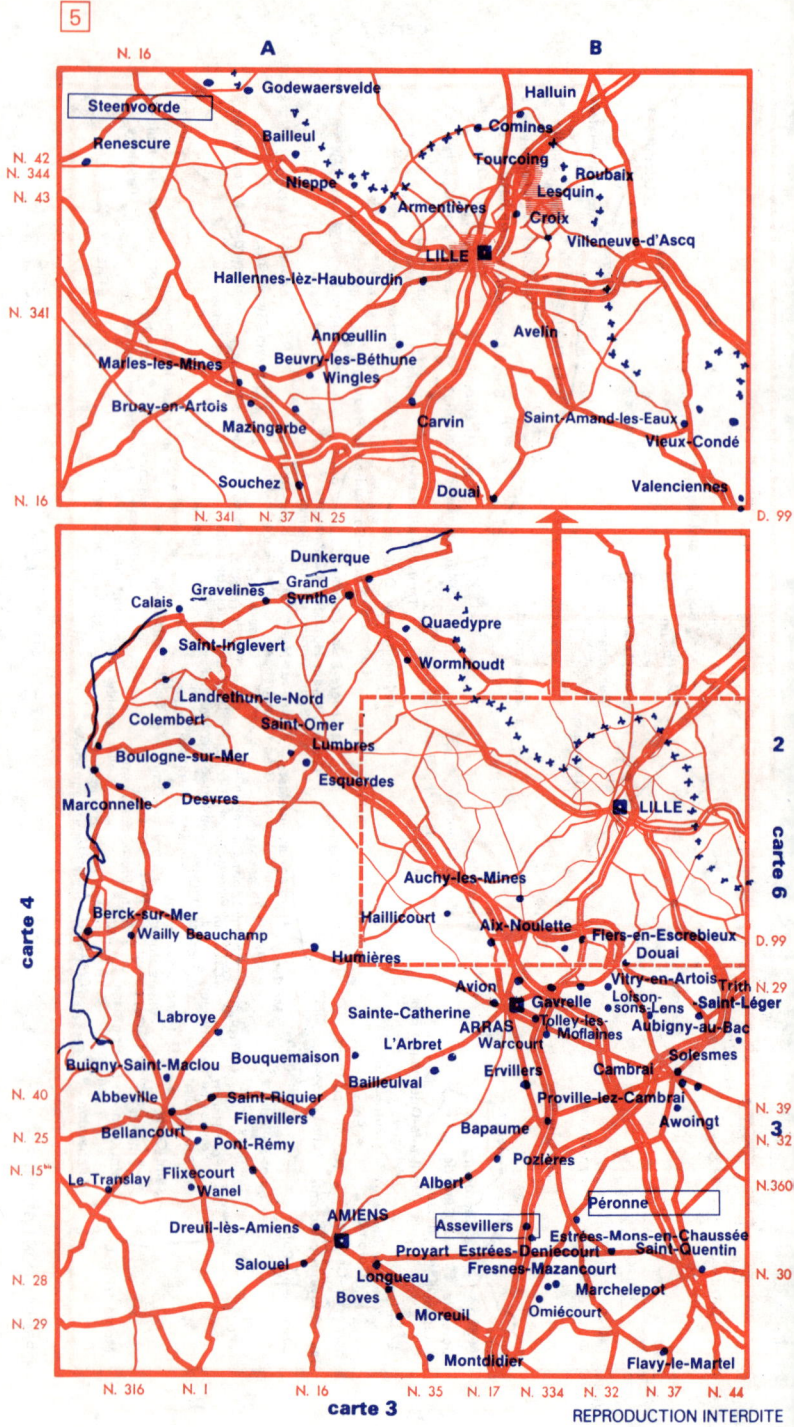

5

N. 16

A　　　　　　　　　**B**

Godewaersvelde　　　Halluin

Steenvoorde

Bailleul　　　Comines

Renescure

N. 42　　　　　　　　　Tourcoing

N. 344　　　　　　Nieppe　　　Roubaix

N. 43　　　　　　　　　Lesquin

Armentières　　　Croix

LILLE　　　Villeneuve-d'Ascq

Hallennes-lèz-Haubourdin

N. 341

Anneeullin　　　Avelin

Marles-les-Mines　　Beuvry-les-Béthune

Wingles

Bruay-en-Artois

Mazingarbe　　　Carvin　　　Saint-Amand-les-Eaux

Vieux-Condé

Souchez

N. 16　　　　　　　　　Douai

Valenciennes

N. 341　N. 37　N. 25　　　　　　　　D. 99

Dunkerque

Gravelines　Grand

Calais　　　Synthe　　　Quaedypre

Saint-Inglevert　　　Wormhoudt

Landrethun-le-Nord

Colembert　　Saint-Omer

Boulogne-sur-Mer　Lumbres

Esquerdes

Marconnelle　Desvres

Auchy-les-Mines

Berck-sur-Mer　　Haillicourt

Wailly Beauchamp　　Aix-Noulette　　Flers-en-Escrebieux

Humières　　　　　Douai　　D. 99

Avion　　Vitry-en-Artois　Trith　N. 29

Labroye　　　　　　Loison-　　Saint-Léger

Sainte-Catherine　Gavrelle　sous-Lens

Buigny-Saint-Maclou　Bouquemaison　L'Arbret　ARRAS　Tolley-les-　Aubigny-au-Bac

Warcourt　　Moflaines

Bailleulval　Ervillers　　　　Cambrai　Solesmes

Abbeville　Saint-Riquier　　Proville-lez-Cambrai

Fienvillers　　　　Bapaume　　Awoingt　N. 39

Bellancourt　Pont-Rémy　　　　　　　　N. 32

N. 25　　　　　　　Pozières

N. 15bis　Le Translay　Flixecourt　Albert　　　Péronne　N.360

Wanel

Dreuil-lès-Amiens　AMIENS　　Asservillers　Estrées-Mons-en-Chaussée

Salouel　　　Proyart Estrées-Deniécourt　Saint-Quentin

N. 28　　　Longueau　Fresnes-Mazancourt　　Marchelepot　N. 30

N. 29　　　Boves　　Moreuil　Omiécourt

Montdidier　　　Flavy-le-Martel

N. 316　N. 1　N. 16　N. 35　N. 17　N. 334　N. 32　N 37　N. 44

carte 4　　　carte 3　　　REPRODUCTION INTERDITE

carte 2

carte 6

carte 3

22

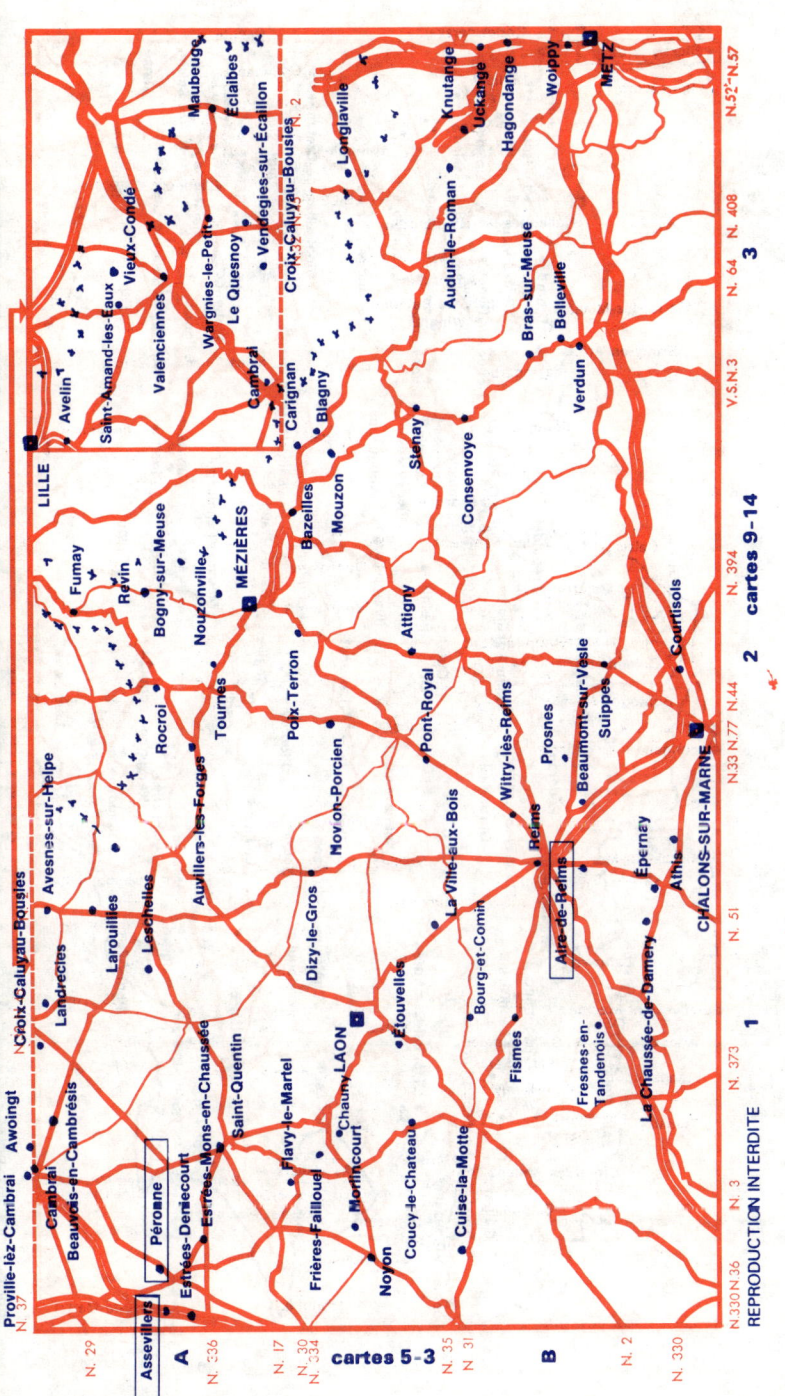

6

23

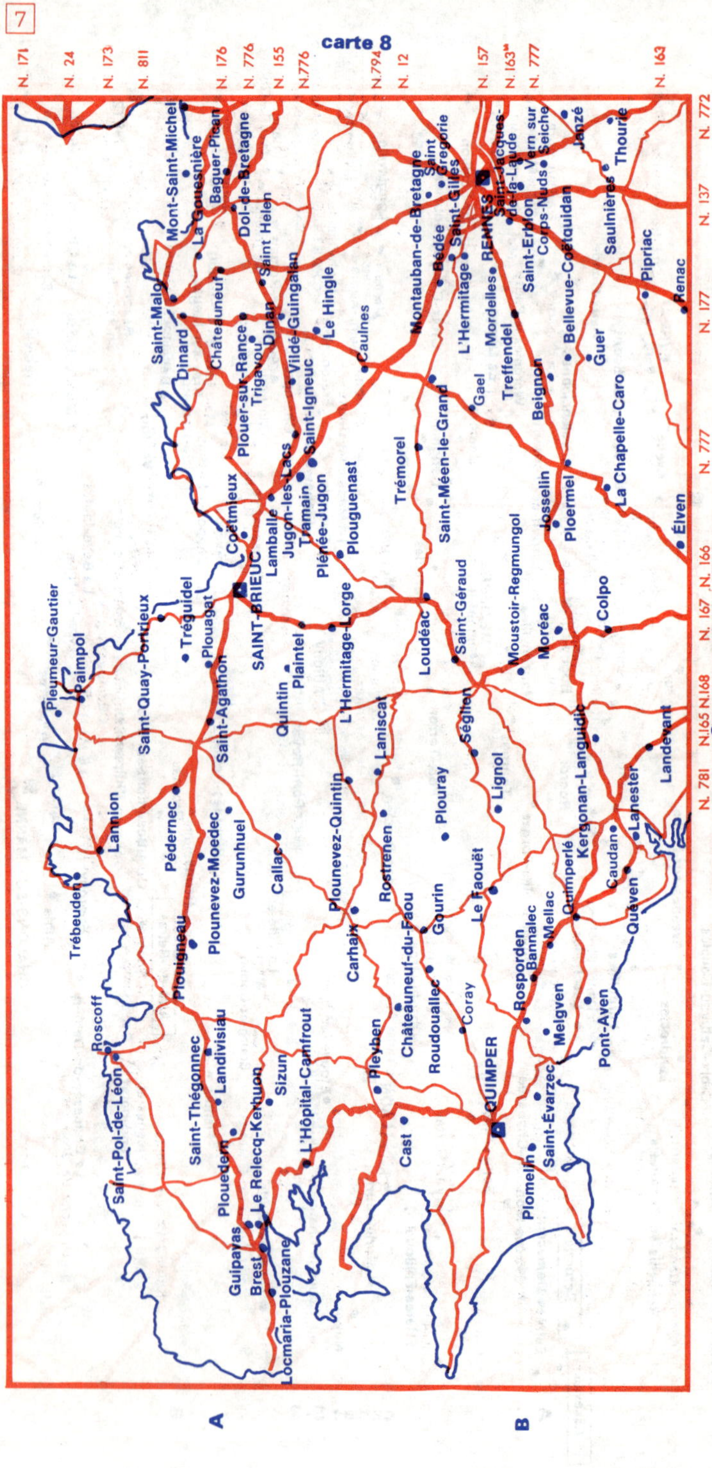

carte 8

N. 171 N. 24 N. 173 N. 811 N. 176 N. 776 N. 155 N.776 N.794 N. 12 N. 157 N.163° N. 777 N. 163

N. 772
N. 137
N. 177
N. 777
N. 166
N. 167 .N. 166
N.165 N.168
N. 781

Mont-Saint-Michel
La Gouesnière
Baguer-Pican
Dol-de-Bretagne
Saint Hélen
Montauban-de-Bretagne
Médée
Saint-Gilles
RENNES
Saint-Jacques
Le Verger-Laude
Saint-Grégoire
Saint-Erblon
Vern-sur-Seiche
Corps-Nuds
Bellevue-Coëtquidan
Janzé
Saulnières
Thourie
Pipriac
Renac

Saint-Malo
Dinard
Châteauneuf
Plouer-sur-Rance
Trigavou
Dinan
Vildé-Guingalan
Saint-Igneuc
Le Hingle
Caulnes
L'Hermitage
Mordelles
Gaël
Treffendel
Béignon
Guer
La Chapelle-Caro
Éven

Pleumeur-Gautier
Paimpol
Tréguidel
Plouagat
Coëtmieux
Lamballe
Jugon-les-Lacs
Trémain
Plénée-Jugon
Plouguenast
Trémorel
Saint-Méen-le-Grand
Josselin
Ploërmel

Saint-Quay-Portrieux
SAINT-BRIEUC
Plaintel
Quintin
L'Hermitage-Lorge
Loudéac
Saint-Géraud
Moustoir-Regmungol
Noréac
Colpo

Trébeudet
Lannion
Pédernec
Plounevez-Moedec
Gurunhuel
Callac
Plounevez-Quintin
Lanfscat
Rostrenen
Plouray
Ségilen
Lignol
Kergonan-Languidic
Landevant
Lanester

Roscoff
Plouigneau
Plounevez-Moedec
Le Faouët
Quimperlé
Caudan
Quéven

Saint-Pol-de-Léon
Saint-Thégonnec
Landivisiau
Sizun
L'Hôpital-Camfrout
Le Relecq-Kerhuon
Ploudem
Pleyben
Châteauneuf-du-Faou
Carhaix
Gourin
Coray
Roudouallec
Rosporden
Bannalec
Mellac
Pont-Aven

Guipavas
Brest
Locmaria-Plouzané
Cast
Plomelin
QUIMPER
Saint-Évarzec
Melgven

A

B

1

2

3

REPRODUCTION INTERDITE

24

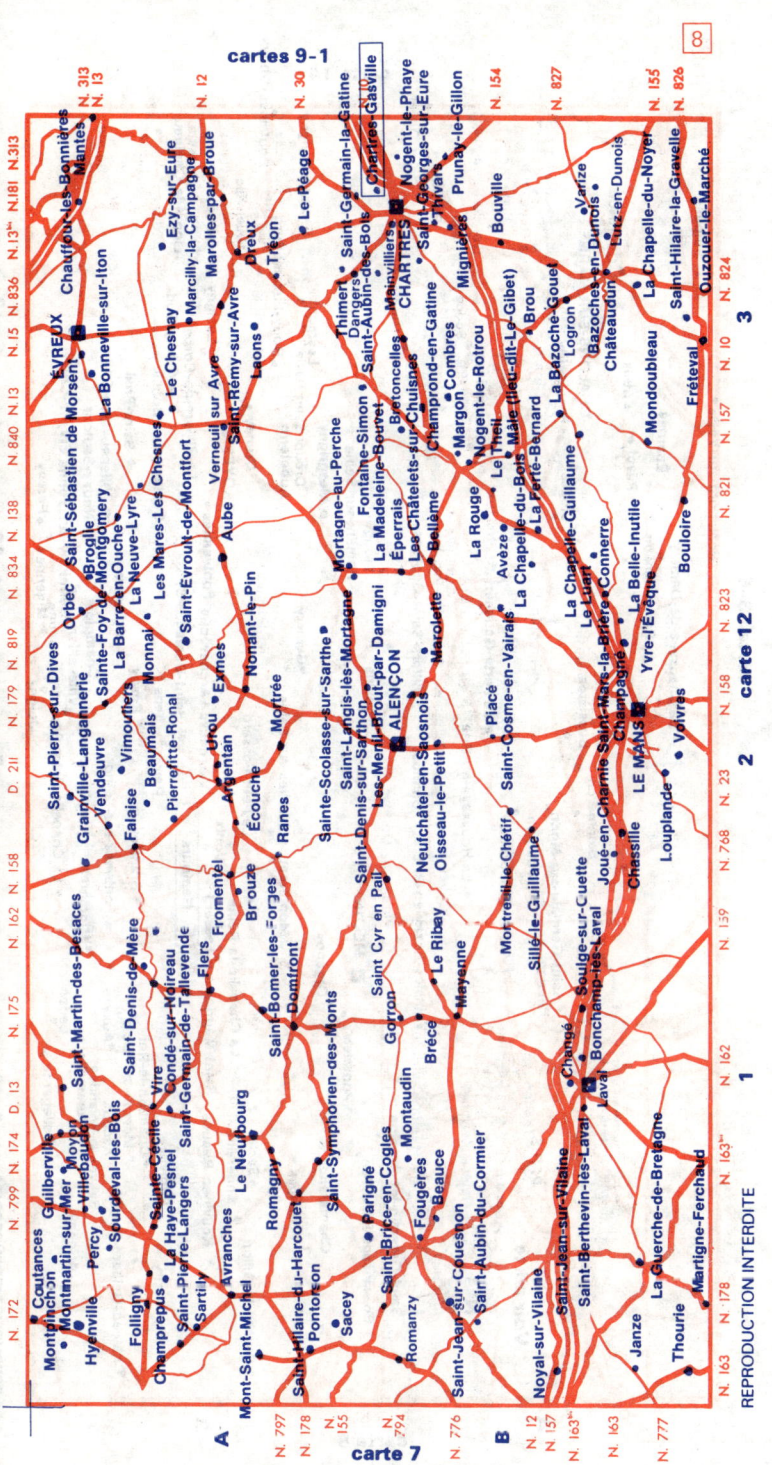

REPRODUCTION INTERDITE

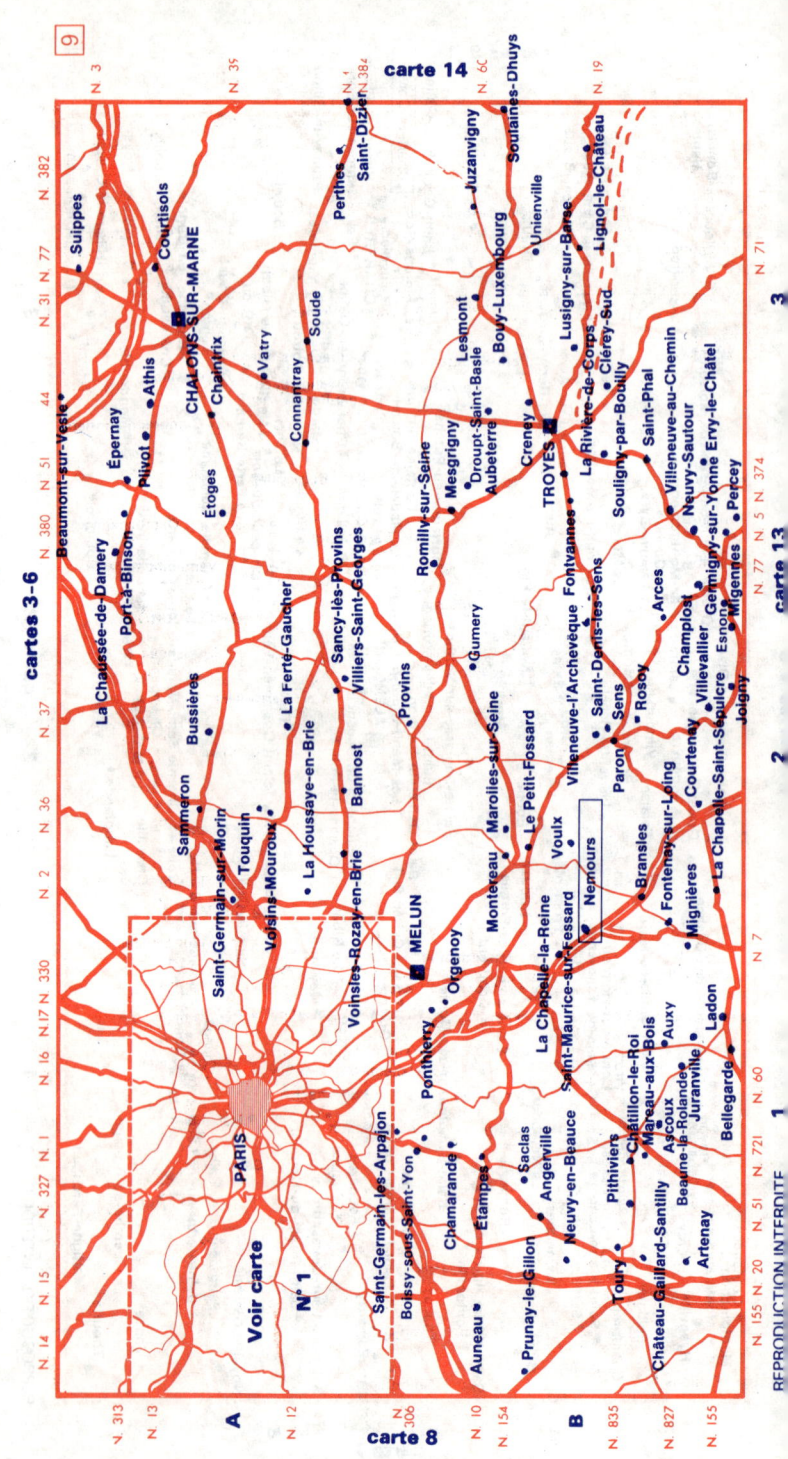

carte 14

cartes 3-6

9

26

REPRODUCTION INTERDITE

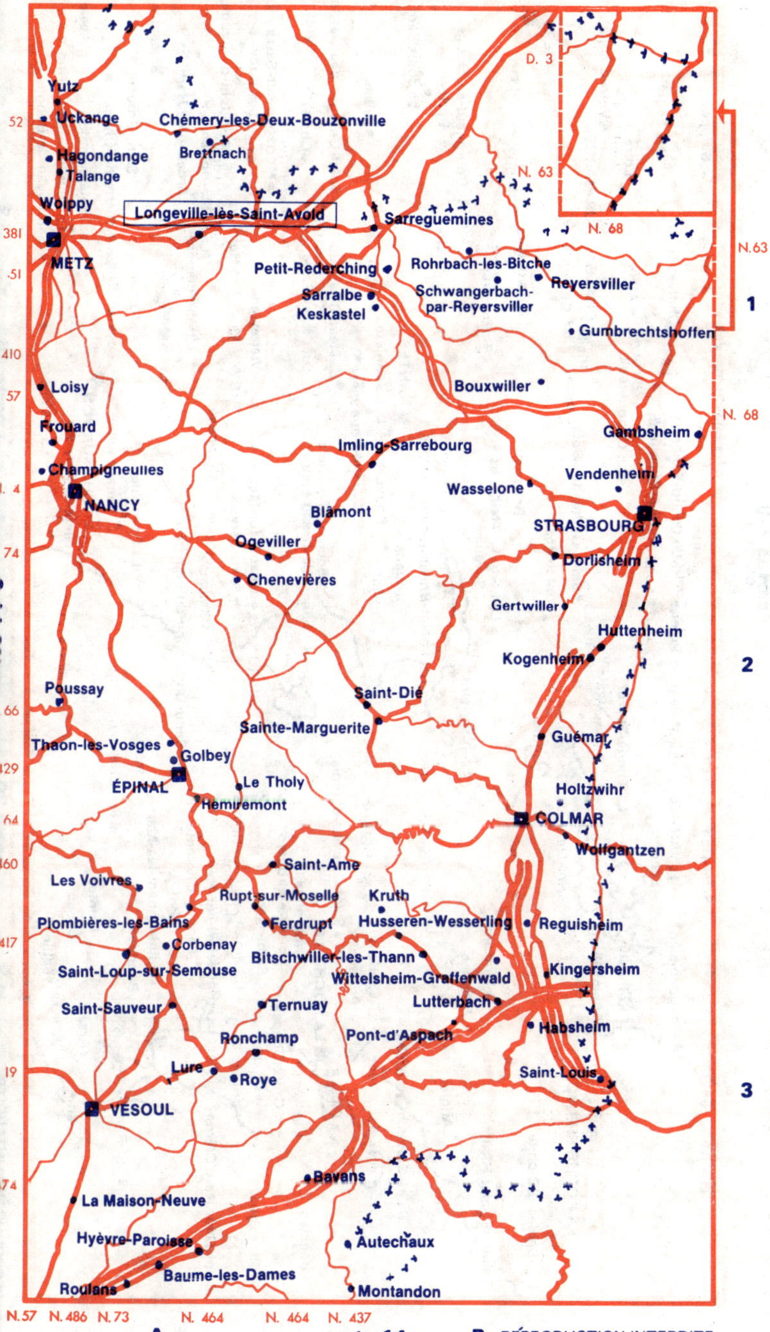

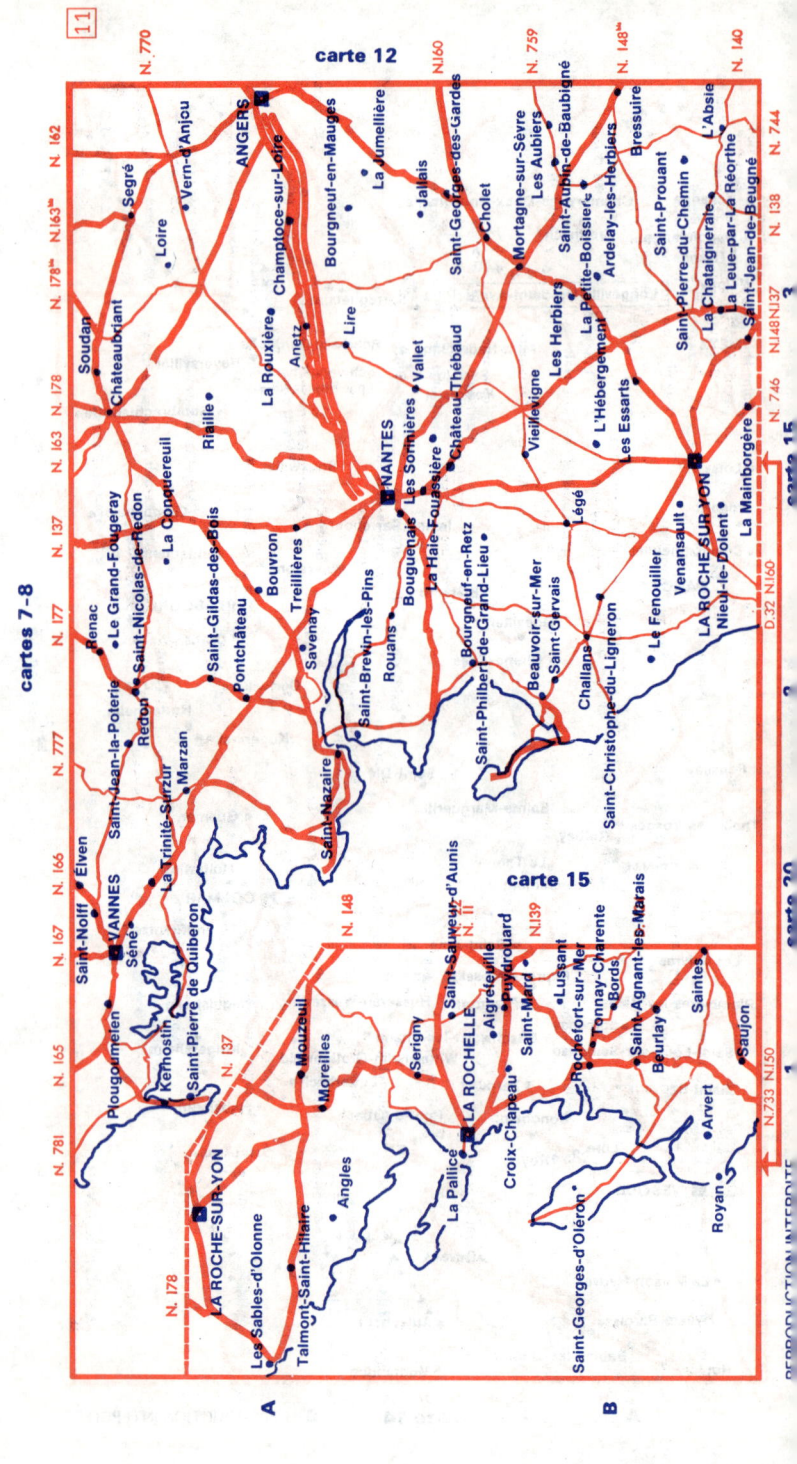

carte 12

cartes 7-8

carte 15

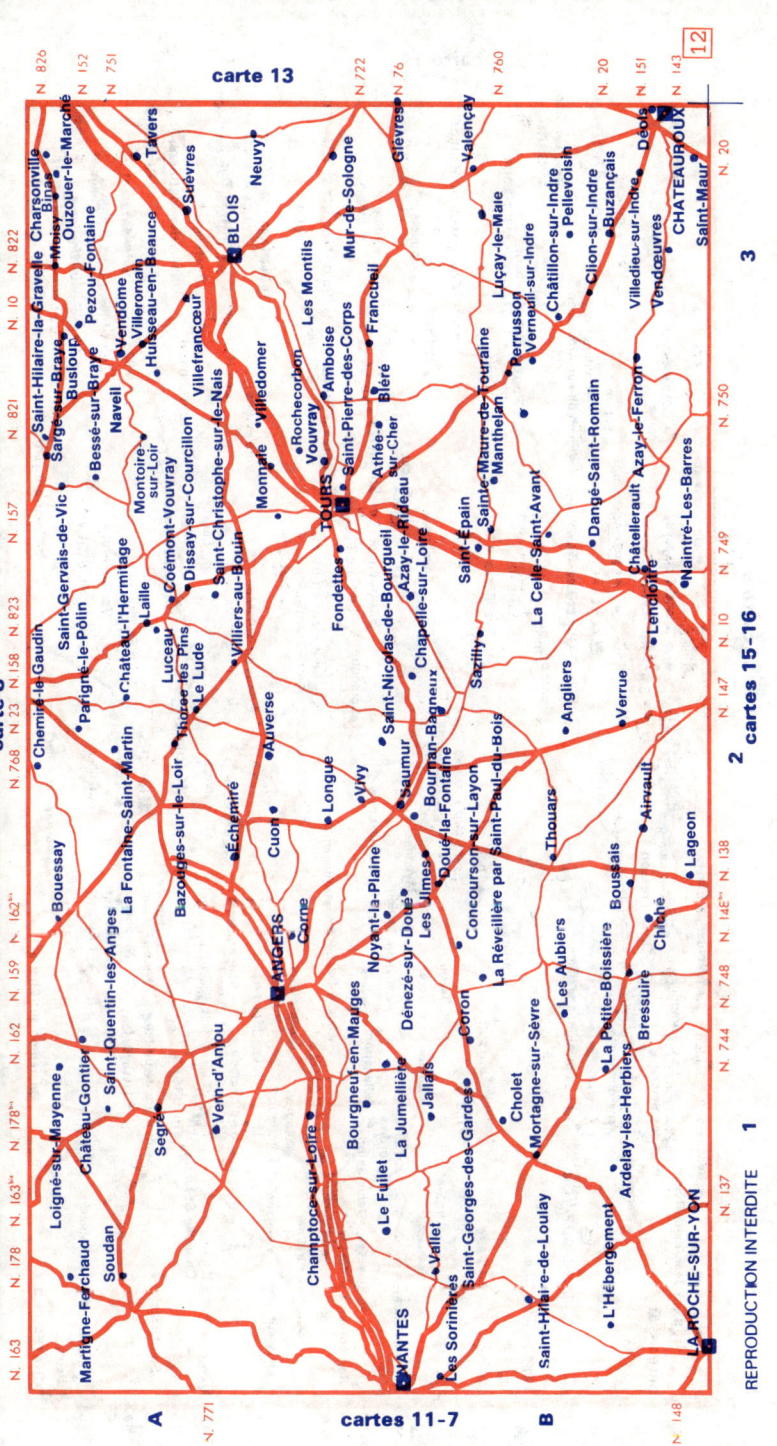

carte 13

carte 8

cartes 15-16

cartes 11-7

REPRODUCTION INTERDITE

12

29

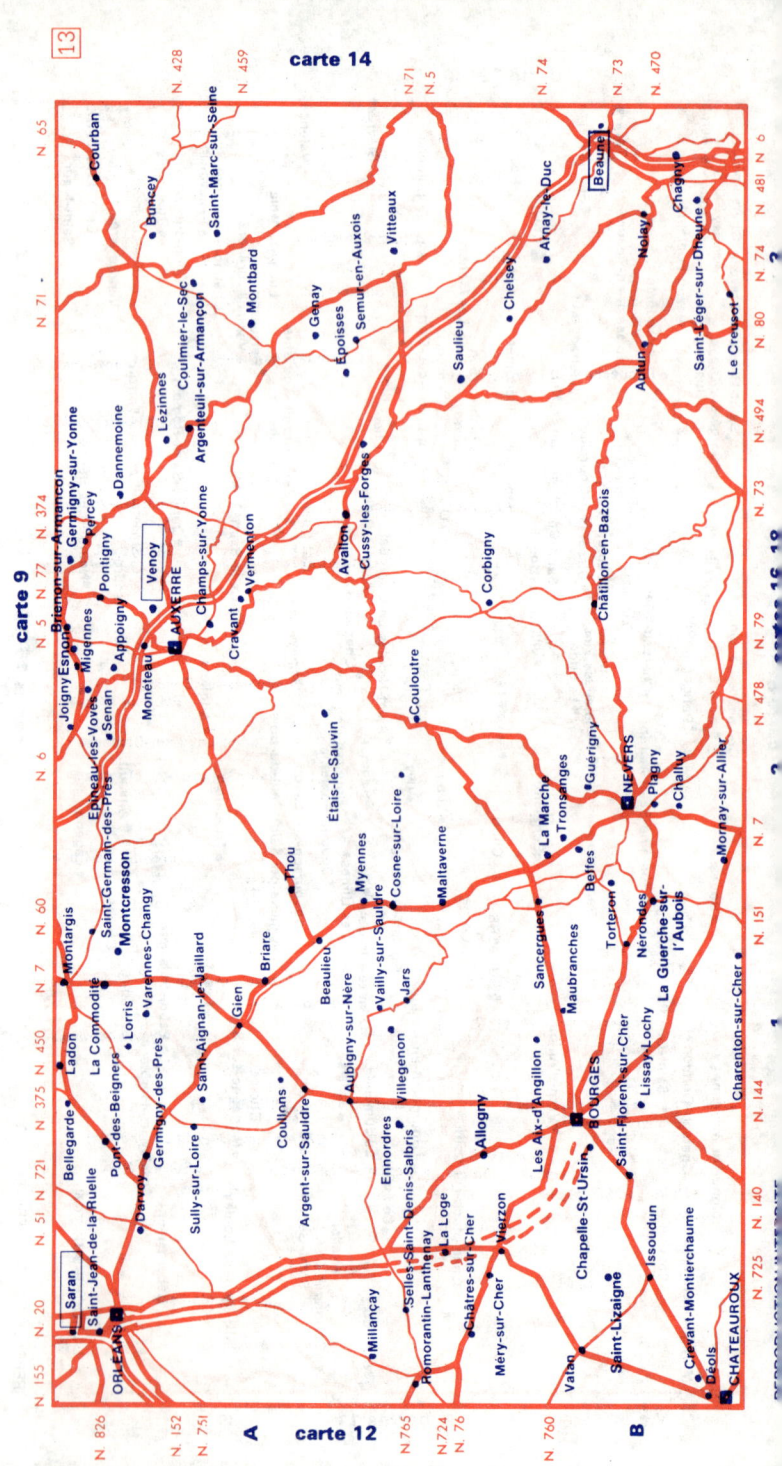

carte 14

carte 9

A carte 12

N 428
N 459
N 71
N 5
N 74
N 73
N 470

N 65
N 71
N 6
N 481
N 2
N 74
N 80
N 494
N 73
N 79
N 478
N 7
N 151
N 151
N 144
N 1
N 140
N 725
N 760
N 155
N 20
N 51
N 721
N 375
N 450
N 7
N 60
N 7
N 77
N 374
N 5
N 826
N 152
N 751
N 765
N 724
N 76

Courban
Buncey
Saint-Marc-sur-Seine
Beaune
Chagny
Aignay-le-Duc
Viteaux
Montbard
Semur-en-Auxois
Chelsey
Nolay
Autun
Saint-Leger-sur-Dheune
Le Creusot
Genay
Epoisses
Saulieu
Coulmier-le-Sec
Argenteuil-sur-Armançon
Lézinnes
Percey
Gerbigny-sur-Yonne
Dannemoine
Pontigny
Venoy
Champs-sur-Yonne
Chablis-en-Bazois
Corbigny
Avallon
Cussy-les-Forges
Vermenton
Cravant
Joigny
Esnon
Brienon-sur-Armançon
Migennes
Epineau-les-Voves
Senan
Appoigny
AUXERRE
Monéteau
Couloutre
Etais-le-Sauvin
NEVERS
Plagny
Challuy
Moiray-sur-Allier
Guerigny
Tronsanges
La Marche
Belfes
Maltaverne
Cosne-sur-Loire
Myennes
Thou
Sancergues
Néronctes
Torteron
Maubranches
La Guerche-sur-l'Aubois
Charenton-sur-Cher
Montargis
La Commodité
Ladon
Lorris
Varennes-Changy
Saint-Germain-des-Prés
Montcresson
Briare
Beaulieu
Vailly-sur-Sauldre
Jars
Aubigny-sur-Nère
Villegenon
Coullons
Argent-sur-Sauldre
Gien
Saint-Aignan-le-Jaillard
Germigny-des-Prés
Pont-des-Beignes
Bellegarde
Saran
Saint-Jean-de-la-Ruelle
Darvoy
Sully-sur-Loire
ORLEANS
Millançay
Romorantin-Lanthenay
Selles-Saint-Denis-Salbris
La Loge
Châtres-sur-Cher
Méry-sur-Cher
Vierzon
Ennordes
Allogny
Les Aix-d'Angillon
BOURGES
Saint-Florent-sur-Cher
Lissay-Lochy
Saint-Germain-St-Ursin
Chapelle-St-Ursin
Issoudun
Vatan
Saint-Lizaigne
Crevant-Montierchaume
Déols
CHATEAUROUX
B

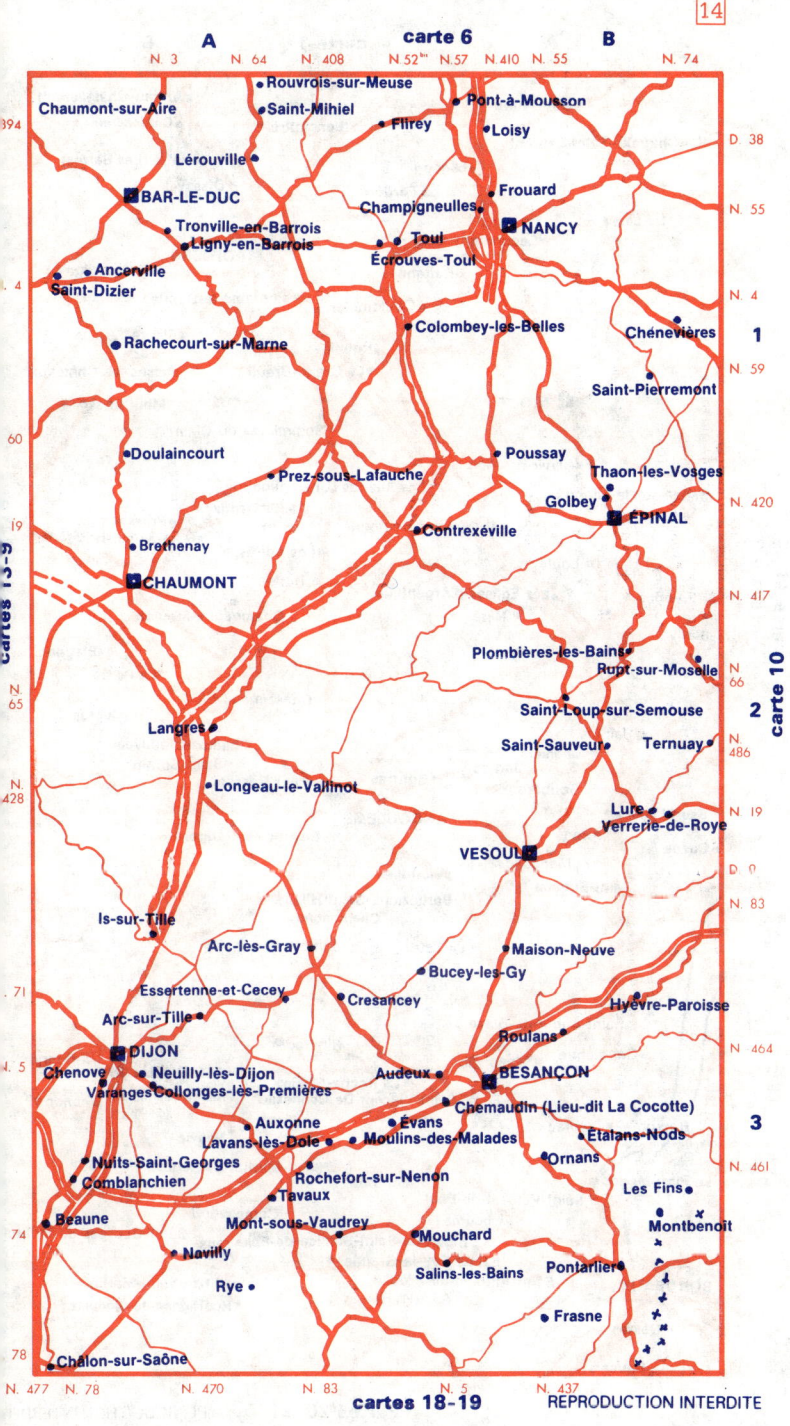

carte 6

A   B

N. 3   N. 64   N. 408   N. 52ᵇⁱˢ N.57   N. 410   N. 55   N. 74

Rouvrois-sur-Meuse
Chaumont-sur-Aire
Saint-Mihiel
Pont-à-Mousson
Flirey
Loisy
Lérouville
D. 38
Frouard
N. 55
BAR-LE-DUC
Champigneulles
NANCY
Tronville-en-Barrois
Ligny-en-Barrois
Toul
Écrouves-Toul
N. 4
Ancerville
Saint-Dizier
Colombey-les-Belles
Chénevières
1
N. 59
Rachecourt-sur-Marne
Saint-Pierremont
Doulaincourt
Poussay
Thaon-les-Vosges
60
Prez-sous-Lafauche
Golbey
N. 420
Contrexéville
ÉPINAL
Brethenay
CHAUMONT
N. 417
Plombières-les-Bains
Rupt-sur-Moselle
N. 66
Saint-Loup-sur-Semouse
2
N. 65
Langres
Saint-Sauveur
Ternuay
N. 486
N. 428
Longeau-le-Vallinot
Lure
N. 19
Verrerie-de-Roye
VESOUL
D. 9
N. 83
Is-sur-Tille
Arc-lès-Gray
Maison-Neuve
Bucey-les-Gy
71
Essertenne-et-Cecey
Cresancey
Hyèvre-Paroisse
Arc-sur-Tille
Roulans
N 464
DIJON
Audeux
BESANÇON
Chenôve
Neuilly-lès-Dijon
Chemaudin (Lieu-dit La Cocotte)
3
Varanges Collonges-lès-Premières
Auxonne
Evans
Etalans-Nods
Lavans-lès-Dole
Moulins-des-Malades
Ornans
N. 461
Nuits-Saint-Georges
Rochefort-sur-Nenon
Comblanchien
Tavaux
Les Fins
Beaune
Mont-sous-Vaudrey
Montbenoit
Navilly
Mouchard
Rye
Salins-les-Bains
Pontarlier
78
Chalon-sur-Saône
Frasne

N. 477 N. 78   N. 470   N. 83   N. 5   N. 437

cartes 18-19   REPRODUCTION INTERDITE

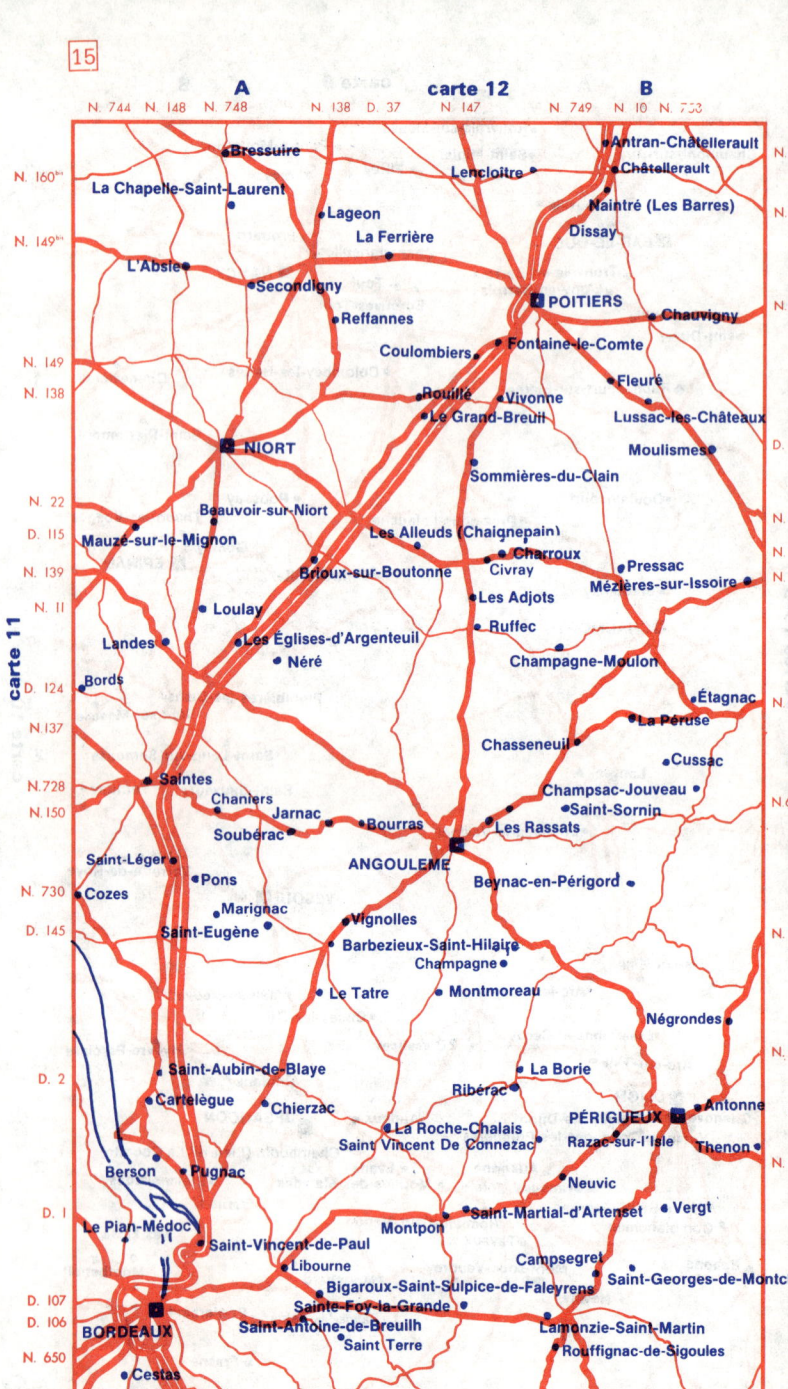

carte 12

A
N. 744 N. 148 N. 748   N. 138 D. 37   N. 147   N. 749 N. 10 N. 733   B

N. 160ᵇⁱˢ

Bressuire

La Chapelle-Saint-Laurent

Lencloître

Antran-Châtellerault
Châtellerault
Naintré (Les Barres)

N. 149ᵇⁱˢ

Lageon
La Ferrière

Dissay

L'Absie
Secondigny

Reffannes

POITIERS

Chauvigny

N. 149
N. 138

Coulombiers

Fontaine-le-Comte

Rouillé
Le Grand-Breuil

Vivonne

Fleuré

Lussac-les-Châteaux

NIORT

Moulismes

N. 22
D. 115

Beauvoir-sur-Niort

Mauzé-sur-le-Mignon

Sommières-du-Clain

Les Alleuds (Chaignepain)

Charroux

Pressac

N. 139

Brioux-sur-Boutonne

Civray

Mézières-sur-Issoire

N. 11

Loulay

Les Adjots

Ruffec

Landes

Les Églises-d'Argenteuil

D. 124

Néré

Champagne-Moulon

Bords

Étagnac

N. 137

La Péruse

Chasseneuil

N.728

Saintes

Cussac

N. 150

Chaniers
Jarnac

Bourras

Champsac-Jouveau
Saint-Sornin

Soubérac

Les Rassats

Saint-Léger

Pons

ANGOULEME

N. 730

Cozes

Beynac-en-Périgord

D. 145

Marignac

Saint-Eugène

Vignolles

Barbezieux-Saint-Hilaire
Champagne

Le Tatre

Montmoreau

Négrondes

D. 2

Saint-Aubin-de-Blaye

La Borie

Cartelègue

Chierzac

Ribérac

PÉRIGUEUX

Antonne

La Roche-Chalais
Saint Vincent De Connezac

Razac-sur-l'Isle

Thenon

Berson

Pugnac

Neuvic

D. 1

Le Pian-Médoc

Montpon

Saint-Martial-d'Artenset

Vergt

Saint-Vincent-de-Paul

Campsegret

D. 107
D. 106

Libourne

Bigaroux-Saint-Sulpice-de-Faleyrens

Saint-Georges-de-Montcl

Sainte-Foy-la-Grande

BORDEAUX

Saint-Antoine-de-Breuilh

Saint Terre

Lamonzie-Saint-Martin
Rouffignac-de-Sigoules

N. 650

Cestas

N. 10

Saucats

N. 651   N.113 D.10   N.672 N.670   N. 668   N. 133   N. 21   D. 2

cartes 20-21

REPRODUCTION INTERDIT

carte 11

32

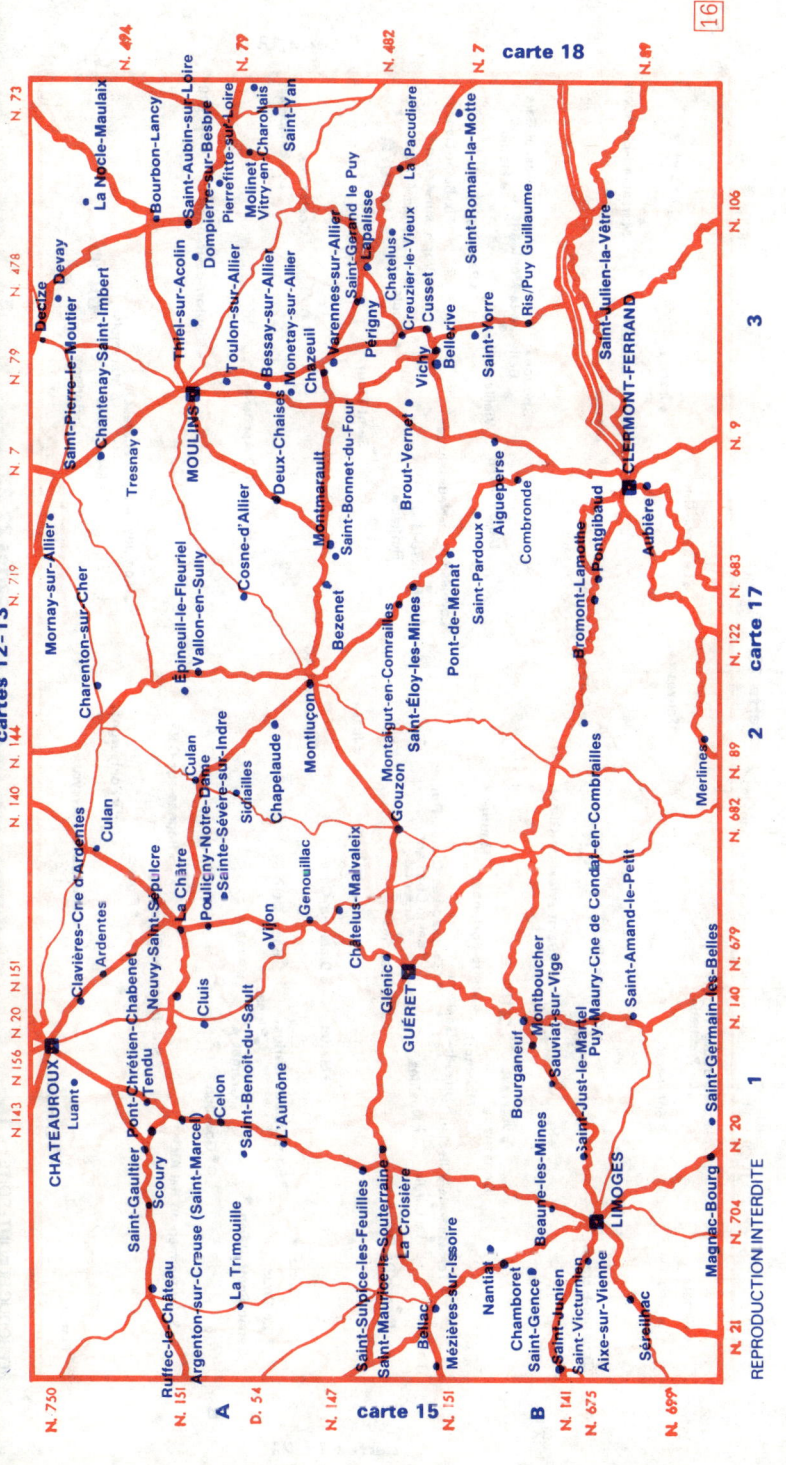

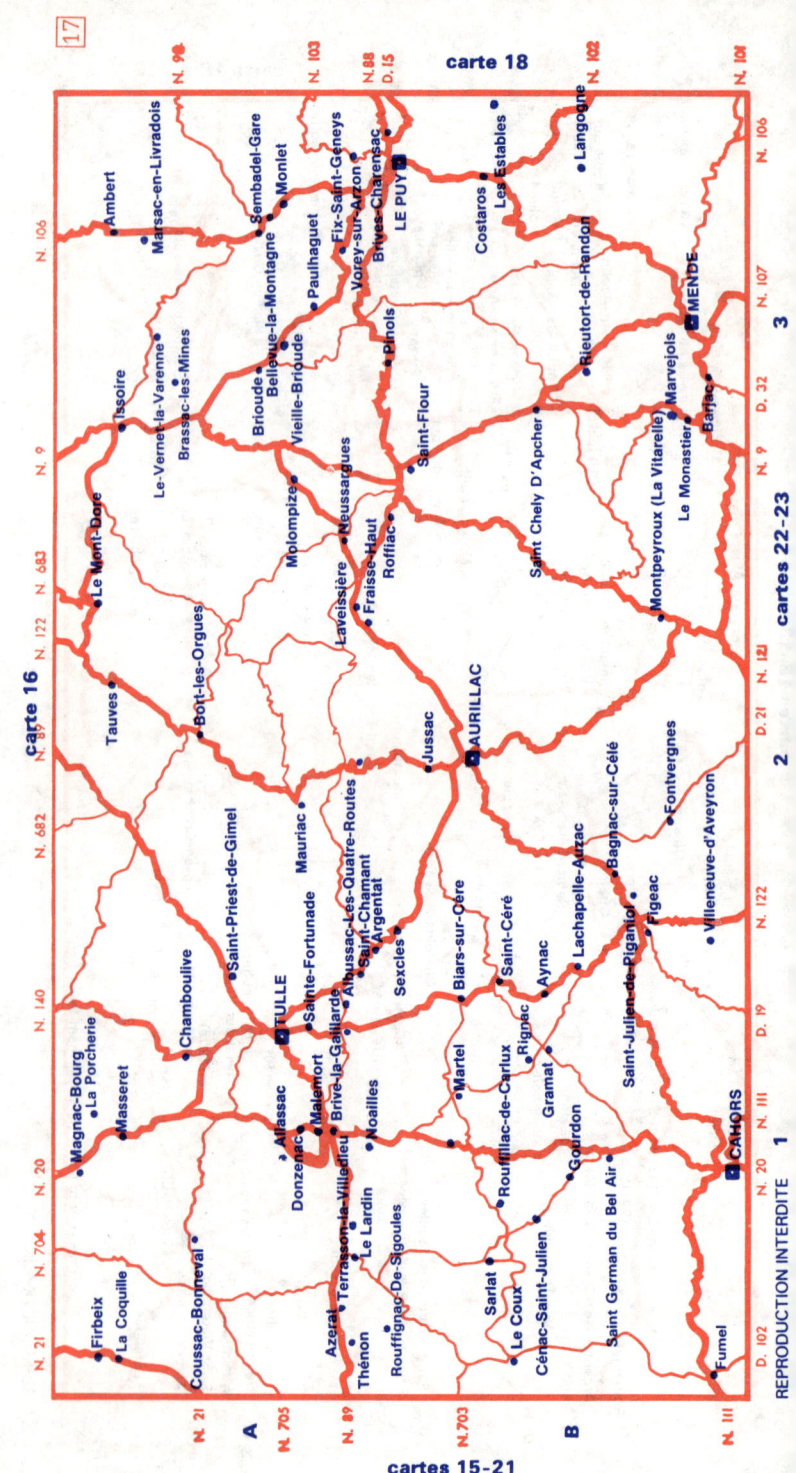

carte 18

carte 16

cartes 15-21

cartes 22-23

REPRODUCTION INTERDITE

N. 98 N. 103 N. 88 D. 15 N. 102 N. 104

N. 106 N. 106 N. 107

N. 9 D. 32

N. 683 N. 9

N. 122

N. 682

N. 87

N. 140

N. 20

N. 704

N. 21

N. 705

N. 89

N. 703

N. 102

N. 20 N. III N. III

D. 21 N. 121

D. 19 N. 122

A B 1 2 3

Ambert
Marsac-en-Livradois
Sembadel-Gare
Monlet
Fix-Saint-Geneys
Vorey-sur-Arzon
Paulhaguet
Brives-Charensac
LE PUY
Costaros
Les Estables
Langogne
Issoire
Le Vernet-la-Varenne
Bellevue-la-Montagne
Brassac-les-Mines
Brioude
Vieille-Brioude
Pinols
Saint-Flour
Rieutort-de-Randon
MENDE
Molompize
Neussargues
Laveissière
Fraisse-Haut
Roffiac
Saint Chely D'Apcher
Montpeyroux (La Vitarelle)
Marvejols
Le Monastier
Barjac
Le Mont-Dore
Tauves
Bort-les-Orgues
AURILLAC
Jussac
Fontvergnes
Saint-Priest-de-Gimel
Mauriac
Bagnac-sur-Célé
Villeneuve-d'Aveyron
Magnac-Bourg
La Porcherie
Masseret
Chamboulive
Saint-Fortunade
TULLE
Argentat
Saint-Chamant
Aubazac-Les-Quatre-Routes
Sexcles
Biars-sur-Cère
Saint-Céré
Aynac
Lachapelle-Auzac
Figeac
Saint-Julien-de-Piganol
Firbeix
La Coquille
Coussac-Bonneval
Malemort
Donzenac
Aixassac
Brive-la-Gaillarde
Noailles
Martel
Rouffillac-de-Carlux
Gramat
Gourdon
CAHORS
Azerat
Terrasson-la-Villedieu
Le Lardin
Thénon
Rouffignac-De-Sigoules
Sarlat
Le Coux
Cénac-Saint-Julien
Saint German du Bel Air
Fumel

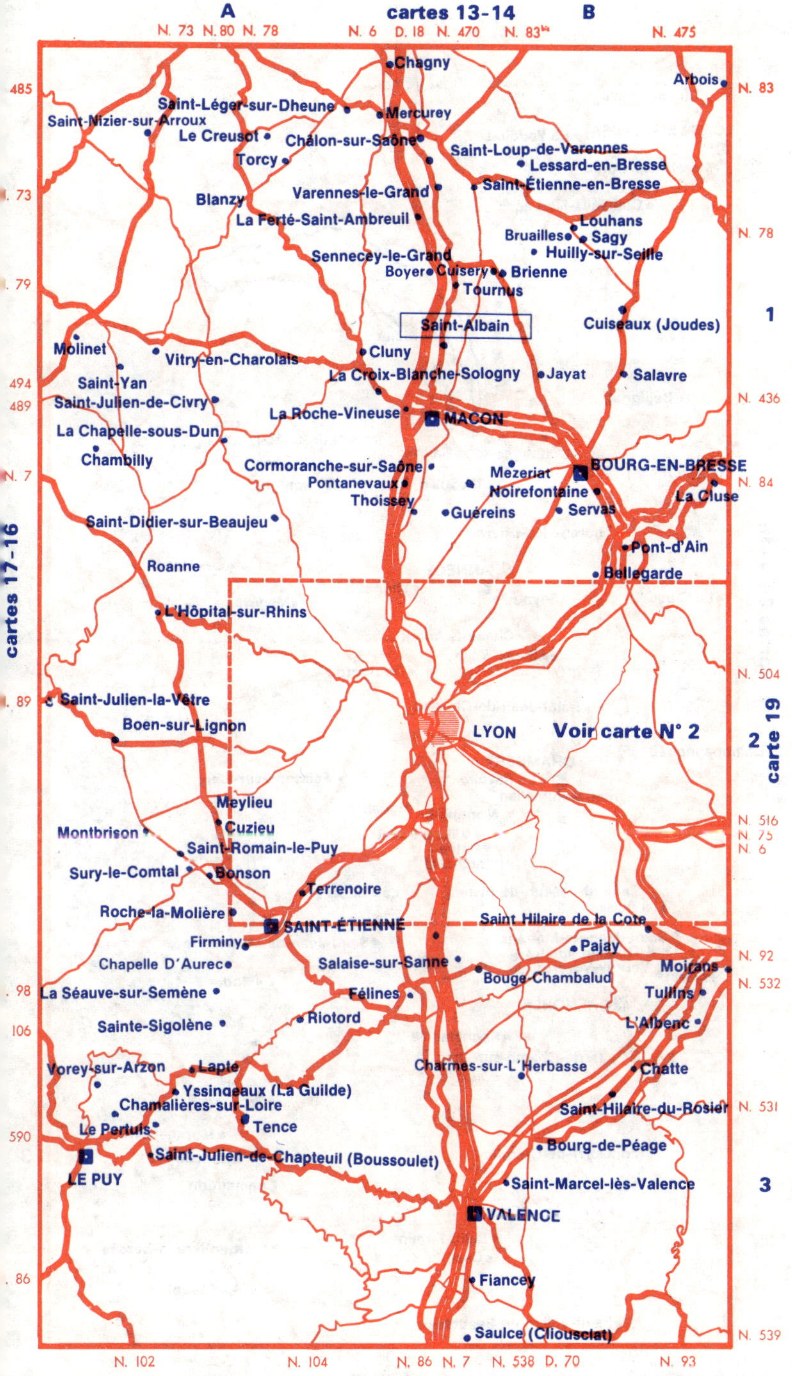

cartes 13-14

A   B

N. 73 N. 80 N. 78   N. 6   D. 18 N. 470   N. 83ᵇⁱˢ   N. 475

Chagny

485   Arbois •   N. 83

Saint-Léger-sur-Dheune •
Saint-Mizier-sur-Arroux •   • Mercurey
Le Creusot •   Châlon-sur-Saône •
Torcy •   Saint-Loup-de-Varennes •
                                             Lessard-en-Bresse •
Blanzy •   Varennes-le-Grand •   Saint-Étienne-en-Bresse •
La Ferté-Saint-Ambreuil •
                                             Louhans •   N. 78
                                    Bruailles • Sagy •
Sennecey-le-Grand •   Huilly-sur-Seille •
                Boyer • Cuisery •
                      • Brienne •
                    Tournus •   1
         Saint-Albain
                                             Cuiseaux (Joudes) •

Molinet •   Vitry-en-Charolais •   Cluny •
494   Saint-Yan •   La Croix-Blanche-Sologny • Jayat •   • Salavre
489 Saint-Julien-de-Civry •   N. 436
     La Chapelle-sous-Dun •   La Roche-Vineuse •
     Chambilly •   ■ MÂCON

N. 7   Cormoranche-sur-Saône •   BOURG-EN-BRESSE ■
                                  Pontanevaux •   Mézeriat •   N. 84
                        Thoissey •   Noirefontaine •   • La Cluse
     Saint-Didier-sur-Beaujeu •   Guéreins •   Servas •
                                                         Pont-d'Ain •
     Roanne •
                                                         Bellegarde •
         L'Hôpital-sur-Rhins •

N. 89   N. 504

     Saint-Julien-la-Vêtre •
         Boen-sur-Lignon •   LYON   Voir carte N° 2   2   carte 19

         Meylieu •
Montbrison •   Cuzieu •   N. 516
         Saint-Romain-le-Puy •   N. 75
Sury-le-Comtal • Bonson •   N. 6
Roche-la-Molière •   Terrenoire •
                                             Saint-Hilaire-de-la-Côte •
     Firminy •   ■ SAINT-ÉTIENNE •
Chapelle D'Aurec •   Salaise-sur-Sanne •   • Pajay •   N. 92
98   Bougé-Chambalud •   Moirans •
La Séauve-sur-Semène •   Tullins •   N. 532
106 Sainte-Sigolène •   • Riotord   Félines •
                                                         L'Albenc •
Vorey-sur-Arzon • • Lapte •   Charmes-sur-L'Herbasse •   • Chatte •
     Chamalières-sur-Loire •
Le Perluis •   • Tence   Saint-Hilaire-du-Rosier •   N. 531
590   Saint-Julien-de-Chapteuil (Boussoulet) •   Bourg-de-Péage •
■ LE PUY   Saint-Marcel-lès-Valence •   3
                                             ■ VALENCE
86
                                    • Fiancey

                        • Saulce (Cliousclat)   N. 539

N. 102   N. 104   N. 86 N. 7 N. 538 D. 70   N. 93

cartes 17-16 (left margin)

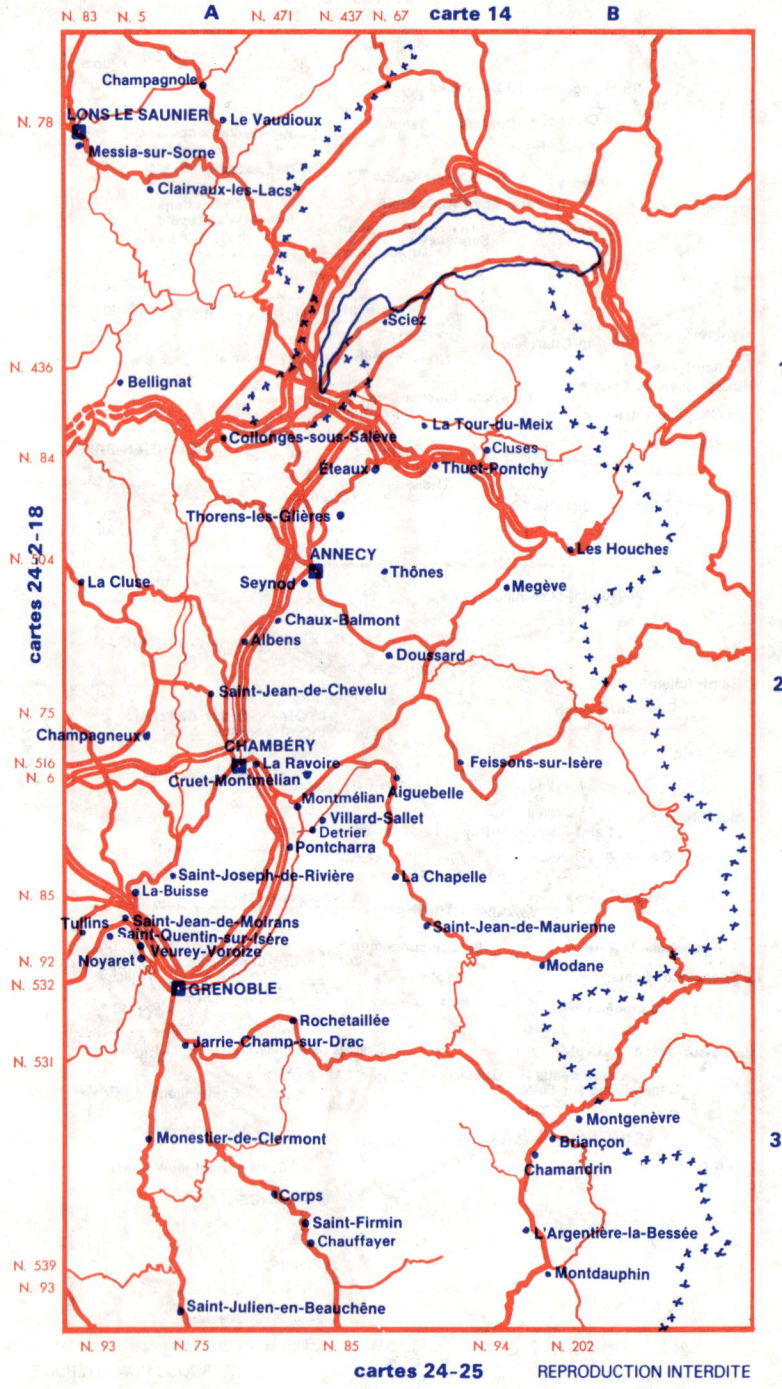

N. 83   N. 5   **A**   N. 471   N. 437   N. 67   **carte 14**   **B**

N. 78   **LONS LE SAUNIER**   • Le Vaudioux

Champagnole

• Messia-sur-Sorne

• Clairvaux-les-Lacs

• Scierz

N. 436   • Bellignat

• La Tour-du-Meix

N. 84   • Collonges-sous-Salève

Cluses

Éteaux   • Thuet-Pontchy

• Thorens-les-Glières

cartes 242-18   N. 504

• Les Houches

ANNECY   • Thônes

• La Cluse   Seynod   Megève

• Chaux-Balmont

• Albens

• Doussard

• Saint-Jean-de-Chevelu

N. 75   • Champagneux

CHAMBÉRY   • La Ravoire

N. 516   Cruet-Montmélian   • Feissons-sur-Isère

N. 6   Montmélian   Aiguebelle

• Villard-Sallet

Detrier

• Pontcharra

• Saint-Joseph-de-Rivière   • La Chapelle

N. 85   • La-Buisse

Tullins   • Saint-Jean-de-Moirans   • Saint-Jean-de-Maurienne

• Saint-Quentin-sur-Isère

N. 92   Noyaret   • Veurey-Voroize   • Modane

N. 532   ■ **GRENOBLE**

• Rochetaillée

• Jarrie-Champ-sur-Drac

N. 531

• Montgenèvre

• Briançon   **3**

• Monestier-de-Clermont   Chamandrin

• Corps

• Saint-Firmin   • L'Argentière-la-Bessée

Chauffayer

N. 539   • Montdauphin

N. 93   • Saint-Julien-en-Beauchêne

N. 93   N. 75   N. 85   N. 94   N. 202

cartes 24-25   REPRODUCTION INTERDITE

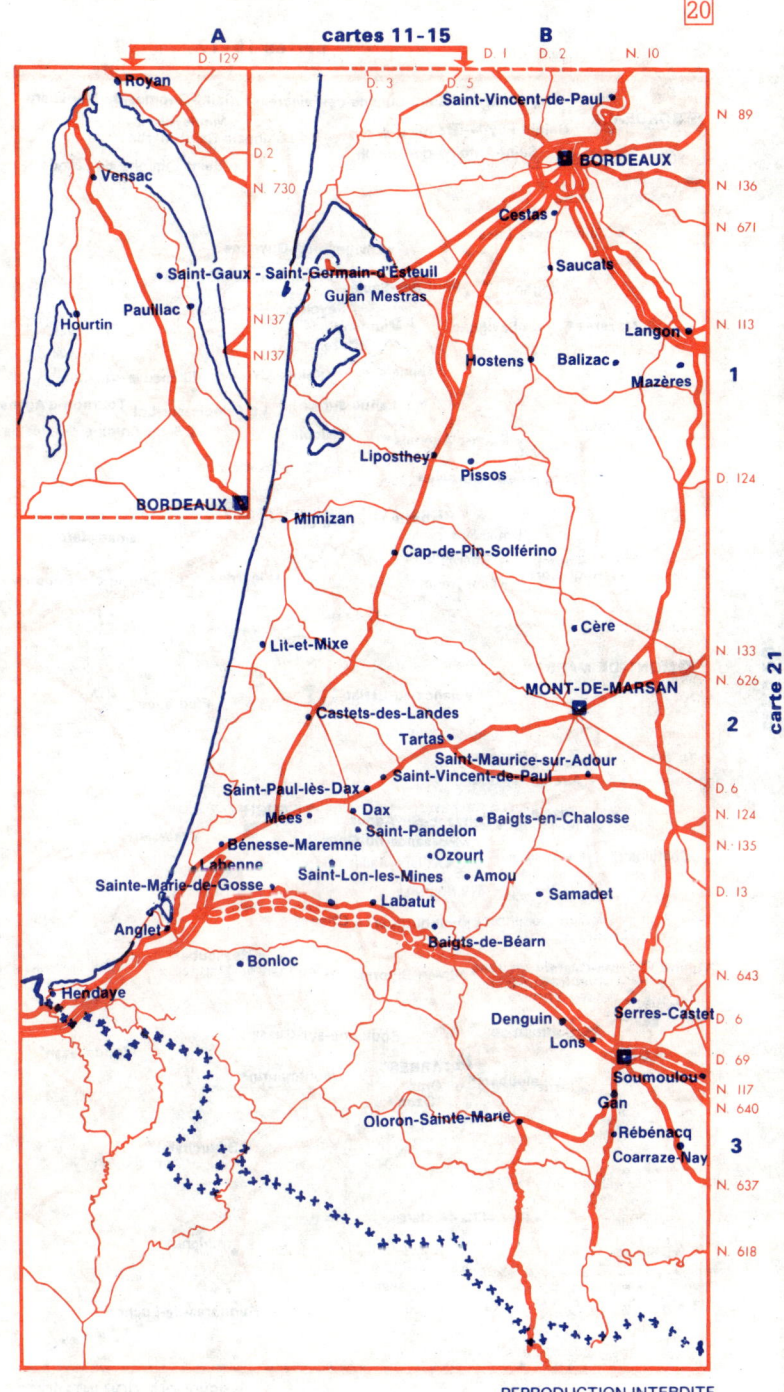

cartes 11-15

A

B

A
D. 129
• Royan
• Vensac
D. 2
N. 730
• Saint-Gaux - Saint-Germain-d'Esteuil
• Hourtin
Pauillac •
N 137
N 137
BORDEAUX

B
D. 1 D. 2 N. 10
D. 3 D. 5
Saint-Vincent-de-Paul •
N 89
BORDEAUX N 136
Cestas • N. 671
Saucats •
Langon • N 113
Hostens • Balizac •
Mazères • **1**
Liposthey • Pissos •
D. 124
Gujan Mestras
• Mimizan
• Cap-de-Pin-Solférino
• Lit-et-Mixe
Cère •
N. 133
MONT-DE-MARSAN N. 626
• Castets-des-Landes **2**
Tartas •
Saint-Maurice-sur-Adour •
Saint-Paul-lès-Dax • • Saint-Vincent-de-Paul
Mées • • Dax D. 6
Saint-Pandelon N. 124
Baigts-en-Chalosse •
Bénesse-Maremne • N. 135
Labenne • Ozourt
Sainte-Marie-de-Gosse • Saint-Lon-les-Mines • Amou D. 13
Labatut • Samadet •
Anglet •
Baigts-de-Béarn •
• Bonloc
N. 643
Hendaye •
Denguin • Serres-Castet • D. 6
Lons •
Soumoulou • D. 69
Gan • N. 117
Oloron-Sainte-Marie • N. 640
Rébénacq • **3**
Coarraze-Nay •
N. 637
N. 618

carte 21

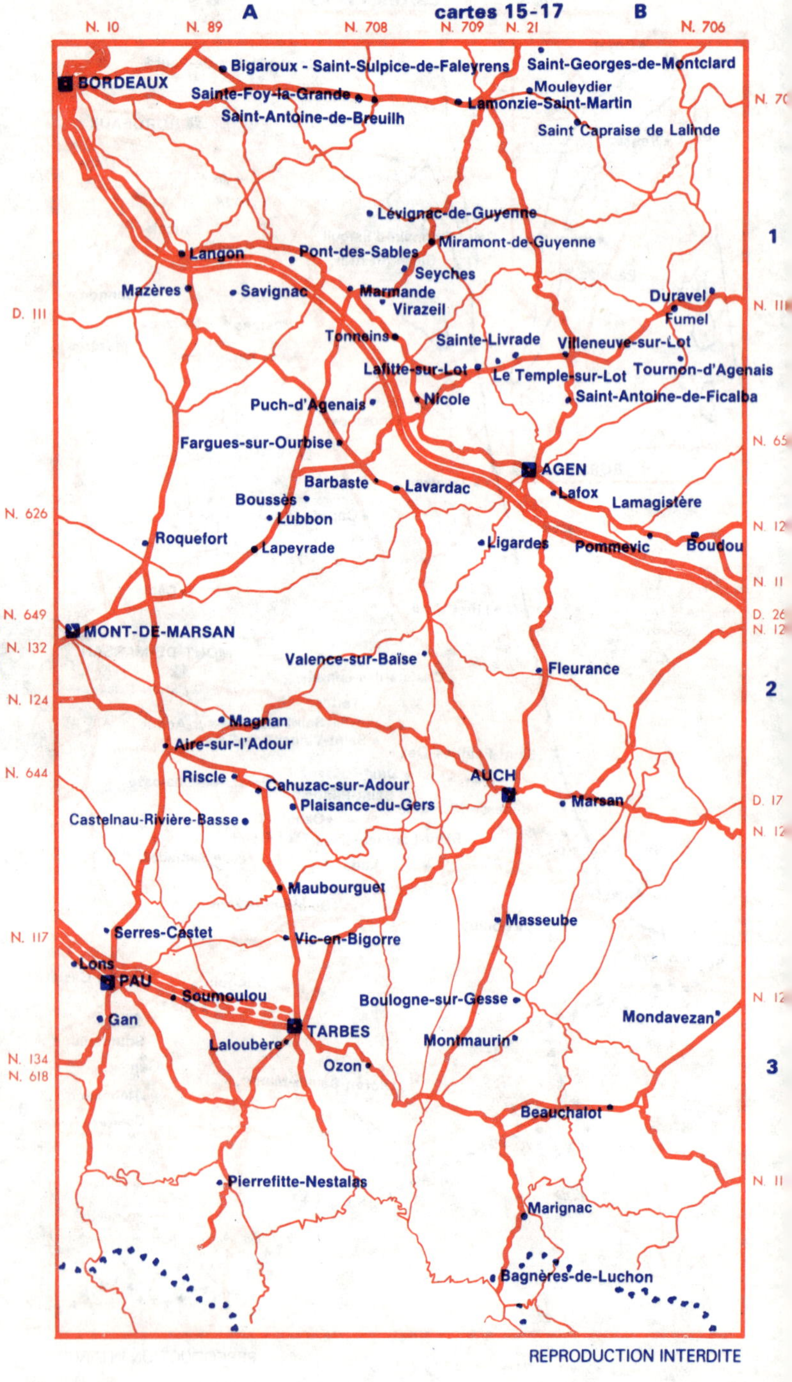

cartes 15-17

A   B

N. 10   N. 89   N. 708   N. 709   N. 21   N. 706

Bigaroux - Saint-Sulpice-de-Faleyrens

Saint-Georges-de-Montclard

BORDEAUX

Sainte-Foy-la-Grande

Mouleydier   N. 70

Lamonzie-Saint-Martin

Saint-Antoine-de-Breuilh

Saint Capraise de Lalinde

Lévignac-de-Guyenne   **1**

Langon   Pont-des-Sables   Miramont-de-Guyenne

Seyches

D. 111   Mazères   Savignac   Marmande   Duravel   N. 118

Virazeil   Fumel

Tonneins   Sainte-Livrade   Villeneuve-sur-Lot

Lafitte-sur-Lot   Le Temple-sur-Lot   Tournon-d'Agenais

Puch-d'Agenais   Nicole   Saint-Antoine-de-Ficalba

Fargues-sur-Ourbise   N. 65

AGEN

Barbaste   Lavardac   Lafox

Bousses   Lamagistère   N. 12

N. 626   Lubbon   Ligardes   Pommevic   Boudou

Roquefort   Lapeyrade   N. 11

N. 649   D. 26

N. 132   **MONT-DE-MARSAN**   N. 12

Valence-sur-Baïse   Fleurance   **2**

N. 124

Magnan

Aire-sur-l'Adour

N. 644   Riscle   Cahuzac-sur-Adour   **AUCH**   D. 17

Plaisance-du-Gers   Marsan   N. 12

Castelnau-Rivière-Basse

Maubourguet

N. 117   Serres-Castet   Masseube

Vic-en-Bigorre

Lons

PAU   Soumoulou   Boulogne-sur-Gesse   Mondavezan   N. 12

Gan   **TARBES**

Laloubère   Montmaurin

N. 134   Ozon   **3**
N. 618

Beauchalot

Pierrefitte-Nestalas   N. 11

Marignac

Bagnères-de-Luchon

carte 20

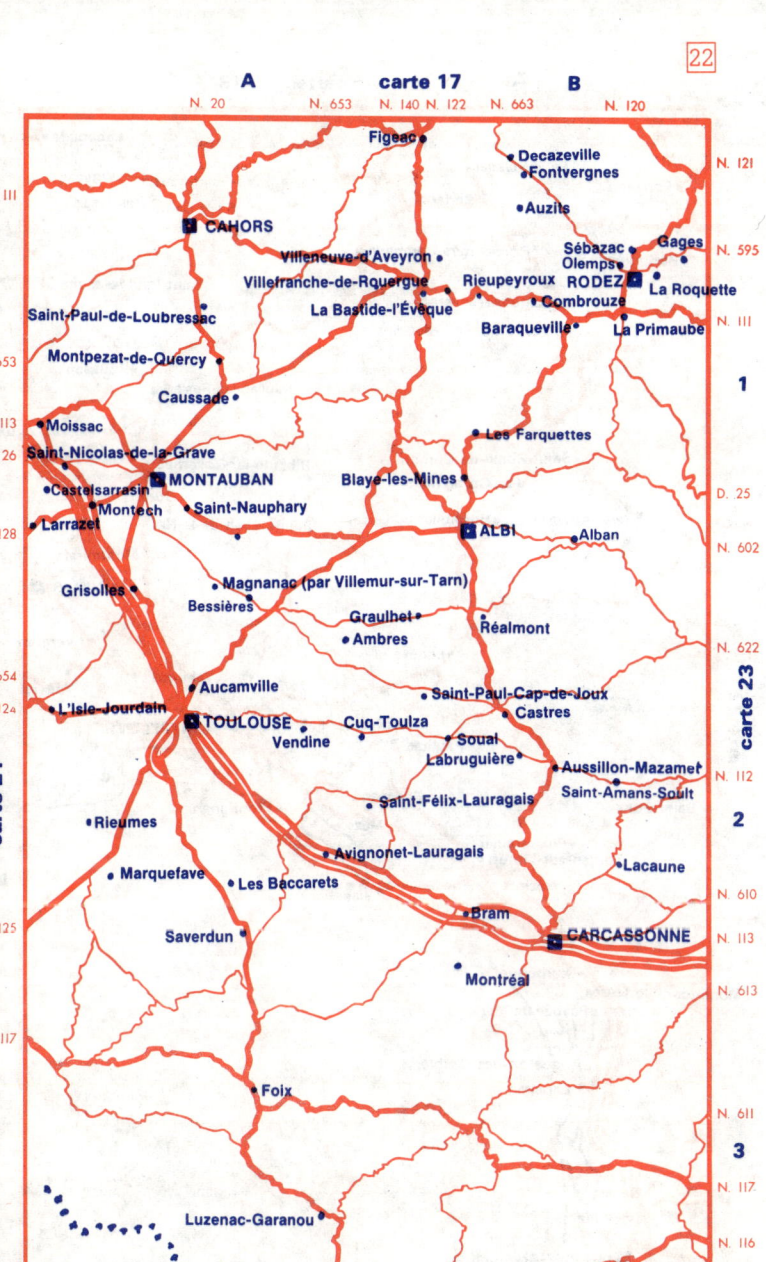

N. 20   N. 653   N. 140 N. 122   N. 663   N. 120

N. 111

N. 121

Figeac

Decazeville
Fontvergnes

Auzits

CAHORS

N. 595

Sébazac
Olemps   Gages

Villeneuve-d'Aveyron

Villefranche-de-Rouergue   Rieupeyroux   RODEZ   La Roquette

Combrouze

La Bastide-l'Évêque

Saint-Paul-de-Loubressac   N. 111

Baraqueville   La Primaube

Montpezat-de-Quercy

653

Caussade   1

Moissac

113

Les Farquettes

26   Saint-Nicolas-de-la-Grave

Castelsarrasin   MONTAUBAN   Blaye-les-Mines   D. 25

Montech   Saint-Nauphary

128   Larrazet   ALBI   N. 602

Alban

Grisolles   Magnanac (par Villemur-sur-Tarn)

Bessières

Graulhet   Réalmont

Ambres   N. 622

654   Aucamville

12a   L'Isle-Jourdain   Saint-Paul-Cap-de-Joux

TOULOUSE   Cuq-Toulza   Castres

Vendine   Soual

Labruguière   Aussillon-Mazamet   N. 112

Saint-Amans-Soult

Saint-Félix-Lauragais

Rieumes   2

Avignonet-Lauragais

Marquefave   Les Baccarets   Lacaune   N. 610

Saverdun   Bram   CARCASSONNE   N. 113

125

Montréal   N. 613

117

3

Foix   N. 611

N. 117

Luzenac-Garanou   N. 116

N. 612

N. 115

carte 21

carte 23

A   B

N. 121   N. 587   N. 9   N. 107   N. 88   N. 102

Labégude

N. 120   Espalion   Le Monastier   Vinezac
   Rosières

Barjac

N. 88
N. 595   Bertholène   Bonsecours-Campagnac   Saint-Paul-le-Jeune

N. 111   Lapanouse-Sévérac

   Rousson

Saint-Julien-les-Rosiers

D. 6
   Saint-Privat-des-Vieux

N. 602
D. 25   Saint-Rome-de-Cernon   Ribaute-les-Tavernes   Vézébobres
   La Cavalerie   Durfort
   Saint-Affrique   Hospitalet du Larzac   La Calmette
   Saint-Julien-de-la-Nef
   Montmirat

NÎMES

N. 622   Lodève   Vergèze

   Valergues   Vauvert

carte 22

   Montpellier-Fabrègues   MONTPELLIER
   Paulhan
D. 6
   Fabrègues

N. 112   Poussan   Frontignan
   Saint-Pons   Mèze
   Sète
   Puisserguier
   Boujan-sur-Libron
   Béziers   Vias

N. 610

N. 113   Narbonne
Montredon-Corbières
N. 613   Peyriac-de-Mer

   Roquefort-des-Corbières
   Lapalme

   Fitou

N. 611
N. 117

   Pia

N. 116
N. 612   PERPIGNAN

   Banyuls-dels-Aspres

N. 115

40

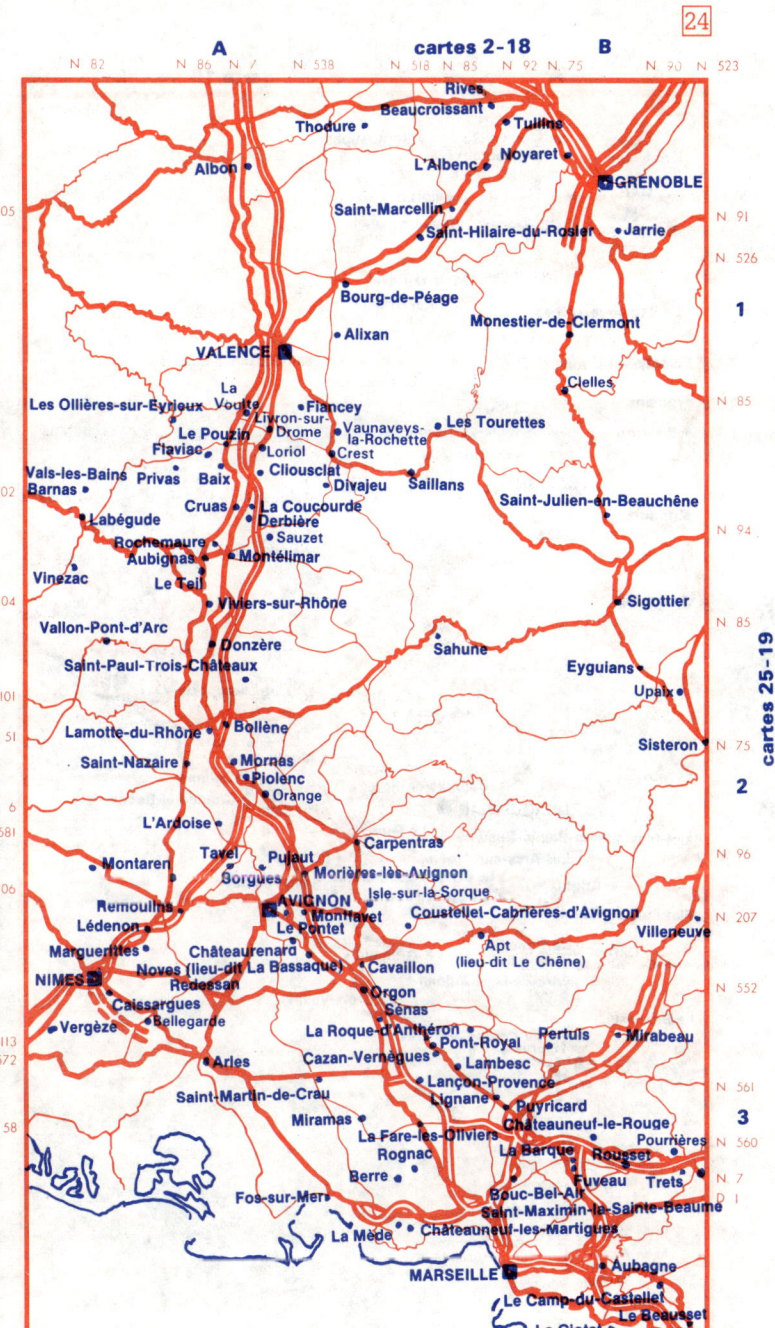

carte 24

Montdauphin

Châteauroux

GAP

Embrun

Chorges

N. 94

Méolans-Revel

Les Thuiles

La Saulce-les-Alpes

Valenty-Ventavon

Eygulans

N. 75

Sisteron

DIGNE

Montfort

Mézel

Puget-Théniers

Blausasc

Villeneuve

N. 96

N. 207

N. 552

Saint-Laurent-du-Var

NICE

N. 554

N. 561

Montauroux

Cannes

Bagnols-en-Forêt

Cannes-la-Bocca

DRAGUIGNAN

Saint-Maximim-la-Sainte-Beaume

Le Muy

N. 7

Les Arcs-sur-Argens

Fréjus

N. 560

Brignoles

Le Cannet-des-Maures

Saint-Raphaël

D. 1

Le Luc

Flassans-sur-Issole

Carnoules

Grimaud

Cogolin

La Croix-Valmer

N. 8

Le Beausset

Hyéres

N. 559

TOULON

La Seyne-sur-Mer

FRENCH DEPARTMENTS

Paris

Key to Departments of France

01	Ain
02	Aisne
03	Allier
04	Alpes-de-Haute-Provence
05	Hautes Alpes
06	Alpes Maritimes
07	Ardèche
08	Ardennes
09	Ariège
10	Aube
11	Aude
12	Aveyron
13	Bouches-du-Rhône
14	Calvados
15	Cantal
16	Charente
17	Charente-Maritime
18	Cher
19	Corrèze
2A	Corse-du-Sud
2B	Haute-Corse
21	Côte-d'Or
22	Côtes-du-Nord
23	Creuse
24	Dordogne
25	Doubs
26	Drôme
27	Eure
28	Eure-et-Loir
29	Finistère
30	Gard
31	Haute-Garonne
32	Gers

33	Gironde
34	Hérault
35	Ille-et-Vilaine
36	Indre
37	Indre-et-Loire
38	Isère
39	Jura
40	Landes
41	Loir-et-Cher
42	Loire
43	Haute-Loire
44	Loire-Atlantique
45	Loiret
46	Lot
47	Lot-et-Garonne
48	Lozère
49	Maine-et-Loire
50	Manche
51	Marne
52	Haute-Marne
53	Mayenne
54	Meurthe-et-Moselle
55	Meuse
56	Morbihan
57	Moselle
58	Nièvre
59	Nord
60	Oise
61	Orne
62	Pas-de-Calais
63	Puy-de-Dôme
64	Pyrénées-Atlantiques
65	Hautes-Pyrénées

66	Pyrénées-Orientales
67	Bas-Rhin
68	Haut-Rhin
69	Rhône
70	Haute-Saône
71	Saône-et-Loire
72	Sarthe
73	Savoie
74	Haute-Savoie
75	Paris
76	Seine-Maritime
77	Seine-et-Marne
78	Yvelines
79	Deux-Sèvres
80	Somme
81	Tarn
82	Tarn-et-Garonne
83	Var
84	Vaucluse
85	Vendée
86	Vienne
87	Haute-Vienne
88	Vosges
89	Yonne
90	Territoire-de-Belfort
91	Essonne
92	Hauts-de-Seine
93	Seine-St-Denis
94	Val-de-Marne
95	Val-d'Oise

MANCHE

OCEAN ATLANTIQUE

Cherbourg
LE HAVRE
ROUEN
Richev
Boulogne
Ca

Saint-Martin-des-Besaces
Bayeux
Caen
Vendeuvre
Nonant-le-P
Saint Pellerin
Coutances
Folligny
Moyon Vire
Saint-Pierre-Langers
Domfront
Marolles
Char
Mignière
Landivisiau
Lamballe
Saint-Brienc
Montauban-de-Bretagne
Brest
Sizun Dinan
Bédée
Saint-Symphorien-des-Monts
Cast
Pont-Aven
RENNES
La Guerche-de-Bretagne
Le Mans
Orléa
Elven
Redon
Landevant
Pontchâteau
Saint-Gildas-des-Bois
La L
(par Theil
Villedome
Suèvre
Sene
Saint-Brevin-les-Pins
NANTES
Jallais
Saumur
Vivy
La Trimouille
Poitiers
La C
La Rochelle
Limoges
Royan
Beynac-en-Perigord
Barbezieux-Saint
Roche-Chalais
Albussac
Saint-Martial-d'Artenset
Cénac-Saint-Julien
BORDEAUX
Sainte-Terre
Cénac-Saint-Julien
G
Langon
Pommevic
Saint-Paul-de-Loubre
Marmande
Mois
Cap-de-Pin
Bayonne
Biarritz
Sainte-Marie-de-Gosse
TOULOUSE

Casserole relais
Main town
Trunk road

Scale

0   100 km

Bastia
calvi
Ajaccio
Bonifacio

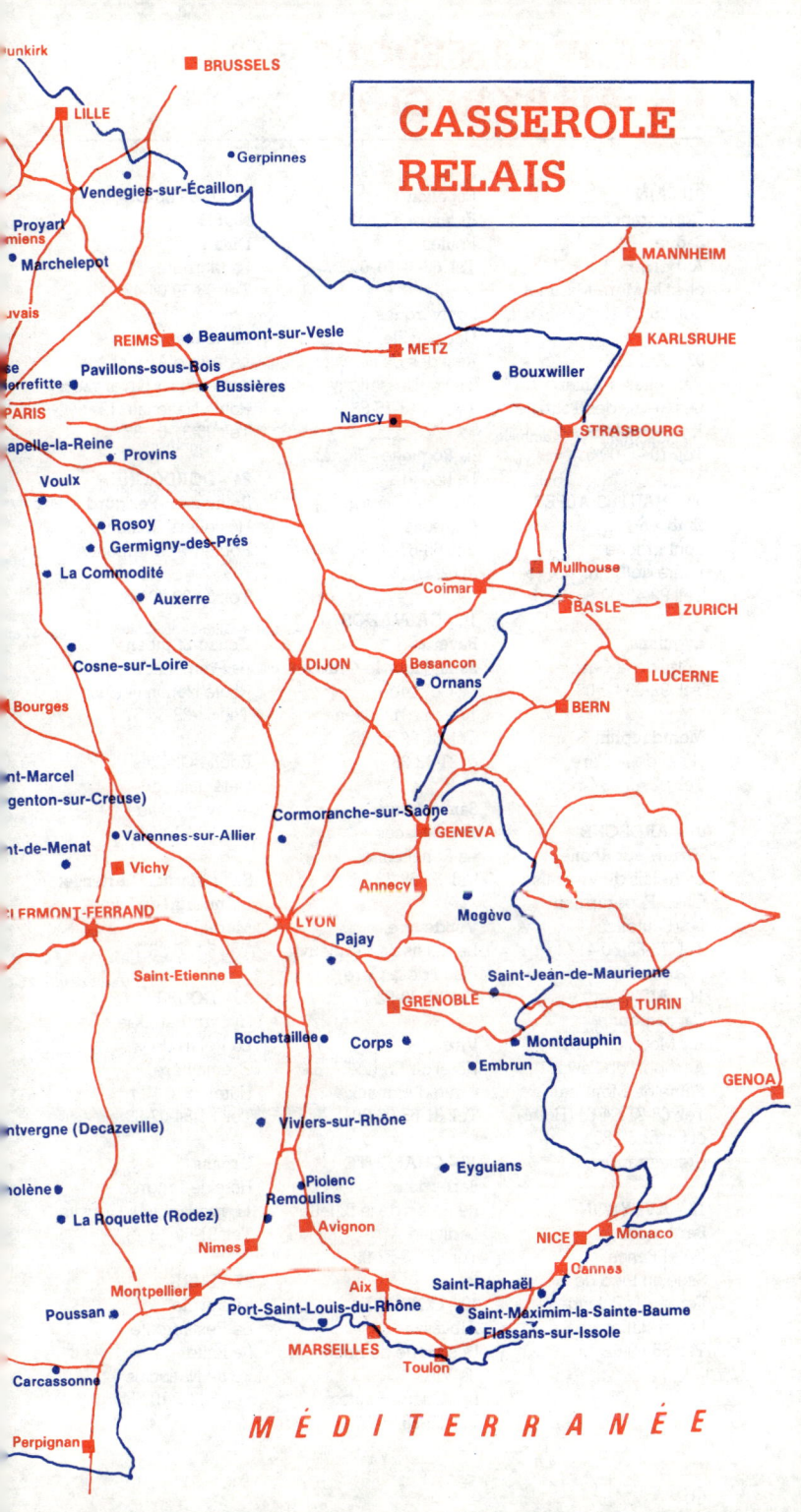

LIST OF CASSEROLE RELAIS BY REGION

01 – AIN
Cormoranche-s-Saône
Auberge
chez la Mère Martinet
Tel: 85-36-20-40

03 – ALLIER
Varennes-s-Allier
Les Relais des Touristes
1, rue des halles
Tel: 70-45-00-51

05 – HAUTES-ALPES
Embrun
Font Frache
Route de Briançon
Tel: 92-43-00-86

Eyguians
Hôtel de la Gare
Tel: 92-66-20-08

Montdauphin
Hôtel de la Gare
Tel: 92-45-03-08

07 – ARDÈCHE
Viviers sur Rhône
Le Relais du Vivarais
Chez-Espérardieu
Les Sautelles
Tel: 75-52-60-41

11 – AUDE
Carcassonne
Air Motel Salvaza
Aéroport de Salvaza
Route de Montréal
Tel: 68-71-64-64 (Hôtel)
et 68-72-52-89
(Restaurant)

12 – AVEYRON
Bertholène
Hôtel Bancarel
Situé au Pied de la
Forêt des Palanges
Route Nationale 88
Tel: 65-69-62-10

Espalion
Relais des Quatre
Routes
Tel: 65-44-01-69

Fontvergnes-Decazeville
Rest des Usines
23, Fg. Desseligny
Tel: 65-43-15-88

La Roquette – Rodez
La Rocade
Anet-le-Château-
4 Saisons
Tel: 65-67-10-44
et 67-17-12

14 – CALVADOS
**Bayeux –
Saint-Vigor-le-Grand**
La Colombe
13, route de Caen
Tel: 31-92-13-65
et 21-12-28

Saint-Martin-des-Besaces
La Renaissance
Tel: 31-68-72-65

Vendeuvre
Le Relais de Vendeuvre
Place de la Gare
Tel: 31-40-92-77

Vire
Hôtel de France
4, rue d'Aignaux
Tel: 31-68-00-35

16 – CHARENTE
Barbezieux
Le Relais de la Billette
Ladiville
Tel: 45-78-57-09

19 – CORRÈZE
Albussac
Hostelerie de Roche
de Vie
Les Quatre Routes
Tel: 55-28-15-87

22 – COTES-DU-NORD
Dinan
La Marmite
Tel: 96-39-04-42

Lamballe
La Tour d'Argent
2, rue du Dr Lavergne
Route Nationale 12
Tel: 96-31-01-37

24 – DORDOGNE
Beynac-en-Périgord
Hôstellerie Maleville
Route Départementale
703
Tel: 53-29-50-06

Cenac-St-Julien
La Promenade
Route Nationale 703
Tel: 53-28-36-87

Roche-Chalais
Café du Midi
32, av. du Stade
Tel: 53-91-43-65

Saint-Martial D'Artenset
L'Auberge de Saint-Martial
Tel: 53-80-35-74

25 – DOUBS
Hyèvre-Paroisse
Le Relais de la
Crémaillère
Hôtel Riss
Tel: 81-84-07-88

Ornans
Hôtel le Progrès
11, rue Jacques-Gervais
Tel: 81-62-16-79

27 – EURE
Richeville
Le Restauroute
Le Balto
Route Nationale 14
Tel: 32-27-10-55

28 – EURE-ET-LOIR
Chartres-Mignières
Le Relais Beauceron
Situé à l'embouchure de
l'autoroute de Chartres
et de la RN 10
Tel: 37-26-46-21

Marolles
Au Relais de Marolles
44 rue Georges Bréant
Route Nationale 12
Tel: 37-43-20-50

Mignières
Le Relais Beauceron
Situated at junction of
Chartres autoroute
and the RN10
Tel: 37-26-46-21

29 –FINISTRÈRE
Cast
Le Relais Saint-Gildas
11 et 13, rue de Kreisker
Tel: 98-73-54-76
ou 73-55-43

Landivisiau
Le Terminus
94, Av. Foch
Tel: 98-68-02-00

Pont-Aven
Chez Mélanie et
Monique
Lieu-dit Croissant-Kogoz
Tel: 98-06-03-09

Sizun
Hôtel des Voyageurs
2, rue de l'Argoat
Tel: 98-68-80-35

30 – GARD
Remoulins
Auberge Les Platanes –
Castillon-du-Gard
Les Croisées
Tel: 66-37-10-69

33 – GIRONDE
Langon
Hôtel Restaurant
Darlot
10, rue Dotézac
Tel: 56-63-01-36

Sainte-Terre
Rest. chez Régis
Av. Du Général de Gaulle
Tel: 57-47-16-21

34 – HÉRAULT
Poussan
Le Chalet
Chez Castor 05
La Moulière - RN 113
Tel: 67-78-33-29

35 – ILLE-ET-VILAINE
Bédée
Hôtel du Commerce
14, place de l'Église
Tel: 99-07-00-37
et 07-00-76

La Guerche-de-Bretagne
Relais du Pont
d'Anjou
11, Faubourg d'Anjou
Tel: 99-96-23-10

Montauban-de-Bretagne
L'Hôtel de France
34, av. du Gl-de-
Gaulle
Tel: 99-06-40-19

Sel de Bretagne
La Taverne Bretonne
Bourg de Saulnières
Tel: 00 44-70-01

36 – INDRE
Argenton-sur-Creuse
Lieu-di Saint-Marcel
Le Relais de Routiers
7, route de
Châteauroux
Tel: 54-24-01-77

Châtre (La)
SARL du Lion d'Argent
2, av. du Lion d'Argent
Tel: 54-48-11-69

37 – INDRE-ET-LOIRE
Villedomer
Le Relais des grands
vins de Touraine –
La Grande Vallée
Route Nationale 10
Tel: 47-55-01-05

38 – ISÈRE
Corps
Hôtel du Tilleul
Rue des Fossés
La Salette
Tel: 76-30-00-43

Pajay
Ma Petite Auberge
La Côte Saint-Audré
Tel: 74-54-26-06

Rochetaillée
Hôtel Belledonne
Route Nationale 91
Tel: 76-80-07-04

40 – LANDES
Cap de Pin
Au Routier
Route Nationale 10
Tel: 58-07-20-54

Sainte-Marie-de-Gosse
Les Routiers
Route Nationale 117
Tel: 59-56-32-02
et 56-34-17

41 – LOIR-ET-CHER
La Loge par Theillay
Relais de la Loge
Route Nationale 20
Tel: 54-83-37-20

Suèvres
La Providence
Chez Jacques
1, Place de la Mairie
Tel: 54-87-80-88

44 – LOIRE-ATLANTIQUE
Pontchâteau
Auberge du Calvaire
6, route de la Brière
Lieu-dit Le Calvaire
Tel: 40-01-61-65

Pontchâteau
Le Relais de Beaulieu
Tel: 40-01-60-58
et 01-63-58

Saint-Brévin-les-Pins
Le Relais du Marche
Place Henri-Basle
Tel: 40 27-22-21

**Saint-Gildas-
des-Bois**
Le Relais des Routiers
27, rue du Pont
Tel: 40-01-42-15
et 01-44-70

**45 – LOIRET
Commodité (La)
(par Solterre)**
Auberge de la Route
Bleue - RN 7
Tel: 38-94-90-04

Germigny-des-Prés
Hôtel de la Place
Le Bourg
Châteauneuf-sur-Loire
Tel: 38-58-20-14

**46 – LOT
Gramat**
Le Relais du Centre
(S.A.)
Place de la
République
Tel: 65-38-73-37

**Saint-Paul-de-
Loubressac**
Le Relais de la
Madeleine
Tel: 62-21-98-08

**47 – LOT-
ET GARONNE
Marmande**
Le Relais du Lion d'Or
1, rue de la République
Tel: 53-64-21-30

**49 – MAINE-ET-
LOIRE
Jallais**
Le Relais de la Croix-
Verte
Hôtel du Vert Galant
1, rue Jean-de-
Sagmond
Tel: 41-64-10-12
et 64-20-22

Saumur
Hôtel de la Gare
16, av. David-
d'Angers
Tel: 41-67-34-24

Vivy
Le Relais Saint-Paul
30, Rue Nationale
Tel: 41-52-50-13
et 52-51-65

**50 – MANCHE
Coutances**
Le Relais du Viaduc
25, avenue de Verdun
Tel: 33-45-02-68

Folligny
Le Lion d'Or
Lieu-dit - Le Repas
Tel: 33-61-32-77

Moyon
Le SuperRoutiers
Carrefour Paris
Départementale 999
Tel: 33-05-59-74

Saint-Pellerin
Auberge de la
Fourchette
Carantan
Tel: 33-42-16-56

Saint-Pierre-Langers
A la Grillade
La Havaudière
Tel: 33-48-83-71

**Saint-Symporien-
des-Monts Lapenty**
Le Relais
du Bois Léger
Tel: 33-49-01-43

**51 – MARNE
Beaumont sur-Vesle**
La maison du
Champagne
2, rue du Port - RN 44
Tel: 26-03-92-45

**54 – MEURTHE-
ET-MOSELLE
Nancy**
Le Relais du Port
Chez Claude
5, rue Henri-Bazin
Tel: 83-35-49-85

**56 – MORBIHAN
Elven**
Le Relais de l'Argouët
36, rue de l'Argouët
Tel: 97-53-32-98

Landevant
Le Pelican
14, Route Nationale 165
Tel: 97-56-93-12

Sene
Le Poulfanc
Route de Vannes
Route Nationale 165
Tel: 97-47-47-97

**58 – NIÈVRE
Cosne-sur-Loire**
Les Trois Couleurs
21, rue Saint-Agnan
Tel: 86-28-23-50

**59 – NORD
Vendegies s/Écaillon**
Relais des Belles Filles
1111 Rte de Solesmes
Tel: 27-27-12-47

**61 – ORNE
Domfront**
Le Relais St-
Michael
5, rue du Mont-
Saint-Michel
Place de La Gare
Route Nationale 176
Tel: 33-38-64-99

Nonant-le-Pin
Le Relais des Haras
Grande-Rue
Tel: 33-39-93-35

**63 – PUY-DE-DOME
Pont-de-Menat**
Chez Roger
Tel: 73-85-50-17

**67 – BAS-RHIN
Bouxwiller**
Le Soleil
71, Grande-Rue
Tel: 88-70-70-06

**73 – SAVOIE
St-Jean-
de-Maurienne**
Restaurant du Relais R
Pl. du Champ-de-Foire
66 rue Louis Sibué
Tel: 79-64-12-03

74 – HAUTE-SAVOIE
Mégève
Le Chalet des Fleurs
Rte Sallanches
Pont d'Arbon
Tel: 50-21-21-46

77 – SEINE-ET-MARNE
Bussières
Au Sans-Gêne
32, rue de la Ferte-sous-Jouarre
Route Nationale 33
Tel: 60-22-50-18

Chapelle-la-Reine (La)
Le Relais
de la Salamandre
5, rue du Dr Battesti
Tel: 64-24-30-03

Provins
La Cure d'Air
54, av. du Gl-de-Gaulle
Tel: 64-00-03-21

Voulx
La Bruyère
72, Grande-Rue
Tel: 64-31-92-41

80 – SOMME
Marchelepot
Restaurant oriental
Chez Dahmane
Route Nationale 17
Tel: 22-84-04-85

Proyart
La Raperie
Tel: 22-85-37-30

82 – TARN-ET-GARONNE
Moissac
Le Relais Auvergnat
31, bd. Camille-Delthil
Place du Palais
Tel: 63-04-93-02
et 63-04-02-58

Pommevic
A La Bonne Auberge
Route Nationale
Tel: 63-39-56-69

83 – VAR
Flassans-sur-Issole
La Nocturne
Quartier de la Bourette
Nationale 7
Tel: 94-69-71-33

Saint-Maximin-La-Seine-Balime
Le Relais du Carillon
5, rue de la République
Tel: 94-78-00-38

St. Raphael
Relais Bel-Azur
247, Bld. de Provence
Tel: 94-95-14-08

84 – VAUCLUSE
Piolenc
Bar Restaurant
Le Commerce
Place Cours Coursin
Tel: 90-37-60-14

86 – VIENNE
Trimouille
Auberge Fleurie
Rue Octave-Bernard
Tel: 49-91-60-64

89 – YONNE
Auxerre
Le Saint-Nitasse
Route de Lyon-Auxerre
Tel: 86-46-95-07

Rosoy
La Maison Blanche
Route Nationale 6
Tel: 86-97-13-01

93 – SEINE-SAINT-DENIS
Pierrefitte
Le Normandie
105, av. Gallieni
Tel: 48-26-55-62

95 – VAL D'OISE
Pontoise
Restaurant de la Poste
68, rue Pierre Butin
Tel: 30-32-47-72

Calais

Boulogne

Cherbourg

LE HAVRE   ROUEN

Cagny   Bosguérard
Villers-sur-Mer   de-Marcouv
Caen
Coutances   Saint-Martin-des-Besaces
Vire
Montmartin-sur-Mer
Saint-Hilaire-du-Harcouet   Mortagne-au-Pere
Saint-Agathon   Saint-Symphorien-des-Monts
Brest   Sizun   Lamballe   Fougères   Domfront
Saint-Brienc   Gorron   Chartres
Montauban-de-Bretagne   Bédée   Saint-Berthevin-lès-Laval   Ymonv
Loudeac   RENNES   La Loge   Orleans
Cast   Elven   Joué-en-Charnie   Le Mans   La Belle-Inutile
Saint-Évarzec   Pipriac   Ouzouer-le-March
Lanester   Vannes   Redon   Le Grand-Fougeray   Romorantin
Séné   Pontchâteau   Besse-sur-Braye
Villiers-au-Bouin
Saint-Brevin-les-Pins   NANTES   Vivy
Saint-Philbert-de-Bouaine   Jallais   Saumur
Les Herbiers   Ardelay-les-Herbiers
Venansault   La Châtre
La Roche-sur-Yon   Poitiers   Châtea
Chaunay
Moulismes

O C E A N

La Rochelle
Saint-Georges-d'Oleron
Champagne-Mouton
Sauviat-sur-Vige

A T L A N T I Q U E   Saujon   Limoges
Royan
Beynac-en-Périgord

• Tourist hotels
■ Main town   Cartelègue   Albu
Trunk road
Gr
BORDEAUX   Saint-Vincent-de-Paul
Scale   Rouffillac-de-Carlux
Tournon-   Cahors
0   100 km   d'Agenais   Saint-   Rieupe
Lévignac-de-Guyenne   Paul-de-Loub
Miremont de Guyenne   Cau
Sainte-Livrade
Montpezat-de-Quercy
Lafox • Moissac
Castelsarrasin
Bénesse-Maremne   Ambres
Saint-Lon-les-Mines   Aire-sur-l'Adour
Bayonne   Riscle   Auch   TOULO
Biarritz   Sainte-Marie-de-Gosse
Denguin   Marquefave
Pau   Tarbes
Gan   Laloubère
Oloron-Sainte-Marie   Marignac
Bagnères-de-Luchon

Bastia
calvi
Ajaccio
Bonifacio

TOURIST HOTELS

Dunkirk
Bailleul
BRUSSELS
LILLE
ruay-en-Artois Fumay
Amiens
eauvais
Knutange
REIMS Beaumont-sur-Vesle
Chaussee-de-Damery
METZ
Rohrbach-les-Bitche
Bouxwiller
PARIS
Ancerville Keskastel
Nancy Gambsheim
KARLSRUHE
MANNHEIM
théry Corbeil-Essonne
Chamarande
rtenay
Souligny
Doulaincourt
Kogenheim STRASBOURG
Saint-Pierremont
Plomieres-les-Bains
Sainte-Marguerite
Bellegarde
Arce
Auxerre
Corbenay Kruth
Ronchamps Mullhouse
Cosne-sur-Loire
Hyèvre-Paroisse
BASLE ZURICH
Bourges
DIJON Besancon
Chenove Ornans
Nuits-Saint-Georges
LUCERNE
Nérondes
Ivry-en-Montagne Nolay Mercury
Varenne-le-Grand
BERN
Lapalisse
Cormoranche-sur-Saône
Jayat Sciez
Clairvaux-les-Lacs GENEVA
Cluses
Vichy
Seynod Meythet
Chaux-Dalmont Annecy
Albens Thones
CLERMONT-FERRAND
LYON Décines
Bonson
Veyrins-Thuellin Doussard
Megève
Aiguebelle
arsac-en-Livradois
Saint-Etienne
Saint-Sigolene
Monlet (près d'Allègre) Vieille-Brioude
GRENOBLE
Corps
TURIN
riac Fraisse-Haut
Le Pouzin
Rochetaillée (par le Bourg-d'Oisans
Boussoulet
Saint-Firmin
Le Puy-en-Velay
Langogne
Félines
Viviers-sur-Rhone
Montdauphin
GENOA
Chateauroux Embrun
Rosières
Chorges
Marvejols
palion Le Monastier
ages Bertholène Balsièges
Alixan
Sahune La Saulce-les-Alpes
a Roquette
Olemps Saint-Nazaire
Le Lauzet
aqueville Saint-Jullen-de-la-Nef Remoulins
Eyguians
Bollène
Montauroux
L Hospitalet Avignon
du Larzac Nimes Montfavet
Mézel
NICE
Saint-Pons
Pont-Royal
Fréjus Cannes
Cuq-Toulza Montpellier
Rognac Aix Saint-Maximim-la-Sainte-Baume
Saint-Raphaël
Labruguière
Les Arcs-sur-Argens
arcassone Narbonne
Fos-sur-Mer MARSEILLES
Toulon
Fitou
Perpignan

MÉDITERRANÉE

LIST OF TOURIST HOTELS BY REGION

01 – AIN
**Cormoranche-s-
Saône**
Auberge Chez le Mère
Martinet
★★NN
Le Bourg
Tel: 85-36-20-40

Jayat
Le Relais de Jayat
★NN
Montrevel-en-Bresse
Tel: 74-30-84-69

03 – ALLIER
Lapalisse
Le Chapon Doré
★NN
Avenue du 8 Mai 1945
Route Nationale 7
Tel: 70-99-09-51

**04 – ALPES DE
HAUTE-PROVENCE**
Mezel
Le Relais de la Place
★NN
Tel: 92-35-51-05

05 – HAUTES-ALPES
Châteauroux
Hôtel Dauphinois
L'Assiette
Gourmande
★NN
rue Centrale
Tel: 92-43-22-01

Chorges
Le Relais des Alpes
★NN
Route Nationale 94
Tel: 92-50-60-08

Embrun
Pont Frache
★NN
Route de Briançon
Tel: 92-43-00-86

Eyguians
Le Relais de la Gare
★NN
Tel: 92-66-20-08

Mont-Dauphn
Hôtel de la Gare
★NN
Tel: 92-45-03-08

La Saulce-les-Alpes
Le Relais de France
★NN
Tel: 92-54-20-08

Saint-Firmin
Le Relais
de la Trinité
★NN
Tel: 92-55-21-64

07 – ARDÈCHE
Felines
Relais de la Remise
★NN
Route Nationale 82
Tel: 75-34-82-22

Le Pouzin
Les Routiers
★NN
64, rue Olivier de
Serres
Tel: 75-63-83-45

Rosières
Les Cévennes
★NN
CD 104
Tel: 75-39-52-07

Vivieres Sur Rhône
Le Relais du Vivarais
Chez Esperandieu
★NN
Rte Nle 86
Lieu-dit les Sautelles
Tel: 75-52-60-41

08 – ARDENNES
Fumay
Le Relais du Lion
★NN
41, Rue de la Gare
Tel: 24-41-10-27

10– AUBE
Souligny par Bouilly
Le Relais de Montaigu
★NN
30, rue aux Fèbres
Tel: 25-40-20-20

11 – AUDE
Carcassone
Air Motel Salvaza
★★NN
Aéroport de Salvaza
Route de Montréal
Tel: 68-71-64-84
(Hôtel)
et 68-72-52-89
(Restaurant)

Fitou
Le Relais Le Parador
★NN
Cabanne de Fitou
Tel: 68-45-79-11

Narbonne
Le Relais des Deux-
Mers
★NN
Route de la Nautique
Croix-du-Sud
de Narbonne
Tel: 68-41-00-21

12 –AVEYRON
Baraqueville
Le Relais Palous
★N
Tel: 65-69-01-89

Bertholène
Hôtel Bancarel
★NN
Tel: 65-69-62-10

Espalion
Le Relais de Quatre
★NN
Tel: 65-44-01-69

Gages
Relais de la Plaine
★NN
Tel: 65-42-29-03

Hospitalet du Larzac (L')
Relais Espace
  62★NN
Route Nationale 9
Aérodrome Millau-Larzac
Tel: 65-62-76-22

Olemps
Relais du Pas
★NN
Le Pas Druelle
Tel: 65-69-39-11

Rieupeyroux
Ches Pascal
★NN
Rue de l'Hom - RD 205
Tel: 65-65-51-13

Roquette par Rodez
Le Relais de la Rocade
★NN
Tel: 65-67-10-44
ct 67 17-12

13 – BOUCHES-DU-RHONE
Fos-sur-Mer
Ma Campagne
★NN
42, avenue Jean-Jaurès
Tel: 42-05-01-66
et 42-05-00-11

Marseille
Beaulieu Glaris
★NN
1/3 place
des Marseillaises
Tel: 01 00 70-50

Pont-Royal
Le Relais Provençal
★NN
Tel: 90-57-40-64

Rognac
Cade Roussel
★★NN
Tel: 42-87-00-33

14 – CALVADOS
Cagny
Hôtel des Routiers
★NN
22, Route de Paris
Tel: 31-23-41-27

Saint-Martin-des-Besaces
La Renaissance
★NN
Tel: 31-68-72-65

Villiers-sur-Mer
Le Normand
★NN
44, Re de Maréchal Foch
Tel: 31-87-04-23

Vire
Hôtel de France
★★NN
4, rue d'Aignaux
Tel: 31-68-00-35

15 – CANTAL
Fraisse-Haut
Hôtel des Cimes
★NN
Tel: 71-20-07-42

Mauriac
Les Routers
★NN
27, rue St-Mary
Tel: 71-68-00-79

16 – CHARENTE
Champagne-Mouton
Le Relais de Plaisance
★NN
Tel: 45-31-80-52
et 31-98-19

17 – CHARENTE-MARITIME
Saujon
Hôtel de la Gare
★NN
2 Rue Clemenceau
Tel: 46-02-80-33

Sainte-georges d'Oléron
Relais de la Petite Plage
★NN
Route de l'Océan
Domino
Tel: 46-76-52-28

18 – CHER
Nérondes
Le Lion d'Or
★NN
Place de la Mairie
Tel: 48-74-87-81

19 – CORRÈZE
Albussac
Aux Quatre-Routes
★★NN
L'Hostellerie de la Roche du Vic
Tel: 55-28-15-87

21 – COTE-D'OR
Chenove
Au Bon Coin
★NN
54, Route de Dijon
Tel: 80-52-58-17

Nolay
Hôtel du Chevreuil
★★NN
Place de l'Hôtel-de-Ville
CD 973
Tel: 80-21-71-89

Nuits-Saint-Georges
Les Cultivateurs
★★NN
12, rue du Général de Gaulle
Tel: 80-61-10-41

22 – COTES-DU-NORD
Lamballe
La Tour d'Argent
★★NN
2, rue du Dr Lavergne
Tel: 96-31-01-37

Loudéac
Hôtel Les Routiers
7 rue Lavergne
Tel: 96-28-01-44

Saint-Agathon
Hôtel Bellevue
★NN
Bel-Orme RN 12
Tel: 96-43-80-53

Saint-Breiuc
Le-Beaufeuillage
★NN
2, rue de Paris
Tel: 96-33-09-16

24 – DORDOGNE
Beynac-en-Périgord
Hôstellerie Maleville
★★NN
RD 703
Tel: 53-29-50-06

Rouffillac-de-Carlux
Aux Poissons Frais
★★NN
Tel: 53-29-70-24

25 – DOUBS
Hyèvre-Paroisse
Le Relais de la
Crémaillère
Hôtel Ziss
★★★NN
Tel: 81-84-07-88

Ornans
Hôtel le Progrès
★NN
11, rue Jacques-
Gervais
Tel: 81-62-16-79

26 – DROME
Alixan
Alpes Provence
★★NN
Route Nationale 532
Tel: 75-47-02-84

Sahune
Le Relais Dauphine-
Provence
★NN
Tel: 75-27-40-99

27 – EURE
Bosguérard-de-
Marcouville
La Tête d'Or
★NN
Route de Lisieux
RN 138
Tel: 35-87-60-24

28 – EURE-ET-LOIR
Chartres
Le Relais Beauceron
Mignières
★★NN
est situé à
l'embouchure
de l'autoroute de
Chartres et de
la RN 10
Tel: 37-26-46-21

Ymonville
Le Relais de l'Étoile
★NN
31, rue du Haut-Chemin
Tel: 37-32-25-67

29 – FINISTÈRE
Cast
Le Relais Saint-Gildas
★NN
11 et 13 rue Kreisker
Tel: 98-73-54-76
et 73-55-43

Sizun
Hôtel des Voyageurs
★NN
2, rue de l'Argoat
Tel: 98-68-80-35

Saint-Évarzec
Au Bon Repos
★NN
Poullogoden
Tel: 38-56-20-09

30 – GARD
Saint-Julien-de-
La-Nef
Auberge de la
Cascade d'Aigues
Folles
Sarl 6
★★NN
Entre Ganges et
Le Sumene
Tel: 67-82-42-78

Saint-Nazaire
Les Terailles
★NN
Route Nationale 86
Tel: 66-89-66-14

Remoulins
Auberge des Platanes
★NN
Castillon du Gard
des Croisées
Tel: 66-37-10-69

31 – HAUTE-
GARONNE
Bagnères-de-Luchon
L'Escapade
★NN
27, av. Jean-Jaurès
Tel: 61-79-01-85

Bessières
Le Bessiérain
★NN
Avenue de Montauban
Tel: 61-84-00-95

Marignac
Le Pic du Gar
★NN
Rue Jean Jaurès
Tel: 61-79-50-57

Marquefave
Chez Roger
★NN
RN 117
Tel: 61-87-85-07

32 – GERS
Auch
Modern Hôtel
★NN
10 bis, avenue
Pierre
Mendis France
Tel: 62-05-03-47

Riscle
Le Relais de
l'Auberge
★NN
Place de la Mairie
Tel: 62-69-70-49

33 – GIRONDE
Cartelègue
L'Escale
⋆NN
Tel: 56-42-71-18

**Saint-Vincent-
de-Paul**
Chez Anatole
⋆NN
Route Nationale 10
Ambarès
Tel: 56-38-95-11

34 – HÉRAULT
Saint-Pons
Le Somail
⋆NN
2, avenue de Castre
Tel: 67-97-00-12

**35 – ILE-ET-
VILLAINE**
Bedee
Hôtel du Commerce
⋆NN
14, place de l'Eglise
Tel: 99-07-00-37
and 07-00-76

Fougères
Aux Amis de la Route
⋆NN
6. Bd. St-Germain
Tel: 99-99-07-62

Le Grand-Fougeray
Relais de la Belle
Ètoile – La Belle Étoile
⋆NN
Tel: 99-08-42-59

**Montauban-de-
Bretagne**
Le Relais de France
⋆⋆NN
34, av. du Gl-de-
Gaulle
Tel: 99-06-40-19

**Montauban-de-
Bretagne**
Relais de la
Hucherais
⋆⋆NN
Tel: 99-06-40-29
et 06-54-31

Pipric
Hôtel de la Tour
d'Auvergne
⋆NN
7, rue de l'Avenir
Tel: 99-34-41-34

Redon
Le Relais
⋆NN
Route de Rennes
Tel: 99-71-46-54

36 – INDRE
Châteauroux
La Rallye
⋆NN
9, rue Bourdillon
Tel: 54-34-37-41

La Châtre
SARL du Lion
d'Argent
⋆⋆NN
2, av. du Lion-
d'Argent
Tel: 54-48-15-67
et 49-11-69

**37 – INDRE-ET-
LOIRE**
Tours
Le Relais de Sainte
Radegonde
⋆NN
178, quai Paul Bert
Tel: 47-51-28-45

Villiers-au-Bouin
Le Grand Cerf
⋆⋆NN
La Porrerie
Tel: 47-24-11-06

38 – ISÉRE
Corps
Le Relais des Tilleuls
⋆NN
Rue des Fossés
Tel: 76-30-00-43

**Rochetaillee, par Le
Bourge-d'Oisans**
Le Relais de
Belledonne
⋆NN
Tel: 76-80-07-04

Veyrins Thuellin
La Bonne Auberge
⋆NN
15, Grande-Rue
Tel: 74-33-94-27

39 – JURA
Clairvaux-les-Lacs
L'Hôtels de l'Horloge
⋆NN
15, Grande Rue
Tel: 84-48-30-09

40 – LANDES
Aire-sur-l'Adour
Les Routiers
Chez Pierrett
⋆NN
15, rue du 4-
Septembre
Tel: 58-71-63-01

Benesse-Marenne
Hôtel des Pins
⋆NN
Tel: 58-72-56-41
et 72-50-80

Saint-Lon-les-Mines
Hôtel du Fronton
⋆NN
Au Bourg
Tel: 58-57-80-45

**Sainte-Marie-
de-Gosse**
Les Routiers
⋆NN
Route Nationale 117
Tel: 59-56-32-02

41 – LOIRE-ET-CHER
La Loge
Le Relais de la Loge
⋆NN
Theillay
Tel: 54-83-37-20

Ouzourer-le-Marché
(rattaché Tourisme)
La Halte Beauceronne
18, Place de l'Eglise
Tel: 54-82-41-26

Romorantin
Les Aubiers
⋆NN
1, avenue de Blois
Tel: 54-76-05-59

42 – LOIRE
Bonson
Le Relais des Sports
★NN
14, avenue St Rambert
Tel: 77-55-20-12

43 – HAUTE-LOIRE
Boussoulet
Auberge du Meygal
★NN
Saint-Julien-
Chapteuil
Tel: 71-08-71-03

Monlet près Allègre
Le Roulis
★NN
Le Bourg
Tel: 71-00-73-54

Le Puy-en-Velay
La Verveine
★NN
6, place Cadelade
Tel: 71-02-00-77
et 02-14-66

Ste Sigolène
Le Relais de la poste
★NN
2, place Leclerc
Tel: 71-61-61-33

Vieille-Brioude
Les Glycines
★★NN
Aveneu de Versailles
Tel: 71-50-91-80

**44 – LOIRE-
ATLANTIQUE**
Pontchâteau
L'Auberge du
Calvaire
★NN
6, route de la Brière
Lieu-dit - Le Calvaire
Tel: 40-01-61-65

**Saint-Brévin-les-
Pins**
Relais du Marché
★NN
Place Henri Basle
Tel: 40-27-22-21

45 – LOIRET
Artenay
Relais d'Artenay
★★NN
Rue de Chartres
Tel: 38-80-40-78

Bellegarde
Le Relais du
Commerce
★NN
1, rue de la
République
Tel: 38-90-10-45

46 – LOT
Gramat
Le Relais du Centre
★★NN
Place de la
République
Tel: 65-38-73-37

**Saint-Paul de
Loubressac**
Le Relais de la
Madeleine
★NN
Tel: 65-21-98-08

**47 – LOT-ET-
GARONNE**
Lafox
Au Relais
Toulousain
★NN
113, Route de
Toulouse
Tel: 53-68-54-83

**Lévignac-de-
Guyenne**
Chez Denise
★NN
Allée des
Promenades
Tel: 53-83-72-12

Marmande
Le Relais du Lion
d'Or
★★NN
1, rue de la
République
Sortie Autoroute
Marmande
Tel: 53-64-21-30

Miramont
L'Étape des Routiers
★★NN
Route de Paris
Saint-Pardoux-Issac
Tel: 53-93-20-76

Saint-Livrade
Au Bon Accueil
★NN
Route de Villeneuve
Tel: 58-01-02-34

Tournon-d'Agenais
Le Relais des
Voyageurs
★NN
Rue de Cahors
Tel: 58-71-70-28

48 – LOZÉRE
Langogne
Le Relais du
Luxembourg
★NN
Place de la Gare
Tel: 66-69-00-11

Marvejols
Hôtels de la Paix
★★NN
2, avenue Brazza
Tel: 66-32-10-17

Le Monastier
Les Ajustons
★NN
Carrefour Nles 9 and
88
Marvejols
Tel: 66-32-70-35

**49 – MAINE-ET-
LOIRE**
Jallais
Le Relais de la
Croix-Verte
Hôtel du Vert Galant
★★NN
1, rue Jean de
Sagmond
Place de la Mairie
Tel: 41-64-10-12
et 64-20-22

Saumur
Hôtel de la Gare
★★NN
16, av. David
d'Angers
Tel: 41-67-34-24

Vivy
Le Relais Saint-Paul
★NN
30, Rue Nationale
Tel: 41-52-50-13
et 52-51-65

50 – MANCHE
Coutances
Le Relais du Viaduc
★NN
25, avenue de Verdun
Tel: 33-45-02-68

Montmartin-sur-Mer
L'Hôtellerie du Bon
Vieux Temps
★★NN
Tel: 33-47-54-44

St-Hilaire-du-Harcouet
Les Routiers
Chez Jacques
Le Relais due
Chemin de Fer
★NN
La Gare
Tel: 33-49-10-55

Saint-Symphorien-des-Monts
Relais du Bois Léger
★NN
Tel: 33-49-01-43

51 – MARNE
Beaumont-sur-Vesle
La Maison du
Champagne
★★NN
2, rue du Port
Tel: 26-03-92-45

Chaussée-de-Damery
Auberge du
la Chaussée
★NN
5, av de Paris
(à 5 km d'Épernay)
Tel: 26-58-40-66

52 – HAUTE-MARNE
Doulaincourt
Hôtel de Paris
★NN
Place du Général-de-
Gaulle
Tel: 25-94-61-18

53 – MAYENNE
Gorron
Au Rendez-vous des
Routiers
★NN
9, rue Corbeau-Paris
Tel: 43-08-61-74

St. Berthevin-lès-Laval
Restaurant de l'Aulne
L'International
★★NN
Lieu-dit L'Aulne
RN 157
Tel: 43-69-31-74

55 – MEUSE
Ancerville
Le Relais
★NN
59, route de Saint
Dizier
Tel: 29-75-30-13

56 – MORBIHAN
Elven
Le Relais de l'Argouet
★NN
36, rue de l'Argouët
Tel: 97-53-32-98

Lanester
Le Relais de la
Rotonde
★NN
120, rue Jean-Jaurès
Tel: 97-76-06-37

Séné
Le Poulfanc
★NN
Rte de Vannes
Tel: 97-47-47-97

Vannes
Le Relais de Lus
canen
★NN
Rouite d'Auvay
Tel: 97-63-45-92

57 – MOSELLE
Knutange
Relais du Stade
★NN
180, rue Victor-Rimmel
Tel: 87-84-12-47

Rohrbach-les-Bitche
L'Auberge de la
Croix d'Or
★NN
6, rue de la Libération
Tel: 87-09-73/01

58 – NIÈVRE
Cosne-sur-Loire
Relais des Trois
Couleurs
★NN
21, Rue Saint Agnes
Tel: 86-28-23-50

59 – NORD
Bailleul
Auberge du Seau
★NN
CD 933
Tel: 20-48-62-00

61 – ORNE
Domfront
Relais St-Michel
★NN
5, r. du Mont-St-
Michel
Place de la Gare
RN 176
Tel: 33-38-64-99

Mortagne-au-Perche
Hôtel des
Voyageurs
★NN
60, Fg. St.-Éloi
Tel: 33-25-25-46

62 – PAS-DE-CALAIS
Bruay-en-Artois
Restaurant
★NN
114, rue Raoul
Briquet
Tel: 21-53-42-07

63 – PUY-DE-DOME
Clermont-Ferrand
Le Relais des
Routiers
Auvergne-Pyrénées
∗NN
12 Bis, place Carme
Tel: 73-92-35-73

Marsac en Livradois
Hôtel le Kallisté
∗NN
Tel: 73-95-60-78

64 – PYRÉNÉES-ATLANT
Denguin
Les Routiers de
Denguin
∗∗NN
Tel: 59-68-85-15

Gan
L'Hôtel Moderne
∗NN
43, Place de la
Mairie
Tel: 59-21-54-98

Oloron-Sainte-Marie
Le Terminus
∗NN
Place de la Gare
Tel: 59-39-01-72

Pau
Hostellerie du Bois
Louis
∗NN
18, av. Gaston-Lacoste
Tel: 59-27-34-98

65 – HAUTES-PYRÉNÉES
Laloubère
Hôtel des
Pyrénées
∗NN
13, rue du Mi-Foch
Tel: 62-93-19-62

Tarbes
Le Relais Victor-Hugo
∗NN
52, Rue Victor-Hugo
Tel: 62-93-36-71

67 – BAS-RHIN
Bouxwiller
Le Soleil
∗∗NN
71, Grande-Rue
Tel: 88-70-70-06

Gambsheim
Europ Relais
∗∗NN
Route du Rhin
Tel: 88-96-43-33

Keskastel
Le Relais d'Alsace
∗NN
11, rue de Faubourg
Tel: 88-00-11-04

Kogenheim
A l'Etoile
∗NN
36, Rte de Strasbourg
Tel: 88-74-70-02

68 – HAUT-RHIN
Kruth
Auberge de France
∗∗NN
20, Grande-Rue
Tel: 89-92-28-02

69 – RHONE
Decines
Le Relais de la Poste
∗∗NN
11, rue d'Alsace
Tel: 78-49-19-03

70 – HAUTE-SAONE
Corbenay
Au P'tit Chariot
∗∗NN
1, rue des Cannes
Route de Fugerolles
Tel: 84-94-13-60

Ronchamp
La Pomme d'Or
∗NN
Rue Le Corbusier
Tel: 84-20-62-12

71 – SAONE-ET-LOIRE
Mercurey
Le Mercurey
∗NN
Grande-Rue
Tel: 85-45-13-56

Varennes-le-Grand
Relais de la Gare
∗NN
Tel: 85-44-22-76

72 – SARTHE
La Belle Inutile
La Biche Dorée
∗NN
RN 23
Tel: 43-76-70-45

Besse-sur-Braye
Le Relais de la Gare
∗NN
19, avenue de la Gare
Tel: 43-35-30-22

Joué-en-Charnie
Restaurant du Cheval
Blanc
∗NN
RN 157
Tel: 43-88-42-13

73 – SAVOIE
Aiguebelle
Le Relais de la Poste
∗∗NN
Grande-Rue
Tel: 79-36-20-05

Albens
Hôtel de France
∗NN
Rue du 8 Mai 1945
Tel: 79-54-17-04

74 – HAUTE SAVOIE
Chaux-Balmont
L'Auberge
∗NN
RN 201
Tel: 50-46-71-02

Cluses
Le Restoport du
Monte-Blanc
Autoport du Mont-Blanc
La Maladière
Tel: 50-96-01-08

Doussard
La Tour du Lac
★NN
Nle 508 La Gare
Tel: 50-44-30-37

Megève
Le Chalet des Fleurs
★★NN
Route de Sallanches
Pont d'Arbon
Tel: 50-21-21-46

Meythet
Les Routiers
★NN
22, route de Frangy
Tel: 50-22-02-93

Sciez
Le Leman
★NN
Bonatrait
Tel: 50-72-60-04

Seynod
Le Relais
Sainte-Catherine
★NN
181, route d'Aix
Tel: 50-59-00-86

Thones
L'Hermitage
Avenue du Vieux Pont
Tel: 50-02-00-31

81 – TARN
Ambres
Les Pommiers
★NN
Le Grès
Tel: 63-58-05-56

Cuq Toulza
Chez Alain
La Bombardière
★NN
Tel: 63-75-70-36

Labrugière
La Marmite
★NN
35, avenue Henri Simon
Tel: 63-50-21-19

82 – TARN-ET-GARONNE
Castelsarrazin
Chez Maurice
★NN
35, route de Toulouse
Tel: 63-32-30-83

Caussade
Relais d'Auvergne
ZI. de Meaux
Tel: 63-93-03-89

Moissac
Relais Auvergnat
★NN
31, bd. Camille-Delthil
Place du Palais
Tel: 63-04-93-02
ou 63-04-02-58

Montpezat-de-Quercy
Le Relais de l'etape
Quercy
★NN
RN 20
Tel: 63-02-07-58

83 – VAR
Arcs sur Argens (Les)
Hôtel de l'Avenir
★NN
Rue Jean Jaurès
Quartier de la Gare
Tel: 94-73-30-58

Fréjus
Les Trois Chènes
★NN
Route de Cannes
RN 7
Tel: 94-53-20-08

Montauroux
Le Relais du Lac
★★NN
Tel: 94-76-43-65

Sainte-Maximin-la-Sainte-Baume
Le Relais du Carillon
Attaché de Tourisme
5, rue de la République
Tel: 94-78-00-38

Saint-Raphael
Le Relais Bel Azur
★NN
247, Bd. de Provence
Tel: 94-95-14-08

Saint Raphael
Hotel Moderne
★★NN
329, Av. du Gl Leclerc
Tel: 94-51-22-16

84 – VAUCLUSE
Avignon
Le Relais d'Avignon
★★NN
Montfavet
Tel: 90-88-18-06

Bollène
La Croisière
★NN
Tel: 90-30-20-05

Montfavet
Relais de Bonpas
★NN
Lieu-dit
Pont de Bonpas
RN 7
Tel: 90-23-07-01

85 – VENDÉE
Ardelay-les-Herbiers
Chez Camilles
★★NN
2, rue Monseigneur Massé
Tel: 51-91-07-57

Les-Herbiers
L'Orée des Bois Verts
★NN
Route des Sables
RN 160
Tel: 51-91-00-18

La Roche-sur-Yon
Hôtel Sully
★★NN
Boulevard Sully
Tel: 51-37-54-02
et 51-37-18-21

Saint-Hilaire-de-Loulay
Le Relax
★**NN**
Les Landes de
Roussais
Tel: 51-94-02-44
ou 51-06-39-41

Venansault
Le Moulin de la
Bergerie
★**NN**
Carrefour de la Grolle
Route de Landeronde
Tel: 51-40-39-64

86 – VIENNE
Moulisme
La Table Ouverte
★**NN**
Route Nationale 147
Montmorillon
Tel: 49-91-90-68

87 – HAUTE-VIENNE
Sauviat-sur-Vige
Hôtel 400 de la Poste
★**NN**
Tel: 55-75-30-12

88 – VOSGES
Plombières-les-Bains
Le Relais
Strasbourgeois
★**NN**
3, place Beaumarchais
Tel: 29-66-00-70

St Pierremont
Le Relais Vosgien
★★**NN**
Tel: 29-65-02-46

Sainte-Marguerite
Le Relais des Amis
★**NN**
486, rue d'Alsace
Tel: 29-56-17-23

89 – YVONNE
Arces
Le Relais de la Forêt
d'Othe
★**NN**
Tel: 86-88-10-44

Auxerre
Le Sainte-Nitasse
★**NN**
Route de Lyon/
Auxerre
Tel: 86-46-95-07

91 – ESSONNE
Chamarande
Le Relais de
Montfort
★**NN**
Route Nationale 20
Tel: 60-82-20-80

Corbell-Essonne
Relais de l'Hermitage
★**NN**
137, Bd de
Fontainebleau
Tel: 64-96-29-42

Montlhéry
Le Sologne
★**NN**
65, route d'Orléans
Tel: 69-01-00-98

MOTORWAY RELAIS ROUTIERS

AUTOROUTE – A1

Vemars
95470 Val-d'Oise
Tel: 34-68-39-20

Assevillers par Péronne
80200 Somme
Towards Sens
Provence/Paris
Tel: 22-85-20-35

Péronne
80200 Somme/
Provence
Tel: 22-85-26-08
Telex: 140828

Wancourt
62128 Pas-de-Calais
Tel: 21-55-97-83

AUTOROUTE – A4

**Rheims –
Aire de Rheims
Champagne**
51400 Marne
Tel: 26-61-63-57

Verdun Saint-Nicolas
55100 Meuse
Tel: 29-86-41-18

Le Fère-en-Tardenois
Relais du Tardenois
02130 Fresnes-en-
Tardenois
Tel: 23-70-23-16

AUTOROUTE – A6

Les Lisses par Villabe
91100 Essonne
Tel: 60-86-22-31

Nemours
77140 Seine-et-Marne
Tel: 64-28-11-97

Venoy par Auxerre
8900 Yonne
Towards Paris/
Provence
Tel: 86-52-31-71

**Venoy/Auxerre
(Venoy 2)**
8900 Yonne
Towards Provence/
Paris
Tel: 86-52-35-52
Telex: 800921

Guillon
89420 Yonne
Tel: 86-32-11-34

**La Ferté Saint-
Ambreuil par
Sennecy-le-Grand**
71240 Saône-et-Loire
Towards Provence/
Paris
Tel: 85-44-20-64

La Ferté-St-Ambreuil
71420 Saône-et-Loire
Towards Paris/
Provence
Tel: 85-44-21-79

**Saint-Albain par
Mâcon**
71260 Saône-et-Loire
Tel: 85-33-19-00

AUTOROUTE – A7

Solaize
69360 Rhône
Tel: 78-02-82-63

Montélimar
26200 Drôme
Tel: 78-46-60-00

Lancon de Provence
13680 B.-du-R.
Tel: 90-53-90-25

Morières-les-Avignon
84310 Vaucluse
Tel: 90-22-59-68

Mornas
84420 Vaucluse
Towards Paris/
Provence
Tel: 90-37-03-09

AUTOROUTE – A7

Sorgues
84700 Vaucluse
Tel: 90-39-10-72

AUTOROUTE – A9

Tavel
30126 Gard
Tel: 66-50-04-19

**Montpellier –
Fabrègues**
34690 Hérault
Towards Passerelle
Tel: 67-85-15-06

AUTOROUTE – A10

**Antran –
Châtellerault**
86100 Vienne
Towards Provence/
Paris
Tel: 49-02-72-04

**Fleury-les-Aubrais
Aire de Bais Picard**
45400 Loiret
Tel: 38-73-34-89
Telex: 780959

Saran par Orléans
45400 Loiret
Tel: 38-91-30-12

Tours
3700 Indre-et-Loire
Towards Passerelle
Tel: 47-56-15-49

**Pons
Aire de Saint-Léger**
17800 Charente
Maritime
Tel: 46-94-25-30

Briis-sous-Forges
91640 Essonne
Tel: 64-90-77-18

Blois
41000 Loir-et-Cher
Tel: 54-46-84-73

AUTOROUTE – A11

**Chartes –
Aire de la Fosse
Blanche**
28300 Eure-et-Loire
Tel: Paris/Provence
37-31-62-41
Tel: Provence/Paris
37-31-62-41

La Ferté-Bernard
72400 Sarthe
Tel: 43-93-41-02

AUTOROUTE – A13

**Morainvilliers par
Orgeval**
78630 Yvelines
Tel: 39-75-92-25

Vironvay
27400 Eure
Towards Passerelle
Tel: 32-40-21-51

AUTOROUTE – A25

Steenvoorde
59114 Nord
Towards Paris/
Provence
and Provcence/Paris
Tel: 28-42-04-67

AUTOROUTE – 31

Loisy
Aire de Pont-á-
Mousson
54700 Meurthe-et-
Moselle
Tel: 83-81-18-89

AUTOROUTE – A32

Longeville-les-
St-Avold
57740 Moselle
Tel: 87-92-23-89

AUTOROUTE – A43

L'Isle d'Abeau
par Bourgoin-Jallieu
38300 Isère
Towards Passerelle
Tel: 74-27-27-91

AUTOROUTE – A63

Cestas
33610 Gironde
Tel: 56-21-80-68

THE ROUTIERS SIGN

The red and blue les Routiers sign is recognised internationally as a mark of quality and value and is awarded annually to restaurants and hotels which pass the strict Routiers inspection.

In order to maintain the right to be listed and display the sign establishments are reinspected regularly. For the most part, standards are maintained; however, there are inevitably a few who let their standards drop and have to be withdrawn. There may have been a change of ownership or reinspection following a complaint.

In spite of our efforts, some establishments continue to display the sign after they have been withdrawn. Authentic Relais Routiers are issued with an annual certificate which should be displayed on the premises, and only if this certificate is valid should this sign be displayed.

If you visit an establishment displaying the Routiers sign without an entry in the Guide or a valid certificate, please write and tell us and we will investigate. Finally, if you have any comments or complaints about a current Relais Routiers, then please let us know – you will find a questionnaire on pages 65 and 66.

YOUR RECOMMENDATION

If you know of an establishment not already
a Relais Routiers but worthy of nomination,
please send us details on the form below.
We will arrange for an inspector to call

Send to: ROUTIERS, 354 Fulham Road,
LONDON SW10 9UH

Name of Establishment:

_____

Address

_____

_____

Name of Proprietor (if known):

_____

Restaurant/Pub/Hotel/Bed and breakfast
(Please delete as applicable)

Comments

_____

_____

_____

_____

_____

_____

_____

Your Name:

_____

Address:

_____

_____

YOUR OPINION

If you are dissatisfied or alternatively would like to praise a Relais Routiers, please write and tell us. Although our establishments are reinspected regularly, your comments help us maintain Routiers' high standards. All correspondence will be treated in confidence.

Send to: ROUTIERS, 354 Fulham Road, LONDON SW10 9UH

Name of Relais Routiers:

_____

Address

_____

_____

_____

on (date) ____ for lunch/dinner/bed and breakfast

Comments

_____

_____

_____

_____

_____

_____

Your Name:

_____

Address:

_____

_____

A

ABBEVILLE 80100 Somme **RN 1 Map 5-A3**
♀ ⊗ **AUBERGE FLEURIE** (N° RR OCT 25 672) (M. and Mme Michel
Rubin) 294, Côte de la Justice ☎ 22-24-88-80 ⊸ 3 Showers.
Closed Sun; July. Good parking.

ABBEVILLE 80132 Somme **RN 25 Map 5-A3**
♀ ⊗ **AU CHEVAL NOIR** (N° RR JANV 26 779) (M. and Mme Bernard
Lafargue-Fortier) Petit Miannay ☎ 22-24-20-17 Closed Fri and
Sat. afternoons and the last week of August. Coaches welcome
(rest. seats 100 places). A little English spoken.

ABSCON 59215 Nord **RN 45 Map 5-B3**
♀ ⊗ ⌂ **LE MOULIN D'OR** (N° RR MAR 25 846) (Mme Monique
Bauduin) 17, place de Gaulle ☎ 27-36-30-33 ⊸ 9 Closed Aug.
Coaches welcome (rest. seats 80). Evening meals.

ABSIE (L') 79240 Deux-Sèvres **Maps 11-B3, 15-A1**
♀ ⊗ **BAR RESTUARANT DE LA POSTE - LES ROUTIERS** (N° RR
AOU 26 984) (M. Eugène **Bignon**) 21, rue de la Poste ☎ 49-95-90-
21 Closed Sun. Filling stations near.

ACQUEDUCS DE BEAUNANT 69110 Rhône **Map 1-A1**
♀ ⊗ **MARYSE ET ANNIE** (N° RR JUL 25 053) (Mme Maryse **Bert**) 66,
av. de la Libération Ste-Foy-Lès-Lyon ☎ 78-59-03-05 Closed Sat,
Sun; 15 July to 15 Aug. Italian spoken.

ADJOTS (LES) 16700 Charente **RN 10 Map 15-B2**
♀ ⊗ **PARIS-IRUN-CHEZ BRANGE** (N° RR JUN 19 796) (M. Jacky
Sommier) ☎ 45-31-02-44 Closed midday Sat to Sun.

AGEN 47000 L.-et-G. **RN 21 and 113 Map 21-B1**
♀ **CHEZ MARIO - Snack bar** (N° RR JUN 24 614) (M. Mario
Ghibaudo) 30, bd de la Liberté ☎ 53-96-89-42 **Minitel** Closed
Sun; Aug.

AIGREFEUILLE D'AUNIS 17290 Charente-Maritime **RD 939 Map 11-
B1**
    (see PUYDROUARD)

AIGUEBELLE 73220 Savoie **RN 6 Map 19-A2**
♀ ⊗ ⌂ **2 Stars NN LE RELAIS DE LA POSTE** (N° RR AOU 18 816)
(Mme Germaine **Vincent**) Grande-Rue ☎ 79-36-20-05 ⊸ 21
Closed Sat; 20 December to 1 February.
♀ ⊗ **LA CHAPELLE** (N° RR OCT 26 353) (Mme Christiane Magnin)
Restoroute La Chapelle ☎ 79-36-17-09 **Minitel** Coaches wel-
come (rest. seats 80). Evening meals until 11pm. German,
English, Italian spoken.

AIGUEPERSE 63260 P.-de-D. **RN 9 Map 16-B3**
♀ ⊗ **LE ROUTIER DE ST-GENEST** (N° RR JUN 22 396) (M. Camille
Chalbos) Les Littes **Saint-Genest-du-Retz** ☎ 73-63-68-35 Closed
Sun; Aug.

A

AIRE-sur-L'ADOUR 40800 Landes **RN 134 Map 21-A2**
♀ ⊗ 🏠 **1 Star NN LES ROUTIERS-CHEZ PIERRETTE** (N° RR OCT 24 377) (M. Joël **Daste**) 15, rue du 4 septembre ☎ 58-71-63-01 ⊷ 10 from 70 to 110F. Breakfast from 12 to 15F. Holiday terms (full board 160 to 180F). Coaches welcome (rest. seats 150). Evening meals until 9.30. Parking, bar. Dogs allowed.

AIRVAULT 79600 Deux-Sèvres **RD 46 Map 12-B2**
♀ ⊗ 🏠 **HOTEL DE LA GARE** (N° RR FEV 26 818) (Mme Anne-Marie **Bourgois**) 26, rue Sablières ☎ 48-64-70-16 ⊷ 7. Closed Sun; Aug.

AIX-D'ANGILLON (LES) 18220 Cher **Map 13-B1**
♀ ⊗ 🏠 **LE PARISIEN** (N° RR JANV 26153) (M. Jacques **Blanchet**) 20, Place du Général-de-Gaulle ☎ 48-64-43-62 ⊷ 4 Closed Sun; Aug. Full board 140F. Coaches welcome (rest. seats 90). Meals served till 9 pm.

AIXE-SUR-VIENNE 87700 Hte-Vienne **RN 21 Map 16-B1**
♀ ⊗ 🏠 **LE RELAIS DE LA CHAUMIERE** (N° RR JUL 15 314) (M. J.-L. **Pechalat**) 5, avenue de la Gare ☎ 55-70-12-12 **Minitel** ⊷ 5 Closed Wed; 15 Aug to 7 Sept. Coaches welcome (rest. seats 35). Evening meals.

AIX NOULETTE 62160 Pas de Calais **Map 5-B2/3**
♀ ⊗ **RELAIS D'EPINETTE** (N° RR JUIL 26 963) (M. and Mme François **Lefebvre**) 181, route de Béthunes ☎ 21-29-93-48 Filling stations near.

ALBAN 81250 Tarn **CD 999 Map 22-B1**
♀ ⊗ **LES QUATRE SAISONS** (N° RR DEC 27 127) (M. Jean-François **Galvan**) 2, Grande-Rue ☎ 63-55-83-22 Arabic, Spanish and Italian spoken. Filling stations near. Open 6.30 to 11.

ALBENC (L') 38470 Isère **Maps 24-B1 and 18-B3**
♀ ⊗ **AUBERGE DU VERCORS** (N° RR MARS 25 335) (Mme Claudette **Torri**) Place Jean-Vinay ☎ 76-64-75-17 Closed Sun. Evening meals.

ALBENS 73410 Savoie **RN 201 Map 19-A2**
♀ ⊗ 🏠 **1 Star NN HOTEL DE FRANCE** (N° RR JAN 25 773) (M. Robert **Stacchetti**) rue du 8 Mai 1945 ☎ 79-54-17-04 ⊷ 9 Closed Wed except in Jul/Aug. Full-board 150-160 F per night. Coaches welcome (rest. seats 40). Evening meals. German, English, Italian spoken.

ALBERT 80300 Somme **Map 5-B3**
♀ ⊗ 🏠 **LA CLOCHE D'OR** (N° RR SEPT 27 009) (M. Daniel **Macarez**) 53, rue Victor Hugo ☎ 22-75-09-68 ⊷ 6 Englifh spoken. Filling station near. Open 24 hours.

ALBI 81000 Tarn **RN 88 and D 81 Map 22-B1**
♀ ⊗ **LE RELAIS FLEURI** (N° RR DEC 25 225) (M. Pedro **Casado**) 25, av. François-Verdier ☎ 63-54-07-09 ⊷ 3 Closed Sun. Full board

160-180F per night. Coaches welcome (rest. seats 60). Meals served till 10. Spanish spoken.

℞ ⊗ **RELAIS CATALAN** (N° RR AVR 26 878) (M. Raymond **Tharreau**) RD 999 Route de Millau (Barrière de Montplaisir) ☎ 63-60-27-00 **Minitel** ⊸ 3 Evening meal. Closed Sat, Sun.

℞ ⊗ **AUBERGE LANDAISE DE CHEZ MARCEL** (N° RR FEV 27 189) (M. Marcel **Gauzère**) Rte de Montplaisir La Rivayrolle ☎ 63-45-03-11 Closed Sun. Filling station near.

ALBON 26140 Drôme **N7 Map 24-A1**

℞ ⊗ 🏠 **RELAIS DE LA TOUR ALBON** (N° RR DEC 26 745) (M. Camille **Bertrand**) Nationale 7 ☎ 75-03-11-22 **Minitel** ⊸ 13 Closed Sun (unless by arrangement). Full board 150F. Coaches welcome (rest. seats 230). Evening meals.

ALBUSSAC-AUX-QUATRE-ROUTES 19400 Corrèze **D 940 RN 121 Map 17-A1**

℞ ⊗ 🏠 **2 Stars NN HOSTELLERIE DE ROCHE-DE-VIC** (N° RR MAI 11 509) (Mme **Pailler**) Les Quatre Routes ☎ 55-28-15-87 **Minitel** ⊸ 14 (85-210F) Closed Mon low season; Feb. Full-board 170-200F per night. Bed ☎ & TV & breakfast 20F. Coaches welcome (rest. seats 100). Evening meals. Parking, terrace, grill, bar, dogs allowed. Places to visit: Roche-de-Vic, Collonges la Rouge,
⚓ Meyssac Turenne. English spoken. Tennis, numerous lakes, swimming, golf.

ALFORTVILLE 94140 Val de Marne **Map 1-B2/3**

℞ ⊗ **LA TERRASSE** (N° RR OCT 27 059) (M. Boualem **Belamri**) 173, rue Etienne Dolet ☎ 43-75-17-02 Closed Sun and 15/8 to 15/9. English spoken.

ALIXAN 26300 Drôme **RN 532 Map 24-A1**

℞ ⊗ 🏠 **2 Stars NN ALPES PROVENCE** (N° RR JUN 25 462) (M. Jean-Claude **Bocaud**) RN 532 Bourg de Péage ☎ 75-47-02-84 ⊸ 22 Closed 15 Nov to 5 Dec. Full-board 140-260F per night. Breakfast (15–35F). Coaches welcome (rest. seats 190) Evening meals. English, German spoken. ☎ & TV optional. Parking, bar, dogs allowed. Games bowls. Shaded park. Places to visit, Museum de la chaussure à Roman, trips to Vercors.

ALLASSAC 19240 Corréze **CD 901 Map 17-A1**

℞ ⊗ **RELAIS CHEZ BABETTE** (N° RR NOV 27 079) (Mme Elisabeth **Dublanche**) Varetz ☎ 55-84-21-79 Spanish and English spoken. Filling station near. Open 7am to 7pm.

ALLEUDS (LES). Lieu-dit Chaignepain 79190 D.-Sèvres **RN 148 Map 12-A1 (see SAUZE-VAUSSAIS)**

ALVIMARE 76640 S.-Mme **RN 15 Map 4-A3**

℞ ⊗ **CHEZ DENISE** (N° RR MAI 26 545) (Mme Denise **Letailleur**) **Fauville-en-Caux** ☎ 35-96-01-50 Closed Sat afternoon, Sun; 15 days in summer and 15 days in winter. Coaches welcome (rest. seats 80).

A

AMBENAY 27250 Eure
♀ ⊗ ⌂ **HOTEL DE LA RISLIE** (N° RR JAN 27 507) (M. Jean-Louis **Marcilly**) 9, rue Guy-Lacombe ☎ 32-24-63-45 ⊸ 6 Closed Sunday. Evening meals until 9.30pm.

AMBERIEU-EN-BUGEY 01500 Ain **RN 504 Map 2-A2**
♀ ⊗ **RELAIS DU GUBEY HUBERT-CHEZ DENISE** (N° RR FEV 25 309) (Mme Denise **Hubert**) 84, au Jules-Pellaudin ☎ 74-38-10-27. **Minitel** Closed on Sun. Aug. Holiday terms. Coaches welcome (rest. seats 42). Evening meal to 12.

AMBERT 63600 P.-de-D **RN 106 Map 17-A3**
♀ ⊗ ⌂ **LE RELAIS DES ROUTIERS** (N° RR MAI 16 065) (M. Robert **Pichoir**) 4, place du Général-Courtial ☎ 73-82-15-82 ⊸ 10 Closed Oct. Coaches welcome (rest. seats 30). Evening meals.

AMBLAINVILLE 60110 Oise **RN 327 Map 3-B2**
♀ ⊗ ⌂ **CHEZ MARIE ODILE** (N° RR JUL 23 393) (Mme Marie-Odile **Prunier**) 40, rue Nationale ☎ 44-52-03-10 Closed Sun.

AMBOISE 37400 I.-et-L. **RD 151 Map 12-A3**
♀ ⊗ ⌂ **LE CHANTECLERC** (N° RR DEC 26 773) (M. Eric **Boitelle**) 34, Avenue de Tours ☎ 47-57-11-94 ⊸ 5 Closed Sun in winter. English spoken.

AMBRES 81500 Tarn **RD 87 Map 22-A2**
♀ ⊗ ⌂ **1 star NN AUBERGE LES POMMIERS** (N° RR MAI 26 887) (M. Alain **Sore**) Le grès ☎ 63-58-05-56 ⊸ 8 (70–110F) Breakfast 15–25F). Closed Fri evenings and February or March. Spanish and English spoken. Holiday terms (full board 160–200F). Coaches welcome (rest. seats 150). Parking, bar. Dogs allowed. TV. Tourist train.

AMFREVILLE LA MI VOIE 76920 S-Mme **RN 13 bis Map 3-A1**
♀ ⊗ **LE BOUT DU MONDE** (N° RR AOUT 26 979) (M. Rémy **Piquot**) 2, route de Paris ☎ 35-23-31-47. Filling stations near. Coaches welcome (rest. seats 50). Evening meals to 11. Parking.
♀ ⊗ **LE RELAIS CHANTECLAIR** (N° RR SEPT 26 636) (M. Roger **Ridel**) 19, route de Paris ☎ 35-23-70-24.

AMIENS 80000 Somme **RN 16 Map 5-A3**
♀ ⊗ ⌂ **SAINT ROCH** (N° RR FEV 21 411) (Mme **Halter**) 2, place Foch ☎ 22-91-38-69 ⊸ 7 Closed Friday evenings and Sun pm. English spoken. Holiday terms (full board 150–190F). Coaches welcome (rest. seats 60).

AMILLY 45200 Loiret **RN 443 Map 13-A1/2**
♀ ⊗ **LE RELAIS DU GROS-MOULIN** (N° RR SEP 19 905) (Mme Bernadette **Grégoire**) 371, rue du Gros-Moulin ☎ 38-85-46-62 Closed Sun; 15 to 31 Aug.

AMOU 40330 Landes **RD 15 Map 20-B2**
♀ ⊗ ⌂ **AU FEU DE BOIS** (N° RR JANV 26 430) (M. Joël **Martinet**)

Avenue des Pyrénées ☎ 58-89-00-86 ⊸ 5 Closed Fri evenings, midday Sat and Jan. Evening meals.

AMPUIS 69420 Rhône **RN 86 Map 2-B1/2**
♈ ⊗ ⌂ **AUX PORTES DE PROVENCE** (N° RR JUN 20 215) (M. Maurice **Terpend**) RN 86 Les Allées ☎ 74-56-10-31 **Minitel** ⊸ 11 Closed Wed and the last 2 weeks of Feb. Aug. Holiday terms (full board 150–220F). Coaches welcome (rest. seats 100). Evening meals to 9. Parking.

ANCERVILLE 55170 Meuse **RN 4 Map 14-A1**
♈ ⊗ ⌂ **1 Star NN LE RELAIS** (N° RR JUN 25 958) (Mme Renée **Lange**) 59 Rte de St-Dizier ☎ 29-75-30-13 ⊸ 10 Closed Sat afternoon and Sun mornings and part of Sept or Oct. Full board 150–220F. Coaches welcome (rest. seats 80). Evening meals.

ANETZ 44150 Loire-Atlantique **RN 23 Map 11 A3**
♈ ⊗ **LE RELAIS DE LA BARBINIÈRE** (N° RR JANV 27 169) (Mme Sylvie **Dronet**) La Barbinière ☎ 40-83-11-25 ⊸ 4 Closed Sun, and between Christmas and New Year. English spoken. Filling station 500m. Open 7.30am to 9pm.

ANGERS 49000 M.-et-L. **RN 31 Maps 12-A1 and 11-A3**
♈ ⊗ ⌂ **CHEZ GEORGES** (N° RR AVR 24 926) (M. Georges **Janneau**) 47, rue Guillaume-Lekeu ☎ 41-43-86-25 ⊸ 7 Evening meals.
♈ ⊗ ⌂ **CHEZ MICHEL** (N° RR MAI 26 836) (M. Michel **Guerin**) 7, bld Ayrault ☎ 41-43-82-43 ⊸ 11 Closed Sat and Aug. English spoken.

ANGERVILLE 91670 Essonnes **RD 838 Map 9-B1**
♈ ⊗ **RESTO-RAPIDE** (N° RR MARS 26 486) (M. Daniel **Saragosa**) Rte d'Authon-la-Plaine ☎ 64-95-29-40 Open 24 hours. English, Spanish, Portuguese, Arabic spoken.

ANGLES 85750 Vendée **RN 747 Map 11-A1**
♈ ⊗ **AUBERGE DU BON ACCUEIL Chez Cathy** (N° RR MAR 21 816) (Mme Catherine **Gaborit**) 5 Rue Nationale ☎ 51-97-52-20 Closed 3 weeks in Sept. Coaches welcome (rest. seats 160). Evening meals. English spoken.

ANGLET 64600 Pyr.-Atl. **RN 10 Map 20-A3**
♈ ⊗ ⌂ **LES MOUETTES** (N° RR AVR 24 180) (M. Reñe **Anneix**) 5, avenue de l'Adour ☎ 59-52-46-08 ⊸ 7 Closed Sat, Sun; 15 Aug to 30 Aug. Evening meals.

ANGLIERS 86330 Vienne **RN 147 Map 12-B2**
♈ ⊗ **LA GALUCHE** SARL (N° RR NOV 25 729) (M. Claude **Poupard**) ☎ 40-98-19-20 Closed Sat afternoon. Coaches welcome (rest. seats 55). Evening meals. English spoken.

ANNOEULLIN 59112 Nord **Map 5-A1**
♈ ⊗ **CHEZ MAUMO** (N° RR JUL 26 006) (M. Maurice **Desailly**) 32, Rue de Touraine ☎ 20-85-75-92 Closed Sun; Aug. Coaches welcome (rest. seats 50).

A

ANTONNE 24420 Dordogne **RN 21 Map 15-B3**
♈ ⊗ ⌂ **LE RELAIS DE LAURIÈRE** (N° RR MAI 26 899) (M. Jean-Claude **Condaminas**) Laurière ☎ 53-06-00-28 ⊷ 5 Closed Sun and 1/5 to 15/5. Full board 140 to 160F. Coaches welcome (rest. seats 80). Evening meal. Filling station near. Italian/Spanish spoken.

ANTONY 92160 Hauts-de-Seine **Map 1-B2**
♈ ⊗ **LES ROUTIERS** (N° RR OCT 13 147) (MME Ginette **Laurence**) 86, av. de la Division Leclerc ☎ 46-66-02-62 Closed Sun.

ANTRAN see **CHATELLERAULT**

APPEVILLE (called ANNEBAULT) 27290 Eure **Map 4-B3**
♈ ⊗ **LE RELAIS DE LA POSTE** (N° RR AVR 26 503) (M. Eric **Duchumin**) Rte de Pont-Audemer ☎ 32-56-11-13 Closed Mon. Coaches welcome (rest. seats 60).

APPOIGNY 89380 Yonne **RN 6 Map 13-A2**
♆ **Les Routiers Shell Service Station LE RELAIS DE L'AMITIE** (N° RR OCT 55 0000 101) (M. Philippe **Saur**) 21, Rte d'Auxerre ☎ 86-53-21-76 Open 24 hours. Closed Sat Sun and 2 weeks Nov. Coaches welcome (rest. seats 25). Evening meals to 12. Parking.

APT 84400 Vaucluse **Map 24-B2/3**
♈ ⊗ **LE RELAIS DU LAC** (N° RR JUL 27 337) (M. Michel **Borde**) Le Chêne ☎ 90-74-01-10 Closed Sun. evening. Evening meals. English/Spanish spoken.

ARBOIS 39600 Jura **Map 18-B1**
♈ ⊗ **LA GRANGE DE VAIVRE** (N° RR JUL 27 342) (Mme Chantal **Vincentz**) La Grange de Vaivre ☎ 84-37-88-06 Closed Sunday. Evening meals to 9.30. English spoken. Filling station 5km. Open 24 hours. Parking.

ARBRESLE (L') 69210 Rhône **RN 7 Map 2-A1**
♈ ⊗ **LES ROUTIERS** (N° RR NOV 22 989) (Mme M.-A. **Durix-Michaud**) 91, rue Gabriel-Péri ☎ 74-01-05-81 Closed Sat afternoon. Meals served until 8.00 pm.
♈ ⊗ **LE RELAIS DES ROUTIERS** (N° RR NOV 26 364) (Mme Monique **Giraudier**) 27 Rte de Paris ☎ 74-01-07-59 Closed Sat. Sun 23rd Dec–8th Jan. English, Spanish spoken. Coaches welcome (rest. seats 55).
♈ ⊗ **AUX VOSIGIENS** (N° RR MARS 27 283) (M. Évelyne **Péchard**) 49, rue Gabriel-Péri ☎ 74-01-00-13 Closed pm and Sun. Filling station near. Open 7–8.

ARBRET (L') 62158 P.-de-C. **RN 25 Map 5-B3**
♈ ⊗ **LE RELAIS DE LA GARE** (N° RR JUN 17 290) (M. Maurice **Vicart**) 44, route Nationale ☎ 21-48-24-33 Open 24 hours, except Sat, Sun. Closed Sat, Sun. Full board 145-150F per night. Coaches welcome (rest. seats 80).

ARC-LES-GRAY 70100 Haute-Saône **Map 14-A3**
Ⓨ ⓧ **LES ROUTIERS** (N° RR SEP 23 928) (Mme Henriette **Demoulin**) 4, place Aristide-Briand La Croisée ☎ 84-65-37-23 Closed Sun. Coaches welcome (rest. seats 60). Evening meals.

ARC-SUR-TILLE 21560 Côte-d'Or **Map 14-A3**
Ⓨ ⓧ ⌂ **LE POELON** (N° RR MAR 25 850) (Mme Roberte **Gauthey**) 13 Rte Nationale ☎ 80-37-21-52 ⊷ 5 Closed Sat afternoon; Aug. Evening meals.

ARCS-SUR-ARGENS (LES) 83460 Var **Map 25-A2**
Ⓨ ⓧ ⌂ **1 Star NN SARL BAR HOTEL RESTAURANT DE L'AVENIR** (N° RR AVR 25 902) (Mme Marie-Jeanne **Hortal**) rue Jean-Jaurès. Quartier de la Gare ☎ 94-73-30-58 ⊷ 9 Closed Sat low season, last 2 weeks Aug. Full board 160F per night. Coaches welcome (rest. seats 180). English, Italian spoken.

ARCES 89320 Yonne **RD 905 Map 9-B2**
Ⓨ ⓧ ⌂ **1 Star NN LE RELAIS DE LA FORET D'OTHE** (N° RR JUN 18 747) (Mme Yolande **Misura**) 15, Place de l'Eglise. ☎ 86-88-10-44 ⊷ 8. Full board 150-200F per night. Coaches welcome (rest. seats 100).

ARDELAY-LES-HERBIERS 85500 Vendée **RD 38 Maps 12-B1 and 11-B3**
Ⓨ ⓧ ⌂ **2 Stars NN CHEZ CAMILLE** (N° RR JAN 20 079) (M. Camille **Masse**) 2, rue Monseigneur-Massé ☎ 51-91-07-57 ⊷ 13 Full-board 200-250F per night. Coaches welcome (rest. seats 200). Evening meals.

ARDENTES 36120 Indre **Map 16 A1**
Ⓨ ⓧ ⌂ **CAFÉ DES SPORTS** (N° RR MAI 27 287) (Mme Cécile **Pascaud**) 21, avenue de Verdun ☎ 54-36-21-19 ⊷ 5 Evening meals served until 9pm. Filling station near open 7–10.
Ⓨ ⓧ ⌂ **LE RELAIS DE CLAVIERESN** (N° RR SEPT 27 377) (Mme Pascale **Portrait**) Clavières ☎ 54-26-98-46 ⊷ 4 Evening meals. Filling station 1km.

ARDOISE (L') 30290 Gard **Map 24-A2**
Ⓨ ⓧ ⌂ **LE CHALET** (N° RR OCT 26 350) (M. Jacky/Martine **Charmasson**) Rte d'Avignon ☎ 66-50-22-22 **Minitel** ⊷ 7 Closed Sun, Christmas, New Year. Half-board 140-180F per night. 15% group discount. Coaches welcome (rest. seats 55). Evening meals until 12 pm.

ARGENLIEU 60130 Oise **D916 Map 3-A3**
Ⓨ ⓧ **LE RELAIS D'ARGENLIEU** (N° RR MARS 26 860) (M. Alain **Meyer**) 45, rue Thierry d'Argenlieu, Avrechy ☎ 44-51-72-18 Closed Sun 3 weeks in Aug. English spoken. Evening meal. Parking (900m^2).

ARGENT-SUR-SAULDRE 18410 Cher **RD 940 Map 13-A1**
Ⓨ ⓧ **AUBERGE DES BRUYÈRES** (N° RR JUN 25 959) (M. Jean-Yves

A

Argent-sur-Sauldre continued
Muelle) 10, Rue Nationale ☎ 48-73-60-20. Evening meals. Closed Sun.

ARGENTAN 61200 Orne **RN 24 Bis and 158 Map 8-A2**
Ⓨ ⊗ 🏠 **LE NORMANDY** (N° RR AVR 21 870) (M. René **Dutertry**) 35, avenue de la 2e Division Blindée ☎ 33-67-05-87 ⇥ 20 Closed Sat, Sun and Aug. Full board 120–160F per night. Coaches welcome (rest. seats 80). Evening meals until 11 pm.

ARGENTAT 19400 Corrèze **RN 120 Map 17-A1/2**
Ⓨ ⊗ 🏠 **CHEZ RAYMOND** (N° RR MAI 22 325) (Mme Monique **Pouzaud**) Place du 14 Juillet ☎ 55-28-01-97 ⇥ 7 Closed Sun; Jun. Full board 150-180F per night Coaches welcome (rest. seats 160). Evening meals.

ARGENTEUIL-SUR-ARMANÇON 89160 Yonne **CD 118 Map 13-A3**
Ⓨ ⊗ **CAFÉ DE LA MARE** (N° RR OCT 27 052) (Mme Marie-Madeleine **Mestanier**) ☎ 86-75-08-60 Closed Fri.

ARGENTIÈRE-LA-BESSEE(L') 05120 Hautes-Alpes **Map 19-B3**
Ⓨ ⊗ 🏠 **HOTEL DE LA MAIRIE** (N° RR JANV 27 138) (Mme Thérèse **Talandier**) 32, avenue Charles de Gaulle ☎ 92-23-10-36 ⇥ 8 Closed Sun. Low season. Full board 180–195F. Coaches welcome (rest. seats 35). Evening meals to 10. Parking. English spoken. Filling station near open 6–10.30.

ARGENTON-SUR-CREUSE 36220 Indre **RN 20 Map 16-A1**
Ⓨ ⊗ 🏠 **LE RELAIS DES ROUTIERS** (N° RR NOV 17 413) (Mme Mauricette **Calmel**) Saint-Marcel, 7, Rte de Châteauroux ☎ 54-24-01-77 ⇥ 6 Closed Sun. Menus 45-80F; specialties: *coq au vin, coquilles de crabes, andouilettes grillées*. English, Spanish spoken. Full board 140–160F. Coaches welcome (rest. seats 60). Evening meal to 9.00.

ARGENTRE-DU-PLESSIS 35370 Ille et Vilaine
Ⓨ ⊗ **KRAMPOUZ-MAD** (N° RR DEC 27 486) (M. Laurent **Thuillier**) Le Bois de Cherbault ☎ 99-96-76-94 Closed Monday. English, Spanish, some German, some Portuguese spoken. Evening meals.

ARLES 13200 B.-du-R. **RN 113 Map 24-A3**
Ⓨ ⊗ 🏠 **LE RELAIS DU PASSAGE A NIVEAU** (N° RR AVR 25 893) (Antoine and Laurence **Pech-Faure**) Route de Tarascon 31, av. de la Libération ☎ 90-96-06-64 ⇥ 8 Closed Sun. Full-board 165-185F per night. Coaches welcome (rest. seats 52). Evening meals. English, Italian, German, Spanish spoken.

ARMENTIERES 59280 Nord **RN 42 Map 5-A1**
Ⓨ ⊗ **AUBERGE DE LA LYS** (N° RR FEV 26 183) (Mme Jacqueline **Leflon**) 110, rue des Résistants ☎ 20-77-21-83 Closed Sun. Evening meals. Coaches welcome (rest. seats 120).
Ⓨ ⊗ **Café-Restaurant LA TERRASSE** (N° RR OCT 27 207) (Mme

A

Jocelyne **Dubar**) 112, rue des Résistants ☎ 20-35-44-80 Evening meals to 10.30. Filling station near. English/Dutch spoken.

ARNAY-LE-DUC 21250 Côte-d'Or **RN 6 Map 13-B3**
Ⓨ ⊗ **RELAIS DU ST-PRIX** (N° RR AVR 26 510) (M. Robert **Tonelli**) ☎ 80-84-81-74 Closed Sat afternoon, Sun. Evening meals. Italian spoken. Parking.

ARRAS 62000 P.-de-C. **RN 25 Map 5-B3**
Ⓨ ⊗ ⌂ **AU POINT DU JOUR** (N° RR OCT 24 707) (SARL M. Patrick **Renier**) 13, avenue Michonneau ☎ 21-59-96-42 ◄ 3 Closed Sat 2pm, Sun. Coaches welcome (rest. seats 120). Evening meals.

ARTENAY 45410 Loiret **RN 20 Map 9-B1**
Ⓨ ⊗ ⌂**2 stars NN RELAIS D'ARTENAY** (N° RR SEPT 26 670) (M. Lucian **Lichet**) rue de Chartres ☎ 38-80-40-78 ◄ 33 English spoken. Breakfast 26F (Buffet) T.V. ☎. Access for disabled. Open all year. Coaches welcome (rest. seats 100). Evening meals to 11.00. Parking, Bar. Dogs allowed. Sites to visit Châteaux de la loire 20km.

ARVERT 17530 Chte-Marit. **RD 14 Map 11-B1**
Ⓨ ⊗ ⌂ **LE RELAIS DES 3 CANARDS** (N° RR JUIL 26 938) (Mme Pascale **Branco**) Rue dos Saunier ☎ 46-36-40-43 ◄ 5 + 8 bungalows Closed Fri afternoons, Sat mornings Feb. English spoken. Coaches welcome (rest. seats 160).

ASCOUX 45300 Loiret **RN 721 Map 9-B1**
Ⓨ ⊗ **AUBERGE SAINT-ELOI** (N° RR MAI 26 543) (SDF **Robillard-Daroux**) 1, rue de Pithiviers ☎ 38-33-00-20 ◄ 3 Closed Sun; 15-31 July. Coaches welcome (rest. seats 140).

ASSEVILLERS 80200 Somme **Autoroute A1 Maps 5-B3 and 6-A1 see PERONNE**

ASTAFFORT 47200 Lot et Garonne
Ⓨ ⊗ **LES RELAIS DES PYRÉNÉES** (N° RR DEC 27 466) (M. Claude **Parma**) Barbonvièle ☎ 53-67-14-57. Closed Sunday. Evening meals. Spanish, Italian spoken. Nearby service station open 7am–10pm.

ATHÉE-SUR-CHER 37270 Indre-et-loire **Map 12-B3**
Ⓨ ⊗ **L'ESCALE** (N° RR NOV 27 444) (M. Gerard **Ramazeilles**) Les Ruelles ☎ 47-56-67-29 Closed Sun. 15 Aug – 1st Sept. German/English spoken. Evening meals to 10.00. Filling station near open 7.30 to 9.00.

ATHIS 51150 Marne **RN 37 Map 6-B2**
Ⓨ ⊗ ⌂ **AU BON ACCUEIL** (N° RR SEP 17 895) (Mme Ginette **Bourscheidt**) 12, Route Nationale ☎ 26-57-62-61 ◄ 4 Full board 150–160F. Closed Sat and Sun Aug. Coaches welcome (rest. seats 48). Evening meals to 9.00.

A

ATTIGNY 08130 Ardennes **Map 6-B2**
♀ ⊗ ⌂ **SPORT BAR** (N° RR JANV 26 792) (Mme Nicole **Pienne**) 16, place Charlemagne ☎ 24-71-20-69 ⇀ 3.

AUBAGNE 13400 B. du R **RN 8 Map 24-B3**
♀ ⊗ ⌂ **LES ROUTIERS** (N° RR 0CT 26 058) (M. Saïd **Sidi Boucif**) La Tourtelle ⇀ 5 Closed Sun afternoon. Arabic spoken. Evening meal to 9.00.

AUBE 61270 Orne **RN 26 Map 8-A2**
♀ ⊗ **LE PETIT QUEBEC** (N° RR MAI 26 903) (M. Jean-Claude **Rialland**) 47, route de Paris ☎ 33-24-55-34 Closed Sun and Aug. English and Spanish spoken.

AUBERGENVILLE 78410 Yvelines **RN 13 and 190 Map 1-A1**
♀ ⊗ **L'AMI RENÉ** (N° RR DEC 27 123) (M. Freddy **Harbiot** M. **Bouchard**) 21, rue Gaston Jouillerat ☎ 30-95-70-07 Closed Sun. Showers and dryer facilities. Coaches welcome (rest. seats 120 and summer terrace). German/English and Arabic spoken.

AUBERIVES-SUR-VARÈZE 38550 Isère **RN 7 Map 18-B3**
♀ ⊗ ⌂ **LE RELAIS DES ROUTIERS — Chez François et Marie-Hélène** (N° RR AVR 21 498) (Mme Marie-Hélène **Graziano**) ☎ 74-84-90-71 ⇀ 8 Closed Sun afternoon; 1-15 Sept. Full board 155–170F per night. Coaches welcome (rest. seats 60). Evening meals.

AUBERVILLIERS 93300 S.-St-Denis **Porte d'Aubervilliers Map 1-A2**
♀ ⊗ **LE RELAIS CRÉOL** (N° RR AOUT 26 623) (M. Alain **Mercien**) 119, avenue Victor Hugo ☎ 48-33-68-99.
♀ ⊗ **AU RENDEZ-VOUS DES CAMIONNEURS** (N° RR SEP 24 330) (M. Akil **Ayadi**) 17, rue de la Haie-Coq ☎ 43-52-09-15.

AUBETERRE 10150 Aube **RN 77 Map 9-B3**
♀ ⊗ **LES TILLEULS** (N° RR DEC 26 401) (M. Raymond **Mielle**) ☎ 25-37-51-11 Closed Sun.

AUBEVOYE 27940 Eure **Map 3-B1**
♀ ⊗ ⌂ **HOTEL DE LA GARE** (N° RR JUIL 27 326) (Mme Michelle **German**) Place de la Gare ☎ 32-53-28-88 ⇀ 10 Filling station near.

AUBIÈRE 63170 Puy-de-Dôme **Map 16-B3**
♀ ⊗ ⌂ **L'EUROPE** (N° RR OCT 27 069) (M. Michel **Mouestier**) SARL, 41 av. du Roussillon ☎ 73-26-34-61 ⇀ 10 Closed Sat afternoon and Sun. English spoken. Service Station open 6am to 10pm.

AUBIERS (LES) 79250 Deux-Sèvres **RN 759 Maps 12-B1 and 11-B3**
♀ ⊗ **HOTEL DU CHEVAL BLANC** (N° RR JUN 11 565) (M. Claude **Sauer**) 9, place St-Melaine ☎ 49-65-60-51 ⇀ 2 Closed Sat afternoon; Sun afternoon; Aug.

AUBIGNAS 07400 Ardeche **RN 120 Map 24-A2**
♀ ⊗ ⌂ **RELAIS DE LA GARE** (N° RR NOV 26 392) (Melle **Borne**)

Quartier de la Gare ☎ 75-52-43-89 ⊷ 5 Closed Sundays. Full-board from 160F inc. 1 bed and 1 meal for 2 persons. (1 room + dinner 2 pers 190F). Coaches on request (rest. seats 60). Evening meals to 1am. English, Spanish spoken.

AUBIGNY-AU-BAC 59265 Nord **RN 17 RN 43 Map 5-B3**
♀ ⊗ ⌂ **LE BERTREISIEN** (N° RR JUL 25 990) (M. Didier **Wattelet**) 21, route Nationale ☎ 27-80-96-40 **Minitel** pointphone ⊷ 5 Full-board 165-195F per night. Coaches welcome (rest. seats 140). Evening meals. English spoken.

AUBIGNY-SUR-NÈRE 18700 Cher **RD 940 Map 13-A1**
♀ ⊗ ⌂ **LE RELAIS DES ROUTIERS** (N° RR JAN 17 168) (M. Bernard **Ollier**) 17, av. Charles Lefebvre ☎ 48-58-01-42 ⊷ 9 Closed Sun; Sat midday; public holidays; August. Full board 140-160F per night. Evening meals until 9.30. Coaches welcome (rest. seats 64).

AUCAMVILLE 31140 Haute-Garonne **Map 22-A2**
♀ ⊗ **REST LE TOIT** (N° RR JUIN 26 259) (M. Jean-Pierre **Lablanchi**) 50 Chaussée des Mazuries ☎ 61-70-46-37 Coaches welcome (rest. seats 150). Spanish spoken.

AUCH 32000 Gers **RN 124 Map 21-B2**
♀ ⊗ ⌂ **1 Star NN MODERN HOTEL** (N° RR SEP 19 908) (M. Henri **Thibault**) 10 bis, avenue Pierre Mendis-France ☎ 62-05-03-47 ⊷ 13 from 80-200F, breakfast 16-25F, telephone in room, access for disabled. Closed Sat. Restaurant and bar closed Sat lunchtime. Meals served until 9 pm. Parking, dogs allowed. Places to visit: Museum, Cathedral. Some English spoken.

AUCHY AU BOIS 62190 Pas de Calais
♀ ⊗ **LE VERT DRAGON** (N° RR JAN 27 503) (Mme Marie-France **De Greef**) 3, rue d'Hesdin ☎ 21-26-64-29. Closed Saturday morning and Sunday morning. Evening meals.

AUCHY-LES-MINES 62138 P.-de-C **RN 41 Map 5-B1**
♀ ⊗ **ROUTIERS ARTÉSIENS** (N° RR MAR 26 832) (M. Daniel **Fontaine**) 120, Route Nationale ☎ 21-66-74-81.

AUDEUX 25170 Doubs **CD 67 Map 14-B3**
♀ ⊗ **LE CHANAT** (N° RR SEPT 26 986) (M. Bernard **Jeandenant**) 6, Grande Rue-Au Village ☎ 81-58-05-87 English spoken. 5km from filling station.

AUDUN-LE-ROMAN 54560 M.-et-M. **RD 156 Map 6-B3**
♀ ⊗ ⌂ **HOTEL DE LA POSTE** (N° RR DEC 26 244) (M. Patrick **Schwarz**) 25/27, rue Albert Lebrun ☎ 82-21-61-53 ⊷ 8 Closed Sun. German, Italian spoken.

AUFFERVILÉL 77570 Seine-et-Marner
♀ ⊗ **SARL AUBERGE DE LA DICIGENCE** (N° RR JAN 27 515) (M. **Vincent**) 9, Route Nationale ☎ 44-28-75-91. Evening meals.

A

AULNAY-SOUS-BOIS 93600 S.-St-Denis **Autoroute A1 Map 1-A3**
⟡ ⊗ ⌂ **BISTRONORD** (N° RR AVR 24 923) (M. Jean-Claude **Pradaller**) Garonor BP 660 ☎ 48-65-63-41 **Minitel** ⊸ 14 Closed Sat, Sun. English spoken. Coaches welcome (rest. seats 160). Evening meal.

AUMONE (L') par MOUHET 36490 Indre **RN 20 Map 16-A1**
⟡ ⊗ ⌂ **A L'ARRET DES ROUTIERS** (N° RR OCT 21 658) (M. Pierre **Boussely**) ☎ 54-47-55-11 ⊸ 6 Closed Sun. Evening meals to 11.00. English, German spoken. Coaches welcome (rest. seats 70).

AUMETZ 57710 Moselle **RN 52 Map 6-B3**
⟡ ⊗ ⌂ **CAFÉ DE LA POSTE** (N° RR JANV 27 145) (Mme Linda **Cossa**) 15, rue Foch ☎ 82-91-91-71 ⊸ 6 Closed Tues pm. Italian spoken. Filling station near open 8–8.

AUNEAU 28700 E.-et-L. **RD 177 Map 9-B1**
⟡ ⊗ ⌂ **HOTEL DES TROIS MARCHES** (N° RR FEV 27 195) (M. **Gasnier**/Mme **Sèttaoui**) 2, rue Emile-Labiche ☎ 37-31-70-49 ⊸ 8 Closed Sun. Filling station near.

AURILLAC 15000 Cantal
⟡ ⊗ **BAR DE L'ESCUDILLIER** (N° RR JAN 27 496) (M. Robert **Montburg**) Place du 8 Mai ☎ 71-63-79-30 Closed Sunday. Evening meals. Nearby service station open 7am to 10pm.

AURILLAC 15000 Cantal **RN 126 Map 17-B2**
⟡ ⊗ **L'ÉTAPE DU ROUTIER** (N° RR MARS 26 219) (M. Michel **Muller**) Rue des Frères Lumières Zl de Sistrières ☎ 71-64-66-70 Closed Sun; Sat afternoon. Coaches welcome (rest. seats 150). Evening meals.

AUSSILLON MAZAMET 81200 Tarn-et-Garonne **RN 112/118 Map 22-B2**
⟡ ⊗ **LE RELAIS DU COMMERCE CHEZ LOULOU** (N° RR JUL 25 991) (M. Louis **Blavy**) 21, av. Charles-Sabatié ☎ 63-61-26-16 **Minitel** Closed Sun; Aug. Coaches welcome (rest. seats 120). Spanish spoken. Evening meals to 9.00.

AUTECHAUX 25110 Doubs **near to the Péage de Beaume-les-Dames motorway Map 10-A3**
⟡ ⊗ **RELAIS DE L'AUTOROUTE LA DÉTENTE** (N° RR DEC 26 112) (Mme Simone **Courtial**) Beaume-les-Dames ☎ 81-84-01-14 Closed Sun afternoons. Full board. Coaches welcome (rest. seats 60). Meals until 2 am. Showers free. TV Channel.

AUTHEUIL 27490 Eure **RN Map 3-B1**
⟡ ⊗ **LA MARMITE** (N° RR OCT 26 075) (M. André **Person**) 17, Rue de Pacy ☎ 32-34-67-67 Closed Sat; Aug.

AUTHIEUX (LES) 27220 Eure **RD 835 Map 8-A3**
⟡ ⊗ **LE RELAIS DES AUTHIEUX** (N° RR NOV 22 569) (M. Claude

Lecomte) St-André-de-l'Eure ☎ 32-37-31-03 Evening meals. Closed 22 Dec–3 Jan.

AUTUN 71400 S.-et-L. **Map 13-B3**
♀ ⊗ **LE CLUB** (N° RR NOV 25 169) (Mme Eva **Rizzo**) **Pizzeria** 13, route de Beaune Pont-l'Evêque ☎ 85-52-27-72 ⊸ 4 Closed Sun. Closed Fri and Sat night. Coaches welcome (rest. seats 80). Evening meals to 10.00.

AUVERSE 49490 M. et L. **Map 12-A2**
♀ ⊗ **LES ROUTIERS** (N° RR AOUT 26 030) (M. Michel **Chasseau**) Route de Noyant à Beauge ☎ 41-82-20-13 Closed Sat, Sun; 15 days in Oct. Evening meals until 9.30pm.

AUVILLERS-LES-FORGES 08260 Ardennes **RN 43 Map 6-A2**
♀ ⊗ ⌂ **ARRET DES ROUTIERS** (N° RR JAN 23 608) (Mme Nicole **Bonnaire**) Mon Idée ☎ 24-36-32-77 **Minitel** ⊸ 6 Coaches welcome (rest. seats 50). Meals served until 10pm.

AUXERRE 89000 Yonne **RN 6 Map 13-A2**
♀ ⊗ ⌂ **1 Star NN LE SAINTE-NITASSE** (N° RR JUIN 26 916) (Mme Corinne **Courault**) Rte de Chablis ☎ 86-46-95-07 ⊸ 31 from 95-160F; breakfast 17–18F. Closed at weekends in winter (permanently May–Sept); 20 Dec to 5 Jan. Coaches welcome (rest. seats 150). Meals served until 10.30 pm, menus from 48F. Parking, dogs allowed. Sites to visit: medieval Auxerre. English spoken. (Full board 165–290F)
♀ ⊗ **LA PETITE VITESSE** (N° RR OCT 26 697) (M. Frédéric **Gouret**) 44, av de la Puisaye ☎ 86-52-35-29 Closed Sunday. English spoken. See also **VENOY.**

AUXONNE 21130 Côte de Or **RN 5 Map 14-A3**
♀ ⊗ **LE MICADO** N° RR OCT 26 696) (Mme Martine **Seurre**) Rte de Dôle ☎ 80-31-00-45 Coaches welcome (rest. seats 80). Evening meal to 3.00.

AUXY 45340 Loiret **RN 375 Map 9-B1**
♀ ⊗ **AUBERGE DU PUITS** (N° RR JANV 26 419) (Mme Marie-Madeleine **Delteil**) 21, rue Principale ☎ 38-96-70-05 Closed Wed; half of Feb; 8 days in Sept. Restaurant closed Sat, Sun evenings. Coaches welcome (rest. seats 50).

AUZITS 12390 Aveyron **RN 140 Map 22-B1**
♀ ⊗ **IGUE DU MOULIN** (N° RR JUIL 26 957) (Mme Brigitte **Felzines**) Rignac ☎ 65-63-90-90 Open 24 hours. Evening meals.

AVALLON 89200 Yonne **RN 6 Map 13-A2/3**
♀ ⊗ **RELAIS SAINT-CHRISTOPHE** (N° RR OCT 27 053) (M. Rémy **Vernier**) 13, route de Paris ☎ 86-34-07-17 Closed Sun. Filling station near.

AVELIN 59710 Nord **RN 353 Map 5-B1 6-A3**
♀ ⊗ **A L'EMBUSCADE** (N° RR AOU 14 906) (Mme **Lemoine**) 14,

Avelin continued
Route de Seclin ☎ 20-32-90-33 **Minitel** Closed Sat, Sun, Fri evening. Meals until 9.30pm.

AVESNES-SUR-HELPE 59440 Nord **RN 2 Map 6-A1**
♟ ⊗ **LE RELAIS MARGUERITE** (N° RR JUL 14 444) (M. Marguerite **Sorriaux**) 22, avenue de la Gare ☎ 20-61-17-88 Closed 1 to 15 Aug.

AVÈZE 72400 Sarthe **Map 8-B3**
♟ ⊗ **AUBERGE DU CHEVAL BLANC** (N° RR JANV 27 156) (M. Bernard **Joly**) La Ganche locality. ☎ 43-93-17-05 ⊷ 4 Closed Sun evening. Filling station 5km.

AVIGNON (84000 Vaucluse) **RN 7 Map 24-A2**
♟ ⊗ ⌂ **2 Stars NN LE RELAIS D'AVIGNON – SARL d'Exploitation** (N° RR NOV 22 100) (M. Henri **Savry**) Montfavet ☎ 90-88-18-06 **Minitel** ⊷ 19 Restaurant – 200 seats. Parking – 9000m^2 – with loudspeaker. Full-board 200–250F per night. Coaches welcome (rest. seats 500). Evening meals to 11.30. English, Spanish spoken.

AVIGNONET DE LAURAGAIS 31290 Hte-Garonne **RN 113 Map 22-A2**
♟ ⊗ ⌂ **LA PERGOLA** (N° RR MAI 22 329) (M. Etienne **Batan**) ☎ 61-81-63-54 **Minitel** ⊷ 6 Closed Sat and Sun evening; from 15 Nov to 30 Nov; 15 days in Feb. Coaches welcome (rest. seats 170). Evening meals. Spanish spoken.
⚑ **Total Station Service LE RELAIS DE NAUROUZE** (N° RR JUL 25 060) (Mme Christiane **Fernandez**) Aire du Lauragais ☎ 61-81-68-23 Open 24 hours. English, Spanish spoken.

AVION 62210 P.-de-C. **RN 43 Map 5-B3**
♟ ⊗ **LE PTI-POT** (N° RR FEV 23 655) (M. and Mme Pierre **Milleville**) 276, Bld H.-Martel ☎ 21-43-14-12 **Minitel** Closed Sat and Sun afternoon. Coaches welcome (rest. seats 45). Evening meals until 8.30pm.

AVRANCHES 50300 Manche **RN 176 Map 8-A1**
♟ ⊗ **LE RELAIS DES ROUTIERS** (N° RR OCT 27 398) (M. George **Hippolyte**) 70, rue de la Constitution ☎ 33-58-01-13 Closed Sun, except Jul, Aug. Evening meals until 8.30pm low season, 11.30. English spoken.
♟ ⊗ **LES ROUTIERS Chez Jean-Pierre et Joëlle** (N° RR SEPT 27 030) (M. Jean-Pierre **Lambert**) 107, rue de la Liberté ☎ 33-58-19-30 Closed Sun and 1st to 20th August. Filling station near.

AWOINGT près CAMBRAI 59400 Nord **RN 39 Maps 6-A1 and 5-B3**
♟ ⊗ ⌂ **AU CHANT DES OISEAUX** (N° RR DEC 22 594) (M. **Plouquet**) 3, route du Cateau ☎ 27-81-31-05 **Minitel** ⊷ 14 Closed Sun; 10 to 20 Aug. Full-board 160F per night. Coaches welcome (rest. seats 70). Evening meals.

A

AYNAC 46120 Lot **RD 940 Map 17-B1**
☥ ⊗ **RELAIS DU QUERCY** (N° RR MARS 27 200) (Mme Christine **Elcheverria**) Grande Rue ☎ 65-38-98-15 Closed Monday afternoon.

AZAY-LE-FERRON 36290 Indre **Map 12-B3**
☥ ⊗ **L'UNION** (N° RR JUL 26 971) (M. Thierry **Audoin**) Place de l'Église ☎ 54-39-20-88 Filling station near. Coaches welcome (rest. seats 145). Evening meals to 9.00.

AZAY-LE-RIDEAU 37190 I.-et-L. **RN 751 and RD57 Map 12-B2**
☥ ⊗ **LE RELAIS DE LA GARE** (N° RR MARS 27 229) (M. Patrick **Vitel**) 59, avenue de la Gare ☎ 47-43-40-60. Closed Sun. English spoken. Filling station near open 9.00–7.00.

AZERAT 24210 Dordogne **RN 89 Map 17-A1**
☥ ⊗ ⌂ **LE RELAIS D'ARGENT** (N° RR SEP 12 424) (Mme **Debord**) ☎ 53-05-21-05 ⊷ 4 Closed end Aug. Closed Sat. Full board. Coaches welcome (rest. seats 70).

B

BACCARETS (LES) 31550 Hte-Gar. **RN 20 Map 22-A2**
☥ ⊗ ⌂ **LA CHAUMIÈRE** (N° RR JUN 26 933) (M. Daniel **Laroche**) ☎ 61-08-90-70 ⊷ 12 Closed Sun. Coaches welcome (rest. seats 120).

BAGNAC-SUR-CELÉ 46270 Lot **RN 122 Map 12-B2**
☥ ⊗ ⌂ **LA PLANQUETTE** (N° RR JUIL 27 340) (Mme Micheline **Claudon**) Route d'Aurillac ☎ 65-34-93-50 ⊷ 4 Evening meals. Filling station near open 7–10. Parking.

BAGNÈRES-DE-LUCHON 31110 Hte-Garonne **Map 21-B3**
☥ ⊗ ⌂ **1 star NN L'ESCAPADE** (N° RR FEV 25 831) (Mme Michèle **Luzent**) 27, av. Jean-Jaurès ☎ 61-79-91-85 **Minitel** ⊷ 11 from 70-90F, breakfast 10–15, 50F Closed low season; Sat, Sun; mid-Dec to mid Jan. Parking, bar, dogs allowed. Sites to visit: Basilique. Some Spanish, English spoken. Evening meals to 9.30.

BAGUER PICAN 35120 Ille-et-Vilaine **Map 7-A3**
☥ ⊗ ⌂ **LE SAINT-MICHEL** (N° RR OCT 27 433) (M. Michel **Robert**) 12, rue de Paris ☎ 99-48-37-48 ⊷ 2 Open all week. Evening meals to 12.

BAGNOLS-EN-FORET 83600 Var **Map 25-B2**
☥ ⊗ ⌂ **LE RELAIS DU COMMERCE** (N° RR AVR 24 901) (M. Serge **Ghigo**) Grande Rue ☎94-40-60-05 ⊷ 8 Closed Tues low season. Italian Spoken. Full board 200–300F. Coaches welcome (rest. seats 100). Evening meals to 9.30.

B

BAIGTS-DE-BÉARN 64650 Pyr.-Atl. **RN 117 Map 20-B2/3**
♉ ⊗ ⌂ **LE RELAIS DE BAIGTS** (N° RR MAI 19 349) (Mme **Austruy**)
☎ 59-69-15-05 **Minitel** ⌐ 15 Full-board 150–180F per night.
Coaches welcome (rest. seats 170). Evening meals. English,
Spanish spoken.

BAIGTS-EN-CHALOSSE 40380 Landes **RD 2 Map 20-B2**
♉ ⊗ **AU CARREFOUR** (N° RR MAR 24 178) (M. Jean **Bonnot**) ☎ 58-
98-63-05 **Minitel** ⌐ 4 Closed Mon. Full-board 110F per night.
Coaches welcome (rest. seats 100). Evening meals.

BAILLEUL 59270 Nord **CO 933 Map 5-A1**
♉ ⊗ ⌂ **1 star NN AUBERGE LE SEAU** (N° RR MAI 23 786) (M. Joël
Dequidt) Le Seau ☎ 20-48-62-00 **Minitel** ⌐ 14 from 110-140F,
breakfast to 23F. Full-board 170–190F. Coaches welcome (rest.
seats 60). Meals until 10pm. Parking; bar; dogs admitted only to
restaurant; pool table; pinball; sites: Museum; Mont de Flandres.
♉ ⊗ **CHEZ ANDRÉ** (N° RR MARS 27 222) (M. André **Nooreberghe**)
Rte Nle 4671 Rte de Lille RD 333 ☎ 28-49-29-14 Filling station
4km.

BAILLEUL-SUR-THERAIN 60930 Oise **RD 12 and RD 620 Map 3-A2**
♉ ⊗ **L'ALOUETTE** (N° RR MAI 26 902) (Mme Mireille **Lemaire**) 4,
rue de Villers ☎ 44-07-66-26.

BAILLEULVAL 62123 Pas de Calais **RN 25 Map 5-B3**
♉ ⊗ ⌂ **BAC DU SUD** (N° RR JUIL 26 958) (M. Yves **Sanson**) ☎ 21-58-
79-12 ⌐ 7 Flemish, Dutch, English spoken. Closed on Sun. 1
week in Aug. Full board 190F. Coaches welcome (rest. seats
100). Evening meal.

BAIX 07210 Ardèche **RN 86 Map 24-A1**
♉ ⊗ **A MA CAMPAGNE** (N° RR MAI 19 790) (Mme Nara **Arsac**)
Quartier des Lilas ☎ 75-85-80-26 Closed Sun evening. Coaches
welcome (rest. seats 100). Evening meals.

BALAN-LA-VALBONNE 01120 Ain **Map 2-A2**
♉ ⊗ ⌂ **FRONT DE BANDIÈRE SARL** (N° RR JANV 27 136) (M. Henri
Bouvard) Route de Balan ☎ 78-06-35-61 ⌐ 8 Closed Sat and Sun.
Filling station near open 7–10.

BALARAUC-LE-VIEUX 34770 Hérault **RN 113 Map 23-B2**
(Voir Issanka)

BALIZAC 33730 Gironde **RD 110 and 111 Map 20-B1**
♉ ⊗ **LE RELAIS BASQUE** (N° RR MAI 22 809) (Mme Jeanne **Des-
claux**) ☎ 56-25-36-71 Closed Mon; Oct. Coaches welcome (rest.
seats 125). Evening meals.

BANNALEC 29114 Finistère **Map 7-B1**
♉ ⊗ **LOGE-BEG** (N° RR AOUT 27 364) (M. Denis **Hulban**) Loge
Begoarem ☎ 98-39-81-00 Evening meal to 11.00. German and
English spoken. Filling station near.

B

BANNOST 77155 S.-et-M. **RN 4 Map 9-A2**
♈ ⊗ **LE RELAIS DE LA GARE** Chez Huguette (N° RR FEV 14 215)
(M. Georges **Fontaine**) ☎ 64-01-02-07 Closed Sat, Sun; Aug.

BANYULS DELS ASPRES 66300 Pyr. Orientales **RN 9**
♈ ⊗ 🏠 **L'HOSTAL DE CATALUNYA** Sarl (N° RR JUIN 26 909) (M.
Robert **Fanon**) Route de Pérthus ☎ 68-21-81-60 ⊷ 11

BAPAUME 62450 P.-de-C. **RN 17 Map 5-B3**
♈ ⊗ 🏠 **CHEZ BERNADETTE** (N° RR MAR 24 892) (Mme Bernadette
Molle) 45, faubourg de Péronne ☎ 21-07-12-78 pointphone and
21-07-46-83 ⊷ 7 Closed Sat 8pm to Sun 10pm; Christmas to New
Year. Full-board. Coaches welcome (rest. seats 50). Evening
meals.

BARAQUEVILLE 12160 Aveyron **RN 88 and 111 Map 22-B1**
♈ ⊗ 🏠 **1 star NN LE RELAIS PALOUS** (N° RR FEV 21 398) (M.
Edmond **Palous**) ☎ 65-69-01-89 ⊷ 14 with ☎ Closed Sun; 24 Dec
to 2 Jan. Full-board 130–190F per night. Coaches welcome (rest.
seats 120). Evening meals until 11/12pm.

BARBASTE 47230 L.-et-G. **RN 655 Map 21-A2**
♈ ⊗ **LES PALMIERS** (N° RR AVR 21 891) (Société **Gineste et Fils**) ☎
53-65-55-02 Closed Sat in winter, Mon evening; Jan. Coaches
welcome (rest. seats 70). Evening meals (special group menus
min 10 per). Spanish spoken. Parking. Covered terrace (rest.
seats 50).

BARBEZIEUX-ST-HILAIRE 16120 Charente **RN 10 Map 15-A2**
♈ ⊗ **LE RELAIS DES ROUTIERS DE LA BILLETTE** (N° RR AOU 22
018) (Mme **Houdusse**) Route Nationale 10, Châteauneuf ☎ 45-78-
57-09 Closed Sun and 1 week Aug. Open 24 hours. Coaches
welcome (rest. seats 200). Evening meals. Menus from 58-85F.
⊷ Specialities: *confit de canard, escalope à la charentaise, magret
de canard. Confit de lapin*. Spanish spoken.

BARJAC 48000 Lozère **Map 23-A1**
♈ ⊗ **PARADIS HOTEL** (N° RR FEV 18 956) (M. **Paradis**) ☎ 66-47-01-
09.

BARNAS 07330 Ardèche **RN 102 Map 24-A1**
♈ ⊗ 🏠 **LE RELAIS DES ROUTIERS** (N° RR AVR 16 028) (Mme
Marthe **Cellier**) ☎ 75-36-40-78 ⊷ 12 Full-board 185–190F. Closed
on Sunday. Coaches welcome (rest.seats 50). Evening meals.

BARNEVILLE-CARTERET 50270 Manche **RN 803 Map 4-B1**
♈ ⊗ 🏠 **HOTEL DES SPORTS** (N° RR SEPT 27 383) (M. Jacky
Hennequin) 1 et 2, Place du Docteur Aubret ☎ 33-53-84-76 ⊷ 12
Closed Sun. Evening meals to 8.30. English spoken. Filling station
near.

BARQUE (LA) 13970 B.-du-R. **RN 96 and RD 6 Map 24-B3**
♈ ⊗ **LE RELAIS DES QUATRE CHEMINS** (N° RR MAR 26 207)

B

Barque (La) continued
(Mme Colette **Girardi**) ☎ 42-58-60-03 Closed Sat, Sun low season. Italian spoken.

BARRE-EN-OUCHE (LA) 27330 Eure **RN 833 Map 8-A3**
♀ ⊗ **CHEZ JACKY ET CORINNE** (N° RR OCT 25 144) (M. and Mme Jacky **Scipion**) Grande Rue ☎ 32-44-35-28 Coaches welcome (35 seats). Evening meals to 9.00. Closed 20th Dec–1st Jan.

BASSE-INDRE 44160 L.-Atl. **RD 107 Map 11-42**
♀ ⊗ ⌂ **HOTEL BRETON** (N° RR MAI 25 415) (M. Yannick **Jaheny**) 10, Quai Langlois ☎ 40-86-01-65 ↤ 12 Closed Sat, Sun; Aug. Evening meals.

BASTIDE-L' EVEQUE (LA) 12200 Aveyron **RD 911 Map 22-B1**
♀ ⊗ **RELAIS DE L'HERMET** (N° RR FEV 26 810) (M. Yvon **Bourdon-cle**) Villefranche-de-Rouergue ☎ 65-65-61-41 Closed Sun, Mon evenings. Coaches welcome (rest. seats 100). Parking.

BAUDRE 50000 Manche **Map 4-B1**
♀ ⊗ **TABAC-ÉPICERIE L'INCOGNITO** (N° RR JUIL 27 317) (M. Lionel et Mme Monique **Maris-Bret**) Le Bourg ☎ 33-57-89-58 **Minitel** Closed Sun. English spoken. Evening meals. Filling station near.

BAUME-LES-DAMES 25110 Doubs **RN 83 Maps 10-A3 and 14-B3**
♀ ⊗ ⌂ **3 Stars NN HOTEL ZISS REST LA CREMAILLÈRE** (N° RR JUL 13 903) (M. Alfred **Ziss**) ☎ 81-84-07-88 **Minitel** Hyèvre-Paroisse ↤ 21 3 star rooms, 10 for lorry drivers. Closed Sat; Oct. Menus from 55-155F. Specialities: *coq au vin, canard à l'orange*
☞ *fritures.* German, English spoken. Special price lorry drivers.

BAVANS 25550 Doubs **RN 463 Map 10-A3**
♀ ⊗ ⌂ **LE RELAIS DES MARRONNIERS** (N° RR AOU 15 757) (M. Louis **Garnier**) Rue des Cerisiers ☎ 81-96-26-54 ↤ 5 Closed 2nd/3rd weeks of Sept. Open all days.

BAYEUX 14400 Calv. **RN 13 Map 4-B2**
♀ ⊗ **LA COLOMBE** (N° RR MAR 22 274) (M. **Hardy**) 13, route de Caen, Saint-Vigor-le-Grand ☎ 31-92-13-65 and 31-21-12-28 **Minitel** ↤ 3 (furnished) Closed evening, Sun. Full-board 150F per
☞ night. Coaches welcome (rest. seats 120). Evening meals.
♀ ⊗ ⌂ **LE COUP-FRANC** (N° RR AOÛT 27 363) (M. Alain **Belka-cemï**) 3, rue du Pond Trubert St-Vigor-Le-Grand ☎ 31-92-98-64 **Minitel** ↤ 4 English/Spanish spoken. Evening meals. Filling station near.

BAZAINVILLE 78123 Yvelines **RN 12 Map 1-B1**
♀ ⊗ **LA PETITE AUBERGE** (N° RR NOV 18 231) (Mme Sonia **Herluison**) Place de l'Église ☎ 34-87-61-40.

BAZEILLES 08140 Ardennes **RN 381 Map 6-A2**
♀ ⊗ ⌂ **LA GIVONNE** (N° RR MARS 21 843) (Mme Elisabeth **Huem-er**) 15, avenue du Général Lebrun ☎ 24-27-05-74 **Minitel** ↤ 5

Closed Mon; Feb. Full-board 150–180F per night. Coaches welcome (rest. seats 120). Evening meals. German, English, Dutch, Italian spoken.

BAZOCHE-GOUET (LA) 28330 E.-et-L. **RD 927 Map 8-B3**
♈ ⊗ **LA BONNE AUBERGE** (N° RR AVR 22 787) (M. Jean-Paul **Thierry**) 54, avenue du Général Leclerc ☎ 37-49-21-61 Closed fortnight in Feb and July. Evening meals for lorry drivers only.

BAZOCHES-EN-DUNOIS 28140 E.-et-L. **RN 827 and RD 27 Map 8-B3**
♈ ⊗ **AU BON ACCUEIL - CHEZ MARIE-CLAUDE** (N° RR DEC 21 717) (Mme Marie-Claude **Boucher**) 7, rue de l'Église ☎ 37-22-08-30. Coaches welcome (rest. seats 50). Evening meals to 10pm.

BAZOUGES SUR LE LOIR 72200 Sarthe **RN 23 Map 12-A2**
♈ ⊗ **AUBERGE DU SOLEIL LEVANT** (N° RR SEPT 26 996) (M. Denis **Borée**) 79, Avenue du Maine ☎ 43-45-33-47. Filling station near. English spoken. Closed Sun. Evening meals to 9.30.

BEAUCE 35133 Ille-et-Villaine **RN 12 Map 8-B1**
♈ ⊗ **BEC FIN LES ROUTIERS** (N° RR JAN 26 789) (Mme Nicole **Vandevelde**), 19, rue de Paris ☎ 99-99-08-00 Closed Suns; Aug. Evening meals to 9pm.

BEAUCHALOT par SAINT-MARTORY 31360 Hte-Gar. **RN 117 Map 21-B3**
♈ ⊗ ⌂ **AUX BEARNAIS** (N° RR SEP 20 540) (M. René **Frechou**) ☎ 61-90-23-44 ⇥ 5 Closed Mon; 15–30 Sept. Full board 220F. Coaches welcome (rest. seats 100). Evening meals to 9.00pm. English, Spanish, German spoken.

BEAUCHAMPS 80770 Somme **RN 15 Bis Map 4-A2**
♈ ⊗ ⌂ **LES ROUTIERS CHEZ MICHEL** (N° RR MAI 21 913) (M. Michel **Blot**), 44, Grande Rue ☎ 22-26-13-12 ⇥ 9 Closed Sun; end Dec. Full board 120–150F. Coaches welcome (rest. seats 90). Evening meals to 10pm.

BEAUCROISSANT 38140 Isère **RD 159 Map 24-B1**
♈ ⊗ **LE RELAIS DU CHAMP DE FOIRE** (N° RR MAR 24 889) (Mme Marie-Thérèse **Blain**) Le Bain - Rive-sur-Fure ☎ 76-91-05-17. Closed Sun; fortnight in May and fortnight in Oct. Coaches welcome (rest. seats 70).

BEAULIEU 45630 Loiret **RD 926 and 951 Map 13-A2**
♈ ⊗ ⌂ **HOTEL DU LOIRET** (N° RR JAN 22 639) (M. Roland **Goury**) Place du Général-de-Gaulle ☎ 38-35-83-34 ⇥ 7 Closed Palm Sun and end Sept. Evening meals.

BEAUMAIS 14620 Calvados **RD 148 Map 8-A2**
♈ ⊗ **LE RELAIS DES ROUTIERS** (N° RR JUN 21 571) (Mme Bernadette **Saillanfait**) ☎ 31-90-70-88.

BEAUMONT-SUR-VESLE 51360 Marne **RN 44 Map 6-B2 and 9-A3**
♈ ⊗ ⌂ **2 stars NN LA MAISON DU CHAMPAGNE** (N° RR MAR 2

B

Beaumont-sur-Vesle continued

227) (M. Marc **Boulard**) 2, rue du Port ☎ 26-03-92-45 ⊷ 10 from 75-200F, breakfast to 22F. Closed Sun evening, Mon; 2 weeks in Feb; 2 weeks in Oct. German, English, Luxemburg spoken. Coaches welcome (rest. seats 170). Evening meals. Menus from 38-130F. Specialities: *terrines du chef, rognons de veau au ratafia, canard aux griottes*. Sites to visit: Vineyards, 1st World War battlefields. Parking. Bar.

BEAUNE 21200 Côte-d'Or **RN 74 Map 13-B3**

♉ ⊗ 🏠 **AUBERGE DE LA GARE SARL** (N° RR SEPT 26 655) 11, avenue des Lyonnais ☎ 80-22-11-13 ⊷ 6 Closed Sun, public holidays; Aug. Coaches welcome (rest. seats 50). Evening meals to 8.30pm.

♉ ⊗ **CAFÉ DE FRANCE** (N° RR NOV 24 023) (M. Jean-Pierre **Le Payen**) 13, Faubourg Bretonnière ☎ 80-22-25-44 Coaches welcome (rest. seats 120). Closed Sun; Aug.

♉ ⊗ **LE MALMEDY** (N° RR DEC 21 315) (Mme Yvette **Pecout**) 6, rue du Lieutenant-Dupuis ☎ 80-22-14-74 Coaches welcome (rest. seats 90). Closed Sun.

♉ **TRUCKSTORE CAFÉ BEAUNE** BP 134 ☎ 80-21-40-78 Télex: 352 105.

BEAUNE-LA-ROLANDE 45340 Loiret **Map 9-B1**

♉ ⊗ 🏠 **LE CYRNOS** (N° RR JUIL 27 354) (Mme Valérie **Topalian**) 40 avenue de la Gare ☎ 38-33-20-16 ⊷ 7 Closed Mon afternoon. English, Arabic, Spanish spoken. Evening meals to 10.30. Filling station near open 6–8pm. Parking.

BEAUNE-LES-MINES 87830 Haute-Vienne **RN 20 Map 16-B1**

♉ ⊗ 🏠 **LA TERRASSE** (N° RR MAI 13 721) (Mme Rachel **Barelaud**) ☎ 55-39-90-58 ⊷ 16 Closed Sun and August. English spoken.

BEAUSSET (LE) 83330 Var **RN 8 Map 24-B3 25-A3**

♉ ⊗ **TERRASSE OMBRAGÉE SUR L'AÉRODROME** (N° RR NOV 25 207) (Mme Marie-France **Gautier**) RN 8 circuit Paul-Ricard Le Camp du Castellet ☎ 94-90-71-48 Closed Sat; 22 Dec to 8 Jan. Coaches welcome (rest. seats 200). English, Portuguese spoken. Evening meals to 8pm.

BEAUVOIR-EN-LYONS 76220 Seine-Maritime **Map 3-B1**

♉ ⊗ 🏠 **RELAIS NORMAND CHEZ FRANÇOISE ET JULIEN** (N° RR JUIL 27 327) (M. Julien **Jué**) Les Carreaux ☎ 35-90-17-20 **Minitel** Closed Sat, Sun and Bank holidays. Menus at 50F. Filling station 5km. Parking.

BEAUVOIR-SUR-MER 85230 Vendée **RN 148 Map 11-B2**

♉ ⊗ **AU RELAIS DU GOIS** (N° RR JUN 14 383) (M. Gilles **Grondin**) ☎ 51-68-70-31 Closed 1 to 31 Dec. Coaches welcome (rest. seats 150). Evening meals (Jul, Aug).

BEAUVOIR-SUR-NIORT 79360 Deux-Sèvres **RN 138 Map 15-A1**

♉ ⊗ **L'ETAPE** (N° RR FEV 27 199) (Mme Annick **Duverne**) 7, place de l'Hôtel de Ville ☎ 49-09-70-17 Closed Sun afternoon. Some English spoken. Filling station near 8–8pm.

BEAUVOIS-EN-CAMBRESIS 59157 Nord **Map 6-A1**
♀ ⊗ **Service Station ELF LE JEUNE BOIS** (N° RR FEV 26 816) (M. Louis **Haesart**) Caudry ☎ 27-85-62-34. English, Dutch, German spoken.

BEDEE 35160 I.-et-V. **RN 12 Map 7-B3**
♀ ⊗ ⌂ **1 Star NN HOTEL DU COMMERCE** (N° RR SEP 13 987) (M. Jean-Louis **Rigoreau**) 14, Place de l'Eglise ☎ 99-07-00-37 and 99-07-00-76 **Minitel** ⇁ 22 86–105F, breakfast 15–18F. Restaurant closed Sun; 5–26 Aug. Full board 170-200F per night. Coaches welcome (rest. seats 360). Evening meals to 10pm. English spoken. Bar. Dogs allowed. TV room. Parking. Menu 40–90F.
⌣ Specialities: *Coquillos St. Jacques à la Brefonro, Gibelotle au cidre. Magrer de canard au vinaigro de jamboises.*

BEFFES 18560 Cher **RN 45 Map 13-B2**
♀ ⊗ ⌂ **LE JACK LONDON** (N° RR JUIL 26 961) (M. Jany **Ombre-dane**) rue du Château Gaillard ☎ 48-76-54-91 ⇁ 8 English spoken. Filling station near.

BEIGNON 56300 Morbihan **RN 24 Map 7-B3**
♀ ⊗ ⌂ **LE RELAIS DES ROUTIERS** (N° RR MAR 14 268) (M. Pierre **Labbe**) 40 km from Rennes – 60 km from Vannes ☎ 97-75-74-37 ⇁ 6 Closed Sat afternoon. Coaches welcome (rest. seats 80). Full board 150-180F per night. Evening meals until 9.30pm.

BELLAC 87300 Haute-Vienne **Map 16-B1**
♀ ⊗ **LE RELAIS** (N° RR AVR 26 906) (M. Henri **Cotte**) 3, rue Fernand Fourreau ☎ 55-68-00-22 Closed Sun; Sept. Evening meals.

BELLANCOURT 80100 Somme **RN 35 Map 5-A3**
♀ ⊗ **CHEZ ALINE ET MICHOU** (N° RR JUL 25 477) (M. Jean-Michel **Hoflack**) 2, Rte Nationale ☎ 22-24-35-13 **Minitel** Closed Sun in winter; 15 days in Sept/15 days Dec. Coaches welcome (rest. seats 60).

BELLEGARDE 01200 Ain **RN 101 Map 18-B2**
♀ ⊗ **LES PLATANES** (N° RR JUL 26 588) (Mme Bruno **Lorenzati**) 5, rue Centrale ☎ 50-48-15-05. Closed Sun; Aug. Italian spoken.

BELLEGARDE 45270 Loiret **RN 60 Maps 9-B1 and 13-A1**
♀ ⊗ ⌂ **1 Star NN LE CAFÉ DU COMMERCE** (N° RR AOU 9 843) (Mme Nelly **Grégoire**) 1, rue de la République ☎ 38-90-10-45 ⇁ 12 (5 with shower) from 86 120F, breakfast from 18-20F. Closed Fri evening, Sat; the last 2 weeks Aug. 25 Dec–15th Jan. Full-board 150–180F per night. Coaches welcome (rest. 3 rooms 170 seats). Evening meals. Parking; bar; dogs allowed. Sites to visit: Châteaux, Churches.

BELLEGARDE 30127 Gard **RN 113 Map 24-A3**
♀ ⊗ **LE LOU FÉLIBRE** (N° RR DEC 27 119) (Sarl Cabinet Pierre

B

Bellegarde continued

Curie) ☎ 66-01-15-21 Closed Sun (low season) German, English, Spanish and Italian spoken. Filling station near open 24 hours.

BELLE-INUTILE (LA) par CONNERRE 72160 Sarthe **RN 23 Map 8-B2**

♀ ⊗ ⌂ **1 Star NN LA BICHE DOREE** (N° RR AOUT 27 370) (M. Dominique **Herault**) RN 23 ☎ 43-76-70-45 ⊷ 10 from 90-120F, breakfast from 11.50-16F. Closed Sat, Sun unless booked. Parking (1 hectare). Sites to visit: Sarthe and surroundings. English spoken. Evening meals to 11pm. Filling station near.

BELLEME 61130 Orne **RN 155 and RD 938 Map 8-B2**

♀ ⊗ ⌂ **SARL LE CHAMP DE FOIRE** (N° RR MARS 27 236) (Mlle **Baire**) 4, place du Gl-Leclerc ☎ 33-73-00-38 ⊷ 6 Closed Sun except 1/5 to 31/8. Spanish and English spoken.

♀ ⊗ **LE GUÉ ROUTIER** (N° RR DEC 26 762) (M. and Mme Bernard **Herouin**) Le Bourg, Le Gué de la Chaine ☎ 33-73-02-66 Closed Sun. Full board. Coaches welcome (rest. seats 56+).

BELLENGREVILLE 14370 Calv. **RN 13 Map 4-B2**

♀ ⊗ **HOTEL DE LA PLACE** (N° RR MAI 26 253) (M. Désiré **Desmeulles**) 16, rue de Paris ☎ 31-23-61-50 Closed Sat afternoon, Sun. Evening meals.

BELLERIVE 03700 Allier **Map 16-B3**

♀ ⊗ ⌂ **LE BOIS DE BOULOGNE** (N° RR JUIN 26 930) (Mme Edith **Moliner**) 130, avenue de Vichy ☎ 70-32-38-11 ⊷ 6 English and Spanish spoken.

BELLEVILLE 55100 Meuse **Map 6-B3**

♀ ⊗ **CHEZ DÉDÉ** (N° RR MAI 25 417) (M. **Buffelo**) 164, av. du Gl-de-Gaulle ☎ 29-84-57-85 Verdun Italian spoken. Closed Sun and 1st two weeks in Sept. Coaches welcome (rest. seats 25–40).

BELLEVUE-COETQUIDAN 56380 Morbihan **Map 7-B3**

♀ ⊗ ⌂ **L'UNION** (N° RR MARS 20 131) 3, avenue de Brocéliande ☎ 97-75-71-46 ⊷ 5 Closed Sun; Aug. Showers, shared bathroom.

BELLEVUE-LA-MONTAGNE 43350 Hte-Loire **RD 906 Map 17-A3**

♀ ⊗ ⌂ **HOTEL DES VOYAGEURS** (N° RR MARS 26 217) (Mme Odette **Chapon**) ☎ 71-00-50-15 ⊷ 12. Full board available. Coaches welcome (rest. seats 110). Evening meals.

BELLEVUE-par-MORNANT 69440 Rhône **RD 42 Map 2-B1**

♀ ⊗ **LE RELAIS DE BELLEVUE** (N° RR MAR 18 045) (M. Georges **Guyot**) ☎ 78-81-22-26 Closed Sun; 2 weeks in Aug. Coaches welcome (rest. seats 70). Meals served until 11pm.

BELLEY 01300 Ain **RN 504 Map 2-A3**

♀ ⊗ **REST DE LA GARE** (N° RR AOUT 25 614) (Mme Elisabeth **Bavu**) Avenue de la Gare ☎ 79-81-06-60. Full board 140-160F per night. Coaches welcome (rest. seats 80). Evening meals served until 10pm. Closed 15th Dec–2nd Jan.

B

BELLIGNAT 01810 Ain **RN 840 Map 19-A1**
♀ ⊗ **A LA BONNE AUBERGE DES ROUTIERS** (N° RR DEC 18 911)
(M. Michel **Detouillon**) 11, avenue Oyonnax ☎ 74-78-24-18 ↦ 4
Closed Aug; Sun. Evening meals to 8.30. Parking.

BENESSE-MARENNE 40230 Landes **RN 10 Map 20-A2**
♀ ⊗ ⌂ **1 star NN HOTEL DES PINS** (N° RR JUN 25 023) (M. Jean-
Claude **Bernettes**) ☎ 58-72-56-41 & 72-50-80 ↦ 5 Closed Sun; 20
Sept to 10 Oct. Coaches welcome (3 dining rooms of 120 places).
Evening meals served until 9.30pm. Full board (125–160F).

BERCK-SUR-MER 62600 Pas-de-Calais **Map 5-A2/A3**
♀ ⊗ ⌂ **RELAIS D'ARTOIS** (N° RR MARS 26 826) (M. Raoul **Postell**)
20, rue Alfred-Lambert ☎ 21-09-29-35 **Minitel** ↦ 14. Full board
135–150F. Coaches welcome (rest. seats 40 places). Evening
meals.

BERNES-SUR-OISE 95340 Val d'Oise **Map 3-B3**
♀ ⊗ **CHEZ CLAUDINE** (N° RR DEC 27 124) (Mme Claudine **Diehl**)
1, rue de Creil ☎ 34-70-04-00 ↦ 4. Closed Sat, Sun and August.
Filling station near.

BERSON 33390 Gironde **RN 137 Map 15-A3**
♀ ⊗ **LA REIGNIERE** (N° RR MAR 18 035) (M. Liliane **Demel**) ☎ 57-
64-35-36 Closed Sat, Sun. Coaches welcome (rest. seats 60).
Evening meals.

BERRE 13130 Bouches-du-Rhône **Map 24-B3**
♀ ⊗ **CHEZ MIMI ET DONAT REST DE L'ENTENTE** (N° RR DEC 24
801) (M. Donat **Le Guennec**) Rte du Moulin Vieux ☎ 42-85-37-44
Closed Sat, Sun; Aug. German, English spoken.

BERTHOLENE-par-LAISSAC 12310 Aveyron **RN 88 Map 23-A1**
♀ ⊗ ⌂ **1 Star NN HOTEL BANCAREL** (N° RR AVR 21 480) (M. Jean
Brun) Situated on outskirts of Palanges forest ☎ 65-69-62-10
Minitel ↦ 13 from 100-140F, breakfast to 18F. Closed 25/9–15/10.
Full-board 170–190F per night. Coaches welcome (rest. seats
150). Evening meals. Parking (individual lockable garages); bar;
dogs allowed; Grand Terrasse. Menus 72-100F. Specialities:
Feuilleté Roquefort, Confit de canard à l'ancienne, Tripoux du
⌂ *Rouergue*. Sites: Trou de Bozouls, Gorges du Lot. Montagne de
Laves.

BESSAY-SUR-ALLIER 03340 Allier **RN 7 Map 16-A3**
♀ ⊗ **LE BAR DE LA ROUTE BLEUE** (N° RR JAN 20 633) (M. Francis
Blanche) rue Charles-Louis-Philippe ☎ 70-43-01-59 Closed Sat
afternoon and Sun. Evening meals. Filling station near.

BESSE-SUR-BRAYE 72310 Sarthe **RN 821 Map 12-A3**
♀ ⊗ ⌂ **1 Star NN LE RELAIS DE LA GARE** (N° RR OCT 13 181)
(Mme Marguerite **Lenoir**) 19, avenue de la Gare ☎ 43-35-30-22
↦ 12. Meals served in evening to 10pm. Full board 140–160F.
Closed Sun; Aug.

B

BESSIÈRES 31660 Haute-Garonne **Map 22-A2**
⏽ ⊗ 🏠 **1 Star NN LE BESSIÉRAIN** (N° RR NOV 27 101) (M. Philippe **Turmo**) avenue de Montauban ☎ 61-84-00-95. Rest. closed August. ⊷ 12. Filling station close.

BEURLAY 17250 Chte-Mme **RN 137 Map 11-B1**
⏽ ⊗ **LE RELAIS D'ARY** (N° RR SEPT 26 631) (M. Yves **Mariaud**) L'Olivière- Saint-Porchaire ☎ 46-95-01-39 Coaches welcome (rest. 3 rooms of 75 places). Meals served until midnight. Spanish spoken.

BEUVRY-LES-BETHUNE 62660 P.-de-C. **RN 41 Map 5-A1**
⏽ ⊗ **AU BON ACCUEIL** (N° RR MAR 26 833) (Mme Madiana **Thurlure**) 32, route Nationale ☎ 21-65-15-60.

BEUZEVILLE 27210 Eure **RN 175 and CD 22 Map 4-B2**
⏽ ⊗ **CAFÉ DE L'ESPÉRANCE** (N° RR DEC 27 125) (Mme Denise **Deguine**) 4, rue Pasteur ☎ 32-57-70-60 Closed Sun pm and 2 weeks of August. English spoken. Filling station near.

BEYNAC-EN-PÉRIGORD 24220 Dordogne **RN 703 Map 15-B2**
⏽ ⊗ 🏠 **2 Stars NN SARL HOSTELLERIE MALEVILLE** (N° RR FEV 25 804) (M. Jacques Maleville) ☎ 53-29-50-06 ⊷ 20 Closed Mon from Oct to Easter. English spoken. Full board 195 to 250F. Coaches welcome (rest. seats 150). Evening meals until 11.30pm.

BEZENET 03170 Allier **RN 145 Map 16-A2**
⏽ ⊗ 🏠 **RESTAURANT DU MIDI** (N° RR MAR 23 154) (M. Michel **Destainville**) Route Nationale ☎ 70-07-72-15 **Minitel** ⊷ 4 Closed Sat; 1 week May, 1 week Oct or Nov. English, Spanish, Italian spoken.

BEZIERS 34500 Hérault **RN 113 Map 23-A2**
⏽ ⊗ 🏠 **LE RELAIS DE LA GRANDE VITESSE** (N° RR MAI 19 050) (Mme Anne-Marie **Prome**) 23, boulevard de Verdun ☎ 67-76-26-30 Closed Wed. Coaches welcome (rest. seats 40). Evening meals.
⏽ ⊗ **LE KING** (N° RR JUIL 27 350) (M. Hasni **Idrici**) Rue quai port Notre-Dame ☎ 67-28-78-48. Closed Sun (low season). Arabic/Spanish spoken. Filling station near open 24 hrs.

BIARS-SUR-CERE 46130 Lot **RN 140 Map 17-B1**
⏽ ⊗ 🏠 **CHEZ ALAIN RELAIS ROUTIERS** (N° RR AVR 23776) (M. Alain **Cavalhac**) 16, av. de la République ☎ 65-38-42-30 ⊷ 4 Closed Sun; Aug. Coaches welcome (rest. seats 110). Evening meals.

BIGAROUX-SAINT-SULPICE-DE-FALEYRENS 33300 Gironde **RN 670 Map 15-A3**
⏽ ⊗ 🏠 **LE RELAIS CHEZ LA PUCE** (N° RR SEP 10 992) (Mme Renée **Forillière**) ☎ 57-24-71-18 ⊷ 5 Closed Sat, Sun. Coaches welcome (rest. seats 70).

B

BINAS 41240 L.-et-C. **RN 157 Map 12-A3**
♟ ⊗ **LE SAINT CHRISTOPHE** (N° RR AVR 24 930) (M. Philippe **Duvernet**) 17, place St-Maurice ☎ 54-82-40-26 ⚊ 5 Closed Sun afternoon in summer, all day winter. Full-board 160–180F per night. Evening meals.

BITSCHWILLER-LES-THANN 68620 Ht-Rhin **RN 66 Map 10-B3**
♟ ⊗ ⌂ **LE RELAIS DE LA VILLE DE THANN** (N° RR JAN 10 268) (M. Alain **Bannwarth**) 12, rue du Rhin ☎ 89-37-02-64 ⚊ 5 Closed Sat; Sept. German, English spoken.

BIVILLE-LA-BAIGNADE 76890 S.Mme **RN 27 Map 3-A1**
♟ ⊗ **LA CUILLERE EN BOIS** (N° RR NOV 24 021) (Mme Yvette **Guerillon**) ☎ 35-32-88-81 Closed Wed. Evening meals.

BLAGNY 08110 Ardennes **RN 381 Map 6-A3**
♟ ⊗ **LE RELAIS DES CITES** (N° RR FEV 17 463) (M. Gérard **Lemaître**) 37, Rte Nationale ☎ 24-22-00-23 Closed Sat; Aug. Evening meals.

BLAMONT 54450 Meurthe-et-Moselle **Map 10-A2**
⛽ **Total Service Station RELAIS D'OGEVILLER** (N° RR FEV 24 862) (M. Christian **Perrette**) Rte Nle 4 ☎ 83-72-27-82 Closed Sun. German spoken.

BLANC-MESNIL (LE) 93150 Seine-St-Denis **RN 2 Map 1-A3**
♟ ⊗ **LA TRAVERSEE DE L'ATLANTIQUE** (N° RR JAN 9 225) (M. Auguste **Lemore**) 178, rue de Flandre ☎ 48-66-89-24 Closed Sun.
♟ ⊗ **LE BON ACCUEIL** (N° RR SEP 26 663) (M. André **Seban**) 58, avenue du 8-Mai-1945 ☎ 48-67-19-88. Open 8am–2am daily. Coaches welcome (rest. seats 123 in 3 rooms). English spoken.

BLANZY 71450 Saône-et-Loire **Map 18-A1**
♟ ⊗ **BAR RESTAURANT DE LA GARE** (N° RR OCT 27 043) (M. Bernard **Borowski**) 16, rue de la Gare ☎ 85-68-03-05 English spoken. Coaches welcome (rest. seats 60). Evening meal to 10pm. Filling station near.

BLAUSASC 06440 Alpes-Maritimes **Map 25-B2**
♟ ⊗ **LE RELAIS CAMPAGNARD** (N° RR JUIL 27 323) (Mme Marie **Negri**) Pointe de Blausasc ☎ 93-91-13-14 English spoken. Evening meals served until 9pm.

BLAYE-LES-MINES 81400 Tarn **RN 88 Map 22-B1**
♟ ⊗ ⌂ **RELAIS SAINTE MARIE** (N° RR MARS 26 847) (M. Jacky **Lacroix**) 53, Bois Redon, Carmaux ☎ 63-76-53-81. ⚊ 7 Closed Sat, Sun.

BLENOD-LES-PONT-A-MOUSSON 54700 M.-et-M. **RN 57 Map 14-B1**
♟ ⊗ **CHEZ FERNANDE** (N° RR DEC 23 056) (SARL Chez Fernande) 88, avenue Victor-Claude ☎ 83-81-03-54 ⚊ 2 Closed Sat afternoon; Sun; Aug. Evening meals to 10pm.

B

BLÉRÉ 37150 I.-et-L. **RN 76 Map 12-B3**
♀ ⊗ **LE RELAIS** (N° RR DEC 17 964) (Mme Paulette **Rossignol**) 48, route de Tours ☎ 47-57-92-31 **Minitel** Full board 200F. Closed Sat; Sept. Coaches welcome (rest. seats 140). Evening meals.

BLOIS 41000 L.-et-C. **RD 951 Map 12-A3**
♀ ⊗ **BAR DE LA CITÉ** (N° RR MARS 26 862) (M. Didier **Moreau**) 55, avenue de Vendôme ☎ 54-43-48-54 Closed Sat and Sun. Coaches welcome (rest. seats 60). Evening meals.
♀ ⊗ **CAFÉ-ROUTE** (M. Jean-Louis **Pignot**) Autoroute A10 ☎ 54-46-84-73 Self-service café open 6am to 11pm.

BLYES 01150 Ain **Autoroute A42 Map 2-A2**
♀ ⊗ ⌂ **AUBERGE DE BLYES** (N° RR DEC 25 237) (M. Georges **Durand**) Lagnieu ☎ 74-61-50-15 ⊷ 4 Closed Sun. Full-board 150–180F per night. Coaches welcome (rest. seats 180). Evening meals until midnight.

BOEN-SUR-LIGNON 42130 Loire **RN 89 Map 18-A2**
♀ ⊗ **BAR RELAIS ROUTIERS** (N° RR JUN 26 921) (Mme Laurence **Carton**) 83, rue de Lyon ☎ 77-24-44-76. Closed Sun. Coaches welcome (rest. seats 33). Evening meals.

BOGNY-SUR-MEUSE 08120 Ardennes **Map 6-A2**
♀ ⊗ **LE RELAIS DE LA GARE CHEZ COCO** (N° RR JUL 24 619) (M. Enrique **Herraiz**) 1, rue de la Vallée ☎ 24-32-03-51 Closed Sun; Aug.

BOISNEY 27300 Eure **RN 13 Map 4-B3**
♀ ⊗ ⌂ **CHEZ MARC** (N° RR SEP 25 099) (M. Jean-Pierre **Thomas**) Rte Nle 13 ☎ 32-43-23-43 ⊷ 7.

BOIS D'OINGT (LE) 69620 Rhône **Map 2-A1**
♀ ⊗ **LE RELAIS DU LAC** (N° RR AVR 24 917) (Mme Christiane **Sibourg**) Les Petits Ponts ☎ 74-71-60-01 Closed Tue afternoon. Last 2 weeks Aug.

BOIS-PARIS see MAINVILLIERS

BOISSY-SOUS-ST-YON 91-Essonne **RN 20 Map 9-B1**
♀ ⊗ **LA RELAIS DE TORFOU** (N° RR FEV 27 181) (M. Mohamed **Toufahi**) RN 20 30, av. de Paris ☎ 64-91-30-50 English, German and Spanish spoken.

BOLLENE 84500 Vaucluse **RN 7 Map 24-A2**
♀ ⊗ ⌂ **1 Star NN LE RELAIS DE LA CROISIERE** (N° RR AOUT 27 374) (Mme Jeanine **Gilles**) ☎ 90-30-20-05 ⊷ 17 from 105–205F, access for disabled. 4 for drivers at 60F. Evening meals. Parking; English spoken.

BONCHAMP-LES-LAVAL 53210 Mayenne **RN 157 Map 8-B1**
♀ ⊗ ⌂ **LE RELAIS DE LA CORBINIERE** (N° RR JAN 17 733) (M. Roger **Dessaint**) ☎ 43-90-36-04 ⊷ 7 Closed Sat evening, Sun

from end March to beginning Nov. Coaches welcome (rest. seats 60). Evening meals until 10pm.

BONLOC 64240 Pyrénées-Atlantiques **RD 21 Map 20-A3**
♈ ⊗ **LILI PEAN** (N° RR NOV 25 190) (M. Gaston **Fouché**) **Hasparren** ☎ 59-29-51-48 **Minitel** Closed Sat low season; 15 Dec to 15 Jan. Coaches welcome (rest. seats 150). Evening meals to 10.30. English spoken and covered terrace 200 seats.

BONNEVILLE-SUR-ITON (LA) 27190 Eure **RD 129 and RN 830 Map 3-B1 and 8-A3**
♈ ⊗ **CAFÉ DES SPORTS** (N° RR NOV 8 068) (M. Roland **Fontaine**) 45, rue Jean-Maréchal ☎ 32-37-10-16 ⏤ 4 Closed Sun; Christmas, New Year. Evening meals to 10pm.
♈ ⊗ **CAFÉ DE L'ÉGLISE** (N° RR SEP 26 999) (M. and Mme Sylvain **Dareau** and Olida **Vasseur**) 23, rue Jean-Maréchal ☎ 32-37-11-90 ⏤ 3 Filling station near. Closed Sun; Aug.

BONSECOURS 12560 Aveyron **Map 23-A1**
♈ ⊗ **LES ROUTIERS** (N° RR AOU 25 072) (Mme Thérèse **Vayssie**) **Campagnac** ☎ 65-47-64-77 Closed Sat. Evening meals to 11pm.

BONSON 42160 Loire **RD 82 Map 18-A2**
♈ ⊗ ⌂ **1 Star NN LE RELAIS DES SPORTS** (N° RR FEV 23 679) (Mme Arlette **Pasca**) 14, avenue de la Gare ☎ 77-55-20-12 ⏤ 7 at 60–85F. Full-board 135–145F per night. Coaches welcome (rest. seats 45). Evening meals until 8.30pm. German, Italian spoken. Parking. Bar.

BORDEAUX 33000 Gironde **RN 10 Maps 15-A3, 20-B1 and 21-A1**
♈ ⊗ ⌂ **L'ALBATROS** (N° RR JAN 27 500) (M. Rcnc **Fucho**) 190, avenue de Labarde ☎ 56-50-97-83. Closcd Saturday, Sunday; August. Evening meals until 7pm. English spoken. Service station open 24 hrs.
♈ ⊗ **LE RELAIS DU BON COIN – Chez Georgette** (N° RR JAN 27 157) (Mme Sandine **Nouts**) 142, rue Lucien-Faure ☎ 56-39-40-13 Closed Sat, Sun; Aug. Fri evening. Filling station 1 km open 24 hrs.
♈ ⊗ **RESTAURANT DE L'UNION** (N° RR AVR 27 255) (M. Dominique **Depeyris**) 116, rue Lucien-Faure ☎ 56-50-05-77 Closed Sat pm, Sun and August. English spoken. Filling station 1km.
♈ ⊗ ⌂ **LE PORTO** (N° RR DEC 24 771) (Mme Rosa-Maria **Pereira**) 202 bis, quai de Brazza ☎ 56-86-15-93 ⏤ 6 Closed Sat, Sun; Aug. Bank holidays. Evening meals. Portuguese, Spanish spoken.
♈ ⊗ **CHEZ PIERRETTE** (N° RR AOU 26 973) (M. Alain **Debot**) 186, av de Labarde ☎ 56-39-66-70 Closed Sat, Sun; July. Some English, German spoken. Filling stations near. Evcning meals to 10pm.

BORDS 17430 Chte-Mme **Map 11-B1 15-A2**
♈ ⊗ **CAFÉ DU CENTRE** (N° RR OCT 26 361) (M. Martial **Perrocheau**) Place de l'Eglise ☎ 46-83-84-31 Evening meals served until 8.30pm. German spoken. Coaches welcome.

LA BORIE see RIBERAC 24600 Dordogne

B

BORT-LES-ORGUES 19110 Corrèze **RN 122 Map 17-A2**
⚗ ⊗ ⌂ **LE RELAIS DES ROUTIERS – CHEZ ANTOINETTE** (N° RR
SEP 14 954) (Mme Antoinette **Cheriex**) 9 place du Champ-de-
Foire ☎ 55-72-00-42 ⏤ 5.

BOSQUÉRARD DE MARCOUVILLE 27520 Eure **RN 138 Map 4-B3**
⚗ ⊗ ⌂ **1 Star LA TÊTE D'OIR** (N° RR MARS 26 844) (M. Gérard
Anquetin) Route de Lisieux ☎ 35-87-60-24 ⏤ 14. Rooms 103 to
135F. Breakfast 16 to 23F. Wheelchair access. Closed at end of
January. Dogs allowed. Horse riding and forest walking close by.
Parking. Bar. English spoken.

BOUC-BEL-AIR 13320 B.-du-R. **RN 8 Map 24-B3**
⚗ ⊗ **LE RELAIS DE LA MALLE** (N° RR JUL 24 276) (M. Jean-Louis
Zanon) ☎ 42-22-08-84 Closed Sat, Sun. Evening meals served
until 8pm. Coaches welcome (rest. seats 50).

BOUDOU 82200 T.-et-G. **RN 113 Map 21-A2**
⚗ ⊗ **LE MAQUISARD** (N° RR AOUT 25 619) (Mme Flora **Leghima**)
RN 113 Moissac ☎ 63-39-66-38 Spanish, German spoken.

BOUESSAY 53290 Mayenne **RN 159 Map 12-A2**
⚗ ⊗ **LE RELAIS DES ROUTIERS** (N° RR JUN 19 824) (M. Brigitte
Boivin) Rte de Sablé ☎ 43-70-82-05 Closed Sat afternoon, Sun.
Evening meals. Filling station 2km open 6–10pm.

BOUGE-CHAMBALUD 38150 Isère **Map 18-B3**
⚗ ⊗ **LE VERRE SOT** (N° RR OCT 27 414) (M. Dominique **Duchêne**) ☎
74-84-05-88 Closed Wed. Nov. Evening meals to 10pm. Parking.

BOUGUENAIS 44340 L.-Atl. **RN 751 Map 11-A3**
⚗ ⊗ **A LA FERME** (N° RR JANV 25 786) (M. Yvon **Burlot**) 65, rue de
la Pierre face Zl de Chevire ☎ 40-65-23-58 Closed Sat, Sun.
Showers. Coaches welcome (4 rooms of 30 seats).

BOUJAN SUR LIBRON 34760 Hérault **RN 113 Map 23-A2**
⚗ ⊗ ⌂ **LE CARRY** (N° RR SEP 27000) (Mme Patricia **Michavila**) ☎
67-31-63-48 ⏤ 10 Closed Sun. English spoken. Filling station 2
kms distant.

BOULAY-LES-BARRES 45140 Loiret **RN 155 Map 13-A1**
⚗ ⊗ ⌂ **L'AUBERGE DE LA ROUTE** (N° RR JUN 22 389) (M. and Mme
Jacky **Gasnot**) 21, rte d'Orléans ☎ 38-75-34-90 ⏤ 7 Closed Sat;
Aug. Evening meals until 10pm.

BOULOGNE SUR GESSE 31350 Haute Garonne **Map 21-B3**
⚗ ⊗ **Snack Bar LA GUINGUETTE** (N° RR MAI 19 356) (M. Pierre
Favre) Route de Blojan ☎ 61-88-11-64. Open 24 hrs. Italian,
Spanish, Portuguese, English spoken. Near to filling station.

BOULOGNE-SUR-MER 62200 P.-de-C. **RN 1 Map 5-A2**
⚗ ⊗ ⌂ **LE RELAIS DES DEUX GARAGES** (N° RR OCT 25 673) (M.
Maurice **Lachère**) 54, avenue John-Kennedy ☎ 21-91-12-96 ⏤ 14

Closed Sat afternoon, Sun. Full-board 107–137F per night. Evening meals. English spoken.

BOULOIRE 72440 Sarthe **RN 157 Map 8-B3**
℣ ⊗ **LE P'TIT MARCHE** (N° RR JUN 26 573) (M. Francis **Hemonnet**), 82, rue Nationale ☎ 43-35-40-04 Closed Thur. Coaches welcome (rest. seats 130).

BOUQUEMAISON 80600 Somme **RN 16 Map 5-A3**
℣ ⊗ **LA CHAUMIÈRE** (N° RR OCT 27 391) (M. Hubert **Payen**) 15, route de Saint Pol ☎ 22-77-32-17. Closed Sat pm and 1st 2 weeks Aug. Evening meals to 10pm. English spoken.
℣ ⊗ **LE RELAIS DES ROUTIERS – Chez Josette** Tobacconist (N° RR SEP 14 943) (Mme Josette **Doal**) 60, rue Saint-Pol ☎ 22-77-02-18 Closed 10 to 31 Aug. Coaches welcome (rest. seats 48).

BOURBON-LANCY 71140 S.-et-L. **RN 73 Map 16-A3**
℣ ⊗ ⌂ **HOTEL DE L'UNION** (N° RR SEPT 26 056) (M. Michel **Fleury**) Le Fourneau ☎ 85-89-15-07 ⊷ 6 Closed end Dec. Full-board 130F per night. Coaches welcome (rest. seats 60). Evening meals to 9pm.

BOURG-EN-BRESSE 01250 Ain **RN 75 Map 18-B1**
℣ ⊗ **LE PUB** (N° RR JAN 26 796) (Mme Paulette **Sueur**) Noirefontaine ☎ 74-23-05-40 Italian spoken.

BOURG-ET-COMIN 02160 Aisne **RS 967/925 Map 6-B1**
℣ ⊗ **L'ESCALE** (N° RR MARS 27 203) (M. Jacques **Pate**) 1, rue de Laon ☎ 23-24-40-44 Closed Mon pm. Filling station near open 7.30–7.

BOURG-DE-PÉAGE 26300 Drôme **RD 532 Maps 18-B3 and 24-A1**
℣ ⊗ **LE RELAIS DU VERCORS** (N° RR FEV 23 646) (M. Raphaël **Sanchez**) L'Écancière ☎ 75-48-83-44 **Minitel** Grill Pizzeria Wedding receptions, banquets. Coaches welcome (rest. seats 90). Evening meals. English spoken. Closed Sun.

BOURGANEUF 23400 Creuse **RN 140, 141 and RD 8 Map 16-B1**
℣ ⊗ ⌂ **LE RELAIS DE LA COUPOLE** (N° RR FEV 16 891) (M. Gérard **Paquet**) 17, avenue Turgot ☎ 55-64-08-99 ⊷ 13 Closed Sat; 25 Nov to 20 Dec. English spoken.
℣ ⊗ ⌂ **AU RENDEZ-VOUS DES CHASSEURS** (N° RR FEV 22 656) (Mme Monique **Feisthammel**) lieu-dit Puy-La-Croix – Saint-Pardoux-Morterolles ☎ 55-64-12-42 ⊷ 16 Closed Sun.

BOURGES 18000 Cher **RN 151 Map 13-B1**
℣ ⊗ ⌂ **LES AILES** Sarl (N° RR OCT 27 038) 147, avenue Marcel Haegelen ☎ 48-21-57-86 ⊷ 16 Closed Sat night Sun. English and German spoken. Full board 110–135F. Coaches welcome (rest. seats 86). Evening meals to 11pm. Filling station near 6–12pm.

BOURGNEUF-EN-MAUGES 49290 M.-et-L. **RN 762 Maps 12-A1 and, 11-A3**
℣ ⊗ ⌂ **LE RELAIS DES ROUTIERS** (N° RR AOU 16 174) (M. Étienne

B

Bourgneuf-en-Mauges continued

Albert) 6, rue Notre-Dame ☎ 41-78-03-61 ⊷ 5 Closed Sun. Coaches welcome (rest. seats 90). Evening meals.

BOURNEUF-EN-RETZ 44580 Loire-Atlantique **Map 11-B3**

♈ ⊗ ⌂ **HÔTEL DES TRADITIONS LE BOIRAT** (N° RR OCT 27 429) (M. Noël **Rousselot**) 11, Avenue de la gare ☎ 40-21-91-44 ⊷ 6 Closed Sat. A little English spoken. Evening meals to 9pm. Filling station 1km open 8–9pm. Parking.

BOURGOIN-JALLIEU 38920 Isère **RN 85 Map 2-B2**

♈ ⊗ **SARL LA MAISON BLANCHE** (N° RR AVR 26 493) (M. Andre **Piloz**) RN 85 Nivolas-Vermelle ☎ 74-27-92-86 **Minitel** Closed Sat, Sun; Aug (3 weeks). Evening meals.

BOURNAN-BAGNEUX 49400 M.-et-L. **RN 160 Map 12-B2**

♈ ⊗ **LE RELAIS DE COTE DE BOURNAN-BAGNEUX** (N° RR JUN 16 601) (M. Claude **Sanzay**) 288, rue du Pont-Fouchard ☎ 41-50-18-02 Closed Sun. Coaches welcome (rest. seats 48). Evening meals.

BOURRAS 16200 Charente **RN 141 Map 15-A2**

♈ ⊗ **LE RELAIS DES VIGNES** (N° RR FEV 25 801) (Mme Monique **Delavoie**) RN 141 Commune de Mérignac ☎ 45-35-83-16 or 45-35-81-62 **Minitel** Closed Sun; Sept. Evening meals until 10pm. Parking.

BOUSSAIS 79600 Deux-Sèvres **RD 725 Map 12-B2**

♈ ⊗ **LE VERRE A SOI Tobacconist** (N° RR SEP 25 656) (M. Loïc **Boisselet**) **Airvault** ☎ 49-69-71-69 Closed Wed afternoon; 15 to 30 Aug.

BOUSSES 47420 Lot-et-Garonne **RD 665 Map 21-A2**

♈ ⊗ **AUBERGE DES RELAIS – Chez Nicole** (N° RR JUL 21 592) (Mme Nicole **Guillygormar'ch**) Au Bourg ☎ 53-89-11-62 Coaches welcome (rest. seats 60). Evening meals.

BOUSSOULET 43260 Haute-Loire **RD 15 Map 18-A3**

♈ ⊗ ⌂ **1 Star NN AUBERGE DU MEYGAL** (N° RR FEV 24 840) (M. René **Chapuis**) **St Julien de Chapteuil** ☎ 71-08-71-03 ⊷ 12 (5 with own WC) from 70-85F. Full-board 130F per night. Coaches welcome (rest. seats 170). Evening meals. Parking; bar; dogs allowed. Lakes and forests to visit. Bungalows and Chalets on weekend lets.

BOUVILLE 28800 E.-et-L. **RN 10 Map 8-B3**

♈ ⊗ **LE RELAIS DU BOIS DE FEUGERES** (N° RR JAN 15 914) (M. **Coatrieux**) ☎ 37-47-23-01 Closed Sat evening.

BOUVRON 44130 L. Atl. **RN 771 and D 16 Map 11-A2**

♈ ⊗ **LE BRETAGNE** (N° RR MARS 26 209) (M. Christian **Biard**) 1, Rue Louis Guihot, Blain ☎ 40-56-31-05 Closed Sun afternoon. Coaches welcome (rest. seats 170). Evening meals. English spoken.

B

BOUXWILLER 67330 Bas-Rhin **RD 6 and 7 Map 10-B1**
♓ ⊗ ⌂ **2 Stars NN LE RELAIS DU SOLEIL PMU** (N° RR AOU 15 750)
(M. Charles **Jaeger**) 71, Grand'Rue ☎ 88-70-70-06 ➼ 15 60–160F
breakfast 18–22F. Telephone. Closed Wed, Sun evening, beginning July to end school holidays; February '89. Full-board 150–
210F per night. Menus 58–120F. Specialities: *Chaucroute Coq au
Riesling Sandre à l'oseille.*Coaches welcome (rest. 3 rooms with
120 seats). Evening meals. German, English spoken. Parking.
Bar. Dogs allowed. Chateaux, lake, forest to visit.

BOUY-LUXEMBOURG 10220 Aube **Map 9-B3**
♓ ⊗ **CHEZ RAYMONDE** (N° RR OCT 25 143) (Mme Raymonde
Bouvron) **Tobacconist** ☎ 25-46-33-80 Closed Tue.

BOUZONVILLE 57320 Moselle **RN 418 Map 10-A1**
see **CHEMERY-LES-DEUX**

BOVES 80440 Somme **RN 334 Motorway Amiens-Roye Map 5-B3**
♓ ⊗ **LA GRENOUILLÈRE** (N° RR MAI 25 939) (M. Bouhou **Ouan-
noune**) La Grenouillère ☎ 22-09-31-26 **Minitel** Closed Sun
(except for banquets); 3 weeks Aug. Coaches welcome (rest.
seats 50). Evening meals. English, Algerian spoken.

BOYER 71700 Saône-et-Loire **RN 6 Map 18-B1**
♓ ⊗ **RELAIS ROUTIERS DU JONCHET** (N° RR AOÛT 27 359) (M.
Patrick **Bouillin**) ☎ 85-57-09-3 Closed Sat pm Sun. 24hr Filling
station nearby. Parking.

BRAM 11150 Aude **RN 113 Map 22-B2**
♓ ⊗ ⌂ **AUBERGE MONTPLAISIR – Chez Alain** (N° RR DEC 21
332) (M. Alain **Albecq**) ☎ 68-76-12-75 & 68 76 53-16 ➼ 10 Closed
Sat, Sun; 1 to 31 Aug; 24 Dec to 1 Jan. Evening meals to 11pm. Full
board 180–220F. Coaches welcome (rest. seats 130).

BRANSLES 77620 S.-et-M. **RN 219 Map 9-B2**
♓ ⊗ ⌂ **LE LION D'OR** (N° RR OCT 25 156) (M. Philippe **Vercruys-
sen**) 2, av. du Gâtinais ☎ 64-29-55-05 ➼ 7 Closed Tue. Coaches
welcome (rest. seats 30).
♓ ⊗ ⌂ **LE RELAIS DE L'UNION** (N° RR AVR 27 249) (Mme
Françoise **Lemairie**) 2, place A.-Briand ☎ 64-29-59-14 ➼ 11
Closed Wed. Evening meals. English spoken.

BRAS-SUR-MEUSE 55100 Meuse **RD 964 Map 6-B3**
♓ ⊗ **LE RELAIS DE LA PAIX** Petrol, tobacconist (N° RR JUN 25 976)
(Mme Anny **Renard**) 8, rue Raymond-Poincaré ☎ 29-83-90-13
Closed Tue. Coaches welcome (rest. seats 55). Evening meals.

BRASSAC-LES-MINES 63570 P.-de-D.) **RD 34 Map 17-A3**
♓ ⊗ **LE BRASSAC** (N° RR FEV 27 175) (M. Édouard **Kaluza**) 6, av. du
Château ☎ 73-54-29-23 Closed Tues pm and Sun pm. Filling
station near 6–8pm.

BRAY 27170 Eure **D 133 Map 4-B3**
♓ ⊗ **AUX AMIS** (N° RR DEC 26 765) (Mme Margaret **Herils**)

B

Bray continued
Beaumont-Le-Roger ☎ 32-35-05-26 Closed Sun.

BRÈCE 53120 Mayenne **Map 8-B1**
♈ ⊗ **LE DOMINO** (N° RR JAN 26 428) (M. **Carlin**) Le Bourg ☎ 43-08-62-72 **Minitel** Closed Sunday.

BRESSUIRE 79300 Deux-Sèvres **RN 748 Maps 11-B3, 12-B1 and 15-A1**
♈ ⊗ **LE FOCH** (N° RR FEV 25 822) (M. Marcel **Chailloux**) 51, bd du Ml-Foch ☎ 49-65-01-69 Closed Sat evening, Sun.

BRETHENAY 52000 Hte-Marne **RN 67 Map 14-A2**
♈ ⊗ ⌂ **BELLEVUE** (N° RR AOUT 7903) (Mme Micheline **Bourgoin**) Chaumont ☎ 25-32-51-02 ⊷ 8 Closed Sun and September. Filling station near 6–10pm.

BRETONCELLES 61110 Orne **Map 8–B3**
♈ ⊗ ⌂ **HOTEL DE LA GARE** (N° RR OCT 26 335) (M. **Alloteau**) 17, rue Ernest Sagot ☎ 37-37-20-13 ⊷ 6 Closed Sun. Full-board 135F per night.

BRETTEVILLE-L'ORGUEILLEUSE 14740 Calvados **RN13 Map 4-B2**
♈ ⊗ ⌂ **AU GRAND MONARQUE** (N° RR OCT 10 066) (Mme Madeleine **Laurent**) 37, Rte de Caen ☎ 31-80-70-35 ⊷ 5 Closed Sat, Sun afternoon; Sept. Evening meals served except on Sat, Sun.

BRETTNACH 57320 Moselle **Map 10-A1**
♈ ⊗ **AU RELAIS LORRAIN** (N° RR SEPT 27 388) (Mme Marie-Madeleine **Geyer**) 95, route de Bouzonville ☎ 87-35-97-36 German spoken. Evening meals.

BRIANÇON 05100 Htes-Alpes **Map 19-B3**
♈ ⊗ **LA LANTERNE** (N° RR NOV 24 424) (M. René **Parisot**) (2 km from Sud Briançon RN 80) Chamandrin ☎ 92-21-12-33 Closed 15/9–30/5. Coaches welcome (rest. seats 100). Evening meals. English, Spanish spoken.

BRIARE 45250 Loiret **RN 7 Map 13-A1/2**
♈ ⊗ ⌂ **SARL LE RELAIS** (N° RR OCT 26 685) (M. Eric **Bourgouin**) Gare de Chatillon-sur-Loire ☎ 38-31-44-42 ⊷ 10 Closed Sat afternoon, Sun. German and English spoken. Full board 180F. Coaches welcome (rest. seats 125 + entertainment room). Evening meals. Parking.

BRIENNE 71290 Saône-et-Loire **Map 18-B1**
♈ ⊗ **AUX AMIS DE LA ROUTE** (N° RR OCT 27 041) (Mme Elsa **Busca**) Bas de Brienne ☎ 85-40-04-18 Closed Mon and August. Italian and English spoken. 24 hr filling station 7km also local filling station open 7–10pm.

BRIENON-SUR-ARMANÇON 89210 Yonne **Map 13-A2**
♈ ⊗ ⌂ **LES ROUTIERS** (N° RR MARS 27 239) (M. Christian **Dussart**)

21, rte de Joigny ☎ 86-43-00-63 Polish, Russian and English spoken. Filling station nearby 6–8pm.

BRIGNOLES 83170 Var **RN 7 and RD 554 Map 25-A2**
⊗ **LA MAMMA AUBERGE LA REINETTE** (N° RR NOV 28 081) (Mlle Santina **Sepilesu**) RN 7 ☎ 94-59-07-46. Closed Sun and August. German, Italian, Spanish and English spoken. Filling station 3km.

BRIIS-SOUS-FORGES 91640 Essonne **Autoroute A 10 Map 1-A2**
⍦ **CAFÉ ROUTE** Motorway A10 (M. Yannick **Foucault**) Limours-Janvry ☎ 64-90-77-18 Open 6am to 10.30pm.

BRIONNE 27800 Eure **RN Map 4-B3**
⍦ ⊗ ⌂ **HOTEL DU HAVRE** (N° RR MARS 26 484) (M. **Kopacz**) Place Fremont-des-Essarts ☎ 32-44-80-28 **Minitel** ⊸ 16 English, Polish, German spoken. Full board available. Coaches welcome (rest. seats 120). Evening meals served.

BRIOUDE 43100 Haute-Loire **RN 102 Map 17-A3**
⍦ ⊗ **LES ROUTIEDS** (N° RR AVR 16 506) (M. Roger **Devins**) Route de Clermont ☎ 71-50-14-39 ⊸ 4 (for drivers only). Closed Sun; 15 Aug to 1 Sept. Coaches welcome (rest. seats 52). Evening meals.

BRIOUX-sur-BOUTONNE 79170 Deux-Sèvres **RN 150 Map 15-A1/2**
⍦ ⊗ **AUBERGE DU CHEVAL BLANC** (N° RR MARS 27 234) (Mme Catherine **Richard**) Place du Champ-de-Foire ☎ 49-07-50-52. English, German spoken. Filling station 24hrs nearby.

BRIOUZE 61220 Orne **RN 24 Bis Map 8-A2**
⍦ ⊗ ⌂ **LE RELAIS DE LA POSTE** (N° RR FEV 3 369) (Mme **Maupas**) ☎ 33 66 03 16 ⊸ 10 Evening meals until midnight.

BRIVE 19100 Corrèze **RN 89 and D Map 17-A1**
⍦ ⊗ ⌂ **NOUVEL HOTEL** (N° RR JAN 26 159) (M. Patrick **Lomey**) 2, Rue Desgenettes ☎ 55-86-01-66 **Minitel** ⊸ 6 Closed Sat afternoon, Sun; Aug. Evening meals.

BRIVE-LA-GAILLARDE 19100 Corrèze **RN 89 Map 17-A1**
⍦ ⊗ ⌂ **CHEZ MONIQUE** (N° RR MAR 23 187) (Mme Monique **Richard**) Varetz ☎ 55-85-02-07 ⊸ 8.

BRIVE-CHARENSAC 43700 Hte-Loire **RN 88 and 535 Map 17-A3**
⍦ ⊗ ⌂ **LE RELAIS DU COMMERCE** (N° RR DEC 23 561) (MM. **Ferret-Masson**) 2, route de Lyon (on the banks of the Loire). ☎ 71-09-16-16 ⊸ 10 Full-board 150–170F per night. Coaches welcome (rest. seats 90). Evening meals to 11pm.

BROGLIE 27270 Eure **RN 138 Map 8-A2 4-B3**
⍦ ⊗ ⌂ **LES TOURISTES ET LES ROUTIERS – RELAIS DE BROG-LIE** (N° RR JUN 17 824) (Mme Julienne **Vannier**) Côté de Bernay à Broglie, 47, rue Augustin-Fresnel ☎ 32-44-60-38 ⊸ 5 Closed 10 days end Jan early Feb. Coaches welcome (rest. seats 80). Evening meals to 12pm. Full board 180–200F.

B

BROMONT-LAMOTHE 63230 P.-de-D. **RD 941 Map 16-B2**
⊗ **LE RELAIS DE BOISSY** (N° RR FEV 14 203) (Mme **Boissy**) ☎ 73-88-71-04.

BROU 28160 Eure-et-Loire **RN 155 Map 8-B3**
♀ ⊗ ⌂ **LE RELAIS DE LA GARE – LE RELAIS DE L'ARC-EN-CIEL** (N° RR MAR 16 915) (M. Alain **Duparc**) 76, avenue du Gl-de-Gaulle ☎ 37-47-00-81 ⊷ 8 Closed Sun; Aug. Coaches welcome (rest. seats 72). Evening meals. Full board 170–200F.

BROUT-VERNET 03110 Allier **Rn 9 Map 16-B3**
♀ ⊗ ⌂ **CENTRE ROUTIERS – SARL** (N° RR JANV 24 475) (Mme **Roux**) Rte Nle 9, ☎ 70-58-24-61 **Minitel** ⊷ 14. Closed Sun. Full board 150F per night. Coaches welcome (rest. seats 70). Evening meals.
♀ ⊗ ⌂ **LES 3 CANARDS SARL** (N° RR NOV 26 730) (M. Patrick **Peltier**) RN 9 Escurolles ☎ 70-58-20-88 Closed Sun. English, Spanish spoken. Evening meals.

BRUAILLES 71500 S. et L. **RD 972 Map 18-B1**
♀ ⊗ ⌂ **REST. DES 4 CHEMINS** (N° RR MARS 27 225) (M. Thierry **Rousse**) Les Quatre Chemins, Louhans ☎ 85-75-15-81 ⊷ 5 Closed Tue evening. Filling station near open 7–8pm.

BRUAY-EN-ARTOIS 62700 Pas-de-Calais near Nle 41 **Map 5-A1**
♀ ⊗ ⌂ **1 Star NN LA LOUETTE (formerly CHEZ MICHEL) Sarl Cali** (N° RR MARS 26 835) (M. Serge **et Dany**) 114, rue Raoul Briquet, Place de la Gare ☎ 21-53-42-07 ⊷ 15 from 75-135F, breakfast 10-18F; TV (optional). Parking; bar; dogs allowed. Amusements: pin ball, darts, pool. Sites: Base d'Olhain, Colinne de l'Artois, châteaux. Full board 170F. Coaches welcome (rest. seats 250). Evening meals. English/German spoken.

BUCEY-LES-GY 70700 Haute-Saône **RD 474 Map 14-B3**
♀ ⊗ **CAFÉ DE LA GARE** (N° RR MAI 25 921) (Mme Yvette **Bole-Besancon**) Pizzeria Rue de la Gare ☎ 84-32-92-02 Coaches welcome (rest. seats 48/50). Evening meals until midnight.

BUIGNY-ST-MACLOU 80100 Somme **RN 1 Map 5-A3 4-A2**
♀ ⊗ ⌂ **LE RELAIS DES ROUTIERS** (N° RR JUN 16 117) (M. Marc **Caron**) ☎ 22-24-20-47 ⊷ 5 Closed Sat afternoon.

BUISSE (LA) 38500 Isère **RN 75 Map 19-B3**
♀ ⊗ **RELAIS DES ROUTIERS CHEZ ANNIE** (N° RR MARS 27 219) (Mme Annie **Revigliono**) Le Village Voiron ☎ 76-55-00-67 Italian spoken. Filling station near by open 6–9pm.

BUNCEY 21400 Côte d'Or **RN 71 Map 13-A3**
♀ ⊗ **LE CHARIOT** (N° RR JUN 26 555) (Paulette and Nadine **Lacroix**) Chatillon/Seine ☎ 80-91-09-82 Night bell for drivers. Closed Sunday; 15-days July. Coaches welcome (rest. seats 60). English spoken.

B

BUSLOUP 41160 Loirie-et-Cherl **RN 157 Map 12-A3**
 ⦸ **CAFÉ DU COMMERCE** (N° RR JUIN 26 927) (M. Gérard **Lefevre**) le Bourg Morée ☎ 54-23-43-41 Closed Aug; 24 Dec-1st Jan. Coaches welcome (rest. seats 90).

BUSSIÈRES 77750 Seine-et-Marne **RN 33 Map 9-A2**
 ⦸ **LE RELAIS AU SANS-GENE** (N° RR SEP 19 941) (M. Raymond **Tixier**) 32, Rte de la Ferté-sous-Jouarre ☎ 60-22-50-18 Closed Tue in Feb, Jul. Coaches welcome (rest. seats 80). Evening meals on request. German, Polish spoken. Menus from 55-120F. Specialities: *Andouillette au champagne, Filet de canard à l'orange ou aux pruneaux.*

BUZANÇAIS 36500 Indre **RN 143 Map 12-B3**
 ⦸ ⌂ **LE RELAIS DES ROUTIERS** (N° RR NOV 17 676) (M. Serge **Imbert**) 19, rue des Hervaux ☎ 54-84-07-37 ⊷ 8. Closed Sun; 15 days Aug. Coaches welcome (rest. seats 120). Evening meals to 10pm.
 ⦸ **LES ROUTIERS** (N° RR JANV 26 133) (M. Bernard **Souadet**) 48, rue des Hervaux ☎ 54-84-05-16 Closed Mon afternoon. Evening meals to 9pm.

C

CABOURG 14390 Calvados **RN 813 Map 4-B2**
 ⦸ ⌂ **HOTEL DE LA MER** (N° RR AOUT 26 023) (Mme Suzanne **Cottineau**) 42, av. René Coty Le Home Varaville ☎ 31-91-27-77 **Minitel** ⊷ 10 Closed Sun; 1 Oct to 15 Mar; 15 Dec to 2 Jan. Full-board 160–180F per night. Coaches welcome (rest. 2 rooms, 62 seats) + 62 seats on terrace. Evening meals to 9.30.
 ⦸ **LE COLOMBIER** (N° RR NOV 26 103) (M. Gérard **Baudel**) Route de Cabourg, Petiville ☎ 31-78-00-67 Closed Sun; Dec. Evening meals to 8.30pm.

CAEN 14000 Calvados **RN 13 Map 4-B2 and 8-A1**
 ⦸ ⌂ **1 Star NN LA RENAISSANCE** (N° RR FEV 20 652) (M. **Lehericey**) **Saint-Martin-des-Besaces** ☎ 31-68-72-65 ⊷ 8 Closed Mon, except in Summer; Jan. English spoken.

CAEN VENOIX 14000 Calvados **RN 175 Map 4-B2**
 ⦸ ⌂ **LE VELODROME** (N° RR MARS 26 195) (M. Daniel **Levigoureux**) 9, av. Henri Cheron ☎ 31-74-40-71 ⊷ 5 Closed Sat evening, Sun; Aug. Evening meals.

CAGNY 14630 Calvados **RN 13 Map 4-B2**
 ⦸ ⌂ **1 Star NN HOTEL DES ROUTIERS Chez Jean-Louis et Monique** (N° RR FEV 25 806) (M. Louis **Charpentier**) 22, Rte de Paris ☎ 31-23-41-27 ⊷ 10 Closed Sat, Sun; Aug. Full board 160F

C

Cagny continued
per night; half board 120F per night. Evening meals. English spoken.

♈ ⊗ ⌂ **HOTEL DE LA POSTE** (N° RR JUL 26 602) (M. Dominique **Klaczak**) 32, Rte de Paris ☎ 31-23-41-26 ⊷ 5. Full board 140F per night. Coaches welcome (rest. seats 50). Evening meals. Closed Sunday pm.

CAHORS 46000 Lot **RN 20 Map 22-A1 17-B1**
♈ ⊗ ⌂ **LE RELAIS DE LA BOURSE** (N° RR MAR 23 721) (M. Jean-Henri **Lebouvier**) 7, place Rousseau ☎ 65-35-17-78 ⊷ 12 Closed Sun; Aug. Full board 140–150F per night. Coaches welcome (rest. seats 90). Evening meals.

CAHUZAC-SUR-ADOUR 32400 Gers **RD 935 Map 21-A2**
♈ ⊗ ⌂ **LE RELAIS DES PYRÉNÉES** (N° RR OCT 14 016) (M. **Pozzobon**) ☎ 62-69-22-11 ⊷ 7 Closed Sat; Oct. Full-board 160F per night. Coaches welcome (rest. seats 50). Evening meals to 9.30 in season.

CAISSARGUES 30132 Gard **RN 113 – Nîmes St-Gilles Map 24-A3**
♈ ⊗ **LE MIRMAN** (N° RR FEV 26 446) (SNC Denis **Amigo**) Rte de Saint-Gilles Les Portes de Mirman ☎ 66-29-54-87. Closed Sat evening, Sun.

CALLAC 22160 C. du N **RN 787 Map 7-A2**
♈ ⊗ ⌂ **LES ROUTIERS** (N° RR OCT 26 064) (Mme Marie Yvonne **Richard**) 21, Rue de la Gare ☎ 96-45-51-10 ⊷ 7 Closed Sun. Full board 150F per night. Evening meals until 8.30pm.

CALLENGEVILLE 76270 Seine-Maritime **Map 4-A3**
♈ ⊗ ⌂ **AUBERGE NORMANDE** (N° RR NOV 24 750) (Mme Françoise **Foulny**) Rte Nle 28 Neufchâtel ☎ 35-93-74-07 ⊷ 6. Closed Sat. Full board 150–200F per night. Coaches welcome (2 rooms, 70 places). Evening meals until 11pm.

CALMETTE (LA) 30190 Gard **RN 6 Map 23-A1**
♈ ⊗ **RELAIS DE L'ESCALETTE** (N° RR JUIL 27 332) (M. Georges **Apostolakis**) ☎ 66-63-13-63 English spoken. Evening meals to midnight. Filling station.

CAMBRAI 59400 Nord **RN 17 Maps 5-B3, 6-A1 and A3**
♈ ⊗ ⌂ **LE RELAIS DES ROUTIERS** (N° RR MAI 7 690) (M. Roger **Guisgand**) 1084, av. du Cateau ☎ 27-81-35-82 ⊷ 4 Closed Sun; Aug. Full-board 140–250F. Evening meals. Coaches welcome (rest. seats 40).
♈ ⊗ **LA GARGOTE - Chez Jean** (N° RR MAI 25 401) (M. Claude **Bedu**) 136, bld Jean-Bart ☎ 27-81-07-18 **Minitel** Closed Sun. Coaches welcome (3 rooms – 140 seats).
♈ ⊗ ⌂ **CHEZ ROGER** (N° RR MARS 27 204) (M. Roger **Leprince**) 10, rue des Docks ☎ 27-83-26-05 ⊷ 6 Closed Sat pm, Sun and August. Filling station open 6–11pm.

CAMBRAI 59400 Nord **see AWOINGT**

CAMBRES 76570 S. Mme **Map 3-A1**

♀ ⊗ **LES AMIS DE LA ROUTE** (N° RR FEV 26 182) (Mme Denise **Ponthieux**) RN 27, Pavilly ☎ 35-32-51-98 Closed Sat, Sun. Coaches welcome (rest. seats 120). Evening meals before 8.30pm. English spoken.

CAMP DU CASTELLET (LE) 83330 Var **RN 8 Map 24-B3**

♀ ⊗ **LE RELAIS CHEZ MIMI** (N° RR AVR 25 890) (Mme Francine **Ponche**) ☎ 94-90-70-53 Closed Friday evening, Sat, Sun between Christmas and New Year. Coaches welcome (rest. seats 120 and terrace). Evening meals to midnight. Sat. English, Italian spoken. Parking.

CAMPSEGRET 24140 Dordogne **Nle 21 Map 15-B3**

♀ ⊗ **LE TAMARIS** (N° RR JUN 26 570) (M. Claude **Boetsh**) Lacroix/ Villamblard ☎ 53-24-21-75. Coaches welcome (rest. seats 60 + 2 terraces at 50 seats). Evening meals.

CANNES 06400 Alpes-Maritimes **Map 25-B2**

♀ ⊗ ⌂ **1 Star NN CHALET DE LISÈRE** (N° RR OCT 27 422) (M. Claude **Santoro**) 42 Avenue de Grasse ☎ 43-38-50-80 ⇥ 8 (all with showers, WC. TV) at 165–180F. Italian spoken. A little English/German. Filling station near open 8–8pm.

CANNES-LA-BOCCA 06150 Alpes-Mmes **Map 25-B2**

♀ ⊗ **PARIS-PROVENCE** (N° RR AVR 25 903) (M. Joaquim **Roldan**) 68, rue Francis Tonner ☎ 93-47-10-48 ⇥ 15 Closed Sun (low season) Spanish spoken.

♀ ⊗ **CAVE DE LA ROUBINE** (N° RR SEPT 26 313) (Mme **Pelletier**) 40, avenue de la Roubine ☎ 93-47-77-10 Closed Sun. Bank holidays. Italian spoken. Evening meal to 11pm.

CANNET-DES-MAURES (LE) 83340 Var **RN 7 Map 25-A2**

♀ ⊗ **AUX QUATRE VENTS** (N° RR JUIN 26 273) (M. Daniel **Lemaire**) Quartier La Forge ☎ 94-60-73-05 Closed Fri eve, all day Sat. Evening meals. English, German spoken.

CAP-DE-PIN par ESCOURCE 40210 Landes **RN 10 Map 20-B2**

♀ ⊗ ⌂ **AU ROUTIER** (N° RR MAR 9 439) (M. Jean-Pierre **Fortinon**) ☎ 58-07-20-54 ⇥ 15 Closed Sat (except high season); Christmas; Feb. Full board 190–220F per night. Menus from 50–190F. Specialities: *Salade de foie de canard frais, Ris de veau Madère, Magret grillé.* Coaches welcome (rest. seats 300). Evening meals.

CAPENDU 11700 Aude **RN 113 Map 22-B2**

♀ ⊗ **LA CAVE DES ARTS** (N° RR JANV 26 431) (M. Yves **Peyra-mayou**) RN 113 ☎ 68-79-09-30 Closed Wed, Sun evenings in winter (1 Nov to 1 May). Coaches welcome (rest. seats 60). Evening meals to 9.30pm.

CAPPELLE-EN-PEVELE 59242 Nord **RN 393 Map 5-B1**

♀ ⊗ **L'AS VEGAS** (N° RR SEP 26 666) (Mme. Eliane **Duquesnoy**) 13,

C

Cappelle-en-Pevele continued
rue de l'Obeau ☎ 20-61-83-10 Closed Sun. Evening meals to 8.30pm.

CARCASSONNE 11000 Aude **RN 113 Map CO 119 22-B2**
♈ ⊗ ⌂ **LE RELAIS DE L'AVENIR** (N° RR MAR 1 824) (Mme Madeleine **Pesez**) 93, avenue Francklin-Roosevelt ☎ 68-25-09-39 ⊸ 12 Closed Sun; public holidays.
♈ ⊗ ⌂ **2 étoiles NN AIR MOTEL SALVAZA** (N° RR NOV 27 096) (Mme ina **Preiffer**) Aéroport de Salvaza Route de Montréal ☎ 68-71-64-64 (hôtel) 68-72-52-89 (restaurant) ⊸ 24 German and English spoken. Full board. Coaches welcome. Evening meals. Filling station nearby.

CARENTAN 50500 Manche **RN 13 Map 4-B1**
♈ ⊗ **LE DERBY** (N° RR SEPT 26 993) (Maurice **Le Guélinet**) 21, rue de la 101 Airborne ☎ 33-42-04-77 Closed Sat afternoon, Sun and public holidays. Meals served until 9pm. Filling station near. Coaches welcome (rest. seats 36).

CARHAIX 29270 Finistère **RN 164 Map 7-A/B2**
♈ ⊗ ⌂ **AU CHEVAL BRETON** (N° RR SEP 16 715) (M. Louis **Le Mignon**) 2, boulevard de la République ☎ 98-93-01-38 ⊸ 10 at l'Hôtel du Cheval Breton. Closed Sat; Aug.

CARIGNAN 08110 Ardennes **Map 6-A3**
♈ ⊗ **LE RELAIS** (N° RR AVR 26 500) (M. Fabrice **Fossani**) 33, rte de Sedan ☎ 24-22-08-78 ⊸ 6 Coaches welcome (rest. seats 60). Evening meals.

CARMAUX 81190 Tarn **RN88 Map 22-B1**
see MIRANDOC

CARNOULES 83600 Var **Map 25-A2**
♈ ⊗ ⌂ **CHEZ DOUDOU** (N° RR JUN 25 025) (M. Adrien **Piasco**) 20, rue Pierre-Sémard ☎ 94-28-33-15 **Minitel** ⊸ 4 Closed Sat, 15 days Sept. Full-board 170F per night. Coaches welcome (rest. seats 150). Evening meals until 9pm (10.30 in summer). Italian spoken.

CARPENTRAS 84200 Vaucluse **RN 538 Map 24-A2**
♈ ⊗ **BAR DU MARCHE GARE** (N° RR AVR 24 922) (M. Bernard **Gil**) Marché Gare ☎ 90-63-19-00 Closed Sun. Coaches welcome (rest. seats 220). Spanish spoken.

CARPIQUET 14650 Calvados **Map 4-B2**
♈ ⊗ **LE POURQUOI PAS?** (N° RR JUIN 27 312) (M. Didier **Prempain**), 33, route de Bayeux Bellevue ☎ 31-73-84-84 Closed Sat evening, Sun and August. Local filling station.

CARSIX 27300 Eure **RN13 Map 4-B3**
♈ ⊗ ⌂ **L'ESCALE** (N° RR OCT 26 711) (M. Michel **Silliau**) Carre four de Malbrouck Bernay ☎ 32-44-79-99 ⊸ 4 Closed Sun. Coaches welcome (2 rooms of 35 seats). Evening meals to 10.30pm.

C

CARTELEGUE 33390 Gironde **RN 137 Map 15-A3**
- ⌦ 🏠 **1 Star NN CHEZ OLGA - LE RELAIS DE L'ESCALE** (N° RR AOU 9 840) (M. and Mme Alban **Durand**) Le Bel Ormeau ☎ 56-42-71-18 ⊷ 12 Closed Sat; 15 Dec to 15 Jan. English, German, Spanish spoken.

CARVIN 62220 P.-de-C. **RN 25 Map 5-A/B1**
- 🍷 ⌦ 🏠 **A L'ARRET DES ROUTIERS - AUX COPAINS** (N° RR JUN 18 427) (Mme Micheline **Dujardin**) 31, rue d'Arras ☎ 21-37-00-35 ⊷ 6 Closed Sun. Evening meals.

CAST 29150 Finistère **RD 7 and 107 Map 7-B1**
- 🍷 ⌦ 🏠 **1 Star NN LE RELAIS SAINT-GILDAS** (N° RR MAR 22 727) (Mme Marie **Philippe** for l'Hôtel and M. Patrice **Philippe** for restaurant) 11 and 13, rue du Kreisker ☎ 98-73-54-76 or 73-55-43 **Minitel** ⊷ 15 from 90–180F, breakfast 15–18F. Closed Sat; 1 month low season. Full-board 150–200F per night. Coaches welcome (rest. seats 100). Evening meals until 9pm. Parking; bar; dogs allowed; private garden. Menus 40–170F. Specialities: ⌐ seafood platter, homemade couscous. Places to visit: chapels, crucifixes. English spoken.

CASTELNAU-RIVIÈRE-BASSE 65700 Htes-Pyrénées **Map 21-A2**
- 🍷 ⌦ **LE MILLEPATTE** (N° RR MAI 27 285) (M. André **Zanardo**) Route de Bordeux ☎ 62-31-97-99 **Minitel** Local filling station.

CASTELSARRASIN 82100 T.-&-G.) **RN 113 Map 22-A1**
- 🍷 ⌦ 🏠 **1 étoille NN CHEZ MAURICE** (N° RR JANV 27 152) (M. Jean-Pierre **Boissier**) 35, rte de Toulouse ☎ 63-32-30-83 ⊷ 15 Closed Sat, pm, Sun; 1st to 22nd August. Specialities: Cassoulet, Duck Breasts and Preserved Duck. Local filling station 7–12pm.

CASTETS-DES-LANDES 40260 Landes **RN 10 Map 20-A2**
- 🍷 ⌦ **LE STUC** (N° RR SEPT 18 528) (Mme **Calleja**) ☎ 58-89-40-62 Closed Sun. Oct. Evening meals. Spanish spoken.
- 🍷 ⌦ **LE CARRIOU DE CHANCHON** (N° RR DEC 25 766) (Mme Josiane **Lataste**) RN 10 ☎ 58-89-40-63 Closed Mon in winter; Oct. English/Spanish spoken. Evening meal to 9.30. Local filling station.

CASTRES 81100 Tarn **RN 622 Map 22-B2**
- 🍷 ⌦ 🏠 **AUX AMIS DE LA ROUTE** (N° RR OCT 17 391) (M. Michel **Labessouille**) av. Charles-de-Gaulle ☎ 63-35-54-38 ⊷ 8 Coaches welcome (rest. seats 70). Evening meals to 9.30pm.

CAUDAN 56850 Morbihan **RD 81 (ZA de Kergoussel) Map 7-B2**
- ⌦ **LE BOUTON D'OR** (N° RR FEV 27 179) (Mme Joëlle **Le Bail**) ☎ 97-81-16-01 Closed Sat, Sun; English spoken. Local filling station.

CAUDEBEC-LES-ELBEUF 76320 S.-Maritime **RN 321 Map 3-B1**
- 🍷 ⌦ **LE RELAIS TIVOLI** (N° RR AVR 25 908) (M. André **Jean**) 43, rue Félix-Faure ☎ 35-77-16-94 **Minitel** Closed Sat, Sun; public holidays; Aug. Meals at all times.

C

CAULNES 22350 C.-du-N.) **Map 7-B3**
♀ ⊗ **LES ROUTIERS** (N° RR MARS 22 726) (Mme **Gaudrel**) 40, rue de la Gare ☎ 96-83-94-14.

CAUNEILLE 40300 Landes **RN 117 Map 20-A2**
♀ ⊗ **AU HAOU** (N° RR MARS 26 836) (Mme Henriette **Lalanne**) ☎ 58-73-04-60 Closed 20 Dec–5 Jan. Coaches welcome (rest. seats 120).

CAUSSADE 82300 Tarn-et-Garonne **RN 20 Map 22-A1**
♀ ⊗ ⌂ **Restuarant (rattaché de tourisme) RELAIS D'AUVERGNE** (N° RR JUIL 25 040) (M. Antoine **Noualhac**) Zl de Meaux ☎ 63-93-03-89 ⇀ 14 Closed Sun. Full board 165 to 193F. Coaches welcome (rest. seats 120). Evening meals. Local filling station 24hr.

CAUVERVILLE-EN-ROUMOIS 27350 Eure **RN 175 Map 4-B3**
♀ ⊗ **LE MEDINE** (N° RR NOV 27 462) (M. Jean-Pierre **Ferrette**) ☎ 32-57-01-55 **Minitel** Closed Sat, Sun. Aug. Evening meal. Local filling station.

CAVAILLON 84300 Vaucluse **RN 538/573 Map 24-A3**
♀ ⊗ **LE RELAIS SAINT-JACQUES** (N° RR NOV 24 024) (Mme Jeannine **Raoux**) 649, avenue de la Libération ☎ 90-71-42-02 Closed Sat evening, Sun. Italian, some English spoken.
♀ ⊗ **LES ROUTIERS** (N° RR OCT 27 440) (M. Claude **Liard**) 21, Avenue de Verdun ☎ 90-71-39-41 Closed Sun. Evening meals. 24hr local filling station.

CAVALERIE (LA) 12230 Aveyrôn **RN 9 Map 23-A1**
♀ ⊗ ⌂ **RELAIS DES INFRUTS** (N° RR SEPT 27 034) (M. Jeannot **Cazabonne**). Commune La Couvertoirada ☎ 65-62-70-82 ⇀ 7 Spanish spoken.

CAZAN 13116 B. du R. **RN 7 Map 24-B3**
⊗ **L'ESCALIER CHEZ ALEXANDRE** (N° RR JUL 25 473) (M. Alexandre **Ghigo**) RN 7 Vernègues ☎ 90-59-13-15 Closed Sun.

CELLE-SAINT-AVANT (LA) 37610 Indre-et-Loire **Map 12-B2**
♀ ⊗ ⌂ **LA CARAVANE** (N° RR DEC 24 440) (M. Serge **Judes**) Descartes ☎ 47-65-07-82 ⇀ 7. Meals served until 1am. Closed Sun. 15 days in Aug. Coaches welcome (rest. seats 50).

CELON 36200 Indre **RN 20 Map 16-A1**
♀ ⊗ **LA BROUETTE** (N° RR NOV 22 991) (Mme Yvette **Dufour**) ☎ 54-25-32-08 Closed Sun. Evening meals to 9.30.

CENAC-SAINT-JULIEN 24250 Dordogne **RN 703 Map 17-B1**
♀ ⊗ **LA PROMENADE** (N° RR OCT 25 153) (M. Pascal **Thomas**) RN 703 ☎ 53-28-36-87 ⇀ 4. Full board 140–180F. Coaches welcome (rest. seats 65). Evening meals to 8.30.

CERE 400900 Landes **Map 20-B2**
♀ ⊗ **RELAIS DE L'ECUREUIL** (N° RR SEPT 26 674) (Mme Martine

C

Belmonte) Au Bourg ☎ 58-51-49-33 Closed Wed. Some English, Portuguese, Spanish spoken. Coaches welcome (rest. seats 110). Evening meals.

CESTAS 33610 Gironde **RN 10 Maps 15-A3 and 20-B1**
♟ ⊗ **LE TAHITI** (N° RR JUN 25 024) (Mme Marie-France **Debacker**) Rte de Bayonne ☎ 56-78-27-25 Closed Sat afternoon, Sun; public holidays (unless reserved for group/coach); Christmas to New Year. Coaches welcome. Evening meals.

CHAGNY 71150 Saône-et-Loire **RN 74 Maps 13-B3 and 18-A/B1**
♟ ⊗ ⌂ **LE RELAIS TERMINUS** (N° RR JUL 21 575) (M. Jean-Louis **Potsimeck**) 1, avenue de la Gare ☎ 85-87-18-13 ⊷ 15 Closed Sun; Dec. Full-board 160–180F per night. Coaches welcome (rest. seats 60). Evening meals to 10pm. English, Polish spoken.

CHAIGNES 27120 Eure **Map 3-B1**
♟ ⊗ ⌂ **MA NORMANDIE** (N° RR AVR 25 920) (M. Gérard **Ducoat**) Rte Nle 13 ☎ 32-36-95-52 ⊷ 14 Closed Sat evening, Sun. English spoken.

CHAINGY 45161 Loiret **RN 152 Map 13-A1**
♟ ⊗ **RELAIS DE FOURNEAUX** (N° RR MAI 26 548) (M. Carlos **De Sousa**) Rte Nle 152 ☎ 38-80-69-12 Closed Sun. English spoken.

CHAINTRIX 51130 Marne **RN 33 Map 9-A3**
♟ ⊗ **LE RELAIS DE LA SOUDE** (N° RR DEC 26 113) (SARL Mme Françoise **Andrieu**) Vertus ☎ 26-66-43-80 Evening meals until mid-night. German spoken. Closed on Mon.

CHALAIS (ou CHALEIX) 24800 Dordogne **RN 21 Map 17-A1**
Voir **THIVIERS**

CHALAIS 24800 Dordogne
♟ ⊗ **LES JARDINS DE LA TUILIERE** (N° RR JAN 27 491) (Mme Suzette **Deschamps**) Mavaleix ☎ 53-52-03-85. Evening meals until 9.30pm. English, Spanish spoken.

CHALLANS 85300 Vendée **RN 148 Map 11-B2**
♟ ⊗ **LE RELAIS DE LA NOUE** (N° RR AVR 24 209) (Mme Monique **Menez**) Place Victor-Charbonnel ☎ 51-93-20-20 Closed Sat night; Sun. Aug.

CHALLUY 58000 Nièvre **RN 7 Map 13-B2**
♟ ⊗ **LE RELAIS DU PONT CARREAU** (N° RR AVR 22 283) (Mme Fernande **Taillemitte**) ☎ 86-21-00-02 ⊷ 4.

CHALONS-SUR-MARNE 51000 Marne **RN 3 and 33 Maps 6-B2 and 9-A3**
⊗ **AU MONT SAINT-MICHEL** (N° RR JUN 15 689) (SNC-**Queige, Mazeau et C**ⁱᵉ) 31, route de Troyes RN 77 ☎ 26-68-05-08 **Minitel** Closed Sun evening. Coaches welcome (rest. seats 160). Evening meals. English, Spanish spoken. 3 parking areas. Full board 160–200F.

C

Chalons-sur-Marne continued
♟ ⊗ 🏠 **LE DELKO** (N° RR SEP 25 101) (M. Christian **Sinot**) rue de Douanes **La Veuve** ☎ 26-67-30-68 **Minitel** ➛ 8 Closed Sun.

CHALON-SUR-SAONE SUD 71240 S.-et-L. **Map 18-B1 14-A3**
⛽ **Total Service Station LE RELAIS DE SEVREY** (N° RR FEV 24 090) (M. Hervé **Bouvier**) RN 6 ☎ 85-48-30-24 Closed Sat 10.30pm to Sun 8.00am. Open 24 hours.

CHAMALIERES-SUR-LOIRE 43800 Haute-Loire **Map 18-A3**
♟ ⊗ **LES ROUTIERS** (N° RR MARS 26 289) (Mme Françoise **Gentes**) Vorey ☎ 71-03-42-10 ➛ 4. Filling station 4.5 kms. Closed in Oct.

CHAMANDRIN 05100 Htes-Alpes **RN 94 Map 19-A3 see BRIANÇON**

CHAMARANDE 91730 Essonne **RN 20 Map 9-B1**
⊗ 🏠 **1 Star NN SARL LE RELAIS DE MONTFORT** (N° RR FEV 17 740) (M. Roland **Cottin**) Rte Nle 20 ☎ 60-82-20-80 **Minitel** ➛ 31 Closed Sat afternoon, Sun; Aug; last week in Dec. Coaches welcome (rest. seats 120). Evening meals until 12pm. English spoken. Parking.

CHAMBERY 73000 Savoie **RN 6 Map 19-A2**
♟ ⊗ **LE RELAIS DES ABATTOIRS – Clara et Chantal** (N° RR FEV 26 456) (Mmes **Vallifuoco-Véronèse**) Place Pierre-de-Coubertin ☎ 79-69-03-97 Closed Sat afternoon, Sun. Italian, Spanish spoken. Coaches welcome (rest. seats 46).

CHAMBILLY 71100 Saône-et-Loire **Map 18-A1**
♟ ⊗ 🏠 **LE RELAIS DU COMMERCE ET DES SPORTS** (N° RR MAI 20 727) (M. Paul and Monique **Prioris**) rue du Gl-de-Gaulle ☎ 85-25-03-62 ➛ 6 Closed Sat afternoon. Italian spoken. Shaded terrace, 'boule' played.

CHAMBLY 60230 Oise **Map 3-B2**
♟ ⊗ 🏠 **LE RELAIS DE CHAMBLY** (N° RR DEC 26 130) (Mme Françoise **Violette**) 660 av. A.-Briand ☎ 34-70-50-37 **Minitel** ➛ 14 Closed Sat, Sun (only res); The week of 15 Aug; 20 Dec–20 Jan. Full-board 150–190F per night. Evening meals to 9pm. Filling station near. Coaches welcome (rest. seats 50).

CHAMBORET 87140 Haute-Vienne **RN 147 Map 16-B1**
♟ ⊗ **LA BERGERIE** (N° RR AVR 27 241) (M. Francis **Albenque-Moreau**) ☎ 55-75-78-21. Local filling station 7–8pm.
♟ ⊗ **LE COMPOSTEL** (N° RR OCT 27 425) (M. Jacques **Caenon**) La lande ☎ 55-08-50-16 or 53-44-05 English/Spanish, Italian, Dutch spoken. Evening meals. Local filling station 7–8pm.

CHAMBOULIVE 19450 Corrèze **D 940 Map 17-A1**
♟ ⊗ 🏠 **RELAIS DU GOZEE** (N° RR JAN 26 793) (Mme Lina **Mazurier**) Route de Tulle ☎ 55-21-60-90 ➛ 5 Closed 24 Aug–8 Sep. Portuguese spoken.

C

CHAMBOURCY 78240 Yvelines **RN 13 Map 1-A2**
♀ ⊗ **LES ROUTIERS** (N° RR MAI 22 814) (Mme Denise **Pettinotti**) 63, route de Mantes ☎ 39-65-43-19 Closed Sun; Aug. Spanish spoken.

CHAMP-SUR-DRAC 38560 Isère **RN 85 Map 19-A3 see JARRIE**

CHAMPAGNE 24650 Dordogne **Map 15-B3**
♀ ⊗ **RELAIS DE CHANCELADE** (N° RR JUIL 27 346) (Mme Huguette **Mazière**) Route d'Angouleme ☎ 53-04-88-69 Closed Sat evening. Sun am. Evening meals to 12.00. Local filling station 7–10pm.

CHAMPAGNE 72470 Sarthe **RN 157 Map 8-B2**
♀ ⊗ **LE RELAIS DES FOUGERES** (N° RR JUL 26 594) (M. Hubert **Gehan**) RN 157 ☎ 48-89-50-96 Closed Sun. Coaches welcome (rest. seats 50). Meals served until 10pm.

CHAMPAGNE-MOUTON 16350 Charente **RN 740 Map 15-B2**
♀ ⊗ ⌂ **1 Star NN LE RELAIS DE PLAISANCE** (N° RR SEP 15 354) (Mme Denise **Delhoume**) ☎ 45-31-80-52 and 45-31-98-19 ⊨ 15 Full-board 180–200F per night. Coaches welcome (rest. seats 140). Evening meals served until 9pm.

CHAMPAGNEUX 73240 Savoie **RN 516 Map 19-A2**
♀ ⊗ ⚑ **RELAIS DES TROIS PROVINCES - CHEZ NICOLE** (N° RR FEV 26 459) (Mme Nicole **Curtillat**) ☎ 76-31-83-22 Closed Aug.

CHAMPAGNOLE 39300 Jura **Map 19-A1**
♀ ⊗ **LES ROUTIERS** (N° RR AVR 25 873) (M. Georges **Chagre**) La Billaude ☎ 84-52-07-95 Closed Sun. Evening meals.

CHAMPIGNOLLES 54520 M.-et-M **RN 4 Maps 10-A2 and 14-B1**
♀ ⊗ **AUBERGE FLEURIE** (N° RR MAR 24 891) (Mme Nathalie **Cheikh**) FONDS DE TOUL Les Baraques Nancy Ouest ☎ 83-98-27-30 Closed Sat, Sun; 15 days in Feb; Jul. English, German spoken.

CHAMPLOST 89210 Yonne **Map 9-B2**
♀ ⊗ **CHEZ MARIE-CLAUDE** (N° RR OCT 26 356) (Mme Marie-Claude **Lauvin**) 23 Rte de Paris ☎ 86-43-14-71 Closed Wed. 15 days in Feb and 15 days in Aug. Coaches welcome (rest. seats 70). Evening meals to 10pm.

CHAMPREPUS 50800 Manche **Map 8-A1**
♀ ⊗ **LE RELAIS DE CHAMPREPUS** (N° RR AOÛT 27 368) (M. Patrick **Jouaudin**) Le Bourg Villedieu-les-Poêles ☎ 33-51-42-32 Closed Wed; Oct to May.

CHAMPROND-EN-GATINE 28240 E.-et -L. **RN 23 Map 8-B3**
♀ ⊗ **LE RELAIS DE CHAMPROND** (N° RR OCT 23 997) (M. Michel **Jonnier**) 5, Grande-Rue ☎ 37-49-82-18 Closed Sun; 15 to 30 Aug.

CHAMPROND-EN-PERCHET 28400 Eure-et-Loir **see NOGENT-LE-ROTROU**

C

CHAMPS-SUR YONNE 89290 Yonne **Autoroute A 6 Sens Paris-Lyon Map 13-A2**
⊗ **LE RELAIS VENOY** (M. Philippe **Tonic**) Autoroute A 6 ☎ 86-52-35-53 Self-service restaurant.

CHAMPSAC-JOUVEAU 87230 Hte-Vienne **Map 15-B2**
⊗ **LE RELAIS DU TILLEUL** (N° RR OCT 24 710) (Mme Renée **Astier**) ☎ 55-78-44-06.

CHAMPTOCE-SUR-LOIRE 49170 Maine-et-Loire **Maps 11-A3 and 12-A1**
⊗ **HOTEL LES RIVETTES** (N° RR NOV 26 373) (Mme Agnès **Chêne**) Rte de Montjean ☎ 41-39-91-75 **Minitel** ⊸ 4 Closed Sat, Sun; 15th July–15th Aug. English, Spanish spoken.

CHANGÉ 53810 Mayenne **Map 8-A1**
⊗ **LE RELAIS DE NIAFLES** (N° RR FEV 27 187) (M. Pierre **Dabet**) Niafles ☎ 43-53-76-15 Closed Sat, Sun, July and August.

CHANIERS 17610 Charente-Maritime **Map 15-A2**
⊗ **AUBERGE DE LA BOISERIE** (N° RR MAI 27 294) (M. Jean-Pierre **Lorillon**) Le Maine Alain ☎ 46-91-11-78 Evening meals. Local filling station.

CHANTENAY-SAINT-IMBERT 58240 Nièvre **RN 7 Map 16-A3**
⊗ **AU BON ACCUEIL** (N° RR DEC 9 101) (Mme Lucette **Vacher**) RN 7 St-Pierre-le-Moutier ☎ 86-38-61-95 Closed Sat midday, Sun; 15 Aug to 8 Sept. Evening meals to 10pm.
⊗ **RELAIS SAINT-IMBERT** (N° RR JANV 27 150) (Mlle **Fressie**) St-Pierre-le-Moutier ☎ 86-36-61-65 Closed Sun. German spoken. Specialities Sauerkraut and Potee (veg cooked with meat and beans). Local filling station 8–12pm.

CHAPELAUDE 03530 Allier **RN 143 Map 16-A2**
⊗ **LE RELAIS DES TARTASSES** (N° RR MAR 24 873) (Mme Colette **Boutillon**) **Huriel** ☎ 70-06-45-06 **Minitel** ⊸ 4 Coaches welcome (rest. seats 50). Evening meals.

CHAPELLE (LA) 73220 Savoie **RN 6 Map 19-A2**
⊗ **RESTOROUTE LA CHAPELLE** (N° RR OCT 26 353) (M. Gilbert **Martoia**) Aiguebelle ☎ 79-36-17-09 German, English, Italian spoken.

CHAPELLE-CARO (LA) 56460 Morbihan **RN 166 Map 7-B3**
⊗ ⌂ **LE RELAIS DES ROUTIERS** (N° RR MAR 23 725) (Mme Marie-Claire **Boulvais**) La Gare ☎ 97-74-93-63 **Minitel** ⊸ 4 Coaches welcome (rest. seats 90). Evening meals until 11pm.

CHAPELLE D'AUREC (LA) 43120 Haute-Loire **Map 18-A3**
⊗ ⌂ **RELAIS DE LA CHAPELLE** (N° RR JUIN 27 295) (M. Gabriel **Colombet**) La Mioulaterre ☎ 71-66-53-55 ⊸ 4 Closed Sun pm. Evening meals. Parking.

C

CHAPELLE DU BOIS (LA) 72400 Sarthe **Map 8-B2 Axe Alençon – Mamers – St Cosmes – La Ferté – Bernard – Aut A11 – RD2**
Ⓨ ⊗ **LA CROIX BLANCHE** (N° RR MAI 26 886) (Mme Annick **Boudet**) Le Bourg ☎ 43-93-18-01 Closed Aug.

CHAPELLE-GUILLAUME (LA) 28330 E. et L. **Map 8-B3**
Ⓨ ⊗ **REST DE L'UNION** (N° RR AOUT 22 436) (M. Michel **Galupeau**) Place de l'Église ☎ 37-49-20-88 Closed Mon afternoon.

CHAPELLE-LA-REINE (LA) 77760 S.-et-M. **RN 152 Map 9-B1/2**
Ⓨ ⊗ **LE RELAIS DE LA SALAMANDRE** (N° RR MAI 27 283) (Mme Marie-Claude **Gachet**) 5, rue du Docteur Battesti ☎ 64-24-30-03 ⊷ 2 Open 24 hours. Closed Sat. Sun. Aug. Coaches welcome (rest. seats 44). Evening meals.

CHAPELLE-SAINT-LAURENT (LA) 79430 Deux Sèvres **RN 748 Map 15-A1**
Ⓨ ⊗ **RELAIS DES SPORTS** (N° RR AVR 26 231) (Mme Louisette **Guérin**) 6 Route de Bressuire ☎ 49-72-05-64 Coaches welcome (rest. seats 110). Evening meals.

CHAPELLE-SAINT-SEPULCRE (LA) 45210 Loiret **RN 60 Map 9-B2**
Ⓨ ⊗ **LA POTENCE** (N° RR FEV 25 825) (Mme Liliane **Visier**) RN 60 ☎ 38-92-03-10 **Minitel** Closed Sat.

CHAPPELE-ST-URSIN (LA) 18570 Cher **RN 151 Map 13-B1**
Ⓨ ⊗ **RELAIS 151** (N° RR JANV 27 148) (Mme Claudine **Maslarde**) Le Subdray Les Tailles Heurtault ☎ 48-55-12-47 Closed Sun, open 5.30 to 12.30am. English spoken. Private parking.

LA CHAPELLE SOUS DUN 71800 Saône-et-Loire **Map 18-A2**
Ⓨ ⊗ **BAR RESTAURANT DE LA MINE** (N° RR SEPT 26 660) (Mme Ariette **Champiaux**) ☎ 85-28-16-15. Closed Sat. 15 days at Christmas and 15 days in Feb. Full board 190–220F. Coaches welcome (rest. seats 90). Evening meals to 9.30pm.

CHAPELLE-SUR-LOIRE (LA) 37140 Indre-et-Loire **RN 152 Map 12-B2**
Ⓨ ⊗ ⌂ **LE RELAIS DE LA MAIRIE** (N° RR AVR 21 509) (M. Jacques **Joyeau**) Place Albert Ruelle ☎ 47-97-34-07 ⊷ 12 Full-board 160–180F per night. Coaches welcome (rest. seats 70). Evening meals.

CHARENTON 94220 Val-de-Marne Porte de Charenton **Map 1-B3**
Ⓨ ⊗ **Aux Armes de Normandie et d'Auvergne – L'ALLIANCE** (N° RR AOU 19 120) (M. Albert **Series**) 121, rue de Paris ☎ 43-68-03-71 Closed Wed; Aug. Meals served until 9pm on Sat and Sun.
Ⓨ ⊗ **PARIS-LISBONNE** (N° RR MAI 24 229) (SARL **Le Paris-Lisbonne/Durarte**) 195, rue de Paris ☎ 43-68-32-29 Closed Aug. Evening meals until 10pm. Portuguese, Spanish spoken.

CHARENTON-SUR-CHER 18210 Cher **RN 151 Bis Maps 13-B2 and 16-A2**
⊗ **A LA BONNE TABLE** (N° RR NOV 18 554) (Mme Antoinette

C

Charenton-sur-Cher continued
Frège) ☎ 48-60-72-73. Closed Aug. Coaches welcome. Evening
meals to 10pm.

CHARMES-SUR-L'HERBASSE 26260 Drôme **Map 18-B3**
♟ ⊗ **LE CABARET NEUF** (N° RR AVR 27 253) (M. Michel **Deveton**)
☎ 75-45-65-65 Closed Tues and 15th Sept. to 1st Oct. Local filling
station 6–8pm.

CHARROUX 86250 Vienne **CD 148 Map 15-B1/2**
♟ ⊗ ⌂ **LE RELAIS DE LA CROIX-BLANCHE** Sarl (N° RR OCT 27
072) (M. Philippe **Jansen**) Place Saint-Pierre ☎ 49-87-50-41 ⊷ 7
Closed Sat and Sun. Local filling station 6–10pm.

CHARSONVILLE 45130 Loiret **RN 157 Map 12-A3**
♟ ⊗ **Tobacconist LE RELAIS DES ROUTIERS** (N° RR DEC 27 120)
(M. Patrick **Biliard**) 15, rue de la Libératon ☎ 38-74-23-00 Closed
Sun. Local filling station (petrol only) 7.30–9pm.

CHARTRES 28000 Eure-et-Loire **RN 10 Map 8-B3**
♟ ⊗ ⌂ **2 Stars NN LE RELAIS BEAUCERON** (N° RR AVR 19 743)
(M. **Lichet**) Mignières. This hotel, in the centre of Beauce, is
200m from the Thivars exit of Autoroute Océane A11, and near
Nationale No 10: 10 km from Chartres, 100km from Paris. ☎ 37-26-
46-21 **Minitel** ⊷ 30 from 165–196F, breakfast 19–28F, bath,
shower, own WC, colour TV. Open 5am to mid-night. Restaurant
Closed Sun. Coaches welcome (rest. seats 60). Evening meals.
English, Spanish spoken. Menus from 46–98F. Specialities:
*Andouille de Boilleau aux flageolets, Sauté de veau orléannis
Pâté en croûte maison.* Parking, bar, dogs allowed. Sites to visit:
⌐ Valleys of the Eure and Loire, windmills of Beauce.

♟ ⊗ **LE RELAIS DES BEAUMONTS** (N° RR MAI 25 392) (M. Jean-
Claude **Esnault**) Rocade Sud de Chartres Av. François Arago ☎
37-28-22-00 Closed Sat, Sun; Aug. Evening meals until 10.30.
Coaches welcome (rest. seats 70).

CHARTRES 28000 Eure-et-Loire **RN10 Map 8-B3**
♟ ⊗ **RESTAURANT LE PALMIER** (N° RR FEV 26 803) (M. Boussad
Naar) 20, the Saint-Maurice ☎ 37-21-13-89. Coaches welcome
(rest. seats 60). Evening meals.

CHARTRES 28300 GASVILLE-MAINVILLIERS – Eure-et-Loir **Autoroute A-11 Océane Map 8-B3 Sens Paris-Province**
♟ ⊗ **Café-Route** (N° RR RA-1) Aire de Service de la Fosse Blanche ☎
37-31-62-42 Routier menus in self-service restaurant in winter
7.00am to 10.30pm; summer 6.30am to 11.30pm. Shop.
♟ ⊗ **CAFÉ ROUTE** Sens Province/Paris Autoroute A11 ☎ 37-31-62-42
Self-serbive restaurant open in winter 7.00am to 10.30pm; summer 6.30am to 11.00pm. English, German, Spanish spoken. Shop.

CHARVIEU (38230 Isère) **RD 98 Map 2-A2**
♟ ⊗ **LES ROUTIERS** (N° RR NOV 27 454) (Mme Pierrette **Dubour-**

guais) Rte de Lyon – La Léchère – Pont de Cheruy ☎ 78-32-23-27 Evening meals. 24hr Local filling station.

CHASSENEUIL 16260 Charente **RN 141 Map 15-B2**
⦻ ⦻ ⌂ **LE RELAIS DES TILLEULS** (N° RR MAR 18 063) (Mme **Bonneau**) 20, rue du Temple ☎ 45-39-57-90 **Minitel** ⊶ 7 Full-board 140–200F per night. Coaches welcome (rest. seats 120). Evening meals served until 12.15am.

CHASSE-SUR-RHONE 38670 Isère **CD 12 Map 2-B1**
⦻ ⦻ **CENTRAL BAR CHEZ MEDA** (N° RR AOU 20 804) (M. Jean-Luc **Merandat**) 5, rue Pasteur ☎ 72-24-00-88 Closed Sun evening. Coaches welcome (rest. seats 370). Spanish, English spoken. Full board 220F. Evening meals to 9.30pm.

CHASSILLE 72910 Sarthe **RN 157 Map 8-B2**
⦻ ⦻ ⌂ **LE PETIT ROBINSON** (N° RR NOV 26 740) (M. **Fournigault**) ☎ 43-88-92-01 ⊶ 4 Closed Fri night. Sat. Coaches welcome (rest. seats 215). Evening meals to 12pm.

CHATAIGNERAIE (LA) 85120 Vendée **RD 949 Map 11-B3**
⦻ ⦻ ⌂ **HOTEL DU CHEVAL BLANC** (N° RR JUIL 26 940) (M. Ramond **Retailleau**) Le Bourg Breuil-Barret ☎ 51-69-67-64 ⊶ 7 Closed Mon.

CHATEAU BERNARD 38650 Isère **Map 15-A2**
⦻ ⦻ **PENSION BAR DU CAMP** (N° RR NOV 25 726) (M. Jean-Louis **Bruno**) Rte de Barbezieux La Pointe A Rullaud ☎ 45-82-09-47 ⊶ 3 Closed Fri evening, Sat, Sun (can open for pre booked groups). Full-board 170F per night. Coaches welcome (rest. seats 90). Evening meals to 11pm. Spanish spoken.

CHATEAUDUN 28000 Eure-et-Loir **RD 955 Map 8-B3**
⦻ ⦻ **LE SAINT JEAN** (N° RR MAI 27 276) (M. Pierre **Thomas**) 1, route de Brou ☎ 37-45-56-75 Local filling station.

CHATEAU-GAILLARD-SANTILLY 28310 Eure-et-Loir **RN 20 Map 9-B1**
⦻ ⦻ **RELAIS 20** (N° RR JUIN 27 304) (M. Dahmani **Frères**) RN 20 ☎ 37-90-07-33 **Minitel** Closed Sat pm, Sun. Evening meals. English, German, Arabic, Yugoslav spoken.
⦻ ⦻ **AU ROUTIER GAILLARD – Chez Lili** (N° RR DEC 21 750) (Mme Liliane **Kieffer**) ☎ 37-90-07-03 Closed Sun. Evening meal to 12pm.

CHATEAU-GONTIER 53200 Mayenne **Map 12-A1**
⦻ ⦻ **L'ÉTOILE** (N° RR JUN 27 313) (M. Norbert **Porúe**) 43, rue Garnier ☎ 43-07-20-80 Closed Sat Sun pm. 1 week at Christmas and 3 weeks in Aug. Evening meal to 10pm. Local filling station.

CHATEAU-L'HERMITAGE 72510 Sarthe **RD 307 Map 12-A2**
⦻ ⦻ **LA BELLE CROIX** (N° RR NOV 26 742) (M. Bruno **David**) Beauregard-Mansigné ☎ 43-46-35-73. Closed Sun. Coaches welcome (rest. seats 160). Evening meal.

C

CHATEAU-THEBAUD 44690 L.-Atl. **RN 137 Map 11-B3**
🍸 ⊗ ⌂ **LA SAUCISSE VOLANTE** (N° RR FEV 25 820) (M. Serge **Violeau**) Le Butay Rte de La Rochelle ☎ 40-06-63-55 ⟞ 5 Closed Sat evening, Sun; 3 weeks June and last week Jan. Evening meals.

CHATEAUNEUF see GERMIGNY-DES-PRES 45110 Loiret

CHATEAUNEUF 35430 I.-et-V. **RN 137 Map 7-A3**
🍸 ⊗ ⌂ **LION D'OR** (N° RR NOV 25 167) (Mme Ginette **Brodbecker**) 137, rue Principale ☎ 99-58-40-11 **Minitel** ⟞ 10 Closed Mon 2pm–5pm. Full-board 120–200F per night. Coaches welcome (rest. seats 80). Evening meals to 10pm. Restaurant + grill, 28 seats, with terrace. English spoken.

CHATEAUNEF-DE-FAOU 29119 Finistère **RN 787 Map 7-B1**
🍸 ⊗ **CHEZ MARIANNE** (N° RR DEC 15 473) (Mlle Marie **Taridec**) 8, rue Jean-Dorval ☎ 98-81-73-67.

CHATEAUNEUF-LE-ROUGE 13790 B.-du-R. **RN 7 Map 24-B3**
🍸 ⊗ **LA CARDELINE** (N° RR MAI 25 425) (M. Michel **Bernard**) RN 7 ☎ 42-58-62-30 Closed first fortnight in Jan. Evening meals until 11pm. English, German spoken. Coaches welcome (rest. seats 130).

CHATEAUNEUF-LES-MARTIGUES 13220 B.-du-R. **RN 568 Map 24-B3**
🍸 ⊗ **L'OASIS** (N° RR NOV 27 456) (Ste Poasis Thierry et Père) Route de Marseille ☎ 42-79-88-35 **Minitel** Closed Sat evening, Sun; Aug. Evening meals to 10pm. Local filling station.

CHATEAURENARD 13160 B.-du-R. **RN 57 Map 24-A3**
🍸 ⊗ **LE PANORAMIQUE** (N° RR FEV 26 448) (M. Alain **Mourier**) Centre nautique ☎ 90-94-79-37 **Minitel** Coaches welcome (rest. seats 50). Showers, swimming pool in summer. English spoken.

CHÂTEAUROUX 05360 Hautes-Alpes **RN 94 Map 25-A1**
🍸 ⊗ ⌂ **1 star NN HÔTEL DAUPHINOIS L'ASSIETTE GOURMANDE** (N° RR JANV 27 141) (M. Michel **Pouypoudat**) rue Centrale ☎ 92-43-22-01 ⟞ 10 Some English spoken. Local filling station.

CHATEAUROUX 36000 Indre **RN 20 Maps 12-B3, 13-B1 and 16-A1**
🍸 ⊗ **BAR DE L'AVENUE** (N° RR OCT 25 147) (M. Laurent **Guillot**) 1, avenue de la Manufacture ☎ 54-34-09-27 Closed Sun. English spoken.
🍸 ⊗ **SARL L'ETAPE** (N° RR FEV 23 681) (Gérant M.D. **Noiret**) Déols ☎ 54-22-02-77 **Minitel** Open 24 hours a day. Coaches welcome (rest. seats 300).
🍸 ⊗ ⌂ **1 Star NN LE RALLYE** (N° RR JANV 26 433) (Mme Françoise **Jasmin**) 9, rue Bourdillon ☎ 54-34-37-41 ⟞ 8 from 59–100F, breakfast from 12.50–16F. Closed Sun; Feb and Bank holidays. Bar, small dogs allowed.

C

CHATELET-SUR-CHUISNES (LES) par COURVILLE 28270 Eure-et-Loir **RN 23 Map 8-B3 see CHUISNES**

CHATELUS 03120 Allier **Map 16-B3**
♈ ⊗ **LES CHEVREAUX** (N° RR MARS 27 209) (M. Joseph **Bernard**) RN 7 Arfeuilles ☎ 70-55-00-79 Spanish and English spoken. Filling station 10km.

CHATELUS-MALVALEIX 23270 Creuse **RN 690 Map 16-A2**
♈ ⊗ 🏠 **LE RELAIS DES VOYAGEURS** (N° RR AOU 23 409) (M. Claude **Brunet**) Route de La Châtre ☎ 55-80-78-11 ⊷ 5 Closed 15.8–4.9 and 23.12 – 4.1. English spoken. Evening meal to 9pm.

CHATELLERAULT 86100 Vienne **Map 15-B1 12-B2**
♈ ⊗ **L'ARCHE DU POITOU** Autoroute A-10 (M. Lionel **Violette**) Aire d'Antran ☎ 49-02-72-04 Self service restaurant.

CHATENOY 45260 Loiret
♈ ⊗ **AUBERGE DE L'ÉTANG** (N° RR DEC 27 481) (M. Laurent **Serestre**) Le Bourg ☎ 38-59-47-50. Closed Monday. Evening meals until 8.30pm. English spoken. Service station 100m.

CHATILLON-EN-BAZOIS 58110 Nièvre **RD 978 Map 13-B2**
♈ ⊗ 🏠 **HOTEL DU RELAIS** (N° RR MAR 22 737) (M. Jean-Jacques **Charprenet**) ☎ 86-84-13-79 ⊷ 7 Closed Sun; public holidays.

CHATILLON-LE-ROI 45480 Loiret **RD 927 Map 9-B1**
♈ ⊗ **LE RELAIS DES FINS GOURMET** (N° RR FEV 26 812) (M. and Mme Joël and Jeanne **Lenglet**) 41, rue du Château ☎ 38-39-97-12 **Minitel** Closed Sun (except in hunting season); 15 days in June 15 days in Sept. Coaches welcome (rest. seats 100). Evening meals.,

CHATILLON-SUR-INDRE 36700 Indre **RN 143 Map 12-B3**
♈ ⊗ 🏠 **LE RELAIS DU MAIL** (N° RR OCT 22 980) (M. **Duluard**) Boulevard du Général-Leclerc ☎ 54-38-71-21 and 38-80-25 ⊷ 11 Closed Sun; 29 Dec to 1 Jan 8. Full-board 145F per night. Coaches welcome (rest. seats 50). Evening meals.

CHATRE (LA) 36400 Indre **RN 143 Map 16-A2**
♈ ⊗ 🏠 **2 Stars NN SARL DU LION D'ARGENT** (N° RR OCT 3 251) (M. Pierre-Marie **Audebert**) 2, avenue du Lion d'Argent ☎ 54-48-11-69 and 48-15-67 ⊷ 26 English spoken.

CHATRES-SUR-CHER 41320 L.-et-C. **RN 76 Map 13-B1**
♈ ⊗ **LES ROUTIERS** (N° RR MARS 25 857) (M. Gérard **Coutaud**) 60, rue du 11-Novembre ☎ 54 98 01 93 Closed Sun. Coaches welcome (rest. seats 40). Evening meals in July/Aug.

CHATTE 38160 Isère **RN 92 Map 18-B3**
♈ ⊗ **LE SIROCCO** (N° RR AVR 26 227) (M. Maurice **Moyroud**) Quartier St Ferreol ☎ 76-64-43-41 Closed Sat afternoon, Sun; 1–15 Aug. Evening meals.

C

CHAUFFOUR-LES-BONNIERES 78270 Yvelines **RN 13 Maps 3-B1 and 8-A3**
♀ ⊗ ⌂ **AU BON ACCUEIL** (N° RR DEC 6 601) (M. Gérard **Magne**) ☎ 34-76-11-29 **Minitel** ⇥ 22 Closed Sat; 14 Jul–14 Aug. Coaches welcome (rest. seats 150). Evening meals to 10pm. Parking.

CHAUMERGY 39230 Jura **RD 468 et 33**
Voir LONS-LE-SAUNIER

CHAUMONT 52000 Haute-Marne **RN 19 Map 14-A2**
♀ ⊗ **CHEZ JEAN** (N° RR MAI 14 804) (M. Jean **Corroy**) 29, avenue Carnot ☎ 25-03-06-57.
♀ ⊗ ⌂ **AUBERGE DES ROUTIERS** (N° RR OCT 22 964) (M. Said **Maames**) 53, av. de la République ☎ 25-03-08-60 ⇥ 7 Closed Wed. English, Italian, German, Arabic spoken.

CHAUMONT-SUR-AIRE 55260 Meuse **RN 35 Map 14-A1**
♀ ⊗ ⌂ **LE RELAIS DE LA RENAISSANCE** (N° RR AVR 20 428) (M. André **Nucci**) ☎ 29-70-66-60 **Minitel** ⇥ 8 Closed Sun; Feb. Italian spoken. Parking for heavy loads. Full board 126–145F. Coaches welcome (rest. seats 130). Evening meal.

CHAUNY 02300 Aisne **Map 6-A/B1**
♀ ⊗ ⌂ **LE CASAMANCE** (N° RR DEC 27 114) (M. Gilles **Claisse**) 92, rue de la Chaussée ☎ 23-52-16-33 Closed Sun. English spoken. ⇥ 6 Full-board 140–160F. Coaches welcome (rest. seats 30). Evening meals to 10pm. Local filling station open 6–10pm.

CHAUSSEE-DE-DAMERY (LA) 51200 Marne **RN 3 Map 9-A3**
♀ ⊗ ⌂ **1 Star NN AUBERGE DE LA CHAUSSEE** (N° RR OCT 11 069) (M. **Lagarde**) 5, avenue de Paris 5 km from Épernay ☎ 26-58-40-66 ⇥ 9 Closed Mon evening; 22 Aug to 15 Sept. Coaches welcome (rest. seats 50). Evening meals to 9pm.

CHAUVIGNY 86300 Vienne **RN 151 Map 15-B1**
♀ ⊗ **LE RELAIS DU MARCHE** (N° RR JUL 25 048) (M. Joël **Torsat**) 8, place du Marché ☎ 49-46-32-34 Closed Thur; 15 Sept to 15 Oct. Coaches welcome (rest. seats 70). Evening meals until 9pm.

CHAUX-BALMONT 74770 Haute-Savoie **RN 201 Map 19-A2**
♀ ⊗ ⌂ **1 Star NN L'AUBERGE** (N° RR SEP 26 310) (M. Louis **Cantagrel**-Monique **Bodin**) ☎ 50-46-71-02 **Minitel** ⇥ 9 from 90–145F breakfast to 19F. Full-board available. Coaches welcome (for breakfast only) (rest. seats 60). Evening meals. Parking, bar, dogs allowed, amusements, terrace. Sites to visit: old town at Annecy, bridge at Alby, gorges of Fier. Closed Sun and end of Dec to mid Jan.

CHAZEUIL 03500 Allier **CD 146 Map 16-A3**
♀ ⊗ **LE RELAIS DU PONT DE CHAZEUIL** (N° RR NOV 26 094) (M. Maurice **Chaduc**) Au Pont Chazeuil – Paray Sous Briailles ☎ 70-45-08-11 Coaches welcome (rest. seats 55). Meals until 10pm. Closed Sat (low season). Parking.

C

CHELLES 77500 Seine-et-Marne **RN 34 Map 1-A3**
ⵏ ⊗ ⌂ **HOTEL DE LA PETITE VITESSE** (N° RR AVR 26 875) (M. Michel **Chea**) 32, avenue du Marais ☎ 64-21-09-47 ⊷ 7 Closed Sun.

CHELSEY 21430 Cote-d'Or **RN 6 Map 13-B3**
ⵏ ⊗ **LE RELAIS DES ROUTIERS** (N° RR JAN 23 630) (M. Bernard **Sentein**) Liernais ☎ 80-84-40-42 Closed Sun; 15 to 25 Aug. Coaches welcome (rest. seats 100/50/45). Meals served until 1am. German spoken.

CHEMAUDIN 25320 Doubs **RN 73 Map 14-B3**
ⵏ ⊗ **LE RELAIS DES ROUTIERS – Chez Cocotte** (N° RR FEV 20 663) (Mme **Grosperrin**) La Cocotte ☎ 81-59-51-92.

CHEMERY-LES-DEUX 57320 Moselle **RD 918 Map 10-A1**
ⵏ ⊗ ⌂ **RELAIS MATHIS** (N° RR DEC 19 601) (Mme Marie **Koch**) ☎ 87-64-91-73 ⊷ 6 Closed Wed. 15 Aug to 30 Sept. German spoken.

CHENEVIERES 54120 M.-et-M. **RN 59 Maps 10-A2 and 14-B1**
ⵏ ⊗ **LE RELAIS DES ROUTIERS – Chez Jean-Lou et Agnès** (N° RR JAN 23 629) (M. Jean-Louis **Rémy**) 10, route Nationale ☎ 83-72-62-75 Closed Sun; Sept. Coaches (50 seats on reservation).

CHENOVE 21300 Cote-d'Or **RN 74 Map 14-A3**
ⵏ ⊗ ⌂ **1 Star AU BON COIN** (N° RR OCT 23 957) (M. Marcel **Marin**) 54, route de Dijon ☎ 80-52-58-17 ⊷ 13 Closed Sat, Sun; Aug.

CHERBOURG 50100 Manche **RN 13 Map 4-A1**
ⵏ ⊗ ⌂ **LES ROUTIERS** (N° RR JUN 26 258) (Mme Viviane **Couvrie**) 10, rue de l'Onglet ☎ 33-53-08-16 ⊷ 11 Closed Fri evening, Sun evening. English, Spanish spoken.
ⵏ ⊗ **CAFETERIA TRUCK-STOP** (N° RR MAR 23 181) (**Société de Catering**) quai de Normandie ☎ 33-44-21-72 and 33-44-18-69 Coaches welcome (rest. seats 100). Evening meals until 11.00pm. English, German spoken.
ⵏ ⊗ ⌂ **A L'HORIZON** (N° RR MAI 24 969) (MM. Yves-Richard **Prunier** Frères) 24, rue Surcouf ☎ 33-93-85-85 ⊷ 8 Closed Sun. English spoken.

CHÈRES (LES) 69380 Rhone A-6 **Map 2-A1**
⛽ **Total Service Station LE RELAIS DU GRAVEYRON** (Sté **Rhodis** M. Claude **Mur**) Autoroute A6 ☎ 78-47-60-36 Open 24 hours. English, German spoken.

CHESNAY 27160 Eure **Map 8-A3**
ⵏ ⊗ **CHEZ CLAUDE** (N° RR MAI 26 244) (M. Claude **Blanfune**) Condé sur Iton ☎ 32-29-89-27 Closed Sun; Aug.

CHEVILLY-LARUE 94150 Val-de-Marne **RN 7 Map 1-B2**
ⵏ ⊗ **LE RELAIS D'AUVERGNE** (N° RR JAN 17 729) (M. **Carayol**) 4, place de la Libération ☎ 46-86-55-32 Closed Sat, Sun; Aug. Coaches welcome (rest. seats 120).

C

CHICHE 79350 Deux-Sevres **RN 149 Bis Map 12-B2**
♀ ⊗ **LE RELAIS CHEZ JACQUES** (N° RR DEC 24 434) (M. Jacques **Vincent**) 27, place St-Martin ☎ 49-72-40-51 **Minitel** Closed Wed evening; Christmas to 1 Jan. Coaches welcome (rest. seats 55). Evening meals.

CHIERZAC par BEDENAC 17210 Chte-Mme **RN 10 Map 15-A3**
♀ ⊗ **AU RENDEZ-VOUS DES ROUTIERS** (N° RR JUN 1922) (M. Robert **Laville**) ☎ 46-04-44-24 Closed Sat evening, Sun evening. Evening meals until 11pm.

CHOISY-LE-ROI 94600 Val-de-Marne **RN 186 Map 1-B3**
♀ ⊗ ⌂ **LE STADE** (N° RR DEC 26 750) (M. J-Claude **Villechenoux**) 134, avenue de Villeneuve-Saint-Georges ☎ 48-90-90-55 ⊷ 6 Closed Sat, Sun; Aug. Evening meals.
♀ ⊗ ⌂ **LE RELAIS DES MILLE PATTES** (N° RR JAN 24 838) (Mme Geneviève **Chenevier**) 98, av. Victor-Hugo ☎ 48-90-93-31 ⊷ 10 Closed Sun. Arabic, English spoken.

CHOLET 49300 M.-et-L. **RN 160 Maps 11-B3 and 12-B1**
♀ ⊗ ⌂ **LE RELAIS DES ROUTIERS** (N° RR JUL 12 347) (M. Michel **Dubillot**) 13, place de la République ☎ 41-62-11-09 ⊷ 19 Closed Sun; 10th July–9th Aug. Evening meals. Coaches welcome (rest. seats 180).
♀ ⊗ **CHEZ DÉDÉ** (N° RR FEVR 25 809) (M. André **Bourgey**) 66, bld de Strasbourg ☎ 41-62-27-79 **Minitel** ⊷ 5 Closed Sat pm, Sun; Aug. (Meals at weekends for booked Routiers.) Meals served until 9.30pm approx.
♀ ⊗ **LE RELAIS DES PRAIRIES** (N° RR SEPT 26 318) (Mme **Albert**) Parc des Prairies, bd du Pont de Pierre ☎ 41-58-09-39 Coaches welcome (rest. seats 170). Meals served in evening to 9pm. Closed Sat ev. Sun ev. English, German spoken.

CHONAS-L'AMBALLAN 38121 Isere **RN 7 Map 2-B1**
♀ ⊗ **L'ETAPE** (N° RR OCT 26 359) (M. Guy **Ailloud**) Grand-Champ ☎ 74-58-87-50 **Minitel** Closed Sun. 1st–15th Aug. Coaches welcome (rest. seats 50). Evening meals to 12pm. Parking.

CHORGES 05230 Hautes-Alpes **RN 94 Map 25-A1**
♀ ⊗ ⌂ **1 Star NN HOTEL DES ALPES** (N° RR NOV 19 996) (M. Roger **Mauduech**) Route Nationale 94 ☎ 92-50-60-08 ⊷ 25 from 90–190F, breakfast from 18–28F. Closed 1 Oct to 20 Nov. Full-board 190–250F per night. Coaches welcome (rest. seats 80). Evening meals to 9pm. Parking. Bar. Dogs allowed. Sites: Hac de Serrie Ponçon, Mountains, Écrins Park.

CHOUAIN 14250 Calvados **RD 6 Map 4-B2**
♀ ⊗ **AUX TROIS ÉCUS** (N° RR AVR 26 870) (Mme Marie-France **Gras**) Tilly-sur-Seulles. English and Spanish spoken.

CHUISNES 28190 Courville-sur-Eure – Eure-et-Loir **RN 23 Map 8-B3**
♀ ⊗ **SARL LES CHATELETS L'ESCALE ROUTIÈRE** (N° RR JUIN 27 305) (M. Gerard **Brulé**) lieu-dit Les Chatelets ☎ 37-23-21-75

C

Closed Sun. Coaches welcome (rest. seats 60). Evening meals. Parking. Filling station 2km.

CIOTAT (LA) 13600 B.-du-R. **Map 24-B3**

⊗ **LOU PITCHOUNET** (N° RR MAR 26 202) (M. Thierry **Guinet**) 8–10, rue Fougasse ☎ 42-08-28-99 Closed Wed; Feb. Coaches welcome (rest. seats 75). Evening meals.

CIVRAY 86400 Vienne **Map 15-B1/2**

♈ ⊗ **RELAIS DES USINES** (N° RR DEC 27 129) (M. Patric **Martel**) 19, route, de Saint-Pierre ☎ 49-87-04-33 Closed Sat 2pm until Sun 8pm and Bank Holidays. Local filling station 8–10.30pm.

CIVRAY DE TOURAINE 37150 Indre et Loire

♈ ⊗ **LE MARCECHAL** (N° RR DEC 24 479) (M. Jean **Jabvenean**) 1, rue de Bléré ☎ 47-23-92-16. Closed Saturday afternoon, Sunday; September. Evening meals until 10pm. Nearby service station open 8am–8pm.

CLAIRVAUX-LES-LACS 39130 Jura **RN 78 et 83 Map 19-A1**

♈ ⊗ **LES ROUTIERS** (N° RR SEPT 27 024) (M. Denis **Perrin**) 4, route de Lons-le-Saunier ☎ 84-25-85-57 ⌫ 10 From 88.50F to 108F, breakfast 20F. Closed Sun (low season) 1st–15th Sept. English and Italian spoken. Evening meals to 10pm. Open 24 hrs. Visit the lakes, grotto and dam.

CLAIX 38640 Isère **RN 75 Map 19-A3**

♈ ⊗ **LE GALION** (N° RR FEV 24 130) (Mme Marcelle **Tronchet**) Cours de la Libération ☎ 76-98-44-26.

CLAMART 92140 Hauts-de-Seine **Porte de Chatillon Map 1-B2**

♈ ⊗ **LE RELAIS DU SOLEIL COUCHANT** (N° RR MAR 10 405) (M. Marc **Trameçon**) 151, avenue du Gal de Gaulle ☎ 46-32-05-94 Closed Sun; Aug.

CLAYE-SOUILLY 77410 S.-et-M. **CD 212 Map 1-A3**

♈ ⊗ **LE RELAIS DE LA ROSEE** (N° RR AVR 25 367) (M. Jean-Claude **Castel**) ☎ 60-26-17-74 Minitel ⛽ **Service Station with HGV garage** Closed Sun. Evening meals. German spoken.

CLELLES 38930 Isère **Map 24-B1**

♈ ⊗ ⌂ **HOSTELLERIE DU TRIÈVES** (N° RR JANV 27 139) (Mme Odlie **Chrétien**) place de la Gare ☎ 76-34-45-40 ⌫ 7. Filling station 2km.

CLERAC 17270 Charente-Maritime **CD 158/134 Map 15-A3**

♈ ⊗ ⌂ **LES BANANIERS** – (N° RR SEP 26 651) (Mme Danielle **Arcay**) Montguyon ☎ 46-04-13-17 Minitel ⌫ 5. Filling station near. Closed Sat. Evening meals to 9pm.

CLEREY SUD 10390 Aube **RN 71 Map 9-B3**

♈ ⊗ **LE RELAIS ROUTIER FRANCO-BELGE** (N° RR AVR 26 504) (M. Bernard **Durville**) RN 71 1, avenue de Bourgogne ☎ 25-46-

C

Clerey Sud
01-50 Closed Sat afternoon, Sun; public holidays; 15 days at end of year. Parking area 2000 sq.m. Coaches welcome (rest. seats 40). Evening meals.

CLERMONT-FERRAND 63000 Puy-de-Dôme **RN 9 Map 16-B3**
♀ ⊗ ⌂ **1 Star NN AUVERGNE PYRÉNÉES - LES ROUTIERS** (N° RR AVR 22 778) (Mme **Laborde**) 12 bis, place des Carme ☎ 73-92-35-73 ⊷ 14 from 93,60–216F, breakfast to 18F, telephone in room. Full-board 170–220F per night. Coaches welcome (rest. seats 80). Evening meals. English, Spanish spoken. Parking; bar; dogs allowed; sports centre nearby.
♀ ⊗ **LE ROUTIER** (N° RR AVR 27 254) (Mme Jocelyne **Sauret**) 12, rue d,'Estaing ☎ 73-90-15-24 Closed Sat and 15/8 to 15/9. Local filling station.

CLERY-EN-VEXIN 95420 Val-d'Oise **Map 3-B2**
♀ ⊗ **AUBERGE DE CLÉRY-EN-VEXIN** (N° RR FEV 27 174) (M. Jean-Guy **Degoul**) Rn 14 n°4 ☎ 34-67-44-15 Closed Sun.

CLICHY 92100 Hauts-de-Seine **Porte de Clichy et Porte d'Asnières Map 1-A2**
♀ ⊗ **AU SOLEIL** (N° RR SEP 26 989) (M. Roger **Queyraud**) 105, bld Victor Hugo ☎ 47-37-15-45. Closed Sun and Aug.

CLION-SUR INDRE 36700 Indre **Map 12-B3**
♀ ⊗ ⌂ **AUBERGE DU PIE DE BOURGES** (N° RR AOU 24 652) (Mme Nicole **Chamton**) 31, Rue Nationale ☎ 54-38-60-90. ⊷ 7 Full board 140–150F. Coaches welcome (rest. seats 120). Evening meals to 9.30. Closed Aug.

CLIOUSCAT 266 30 Drôme **RN7 Map 24-A1 See SAULCE**

CLUIS 36340 Indre **RN 990 and RD 38 Map 16-A1**
♀ ⊗ **LE RELAIS DES ROUTIERS** (N° RR JAN 15 090) (Mme **Mireau**) Rue du Champ-de-Foire ☎ 54-31-23-02. Evening meals until 9pm. Public parking.

CLUNY 71250 S.-et-L. **RN 80 Map 18-A1**
♀ ⊗ **AUBERGE DU CHEVAL BLANC** (N° RR FEV 21 785) (SARL **Bouillin/Papion**) 1, rue Porte-de-Mâcon ☎ 85-59-01-13 Closed Sat; 20 Dec to 5 Jan. Coaches welcome (rest. seats 120). Evening meals.

CLUSE (LA) 01460 Ain **RN 84 Map 19-A2 18-B1/2 19-A2**
♀ ⊗ **AU PETIT BAR** (N° RR JUL 17 022) (M. Jean **Dufour**) 1, rue du Lyonnais ☎ 74-76-03-57 Closed Sun; Aug. Coaches welcome (rest. seats 40).

CLUSES 74300 Haute-Savoie **Map 19-B2**
♀ ⊗ **LE REFUGE** (N° RR AVR 27 257) (M. Serge **Rousseau**) Arraches Cheflieu ☎ 50-90-33-99 English and German spoken. Filling station 2km 8–7pm.

C

♀ ⊗ ⌂ **1 Star LE RESTOPORT DU MONT BLANC** (N° RR OCT 27
411) (Logana S.A.M. Anastase Stauridis) (?) *Autoport* Mont-Blanc
La Maladière ☎ 50-96-01-08 ⇥ 18 at 80–110F. Breakfast 17F.
Closed Sun. English, Greek, Italian spoken. Evening meals. 24hr
local filling station.

COARRAZE-NAY 64800 Pyrénées-Atlantiques **Map 20-B3**
♀ ⊗ **LETERMINUS** (N° RR JUIL 27 353) (Mme Josette **Kohnen**) 3
avenue de Berrejacq ☎ 54-61-02-60 Spanish spoken. Local filling
station 8–8pm.

COEMONT-VOUVRAY 72500 Sarthe **RN 158 Map 12-A2**
♀ ⊗ **LE BON COIN** (N° RR SEP 19 886) (Mme **Jouanneau**) ☎ 43-44-
04-17.

COETMIEUX 22400 C.-du-N. **Map 7-A23**
☕ **Service Station RELAIS MANCHE ATLANTIQUE** (N° RR AOU
55 000002) (SARL Jean-Louis **Merdrignac**) RN Bel-Air **Lamballe**
Sens Lamballe/St-Brieuc ☎ 96-34-31-23 Bar; buffet; HGV car
park; car wash; Service Station; Shop.

COGOLIN 83310 Var **RN 98 Map 25-A3**
♀ ⊗ **AUBERGE DU GISCLET** (N° RR JUL 26 954) (M. Robert **Vialenc**)
☎ 94-56-40-39 Closed Sun out of season. Italian, Spanish, English
spoken. Coaches welcome (rest. seats 40 + terrace).

COLEMBERT 62142 Pas-de-Calais **RN 42 Map 5-A2**
♀ ⊗ **CAFÉ DU COMMERCE** (N° RR JUL 26 966) (M. and Mme
Gourdin-Duhautoy) Route Nationale ☎ 21-33-31-11 Closed Sun.
Filling station near.

COLLONGES-LES-PREMIERES 21110 Côte-d'Or **RN 5 and RD 116
Map 14-A3**
♀ ⊗ **LA BONNE AUBERGE** (N° RR AVR 26 521) (M. Pierre **Colot**) 8,
avenue de la Gare ☎ 80-31-32-01. Open 7 days a week 6am–
11pm.

COLLONGES-SOUS-SALEVE 74610 Hte-Savoie **RN 206 and 201 Map
19-A2**
♀ ⊗ **LE RELAIS DU COMMERCE** (N° RR AOUT 27 361) (Mme
Marianne **Gougne**) Bas de Collonges St-Julien-en-Genevois ☎
50-43-60-29 Closed Sat. Local filling station 7–8pm. Parking.

COLMAR 68000 Haut-Rhin **RN 83 Map 10-B2**
♀ ⊗ **GARE DES MERCHANDISES** (N° RR DEC 26 770) (Mme
Pascale **Debenath**) 53, route de Roufflach ☎ 89-41-39-95 Closed
Sun. German, English spoken.

COLOMBELLES 14460 Calvados **RD 513 Map 4-B2**
♀ ⊗ ⌂ **HÔTEL DU COMMERCE** (N° RR AVR 26 221) (M. Jean-
Claude **Musson**) 3, route de Cabourg ☎ 31-72-18-89 ⇥ 27 Closed
Sun. Aug. Full-board 110–135F per night. Coaches welcome
(rest. seats 80). Evening meals to 11pm.

C

COLOMBES 92700 Hauts-de-Seine **Porte Maillot Map 1-A2**
Ⓨ ⊗ **BERRY** (N° RR JAN 16 853) (M. **LEROY**) 134, boulevard de
Valmy ☎ 42-42-02-08.

COLOMBEY-LES-BELLES 54170 M.-et-M. **RN 74 Map 14-B1**
Ⓨ ⊗ **AUBERGE LORRAINE** (N° RR AVR 26 234) (M. Claude
Arnould) 71, rue Carnot ☎ 83-52-00-23 Coaches welcome (rest.
seats 70). Evening meals. Closed from Christmas to New Year.

COLOMBY 50700 Manche **RD 2 (Valognes/Avranche) Map 4-B1**
Ⓨ ⊗ **CHEZ MÉMÈNE** (N° RR JUN 26 572) (Mme Germaine
Delacotte) Le Bourg-Valognes ☎ 33-40-10-59 Closed Mon; 2nd
fortnight Aug. Snacks in the evenings. Coaches welcome (rest.
seats 28 + 20 in bar).

COLPO 56390 Morbihan **Map 7-B2**
Ⓨ ⊗ 🏠 **AUX DÉLICES DE L'OCÉAN** (N° RR AVR 25 385) (M. Jean-
Claude **Le Guillan**) 1, avenue de la Princesse ☎ 97-66-82-21 ⊷
13 Closed Sat; 15 June to 8 Jul. Full-board 150–160F per night.
Coaches welcome (rest. seats 180). Evening meals.

COMBLANCHIEN 21700 Côte-d'Or **RN 74 Map 14-A3**
Ⓨ ⊗ 🏠 **AUBERGE DU GUIDON** (N° RR FEV 24 121) (M. André
Vauchez) Rte Nle 74 ☎ 80-62-94-39 ⊷ 8 Closed Sat, Sun; Aug.
Meals served until 11pm.

COMBRES 28480 E.-et-L. CO15 **Map 8-B3**
Ⓨ ⊗ 🏠 **HOTEL DE LA CROIX BLANCHE** (N° RR OCT 27 045) (Mme
Christiane **Vaux**) Place de l'Église ☎ 37-29-59-54 ⊷ 7 Full board
160–180F. Coaches welcome (rest. seats 44). Evening meals to
10pm. English spoken.

COMBRONDE 63460 Puy-de-Dôme **RN 144 et CD 223 Map 16-B3**
Ⓨ ⊗ 🏠 **RELAIS DE L'HERMITAGE** (N° RR NOV 27 107) (Mme
Chantal **Duprat**) 5, Belle-Allée ☎ 73-97-10-57 Local filling station.

COMBROUZE 12240 Aveyron **D 911 Map 22-B1**
Ⓨ ⊗ 🏠 **LE RELAIS BONNET** (N° RR JUL 19 107) (Mme Rolande
Bonnet) ☎ 65-69-93-01 ⊷ 14 Closed Sun. Coaches welcome
(rest. seats 70). Evening meals.

COMINES 59560 Nord **Map 5-B1**
Ⓨ ⊗ **AUX AMIS DE LA ROUTE** (N° RR SEPT 27 015) (Mme
Christiane **Verbeke**) 6, rue de Pont ☎ 20-39-04-67 Closed Tues
2pm to Wed 11am 15 days in July. Dutch spoken. Evening meals
to 10pm.

COMMODITE (LA) par SOLTERRE 45700 Loiret **RN 7 Map 13-A1/2**
Ⓨ ⊗ **AUBERGE DE LA ROUTE BLEUE** (N° RR MAR 2 687) (SNC
Charles et Albert **Rocco**) ☎ 38-94-90-04 Closed Tue evening,
Wed; Aug. Coaches welcome (60/32 seats). Evening meals.
⊷ Some Spanish spoken. Menu 45–92F. Specialities: *Ris de veau
normand Escalope cordon bleu. Escarjots Roquejort.*

C

COMPIÈGNE 60200 Oise **RN 31-32-35 Map 3-A3**
♀ ⊗ **BAR DE LA MARINE** (N° RR JUL 25 993) (M. Bernard **Piat**) 17, rue de l'Estacade ☎ 44-40-15-14 Closed Sat, Sun. Coaches welcome (rest. seats 44). Evening meals until 9pm.

CONCOURSON-SUR-LAYON 49700 M.et-L. **RN 960 Map 12-B2**
♀ ⊗ **AUBERGE DU HAUT LAYON** (N° RR DEC 26 746) (M. Bernard **Battais**) Rte Nationale ☎ 41-59-27-60 Closed Sun evening (winter). English spoken.

CONDÉ-SUR-NOIREAU 14110 Calvados **RN 162 Map 8-A1/2**
♀ ⊗ **LE RELAIS DES PROMENADES** (N° RR JAN 18 594) (M. Michel **Jomat**) 2, rue Motte-de-Lutre Angle rue St-Martin ☎ 31-69-03-36 **Minitel** ⊶ 4 Closed Sun; Aug. Full-board 150–200F per night. Evening meals.

CONDÉ-SUR-VIRE 50890 Manche **Map 4-B1**
♀ ⊗ ⌂ **HOTEL DES ROCHES** (N° RR MAI 26 546) (M. Achour **Mohabeddine**) 12, rue Alfred Duros ☎ 33-55-20-82 ⊶ 8 Closed Sun. Aug. English spoken. Coaches welcome (rest. seats 26).

CONNANTRAY 51230 Marne **RN 4 Map 9-A3**
♀ ⊗ ⌂ **LA ROUTIÈRE** (N° RR OCT 27 415) (M. Michel **Villain**) ☎ 26-42-42-03 ⊶ 8. Open 7 days. Evening meals. 24hr local filling station.

CONNANTRE 51230 Marne **RN 4 Map 9-A3**
♀ ⊗ ⌂ **LA GRAPPE D'OR** (N° RR MARS 26 472) (M. Claude **Longatte**) 1, rue de la Gare ☎ 26-81-04-62 **Minitel** ⊶ 6 Closed Sun; Jan.

CONNERRE 72160 Sarthe **RN 23 Map 8-B2/3**
♀ ⊗ **LE RELAIS DU COMMERCE** (N° RR AVR 11 404) (M. Daniel **Charpentier**) 14, rue de Paris ☎ 43-89-00-55 Closed Sun; Aug. Coaches welcome (rest. seats 120).

CONQUEREUIL (LA) 44290 Loire-Atlantique **RD 124 Map 11-A2**
♀ ⊗ **LE RELAIS DES ROUTIERS – LE BON ACCUEIL** (N° RR NOV 16 350) (Mme Eugénie **Louis**) ☎ 40-87-36-04. Coaches welcome (100 seats reservable). Evening meals.

CONSENVOYE 55110 Meuse **RD 964 Map 6-B3**
♀ ⊗ ⌂ **AUBERGE LORRAINE** (N° RR MAR 26 854) (Mme Denise **Poussant**) Grand Rue ☎ 29-85-80-19 ⊶ 6 Closed Sat; 2nd fortnight Feb. English spoken. Full board 170–205F. Coaches welcome (rest. seats 60 + 150).

CONTREXÉVILLE 88140 Vosges **RN 64 Map 14-B2**
♀ ⊗ **LE BELFORT** (N° RR JUIN 25 957) (M. André **Sundhauser**) 587, av. Division Leclerc ☎ 29-08-04-22 **Minitel** Closed Sat, Sun. Evening meals on Sat.

COQUILLE (LA) 24450 Dordogne **Map 17-A1**
♀ ⊗ **LES PORTES DU PÉRIGORD VERT** (N° RR JUIL 27 348) (M.

C

Coquille (La) continued

Franck **Fauvel**) Les Commuveaux ☎ 53-52-83-46. Evening meals to 10.30pm. Local filling station 7–7pm.

CORAY 29145 Finistère **CD 15 et 36 Map 7–B1**

♈ ⊗ **LE BREIZH RELAIS** (N° RR NOV 27 089) (M. Albin **Le Roux**) Place de l'Église ☎ 98-59-36-26 Closed Monday pm. Local filling station.

CORBEIL-ESSONNES 91100 Essonne **RN 7 Map 1-B3**

♈ ⊗ ⌂ **1 Star NN L'ERMITAGE** (N° RR OCT 27 037) (Mme Suzanne **Gerlache**) 137, boulevard de Fontainebleau ☎ 64-96-29-42 ⊷ 19 Closed Sun.

♈ ⊗ **LA NACELLE** (N° RR OCT 24 701) (Mme Patricia **Sonnet**) 31, rue de la Papeterie ☎ 64-96-21-17 Closed Sun afternoon.

♈ ⊗ **L'ESCALE** (N° RR JUL 18 461) (M. Marcel-André **Gatefait**) 10, rue de Seine ☎ 64-96-26-58 Closed Sun; Sept.

See also Lisses

CORBENAY 70800 Haute-Savoie **Map 10-A3**

♈ ⊗ ⌂ **1 Star NN AU P'TIT CHARIOT** (N° RR OCT 27 427) (M. Thierry **Mougenot**) 1, rue des Cannes Route de Fougerolles ☎ 84-94-13-60 ⊷ 10 at 95–110F. Breakfast 17F. Closed Sunday night. Aug. German/English spoken. Evening meals to 10.30pm. Local filling station 7.45–8.30pm. Showers available to drivers.

CORBIGNY 58800 Nièvre **Map 13-B2**

♈ ⊗ **LES AMIS DES ROUTIERS** (N° RR DEC 24 777) (Mme Colette **Perini**) Rte de Clamecy ☎ 86-20-19-77 Closed Sat pm. Sun. Oct. Coaches welcome (rest. seats 30). Evening meals to 11pm.

CORMEIL-EN-PARISIS 95240 Val-d'Oise **Map 1-A2**

♈ ⊗ **LE BON ACCUEIL** (N° RR OCT 27 436) (M. Granday et Mme **Richard**) 26 bd du Maréchal Juin ☎ 39-78-83-24. Closed Sun. Russian, Polish spoken. Evening meals.

CORMEILLES-EN-VEXIN 95830 Val-d'Oise **Map 3-B2**

♈ ⊗ **LE MONTMARTRE** (N° RR JANV 26 427) (M. Jean-Claude **Lorre**) SNC Le Relaxe 4, rue Jean Jaurès ☎ 34-66-61-18 **Minitel** Closed Mon. Coaches welcome (rest. seats 40). Evening meals.

CORMERY 37320 Indre-et-Loire **RN 143 Map 12-B3**

♈ ⊗ ⌂ **LA CHAUMIERE** (N° RR OCT 22 984) (Mme **Colle**) La Croix-d'Avon ☎ 47-50-20-26 ⊷ 6 Closed Fri evening.

CORMORANCHE-SUR-SAONE 01290 Ain **Map 18-B1**

♈ ⊗ ⌂ **1 Star NN AUBERGE CHEZ LA MÈRE MARTINET** (N° RR JUL 23 864) (Mme Geneviève **Martinet**) ☎ 85-36-20-40 **Minitel** ⊷ 7 at 118–158F. Breakfast 22F. Menu 55–170F. Special sarcisson chaud à la beaujolaise. Grenouilles fraiches aux dines herbies suprême de Volaille Closed Sun ev. Wed; 15 Aug to 10 Sept. Full-board 190F to 250F per night. Coaches welcome (rest. seats 35). Evening meals. Parking. Bar. Dogs allowed. Bowls, leisure lake.

CORNE 49250 M.-et-L. **RN 147 Map 12-A2**

♀ ⊗ **LE RELAIS DE LA CROIX BLANCHE** (N° RR JUL 25 479) (M. Jean-Noël **Pignard**) La Croix Blanche RN 147 ☎ 41-45-01-82 Closed Sat evening; Sun; Christmas to New Year. Evening meals to 10pm. Parking.

CORNEVILLE-SUR-RISLE 27500 Eure **RN 180 Map 4-B3 see PONT-AUDEMER**

CORON 49690 Maine-et-Loire **RD 960 Map 12-B1**

♀ ⊗ ⌂ **LA BOULE D'OR** (N° RR MARS 26 851) (Mme Marie-Claire **Merlet**) 56, rue Joachim du Bellay ☎ 41-55-81-84 ━ 11 Closed Wed from 3.30pm. English spoken.

CORPS 38970 Isère **RN 85 Map 19-A3**

♀ ⊗ ⌂ **LE RELAIS DU TILLEUL** (N° RR JUL 25 979) (M. Claude **Jourdan**) Rue des Fossés ☎ 76-30-00-43 ━ 10 Closed Nov, 1st 2 weeks Dec. Full-board 180–200F per night. Coaches welcome (rest. seats 60). Evening meals. English, German spoken. Menus ⏚ 55–110F. Special Gratin dauphinois. Civet de porcelet, Poulet de écre visses.

CORPS-NUDS 35150 Ille-et-Vilaine **RN 163 Map 7-B3**

♀ ⊗ **LES ROUTIERS** (N° RR FEV 22 676) (Mme Solange **Piel**) Place de l'Eglise ☎ 99-44-00-25 Closed Sat; Aug.

COSNE-SUR-LOIRE 58200 Nièvre **RN 7 Map 13-A/B2**

♀ ⊗ ⌂ **1 Star NN LE RELAIS DES TROIS COULEURS** (N° RR MAR 6 751) (MM. Jean and Pierre **Morfaux**) 21, rue St-Agnan ☎ 86-28-23-50 ━ 25 Closed last week Dec to 2nd week Jan. Full-board ⏚ 130–150F per night. Coaches welcome (rest. seats 120). Evening meals. Menus from 46–90F. Specialities: *coq au vin*, frogs' legs à la provençale.

♀ ⊗ **LA TASSE** (N° RR NOV 24 409) (M. Claude Maurice **Chet**) RN7 Maltaverne ☎ 86-26-11-76 Closed Sun (open for coach bookings) Bank holidays Aug. English spoken. Coaches welcome (rest. seats 70). Evening meals.

COSNE D'ALLIER 03430 Allier **Map 16-A2**

♀ ⊗ **L'ESCALE** (N° RR NOV 27 457) (Mme Marie-Josephe **Sauvat**) 2, place de la liberté ☎ 70-07-21-10 English, Spanish spoken. Evening meals. 24hr local filling station.

♀ .60 **LE LION D'OR** (N° RR MARS 27 207) (M. Jean-Yves **Bernardeau**) 7, place de la Liberté ☎ 70-07-21-20.

COSTAROS 43490 Hte-Loire **RN 88 Map 17-B3**

♀ ⊗ ⌂ **RELAIS ROUTIERS** (N° RR JUN 21 057) (Mme Marie-Thérèse **Rossello**) Rue Principale ☎ 71-57-16-04 ━ 17 Closed Sat afternoon in winter. Coaches welcome (rest. seats 60). Spanish spoken. Full board 140–150F.

COTEAU (LE) 42120 Loire **RN 7 (exit south de Roanne Map 18-A2**

♀ ⊗ ⌂ **LE PARIGNY** (N° RR OCT 24 397) Sarl Le Parigny (Mme Jeanine **Pamurie**) Les Bas de Rhins ☎ 77-62-06-18 ━ 6 Closed on

C

Coteau (Le) continued
Sun and 15th–30th Aug. Evening meal to 9pm.

COUCY-LE-CHATEAU 02380 Aisne **Map 6-B1**
♀ ⊗ ⌂ **LE LION ROUGE** (N° RR NOV 27 450) (M. Patrick **Clavet**) 62, avenue Altenkessel ☎ 23-52-70-13 ⊷ 13 Closed 2 weeks at Christmas. German, English spoken. Evening meals to 9.30. Filling station 2km from 7–9pm.

COULLONS 45720 Loiret
♀ ⊗ **LE PECHEUR** (N° RR JAN 27 511) (Mme Eileen **Barrows**) 45, Rue du Sergent Le Lievre ☎ 38-29-22-32 ⊷ 8 Evening meals. English spoken.

COULLONS 45500 Loiret **RD 51 Map 13-A1**
♀ ⊗ ⌂ **LE ROUSSILLON** (N° RR SEP 25 640) (M. Eric **Vialatte**) 45, rue du Sergent-Lelièvre ☎ 38-36-10-49 ⊷ 11 Closed Sun afternoon. Full-board 155F per night. Coaches welcome (rest. seats 40). Evening meals.
♀ ⊗ **LA BARBE GRISE** (N° RR OCT 25 681) (M. Jean **Poirirer**) Rte Jacques Coeur CD 940 ☎ 38-36-11-27 Closed Mon (except bank holidays) Early Sept and Feb. English spoken.

COULMIER-LE-SEC 21400 Côte-d'Or **RD 980 Map 13-A3**
♀ ⊗ **LE RELAIS DES ROUTIERS** (N° RR JUL 24 267) (M. Jean-Maurice **Terillon**) ☎ 80-93-13-09 Closed Sun; 1st fortnight in Aug; Christmas to New Year. Coaches welcome (rest. seats 60). Evening meals until midnight.

COULOMBIERS 86600 Vienne **RN 11 Map 15-B1**
♀ ⊗ **LE RELAIS DE LA PAZIOTERIE** (N° RR JUL 25 050) (Mme Yvonne **Barrusseau**) **Lusignan** ☎ 49-60-90-59 **Minitel** Coaches welcome (rest. seats 67).

COULOUTRE 58220 Nièvre **RD 1 Map 13-A/B2**
♀ ⊗ **AUBERGE DU NIVERNAIS** (N° RR DEC 24 443) (M. Jean-Bernard **Michel**) Rue Principale ☎ 86-39-32-17 Closed Mon.

COURBAN 21520 Côte d'Or **RD 965 Map 13-A3**
♀ ⊗ ⌂ **LES ROUTIERS – Chez Jaquotte** (N° RR JUN 25 965) (Mme Jacqueline **Aubry**) Montigny-sur-Aube ☎ 80-91-72-81 ⊷ 5 Closed Sun afternoon (unless by previous arrangement). Full-board 130–150F per night. Coaches welcome (rest. seats 80). Evening meals.

COURCELLES-LES-GISORS 60240 Oise **RD 981 Map 3-B2**
♀ ⊗ **AUBERGE DU CARREFOUR** (N° RR DEC 21 716) (M. Daniel **Hillion**) ☎ 32-55-03-16 Closed Sat evening to Sun evening. 1 to 15 Sept. Coaches welcome (rest. seats 60). Evening meals to 9pm.

COURGIVAUX 51310 Marne **RN 4**
♀ ⊗ ⌂ **1 Star AUBERGE DE CHAPERON ROUGE** (N° RR JAN 27 501) (M. Bernard **Moreau**) ☎ 26-81-57-09 ⊷ 14 from 100–130F.

Breakfast 17.50–19.50F. Evening meals until 8.30pm. Closed Saturday. Parking.

COURNEUVE (LA) 93120 Seine-St-Denis **Porte de la Villette Map 1-A2/3**
Ⓨ ⊗ ⌂ **L'ESCALE DES ROUTIERS** (N° RR JAN 26 786) (M. and Mme **Khaled**) 27, avenue Jean-Jaurès ☎ 48-36-43-78 Arabic, English, Italian spoken. ⊷ 3 Coaches welcome (rest. seats 82). Evening meals to 12pm. Closed Sun. 15th July to 15th Aug. Full board 100–120F.
Ⓨ ⊗ ⌂ **CAFE DE L'AVENIR** (N° RR SEP 26 662) (M. Sadid **Hadj-Arab**) 98, ave. P.-V. Couturier ☎ 48-36-37-53 Closed Sun afternoon. Aug. Coaches welcome (rest. seats 42).

COURTENAY 45320 Loiret **RN 60 Map 9-B2**
Ⓨ ⊗ ⌂ **LE RELAIS DES SPORTS** (N° RR MAI 7 681) (M. Armand **Martin**) 38, rue de Villeneuve ☎ 38-97-32-37 ⊷ 9 Closed Sun; 15 to 30 Mar; 15 to 30 Aug. Coaches welcome (rest. seats 60). Evening meals.

COURTHEZON 84350 Vaucluse **RN 7 Map 24-A2**
Ⓨ ⊗ **LE RELAIS DU SOLEIL** (N° RR MAI 27 292) (Mme Marie Ange **Meilloret**) RN 7 ☎ 90-70-74-36 Closed Sat, Sun. Italian, English, German spoken. Evening meals. Local filling station 7–10pm.

COURTISOLS 51460 Marne **RN 3 Maps 6B2 and 9-A3**
Ⓨ ⊗ **LE RELAIS DES TOURISTES** (N° RR NOV 18 551) (M. Gérard **Gaubert**) 57, route Nationale ☎ 26-66-61-42 ⊷ 4 Closed 15 Aug for 3 weeks. Coaches welcome (rest. seats 120). Evening meals.

COUSSAC-BONNEVAL 87500 Haute-Vienne **RN 701 Map 17-A1**
Ⓨ ⊗ ⌂ **LE RELAIS DU GAI COUSSAC** (N° RR DEC 20 051) (Mme Marcelle **Dorion**) Rue du 11 Novembre ☎ 55-75-21-59 **Minitel** Closed Sept. Full-board 130F per night. Coaches welcome (rest. seats 100). Evening meals.

COUSTELLET 84220 Vaucluse **RN 100 Map 24-B2**
Ⓨ ⊗ **LE SARRET** (N° RR MAR 25 336) (M. André **Simonin**) RN 100 **Cabrières d'Avignon** (Gordes) ☎ 90-71-85-58 ⊷ 7 Closed Sun; Feb.

COUTANCES 50200 Manche **RN 171 Map 8-A1 4-B1**
Ⓨ ⊗ ⌂ **1 Star NN LE RELAIS DU VIADUC** (N° RR JUN 16 098) (Mme **Hossin**) 25, avenue de Verdun ☎ 33-45-02-68 **Minitel** ⊷ 10 from 70–150F, breakfast 17–20 F; telephone in room. Closed Fri evening, Sun evening out of season; (restaurant) Sep. Full-board 170–250F per night. Coaches welcome (rest. seats 70/40). Evening meals to 9pm. English, German spoken. Menus from 38–230F. Specialities: *Langouste gratinée, Tripes maison, Gigot d'agneau*. Sites to visit: cathedral.

COUX (LE) 24220 Dordogne **RD 703 Map 17-B1**
Ⓨ ⊗ **LA COTTE DE MAILLES** (N° RR NOV 27 078) (Mme Michelle **Mandler**) Place de l'Église ☎ 53-31-61-04 Closed 15/12 to 15/1.

C

Coux (Le) continued

English and German spoken. Local filling station 7–8pm.

COZES 17120 Chte-Mme **Map 15-A2**

Shell Service Station BEL AIR (N° RR AVR 550 000 08) (M. Jacques **Gadiou**) Rte de Royan ☎ 46-90-84-12 Grezac.

CRAVANT 89460 Yonne **RN 6 Map 13-A2**

LE RELAIS DES DEUX PONTS (N° RR JAN 17 724) (Mme Isabelle **Nogueria**) 17, route de Paris ☎ 86-42-24-01 ⇥ 10 Portuguese spoken.

CREIL 60109 Oise **RN 16 Map 3-B3**

CHEZ PIERROT (N° RR JUL 25 489) (M. Jacques **Bouchart**) 36, rue des Usines ☎ 44-25-37-22 ⇥ 9 Closed Sat, Sun; Aug.

CREMIEU 38460 Isère **RN 157 Map 2-A2**

LE RELAIS DE L'HOTEL DE VILLE (N° RR MAI 24 579) (M. Jean **L'Hopital**) 1, place de la Nation ☎ 74-94-76-09.

CREMIEU 38460 Isère **see SABLONNIÈRES**

CRENEY 10150 Aube **RD 960 Map 9-B3**

LE RELAIS DU CENTRE (N° RR DEC 26 128) (M. Jacques **Jeandon**) 29, route de Brienne ☎ 25-81-39-79 Evening meals to 9pm. Coaches welcome (rest. seats 50).

CRESANCEY 70100 Haute-Saône **Map 14-A3**

AUBERGE DE LA PETITE FRINGALE (N° RR JUIL 27 349) (M. Jean-Paul **Loisel**) ☎ 84-31-56-08 Closed Mon am to Wed pm and Thurs am. English spoken. Evening meal to 9pm. Local filling station. Parking.

CRESPIERES 78121 Yvelines **RN 307 Map 1-A1**

AUBERGE DES ROUTIERS (N° RR DEC 9 124) (Mme Magdeleine **Glatigny**) ☎ 30-54-44-28 Closed Sat. Evening meals to 8pm.

CREST 26400 Drome **Map 24-A1**

LE CHAMPS DE MARS (N° RR AVR 27 259) (M. Bernard **Genthon**) 8, place de la Liberté ☎ 75-40-61-06 Closed Mon. German spoken. Filling station 2km.

CREUSOT (LE) 71200 S.-et-L. **RN 80 Map 18-A1 13-B3**

LE RELAIS DES ROUTIERS (N° RR SEP 22 041) (M. **Beauclair**) 26, rue de l'Yser ☎ 85-55-03-34 ⇥ 14 Closed Sat afternoon. Full-board 155–160F per night. Coaches welcome (rest. seats 50). Evening meals.

CREUZIER-LE-VIEUX 03300 Allier **Map 16-B3**

CHEZ LA MÈRE RIBOULIN (N° RR AVR 27 247) (SARL Marcel **Joly**) 10, rue des Ailes ☎ 70-98-44-88 ⇥ 13 Repas servi le soir.

CREVANT-MONTIERCHAUME 36130 Indre **Map 13-B1**

C

🍷 ⊗ **LE RELAIS DES ROUTIERS** (N° RR DEC 11 180) (Mme **Belouin-Ferre**) ☎ 54-36-00-19 Closed Sun.

CREVECŒUR LE GRAND 60360 Oise **RN 30 and RD 93 Map 3-A2**
🍷 ⊗ **LE RELAX** (N° RR JUIL 26 969) (M. Michel **Dubois**) 12, rue de Breteuil ☎ 44-46-87-65 Closed Sun; Filling station near.

CROISIÈRE (LA) 23300 Creuse **RN 145 and 20 Map 16-B1**
🍷 ⊗ 🏠 **LES ROUTIERS** (N° RR JUIL 26 596) (M. Raymond **Boutet**) La Croisière St-Maurice ☎ 55-63-77-55 and 55-63-30-37 ⬩ 12 Closed 24 Dec–2 Jan. Full-board 140–150F per night. Coaches welcome (rest. seats 50). Evening meals to 9pm.

CROISY-SUR-ANDELLE 76780 S.-Marit **RN 31 Map 3-A1**
🍷 ⊗ **LE RELAIS DU COMMERCE** (N° RR OCT 23 975) (Mme Colette **Belière**) RN 31 ☎ 35-23-61-82 **Minitel** Closed Sun; 15 Dec to 10 Jan. Coaches welcome (rest. seats 80). Evening meals to 9pm. Parking.

CROIX 59170 Nord **RD 14 Map 5-B1**
🍷 ⊗ **LE RELAIS DE L'HOTEL DE VILLE** (N° RR MAR 21 837) (Mme Lucette **Streleki**) 211, rue Jean-Jaurès ☎ 20-70-50-92 Closed Mon afternoon; Jul.
🍷 ⊗ 🏠 **LE RELAIS CHEZ HENRI** (N° RR DEC 24 051) (Mme **Vandesompele**) 53, avenue Georges-Hannart, 188, rue Gustave Dubled ☎ 20-72-59-08 **Minitel** ⬩ 9 Closed Sat, Sun evening; Aug. Full-board 180–220F per night. Coaches welcome (rest. seats 60). Evening meals until 9pm. Flemish spoken.

CROIX-BLANCHE-SOLOGNY (LA) 71960 S.-et-L. **RN 79 Map 18-A1**
Voir BERZÉ-LA-VILLE

CROIX-CALUYAU-BOUSIES 59222 Nord **RD 932 Map 6-A3**
🍷 ⊗ **LE RELAIS DES ROUTIERS** (N° RR JUIL 21 991) (Mme Josette **Verriez**) Le Gué-Fené ☎ 27-84-15-99.

CROIX-CHAPEAU 17220 Chte-Mme **Map 11-B1**
🍷 ⊗ **CAFE-DE-PARIS** (N° RR JAN 27 494) (EURL DM PB – Daniel **Mineur**) 60, Rue de la Libération ☎ 46-35-81-20. Evening meals. English, Spanish spoken.
🍷 ⊗ **RELAIS DE PARIS** (N° RR DEC 26 412) (M. Jean-Paul **Thabault**) 60, avenue de la Libération ☎ 46-35-81-20 Closed Wed.

CROIX-VALMER (LA) 83420 Var **RN 559 Map 25-A3**
🍷 ⊗ 🏠 **LA CIGALE** (N° RR MAI 24 966) (M. Eric **Korhel**) Rte Nle 559 ☎ 94-79-60-41 ⬩ 7. Full board 170–220F. Coaches welcome (rest. seats 50).

CROLLES 38190 Isère **RN 90 Map 19-A3**
🍷 ⊗ 🏠 **1 Star NN HOTEL DU PETIT PONT** (N° RR JUN 25 946) (M. André **Legallais**) RN 90 ☎ 76-08-03-92 Montfort ⬩ 13 from 85–230F Closed Mon; Nov. Full-board 160–280F per night, Coaches welcome (rest. seats 60). Evening meals from 7pm to 8.30pm. Parking; bar; dogs allowed; 'boule' played; ski runs near. Some German spoken.

C

CRUAS 07350 Ardeche **RN 86 Map 24-A1/2**
♀ ⊗ **AUX AMIS DES ROUTIERS** (N° RR JUL 17 322) (Mme Jeannette
Pistoresi) ☎ 75-51-41-12 Coaches welcome (rest. seats 120).
Evening meals until 11pm. Parking.

CRUET-MONTMELIAN 73820 Savoie **RN 6 Map 19-A2**
♀ ⊗ ⌂ **CHEZ MARCEL** (N° RR DEC 26 747) (M. Jean-Noël **Padel**)
Association Solidarité Savoyarde. 142, Rue de Perradière. ☎ 79-
85-25-25 ⊷ 8 Coaches welcome (rest. seats 130). Evening meal to
10pm. Closed Aug. Full board 168F. English, German spoken.

CUIGY-EN-BRAY 60850 Oise **RN 3 Map 3-A2**
♀ ⊗ **RELAIS DE ST-LEU** (N° RR NOV 26 365) (M. Jacques **Delaruel-
le**) ☎ 44-82-53-17 **Minitel** Closed Sat afternoon, Sun, Aug.
Coaches welcome (rest. seats 100). Evening meals to 9pm.

CUISE-LA-MOTTE 60350 Oise **RN 31 Map 6-B1**
♀ ⊗ ⌂ **AUX AS DU VOLANT** (N° RR MAI 26 547) (M. Dominique
Bignet) 23, rue du Dr Moussaud ☎ 44-85-70-51 ⊷ 6 Closed Sat,
Sun; 24 Dec to 2 Jan. Coaches welcome (rest. seats 74). English
spoken. Evening meals to 9pm.

CUISEAUX 71480 Saône-et-Loir **Map 18-B1**
♀ ⊗ **RELAIS FRANC COMTOIS** (N° RR JUL 27 341) (M. Jean-Marc
Girona) Joudes ☎ 85-72-79-79 Evening meals to 10pm. Local
filling station 7–8pm.

CUISERY 71290 S.-&-L. **RD 971 Map 18-B1**
♀ ⊗ **SARL LE JARDIN DE LA COQUELLE** (N° RR JANV 27 157) (M.
Jean-Paul **Fallet**) Zone artisanale du Bois Bernouz ☎ 85-40-06-90
Closed Mon. English spoken. Specialities: regional products
(Chickens, Snails etc) Monkfish in Sauce Armoricaine 39.30F,
Perch Fillet in Chardonnay 41F. Local filling station 7–7pm.

CULAN 18270 Cher **RD 943 Map 16-A2**
♀ ⊗ **HOTEL DU BERRY** (N° RR MAR 27 224) (Mme Chantal **Gallurt**)
Place du Champ de Joire ☎ 48-56-65-93. Closed Sun. Sites to visit:
château, church, museum, dam at Sidiailles. English spoken.

CUON 49150 M.-et-L. **Map 12-A2**
♀ ⊗ **LA POMM'DE PIN** (N° RR AVR 25 904) (Mme Yvette **Pécot**) RN
938 Le Bourg ☎ 41-82-75-74 ⊷ 4 Closed Mon afternoon; Aug.
Coaches welcome (rest. seats 60). Evening meals until 10pm.

CUQ-TOULZA 81470 Tarn **RD 621 Map 22-A2**
♀ ⊗ ⌂ **1 Star NN LE RELAIS CHEZ ALAIN – La Bombardière** (N°
RR MAR 22 271) (M. Alain **Pratviel**) ☎ 63-75-70-36 ⊷ 10 at 160F,
breakfast from 20 to 25F. Full-board 170–185 F per night.
Coaches welcome (rest. seats 400). Evening meals. Parking; bar;
dogs allowed; TV room; walks. Sites to visit: Lake Saint Ferréol,
Cordes, Sidobre. English spoken.

CUSSAC 87150 Hte-Vienne **RD 699 Map 15-B2**
♀ ⊗ **LES BRUYÈRES** (N° RR JAN 25 787) (M. **Morichon**) Place de

C

l'Église ◡ 4 English spoken.
Ᵽ ⊗ 🏠 **LA BARRIÈRE** (N° RR AVR 27 240) (Mme Denise **Barrière**)
☎ 55-70-94-84 ◡ 9 Local filling station 7–8pm.

CUSSET 03300 Allier **Map 16-B3**
Ᵽ ⊗ **HOTEL DE LA GARE LES ROUTIERS** (N° RR JAN 26 421) (M.
Jean **Laroque**) 1, route de Paris ☎ 70-98-26-10 ◡ 3 Closed Sun;
Jul.
Ᵽ ⊗ **LES MONTAGNARDS** (N° RR JUL 26 960) (M. Roger **Pol**) 20, rue
Général Raynal ☎ 70-98-38-60 Closed Sun. Filling station near.
Coaches welcome (rest. seats 40).

CUSSY-LES-FORGES 89420 Yonne **RN 6 Map 13-A3**
Ᵽ ⊗ **LE RELAIS 6** (N° RR FEV 26 805) (M. Hamid **Adjaoud**) Route
nationale 6 ☎ 86-33-10-14 Closed Sun. Coaches welcome (rest.
seats 130). Evening meals.

CUVILLY 60490 Oise **RN17 Map 3-A3**
Ᵽ ⊗ 🏠 **LA CAMPAGNARDE** (N° RR JUN 26 922) (M. Daniel **Hillion**)
5, route de Flandres ☎ 44-85-00-30 ◡ 9 Closed Sun; 1–15 Sept.

CUZIEU 42330 Loire **RN 82 Map 18-A2**
Ᵽ ⊗ 🏠 **REST DE LA MAIRIE** (N° RR AVR 26 225) (Mme Janine
Dard) RN 82, Le Bourg ☎ 77-54-88-21 **Minitel** ◡ 12 Closed Sat
pm, Sun; 1 week at Christmas; 3 weeks in Aug. Evening meals.

D

DAGNEUX 01120 Ain **RN 84 Map 2-A2**
Ᵽ ⊗ **RELAIS DE LA PLACE** (N° RR OCT 26 336) (Mme **Aliu** and M.
Colin) 96, rte de Genève ☎ 78-06-43-70 Spanish, Italian spoken.
Evening meals until mid-night.

DANGERS 28190 Eure-et-Loir **CD 939 Map 8-A/B3**
Ᵽ ⊗ **LE RELAIS** (N° RR DEC 27 134) (M. Patrick **Ollier**) rue de
Chartres ☎ 37-22-90-30 Closed Sun and two weeks in August.
Local filling station 7.15–8.30.

DANGÉ-ST-ROMAIN 86220 Vienne **Map 12-B2**
Ᵽ ⊗ 🏠 **LE NATIONAL CHEZ ARLETTE** (N° RR JUIN 27 296) 120, RN
10 ☎ 49-86-40-14 ◡ 5 Closed Sun. Evening meals. Coaches
welcome.

DANNEMOINE 89700 Yonne **RD 905 Map 13-A3**
Ᵽ ⊗ **A LA BONNE AUBERGE - LES ROUTIERS** (N° RR MAI 21 096)
(Mme Nicole **Verdin**) ☎ 86-55-54-22 Coaches welcome (rest.
seats 65). Evening meals. ◡ 12 from 140 to 150F.

131

D

DARDILLY 69570 Rhône **RD 67 and RD 73 Map 2-A1**
♈ ⊗ ⌂ **LE CHENE ROND** (N° RR FEV 23 144) (M. Emile **Lagoutte**) 87, Rte Nle 7 ☎ 78-87-15-48 ⊸ 6 Closed Sat midday, Sun; Aug. Evening meals for drivers.
♘ **Service Station LES BRUYÈRES** (N° RR FEV 23 649) (M. Norbert **Berton**) Aire de Paisy ☎ 78-35-73-80 sens Lyon/Paris Open 24 hours. German spoken.
♈ ⊗ ⌂ **LE RELAIS DE LA RADIO** (N° RR JAN 27 137) (M, Pierre **Laputo**) lieu-dit Montcourant ☎ 78-48-01-39 ⊸ 8 Closed Sat evening, Sun; 28th Jul to 2 Aug. English/Italian spoken. Filling station 1.5km 7–8pm.

DARVOY 45150 Loiret **RN 751 Map 13-A1**
♈ ⊗ **LE RELAIS DES ROUTIERS** (N° RR DEC 16 348) (Mme Germaine **Girard**) 4, rte d'Orléans ☎ 38-59-71-00 Closed Sun.

DAX 40100 Landes **RN 647 and 124 Map 20-A2**
♈ ⊗ **AUBERGE DE LA CHALOSSE** (N° RR OCT 22 956) (M. **Richaud**) 157, avenue Georges Clemenceau ☎ 58-74-23-08 ⊸ 6 Closed Sun; Aug. Evening meals to 10pm. Parking.

DECAZEVILLE 12300 Aveyron **RN 140 (axe Brive Mediterranée) Map 22-B1 and 17-B2**
♈ ⊗ **REST. DES USINES** (N° RR OCT 25 132) (Mme Régine **Forsse**) 23, faubourg Desseligny Fontvergnes ☎ 65-43-15-88 Closed Sat afternoon. Evening meals. Menus 40–105F. Specialities: *écrevis*
🖛 *ses américaines, cuisses de grenouilles, bavette aux échalottes on request.*

DECINES 69150 Rhône **RN 517 Map 2-A2**
♈ ⊗ ⌂ **2 Stars NN – HOTEL DE LA POSTE – Chez Simone** (N° RR JUL 18 783) (Mme Marcel **Buisson**) 11, rue d'Alsace ☎ 78-49-19-03 **Minitel** ⊸ 34 from 100 to 180F, breakfast to 20F. Restaurant closed Sun, (Hotel open). Car park (area 2000 sq.m.) locked at night. Evening meals. English, Spanish, Italian spoken. Bar; dogs allowed; boule played; track and pool near. Full board 160–285F. Coaches welcome (rest. seats 20).

DECIZE 58300 Nièvre **Map 16-A3**
♈ ⊗ **LE RELAIS BEL-AIR** (N° RR MARS 27 213) (M. and Mme André **Demery**) 164, avenue de Verdun ☎ 86-25-01-86 Closed Sun; Aug.

DENEZE-SUR-DOUÉ 49700 Maine-et-Loire **RD 69 Map 12-B2**
♈ ⊗ **LE RELAIS DES ROUTIERS** (N° RR JAN 23 113) (Mme Onillon) ☎ 41-59-21-56.

DENGUIN 64230 Pyrénées-Atlantiques **RN 117 Map 20-B3**
♈ ⊗ ⌂ **1 star NN LES ROUTIERS DE DENGUIN** (N° RR MARS 26 846) (**Sarl Pyrénées Montagne Océan**) ☎ 59-68-85-15 ⊸ 14 English, Spanish, German spoken. Closed Sat. Evening meals. Parking.

D

DÉOLS 36130 Indre **RN 151, RN 20 and RN 725 Maps 12-B3 and 13-B1**
♼ ⊗ **RELAIS DE L'ESPÉRANCE** (N° RR OCT 26 022) (Mme **Dugué**) route d'Issoudun ☎ 54-22-68-17.

DÉOLS 36130 see **CHATEAUROUX**.

DERBIÈRE 26740 Drôme **RN 7 Map 24-A2**
♼ ⊗ ⌂ **LE RELAIS DES MARRONNIERS** (N° RR AOU 26 022) (M. Dominique **Léorat**) RN 7, La Coucourde ☎ 75-51-06-25 ⊶ 6 Closed Sun in winter.

DESVRES 62240 Pas-de-Calais **RN 341 Map 5-A2**
♼ ⊗ ⌂ **LE RELAIS DE LA BELLE CROIX** (N° RR SEP 23 462) (M. **Grumelart-Mielot**) ☎ 21-91-65-81 Longfosse ⊶ 5 English spoken.

DETRIER 73110 Savoie **RD 925 Map 19-A2**
♼ ⊗ **LES SMOUTANS** (N° RR MARS 19 217) (M. Alain **Sigrand**) La Rochette ☎ 79-25-52-59 Closed Sun afternoon. English spoken. Filling station 1km 6.30–10pm.

DEULEMONT 59890 Nord
♼ ⊗ **LA BOULE D'OR** (N° RR JAN 27 508) (M. Guy **Francois**) 16, Rue de Maréchal Foch ☎ 20-39-24-38. Closed Wednesday. Evening meals.

DEUIL-LA-BARRE 95170 Val-d'Oise **RN 428 Map 1-A2**
♼ ⊗ **LE RELAIS DU COQ HARDI** (N° RR SEP 19 940) (M. and Mme **Lantinier**) 62 bis, avenue de la Division Leclerc ☎ 39-64-16-81 Closed Sat; Sun; Aug. Evening meals to order.

DEUX-CHAISES 03240 Allier **Map 16-A3**
♼ ⊗ **LE RELAIS DE L'AMITIÉ** (N° RR AVR 24 904) (M. Louis **Douge**) RN 145 ☎ 70-47-15-64 **Le Montet**.

DEVAY 58300 Nièvre **Map 16-A3**
♼ ⊗ **L'ETRIER** (N° RR MARS 26 842) (M. Jean-Marc **Boutet**) Route Nationale ☎ 86-25-15-65. German spoken. Closed in Sept. Coaches welcome (rest. seats 60). Evening meals.

DIEPPE 76200 Seine-Maritime **RN 15 Map 4-A2**
♼ ⊗ **L'AVENIR** (N° RR JUN 23 856) (M. Benoît **Pan**) 10, Cours de Dakar Port de Commerce ☎ 35-84-18-10 Closed Sun; Aug.

DINAN 22100 C.-du-N. **RN 166 and 176 Map 7-A3**
♼ ⊗ ⌂ **LA MARMITE** (N° RR AOU 23 004) (M. **Bouillet**) 91, rue de Brest ☎ 96-39-04-42 ⊶ 5 Closed Sat evening, Sun. Full-board 140F per night. Coaches welcome (rest. seats 45). English, German spoken.
⌐

DINARD 35400 I.-et-V. **RN 166 and 168 Map 7-A3**
♼ ⊗ ⌂ **LE CAP HORN** (N° RR MARS 25 837) (M. Jean-Pierre **Treff**) 66, rue de la Gare ☎ 99-46-59-09 ⊶ 4 Closed Christmas to New

D

Dinard continued

Year; 15 to 31 Aug. Coaches welcome (rest. seats 32/20). Evening meals.

DISSAY 86130 Vienne **RN 10 Map 15-B1**

♀ ⊗ **LA MOURANDERIE** (N° RR JUL 25 067) (Mme Colette **Berrier**) **CHEZ COLETTE** ☎ 49-52-40-13 or 12 Coaches welcome (rest. seats 150). Evening meals. TV Room. Shower (in cloakroom).

DISSAY-SUR-COURCILLON 72500 Sarthe **RN 138 Map 12-A2**

♀ ⊗ **RELAIS MAINE-TOURAINE** (N° RR MAI 21 918) (Mme Colette **Petit**) Route Nationale 138 ☎ 43-44-09-08 Restaurant open 24 hours. Room for weddings, banquets. Evening meals to 10pm (high season only).

DIVAJEU 26400 Drôme **RN 538/DLE 26 Map 24-A1**

♀ ⊗ **LES TONNELLES** (N° RR SEPT 26 654) (M. Bernard **Berchaud**) Quartier de Lambres ☎ 75-40-66-82 Closed Sat. Coaches welcome (rest. seats 54 + shaded terrace). Meals served until 10pm. Italian spoken.

DIVES-SUR-MER 14360 Calvados **Map 4-B2**

♀ ⊗ **LE CAFE DU PARKING** (N° RR SEP 26 047) (M. Daniel **Constant**) 2, rue des Frères-Le-Paule ☎ 31-91-24-25 Closed Sun; Aug.

DIZY-LE-GROS 02150 Aisne **RD 336 Map 6-A2**

♀ ⊗ **LE RELAIS FRANCE-EUROPE** (N° RR AOU 19454) (M. Claude **Gantier**) Route de Reims ☎ 23-21-23-15 **Minitel** ⇥ 3 Closed Sun; 15 to 31 Aug. Coaches welcome (3 rooms + heated terrace = 160 seats). Evening meals until 9pm.

DOL-DE-BRETAGNE 35120 Ille-et-Vilaine **RN 12 Map 7-A3**

♀ ⊗ ⌂ **LE RELAIS DE BELLE LANDE** (N° RR OCT 23 999) (M. Jean-Yves **Beubry**) 23 bis, rue de Rennes ☎ 99-48-06-14 **Minitel** ⇥ 2 Coaches welcome (rest. seats 50). Evening meals to 9.30pm.

DOMFRONT 61700 Orne **RN 12 and CD 908 MAP 8-A1**

♀ ⊗ ⌂ **1 Star NN RELAIS ST-MICHEL** (N° RR JAN 10 298) (M. Michel and Claudine **Prod'homme**) 5, rte du Mont St-Michel ☎ 33-38-64-99 **Minitel** ⇥ 19 from 65 to 120F, breakfast 18–22F. Closed Fri evenings low season. 15 days in Feb. Full-board 150–250F per night, 1000F per 7 days. Coaches welcome (rest. seats 120). Evening meals. Some English spoken. Menus from 45 to 85F. Specialities: *Andouillette au poivre, tarte normande, poulet normande.* Sites to visit: church, château, remains of 11th C chapel.

♀ ⊗ **LA CROIX DES LANDES** (N° RR NOV 27 093) (M. Claude **Leveau**) Route de la Ferté La Croix des-Landes ☎ 33-38-51-35 ⇥ 8 Holiday terms coaches welcome (rest. seats 120). Evening meals to 11pm. English, Spanish spoken. Local filling station 7.30–9pm.

D

DOMONT 95330 Val d'Oise **RN 1 Maps 1-A2 and 3-B3**
Ⓨ Ⓧ **LA VIELLE AUBERGE** (N° RR JAN 24 085) (M. Roger **Badaire**)
72, Rte Nle 7 ☎ 39-91-01-66 ⊷ 7 Closed Sat, Sun; Aug. Spanish
spoken. Evening meals until 9pm.

DOMPIERRE-SUR-BESBRE 03290 Allier **RN 79 Map 16-A3**
Ⓨ Ⓧ **LE RELAIS DE LA BESBRE** (N° RR JUN 25 453) (M. Jean-Pierre
Marossa) 207, avenue de la Gare ☎ 70-34-53-69 Closed Sun; half
Sept. Evening meals until 9pm.

DONZENAC 19270 Corrèze **RN 20 Map 17-A1**
Ⓨ Ⓧ **RELAIS DE LA POÊLE D'OR** (N° RR SEPT 26 987) (M. Daniel
Vermand) Av. de Paris ☎ 55-85-72-20. Filling station near.

DONZÈRE 26290 Drôme **RN7 Map 24-A2**
Ⓨ Ⓧ ⌂ **1 star NN AU BON ACCUEIL** (N° RR OCT 26 701) (M. Jacky
Paunon) RN 7 ☎ 75-51-64-58 ⊷ 11 Dutch, Spanish spoken.

DORLISHEIM 67120 Bas-Rhin **RN 392 Map 10-B2**
Ⓨ Ⓧ ⌂ **LE RELAIS DE LA GARE** (N° RR NOV 9 059) (M. René **Jost**)
4, avenue de la Gare ☎ 88-38-14-28 ⊷ 7 Closed Sat, Sun
afternoon; from 28 Aug to 15 Sep; 10 days in Oct. Coaches
welcome (rest. seats 70). Evening meals to 9pm.

DOUAI 59500 Nord **RN 17 and 34 Map 5-B3**
Ⓨ Ⓧ ⌂ **A L'ÉPI D'OR** (N° RR FEV 22 663) (M. Michel **Barjou**) 38,
faubourg d'Arras Lambres ☎ 27-87-04-56 ⊷ 7 Closed Sun. Open
4.30am to midnight. Full board (150F) Coaches welcome (rest.
seats 55).
Ⓨ Ⓧ ⌂ **LE RELAIS** (N° RR MARS 25 844 (Mme Jeanine **Deyredk**)
370, rue d'Aniche ☎ 27-88-12-06 ⊷ 8.
Ⓨ Ⓧ **LA FLAMANDRIÈRE** (N° RR OCT 26 347) (M. **Tison**) 3869 Rte
de Tournai ☎ 27-98-55-28 **Minitel** Closed Sat. Sun. Coaches
welcome (rest. seats 80). Evening meals to 8.30. Parking.

DOUÉ-LA-FONTAINE 49700 M.-et-L. **Map 12-B2**
Ⓨ Ⓧ **CHEZ PAUL** (N° RR 27 118) (M. et Mme Paul et Josette **Type**)
Zone industrielle Route de Montreuil ☎ 41-59-03-33 Open 24
hours, English and Spanish spoken.

DOULAINCOURT 52270 Hte-Marne **RN 67 Map 14-A1**
Ⓨ Ⓧ ⌂ **1 Star NN LE RELAIS DE PARIS** (N° RR JAN 8 214) (M. Denis
Frantzen) Place Charles de Gaulle ☎ 25-94-61-18 ⊷ 10 at 75–
110F. Breakfast 15–16F. Closed Wed (except Jul, Aug); 24 Aug–
14 Sep. Full-board 140–150F per night. Evening meals. Parking,
Bar. Dogs allowed. Billiards, electronic games. Fishing, hunting.
Sites Lar du Der The Cross and Nomb Général de Gaille.

DOUSSART 74210 Hte-Savoie **Map 19-A2**
Ⓨ Ⓧ ⌂ **1 Star NN LA TOUR DU LAC** (N° RR OCT 26 677) (Mme
Lucette **Favre-Bonvin**) SARL Scherfa – La Gare ☎ 50-44-30-37
⊷ 10 Closed Sun. Full board 160F half board 145F. Evening
meals to 10pm.

D

DOZULE 14430 Calvados **RN 175 Map 4-B2**
Ⴟ ⊗ 🏠 **LES CHARMETTES** (N° RR FEV 26 804) (M. Patrice **Tanguy**)
1, route de Rouen ☎ 31-79-21-87 ⊷ 4 Closed Sun evening; Oct.
German spoken.

DRAGUIGNAN 83300 Var **Map 25-A2**
Ⴟ ⊗ **LE PENALTY** (N° RR FEV 26 437) (M. Guy **Chabrand**) Quartier
St Léger, 1, av. de la 1ʳᵉ Armée ☎ 94-68-11-28 **Minitel** Closed
Sun; half Aug.

DREUIL-LES-AMIENS 80730 Somme **RN 235 Map 5-A3**
Ⴟ ⊗ **CHEZ JEAN-MARIE ET CHRISTIANE** (N° RR FEV 23 645) (M.
Jean-Marie **Dumeige**) 285, avenue Pasteur ☎ 22-43-12-95 **Mini-
tel** Closed Sun; Aug. Evening meals.

DREUX 28100 Eure-et-Loire **RN 12 and RN 154 Map 8-A3**
Ⴟ ⊗ **LE RELAIS DE LA POSTE** (N° RR SEP 19 506) (Mme **Sedaine**) 2,
rue du Général-de-Gaulle ☎ 37-42-12-00 Closed Sun.
Ⴟ ⊗ **LE MARCEAU** (N° RR SEPT 26 998) (M. Jean-Pierre **Parent**) 40/
42, av. du Général Marceau ☎ 37-46-05-57 Closed Sun.

DROCOURT 78440 Yvelines **Map 1-A2**
Ⴟ ⊗ **AU RELAIS DU NORD** (N° RR OCT 27 413) (M. Daniel **Tirouard**)
15 Rue Nationale ☎ 34-76-71-23. Closed Sat and Aug. Evening
meals to 10pm.

DROUPT SAINT-BASLE 10170 Aube **Map 9-B3**
Ⴟ ⊗ **LE ROYAL** (N° RR AUG 27 371) (Mme Patricia **Delouette**) 1,
place Royale ☎ 25-21-23-57 Evening meals to 12.30pm. Local
filling station.

DUNKERQUE 59140 Nord **RN 16 Map 5-A2**
Ⴟ ⊗ 🏠 **AU PANIER FLEURI** (N° RR DEC 23 073) (M. **Playe**) 15-17,
rue du Ponceau ☎ 28-66-76-19 ⊷ 8 Closed Sat (from 2pm). Full-
board 200F per night. Coaches welcome (rest. seats 40). Evening
meals to 11pm. English spoken.

DURANVILLE 27230 Eure **RN 13 Map 4-B3**
Ⴟ ⊗ 🏠 **BON ACCUEIL** (N° RR JAN 27 164) (M. Alain **Cauvin**) RN 13
☎ 32-46-83-02 ⊷ 15 Closed Sun; Sept. Local filling station.
Ⴟ ⊗ Tobacconist **LE RELAIS DES ARCADES** (N° RR OCT 25 664)
(M. Claude **Yssambourg**) ☎ 32-46-83-01 Closed Sun; Aug. Even-
ing meals to 1am.

DURAVEL 46700 Lot **Map 21-B1**
Ⴟ ⊗ **LE PIED DE MOUTON** (N° RR DEC 26 417) (M. John **Duberley**)
☎ 65-36-50-39 Closed Mon (low season). Evening meals to
9.30pm. English spoken.

DURFORT 30170 Gard **Map 23-B1**
Ⴟ ⊗ **LE SANTA FE** (N° RR FEV 24 851) (M. Michel **Vallat**) Rte de St-
Hippolyte ☎ 66-77-57-00 Closed Mon. English, German spoken.

E

ECALLES-ALIX 76190 S.-Marit. **RN 15 Bis Map 4-A3**
♈ ⊗ ⌂ **AUBERGE DE LA FOURCHE** (N° RR AVR 25 867) (M. Serge **Vannier**) Tobacconist Hameau de Loumare ☎ 35-95-45-01 **Minitel** ⊸ 5 Closed Sun. Coaches welcome (rest. seats 32). Evening meals.

ECARDENVILLE-LA-CAMPAGNE 27170 Eure **RN 13 Map 4-B3**
♈ ⊗ ⌂ **AUBERGE DU RELAIS** (N° RR JUN 26 928) (Mme Phillippe **Lelièvre**) ☎ 32-35-05-32 ⊸ 10 Closed Sun; 2nd fortnight Aug. English, German spoken. Coaches welcome (rest. seats 100). Evening meals to 12pm.

LES ÉCHELLES 73 360 Savoie **RN 6 Map 2-B3**
♈ ⊗ **L'ESCAPADE** (N° RR JUL 25 997) (M. Jean-Françoise **Daude**) Rte Nle 6 ☎ 79-36-55-99 Closed Sun; last week Aug, 1st week Sept.

ECHEMIRE 49150 M.-et-L. **Autoroute Océane A11 RN 766 Map 12-A2**
♈ ⊗ **LE RELAIS DES ROUTIERS – CHEZ JACQUELINE** (N° RR AOU 20 270) (Mme **Gaillot**) 7, 9, rue Principale Le Bourg ☎ 41-89-19-17 Closed Sun; 1–21 Jun. Coaches welcome (rest. 3 rooms of 45/30 /10 seats). Evening meals to 10pm.

ECLAIBES 59330 Nord **RN 2 Map 6-A3**
♈ ⊗ **LE ROBINSON** (N° RR JUN 26 270) (M. Elhadi **Manseur**) Rte Nle 2 ☎ 27-61-14-63 Coaches welcome (rest. seats 240). Evening meals.

ECHOUCHE 61150 Orne **RD 924 Ex 24 bis Map 8-A2**
♈ ⊗ ⌂ **HOTEL DE L'OUEST** (N° RR MARS 26 206) (M. Dominique **Bodin**) 27, avenue du Gal-Leclerc ☎ 33-35-12-24 **Minitel** ⊸ 4. Closed Sat. Coaches welcome (rest. seats 30/50/100). Evening meals. Full board 165F.

ECROUVES-TOUL 54200 M.-et-M. **RN 4 Map 14-A/B1**
♈ ⊗ ⌂ **LE RELAIS MATHY** (N° RR AOU 13 061) (**Mathy SARL**) 825, avenue du 15ᵉ Génie ☎ 83-43-04-27 ⊸ 16 Closed Fri evening, Sat; 1 week Christmas and New Year. Full-board 180F per night. Coaches welcome (rest. seats 50). Evening meals to 10pm.

ECULLY 69130 Rhone **RN 7 Map 2-A1**
♈ ⊗ **LES ROUTIERS** (N° RR JUIN 26 906) (Mme Sylvie **Taillandier**) 30, Rte de Paris ☎ 78-34-01-40. Closed Sat, Sun and last fortnight Aug. Coaches welcome (rest. seats 30).

ÉGLISES-D'ARGENTEUIL (LES) 17400 Chte-Marit. **CD 950 Map 15-A2**
♈ ⊗ ⌂ **CHEZ VEVETTE** (N° RR SEP 27 023) (M. Joël **Pilot**) Saint-Jean-d'Angély ☎ 46-59-94-21 ⊸ 6 Closed Fri and Sat night Sun pm. Full board 160F. Coaches welcome (rest. seats 110). Evening meals to 8.30pm.

ELVEN 56250 Morbihan **RN 166 Map 7-B2 11-A2**
♈ ⊗ ⌂ **1 Star NN LE RELAIS DE L'ARGOUET** (N° RR AOU 16 177)

E

Elven continued

⌂ (M. and Mme André **Le Douarin**) 36, avenue de l'Argouët ☎ 97-53-32-98 ⊨ 12 from 90 to 150F, breakfast to 18F. Closed Sat except high season; Sept. Full-board 165–170F per night. Coaches welcome (rest. seats 180). Evening meals until 10pm. English spoken. Parking; bar; dogs allowed. Menus from 45 to 120F. Specialities: fish, seafood. Sites to visit: lakes, rivers. Golf.

EMBRUN 05200 Htes-Alpes **RN 94 Map 25-A1**

♀ ⊗ ⌂ **1 star NN PONT FRACHE** (N° RR MAI 26 879) (Mme Simone **Faure**) Route de Briançon ☎ 92-43-00-86 ⊨ 20 English, Italian, ⌂ Spanish, German spoken.

♀ ⊗ **Self-Service Embrunais SUR L'POUCE** (N° RR DEC 25 767) Mme Michèle **Veillon**) Boulevard Pasteur, Réfectoire des Cordeliers ☎ 92-43-27-07 Closed Sun; Christmas holidays. Coach welcome (rest. seats 80). English spoken.

EMONDEVILLE 50310 Manche **RN 13 Map 4-B1**

♀ ⊗ ⌂ **AU COUP DE FREIN** (N° RR MARS 26 825) (Mme Thérèse **Jean**) Montebourg ☎ 33-41-22-74 ⊨ 5 Closed Sat from 2.30pm to Sun evening. Evening meals.

ENNORDES 18380 Cher **RD 30 Map 13-A1**

♀ ⊗ **LE RELAIS DES ROUTIERS** (N° RR JAN 19 620) (Mme Georgette **Champion**) Route Départementale 30 ☎ 48-58-06-36 Closed Sat.

ENTRAN 86100 Vienne **A 10 Map 15-B1**

♀ ⊗ **ACCOR L'ARCHE** Aut. A10 Sens Province/Paris ☎ 49-21-75-58 Self service 7am to 10pm. Shop. English spoken.

EPANNES 79270 Deux-Sèvres **RN 11 Map 15-A1**

♀ ⊗ ⌂ **LE RELAIS SUISSE-OCÉAN** (N° RR MAI 8 479) (M. Jacky **Guilloteau**) On edge of the Poitevin Marais, 10km from A23 exit. ☎ 49-04-80-01 ⊨ 10 Closed Sun low season; Sept. Full-board 150–170F. Coaches welcome (rest. seats 125). Evening meals.

EPERNAY 51200 Marne **RN 3 Map 9-A3 6–B2**

♀ ⊗ ⌂ **AU BON ACCUEIL** (N° RR JAN 16 390) (Mme Marie-Louise **Prejent**) 13, avenue J.-J. Rousseau ☎ 26-55-23-29 **Minitel** ⊨ 5 Closed Sat and Sun; Jan. Full-board 160–200F. Coaches welcome (rest. seats 30/50). Evening meals until 10pm to mid-night. Hotel open 24hrs.

EPERRAIS 61400 Orne **RD 938 Map 8-B2**

♀ ⊗ **LA PETITE VALLÉE** (N° RR MARS 26 839) (Mme Monique **Germond**) La Petite Vallée, Mortagne ☎ 33-83-91-34. Closed Sun. English spoken.

EPINAL 80000 Vosges **Map 10-A2 14-B1/2**

♀ ⊗ **LE RELAIS DE L'ABATTOIR** (N° RR SEPT 26 053) (M. Gérard **Didier**) 63, rue de Nancy ☎ 29-82-32-13 Closed Sun; 14 Jul to 15 Aug. Evening meals.

EPINAY-SUR-SEINE 93800 Seine-Saint-Denis) **RN 14 Map 1-A2**
- ⊗ **AU RENDEZ-VOUS DES COCHERS LIVREURS** (N° RR JUIN 26 924) (M. Jean-Francois **Fremont**) 32, Bld Foch ☎ 48-26-80-03 Closed Sun; public holidays. Evening meals to 10pm.
- ⊗ **LES OISEAUX** (N° RR JANV 27 155) (Mme Jeanine **Lecointe**) 1, rue de l'Yser ou 12, bd Foch ☎ 42-43-91-38 ⊷ 8 Closed Sun.

EPINEAU-LES-VOVES 89400 Yonne **RN 6 Map 13-A2**
- ⊗ ⌂ **LE RELAIS DES 6 BOULES** (N° RR JUL 22 864) (M. Ahmed **Betroune**) 2, route de Chambéry ☎ 86-91-20-45 and 86-91-20-54 Arabic, German spoken.

EPINEUIL-LE-FLEURIEL 18360 Cher **Map 16-A2**
- ⊗ **LES ROUTIERS** (N° RR JAN 26 154) (Mme Hélène **Bergerat**) Saulzais-le-Potier ☎ 48-63-02-81 **Minitel** Closed Mon afternoon. Coaches welcome (rest. seats 90). Evening meals.

EPONE 78680 Yvelines **RN 13 Map 1-A1**
- ⊗ **LE RESTAUVERT** (N° RR MAI 26 891) (**Sarl Restauvert**) Route de Gargenville ☎ 30-95-60-20 **Minitel** Italian spoken.

EPREVILLE-près-LE-NEUFBOURG 27110 Eure **RD 133 Maps 3-B1 and 4-B3**
- ⊗ **LE BRABANT** (N° RR AVR 27 248) (M. Jean-Paul **Goblin**) ☎ 32-35-04-40 Closed Sun night.

EQUEURDREVILLE 50120 Manche **RD 901 Map 4-A1**
- ⊗ ⌂ **RESTAURANT DE LA HAGUE** (N° RR JUN 22 835) (M. Claude **Lamy**) 120, rue de la Paix ☎ 33-53-14-87 ⊷ 17 Closed Sun. 1 to 15 Sept. English spoken.
- ⊗ **À L'HORIZON** (N° RR DEC 27 117) (Mme Christiane **Casrouge**) 24, rue Surcouf ☎ 33-93-85-85 Closed Sun. Filling station near.

ERQUINGHEM-LYS 59193 Nord
- **BRASSERIE AUX LILLOIS** (N° RR DEC 27 489) (Mme Marian **Chicux**) 314, Rue du Bac ☎ 20-77-40-07 Evening meals. English spoken. Nearby service station open 8am–7.30pm.

ERVILLERS 62121 P.-de-C. **Map 5-B3**
- ⊗ **LE RELAIS** (N° RR JUL 26 965) (Mme Muriel **Gillon**) 34, Rte Nationale ☎ 21-55-83-02 **Minitel** English, German spoken.

ERVY-LE-CHATEL 10130 Aube **D 374 Map 9-B3**
- ⊗ **RESTAURANT DE LA GARE** (N° RR FEVR 26 811) (M. Dany **Bordier**) Place de la Gare ☎ 25-70-66-36 Closed Tue at 2pm. 1st–15 Aug. Evening meals. Coaches welcome (rest. seats 60).

ESLETTES (LES) 76710 Seine-Marit. **RN 27 Map 3-A1**
- ⊗ **LE RELAX** (N° RR MAI 21 091) (M. Jean **Sorel**) Route de Dieppe Côte de Malaunay ☎ 35-75-11-70 Closed Sun. Coaches welcome (rest. seats 30).

ESNON 89210 Yonne **RN 443 Map 9-B2 13-A2**
- ⊗ **LE RELAIS DES AMIS** (N° RR FEV 26 806) (Mme Danièle

E

Esnon continued

Ollivon) 20, Route Nationale ☎ 86-56-13-26 **Minitel** Closed Mon and September. Coaches welcome (rest. seats 70). Filling station 3.5km.

ESPALION 12500 Aveyron **RN 120 Map 23-A1**

♈ ⊗ ⌂ **1 Star NN LE RELAIS DES QUATRE ROUTES** (N° RR JAN 26 162) (Mme Marie **Bouteleau**) Quatre Routes ☎ 65-44-01-69 ← 7 Closed Sun. Full-board 150–200F per night. Evening meals. Portuguese, Spanish spoken.

ESQUERDES 62380 P.-de-C. **RD 211 Map 5-A2**

♈ ⊗ ⌂ **CAFE ROUTIERS D'ESQUERDES** (N° RR MAR 6 466) (Mme Justine **Tassart**) 1114, rue Bernard-Chochoy ☎ 21-98-17-35 ← 7 Evening meals. Tearoom.

ESSARTS (LES) 85140 Vendee **RN 160 Map 11-B3**

♈ ⊗ **LE PINIER** (N° RR MAR 20 423) (Mme Jacqueline **Dupont**) ☎ 51-62-81-69 Closed Sun (low season), Sat. Evening meals. Coaches welcome (rest. seats 35).

♈ ⊗ **CAFE RESTAURANT DES TOURISTES** (N° RR MAI 26 544) (Mme Chantal **Rousselot**) 35, rue de Gaulle ☎ 51-62-83-52 Coaches welcome (rest. seats 40). Evening meals to 10pm.

ESSARTS-LE-ROI (LES) 78690 Yvelines **RN 10 Maps 1-B1–9-A1**

♈ ⊗ **LE RELAIS DE L'ARCOAT** (N° RR JAN 25 793) (SARL **ARCOAT**) 39 Rte Nle 10 ☎ 30-41-60-53 Closed Sat evening, Sun. English spoken.

♈ ⊗ **A LA GRACE DE DIEU** (N° RR JUL 25 055) (M. Daniel **Bigot**) Rte Nle 10 ☎ 30-41-60-04 Closed Sat, Sun; Aug. Coaches welcome (rest. seats 100). Evening meals to 11.30pm.

ESSERTENNE-ET-CECEY 70100 Haute-Saône **CD 70 Map 14-A3**

♈ ⊗ **LES ROUTIERS** (N° RR NOV 27 105) (M. Pascal **Roy**) rue de la Gare ☎ 84-67-41-66 Closed Wed pm. afternoon. Coaches welcome (rest. seats 40). Evening meals to 11.00. Filling station 4km 7–7pm.

ESTABLES 43160 Hte-Loire **RN 106 and Dle 35 Map 17-B3**

♈ ⊗ **LE RELAIS D'ESTABLES** (N° RR OCT 26 076) (M. Gérard **Fournerie**) Félines, La Chaise-Dieu ☎ 71-00-92-11 Open 24 hours.

ESTREÉS-DENIECOURT 80660 Somme **RN 336 Maps 5-B3 and 6A1**

♈ ⊗ ⌂ **L'AUBERGE DE LA MAIRIE** (N° RR AVR 21 466) (Mme Claudette **Demuynck-Dehenry**) Péronne exit Autoroute A1 to Amiens ☎ 22-85-20-16 ← 4 Closed Sat, Sun; Aug. Full-board 130–140F. Coaches welcome (rest. seats 100–120). Evening meals.

ESTREES-MONS-EN-CHAUSSEE 80200 Somme **RN 29 Maps 5-B3–6-A1**

♈ ⊗ **A LA POMME D'API** (N° RR FEV 14 686) (M. Albert **Gras**) 28, Route Nationale ☎ 22-85-60-04 Closed Sun; Aug. Coaches welcome (rest. seats 40). Evening meals.

E

ETAGNAC 16150 Chte **RN 141/948 Map 15-B2**
♀ ⊗ **RELAIS D'ÉTAGNAC** (N° RR AVR 25 376) (M. Christian **Labrousse**) ☎ 45-89-21-38 ⊶ 10 Coaches welcome (4 dining rooms). Filling station, tobacconist, newsagent. English spoken. Evening meal.

ETAIS-LE-SAUVIN 89840 Yonne **Map 13-A2**
♀ ⊗ **CAFÉ DE LA PLACE** (N° RR NOV 27 441) (M. Bérard **Dupuy**) rue de la Gare ☎ 86-47-21-46 Evening meals to 10pm. Closed Mon. Local filling station open 7–7pm.

ETALANS-NODS 25580 Doubs **RN 57 Map 14-B3**
♀ ⊗ **AUBERGE DU GOUFFRE DE POUDREY** (N° RR FEV 24 110) (Mme Elisabeth **Gorrissen**) Rte Nle 57 ☎ 81-59-20-43 Closed Jan. Coaches welcome (rest. seats 100). Evening meals. Dutch, English, German spoken.

ETALONDES 76260 S.-Mme **RD 925 Map 4-A3**
♀ ⊗ **LA BAHUTIÈRE** (N° RR JUIN 27 298) (M. Alain **Savelon**). ☎ 35-50-21-10 Closed Sun. Evening meals until 10pm.

ETAMPES 91150 Essonne **RN 20 Map 9-B1**
GARAGE DES ROUTIERS (N° RR JAN 15 508) (M. Roger **David** Unic Agent and Westinghouse brake-fitters RN 20 South of Etampes ☎ 64-94-56-18

ETOGES 51270 Parne **Map 9-A3**
♀ ⊗ **LE CAVEAU DE L'ANCIENNE FORGE** (N° RR AUG 27 357) (Mmes Joffrette Bouezeret Georgette **Jacquart**) Grand Rue ☎ 26-59-32-79 Local filling station 8–10pm.

ETOILE 26800 Drôme **RN 7 Map 24-A1**
♀ ⊗ ⌂ **ROUVEYROL** (N° RR JAN 26 134) (M. Roland **Rouveyrol**) RN 7 ☎ 75-61-62-06 Fiancey ⊶ 13 Closed Sun. Evening meals to 11pm. English, German spoken. Full board 140–160F. Coaches welcome (rest. seats 80). Parking.

ETOUVELLES 02000 Aisne **RN 2 Map 6-B1**
♀ ⊗ **CHEZ JEANNOT** (N° RR MAR 16 908) (M. J.-M. **Serre**) 30, Rue de Paris, D542 ☎ 23-20-63-26 ⊶ 9 Closed Sat, Sun and August. Evening meals. Coaches welcome (rest. seats 120).

ETRELLES 35370 I.-et-V. **see VITRE**

EU 76260 Seine-Maritime **RN 15 Bis Map 4-A2**
♀ ⊗ ⌂ **LE RELAIS DE L'ETOILE** (N° RR JUN 16 132) (M. Maurice **Pajot**) 37, boulevard Thiers ☎ 35-86-14-89 ⊶ 10 Evening meals.

EXMES 61310 Orne **RD 14, 26 Map 8-A2**
♀ ⊗ ⌂ **LE RELAIS DU COMMERCE** (N° RR JUN 21 556) (Mme Fernande **Simon**) Grande-Rue ☎ 33-39-93-04 ⊶ 4 Full-board 140–180F per night. Coaches welcome (rest. seats 200). Evening meals.

E

Exmes continued

♀ ⊗ **LE RELAIS** (N° RR DEC 26 763) (M. Michel **Goulabaille**) Bourg St. Léonard ☎ 33-67-17-63 Closed on Mon. Sept. Coaches welcome (rest. seats 60). Evening meals to 11pm.

EYGUIANS 05300 Hautes-Alpes **RN 75 Maps 24-B2–25-A1**

♀ ⊗ 🏠 **1 Star NN LE RELAIS DE LA GARE** (N° RR NOV 15 439) (Mme Michelle **Robert**) ☎ 92-66-20-08 **Minitel** ⊶ 15 Closed Sat
⊸ (low season) Jan. Full board 180–240F per night. Evening meals to 9.30. Coaches welcome (rest. seats 100).

EYMOUTIER Voir ST-AMAND-LE-PETIT 87120 Hte-Vienne

EZY-SUR-EURE 27530 Eure **RD 143 Map 8-A3**

♀ ⊗ 🏠 **LE RELAIS LE TERMINUS** (N° RR AVR 17 514) (Mme Madeleine **Veisen**) 16, bld Ulysse-Lavertu – place de la Gare ☎ 37-64-73-24 ⊶ 10 Closed Fri 2.00pm, Sat. Open Sun midday. Closed Aug. Evening meals.

F

FABREGUES 34690 Hérault **RN 113 Map 23-B2**

♀ ⊗ **BAR LE 113** (N° RR AOU 24 303) (Mme Josette **Avignon**) 36, avenue Georges-Clémenceau ☎ 67-85-12-86 Closed Sun; Oct. Coaches welcome (rest. seats 45). Evening meals to 10pm.

FALAISE 14700 Calvados **RN 158 Map 8-A2**

♀ ⊗ 🏠 **LE RELAIS CHEZ DURAND** (N° RR OCT 21 674) (M. Christian **Durand**) 33, avenue d'Hastings ☎ 31-90-04-67 **Minitel** ⊶ 5 Closed Sun; public holidays; Jul. Evening meals until 8.30pm. Coaches welcome (rest. seats 35).

FALCK 57550 Moselle **RD 23 Map 10-A1**

♀ ⊗ **KRAUSER** (N° RR AVR 26 220) (M. Guy **Louvet**) 2, rue Hargaten ☎ 87-82-60-69 Evening meals.

FAOUET (LE) 56320 Morbihan **RN 782 Map 7-B2**

♀ ⊗ 🏠 **LE RELAIS DES HALLES** (N° RR MAR 4 067) (M. and Mme **Le Puil**) 19, rue du Soleil ☎ 97-23-07-66 ⊶ 8 Closed Sun; Sept. Evening meals. English spoken.

♀ ⊗ **TY CRAVIC** (N° RR JUIN 27 308) (Mme Josiane **Herbaux**) ☎ 94-23-07-04 Closed Sun and August. Evening meals served to 11pm. Filling station 2km 8–7pm.

FARE-LES-OLIVIERS (LA) 13380 B.-du-R. **RN 113 Map 24-B3**

♀ ⊗ 🏠 **LE RELAIS PROVENÇAL** (N° RR MAI 22 352) (Mme Odette **Camarasa**) Route National 113 ☎ 90-42-65-62 ⊶ 8 Closed Sun; 15

F

Aug to 1 Sept. Spanish, Italian spoken. Full board 150–180F. Evening meal.

FARGUES-SUR-OURBIZE 47700 Lot-et-Garonne **RN 655 Map 21-A1**
♈ ⊗ **LE RELAIS DES ROUTIERS** (N° RR FEV 22 218) (Mme Michèle **Téchene**) ☎ 53-93-04-54 ⊶ 4 Closed Wed from 2–7pm. Half board 95F, full board 125F per night. Coaches welcome (3 dining rooms = 200 seats). Evening meals. Spanish spoken.

FARGUETTES (LES) 81190 Tarn **RN 88 Map 22-B1**
♈ ⊗ **RELAIS DE LA PLAINE** (N° RR OCT 27 049) (Mme Marie-Ange **Feral**) ☎ 63-76-65-89 Closed Sat to 5pm the last two weeks of Aug. Evening meals to 9pm. Local filling station open 6.30 to 10.30pm.

FAVEROLLES-SUR-CHER 41400 L.-and-C.)
Voir MONTRICHARD

FECAMP 76400 Seine-Maritime **RD 925 Map 4-A3**
♈ ⊗ **RELAIS DU CHEMIN DE FER** (N° RR AVR 25 899) (M. Jean-Marie **Lefèbvre**) 29/31 quai-Bérigny ☎ 35-28-06-17 Closed Sat night, (evening only in season) 1st Sept to 30 April. Evening meals until 9pm.

FEISSONS-SUR-ISERE 73260 Savoie **Map 19-B2**
♈ ⊗ **LE RELAIS DES ROUTIERS** (N° RR OCT 24 699) (M. Michel **Ruffier**) between Albertville and Moutiers (take 1st right after Cevins) ☎ 79-22-50-97 **Minitel** Closed Sat pm Sun. Some English, German spoken. Coaches welcome (rest. seats 50).

FELINES 07340 Ardèche **RN 82 Map 24-A1, 18-A/B3**
♈ ⊗ ⌂ **1 Star NN LE RELAIS DE LA REMISE** (N° RR JUN 25 032) (M. Jacky **Laurencin**) Route Nationale 82 ☎ 75-34-82-22 **Minitel** ⊶ 4 Closed Sat, Sun; Dec to Mar. Full-board 135–155F per night. Coaches welcome (rest. seats 130 + 80 on terrace). Evening meals.

FENOUILLER (LE) 85800 Vendée **RD 754 Map 11-B2**
♈ ⊗ ⌂ **LA MADELON** (N° RR JAN 26 137) (M. Fulbert-Gérard **Pouvreau**) 64, rue du Centre, St-Gilles-Croix-de-Vie ☎ 51-55-05-35 ⊶ 20 Coaches welcome (rest. seats 110). Full-board 140–152F per night. Evening meals. English spoken.

FERDRUPT 88360 Vosges **RN 66 Map 10-A3**
♈ ⊗ **PLEIN AIR VOSGES ALSACE** (N° RR AVR 24 566) (M. Michel **Guenot**) ☎ 29-25-03-51 Full-board available. Coaches welcome (rest. seats 65). Evening meals.

FERRIÈRE (LA) 79390 Deux-Sevres **RN 148 bis Map 15-A1**
♈ ⊗ **AU BON ACCUEIL** (N° RR JUN 25 469) (Mmes **Bilheu-Berger**) La Feriere Route Poitiers Nantes ☎ 49-63-03-01 Closed Thur evening; last 2 weeks Jan, end Aug. Coaches welcome (rest. seats 65). Evening meals to 9.30pm.

F

FERRIERES-EN-BRAY 76220 S.Marit **RN 31 Map 3-A2**

♀ ⊗ ⌂ **HOTEL DU CHEMIN DE FER** (N° RR MAI 24 573) (M. Jean **Feret**) 26, av. de la Gare ☎ 35-90-01-61 ⇥ 10 Closed Sat, Sun. Bank holiday. Full-board 120–145F per night. Coaches welcome (rest. seats 90). Evening meals until midnight.

FERTE-BERNARD (LA) 72400 Sarthe **RN 23 Map 8-B3**

♀ ⊗ **ACCOR L'ARCHE** (M. G. **Bisson**) Autoroute A11 ☎ 43-93-41-02 Self-service restaurant 7.00am–11.00pm. Shop.

FERTE-GAUCHER (LA) 77320 S.-et-M. **RN 34 Map 9-A2**

♀ ⊗ **LE RELAIS DE L'EST** (N° RR SEP 19 501) (M. Bruno **Gapillou**) 4, avenue de la Gare ☎ 64-04-01-90 Closed Sun; Aug. Evening meals until 9.30pm. German spoken.

see also SANCY-LES-PROVINS

FERTE-SAINT-AMBREUIL (LA) 71420 Saône-et-Loire **Autoroute A-6 Map 18-B1**

♀ ⊗ **CAFE ROUTE ACCOR** (M. Jean-Jacques **Viau**) Aire de Service de Sennecey-le-Grand Direction Paris-Province ☎ 85-44-21-79 Open 7.00am–10.00pm weekends, 24 hours weekdays. Self-service restaurant. Shop. English spoken.

♀ ⊗ **ACCOR L'ARCHE (Mme Marie-Claude Debrune)** Aire de St-Ambreuil Direction Province-Paris Autoroute A-6 ☎ 85-44-20-64 Self-service restaurant open 24 hours. Shop.

FIANCEY-PAR-LIVRON 26250 Drôme **RN 7 Maps 18-B3 and 24-A1**

♀ ⊗ ⌂ **RELAIS DU SUD-EST** (N° RR MAI 26 552) (M. André **Courbier**) RN 7 ☎ 75-61-61-19 ⇥ 9 English and German spoken. Closed Sun. Evening meals served till 11pm. Coaches welcome (Rest. seats 52).

FIANCEY see ÉTOILE

FIENVILLERS PAR CANDAS 80500 Somme **Map 5-A3**

♀ ⊗ **LE RELAIS FLEURI** (N° RR OCT 27 070) (Mme Sylviane **Doriol**) 66, route Nationale ☎ 22-32-51-78 Closed Sat and Sun. Polish spoken. Filling station 4km. Pay blue card.

FIGEAC 46100 Lot **Map 17-B2**

♀ ⊗ ⌂ **LE RELAIS DES CHASSEURS** (N° RR DEC 27 478) (Mme Veronique **Noyer**) La Vayssière ☎ 65-34-12-33 ⇥ 8 Evening meals to 9pm. Spanish, English spoken. Local filling station.

FIRBEIX 24450 Dordogne **RN 21 Map 17-A1**

♀ ⊗ **LE RELAIS DES SPORTS** (N° RR JUN 21 548) (M. René **Beaubatit**) Nationale 21 ☎ 53-52-82-53 Closed Oct. Coaches welcome (rest. seats 100). Evening meals.

FIRMINY 42600 Loire **Map 18-A3**

♀ ⊗ **AU PETIT BONHEUR** (N° RR SEPT 27 379) (M. Hervé **Salleron**) 9, rue du Prof Calmette ☎ 77-61-29-73 Italian, Spanish spoken. Evening meals to 11pm. Local filling station 6.30–10pm.

F

FISMES 51170 Marne **RN 31 Map 6-B1**
♀ ⊗ ⌂ **LE LION ROUGE** (N° RR AVR 24 200) (M. Michel **Sohier**) 6,
route de Soissons ☎ 26-78-12-63 ⊷ 5 Closed Sun. Evening meals
until 10pm.

FITOU 11510 Aude **RN 9 Map 23-A3**
♀ ⊗ ⌂ **1 Star RELAIS LE PARADOR** (N° RR MAI 27 273) (M. Robert
Morhain) Cabanne de Fitou ☎ 68-45-79-11 ⊷ 50.70 to 170F
Breakfast 18 and 25F. German, Spanish and Italian spoken.
Evening meals served to 12pm. Filling station 7–11pm.
♀ ⊗ ⌂ **RELAIS SAINT-ROCH** (N° RR AUG 27 356) (M. Bernard
Paros) ☎ 68-45-71-75 **Minitel** ⊷ 14 Local filling station. Parking.

FIX-SAINT-GENEYS 43320 Hte-Loire **RN 102 Map 17-A3**
♀ ⊗ **RELAIS DU COL** (N° RR OCT 18 858) (Mme **Gallien**) ☎ 71-57-
02-67 Closed Sun.

FLASSANS-SUR-ISSOLE 83340 Var **RN 7 Map 25-A2**
♀ ⊗ **REST LE NOCTURNE** (N° RR NOV 27 102) (M. Claude **Bouvet**)
Nationale 7, quartier de la Bourette ☎ 94-69-71-33 Closed Sat
⊷ evening, Sun. Coaches welcome (rest. seats 140). English, Italian
spoken. Evening meals. Local filling station.
♀ ⊗ **LE BIEN ÊTRE** (N° RR OCT 27 438) (M. Robert **Mourrat**) Les
Quatre Chemins ☎ 94-59-67-65 Closed Sunday. Italian spoken.
Evening meals. Local filling station 7–8pm.

FLAVIAC 07000 Ardèche **Map 24-A1**
♀ ⊗ **LES ROUTIERS** (N° RR DEC 26 407) (M. Didier **Garrayts**) Place
Émile-Crémière ☎ 75-65-77-57 ⊷ 7 Closed Sun; Sept. Coaches
welcome (rest. seats 50). Evening meals.

FLAVY-LE-MARTEL 02520 Aisne **Maps 5-B3 and 6-A1**
♀ ⊗ **LE RELAIS DES ROUTIERS** (N° RR FEV 26 178) (M. Jean-Paul
Brière) 17, rue André-Brûlé ☎ 23-52-51-31 **Minitel** Closed Sat.
Coaches welcome (rest. seats 40). Evening meals to 9pm.

FLERS 61100 Orne **RD 924 and RD 18 Map 8-A1/2**
♀ ⊗ ⌂ **HÔTEL DES TOURISTES** (N° RR DEC 26 758) (M. Maurice-
Dupont) 80, rue de Paris ☎ 33-65-25-57 ⊷ 12 Closed Sun. 15th
Aug–1st Sept. Evening meal. (Full board 145F). Coaches welco-
me (rest. seats 40).
♀ ⊗ **LE PRIEURÉ** (N° RR JAN 26 795) (M. Lionel **Pailleux**) La Lande
Patry ☎ 33-64-83-12 Coaches welcome. Parking. Evening meals.

FLERS-EN-ESCREBIEUX 59128 Nord **RN 43 Map 51-B2/3**
♀ ⊗ **AU BON CASSE-CROÛTE** (N° RR OCT 27 050) (M. Raymond
Dufour) 59, route Nationale ☎ 27-86-69-41 Closed Sat and Sun.
Coaches welcome (rest. seats 40). Evening meals to 12pm.
Parking. Filling station 3km.

FLEURANCE 32500 Gers **RN 21 Map 21-B2**
♀ ⊗ **REST. DU STADE** (N° RR MAR 22 261) (M. Alphonse **Pujade**)
place de l'Eglise ☎ 62-06-02-23 Closed Sat; June. Coaches
welcome (rest. seats 160). Evening meals.

F

FLEURE 86340 Vienne **RN 147 Map 15-B1**
♀ ⊗ **AUX AMIS DE LA ROUTE** (N° RR JUIN 26931) (Mme Michèle **Gulonnet**) Route de Poitiers ☎ 49-42-60-25 Coaches welcome (rest. seats 60). Evening meals to 10pm.

FLEURIEU-SUR-SAÔNE 69250 Rhône **CD 433 Map 2-A1**
♀ ⊗ **LA CABANE** (N° RR AVR 26 492) (M. Jean-Robert **Richard**) 54, rte de Lyon ☎ 78-91-40-60 **Minitel** Closed Sat, Sun; Aug. Coaches welcome (rest. seats 40). English, Italian spoken.

FLEURY 60240 Oise **Map 3-B2**
♀ ⊗ **LA TABLE DE FLEURY** (N° RR JANV 26797) (M. Yvan **Marie**) Gran-de-Rue ☎ 44-49-04-60.

FLEURY-SUR-ORNE 14000 Calvados **RN 162 Map 4-B2**
♀ ⊗ **RELAIS DE LA POMME D'OR** (N° RR OCT 21 680) (Mme Emilienne **François**) 20, route d'Harcourt ☎ 31-82-36-87 Closed Sun; public holidays; Aug.

FLEVIEU 69300 Rhône **CD 12 Map 2-B1**
♀ ⊗ **LE GAULOIS** (N° RR MARS 27 237) (M. Hen-Pierre **Coursat**) 2, rue Saint-Nicholas Ternay ☎ 78-73-07-34. English spoken. Filling station 3km.

FLIREY 54470 M.-et-M. **RN 958 Map 14-B1**
♀ ⊗ **WARIN LES ROUTIERS** (N° RR MAI 12 261) (M. Jacques **Warin**) ☎ 83-81-15-73 ⊷ 4. Full board 150–200F. Evening meal.

FLIXECOURT 80420 Somme **30 m RN1 Map 5-A3**
♀ ⊗ **LES FLONFLONS DU BAL** (N° RR DEC 26 768) (M. Jean-Marc **Rohaut**), 16 rue Georges- Clémenceau ☎ 22-51-36-34 English spoken. Coaches welcome (rest. seats 70). Open everyday 6–1am. Evening meals.

FOIX 09000 Ariège **RN 20 Map 22-A3**
♀ ⊗ ⌂ **LE RELAIS DU SOLEIL D'OR** (N° RR AOU 20 527) (M. Jean **Coumes**) 57, avenue du Ml-Leclerc ☎ 61-65-01-33 ⊷ 6 Closed Sun Nov to May.

FOLLIGNY 50320 Manche **RD 924 Map 8-A1**
♀ ⊗ ⌂ **LE RELAIS DU LION D'OR** (N° RR OCT 24 716) (Mme **Héon**)
⊷ Le Repas ☎ 33-61-32-77 ⊷ 7 Closed Feb. English spoken.

FONDETTES 37230 I.-et-L. **RN 152 Map 12-A2**
♀ ⊗ **LE BEAU MANOIR** (N° RR MAR 27 330) (Mme Edith **Bouireau**) 6, quai de la Guignière ☎ 47-42-01-02 Closed Sun; Jan. Filling station 1km.

FONTAINE-LE-COMTE 86240 Vienne **RN 11 near to RN 10 Map 15-B1**
♀ ⊗ **AUBERGE DE LA GARENNE** (N° RR AVR 25 386) (Mme Michelle **Guerin**) ☎ 49-57-01-22 **Minitel** Closed Sun; Aug. Coaches welcome (rest. seats 70). Evening meals until 11pm.

F

FONTAINE-SAINT-MARTIN (LA) 72330 Sarthe **RN 23 Map 12-A2**
♈ ⊗ **LE RELAIS DU CHENE VERT** (N° RR FEV 16 890) (Mme
Flameych) ☎ 43-29-80-84 Closed Sun; Aug. Evening meals.
Coaches welcome (rest. seats 70).

FONTAINE-SIMON 28240 E.-et-L. **RD 2 and 25 Map 8-A/B3**
♈ ⊗ ⌂ **AU BON COIN** (N° RR JAN 23 108) (M. **Durand**) rue de la
Mairie La Loupe ☎ 37-81-84-98 ⇥ 10 Closed Fri; Aug. Full-board
130–150F per night. Evening meals.

FONTENAY-SUR-LOING 45210 Loiret **RN 7 Map 9-B2**
♈ ⊗ **LE RELAIS DES CENT BORNES** (N° RR DEC 21 722) (M.
Martin) Nationale 7 ☎ 38-95-82-06 Open 24 hours. Closed 9 to 24
Aug. Coaches welcome (rest. seats 140). Evening meals.

FONTVANNES 10190 Aube **Map 9-B3**
♈ ⊗ ⌂ **AUBERGE DE LA VANNE** (N° RR JAN 26 425) (M. Michel
Dubrulle) 1, rue Léandre-Denis ☎ 25-70 37-60 ⇥ 8 Closed Sun.
Feb. Coaches welcome (rest. seats 35).

FONTVERGNES 12300 Aveyron **RN 140 (main Brive-Méditerranée
road) Maps 22-B1 and 17-B2** see Decazeville
♈ ⊗ **REST. DES USINES** (N° RR OCT 25 132) (Mme Régine **Forsse**)
23, faubourg Desseligny Decazeville ☎ 65-43-15-88 Closed Sun.
⇥ Evening meals served until 11pm.

FORMERIE 60220 Oise **Map 3-A2**
♈ ⊗ ⌂ **CAFE DE LA PAIX** (N° RR MAI 24 576) (Mme Françoise
Merlin) 8, rue Dornat ☎ 44-46-17-08 **Minitel** ⇥ 6 Closed Sun
afternoon; Full-board 135F per night. Coaches welcome (rest.
seats 60). Evening meals.

FOS-SUR-MER 13270 Bouches-du-Rhône **Map 24-A3**
♈ ⊗ **LE MOULIN** (N° RR OCT 25 135) (Mme Gisèle **Lefèbvre**) plage
du Cavaou ☎ 42-05-48-38 **Minitel** Coaches welcome (rest. seats
71). Evening meals to 10.30pm. English spoken.
♈ ⊗ **RELAIS DE LA FOSSETTE — Chez Annie et Guy** (N° RR MAR
25 317) (M. Guy **Hologne**) quartier de la Fossette ☎ 42-05-30-01
Minitel Closed Sat, Sun; Aug. Coaches welcome (rest. seats 80).
Evening meals to 9.30pm.

FOUCARMONT 76340 S.-Mme **RN 28 Map 4-A2**
♈ ⊗ **LE RELAIS ROUTIERS** (N° RR JAN 25 275) (Mme **Bénard**) RN
28 ☎ 35-93-91-50 **Minitel** Closed Sun. Evening meals.
♈ **CHEZ FRANÇOISE** (N° RR JUN 25 458) (Mme Françoise
Maubert) 35, rue Douce ☎ 35-93-70-37 Closed Sat. Evening
meals to 8.30pm.

FOUGERES 35300 Ile-et-Vilaine **RN 12 Map 8-B1**
♈ ⊗ ⌂ **1 Star NN AUX AMIS DE LA ROUTE** (N° RR SEP 23 992) (M.
Michel **Bastien**) 6, bld St-Germain ☎ 99-99-07-62 ⇥ 12 from 100–
120F, breakfast to 20F. Full-board 150–180F per night. Coaches
welcome (rest. seats 90). Evening meals. English, German spo-

F

Fourgeres continued
ken. Parking (1000 vehicles). Bar; dogs allowed; Recreation (fishing, watersports). Sites to visit: Saint-Mâlo, Mont St Michel, countryside and châteaux.

FOUILLOUSE (LA) 42480 Loire **RN 82 Map 2-B1**
♀ ⊗ **LE RELAIS** (N° RR JAN 24 830) (Mme Louise **Bonnet**) locally 'Les Molineaux' ☎ 77-30-13-51 Closed Sat, Sun; 14 Jul to 15 Aug. Evening meals.

FRAISSE-HAUT 15300 Cantal **Map 17-A2**
♀ ⊗ ⌂ **1 Star NN HOTEL DES CIMES** (N° RR SEPT 26 656) (M. Christophe **Cros**) RN 122 Laveissière ☎ 71-20-07-42 **Minitel** ⊷ 20 Full-board 142–152F per night. Coaches welcome (2 dining rooms = 90 places). Evening meals to 8.30pm. Closed Sun. Oct. Nov.

FRASNE 25560 Doubs **RD 471/49 Map 14-B3**
♀ ⊗ **L'ARC-EN-CIEL** (N° RR MARS 26 477) (M. Claude **Guyon**) 94, Gran-du-Rue ☎ 81-49-83-68 Closed Tue. Evening meals.

FRÉJUS 83600 Var **RN 7 Map 25-B2**
♀ ⊗ ⌂ **1 Star NN LES TROIS CHÊNES** (N° RR AVR 16 518) (Mme Monique **Laurent**) Route de Cannes ☎ 94-53-20-08 ⊷ 18 all with showers (5 with own WC) from 140–200F, breakfast 22–25F. Access for disabled. Coaches welcome (rest. seats 100). Evening meals. English, German, Italian spoken. Parking; bar; boules played; recreations (swimming pool, tennis courts near). Sites to visit: Gorges du Verdon, Lakes of Saint Cassien. Full board 170–200F.

FRÉJUS (Tunnel) 73500 Savoir **See MODANE**

FRESNES-EN-TARDENOIS 02130 Aisne **Autoroute A4 Map 6-B1**
♀ ⊗ **RELAIS DU TARDENOIS** (Mme **Pongnan**) Autoroute A4 Fresnes-en-Tardenois ☎ 23-70-23-16 Self-service restaurant open 6.30am to 10.30pm. Entrance cards for lorry drivers. Shop, TV, rest room.

FRESNES-MAZANCOURT 80320 Somme **RN 17 Map 5-B3**
♀ ⊗ **L'ESCALE DES ROUTIERS** (N° RR SEPT 27 010) (M. Jean-Claude **Guerquin**) ☎ 22-85-28-50 Closed Sat and Sun. Jul. Coaches welcome (rest. seats 32). Evening meals to 12pm.

FRETEVAL 41160 Loir-et-Cher **RN 10 Map 12-A3 and 8-B3**
♀ ⊗ **LE PLESSIS** (N° RR OCT 27 404) (Mme Isabelle **Thébault**) ☎ 54-82-65-28 Open Sat 6–10am Sun 10–3.30pm and 7pm–12pm. English, German, Spanish spoken. Evening meals to 12pm. Filling station 1km 6.30–10pm.

FRIÈRES-FAILLOUEL 02700 Aisne **Map 6-A1**
♀ ⊗ **CHEZ MARTINE** (N° RR JUL 26 007) (Mme Martine **Rouillat**) 19, place André-Ruller.

F

FROISSY 60480 Oise **RN 1 Map 3-A2**
♉ ⊗ 🏠 **LE BEAUVAIS BRETEUIL** (N° RR JUIL 26 962) (M. Raymond **Julen**) Bois Saint-Martin ☎ 44-79-13-09 ⊷ 5 Closed Sun and three weeks in August. Evening meals served to 11pm.

FROMENTEL par PUTANGES 61210 Orne **RN 24 Bis and 809 Map 8-A2**
♉ ⊗ **LE RELAIS DE L'AIGLE D'OR** (N° RR AVR 25 365) (M. Didier **Creteau**) D 924 Paris/granville ☎ 33-96-21-00 **Minitel** ⊷ 3 Closed Sat, Sun; Aug. Coaches welcome (rest. seats 40). Evening meals. Italian, English spoken.

FRONTIGNAN (en ville Gare SNCF direction plage) 34110 Hérault **CO 50 Map 23-B2**
♉ ⊗ 🏠 **LE RELAIS DES VOYAGEURS** (N° RR JUL 26 003) (M. Marcel **Rosso**) 12, rue du Puits-Pascal ☎ 67-48-12-34 **Minitel** ⊷ 6 Closed Sun, low season; 20 Dec to 10 Jan. Coaches welcome (rest. seats 40). Evening meals. English, Italian spoken. Full board 185–290F.

FROUARD 54390 M.-et-M **RN 57 Maps 10-A1/2 and 14-B1**
♉ ⊗ **AU RELAIS DES SPORTIFS Chez Raph** (N° RR JAN 14 656) (M. Raphaël **Capezzali**) 1, rue de la Salle ☎ 83-49-03-52 Closed Mon; Sept.
♉ ⊗ **LA GRANDE CHOPE** (N° RR JUL 21 168) (Mme Christiane **Pallagi**) 4, rue de la Gare ☎ 83-49-05-64 Closed Sat, Sun; Aug.

FUILET (LE) 49000 Maine-et-Loire **Map 12-B1**
♉ ⊗ **CHEZ ALPHONSE ET MONIQUE** (N° RR DEC 26 394) (Mme Monique **Bodo**) 1, rue de la Blandinière ☎ 41-70-52-58 Closed Aug. Evening meals until 9.30pm.

FUMAY 08170 Ardennes **RN 51 Map 6-A2**
♉ ⊗ 🏠 **1 Star NN LE RELAIS DU LION** (N° RR AVR 21 465) (Mme Édith **Potier**) 41, rue de la Gare ☎ 24-41-10-27 ⊷ 11 Closed Sun; Sept. Full-board 150F, Half-board 85F per night. Evening meals. Coaches welcome (rest. seats 45).

FUMEL 47500 Lot-et-Garonne **Map 17-A1and B1**
♉ ⊗ **BAR DE LA SOIERIE** (N° RR NOV 27 098) (Mme Liliane **Lafon**) 88, avenue de l'Usine ☎ 53-71-34-22 Closed Sat. Sun. Coaches welcome (rest. seats 35). Evening meals, parking.
⊗ **SALON DE THÈ-CRÈPERIE CHEZ DANIEL** (N° RR DEC 27 113) (M. Daniel **Herranz**) Centre Commercial de Florimont ☎ 53-40-92-60 English spoken. Closed Sun. Local filling station 9–7.30pm. Closed noon.

FUVEAU 13970 B.-du-R. **RN 96 Map 24-B3**
♉ ⊗ **AUBERGE DU CHATEAU** (N° RR JUN 25 962) (Mme Claudette **Charried**) RN 96 ☎ 42-58-60-10 Closed Tue.

G

GAËL 35290 l.-et-V. **Map 7-B3**
♀ ⊗ **LE RELAIS DES SPORTS – REST. CHEZ ANNICK** (N° RR MAI 24 970) (Mme Annick **Rebillard**) Place des Tileuls ☎ 99-07-72-39 **Minitel** ⌐ 4 Closed Fri evening pm. Coaches welcome (rest. seats 150). Evening meals. Full board (151F).

GAGES 12630 Aveyron **RN 88 Map 22-B1 10 Km from Rodez**
♀ ⊗ ⌂ **1 Star NN LE RELAIS DE LA PLAINE** (N° RR DEC 20 920) (Mme Yvonne **Dallo**) ☎ 65-42-29-03 ⌐ 22 at 85–200F. Breaekfast 16–30F. Closed Fri 5pm to Mon am and Oct. Full-board 160–200F per night. Coaches welcome (rest. seats 150). Evening meals to 11pm. Parking, bar, dogs allowed. Sites to visit. Gorges Dams, Lakes.

GALBSHEIM 67760 Bas-Rhin **Map 10-B1/2**
♀ ⊗ ⌂ **2 star NN EUROP RELAIS** (N° RR FEV 22 226) (M. **Lepron**) Route du Rhin ☎ 88-96-43-33 ⌐ 22 Closed Fri, pm, Sat and 15/8 to 31/8. German spoken.

GAMACHES 80220 Somme **Map 4-B2**
♀ ⊗ **LES ROUTIERS** (N° RR FEVR 25 817) (M. Claude **Reffay**) 20, place du Général Lederc ☎ 22-26-16-33. Closed Sun pm. Evening meals.

GAN 64290 Pyr.-Atl **RN 134 Maps 20-B3 and 21-A3**
♀ ⊗ ⌂ **1 Star NN HOTEL MODERNE** (N° RR DEC 23 568) (M. Patrick **Piette**) 41–43, place de la Mairie ☎ 59-21-54-98 ⌐ 15 from 58 to 105F, breakfast to 15F. Closed Sun. Coaches welcome (rest. seats 180). Evening meals until 8.30pm. Bar; dogs allowed. Full board 130–150F.
♀ ⊗ ⌂ **LE RELAIS DES VOYAGEURS** (N° RR OCT 25 710) (M. Jean-Michel **Bonis**) 9, rue Henri IV ☎ 59-21-56-38.

GAP 05000 Hautes-Alpes **Map 25-A1**
♀ ⊗ ⌂ **ALPES DAUPHINE** (N° RR JUN 25969) (M. André **Farizy**) Quartier de la Descente RN 85 (Napoléon) ☎ 92-51-47-15 and 92-57-29-95 ⌐ 5 Closed 1–14th Nov. Coaches welcome (rest. seats 60). English, German, Italian spoken. Full board 165F. Evening meal to 9.30pm.
♀ ⊗ ⌂ **AUX AMIS DE LA ROUTES** (N° RR AUG 27 373) (M. Marcel **Bary**) La Plaine de Lachamp ☎ 92-52-36-94 Closed Sun (low season). Evening meals to 11pm. Local filling station. Parking.

GARGES-LES-GONESSES 95140 Val-d'Oise
♀ ⊗ **AUX VIEUX GARGES** (N° RR DEC 27 485) (Mme Paulette **Aubre**) 37, rue Marcel-Bourgogne ☎ 39-86-30-31 Closed Saturday afternoon and Sunday. Evening meals.

GASVILLE see MAINVILLIERS

GAVRELLE 62580 Pas-de-Calais **Map 5-B3**
♀ ⊗ **RELAIS DE LA CHAUMIÈRE** (N° RR SEPT 27 013) (M. Franck **Courcelle**) 21, route Nationale ☎ 21-58-16-99 English spoken. Local filling station.

G

GENAY par SEMUR-EN-AUXOIS 21140 Côte-d'Or **Map 13-A3**
♀ ⊗ **AU PONT DE GENAY** (N° RR SEP 23 942) (Mme Josette **Goubard**) ☎ 80-97-03-32 Closed Tue.

GENNEVILLIERS 92230 Hauts-de-Seine **Map 1-A2**
♀ ⊗ **LES ROUTIERS** (N° RR SEPT 26 664) (Mme Anne-Maria **Vidalenc**) 39, avenue Marcel-Paul ☎ 47-92-11-70 Closed Fri evening, Sat, Sun; 3 weeks Aug. Evening meals served until 9pm.

GER 64550 Pyrénées-Atlantiques **RN 117 Map 21-A3**
♀ ⊗ ⌂ **A LA CLÉ D'OR** (N° RR AVR 20 706) (M. Robert **Coudert**) ☎ 62-31-50-56 ⌐ 4 Closed Sat afternoon, Sun; 15 Aug–15 Sept. Evening meals.

GERMIGNY-DES-PRÉS 45110 Loiret **RD 60 Map 13-A1**
♀ ⊗ ⌂ **HOTEL DE LA PLACE** (N° RR JAN 25 250) (Mme **Maillard**)
⌐ Le Bourg Châteauneuf ☎ 38-58-20-14 ⌐ 13 Closed Fri; (except in season and booked) end of Jan. Feb. Full-board 150–170F per night. Coaches welcome (rest. seats 90). Evening meals to 9pm. Menus 45–105F. Special on request.

GERMIGNY-SUR-YONNE 89600 Yonne **RN 5 Maps 9-B2 and 13-A2**
♀ ⊗ ⌂ **SARL LE RELAIS DES ROUTIERS** (N° RR MAI 23 806) Rte de Genève ☎ 86-35-06-39 **Minitel** ⌐ 9 Closed Sun.

GERTWILLER 67140 Bas-Rhin **Map 10-B2**
♀ ⊗ **RELAIS DES GOURMETS** (N° RR JUIL 27 324) (M. Hubert **Klein**) 154, route de Strasbourg ☎ 88-08-92-69 Closed Tues and mid Feb to mid March. English and German spoken. Evening meals served until 9.30pm. Local filling station 8.30–7pm.

GHYVELDE 59254 Nord **Map 5-B2**
♀ ⊗ **CAFE ST-SÉBASTIEN** (N° RR OCT 26 712) (Mme Edith **Marie Rubben**) 161, rue Nationale ☎ 28-26-61-95 Closed Tue; 17 Aug–5 Sept. Dutch spoken. Coaches welcome (rest. seats 190). Evening meals to 6pm.

GIBERVILLE 14730 Calvados **RN 175 Map 4-B2**
♀ ⊗ **AU VERT GALANT** (N° RR MAI 26 892) (M. Jean-Luc **Outrequin**) 19, route de Rouen ☎ 31-72-36-52 Closed Sun; last fortnight Aug. English spoken. Full board 200–250F. Coaches welcome (rest. seats 60). Evening meals to 9.30pm.

GIDY see ORLEANS SARAN

GIEN 46600 Loiret **RN 140 Map 13-A1**
♀ ⊗ **AUBERGE DE LA CROIX-BLANCHE** (N° RR NOV 9 042) (Mme Chauvel **Michonnet**) 17, route de Bourges ☎ 38-67-28-95 Closed Fri evening; 24 Dec to 5 Jan. No evening meals.
♀ .60 **CAFÉ DU NORD** (N° RR OCT 27 054) (Mme Suzanne **Botineau**) 51, place de la Victoire ☎ 38-67-32-98 Closed Sun and first 2 weeks of August. English spoken. Local filling station 7–8pm.
♀ .60 ⌂ **AU RELAIS NORMAND** (N° RR OCT 27 055) (M. Pierre **Montceau**) **Sarl,** 64, place de la Victoire ☎ 38-67-28-56 ⌐ 9

151

G

Gien continued
> Closed Sun. Full aboard 140–170F. Coaches welcome (rest. seats 170). Evening meals to 8.30pm. Local filling station 7–8pm.

GIÈVRES 41130 Loir-et-Cher **RN 76 Map 12-B3**
> ☼ ⊗ ⛽ **Petrol/oil LE RELAIS DE NORAY** (N° RR SEP 21 206) (M. Michel **Ribeau**) ☎ 54-98-64-00 **Minitel** Closed Sat afternoon; end Sept/beginning Oct. Evening meals to 10pm. English, German spoken. Coaches welcome (rest. seats 40). Parking.
> ☼ ⊗ **LA BALANCELLE** (N° RR JUL 26 946) (Mme Francine **Brialy**), 1, route de Romorantin ☎ 54-98-64-76. Evening meals to 11pm.

GILOS SUR RISLE 27290 Eure
> ☼ ⊗ **RELAIS DE LA FORGE** (N° RR DEC 27 487) (M. Serge **Langlois**) La Forge ☎ 32-56-16-34 Closed Saturday afternoon. Evening meals until 10pm.

GISORS 27140 Eure **RN 15 Map 3-B2**
> ☼ ⊗ **BAR DE L'AVENUE** (N° RR JUN 26 564) (M. **Roussel**) Sarl Tina, 95, route de Dieppe ☎ 32-27-19-45 Closed Sun; 15–30 Aug. Evening meals served until 9pm. English spoken.

GLACERIE (LA) 50470 Manche **RN 13 Map 4-A1**
> ☼ ⊗ **LE RELAIS DE LA GLACERIE** (N° RR SEPT 26 034) (M. Paul **Roupsard**) near Conforama ☎ 33-44-13-54 **Minitel** Closed Sat, Sun night; 14 Jul to 14 Aug. Coaches welcome (rest. seats 80). Evening meals until 9pm. Parking.

GLENIC 23380 Creuse **RN 140 and RD 940 Map 16-B1**
> ☼ ⊗ 🏠 **LA PERGOLA** (N° RR JUN 25 021) (M. André **Laforme**) Le Pont ☎ 55-52-93-38 ⊷ 14 Closed Oct.

GLOS-SUR-RISLE 27290 Eure **Map 4-B3**
> ☼ ⊗ **RELAIS LAFORGE** (N° RR NOV 24 758) (Mme Micheline **Salm**) La Forge **Montfort-sur-Risle** ☎ 32-56-16-34 Closed Sun.

GODEWAERSVELDE 59270 Nord **RN 348 Map 5-A1**
> ☼ ⊗ **LE CUSTOM** (N° RR JUIL 26 961) (M. Antoine **Trassaert**) "Callicanes" ☎ 28-43-33-87 Service station opposite. Dutch spoken.

GOLBEY 88190 Vosges **RN 66 460 Maps 14-B1 and 10-A2**
> ☼ ⊗ **RELAIS DU PETIT CERF** (N° RR MAI 26 888) (M. Christian **Kuntz**) 63, rue du Gl-Leclerc ☎ 29-34-23-25. Closed Sun. Public holidays. Aug. Evening meals.

GONESSE 95500 Val-d'Oise **Map 1-A3**
> ☼ ⊗ 🏠 **CHEZ COCO** (N° RR JAN 25 265) (M. André **Baugé**) 43, rue de Paris ☎ 39-85-01-26 ⊷ 9 Closed Sun afternoon 2.30 pm.

GONNEVILLE-SUR-HONFLEUR 14600 Calvados **Map 4-B2**
> ☼ ⊗ **LE MERLE BLANC** (N° RR DEC 24 775) (M. **Renault**) Honfleur

☎ 31-89-11-98 Closed Sat; Aug; 20 to 31 Dec. Coaches welcome (rest. seats 58). Evening meals. English spoken.

GORRON 53120 Mayenne **RN 806 Map 8-B1**
Y ⊗ ⌂ **1 Star NN LE RELAIS DU BOCAGE – AU RENDEZ-VOUS DES ROUTIERS** (N° RR FEV 14 232) (Mme **Bibron**) 9, rue Corbeau Paris ☎ 43-08-61-74 ⊷ 10 Full-board 160–200F per night. Coaches welcome (rest. seats 100). Evening meals.

GOUESNIÈRE (LA) 35350 Ile-et-Vilaine **RD 4 Map 7-A3**
Y ⊗ **LE RELAIS DES ROUTIERS** (N° RR JUL 21 599) (Mme M.-T. **Bourgalais**) Le Bourg ☎ 99-58-80-57 ⊷ 16 with showers. Closed Sun; 6–28 Aug. Full-board 145–150F per night. Coaches welcome (rest. seats 180). Evening meals.

GOURDON 46300 Lot **RN 704 Map 17-B1**
Y ⊗ ⌂ **LE RELAIS DE LA MADELEINE** (N° RR JUL 18 770) (Sarl **Barbes**) Boulevard de la Madeleine ☎ 61-41-02-63 **Minitel** ⊷ 16 Closed Sun in winter, Oct. Full-board 165–185F per night. Coaches welcome (rest. seats 55 + covered terrace). Evening meals.

GOURIN 56110 Morbihan **RD 1/769 Map 7-B2**
Y ⊗ ⌂ **AUBERGE DE TOUL-AN-CHY** (N° RR MAI 26 541) (M. Joseph **Hilliou**), 20, rue de la Libération ☎ 97-23-43-77 ⊷ 9 Closed Sat. Evening meals served. English spoken.

GOUSSAINVILLE 95190 Val-d'Oise **Map 1-A3**
Y ⊗ **AUX SPORTS** (N° RR MAR 24 885) (M. Marcel **Dufros**) 22, avenue Albert Sarrault ☎ 39-88-10-84 Closed Sat.

GOUSTRAINVILLE par DOZULE 14430 Calvados **RN 815 Map 4-B2**
Y ⊗ **LE RELAIS DES ROUTIERS** (N° RR DEC 11 933) (M. Daniel **Duval**) ☎ 31-79-21-90 Closed Sun; Aug.

GOUZON 23230 Creuse **Map 16-B2**
Y ⊗ **CHEZ HÉLÈNE** (N° RR NOV 26 380) (Mme Hélène **Kowalski**) Trois Fonds ☎ 55-81-75-98 Polish spoken.

GRAINVILLE 27380 Eure **RN 14 Map 3-A1**
Y ⊗ **LE RELAIS DE GRAINVILLE** (N° RR JUN 26 563) (Mme Edwige **Legatt**) 40, route Nationale ☎ 32-48-06-28 Closed Sun. Coaches welcome (rest. seats 100 in 2 rooms). Evening meals 6pm–8pm.

GRAINVILLE-LANGANNERIE 14190 Calvados **RN 158 Map 8-A2 4-B2**
Y ⊗ **CHEZ DOMINIQUE** (N° RR SEPT 27 031) (M. Dominique **Laine**) Route Nationale ☎ 31-90-51-00 Closed Sun. English spoken. Local filling station.

GRAMAT 46500 Lot **RN 140 and D 677 Map 17-B1**
Y ⊗ ⌂ **2 Stars NN LE RELAIS DU CENTRE** (N° RR FEV 13 419) (Société **Grimal**: M. André **Grimal et Fils**) Place de la Republique ☎ 65-38-73-37 **Minitel** ⊷ 14 from 150 to 250F, breakfast to

G

Gramat continued

24F. Telephone, TV in room. Access for disabled. Closed Sat low season Feb. Coaches welcome (rest. seats 145). Evening meals to 9pm. English spoken. Parking; bar; dogs allowed; TV room; terrace. Menus 60–80F. Specialities: *Foie gras et confit de canard, Cassoulet maison, Salade quercynoise.* Sites to visit: Roc – Amadoux, Gouffre de Padirac (10 kms).

GRAND-BREUIL (LE) par ROUILLÉ 86480 Vienne **RN 150 Map 15-A1**
♈ ⊗ **LE RELAIS DE LA BONNE AUBERGE CHEZ DÉDÉ** (N° RR JUN 19 800) (M. André **Rousseville**) ☎ 49-43-90-62 ⊷ 6 Closed Sun; 22 Dec to 2 Jan. Evening meals to 9pm. Parking.

GRAND-FOUGERAY (LE) 35390 I.-et-V. **RN 137 Map 11-A2**
♈ ⊗ 🏠 1 Star **NN RELAIS DE LA BELLE ÉTOILE** (N° RR MAI 25 407) (M. Roland **Pirot**) Le Belle Étoile ☎ 99-08-42-59 Closed Sun. English spoken.

GRAND QUEVILLY 76120 Seine-Maritime **Map 3-A1**
♈ ⊗ 🏠 **HÔTEL DU CADRAN** (N° RR JUIN 27 301) (M. Phillippe **Delafenestre**) 1, rue Pierre-Corneille ☎ 35-69-69-34 ⊷ 7 English spoken. Evening meals.

GRANDE-AU-BOIS (LA) see SAINTE-MENEHOULD Marne

GRANDE-SYNTHE 59760 Nord **Map 5-A2**
♈ ⊗ 🏠 **LA BIGUINE** (N° RR NOV 26 390) (M. Denis **Jaeger**) 176, route de Spycker ☎ 28-27-88-32 **Minitel** ⊷ 6 Closed Sun. Full-board 140–170F per night. Coaches welcome (rest. seats 60). Evening meals until 11pm. English, German spoken.

GRANDE-VALLÉE (LA) 37110 I.-et-L. **see VILLEDOMER**

GRAULHET 81100 Tarn **RN 631 Map 22-B2**
♈ ⊗ **LE DOMINO** (N° RR OCT 25 146) (Mme Lucienne **Fallières**) Place du Jourdain ☎ 63-34-43-74 Spanish spoken.

GRAVELINES 59820 Nord **RN 40 Map 5-A1**
♈ ⊗ **CAFÉ DE L'AGRICULTURE** (N° RR 24 414) (Mme Raymonde **Blanckaert**) 52, avenue Jean-Jouhaux ☎ 28-23-05-50 Closed Oct.

GRAVIGNY 27930 Eure **RN 154 Maps 3-B1 and 4-B3**
♈ ⊗ 🏠 **HOTEL DES SPORTS** (N° RR OCT 23 513) (Mme Annick **Chrétien**) 109, avenue A.-Briand ☎ 32-33-16-19 ⊷ 7.

GREMONVILLE 76790 Seine-Maritime **RD 20 Map 4-A3**
♈ ⊗ **LA CHAUMIERE** (N° RR JAN 26 776) (M. Christian **Lemasurier**) Motteville ☎ 35-56-45-65 English spoken. Closed Tues night. Wed pm.

GRENOBLE 38100 Isère **Maps 19-A3 and 24-B1**
♈ ⊗ **LE CAFÉ DU NORD** (N° RR AOU 23 415) (Mme Bernadette

G

Bonnet) 44, Grand rue Monestier-de-Clermont ☎ 76-34-03-73
Closed Sun 2.00 pm.
♈ ⊗ **LE CATALPA** (N° RR JUL 27 334) (Mme Denise **Brisset**) 8bd. de
l'Esplanado ☎ 76-47-38-03 Closed Sun. Italian spoken. Evening
meals to 12pm. Local filling station 6.30–8.30pm.

GRIGNY 69250 Rhône **Map 2-B1**
♈ ⊗ **LE PHOENIX** (N° RR JUIL 27 320) (M. Michel **Lelarge**) 80, rue
de Bouteiller ☎ 78-73-03-72 Closed Sat pm, Sun and 7/7 to 15/7.
English, Spanish and Italian spoken. Evening meals. Local filling
station.

GRIMAUD 83360 Var **Map 25-A2**
♈ ⊗ ⌂ **LE RESTAUROUTE** (N° RR JAN 24 815) (M. Bernard **Gentile**)
Rte Nationale 98 **St Pons-les-Murs** ☎ 94-56-03-75 **Minitel** ⊷ 10
Closed Sun; Dec. Coaches, reservations only (rest. seats 60; 150
in season). Evening meals. English, German, Dutch, Italian
spoken. Full board 140–180F.

GRISOLLES 82170 T.-et-G. **RN 20 and 113 Map 22-A2**
♈ ⊗ **LE RELAIS DE LA GARE** (N° RR FEV 25 807) (M. Pierre
Dupuis) RN 20 ☎ 63-67-31-83 Coaches welcome (rest. seats 40).
Evening meals. Closed Fri and Sun night. Pointphone.

GUEMAR 68970 Haut-Rhin **RN 83 Map 10-B2**
♈ ⊗ ⌂ **A L'ANGE** (N° RR MAR 24 173) (M. Claude **Meinrad**) 16, Rte
de Sélestat ☎ 89-71-83-03 ⊷ 14 Closed Sat. 15 Dec to 15 Jan.
Evening meals. German, English, Italian spoken.

GUER near BELLEVUE-COETQUIDAN 56380 Morbihan **RN 772 and 773 Map 7-B3**
♈ ⊗ ⌂ **LE RELAIS DE L'UNION** (N° RR MAR 20 131) (M. Oliver
Guérin) ☎ 97-75-71-46 ⊷ 5 Closed Sun; Aug. Evening meals.
♈ ⊗ ⌂ **LE LION D'OR** (N° RR JANV 27 167) (M. Pierre **Poirier**) 7,
place de la Gare ☎ 97-22-00-26 ⊷ 5 Closed Sun. Local filling
station 8–8pm.

GUERCHE-DE-BRETAGNE (LA) 35130 I.-et-V. **RN 178 Map 8-B1**
♈ ⊗ ⌂ **LE RELAIS DU PONT D'ANJOU** (N° RR JUN 19 813) (M.
Moussu) 11, faubourg d'Anjou ☎ 99-96-23-10 ⊷ 12 Closed Sat
evening. Full-board 145–165F per night. Coaches welcome (rest.
seats 70). Menus 40.50–82.50F. Special Fruits de mer. Couscous
paëlla.

GUERCHE-SUR-L'AUBOIS (LA) 18150 Cher **Map 13-B2**
♈ ⊗ **LE REFUGE** (N° RR OCT 27 409) (M. Dominique **Letin**) La
Chapelle Hugon ☎ 48-74-05-25 Closed Tues, Feb. Evening
meals. Local filling station.

GUEREINS 01090 Ain **RN 17 Map 18-B2**
♈ ⊗ **LA CROISÉE** (N° RR MAI 26 551) (M. Michel **Manains**) La
Croisée de Guereins ☎ 74-66-14-93 Closed Sun; Tue from 4pm; 3
weeks in Aug. Evening meals. 3 parks for one drivers.

G

GUÉRIGNY 58130 Nievre **RD 977 Map 13-B2**
♀ ⊗ ⌂ **HOTEL DU COMMERCE** (N° RR NOV 26 095) (M. Gérard **Page**) ☎ 86-37-32-77 ⌐ 8 Closed Sun in winter; 20 Dec to 5 Jan. Full-board 160–180F per night. Evening meals until 9pm. German spoken.

GUILBERVILLE 50160 Manche **RN 175 Maps 4-B1 and 8-A1**
♀ ⊗ **LE POTEAU** (N° RR MAI 15 941) (M. Fredy **Menant**) Le Poteau ☎ 33-56-73-10 **Minitel** Closed Sat, Sun; Christmas holiday. Evening meals until midnight. English, German spoken. Coaches welcome (rest. seats 45).

GUILLON 89420 Yonne **Map 13-A3**
♀ ⊗ **ACCOR L'ARCHE** (M. **Prioul**) Autoroute Aire de Maison Dieu ☎ 86-32-11-34 Self-service restaurant.

GUIPAVAS 29215 Finistère **CD 712 Map 7-A1**
♀ ⊗ ⌂ **LE RELAIS DU LION D'OR** (N° RR NOV 8 075) (Mme **Troadsec**) 52, rue de Paris ☎ 98-28-00-33.

GUJAN MESTRAS 33470 Gironde **Map 20-A1**
♀ ⊗ **LA MOUCLADE** (N° RR FEV 27 183) (Mme Marcelle **Judas**) 150, avenue de Lattre-de-Tassigny ☎ 56-66-56-00 Closed Tues and 1/12 to 12/12. Local filling station 7–2am

GUMBRECHTSHOFFEN 67110 Bas-Rhin 500m from **RN 62 RD 242 Map 10-B1**
♀ ⊗ **AU SOLEIL – Chez Bernard et Lili** (N° RR AOU 22 020) (Mme Liliane **Peifer**) 30, Rue Principale ☎ 88-72-90-77 ⌐ 3 Closed Sun; Aug. Full-board 100–130F per night. Coaches welcome (rest. seats 130/50). Evening meals to 12pm. German spoken.

GUMERY 10400 Aube **RD 439 Map 9 A/B2**
♀ ⊗ ⌂ **AU RELAIS** (N° RR FEV 27 194) (Mmes Évelyne et Jacqueline **Visse**) 3, rte de Sens ☎ 25-39-16-01 ⌐ 10 Closed Sun afternoon. English spoken.

GURUNHUEL 22390 Côtes-du-Nord **RN 787 Map 7-A2**
♀ **AU RENDEZ-VOUS DES CHASSEURS ET DES PECHEURS – Chez Gilberte** (N° RR JUL 19 429) (M. and Mme Yves **Georgelin**) Kérambellec ☎ 96-21-81-00 **Minitel** Closed Jul. Coaches welcome (rest. seats 50).

H

HABSHEIM 68440 Haut-Rhin **RN 66 Map 10-B3**
♀ ⊗ **A LA VILLE DE MULHOUSE** (N° RR OCT 21 676) (Mme Gabrielle **Lehmann**) 76, rue du Général-de-Gaulle ☎ 89-44-31-33

Coaches welcome (rest. seats 150/50/45). German, English spoken.

HAGONDANGE 57300 Moselle **RN 53 Map 10-A1 and 6-B3**
Y ⊗ ⌂ **LE RELAIS DES AMIS** (N° RR JAN 16 412) Mme Martine **Bognolo**) 36, rue de Metz ☎ 87-71-46-63 — 10 **Hôtel du Centre 1 star NN** 7, rue Anatole-France ☎ 87-71-47-64 Closed Sun; first 3 weeks Aug. Full board 150F. Coaches welcome (rest. seats 40). Evening meals.

HAIE-FOUASSIÈRE (LA) 44690 Loire-Atl Clisson N 359 Map 11-B3
Y ⊗ **LE RABELAIS** (N° RR FEV 26 433 bis) (Mme Ghyslaine **Girard**) 1, rue de Seures ☎ 40-54-87-76 Closed Sun. English, German spoken. Coaches welcome (rest. seats 60). Evening meals to 8pm.

HAILLICOURT 62940 Pas-de-Calais **Map 5-B2**
Y ⊗ **L'ABREUVOIR** (N° RR OCT 25 148) (Mme Suzanne **Lemoine**) 30, rue du 1er Mai ☎ 21-62-26-54 English Spoken.

HALLENNES-LEZ-HAUBOURDIN 59320 Nord **RD 941 Map 5-B1**
Y ⊗ **AUX AMIS DE LA ROUTE** (N° RR MAR 23 705) (Mme Micheline **Masfrand**) 329, rue de Général-de-Gaulle ☎ 20-07-14-24 **Minitel** Showers. Closed Sat, Sun; Aug. Shop. Evening meals for drivers.

HALLUIN 59250 Nord **RN 17 Map 5-B1**
Y ⊗ **AU ROUTIER** (N° RR OCT 26 687) (M. Richard **Kozior**) 196, rue de la Lys ☎ 20-23-88-20 Closed Sat afternoon, Sun; Aug. Polish, Yugoslav, Dutch spoken. Evening meals to 10pm. Parking.

HARDRICOURT 78250 Yvelines **RN 190 Map 1-A1**
Y ⊗ **LA DEVINETTE** (N° RR NOV 26 367) (M. Michel **Lemoine**) 30, boulevard Michelet ☎ 34-74-06-32 Closed Sat, Sun; Aug. Evening meals. Special fruits de mer.

HAVRE (LE) 7660 S,-Marit **RN 13 Bis Map 4-A/B2**
Y ⊗ **LE RELAIS DES ROUTIERS** (N° RR NOV 23 550) (Mme Marie-Pierre **Priser**) 57, rue Marceau ☎ 35-25-06-44.
Y ⊗ **A LA PIPE (S.A. Garonne)** (N° RR OCT 24 367) (M. Didier **Eudes**) 128, Bld de Graville ☎ 35-24-54-48 Closed Sun; 15 days in Sept. Coaches welcome (rest. seats 75/85). Evening meals to 11pm. English spoken.
Y ⊗ **LE P'TIT COMPTOIR** (N° RR JUN 26 558) (M. Bernard **Rondel**) 31, rue du Général Faidherbe ☎ 35-42-78-72 Closed Sun; 20th Dec to New year. Coaches welcome (2 dining rooms = 60 seats). Evening meals to 11pm. English spoken.
Y ⊗ **AU TÉLÉPHONE** (N° RR AVR 27 258) (M. Jean-Claude **Bouillon**) 173, Bld Amiral Mouchez ☎ 35-25-24-73 Closed Sun. English spoken.
Y ⊗ **LA RASCASSE** (N° RR SEPT 27 018) (M. Serge **Pekic**) 2, rue Gustave Nicolle ☎ 35-24-50-05 **Minitel** Closed Sun; Aug. Local filling station.

H

♀ ⊗ **LE CARGO** (N° RR DEC 27 488) (Mme Janine **Contréras**). 1, rue du Generale-de-Lasalle ☎ 35-26-69-50. Closed Saturday after 3pm and Sunday. Evening meals. English spoken.

♀ ⊗ ⌂ **LE WELCOME** (N° RR OCT 27 048) (Mme Marie-Pierre **Priser**) Quai Southampson ☎ 35-43-17-84 ↦ 10 Local filling station.

♀ ⊗ **AU PETIT MOUSSE** (N° RR FEV 27 178) (M. Patrice **Munster**) 19, rue Amiral Courbet ☎ 35-25-13-43 Closed Sat pm and Sun. German spoken. Local filling station.

♀ ⊗ **TANTE-JEANNE** (N° RR MARS 27 232) (M. Claude **Sauvage**) 72/74, rue Paul-Marion ☎ 35-26-40-54 Local filling station.

HAYE-DU-PUITS (LA) 50250 Manche **RN 800 Map 4-B1**
♀ ⊗ **LE RELAIS LES AMIS** (N° RR MAI 24 572) (M. Louis **Le Filliastre**) 16, rue du Château ☎ 33-46-03-42 Closed Sun in winter. Coaches welcome (rest. seats 150).

HAYE-PESNEL 50320 Manche **RD 7 Map 8-A1**
♀ ⊗ **LE RELAIS CHEZ ARMELLE** (N° RR AOU 15 766) (Mme Armelle **Jacquette**) Rue de la Libération ☎ 33-61-50-83 Closed Sat, Sun low season; Dec. Full-board guest rooms. Coaches welcome (rest. 2 rooms seat 50). Evening meals to 10pm. English spoken.

HAYONS-ESCLAVELLES par NEUFCHATEL-EN-BRAY (LES) 76270 Seine-Maritime **RN 28 and 29 Map 3-A1**
♀ ⊗ ⌂ **AUX AMIS DES ROUTIERS** (N° RR AOU 25 620) (M. Pierre **Durieu**) ☎ 35-93-13-15 ↦ 8 Closed Sun; Dec. Car park. English spoken.

HEBERGEMENT (L') 85260 Vendée **RN 763 Maps 11-B3 and 12-B1**
♀ ⊗ **LE RELAIS DES ROUTIERS** (N° RR NOV 24 408) (M. **Bretin**) 17, rue Georges-Clemenceau ☎ 51-42-80-71 Closed Sat; Aug (3 weeks). Evening meals.

HENDAYE 64700 Pyr.-Atl. **RN 10 Map 20-A3**
♀ ⊗ **LE RELAIS DES ROUTIERS CHEZ MARCEL-FRANCO-ESPAGNOL** (N° RR MAI 18 415) (Mme **Mongobert**) Pont International 11, avenue d'Espagne ☎ 59-20-78-95 Closed Sun; Aug. Evening meals to 10pm. German spoken.

♀ ⊗ **BAR-RESTAURANT DE PONT** (N° RR OCT 27 071) (M. Richard **Mas**) 17, avenue d'Espagne ☎ 59-20-73-96 Closed Sun and 15th to 30th August. Spanish spoken. Local filling station.

HERBIERS (LES) 85500 Vendée **RN 160 Map 11-B3**
♀ ⊗ ⌂ **1 Star NN L'ORÉE DES BOIS VERTS** (N° RR OCT 27 044) (M. René **Joulin**) Route des Sables ☎ 51-91-00-18 ↦ 11 70–140F Breakfast 15F Closed Sun pm and Christmas to New Year. All saints day. Full board 170–215F. Coaches welcome (rest. seats 80). Evening meals to 9.30pm. Parking, bar, dogs allowed (except in the restaurant), T.V room. Visit puy du fou, Abbey, Tricherie pool.

H

HERMANVILLE-SUR-MER 148800 Calvados **CD 514 Map 4-B2**
♈ ⊗ **LE LUDO** (N° RR SEPT 27 020) (Mme Josianne **Gueniot**) 37, boulevard de la 3ᵉ D.I.B. ☎ 31-96-84-55. English spoken. Local filling station.

HERMITAGE (L') 35590 I.-et-V. **RD 125 Map 7-B3**
♈ ⊗ **LE VILLAGE** (N° RR JUN 25 964) (Mme **Cosnier**) 23, rue de Rennes ☎ 99-64-03-31 Closed Sun; Aug. Coaches welcome (rest. 3 rooms seat 100). Evening meals to 10.30pm.

HERMITAGE-LORGE (L') 22150 C.-du-N. **RD 168 Map 7-A2**
♈ ⊗ ⌂ **LE SOLEIL D'OR** (N° RR SEPT 26 031) (Mme Huguette **Maillard**) Le Paly ☎ 96-42-11-39 **Minitel** ⇀ 9 Closed Sun. Full-board 140–200F per night. Coaches welcome (rest. seats 125). Evening meals to 9pm.

HEUDEBOUVILLE 27400 Eure **RN 15 Map 3-B1**
♈ ⊗ ⌂ **AU TROU NORMAND** (N° RR AVR 25 387) (M. Guy **Fort**) Louviers ☎ 32-40-18-00 ⇀ 5 Closed Sun; Aug.
♈ ⊗ **LE 100 BORNES** (N° RR OCT 27 419) (M. Marcel **Narcisse**) 15, Route National ☎ 32-40-14-03 Closed Fri night. Sat pm. Evening meals to 10pm.

HINGLE (LE) 22100 C..-du-N. **RN 166 Map 7-A3**
♈ ⊗ ⌂ **LE RELAIS DES ROUTIERS** (N° RR JUL 24 633) (M. Rémy **Pessel**) place de la Gare Les Granits ☎ 96-83-58-45 ⇀ 6 Closed Sat, Sun. Full-board 140–150F. Coaches welcome (rest. seats 100). Evening meals to 9.30pm. English spoken.

HIRSON 02500 Aisne **RN 43 Map 6-A2**
♈ ⊗ **CHEZ JULIANO** (N° RR SEP 26 644) (M. Giulio **Corsini**) 151, avenue Joffre ☎ 23-58-14-03. Closed Sun. Coaches welcome (rest. seats 50). Evening meals to 10pm.

HOLTZWIHR 68320 Haut-Rhin **Map 10-B2**
♈ ⊗ **AU TONNEAU D'OR** (N° RR DEC 76 769) (M. Patrick **Vonders-cher**) 99, rue Principale ☎ 89-47-41-24 Closed Mon; Aug. German spoken. Coaches welcome (rest. seats 80). Evening meals to 10pm.

HOPITAL-CAMFROUT (L') 29224 Finistere **RN 170 Map 7-A1**
♈ ⊗ **LE RELAIS DES ROUTIERS** (N° RR DEC 21 301) (M. Bernard **Hamery**) Le Bourg ☎ 98-20-01-21 and 98-20-03-18 **Minitel** Closed Mon pm 15 Aug to 1 Sept. Coaches welcome (rest. seats 240). Evening meals (Sat, Sun).

HOPITAL-SUR-RHINS (L') par ST-CYR-DE-FAVIERES 42132 Loire **RN 7 Map 18-A2**
♈ ⊗ ⌂ **LE RELAIS DES ROUTIERS** (N° RR MARS 9 420) (M. **Lagoutte**) ☎ 77-64-80-13 ⇀ 7 Closed Sat; Aug. Coaches welcome (rest. seats 35). Evening meals until 9.00pm for drivers.
♈ ⊗ **RELAIS ALSACIEN** (N° RR JUL 26 618) (M. Marcel **Terrier**) Saint- Cyr de Favières ☎ 77-64-81-01 Closed Sat, Sun; Jul. Coaches welcome (rest. seats 25). Evening meals to 11pm.

H

HOSPITALET DU LARZAC (L') 12230 Aveyron **RN 9 Map 23-A1**
Ⓨ ⊗ ⌂ **2 star RELAIS ESPACE** (N° RR AVR 27 243) (Mme Ginette **Gineste**) RN 9 Aérodrome Millau-Larzac ☎ 65-62-76-22 ⊷ 10 TV showers Open 6am to 11pm. English and Spanish spoken. Self service menu. Parking for 120 cars. Filling station 2km 6–11pm.

HOSTENS 33125 Gironde **RN 657 Map 20-B1**
Ⓨ ⊗ **AU BON ACCUEIL** (N° RR NOV 22 561) (Mme **Laouilleau**) ☎ 56-88-50-63 Closed Sun.

HOTTOT LES BAGUES 14250 Calvados **CD9 Map 4-B2**
Ⓨ ⊗ **LE RELAIS DE LA MANCHE** (N° RR JANV 26 794) (M. Roland **Jeanne**) Route de Caumont ☎ 31-80-81-72. Closed Sat afternoon, 1 week in Feb 2 weeks Sept. Coaches welcome (rest. seats 40). Evening meals.

HOUCHES (LES) 74310 Hte-Savoie **RN 205 Map 19-B2**
Ⓨ ⊗ **RELAIS DU CHATELARD** (N° RR JUL 26 593) (M. Bernard **Chibaudel**) Passy Le Chatelard ☎ 50-47-21-62 Closed Sun. Spanish spoken.

HOURTIN 33990 Gironde **Map 20-A1**
Ⓨ ⊗ **LE NOUVEAU NICE** (N° RR NOV 27 100) (M. Phillippe **Roberel**) 6, rue du Médoc ☎ 56-09-21-13 English and Spanish spoken. Local filling station.

HOUSSAYE-EN-BRIE (LA) 77610 S.-et-M. **RN 36 Map 9-A1**
Ⓨ ⊗ ⌂ **AUBERGE DU COUCOU** (N° RR JUL 26 607) (MM. Christian and Jacky **Broust**) La haute-Gonière ☎ 64-07-40-75 English spoken. 1 shower for drivers.

HOUSSOYE (LA) 60390 Oise **RN 181 Map 3-B2**
Ⓨ ⊗ ⌂ **LE RELAIS DU CHEVAL BLANC** (N° RR SEP 15 790) (Mme **Juttier**) 5, rue de Grisors ☎ 44-81-40-23 ⊷ 6 Closed Sun. Sat Dec.

HUILLY-SUR-SEILLE 71290 S, et L. **RN 175 Map 18-B1**
Ⓨ ⊗ ⌂ **CHEZ DAFFY** (N° RR JAN 26 135) (Mme Michel **Roy**) ☎ 85-40-00-65 Closed Wed. Evening meals served.

HUISSEAU-EN-BEAUCE 41310 L.-et-C. **RN 10 Map 12-A3**
Ⓨ ⊗ **LES PLATANES** (N° RR SEPT 27 001) (M. Hubert **Breton**) ☎ 54-82-81-46 Closed Sat afternoon; Sun. Filling station near. Coaches welcome (rest. seats 54). Evening meals to 11.30pm.

HUMIERES 62130 Pas-de-Calais **Map 5-A3**
Ⓨ ⊗ **LA SEMEUSE Fina Station** (N° RR MAR 24 537) (Mme Berthe **Ternisien**) ☎ 21-41-85-77 **Minitel** Coaches welcome (rest. seats 50). Evening meals.

HUSSEREN WESSERLING 68470 Haut-Rhin **RN 66 Map 10-B3**
⊗ **RELAIS DU PONT ROUGE** (N° RR JANV 26 783) (Mme Juliana **Menzione**) 36, route Nationale ☎ 89-82-14-81. Closed Sun. Evening meals on all days. Italian spoken. Parking 40 HGV.

H

HUTTENHEIM 67230 Bas-Rhin **RN 83 Map 10-B2**
♈ ⊗ **AU JARDIN DES ROSES** (N° RR SEPT 27 027) (M. Maurice **Schneider**) Près Benfeld ☎ 88-74-41-44 **Minitel** Closed Sat and mid August. Coaches welcome (rest. seats 60). Evening meals to 9pm. German spoken. Local filling station.

HYENVILLE 50660 Manche **RD 971 Map 8-A1**
♈ ⊗ 🏠 **LE RELAIS DE LA SIENNE** (N° RR MARS 26 481) (Mme Éliane **Mayor**) Le Pont Hyenville-Quettreville-sur-Sienne ☎ 33-07-56-03 **Minitel** ⊷ 7 Closed Sun (in winter). Full board 200F. Evening meals. English spoken.

HYERES 83400 Var **RN 98 Map 25-A3**
♈ ⊗ 🏠 **RELAIS DU GROS PIN** (N° RR MAI 21 935) (Mme Antoinette **Durante**) 15, avenue Paul-Renaudel ☎ 94-97-63-26 ⊷ 8 Closed Sun; Christmas, New Year.

HYERES-PAROISSE 25110 Doubs **RN 73 Maps 10-A3 and 14-B3 see BAUME-LES-DAMES**

I

IMLING SARREBOURG 57400 Moselle **RN 4 Map 10-B2**
♈ ⊗ **RELAIS DE LA FERME** (N° RR DEC 25 757) (M. Jean-Luc **Steiner**) Rte de Sarrebourg RN 4 ☎ 87-23-68-72 Closed 15 days in beginning Aug, 15 days Dec, Jan. Coaches welcome (rest. seats 50). Evening meals. German spoken.

INTVILLE-LE-GUETARD 45300 Loiret **see PITHIVIERS**

ISDES 45620 Loiret
♈ ⊗ 🏠 **LE DAUPHIN** (N° RR DEC 27 463) (M. Lucien **Laurent**) 11 Grande-Rue ☎ 38-29-10-29 ⊷ 10 Evening meals. Service station nearby.

ISLE-ADAM (L') 95290 Val-d'Oise **RN 322 Map 3-B2**
♈ ⊗ **AU RALLYE Chez Paulette** (N° RR FEV 18 325) (Mme Paulette **Combes** 71, rue de Pontoise ☎ 34-09-08-24 Closed Sat evening, Sun evening; Aug.

ISLE-D'ABEAU (L') par BOURGOIN-JALLIEU 38300 Isère **Autoroute A43 Map 2-B2**
♈ ⊗ **L'ARCHE** Autoroute A3, Bourgoin-Jallieu ☎ 74-27-27-91 Self-service restaurant. Open 7.00am to 11.00pm. Shop.

I

ISLE-JOURDAIN (L') 32600 Gers **RN 124 Map 22-A2**
Y ⊗ **L'OLYMPIA** (N° RR SEP 19 912) (M. Michel **Amour**) 5, rue de la République ☎ 62-07-01-35 Closed Sun; Aug. Evenings meals to 10pm. Coaches welcome (rest. seats 90).

ISLES-SUR-LA-SORGUE 84800 Vaucluse **Map 24-A/B-2**
Y ⊗ **Tabac CHEZ L'ANCHOIS** (N° RR OCT 27 439) (M. Jean-Marc **Baudet**) Velorgues ☎ 90-38-01-38 Closed Sat. Evening meals to 9pm.

ISSANKA 34540 Herault **RN 113**
Y ⊗ ⌂ **2 stars LE GARRIGOU** (N° RR DEC 27 471) (Mme Danyelle **Hohmann**) ☎ 67-78-71-30 ◄ 8 from 80–190F. Breakfast 15–18F. Evening meals served. Service station open 7am–8pm.

ISSOIRE 63500 Puy-de-Dôme **RN 9 Map 17-A3**
Y ⊗ **LE CHAPEAU ROUGE** (N° RR FEV 15 540) (M. André **Jouve**) route de St-Germain ☎ 73-89-14-74 Closed Sun; Aug. Evening meals, served until midnight. Coaches welcome (rest. seats 92).
Y ⊗ ⌂ **AU REPOS DES ROUTIERS** (N° RR NOV 25 746) (Mme Ginette **Clauzin**) Veneix ☎ 73-96-62-01 ◄ 7 Full-board 150F per night. Coaches welcome (rest. seats 90). Evening meals.

ISSOUDUN 36100 Indre **RN 151 Map 13-B1**
Y ⊗ ⌂ **LE RELAIS DE LA CROIX-ROUGE** (N° RR AOU 22 432) (M. Claude **Grosyeux**) 14, faubourg de la Croix-Rouge ☎ 54-21-04-91 **Minitel** ◄ 5 Closed Sun. Full board 160F per night. Coaches welcome (rest. seats 97). Evening meals to 8.30. English, German, Italian, Turkish spoken.
Y ⊗ **LE RELAIS DES SPORTS** (N° RR OCT 24 378) (M. and Mme Guy **Bertaud**) 8, route de Bourges ☎ 54-21-50-30 Closed Sat; 10 to 25 Aug. Evening meals.

IS-SUR-TILLE 21120 Côte-d'Or **RN 459 Map 14-A3**
Y ⊗ **LE RELAIS DU MIDI** (N° RR JUL 17 848) (M. **Chalopet**) place Villeneuve ☎ 80-95-07-51 Coaches welcome (rest. seats 60).

IVRY-SUR-SEINE 94200 Val-de-Marne **Map 1-B2**
Y ⊗ **CHEZ PAINDAVOINE** (N° RR JUL 26 598) (M. François **Verdière**) 11, Quai Marcel Boyer ☎ 46-71-36-37 Closed Sun Aug. Evening meals to 11pm.

J

JALLAIS 49510 M./et/L. **RN 756/RD 15 Maps 11-B3 and 12-B1**
Y ⊗ ⌂ **2 Stars NN LE RELAIS DE LA CROIX VERTE Son Restaurant Le Vert Galant** (N° RR MARS 18 345) (M. **Gaillard**) Centre ville 1, rue Jean-de-Sagmond ☎ 41-64-10-12 and 64-20-22

Minitel ⊶ 25 from 148 to 220F, breakfast to 21F, telephone, T.V. Closed Fri. evening off season. Full-board 160–220F per night. Coaches welcome (rest. seats 160). Evening meals. English, German spoken. Car park; bar; dogs allowed. Menus from 59–135F. Specialities: *salade de rillauds d'Anjou chauds, Brochet de Loire au berre blanc, Civet de porcelet Saint-Hubert*. Sites to visit: vineyards of Muscadet and Anjou, Museum of Cholet.

JANZE 35150 I.-et-V. **RN 777 Maps 7-B3 and 8-B1**
Ⓨ ⊗ **LE RELAIS DE ROUTIERS** (N° RR JAN 20 967) (M. Michel **Métayer**) 5, Jean-Marie Lacire ☎ 99-47-05-10 Coaches welcome. (2 dining rooms = 400 places). Evening meals until 8pm.

JARNAC 16200 Charente **RN 141 Map 15-A2**
Ⓨ ⊗ **LES ROUTIERS** (N° RR AOU 22 910) (Mme Maryse **Bouffinie**) 77, rue Pasteur ☎ 45-81-02-40 Closed Sun. Coaches welcome (rest. seats 55). Evening meals to 10pm.

JARRIE 38560 Isere **RN 85 Maps 19-A3 and 24-B1**
Ⓨ ⊗ **LES ROUTIERS Chez Michel and Lucie Relais du Pont** (N° RR AVR 25 378) (M. and Mme **Bellosguardo-Rochas**) ☎ 76-88-85-38 Closed Sun. Evening meal served until 8.30pm.

JARS 18420 Cher **RN 723 Map 13-B1**
Ⓨ ⊗ **LE RELAIS DES ROUTIERS** (N° RR JUL 11 601) (Mme **Castagnie**) ☎ 48-48-70-44 Evening meals.

JAYAT 01340 Ain **CD 975 Map 18-B1**
Ⓨ ⊗ ⌂ **1 Star NN LE RELAIS DE JAYAT** (N° RR DEC 27 132) (M. Jean-Pierre **Rousselle**) Montrevel-en-Bresse ☎ 74-30-84-69 ⊶ 12 English spoken. Local filling station 7–10pm.

JOIGNY 89300 Yonne **RN 943 Maps 9-B2 and 13-A2**
Ⓨ ⊗ **RELAIS DE LA PROMENADE** (N° RR JUL 26 586) (M. Maurice **Deschamps**) 17, avenue Jules Hémery ☎ 86-62-18-13 Closed Sun and last week Aug.

JOSSELIN 56120 Morbihan **RN 24 Map 7-B3**
Ⓨ ⊗ **LA ROCHETTE** (N° RR AOU 22 002) (Mme Annie **Le Corre**) 128, rue Glatinier ☎ 97-22-27-29 Closed Sat, Sun low season. Coaches welcome (rest. seats 110). Evening meals. English spoken. Coaches welcome (rest. seats 160). Evening meals.

JOUE-EN-CHARNIE 72540 Sarthe **RN 157 Map 8-B2**
Ⓨ ⊗ ⌂ **RESTAURANT DE CHEVAL BLANC** (N° RR JUIL 23 400) (M. **Lalande**) ☎ 43-88-42-13 ⊶ 11 Closed Fri night, 15 days in Feb.

JUGON-LES-LACS 22270 Côtes-du-Nord **N12 near Dole exit Map 7-A3**
Ⓨ ⊗ **LES VALLÉES** (N° RR SEPT 26 645) (Mme Paulette **Hervé**) Dole ☎ 96-31-64-62 Closed Sat night Sun night. Evening meals 11pm. English spoken.

J

JUMELLIERE (LA) 49120 M.-et-L. **RD 961 Map 11-A3**
♀ ⊗ **LE RELAIS DE LA BOULE D'OR** (N° RR JAN 12 009) (M. and Mme **Sécher**) 2, rue du Val de Loire ☎ 41-64-33-23 ➞ 4 Closed Sun. Full-board 140–155F per night. Coaches welcome (rest. seats 55). Evening meals.

JURANVILLE 45340 Loire **RN 375 and RD 31 Map 9-B1**
♀ ⊗ **L'AUBERGE DES ROUTIERS** (N° RR JUN 24 611) (M. Maryse **Rocher**) Pavé de Juranville ☎ 38-33-24-61 Closed Sun evening; Evening meals to 9pm. Coaches welcome (rest. seats 60).

JURQUES 14260 Calvados **RN 177 Maps 4-B2 and 8-A1**
♀ ⊗ **AU BON ACCUEIL** (N° RR MARS 27 211) (M. Christian **Lesage**) route de Vire ☎ 31-77-81-17

JUSSAC 15250 Cantal **RN 122 Map 17-B2**
♀ ⊗ **LE RELAIS DES ROUTIERS** (N° RR OCT 19 556) (Mme Denise **Lasgouttes**) Route Nationale ☎ 71-47-65-61 Closed Sun; beginning Aug.

JUVISY-SUR-ORGE 91260 Essonne **RN 7 Map 1-B2**
♀ ⊗ **LE JOFFREY** (N° RR JANV 27 147) (M. Patrick **Thierry**) 45, av. de la Cour-de-France ☎ 69-21-27-50 Closed Sun.
♀ ⊗ **LE RELAIS DE LA MARINE** (N° RR NOV 26 389) (M. François **Sciabbarrasi**) 61, quai J.-P. Thimbault ☎ 69-21-28-65 ➞ 6 Closed Sat afternoon, Sun. Italian spoken.

JUZANVIGNY 10500 Aube **RD 400 Map 9-B3**
♀ ⊗ **CHEZ JACKY ET ROSE** (N° RR FEV 21 789) (M. Jacques **Deflin**) ☎ 25-92-80-57 and 25-92-60-06 ➞ 3. Closed Aug. Evening meals to midnight.

K

KERGONAN-LANGUIDIC 56440 Morbihan **RN 24 Map 7-B2**
♀ ⊗ **LE RELAIS DES ROUTIERS** (N° RR JUL 20 785) (M. **Le Garrec**) 9, rue du Commerce ☎ 97-65-87-03 Closed Sat; end Dec.

KERHOSTIN 56510 Morbihan **D 768 Map 11-A1 see SAINT-PIERRE-QUIBERON**

KESKASTEL 67260 Bas-Rhin **RN 61 Map 10-A/B1**
♀ ⊗ ⌂ **1 Star NN LE RELAIS L'ALSACE** (N° RR JUN 15 259) (Mme **Lenjoint**) 11, rue du Faubourg ☎ 88-00-11-04 ➞ 8 Closed Fri evening, Sat; mid Jul to mid Aug.

KINGERSHEIM 68470 Haut-Rhin **Map 10-B3**
♀ ⊗ ⌂ **AU CHASSEUR VERT** (N° RR JUIN 26 561) (Mme Kheria

K

Mabrouk) 5, rue de Guebwiller ☎ 89-52-36-47. English, German spoken. Full board 125–170F. Coaches welcome (rest. seats 50 + 30). Evening meals.

KNUTANGE 57240 Moselle **RN 52 Map 6-B3**
♇ ⊗ ⌂ **1 Star NN LE RELAIS DU STADE** (N° RR NOV 25 197) (Mme Rada **Radojcic**) 180, rue Victor-Rimmel ☎ 82-84-12-47 ⊷ 15 Closed Sat. German, some Italian spoken.

KOGENHEIM 67230 Bas-Rhin **RN 83 Map 10-B2**
♇ ⊗ ⌂ **A L'ÉTOILE** (N° RR AOUT 26 624) (M. and Mme Robert **Rapp**) 36, route de Strasbourg ☎ 88-74-70-02. **Minitel** Closed Mon (Hotel only) Jan. Coaches welcome (rest. seats 110). Evening meals served until midnight. German spoken.

KRUTH 68820 Haut-Rhin **Map 10-B3**
♇ ⊗ ⌂ **2 Stars NN AUBERGE DE FRANCE** (N° RR OCT 22 987) (M. **Ruffenach**) 20, Grand-Rue ☎ 89-82-28-02 ⊷ 16 Closed Thur; Nov. Full board 200F half-board 160F per night. Coaches welcome (rest. seats 130). Evening meals to 10pm. English, German spoken.

L

LABATUT 40300 Landes **RN 117 Map 20-A/B2**
♇ ⊗ ⌂ **LA GUINGUETTE** (N° RR JUL 26 968) (M. Christian **Begu**) ☎ 58-98-18-82 ⊷ 5 Spanish spoken. Evening meals to 9pm. Closed Sun night. Full board 160–180F. Coaches welcome (rest. seats 47). Local filling station.

LABEGUDE 07200 Ardèche **RN 102 Maps 23-B1 and 24-A2**
♇ ⊗ ⌂ **LE RELAIS DE LA POSTE** (N° RR AVR 8 426) (M. Maurice **Teyssier**) Route Nationale 64 ☎ 75-37-40-25 ⊷ 12 Closed Sun in winter, Sept. Full board 140–155F per night. Coaches welcome (rest. seats 55). Evening meals.

LABENNE 40530 Landes **RN 10 Map 20-A2**
♇ ⊗ ⌂ **HÔTEL BOUDIGAU** (N° RR DEC 25 221) (M. Francis **Begards**) Nationale 10 ☎ 59-31-40-18 ⊷ 6 Closed Sat/Sun; public holiday. Open 6am to 10pm.
⚑ **Esso Service Station** (N° RR MAI 24 589) (Mme Marie-Josephe **Dillenschneider**) Autoroute A63 Aire de Labenne Ouest ☎ 59-31-47-73.

LABROYE par HESDIN 62140 Pas-de-Calais **RD 928 Map 5-A3**
♇ ⊗ **Tobacconist LE RELAIS DES ROUTIERS – Chez Georgette** (N° RR AOU 19 459) (Mme Georgette **Flicourt**) route du Val d'Authie

L

Labroye par Hesdin continued
☎ 21-86-83-10 Closed last 2 weeks Sept. Coaches welcome (rest. seats 95). Evening meals.

LABRUGUIERE 81290 Tarn **RN 621 Map 22-B2**
♈ ⊗ ⌂ **1 Star NN LE RELAIS DE LA MARMITE** (N° RR JAN 24 073) (M. René **Ozanne**) 35, avenue Henri-Simon ☎ 63-50-21-19 ⊷ 16 Closed Sat, Sun; 15 days Aug. Coaches welcome (rest. seats 60). Full board from 130–150F. Evening meals served until 9pm.

LACAPELLE MARIVAL 46320 Lot **CD 940 Map 17-B1/2**
♈ ⊗ ⌂ **LE RELAIS DU SEGALA** (N° RR JAN 26 788) (M. Jean **Cagnac**) Route de Leye ☎ 65-40-81-91. English, Spanish spoken. Full board from 110F–150F. Coaches welcome (rest. seats 210). Evening meals served until 10pm.

LACAUNE 81230 Tarn **RD 622 Map 22-B2**
♈ ⊗ ⌂ **LE CHALET** (N° RR NOV 26 736) (M. Joseph **Delpino**) 14, rue André Théron ☎ 63-37-08-91. ⊷ 7 Closed Sun low season and 22/12–4/1. Full board 150–170F. Evening meals until 8pm.

LACHAPELLE AUZAC 46200 Tarn **RN 20 Map 17-B1**
♈ ⊗ ⌂ **LE RELAIS DE MAURE** (N° RR JAN 26 140) (M. Patrick **Cambroux**) Souillac ☎ 63-37-82-32 ⊷ 6. Full board 120–170F. Coaches welcome (rest. seats 60). Evening meals until 11pm. English, Spanish spoken.

LADON 45270 Loiret **RN 60 Maps 9-B1 and 13-A1**
♈ ⊗ ⌂ **LE RELAIS DE LADON** (N° RR FEVR 25 829) (M. Pierre **Guillaumin** 400, avenue du 24 Novembre ☎ 38-95-51-32 ⊷ 7 Closed Sun; 1/5–25/5. Full board 120F per night. Coaches welcome (rest. seats 55). Evening meals.
♈ ⊗ ⌂ **LES RUCHERS DU PARC** (N° RR JUIL 26 951) (Mme Ghislaine **Thiriau**) 240, route de Bellegarde ☎ 38-95-56-69 Closed Tue afternoon, all day Wed. English spoken.

LAFITTE-LOT 47320 L. et G. **RN D 666 Map 21-B1**
♈ ⊗ **LES AMIS DE LA ROUTE** (N° RR NOV 26 085) (Mme Jeannette **Briot**) Dle 666 ☎ 53-84-08-98 **Minitel** Closed Aug. Evening meals until 10pm. English, Spanish spoken.

LAFOX 47270 L.-et-G. **RN 113 Map 21-B1/2**
♈ ⊗ ⌂ **1 Star NN LE RELAIS TOULOUSAIN** (N° RR JAN 22 155) (M. and Mme **André**) 113, route de Toulouse ☎ 53-68-54-83 **Minitel** ⊷ 27 Closed Sat evening, Sun. 15/8–18/9 and 24/12–2/1. Full board 185–207F per night. Coaches welcome (rest. seats 220). Evening meals until 1.30pm. Spanish, Italian spoken.

LAGEON 79200 Deux-Sèvres **RN 138 and RD 79 Maps 12-B2 and 15-A1**
♈ ⊗ ⌂ **LE RELAIS DES ROUTIERS – Le Sampiero** (N° RR JUIL 12 348) (M. Robert **Garandeau**) ☎ 49-69-82-11 ⊷ 5 Closed Sat, Sun; Aug. Italian spoken. Evening meals.
♈ ⊗ ⌂ **CHEZ MARINETTE** (N° RR SEPT 27 003) (Mme Marie-Reine

Vignaud) ☎ 49-69-86-57 ⟶ Open 5.30 am – 1 am. Italian, some German spoken. Filling station near.

LAISSAC 12310 Aveyron **RN 88 Map 23-A1**
🍷 ⊗ 🏠 **1 Star AUBERGE DU ROVERGUE** (N° RR DEC 27 467) (SARL **Janda**) Route de Rodez ☎ 65-69-60-38 ⟶ 17 at 95–120F. Breakfast 15F. Evening meals. Nearby service station 6am–9pm.

LAILLE 72220 Sarthe **RN 138 Map 12-A2**
🍷 ⊗ 🏠 **LA LISIÉRE DE BERGE** (N° RR AUG 27 367) (Mme Annie **Pennerath**) Marigné ☎ 43-42-12-11 ⟶ 10 English spoken.
🍷 ⊗ **LE BON ACCUEIL** (N° RR OCT 27 401) (M. Jean-Louis **Londiere**) Marigue ☎ 43-42-12-01 Closed Wednesday. Evening meals until 11pm. Nearby service station open 6am–9pm.

LALOUBERE 65310 Htes-Pyr. **RD 135 Map 21-A3**
🍷 ⊗ 🏠 **1 Star NN HÔTEL DES PYRENEES** (N° RR AOU 16 207) (Mme Michelle **Cazamayou**) 13, rue du Ml-Foch ☎ 62-93-19-62 ⟶ 9 from 80–100F, breakfast 18–20F. Access for disabled. Closed Sun. Aug. Full board 155F per night. Evening meals until 9pm. Car park; bar; dogs allowed. Sites to visit: Lourdes (17 kms), Pic du Midi, Pyrenees. English, Spanish, Italian spoken.

LAMAGISTERE 82360 T.-t-G. **RN 113 Map 21-B2**
🍷 ⊗ **CHEZ BOMPA** (N° RR AVR 23 774) (M. Gilbert **Bompa**) 86, avenue Saint-Michel ☎ 63-39-91-56 **Minitel** Closed Sat. 1 to 15 Aug. Coaches welcome (rest. seats 100). Evening meals until 11pm. Spanish, Italian spoken.

LAMBALLE 22400 Côtes-du-Nord **RD 12 Map 7-A3**
🍷 ⊗ 🏠 **2 Stars NN LA TOUR D'ARGENT** (N° RR JAN 3 713) (M. Claude **Mounier**) 2, rue du Docteur Lavergne ☎ 96-31-01 37 ⟶ 15 in 1 Star NN ⟶ 16 in 2 Stars NN. from 95–250F, breakfast 24–30F, telephone, TV. Closed Sat, 15 days in Jun. Coaches welcome (rest. seats 50). Evening meals. English spoken. Car park; bar; dogs allowed; TV room; amusements (pool table, table tennis). Menus 65–150F. Specialities: *crevettes grillées, Canard à l'orange, coquilles Saint-Jacques.* Sites to visit: Saint-Malo, Le Mont St. Michel.

LAMBESC 13410 B.-du-R. **RN 7 Map 24-B3**
🍷 ⊗ **RELAIS DE LA GARE** (N° RR AVR 26 044) (Mme Germaine **Lansac**) Bld des Coopèratives ☎ 42-92-97-60 Closed Sun. Coaches welcome (rest. seats 70). Evening meals. Italian spoken.
🍷 ⊗ **LE VOLTAIRE** (N° RR JUN 26 923) (M. Albert **Reymond**) Cros du Loubon ☎ 42-92-72-19 ⟶ 8 Open 6am–11pm. Italian spoken. Filling station (8 pumps).

LAMONZIE-ST-MARTIN 24130 Dordogne **RD 936 Maps 15-B3 and 21-B1**
🍷 ⊗ **LA POMME D'OR** (N° RR AVR 23 762) (M. Giuseppina **Perna**) La Force ☎ 53-24-04-00 Closed Sat; 3 weeks in Aug. Spanish, English spoken.

L

LAMOTTE-DU-RHONE 84500 Vaucluse **RN 994 Map 24-A2**
ℙ ⊗ **CAFE DE LA PAIX** (N° RR OCT 26 060 (M. Gérard **Dewez**) ☎
90-30-41-89 ⊷ 7 Closed Sun. Full board 150–180F per night.
Coaches welcome (rest. seats 62). Evening meals until 9pm.

LANCON-DE-PROVENCE 13680 B.-du-R. **RN 113 Map 24-B3**
ℙ ⊗ **RELAIS DES FOURCHES** (N° RR FEV 26 166) (M. Vincent
Florio) RN 113 Quartier des Fenage ☎ 90-42-71-21 ⊷ 3 Closed
Sun. Full board 150–200F. Coaches welcome (rest. seats 120).
Evening meals until 9pm. Italian spoken.

LANCON PROVENCE
ℙ ⊗ 🏠 **AUBERGE DU MOULIN** (N° RR JUL 27 388) (M. Huguette
Gouella) ☎ 90-42-71-14. Evening meals until 10pm. Nearby
service station open 24 hours.

LANCON-DE-PROVENCE 13680 B.-du-R. **Autoroute A7**
⊗   **RELAIS DE PROVENCE** (Sté Accor) Autoroute A7 Aire de
Lancon-de-Provence ☎ 90-53-90-25 Self-service restaurant, open
6 to midnight, 24 hours Jun to Sept. Carpark, TV, exchange,
telephones. Tobacconist. Newsagent.
⚑   **Total Service Station – RELAIS DU SENEGUIER** A7 ☎ 90-53-
18-18.

LANDE-SUR-EURE (LA) 61290 Orne **Map 8-A3**
ℙ ⊗ **RELAIS DE LA TOUR** (N° RR FEV 26 808) (M. Edouard **Simon**)
Le Bourg ☎ 33-73-65-00.

LANDES 17380 Charente-Marit. **RN 139 Map 15-A2**
ℙ ⊗ 🏠 **AUX AMIS DE LA ROUTE** (N° RR MARS 26 218) (M. Robert
Picard) Tonnay Boutonne ☎ 46-59-73-12 ⊷ 4 Full board 140F.
Evening meals.

LANDEVANT 56690 Morbihan **RN 165 Map 7-B2**
ℙ ⊗ **LE RELAIS DU PELICAN** (N° RR JUL 6 281) (M. **Bourn**) 14, rte
⊷ Nle ☎ 97-56-93-12 Closed Mon evening/Tue; Oct.

LANDIVISIAU 29230 Finistère **RN 12 Map 7-A1**
ℙ ⊗ 🏠 **LE TERMINUS** (N° RR JUN 17 822) (M. Raymond **Floch**) 94,
avenue Foch ☎ 98-68-02-00 ⊷ 15 Closed Sat; 1 to 31 Aug. Full
board available. Coaches welcome (rest. seats 80). Evening
⊷ meals. Menus 58–75F. Specialities: seafood. English spoken.

LANDRECIES 59550 Nord **RN 45 Map 6-A1**
ℙ ⊗ **LE SAMBRETON** (N° RR AOU 23 896) (M. and Mme Monique
Lacoche SARL) Guise Road. ☎ 27-84-81-58. Closed Sat after-
noon, Sun afternoon; 15–30 Aug.

LANDRETHUN-LE-NORD 62250 Pas-de-Calais **RD 234 and 231 Map
5–A2**
ℙ ⊗ **A LA DESCENTE DES VOYAGEURS** (N° RR JUN 24 244) (Mme
Nelly **Brisbout**) ☎ 21-92-85-55 ⊷ 3 Full board 160F per night.
Coaches welcome (rest. seats 60). Evening meals.

L

LANESTER 56600 Morbihan **RN 24 Map 7-B2**
♈ ⊗ 🏠 **1 Star NN LE RELAIS DE LA ROTONDE** (N° RR NOV 15 440)
(M. **Mercier**) 120, rue Jean-Jaurès ☎ 97-76-06-37 ➡ 14 Closed Sat
afternoon, Sun; 15 days in Aug, Christmas, New Year. Full board
150 per night. Coaches welcome (rest. seats 40). Evening meals
until 8.30pm.
♈ ⊗ **LE RELAIS DU PONT-DU-BONHOMME** (N° RR OCT 23 963)
(M. Lucien **Phillippe**) avenue du Pont-du-Bonhomme ☎ 97-76-
51-23 Closed Aug. Coaches welcome (rest. seats 400/200).

LANGOGNE 48300 Lozère **RN 102 Map 17-B3**
♈ ⊗ 🏠 **1 Star NN HOTEL DU LUXEMBOURG** (N° RR AVR 22 750)
(Mme Adrienne **Chabalier**) place de la Gare ☎ 66-69-00-11 ➡
14 Closed Jan. Full-board 160–190F per night. Coaches welcome
(rest. seats 60). Evening meals.

LANGON 33210 Gironde **RN 113 and RN 132 Autoroute A61 Maps
20–B1 and 21–A1**
♈ ⊗ 🏠 **HÔTEL RESTAURANT DARLOT** (N° RR MAR 14 293) (M.
Jean-Paul **Darlot**) 10, rue Dotézac ☎ 56-63-01-36 ➡ 11 Closed
Sun 15 Aug to 5 Sept. Full-board 160–190F per night. Coaches
welcome (rest. seats 80). English, Spanish spoken. Menus up to
52F. Specialities: *civet de lièvre, cèpes à la bordelaise, Sailmis de
🍴 palombe.*

LANGRES 52200 Haute-Marne **RN 19 Map 14-A2**
♈ ⊗ 🏠 **RELAIS DE LA COLLINIÈRE** (N° RR JUL 26 601) (Mme
Élisabeth **Guerra**) ☎ 25-87-03-27 ➡ 8 Closed Sun. Coaches
welcome (rest. seats 40). Evening meals. Portuguese spoken.
♈ ⊗ 🏠 **A LA BONNE AUBERGE** (N° RR AVR 16 016) (M. Marcel
Baumann) Faubourg de la Collinière ☎ 25-87-09-18 ➡ 6 Closed
Sun; Christmas; beginning May. Full-board 110–140F per night.
Coaches welcome (rest. seats 50/20). Evening meals.

LANISCAT 22 570 C.-du-N. **Map 7-B2**
♈ ⊗ **CHALET DES ROUTIERS** (N° RR SEPT 25 638) (Mme Catherine
Morvan) Gare de Gouarec ☎ 96-24-81-78 Closed Sat evening
and Sun. Evening meals until 8.15pm. English spoken.

LANNION 22300 Côtes-du-Nord **Map 7-A2**
♈ ⊗ 🏠 **LE RELAIS DE LA CROIX ROUGE** (N° RR DEC 23 571)
(Mme **Pasquiou**) Croix Rouge Ploumilliau route de Morlaix ☎ 96-
35-45-08 ➡ 14. Closed last 2 weeks in August. Evening meals
until 9.30pm.

LAONS 28270 Eure-et-Loire **RD 4 Map 8-A3**
♈ ⊗ **LES ROUTIERS** (N° RR JUL 24 649) (Mme Suzanne **Rio**) 2, Place
du Carrefour ☎ 37-38-10-21 Closed Thur afternoon.

LAPALISSE 03120 Allier **RN 7 and RD3 Map 16-A3**
♈ ⊗ 🏠 **1 Star NN LE CHAPON DORÉ** (N° RR FEV 26 814) (M. Jean-
Luc **Lalauze**) 2, avenue du 8 Mai 1945 ☎ 70-99-09-51 ➡ 8. (4 with
shower) from 65–130F, breakfast to 18.50F. Full-board 150–180F.
Closed Sun. Car park; bar; dogs allowed; recreations (*pétan-*

L

Lapalisse continued
que). Places to visit: zoo, *châteaux*. Coaches welcome.
🐾 **Avia Service Station – LES ROUTIERS** (N° RR FEV 23 666) (M. Serge **L'Habitant**) 48, avenue du 8-Mai ☎ 70-99-10-08 Closed Sun (expect summer). English, German spoken.

LAPALME 11480 Aude **RN 9 Map 23-A3**
♀ ⊗ ⌂ **LE CHANTECLAIR** (N° RR AVR 26 867) (M. Maurice **Preigman**) ☎ 68-48-15-03 ➝ 7. Evening meals until 10pm.

LAPANOUSE-SERVERAC 12150 Aveyron **RN 595 Map 23-A1**
♀ ⊗ **LE RELAIS DES ROUTIERS** (N° RR DEC 21 736) (M. Roger **Arnal**) route de Rodez ☎ 65-71-60-44 Closed Sun. Full-board 150–180F. Evening meals until midnight.

LAPEYRADE 40240 Landes **RD 933 Map 21-A2**
♀ ⊗ ⌂ **LE RELAIS DES BRUYÈRES** (N° RR JANV 27 161) (SARL Palm Gérnte Mme Aline **Lallemant**) Labastide d'Armagnac ☎ 58-93-61-16 ➝ 11 Closed Sun evening and Tues morning (except 15/6 to 15/9, and Nov to Dec.) English and Spanish spoken.

LARDIN (LE) 24570 Dordogne **RN 89 Map 17-A1**
♀ ⊗ ⌂ **RELAIS ST-LAZARE** (N° RR MAI 26 248) (Mme Denise **Baril**) La Galibe RN 87 ☎ 43-51-37-45 ➝ 10.

LAROUILLIES 59219 Nord **RN 2 Map 6-A1/2**
♀ ⊗ **L'AVESNOIS** (N° RR MARS 26 834) (M. and Mme Kléber **Moreau**) ☎ 27-59-22-88 English spoken.

LARRAZET 82500 Tarn-et-Garonne **RD 928 Map 22-A1**
♀ ⊗ **AUBERGE DE LA BARBACANE** (N° RR JANV 26 798) (M. Roland **Cancel**) route d'Auch ☎ 63-20-71-29 ➝ 5 Closed Mon afternoon.

LAUSSEIGNAN-BARBASTE 47230 L.-et-G. **RN 655 Map 21-A2 see BARBASTE**

LAVAL 53000 Mayenne **RN 162 and RD 53 Map 8-B1**
♀ **BAR DE LA GARE** (N° RR JUL 25 493) (Mme Claudia **Helbert**) 107, avenue Robert Buron ☎ 43-53-94-88 Coaches welcome (rest. seats 27).

LAVANS-LES-DOLE 39700 Jura **RN 73 Map 14-A3**
♀ ⊗ ⌂ **LE PANORAMIC** (N° RR MAI 26 238) (Mme Nadège **Hardy**) Orchamps ☎ 84-81-21-41 ➝ 10.

LAVARDAC 47230 L.-et-G. **RN 655 Map 21-B1**
♀ ⊗ ⌂ **LE RELAIS** (N° RR FEV 25 299) (M. Patrick **Caillau**) 8, allée des Alliés ☎ 53-65-54-35 ➝ 8 Closed Fri 3.00pm, Sat 3.00pm. English spoken.

LAVEISSIERE 15300 Cantal **RN 122 Map 17-A2**
♀ ⊗ ⌂ **LE ROCHER FLEURI** (N° RR NOV 26 092) (M. Claude **Chevallier**) La Grande-Granilh ☎ 71-20-01-77 ⊷ Closed Sun, Oct.

LAVERSINES 60510 Oise **RN 31 Map 3-A2**
♀ ⊗ **LE RELAIS ROUTIERS** (N° RR MAI 25 416) (Mme Nadine **Fontaine**) 90, rue St-Germain ☎ 44-07-75-80 Closed Sat and Sun.

LEDENON 30210 Gard **RN 86 Map 24-A2**
♀ ⊗ ⌂ **RELAIS DE LEDENON** (N° RR AVR 25 889) (M. **Brunel and Co**) Nationale 86 ☎ 66-37-12-83 ⊷ 7 Closed Sat, Sun; public holidays. No rooms let Fri night. English spoken.

LEGE 44650 Loire-Atlantique **Map 11-B2**
♀ ⊗ **L'ATHÉMA** (N° RR OCT 27 430) (M. Jacky **Michon**) Centre Commercial Super U ☎ 40-04-93-98. Evening meals.

LENCLOITRE 86140 Vienne **RD 725 Maps 15-B1 and 12-B2**
♀ ⊗ **LE CHAMP DE FOIRE** (N° RR AVR 24 552) (Mme Michelle **Guignon**) 18, place du Champ de Foire ☎ 49-90-74-91 ⊷ 4 Closed Sun. Coaches welcome (rest. seats 70). Evening meals.
♀ ⊗ **AU 14** (N° RR JUIL 26 934) (M. André **Pernelle**) 2, place du Champ de Foire ☎ 49-90-71-29 Closed Sun. Filling stations opposite and at 200m. Closed Sun.

LEROUVILLE 55200 Meuse **RD 964 Map 14-A1**
♀ ⊗ **LE RELAIS DE L'HOTEL DE VILLE** (N° RR MAR 24 171) (Mme Hélène **Ruse**) 23, Rue Nationale ☎ 29-91-06-16 Closed Wed. German spoken.

LESCHELLES 02170 Aisne **RN 30 Map 6-A1**
♀ ⊗ **LE RELAIS DES QUATRE CHEMINS** (N° RR OCT 13 164) (M. Pierre **Rousseaux**) ☎ 23-97-04-88 ⊷ 2 Closed Aug. Rest seats 50. Evening meals until 10pm. Coaches welcome.

LESMONT 10500 Aube **RN 60 Map 9-B3**
♀ ⊗ **LA GUINGUETTE** (N° RR FEV 21 002) (M. Paul **Meurville**) ☎ 25-77-26-48 Closed Mon afternoon.
♀ ⊗ ⌂ **LE RELAIS L'AUBE** (N° RR APR 11 402) (M. Pierre **Ternard**) Route Nationale ☎ 25-92-45-08 ⊷ 5 Closed Sunday, 8 days at Easter and the 15 days of August. Evening meals.

LESQUIN 59810 Nord **Map 5-B1**
♀ ⊗ **CHEZ PASCAL** (N° RR MARS 25 854) (Mme Christiane **Montaigne**) 23, rue Voltaire ☎ 20-86-25-84 Closed Sat, Sun. Evening meals until midnight. English spoken.

LESSARD-EN-BRESSE 71440 S-et-L. **RN 78 Map 18-B1**
♀ ⊗ **RELAIS DU SOLEIL** (N° RR MARS 26 857) (Mme Jeanine **Cristofini**) Place de L'Église ☎ 85-96-40-57 English spoken. Filling station near. Closed Sun. Evening meals until 9pm.

L

LEUE (LA) (Commune de la REORTHE) 85210 Vendee **RN 137 Map 11-B3**
♈ ⊗ ⌂ **LE RELAIS DES ROUTIERS** (N° RR AVR 20 714 bis) (MM. **Carbonneau** and **Dariet**) ☎ 51-94-41-46 ⌐ 7 Closed Sat, Sun; Jul. Coaches welcome (rest. seats 56). Evening meals until 10pm.

LÉVIGNAC-DE-GUYENNE 47120 L.-et-G. **708 D green Map 21-A1**
♈ ⊗ ⌂ **1 Star NN CHEZ DENISE** (N° RR OCT 25 675) (M. Jean **Mamie**) Al. des Promenades ☎ 53-83-72-12 **Minitel** ⌐ 10 Full-board 155–165F. Coaches welcome (rest. seats 200). Evening meals.

LEYMENT 01150 Ain **RN 84 Map 2-A2**
♈ ⊗ ⌂ **LE RELAIS DE LA GARE** (N° RR FEV 27 190) (M. Marcel **Bessière**) 34, rue de la Gare ☎ 74-34-94-30 ⌐ 7 Closed Tues pm and Wed pm, 22/12 to 2/1.

LEZINNES 89160 Yonne **RD 905 Map 13-A3**
♈ ⊗ ⌂ **LE RELAIS DES VOYAGEURS** (N° RR OCT 25 701) (M. Serge **Vermeulen**) 41, Route Nle 905 ☎ 86-75-61-49 ⌐ 9. Coaches welcome. Evening meals.

LIBOURNE 33500 Gironde **RN 89 Map 15-A3**
♈ ⊗ **MOULIN BLANC** (N° RR JANV 27 171) (Mme Geneviève **Fernandez**) 132, av. Georges-Clemenceau ☎ 57-25-01-61 ⌐ 9 Spanish, Italian and German spoken. Full-board 185–200F. (Rest seats 120). Evening meals until 1am.

LIGARDES 32650 Gers **RN 131 and RD 36 Map 21-B2**
♈ ⊗ **LE RELAIS CHEZ DUDULE** (N° RR MAR 21 820) (M. Francis **Dulong**) Route d'Agen ☎ 62-28-85-76.

LIGNANE 13540 B.-du-R. **RN 7 Map 24-B3**
♈ ⊗ **LE RELAIS DE LIGNANE** (N° RR MAR 21 453) (M. Christian **Mondin**) Nationale 7 ☎ 42-92-51-15 Coaches welcome (rest. seats 50). Meals served 11.30am to 2pm and evening. HGV parking.

LIGNOL 56150 Morbihan **RD 782 Map 7-B2**
♈ ⊗ ⌂ **RELAIS DES VOYAGEURS** (N° RR DEC 26 126) (M. Bernard **Le Solliec**) 4, rue de la Marie ☎ 97-27-03-48 **Minitel** ⌐ 7 Closed Mon 1.30pm. Coaches welcome (rest. seats 200). Evening meals until 9.30pm. Full-board 120F.

LIGNY-EN-BARROIS 55500 Meuse **Map 14-A1**
♈ ⊗ **RELAIS DE L'EUROP** (N° RR JUIL 26 943) (M. Mario **Fodde**) ☎ 29-78-00-83 Closed Sat and Sun. Filling station near. Evening meals until 1.30pm. Coaches welcome (rest. seats 96).

LILLE 59000 Nord **R 17 Map 5-B1 6-A3**
♈ ⊗ **L'EDEL WEISS** (N° RR MAR 25 332) (Mme Monique **Duthoit**) 205, rue d'Arras ☎ 20-52-45-29 Closed Aug. Dutch spoken.

LIMAY 78520 Yvelines **Map 3-B2**
♀ ⊗ **LA MARMITE** (N° RR AOU 25 617) (M. Claude **Pesta**) 1, rte de
Meulan ☎ 34-78-65-52 **Minitel** Closed Sun. Evening meals ex-
cept Fri. Polish, English, Spanish, Portuguese spoken.

LIMOGES 87000 Haute-Vienne **RN 20 Map 16-B1**
♀ ⊗ **CHEZ BICHON** (N° RR DEC 23 057) (M. **Houard**) 68, avenue de
Lattre-de-Tassigny ☎ 55-30-68-83 Closed Sat. Evening meals
until 9pm. English, Spanish spoken. Coaches welcome (rest.
seats 30).

LINAS-MONTLHÉRY 93310 Essonne **RN 20 Map 1-B2**
♀ ⊗ **LE JUBILÉ** (N° RR SEPT 25 095) (M. Jacques **Boissier**) ☎ 64-90-
64-45 et 90-23-87.

LIPOSTHEY-PISSOS 40410 Landes **RN 10 Map 20-B1**
♀ ⊗ ⌂ **LE RELAIS CHEZ ALINE** (N° RR MAR 10 433) (Mme **Gros**) ☎
58-82-30-30 ⊷ 7 Closed Sat in winter; Christmas holidays; Full-
board 170–180F per night. Coaches welcome (rest. seats 80).
Evening meals until 9pm.

LIRE 49530 M.-et-L. **RN 763 Map 11-A3**
♀ ⊗ **CHEZ ANGÈLE** (N° RR JUL 25 474) (M. Jean-Claude **Gouraud**)
Les Fourneaux ☎ 40-83-13-10 Closed Mon afternoon; Aug.

LISIEUX 14100 Calvados **RN 13 and CD 579 Map 4-B2**
♀ ⊗ ⌂ **RELAIS PARIS-CHERBOURG** (N° RR MAI 21 902) (M. and
Mme **Pestel**) 113, avenue du Six-Juin ☎ 31-62-06-38 ⊷ 6 Closed
Sun evening; Sept for 15 days. Full board 158–80F per night.
Coaches welcome (rest. seats 40). Evening meals.
♀ ⊗ **PILE OU FACE** (N° RR JUN 25 443) (Mme Gisèle **Bellemont**) 68,
Bld Herbert Fournet ☎ 31-62-06-09 Closed Sun. Coaches welco-
me (rest. seats 52). Evening meals. Spanish spoken.
♀ ⊗ **LE RELAIS DE L'AGRICULTURE** (N° RR MARS 27 212) (M.
Andre **Fiaut**) 23, rue du Gal-Leclerc ☎ 31-31-44-18 ⊷ 10 Closed
Sun.

LISSAY LOCHY 18340 Cher **RD 28/73 Map 13-B1**
♀ ⊗ **AUBERGE DES MAISONS ROUGES** (N° RR MARS 26 473) (M.
Robert **Leger**) Levet ☎ 48-64-76-07 **Minitel** Closed Sat; Dec.
Evening meals.

LES LISSES 91100 Villabe Essonne **Autoroute A6 Map 1-B2**
♀ ⊗ **RESTOP DES LISSES** (N° RR RA-4) (M. Jean **Lamotte**), J.-C.
Després) Aire de Service des Lisses ☎ 60-86-22-51 Self-service
restaurant 11.00am to 10.00pm. TV. Showers.

LIT ET MIXE 41170 Landes **CD 652 Map 20-A2**
♀ ⊗ **Grill RESTO GRILL** (N° RR OCT 27 056) (M. Phillippe **Labro**)
route de Mimizan ☎ 58-42-84-91 English spoken.

LIVRON-SUR-DROME 26250 Drôme) **Map 24-A1**
♀ ⊗ ⌂ **AUBERGE MACAMP** (N° RR JUIL 27 136) (Mme Josiane

L

Vocanson) Francy ☎ 75-61-73-91 **Minitel** ⌐ 17 Evening meals.

Ⓨ Ⓧ **BAR DE LA PETANQUE-CHEZ SYLVIE** (N° RR DEC 27 482) (Mme Sylvie **Perey**) 23, Avenue J. Combier ☎ 75-85-62-85 Closed Wednesday. Evening meals. Spanish spoken. Service station open 24 hours 500m away.

LODEVE 34700 Hérault **RN 9 Map 23-A2**

Ⓨ Ⓧ **LE RELAIS DE LA FONTAINE D'AMOUR** (N° RR JUN 21 149) (Mme Renée **Granier**) Nationale 9 ☎ 67-44-02-77. Closed Tue. Evening meals.

Ⓨ Ⓧ **RELAIS DE LA CROIX** (N° RR JUN 26 910) (M. Jean-Dennis **Roig**) Cartels ☎ 67-44-00-72 ⌐ 6 Closed weekends; 10–30 Oct.. Filling station 5kms. Car park (3,300 m^2). Full-board 130–180F. Rest seats 70.

Ⓨ Ⓧ **LE RELAIS DE L'ESCALETTE** (N° RR FEV 24 852) (M. Lucien **Mirman**) Rte Nationale 9 ☎ 67-44-01-14 ⌐ 22 Closed Sat; Oct. Full board 150–170F per night. Coaches welcome (rest. seats 80). Evening meals. English, Italian, Spanish spoken.

LOGE (LA) par THEILLAY 41390 Loir-et-Cher **RN 20 Map 13-B1**

Ⓨ Ⓧ ⌂ **1 Star NN LE RELAIS DE LA LOGE** (N° RR JAN 25 249) (M. Guy **Paillaud**) ☎ 54-83-37-20 ⌐ 40 Open 24 hours. Coaches ⌐ welcome (rest. seats 170). Evening meals. English spoken.

LOGRON 28200 Eure-et-Loire **Map 8-B3**

Ⓨ Ⓧ **AUBERGE SAINT NICHOLAS** (N° RR OCT 27 400) (M. Bruno **Hubert**) 2 Rue des Buigonnotts ☎ 37-98-98-02. Closed Monday pm, Sunday pm and 15 days at New Year. Evening meals until 9pm.

LOIGNE-SUR-MAYENNE 53200 Mayenne **Map 12-A1**

Ⓨ Ⓧ **CAFÉ DES SPORTS** (N° RR JUIN 27 314) (M. José **Atlan**) 2, rue de la Roche-du-Maine ☎ 43-07-19-10 Closed Mon pm and first two weeks of August. English spoken. Evening meals.

LOIRE 49480 Maine-et-Loire **Map 11-A3**

Ⓨ Ⓧ **LE RELAIS DES SPORTS** (N° RR AVR 24 551) (M. Phillippe **Audouin**) Bourg ☎ 41-92-20-64 Evening meals.

LOISON-SOUS-LENS 62218 P.-de-C **Map 5-B3**

Ⓨ Ⓧ ⌂ **LE PRESIDENT** (N° RR MARS 27 221) (M. **Fauer**) 7/9, rue de Lille ☎ 21-78-51-95 ⌐ 5 Closed Sun.

LOISY 54700 PONT-A-MOUSSON Meurethe-et-Moselle **Autoroute A-31 Maps 10-A1 and 14-B1**

Ⓨ Ⓧ **RESTAURANT TOURNEBRIDE** Aire de Service de Pont-à-Mousson Loisy ☎ 83-81-18-89 Food served 11.30am to 3.00pm, 7.00pm to 10.00pm. Open 24 hours in summer. English, Spanish spoken.

🏆 **Les Routiers Total Service Station – LE RELAIS DE L'OB-RION** (N° RR AVR 22 779) (**Cogesta**) Autoroute A31 Pont-à-Mousson ☎ 83-81-03-85 Open 24 hours. English, Spanish, Italian spoken.

L

LONGEAU-LE-VALLINOT 52600 Haute-Marne **RN 67 Map 14-A2**
Ɏ ⊗ ⌂ **L'AUBERGE ROUTIERE** (N° RR AVR 17 783) (M. Georges
Groscolas) ☎ 25-88-42-16 ⊷ 10 Closed Sat evening in winter,
Sept. Full-board 140–145F per night. Coaches welcome (rest.
seats 60).
Ɏ ⊗ ⌂ **LE CAFÉ DES ROUTIERS** (N° RR JUL 21 994) (Mme Edwige
Denis) Rte Nle ☎ 25-88-40-51 ⊷ 7 Closed Fri evening. Full-board
150–170F. Coaches welcome (rest. seats 50/25). Evening meals
until 10pm.

LONGEVILLE-LES-SAINT-AVOLD 57740 Moselle **Autoroute A32
Map 10-A1 see ST-AVOLD**
⛽ **Antar Service Station RELAIS SARRE LORRAINE** (N° RR JUL
25 043) (M. Jean-Pierre **Duytschaevel**) Autoroute ☎ 87-92-23-89
Open 24 hours English, German spoken.

LONGAVILLE 54810 M.-et-M. **RN 52 Map 6-A3**
Ɏ ⊗ **LE RELAIS DE LA DOUANE** (N° RR AVR 18 684) (Mme Liliane
Gaudelet-Bonnarue) 8, avenue du Luxembourg Frontière
France-Luxembourg ☎ 82-23-29-19 Closed Aug. English, Ger-
man spoken.

LONGUE 49160 M.-et-L. **RN 138 Map 12-A2**
Ɏ ⊗ **LE RELAIS DES SOUVENETS** (N° RR SEP 25 632) (Mme Réjane
Taugourdeau) RN 147 ☎ 41-52-13-86 Closed Sat afternoon, Sun;
end Aug. Evening meals.
Ɏ ⊗ **RELAIS DE LA GARE** (N° RR AVR 26 499) (M. Pascal **Desert**)
22, rue Michel-Couet ☎ 41-52-10-37.

LONGUEAU 80330 Somme **RN 35 Map 5-A3**
Ɏ ⊗ ⌂ **LE REALIS DE L'HOTEL DE VILLE** (N° RR SEP 23 944) (M.
Konidor **Bellaredj**) 105, avenue Henri-Barbusse ☎ 22-46-16-14 ⊷
10 Closed Sun. English, Arabic spoken.

LONS 64140 Pyr.Atl. **see PAU**

LORIOL 26270 Drôme **RN 7 Map 24-A1**
Ɏ ⊗ **RELAIS SAINT PAUL** (N° RR MARS 26 214) (M. Albert **Begot**)
RN 7 ☎ 75-61-76-31 Closed Mon.

LORRIS 45260 Loiret **RD 961 Map 13-A1**
Ɏ ⊗ **LE RELAIS DES ROUTIERS** (N° RR AOU 16 655) (M. Baptiste
Charbonnier) 21, Grande-Rue ☎ 38-92-40-64. Rest seats 85.
Evening meals until midnight.
Ɏ ⊗ ⌂ **AUBERGE DE LA CROIX ROUGE** (N° RR MARS 26 861) (M.
Jean-Yves **Charrier**) 28, rue Guillaume de Lorris ☎ 38-92-87-03.
Open 7am – 9pm. Filling station at 700 metres.

LOUDEAC 22600 C. du N. **Map 7-B2**
Ɏ ⊗ **RELAIS DU STOP** (N° RR OCT 20 868) (M. **Kerizoret**) Le Haut
Breuil ☎ 96-28-01-76.
Ɏ ⊗⌂ **1 Star NN REST. LES ROUTIERS** (N° RR JANV 26 426) (M.
and Mme Dominique **Le Cozannet**) 7, rue Lavergne ☎ 96-28-01-

L

Loudeac continued

44 ⊸ 40 from 60–110F, breakfast 14F, telephone in room. Closed Sun evening; Aug. Full-board 140–160F per night. Coaches welcome (rest. seats 180). Car park; bar; dogs allowed.

LOUHANS 71500 S.-et-L. **RN 78 Map 18-B1**

♀ ⊗ **LE ROUTIERS** (N° RR MAR 18 031) (Mme **Alexandre**) 19, rue Lucien Guillemot ☎ 85-75-11-75. Closed Sun; Aug. Coaches welcome. Evening meals.

LOULAY 17330 Charente-Marit. **RN 150 Map 15-A2**

♀ ⊗ ⌂ **LE RELAIS CHEZ NENETTE** (N° RR OCT 20 856) (Mme Renée **Rullier**) place de-Gaulle ☎ 46-33-80-59 ⊸ 5 Closed Sun (except by arrangement). Coaches welcome (rest. seats 100/30). Evening meals.

♀ ⊗ **LE COUCOU** (N° RR MAI 26 536) (Mme Antoinette **Couturier**) Tout-y-Faut Vergne ☎ 46-33-90-16 Closed Sat off season.

LOUPE (LA) 28240 Eure-et-Loir **RN 23 Map 8-B3**

♀ ⊗ **LA HURIE CHEZ BEATRICE** (N° RR OCT 26 029) (Mme Béatrice **Collin**) La Hurie St-Victor-de-Buthon ☎ 37-81-30-38 Closed Sun. Evenings meals until 10.30pm. English spoken.

LOUPLANDE 72780 Sarthe **RN 768 Map 8-B2**

♀ ⊗ ⌂ **LE RELAIS DE L'HOTEL DE FRANCE – Les Routiers** (N° RR MAI 11 344) (M. and Mme **Fretault**) ☎ 43-88-52-18 ⊸ 7 Closed Fri, 1pm; Aug. Full-board 120–150F per night. Coaches welcome (rest. seats 160). Evening meals.

LOUVIERS 27400 Eure **RN 154 Map 3-B1**

♀ ⊗ **AU RENDEZ-VOUS DES SPORTIFS Chez Jeannot** (N° RR OCT 22 546) (M. Jean **Hébert**) 27, avenue Winston-Churchill ☎ 32-40-02-00 Closed Sat, Sun; public holidays; Jul.

♀ ⊗ **LE RELAIS DES ROUTIERS** (N° RR MAR 23 714) (Mme **Quesney**) 13, rue de Paris ☎ 32-40-29-22 Closed Sun. Coaches welcome (rest. seats 100). Evening meals until 1am.

LUANT 36350 Indre **Map 16-A1**

♀ ⊗ **RELAIS ROUTIERS** (N° RR SEPT 27 376) (M. Jacky **Michaud**) Lothiers ☎ 54-36-76-43. Service station nearby.

LUART (LE) 72390 Sarthe **near RN23/RD29 Map 8-B2**

♀ ⊗ **LES LABOUREURS** (N° RR SEPT 25 668) (M. **Gay**) 2, Place de L'Eglise, Dollon ☎ 43-93-44-06 Closed Sun afternoons. English spoken. Coaches welcome (rest. seats 70).

LUBBON 40240 Landes **RD 933 Map 21-A2**

♀ ⊗ ⌂ **LE RELAIS CHEZ MAMY** (N° RR FEV 20 116) (M. Louis **Nicoletto**) ☎ 58-93-60-47 ⊸ 9 Closed Sat evening; Oct. Coaches please reserve (rest. seats 70). Evening meals. Full-board 140F. Italian spoken.

LUÇAY LE MALE 36360 Indre **Map 12-B3**

♀ ⊗ ⌂ **LE DAUPHIN** (N° RR MARS 26 843) (M. Patrick **Rebout**) 7,

Place Verdun. ☎ 54-40-41-17 ⟶ 3 Car park (3,000 m²). Filling
station (7.30am–8.30pm). Full-board 100–150F. Coaches welcome
(rest. seats 110).

LUCEAU 72500 Sarthe **RN 138 Map 12-A2**
♀ ⊗ **LA CROIX DE PAILLE** (N° RR OCT 24 744) (M. **Moreau**) Route
du Mans **Château de Loir** ☎ 43-44-05-50 **Minitel** Closed Sun
except for banquets; Aug. Meals served until 1am.

LUDE (LE) 72800 Sarthe **Map 12-A2**
♀ ⊗ **LE RELAIS DES PECHEURS** (N° RR DEC 23 061) (M. **Moire**) 14,
boulevard de l'Hospice ☎ 43-94-61-03 Closed Sun afternoon in
winter. Coaches welcome (rest. seats 40/25). Evening meals.

LUMBRES 62380 Pas-de-Calais **Map 5-A2**
♀ ⊗ **HOTEL MODERNE** (N° RR SEPT 26 271) (M. Pierre **Fichaux**)
18, rue François-Cousin ☎ 21-39-62-87 Closed Sun; Aug. Full-
board 140–170F. Rest seats 70. Evening meals until 9pm.

LURE 70200 Haute-Saône **RN 19 Maps 10-A3 and 14-B2**
♀ ⊗ ⌂ **LE PETIT RELAIS** (N° RR JUL 24 643) (Mme Monique
Carrière) 4, rue Albert Mathiez ☎ 84-30-03-53 ⟶ 8 Closed Sun.
Evening meals. Coaches welcome (rest. seats 30). Full-board
130F.

LUSIGNY-SUR-BARSE 10270 Aube **RN 19 Map 9-B3**
♀ ⊗ ⌂ **AUBERGE DES PRAIRIES** (N° RR NOV 25 173) (Mme
Monique **Mireaux**) ☎ 25-41-20-32 ⟶ 5 Full-board 145–150F per
night. Coaches welcome (rest. seats 60). Evening meals.

LUSSAC-LES-CHATEAUX 86320 Vienne **RN 147 Map 15-B1**
♀ ⊗ **LE CHENE VERT** (N° RR AVR 26 874) (Mme Alexandrine **Dos
Reis Martins**) 14, avenue Léon-Pineau ☎ 49-48-40-30 Closed
Sun. English, Italian, German, Spanish, Portuguese spoken. Car
park (2,000m²) Filling station (7am–12pm). Rest seats 90.

LUSSANT 17680 Charente-Maritime **CD 739 Map 11-B1**
♀ ⊗ ⌂ **CHEZ MOI** (N° RR AOUT 26 983) (SARL **Guerin and Sons**) Le
Bourg ☎ 46-83-42-44 ⟶ 10 English spoken. Filling station near.
Full-board 160–200F. Rest seats 100. Evening meals until mid-
night.

LUTTERBACH 68460 Haut-Rhin **RN 66 Map 10-B3**
⚑ **Elf Service Station – LE RELAIS DES CHEVEREUILS** (N° RR
DEC 24 039) (M. Roland **Heid**) RN 66 ☎ 89-52-14-66 Closed Sun.
German spoken.

LUTZ-EN-DUNOIS 28200 Eure-et-Loire **Map 8-B3**
♀ ⊗ ⌂ **LA RENCONTRE** (N° RR JUIN 27 299) (M. Francis **Berrier**) ☎
37-45-18-08 ⟶ 5 Closed Sun.

LUZENAC-GARANOU 09250 Ariège **RN 20 Map 22-A3**
♀ ⊗ ⌂ **LE RELAIS DES ROUTIERS** (N° RR DEC 24 041) (Mme Marie

L

Luzenac-Garanou continued
Pires) Avenue de la Gare ☎ 61-64-47-13 ➡ 9 Spanish, Portuguese spoken.

LYON 69007 Rhône **RN 6 and 7 Maps 2-A2 and 18-B2**
♀ ⊗ **LES ROUTIERS** (N° RR JUL 21 983) (M. Pierre **Sala**) 21, quai Perrache ☎ 78-37-75-86 Closed Sat, Sun; Aug. Evening meals until 1am. Coaches welcome (rest. seats 40).

M

MABLY 42300 Loire **see ROANNE**

MACHECOUL 44270 Loire-Atlantique
♀ ⊗ ⌂ **LA BICYCLETTE D'ARGENT** (N° RR JAN 27 504) (Mme Marie-Josephe **Baudry**) 6, place du Pont ☎ 40-78-50-48 ➡ 6 Closed Saturday afternoon, Sunday afternoon, 18–25 Feb; 22 Dec–1 Jan. Evening meals until 9.30pm. Parking. English spoken.

MADELEINE-BOUVET (LA) 61110 Orne **RD 920 and 36 Map 8-B3**
♀ ⊗ **LE RELAIS PECHEURON** (N° RR OCT 24 355) (M. Alain **Jouanneau**) Le Bourg ☎ 33-73-93-00 Closed Wed afternoon; 15 days in Feb. English spoken.

MAGNAC-BOURG 87380 Hte-Vienne **RN 20 Map 17-A1**
♀ ⊗ **LE RELAIS PARIS-TOULOUSE** (N° RR JUL 24 629) (M. **Meriadec**) ☎ 55-00-81-53 Closed Wed; (except Jul, Aug). Coaches welcome (rest. seats 35). Evening meals until 1am.

MAGNAN 32100 Gers **CD 6 Map 21-A2**
♀ ⊗ **LE FER À CHEVAL** (N° RR SEPT 27 022) (Mme Melanie **Bolajuzon**) route le Houga-Nogaro ☎ 62-09-04-24 Closed Wednesday pm.

MAGNANAC par VILLEMUR-SUR-TARN 331340 Haute-Garonne **RN 630 Map 22-A2**
♀ ⊗ ⌂ **LE RELAIS DE LA GARE** (N° RR OCT 24 737) (Mme Fabienne **Degoul**) 65, rue de Beauvais ☎ 34-67-20-70 ➡ 10 Closed Sun. Portuguese spoken.
♀ ⊗ ⌂ **CHEZ FRANÇOISE** (N° RR SEPT 26 331) (Mme **Rossi**) ☎ 61-09-01-87 or 61-09-32-72 ➡ 4 Closed Sat evening Sun; 15 to 22 Aug. Evening meals until 9pm. Coaches welcome (rest. seats 85).

MAGNY-EN-VEXIN 95420 Val d'Oise **Map 3-B2**
♀ ⊗ **HOTEL DE LA GARE** (N° RR OCT 24 737) (Mme **Degoul**) 65, rue de Beauvais ☎ 34-67-20-70 Full-board 125–160F per night. Coaches welcome (rest. seats 50). Evening meals until 10.30pm.

M

MAGNY-LA-CAMPAGNE 14270 Calvados **RD 40 Map 4-B2**
♀ ⊗ **A LA VALLÉE D'AUGE – Tobacconist** (N° RR AVR 21 502)
(Mme Marie-Thérèse **Sevin**) ☎ 31-20-04-20 Service station.
Closed Tue; Jul.

MAINBORGÈRE (LA) 85320 Vendée **RD 746 Map 11-B3**
♀ ⊗ **LE RELAIS ROUTIER DE LA MAINBORGÈRE** (N° RR AVR 23
763) (M. Michel **Hémery**) Mareuil-sur-Lay ☎ 51-31-91-24 Closed
Sat, Sun. Evening meals until 8.30pm.

MAINVILLIERS 28300 Eure-et-Loire **Map 8-B3**
♀ ⊗ **CAFÉ ROUTE** Autoroute A11 (M. Philippe **Blanc**) Aire de
Gasville Paris-Province direction ☎ 37-31-62-42 Self-service restaurant open 6.45am to 11.00pm.
♀ ⊗ **CAFÉ ROUTE** (M. Éric **Grujaro**) Autoroute A11 Province-Paris
direction Aire de Bois Paris ☎ 27-31-62-41 Self-service restaurant
open 7.00am to 10.30pm.

MAISON DIEU see GUILLON

MAISON-NEUVE Commune QUENOCHE-par-RIOZ 70190 Haute-
Saône **RN 57 Maps 10-A3 and 14-B2/3**
♀ ⊗ ⌂ **LES ROUTIERS MAISON NEUVE** (N° RR NOV 26 371) (Mme
Marie-Hélene **Moureau**) ☎ 84-91-80-54 ⇥ 9 Closed Sun in
winter; beginning of Jan. Full-board 135–160F per night. Evening
meals until 8.30pm.

MAISONS-LAFITTE 78600 Yvelines **Porte Maillot Map 1-A2**
♀ ⊗ **LE RALLYE** (N° RR FEV 23 650) (M. Jacques **Lalanne**) 17, rue
des plantes ☎ 39-62-44-28 Closed Sun; Aug.

MALAKOFF 92240 Hts-de Seine **RN 306 Map 1-B2**
♀ ⊗ **BAR LE DÉPART** (N° RR OCT 24 399) (M. Armand **Alle**) 64,
avenue Pierre Brossolette ☎ 46-57-76-05 Closed Sun; Aug. Evening meals.

MALE 61260 Orne **RN 23 Map 8-B3**
♀ ⊗ ⌂ **HOTEL DE LA BELLE RENCONTRE** (N° RR OCT 25 129)
(M. André **Carle**) Le Gibet ☎ 37-49-68-85 ⇥ 6 Closed Sun
(except for coaches, banquets) and 15–30 August. Coaches
welcome (rest. seats 130). Evening meals until 8.30pm.

MALEMORT 19360 Corrèze **RN 89 Map 17-A1**
♀ ⊗ **CHEZ PAULETTE** (N° RR JAN 23 604) (Mme Paulette **Vergne**) 2,
avenue Pierre et Marie Curie ☎ 55-24-28-14 Closed Sun; Aug.
Coaches welcome (rest. seats 90).

MALTAVERNE Commune de TRACY-LOIRE 58150 Nièvre **RN 7
Map 13-B2**
♀ ⊗ **LE RELAIS DES ROUTIERS** (N° RR OCT 24 007) (M. **Robillot**) ☎
58-28-15-34 Closed Sat afternoon, Sun; 10 to 31 Aug. Evening
meals.
♀ ⊗ **LA BRISE** (N° RR JIII, 27 330) (Mme Marie-Madeleine **Bous-
touker**) 10 Place de l'Eperon ☎ 43-28-20-52. Closed Saturday.

M

MANS (LE) 72000 Sarthe **RN 23 Map 8-B2**

Y ⊗ **CHEZ GABY** (N° RR MARS 27 235) (Mme Marie-Thérèse **Coutable**) 8, rue du Pied-Sec ☎ 43-84-24-48 Closed Sat pm, Sun and August.

Y ⊗ **L'AUTO-CLUB** (N° RR JUN 23 340) (M. Rémy **Adet**) 239 bis, avenue Bollée ☎ 43-84-70-73 Closed Sun and the week of August 15th. Coaches welcome (rest. seats 60). Evening meals served until 9.30pm.

MANTES-LA-JOLIE 78200 Yvelines **RN 13 Map 1-A1**

Y ⊗ ⌂ **LA CURE D'AIR** (N° RR FEV 26 175) (M. Jean-Claude **Ammar**) 161, bld du Mal-Juin ☎ 30-94-29-15 **Minitel** ⇀ 9 Closed Sat. Coaches welcome (rest. seats 200). Evening meals.

Y ⊗ **LE NOVELTY** (N° RR MAI 26 535) (Mme Marc **Laurent**) 47, rue de la Papeterie ☎ 30-94-03-04 Closed Sun; Aug.

MANTES-LA-VILLE 78200 Yvelines **RN 13 Map 1-A1**

Y ⊗ **LA DEMI-LUNE** (N° RR DEC 26 129) (Mme Nicolas **Petitpas**) 51, boulevard Roger Salengro ☎ 34-77-03-66 Closed Sat afternoon, Sun.

Y ⊗ **LE HOUDAN BAR** (N° RR AVR 23 747) (M. Mohamed **Benariba**) 43, route de Houdan ☎ 34-77-06-11 **Minitel** Closed Sun. Meals served until 9pm.

MANTHELAN 37240 Indre-et-Loire **Map 12-B3**

Y ⊗ **LE RELAIS DE LA CROIX-VERTE** (N° RR SEP 21 626) (Mme **Martin**) 25, rue Nationale ☎ 47-92-80-16 English spoken.

Y ⊗ **RELAIS DE LA PROMENADE** (N° RR MAI 26 243) 5, Mail de la Mairie ☎ 47-92-80-39 Evening meals. English spoken.

MARAIS (AUX) 60000 Oise **RN 181 Map 3-A2**

Y ⊗ **AU GRAND "R"** (N° RR NOV 26 369) (M. Marcel **Boutoille**) 125, route de Gisors ☎ 44-48-18-66 **Minitel** Closed Sun; 5–27 Aug. Evening meals until 9pm.

MARCHE (LA) 58400 Nièvre **RN 7 Map 13-B2**

Y ⊗ **LE RELAIS DES ROUTIERS** (N° RR JAN 22 150) (M. Jany **Larive**) ☎ 86-70-14-11 Closed Wed and 10th to 20th June.

MARCHELEPOT 80200 Somme **Map 5-B3**

Y ⊗ ⌂ **HOTEL DU PARC – Rest. Oriental – Chez Dahmane** (N° RR MAR 24 531) (M. Dahmane **Houady**) Rte Nationale 17 ☎ 22-84-04-85 ⇀ 6.

MARCILY-LA-CAMPAGNE 27320 Eure **Map 8-A3**

Y ⊗ **LE RELAIS EUROPEAN** (N° RR SEPT 27 382) (SNC Mme **Fieneder**) Tivoly ☎ 32-58-31-75 Closed Saturday pm, Sunday; August. English, German spoken.

MARCONNELLE 62140 P.-de-C. **Map 5-A2**

Y ⊗ **LE DAUPHIN** (N° RR MAR 24 870) (Mme Josiane **Dauphin**) 948, Rte Nationale 39 ☎ 21-86-83-64 Closed Wed.

M

MARES (LES) 27160 Eure **RD 840 Map 8-A3**
℗ ⊗ **LE RELAIS DES MARES** (N° RR NOV 26 743) (M. **Guiot**) Les
Chesnes-Breteuil-sur-Iton ☎ 32-29-85-09 Closed Sat pm, Sun.
Coaches welcome (rest. seats 30). Evening meals until midnight.

MAREUIL-SUR-LAY 85320 Vendée **RN 746 Map 11-A1**
℗ ⊗ ⌂ **LE STOP BAR** (N° RR AVR 19 037) (M. Claude **Chavignois**)
rue Principale ☎ 51-30-52-72 ⇒ 5 Closed Sat.

MAREUIL-SUR-OURCQ 60890 Oise **RD 936 Map 3-B3**
℗ ⊗ **RESTAURANT DE ROUTIERS** (N° RR SEP 22 927) (Mme
Huguette **Picard**) 7, rue de Meaux à Bourneville ☎ 23-96-72-11
Evening meals until 8pm.

MARGON 28400 Eure-et-Loir **Map 8-B3**
℗ ⊗ **L'ESPÉRANCE** (N° RR OCT 26 360) (M. Marc **Robinet**) Nogent-
le-Rotrou ☎ 37-52-19-03 **Minitel** Evening meals served until
8.30pm. Closed Sun and New Year. Coaches welcome (rest.
seats 90).

MARIGNAC 31440 Haute-Garonne **Map 21-B3**
℗ ⊗ ⌂ **1 Star NN LE PIC DU GAR** (N° RR MAI 27 289) (M. Henri
Fourment) Rue Jean-Jaurès ☎ 61-79-50-57 ⇒ 25 Rooms 80–130F
Breakfast 15 to 20F. Spanish spoken. Evening meals.

MARGUERITTES 30320 Gard **A9 Map 24-A2/3**
℗ ⊗ ⌂ **LE RELAIS DE LA PINÈDE** (N° RR OCT 26 066) (Mme
Monique **Brouzet**) ☎ 66-26-03-63 Closed Sun low season. Spanish
spoken.

MARLES-LES-MINES 62540 Pas-de-Calais **Map 5-A1**
℗ ⊗ **LE 74** (N° AVR 26 877) (M. Bertrand **Schatt**) 74, rue Jean-Jaurès
☎ 21-65-53-71 English, German spoken. Closed Sun. Evening
meals.

MARMANDE 47200 L.-et-G. **RN 113 and 133 Map 21-A1**
℗ ⊗ ⌂ **2 Stars NN LE RELAIS DU LION D'OR** (N° RR AOU 17 345)
⊖ **(Ets Beaulieu SARL)** 1, rue de la République ☎ 53-64-21-30 ⇒
50 Open 24 hours. English, Spanish, Italian spoken. Full-board
220–280F. Evening meals until 10pm.
℗ ⊗ ⌂ **LE RELAIS** (N° RR FEV 24 860) (M. Hervé **Pouchet**) 93, bld
Ulysse-Casse ☎ 53-64-26-96 ⇒ 8 Closed Sun.

MAROLLES par BROUE 28260 E.-et-L. **RN 12 Map 8-A3**
℗ ⊗ **AU RELAIS DE MAROLLES** (N° RR SEP 18 193 (Mme Viviane
⊖ **Beauvais**) 44, rue Georges-Bréant ☎ 37-43-20-50 Closed Sat
(except for banquets); Sun; 1st fortnight Aug. Coaches welcome
(3 dining rooms = 150 seats). Evening meals until midnight.
Specialities: *Escalope normande, Omelette aux pleurotte,* Grills.
Menus 55–85F.

MAROLLES-SUR-SEINE 77130 S.-et-M. **RN 51 Map 9-B2**
℗ ⊗ **AU RENDEZ-VOUS DES PECHEURS ET DES CHASSEURS**

M

Marolles-Sur-Seine continued
(N° RR NOV 19 566) (Mme **Bodic**) 70, Grande Rue ☎ 64-31-32-20
⊸ 3. Closed Sun. Evening meals.

MAROLLETTE 72600 Sarthe **Map 8-B2**
♀ ⊗ **LE RENDEZ-VOUS DES CHASSEURS** (N° RR SEPT 26 038) (M.
Norbert **Vaidie**) Le Bourg ☎ 43-97-67-00 Closed Tue pm; Aug.
Coaches welcome (rest. seats 80). Evening meals until 10pm.

MARQUEFAVE 31390 Hte-Gar. **RN 117 Map 22-A2**
♀ ⊗ ⌂ **1 Star NN LE RELAIS CHEZ ROGER** (N° RR JUL 13 851) (M.
Roger **Descuns**) ☎ 61-87-85-07 ⊸ 10 from 60 to 80F, access for
disabled. Closed Sun; Oct. Evening meals. Car park; bar; dogs
allowed; recreations (fishing, shooting); sports (*pétanque*).

MARSAC EN LIVRADOIS 63940 Puy-de-Dôme **RN 106 Map 17-A3**
♀ ⊗ ⌂ **1 Star NN LE KALLISTE** (N° RR AVR 26 516) (M. Yves
Graglia) ☎ 73-95-60-78 ⊸ 18 from 80 to 130F, breakfast 15–18F.
Closed Mon pm and Feb. Coaches welcome. Evening meals.
Portuguese and English spoken. Car park; bar; dogs allowed;
recreations (zoo, fishing, walks); museum.

MARSAN 32270 Gers **RN 124 Map 21-B2**
♀ ⊗ **RELAIS 124** (N° RR SEPT 26 990) (M. Fernand **Castaing**) Aubiet
☎ 62-65-63-43 **Minitel** Closed Sat, Sun, bank holidays, one week
in August and December. English spoken. Evening meals served
until 11.30pm. Filling station near.

MARSEILLE 13000 B.-du-R. **RN 8 Map 24-B3**
♀ ⊗ **LE RELAIS DE L'INDEPENDANCE** (N° RR SEP 21 657) (Mme
Potoudis) 234, bld de Paris ☎ 91-91-21-89 Closed Sun.
♀ ⊗ **LE RELAIS DES AMIS** (N° RR JUN 15 693) (M. Raymond
Servière) 188, boulevard de Paris ☎ 91-62-60-76 **Minitel** Closed
Sun; public holidays; Aug. Coaches welcome (rest. seats 60).
Evening meals.
♀ ⊗ **AUX DELICES DE MOUREPIANE** (N° RR OCT 25 136) (M.
Daniel **Barnabon**) 578, chemin du Littoral ☎ 91-46-08-11 Closed
Sun. Coaches welcome (rest. seats 100). Evening meals served
until 11pm. Italian spoken.
♀ ⊗ **LE RELAIS** (N° RR OCT 26 342) (Mlle **Commeau**) 40, quai du
Lazaret ☎ 91-90-93-02 Closed Sat, Sun, 2 weeks in Aug. Coaches
welcome (rest. seats 80). Evening meals served until 11pm.
♀ ⊗ ⌂ **O'ROUTIERS-ANJOLY** (N° RR MAI 27 274) (M. William
Lequem) Centre Routier Z.A. d'Anjoy ☎ 42-75-19-60 **Minitel** ⊸
47 with shower. English, Spanish and Italian spoken. Evening
meals served until midnight.
♀ ⊗ ⌂ **1 star NN BEAULIEU-GLARIS** (N° RR NOV 27 085) (M. Yvon
Garros) 1/3 Place des Marseillaises ☎ 91-90-70-59 **Minitel** ⊸ 35
Closed Sat and Sun (hotel always open). English and Arabic
spoken.

MARTEL 46600 Lot **RD 703 Souillac-Figeac Map 17-B1**
♀ ⊗ **LA FONTANELLE – CHEZ FRANÇOISE** (N° RR OCT 26 073)
(Mme Françoise **Anger**) Avenue de Nassogne ☎ 65-37-31-59 ⊸

4 Closed Wed afternoon in winter; Wed in summer, 2.00pm to 6.00pm. Full-board 140F per night. English spoken.

MARTIGNE-FERCHAUD 35640 I.-et-V. **RN 178 Maps 8-B1 and 12-A1**

☖ ⊗ ⌂ **LE RELAIS DU POT D'ETAIN** (N° RR JAN 10 229) (Mme Yvonne **Bouteiller**) 10, Grand Rue ☎ 99-47-90-12 ⊷ 8 Closed Sun evening and 15th–31st August. Evening meals served.

MARTINCAMP 76270 S.-Mme **RD 915 Map 3-A1**

☖ ⊗ **RELAIS DE LA FORET D'EAWY** (N° RR DEC 26 404) (M. Michel **Yon**) Neufchâtel-en-Bray ☎ 35-93-07-03 Closed Wed; end Aug. Coaches welcome (rest. seats 50). Evening meals. English spoken.

MARVEJOLS 48100 Lozère **RN 9 Map 17-B3**

☖ ⊗ ⌂ **2 stars NN REST DE LA PAIX** (N° RR NOV 26 735) (M. Jean-Jacques **Bourguignon**) 2, ave Brazza ☎ 66-32-10-17 ⊷ 19 English, Spanish spoken. Full-board (160 and 180F). Coaches welcome (rest. seats 70). Evening meals served until 9pm.

MARZAN 56230 Morbihan **Map 11-A2**

☖ ⊗ **LES RIVES DE VILAINE** (N° RR OCT 27 393) M. Gilles **Jouan**) 13 rue de la Fontaine ☎ 99-90-63-22 **Minitel** Evening meals served until 10pm.

MASSERET 19510 Corrèze **RN 20 Map 17-A1**

☖ ⊗ ⌂ **LE RELAIS DES VOYAGEURS** (N° RR DEC 21 714) (M. Michel **Pons**) ☎ 55-73-40-11 Closed Mon. Evening meals served until 10pm.

MASSEUBE 32140 Gers **RN 129 Map 21-B2/3**

☖ ⊗ **LE RELAIS CHEZ YVETTE** (N° RR JUN 12 898) (Mme Yvette **Beyries**) ☎ 62-66-02-14 Closed Sun; and August.

MATHIEU 14920 Calvados **RD 7 Map 4-B2**

☖ ⊗ **RELAIS LA COTE DE NACRE** (N° RR OCT 26 068) (M. Marc **Bedeau de l'Écochère**) 4, rue Auguste-Fresnel ☎ 31-44-10-17 ⊷ 2 Closed Sun and 15 days in December. Full-board 170F per night. Evening meals. Coaches welcome (rest. seats 38).

MAUBEUGE 59600 Nord **RN 2 Map 6-A3**

☖ ⊗ ⌂ **AUX ARCADES Chez Ginette** (N° RR AVR 26 522) (M. Claude **Spittel**) 260, route de Mons ☎ 27-64-60-94 ⊷ 8 Closed Sun afternoon. Full-board 140–180F per night. Coaches welcome (rest. seats 45). Evening meals until 2am (midnight Mon).

☖ ⊗ **AUX ROUTIERS** (N° RR NOV 23 009) (Mme Jeanine **Bla**) 21, ave de la Gare ☎ 27-64-82-98 Closed Sun.

☖ ⊗ **LE BERLIOZ** (N° RR AVR 26 865) (M. René **Dupont**) 27, ave de la Gare ☎ 27-64-68-79 **Minitel** Closed Sun and August.

MAUBOURGUET 65700 Htes-Pyr. **Map 21-A2**

☖ ⊗ **RELAIS DES AUTOBUS** (N° RR FEV 26 185) (Mme Nicole **Dauba**) 87, place de la Libération ☎ 62-96-38-78 **Minitel** Bar

M

Maubourguet continued
open every day. Restaurant closed Sat evening, Sun. Coaches welcome.

MAURIAC 15200 Cantal **RD 678 Map 17-B2**
♈ ⊗ 🏠 **LES ROUTIERS** (N° RR NOV 26 744) (**SARL Laroche-Rongier**) 27, rue St-Mary ☎ 71-68-00-79 ⊷ 10 Closed Fri evening. English spoken. Full-board 150–180F. Coaches welcome (rest. seats 60). Evening meals served until 10pm.

MAUZE-LE-MIGNON 79210 Deux-Sèvres **RN 11 and 22 Map 15-A1**
♈ ⊗ 🏠 **LE RELAIS DU COQ HARDI** (N° RR JUN 22 387) (M. Paul **Bombard**) 41, Grande Rue ☎ 49-26-30-39 ⊷ 10 Closed Sun. Full-board 130–180F per night. Coaches welcome (2 rooms = 230 seats). Evening meals. English spoken.

MAY-SUR-ORNE 14320 Calv. **RD 562 Map 4-B2**
♈ ⊗ 🏠 **L'AMMONITE** (N° RR DEC 26 119) (M. Jean-Claude **Horel**) 2, rue du Canada ☎ 31-79-80-27 ⊷ 8 Closed Sun in winter; 8 days in Feb; 2nd week Aug. Full-board 160–180F. Coaches welcome (rest. seats 95). Evening meals served until 10pm.

MAYENNE 53100 Mayenne **RN 162 and 823-12 Map 8-B1**
♈ ⊗ 🏠 **LE RELAIS L'ESCALE** (N° RR JUN 20 742) (M. and Mme **Fortin**) route du Mans 2, rue Colbert ☎ 43-04-19-14 ⊷ 13 Closed Sat afternoon, Sun. Evening meals until 8.30pm. Full-board 137F. Coaches welcome (rest. seats 142).

MAZAMET 81200 Tarn **RN 112/118 Map 22-B2**
Voir AUSSILLON-MAZAMET

MAZERES 33210 Gironde **RD 932 Map 20-B1 & 21-A1**
♈ ⊗ **LE PASSAGER** (N° RR AVR 18 665) (M. Serge **Garrigues**) route de Pau ☎ 56-63-15-22 Closed Sat, Sun; 2 weeks Aug. Evening meals. Some English, German, Spanish spoken.

MAZINGARBE 62670 Pas-de-Calais **RN 43 Map 5-A1**
♈ ⊗ **AU RELAIS DES ROUTIERS** (N° RR AVR 20 444) (Mme Geneviève **Marcinkowski**) 85, route Nationale 43 ☎ 21-72-00-09 Closed Sun; Aug. Coaches welcome (rest. seats 50). Polish, German spoken.

MEDE (LA) 13220 B.-du-R. **RN 568 Map 24-A/B3**
♈ ⊗ **L'ARC EN CIEL** (N° RR JUL 26 949) (Mme Marie **Courevellis**) 5, avenue Mirabeau ☎ 42-07-04-38 ⊷ 5 Spanish, Greek spoken.

MEES 40990 Landes **RN 124 Map 20-A2**
♈ ⊗ **L'OREE DU BOIS** (N° RR OCT 26 067) (M. Jean-Paul **Gueffier**) Route de Bayonne, Nle 124 ☎ 58-97-57-77 Closed Sun.

MEGEVE 74120 Hte-Savoie **RN 212 Map 19-B2**
♈ ⊗ 🏠 **2 Star NN LE CHALET DES FLEURS** (N° RR JAN 17 730) (M. Georges **Roussel**) route de Sallanches au Pont d'Arbon ☎ 50-21-21-46 ⊷ 27 from 105–185F, breakfast 25F. Closed 15 Sept to 15

Dec; 15 April to 15 June. Full-board 210–275F per night. Coaches welcome (rest. seats 95). Evening meals. English spoken. Car park; bar; dogs allowed; recreations (miniature golf, playground). Menus 73–150F. Specialities: *escargots de Bourgogne maison, omelette norvegienne maison, escalope normande garnie.*

MELGVEN 29140 Finistère **Map 7-B1**
Y ⊗ **KERAMPAOU** (N° RR AVR 23 771) (**SARL Mevellec**) ☎ 98-97-90-18 **Minitel** Closed Sun morning. Video. Coaches welcome. Evening meals. HGV parking. English spoken.

MELLAC 29130 Finistère **Map 7-B2**
Y ⊗ **LE MARLI** (N° RR AVR 27 267) (M. Rodolphe **Dupart**) Z.A. de Keringant ☎ 98-39-31-97 Closed Sun am. Meals served until 10.30pm.

MENIL-BROUT (LE) par DAMIGNI 61250 Orne **RN 12 Map 8-A/B2**
Y ⊗ 🏠 **LE RELAIS A LA BONNE FRANQUETTE** (N° RR AVR 14 764) (Mme **Castelier**) ☎ 33-27-10-03 Auberge rurale Closed Sat, Sun; Aug.

MEOLANS-REVEL 04340 Alpes de Haute-Provence **Map 25-A1**
⊗ **Camping Caravaning Caravaneige RELAIS ROUTIERS DU RIOCLAR** (N° RR JANV 27 140) (SARL Europ Neige et Soleil) ☎ 92-81-10-32 English, Spanish and Italian spoken.

MERCUREY 71540 Saône-et-Loire) **RD 978 Map 18-A1**
Y ⊗ 🏠 **LE MERCUREY** (N° RR AUG 27 372) (Mme Roseline **Goy**) Crande Rue ☎ 85-45-13-56 ⊷ 8 from 90 to 130F. German and English spoken. Evening meals served until 10.30pm.

MERLINES 19340 Corrèze **RN 89 Map 16-B2**
Y ⊗ **RELAIS DU COMMERCE** (N° RR FEV 27 186) (Mmes **Rebaix/Theil**) av. Pierre-Sémard ☎ 55-94-32-31.

MERY-SUR-CHER 18100 Cher **RN 76 Map 13-B1**
Y ⊗ 🏠 **LE RELAIS BERRY-SOLOGNE** (N° RR NOV 16 762) (M. Claude **Carré**) route de Tours ☎ 48-75-20-34 ⊷ 10 Closed Sat, Sun.

MESGRIGNY 10170 Aube **RN 19** and **CD 373 Map 9-B2/3**
Y ⊗ **LA BELLE ÉTOILE** (N° RR FEB 27 196) (Mme Sylvie **Schmutz**) Méry-sur-Seine ☎ 25-21-15-70 English and German spoken.

MESNIL-DURAND 14140 Calvados **RD 579 Map 4-B2**
Y ⊗ **LE RELAIS DE LA FORCE** (N° RR JUL 23 881) (M. Roger **Cardonnel**) Les Forges Mézières ☎ 31-63-52-79 **Minitel** Closed Sun; Aug. German spoken. Coaches welcome (rest. seats 120). Evening meals served until 10pm.

M

MESSIA-SUR-SORNE 39570 Jura **RN 83 Map 19-A1**
 ⅋ ⊗ **LA CHARMILLE** (N° RR JANV 22 618) (M. Patrick **Vaucher**)
 570, route de Lyon Lons-le-Saunier ☎ 84-24-65-92 Closed Sun.
 English spoken.

MEYLIEU 42210 Loire **RN 82 Map 18-B2**
 ⅋ ⊗ **LES OMBRELLES** (N° RR SEPT 26 661) (M. Christian **Chadrin**)
 Montrond-Les-Bains ☎ 77-54-52-44 Closed Sat, Sun and 2 weeks
 in Aug. English spoken. Coaches welcome (rest. seats 32).
 Evening meals served until 10pm.

MEYTHET 74000 Haute-Savoi **Map 19-A2**
 ⅋ ⊗ **1 Star NN LES ROUTIERS** (N° RR SEPT 26 057) (M. Christian
 Garachan) 22 route de Francy ☎ 50-22-02-93 Closed Sun and
 July. English and German spoken. Coaches welcome (rest. seats
 65). Evening meals served until 9pm.

MEZE 34140 Hérault **RN 113 Map 23 A/B2**
 ⅋ ⊗ **LE MARSEILLAIS** (N° RR NOV 26 109) (M. Willie **Rennie**) 8,
 avenue de Montpellier ☎ 67-43-81-29 Closed Sat. Coaches
 welcome (rest. seats 80). Evening meals. English spoken.
 ⅋ ⊗ **LA VITARELLE II** (N° RR 27 261) (M. Daniel **Garcia**) ☎ 67-43-
 53-89 ⇥ 35 Closed Sun evening. English, Spanish and Italian
 spoken. Evening meals served until 10pm.

MEZEL 04270 Alpes-de-Haute-Provence **RD 207 Map 25-A2**
 ⅋ ⊗ ⌂ **1 Star NN LE RELAIS DE LA PLACE** (N° RR JUL 22 884)
 (Mme Christiane **Sarracanie**) Place Victor-Arnoux ☎ 92-35-51-05
 ⇥ 12 Closed Mon (except Jul, Aug; Sept); Oct. Full-board.
 Coaches welcome (rest. seats 30). Evening meals served until
 9pm.

MÉZÉRAIT 01660 Ain **RN 79 Map 18-B1**
 ⅋ ⊗ **RELAIS DE MÉZÉRAIT** (N° RR NOV 27 111) (M. Alain **Darbon**)
 Les Pigots ☎ 74-30-25-87 Closed Sat. Coaches welcome (rest.
 seats 60). Evening meals served until 10pm.

MÉZIÈRES-EN-DROUAIS 28500 Et.-et-L. **Voir MARSAUCEUX**

MEZIERES-SUR-ISSOIRE 87330 Haute-Vienne **RN 151 Bis Maps 15-
B2 and 16-B1**
 ⅋ ⊗ **LE RELAIS DES VOYAGEURS ET DES ROUTIERS** (N° RR MAR
 25 341) (Mme Odette **Daganaud**) ☎ 55-68-34-47 ⇥ 5. Closed Sun;
 Oct. Full-board 130F. Coaches welcome (rest. seats 150).

MIGENNES 89400 Yonne **RN 6 Maps 9-B2 and 13-A2**
 ⅋ ⊗ ⌂ **RELAIS ROUTIER D'EPINEAU-LES-VOVES** (N° RR JUL 22
 864) (M. Ahmed **Betroune**) 2, route de Chambey ☎ 86-73-20-45
 ⇥ 11 German, Arabic spoken.

MIGNIERES 45490 Loiret **RD 94 Map 9-B2**
 ⅋ ⊗ ⌂ **RELAIS DE MIGNIERES** (N° RR AVR 25 916) (Mme Liliane
 Francart) Allee de la Gare ☎ 38-87-82-06 **Minitel** ⇥ 7 Closed
 Sun; 15 Dec–10 Jan. Evening meals.

MIGNIERES 28000 Eure-et-Loir **RN 10 Map 8-B3 see CHARTRES**

MILLANCAY 41210 L.-et-C. **Map 13-A1**
♟ ⊗ **LA TAVERNE SOLOGNOTE** (N° RR NOV 26 382) (Mme Martine **Cottencin**) route d'Orléanes ☎ 54-96-65-38 Closed Sun; Aug or Sept. Evening meals served until 9pm.

MILLAU 12100 Aveyron **RN 9 Map 23-A1**
♟ ⊗ **LES TILLEULS** (N° RR DEC 26 406) (M. Jean **Vernhet**) 17, avenue Martel ☎ 65-60-43-98 Closed Sun; last 2 weeks Sept.

MILLIÈRES 50190 Manche **Map 4-B1**
♟ ⊗ **LE RELAIS DES TOURISTES** (N° RR SEPT 27 381) (M. Gérard **Lunel**) La Bézenterie ☎ 33-46-71-12 Closed Sun. English spoken. Evening meals served until 10pm.

MIMIZAN 40200 Landes **RN 626 Map 20-A2**
♟ ⊗ ⌂ **RELAIS DUCOURT** (N° RR MARS 26 475) (Mme Françoise **Bricard**) 20, avenue de la Plage ☎ 58-82-42-37 **Minitel** ⊸ 35 Closed Sun off season. Full-board 155–170F per night. Coaches welcome (rest. seats 80). Evening meals.
♟ ⊗ **LE RABA** (N° RR JUIN 27 311) (M. Stéphane **Noorkhan**) 28, avenue de la Plage ☎ 58-09-18-60 ⊸ 3 English spoken open 24 hours.

MIONNAY 01390 Ain **RN 83 Map 2-A2**
♟ ⊗ **LE RELAIS BRESSAN** (N° RR MAI 26 550) (Mme Monique **Millet** and Christian **Desmaris**) St-André-de-Corcy ☎ 78-91-82-22 Closed Sun and 2 weeks Aug. Evening meals.

MIRABEAU 84120 Vaucluse **RN 96 Map 24-B3**
♟ ⊗ ⌂ **LOU BOUMIAN** (N° RR JANV 26 138) (M. Marcel **Souliol**) Quartier de la Gare ☎ 90-77-04-50 ⊸ 5 Closed Sun. Coaches welcome (rest. seats 72). Evening meals until 10pm.

MIRAMAS 13140 B.-du-R. **RN 569 Map 24-A3**
♟ ⊗ **LE RELAIS** (N° RR DEC 25 762) (Mme **Bouvier**) 72, avenue Charles de Gaulle ☎ 90-58-05-89 **Minitel** Closed Sun. Coaches welcome (rest. seats 90). Evening meals.

MIRAMONT-DE-GUYENNE 47800 Lot-et-Garonne **CD 933 Map 21-B1**
♟ ⊗ ⌂ **2 star NN L'ÉTAPE DES ROUTIERS** (N° RR NOV 27 097) (Mme Raymonde **Rodes**) Route de Paris **Saint-Pardoux-Isaac** ☎ ⊸ 53-93-20-76 Closed Sat; Spanish and Italian spoken.

MITRY-MORY 77290 S.-&-M. **Map 1-A3**
♟ ⊗ **LE RELAIS DE MITRY** (N° RR FEV 27 197) (Mme Josiane **Thyphonnet**) 3, rue Paul-Vallant-Courturier ☎ 64-27-11-61 Closed Sat, Sun.

MODANE 73500 Savoie **RN 6 Map 19-B3**
♟ ⊗ **LA CROIX DU SUD** (N° RR JUL 26 599) (M. Bernard **Mestrallet**) La Praz ☎ 79-05-34-47 Closed Sun; Aug. Italian spoken. Full

M

Modane continued
board 160–180F ◄ 5. Coaches welcome (rest. seats 120). Evening meals served until 11pm. Bar open until 0030.

♀ ⊗ **LE RESTOPORT DU FREJUS** (N° RR 27 412) (Joana S.A. M Starras **Stauridis**) Autoport du Frejus Le Freney ☎ 79-05-29-98 Closed Sun. English, Greek and Italian spoken. Evening meals.

MOIDIEU-DETOURBE 38440 Isère **RD 502 Map 2-B2**
♀ ⊗ **CHEZ DÉDÉ** (N° RR OCT 26 079) (M. André **Seigle**) St-Jean-de-Bournay ☎ 74-58-13-02 Closed Sat, Sun midday; 15 to 30 Aug; 10 days at Christmas/New Year. Evening meals served until 10pm. Coaches welcome (rest. seats 40).

MOIRANS 38430 Isère **RN 85 Maps 18-B3, 19-A3 and 24-B1**
♀ ⊗ 🏠 **LE VIADUC** (N° RR AOU 23 906) (M Ferland **Barral-Poulet**) 4, route de Grenoble ☎ 76-35-31-01 ◄ 4 Closed Sat, Sun. Evening meals served until midnight.

MOISSAC 82200 T.-et-G. **RD 127 Maps 21-B2 and 22-A1**
♀ ⊗ 🏠 **1 Star NN LE RELAIS AUVERGNAT** (N° RR AOU 15 344) (M. Jacques **Ginisty**) 31, boulevard Camille-Delthil place du Palais ☎ 63-04-02-58 or 63-04-93-02 ◄ 12 80–130F (with bath). Closed Sun evening. Full-board 160–180F per night. Coaches welcome (rest. seats 60). Meals served until 11pm. Menus 45–70F. Specialities: *Magret et confit de canard, Cassoulet.* Spanish spoken. Dogs welcome.

MOISY 41160 L.-&-C. **RD 924 Map 12-A3**
♀ ⊗ **AUX DÉLICES DU PALAIS** SARL Auberge gastronomique de la Vallée du Loir (N° RR MARS 27 205) (Mme Michèle **Normand**) Dle 924 Bourg de Moisy ☎ 54-82-62-40 Closed Tues and Feb. English and German spoken.

MOLINET 03510 Allier **RN 79 Map 16-A3 & 18-A1**
♀ ⊗ **LES ARCADES** (N° RR AVR 25 876) (Mme Anne-Marie **Fongarnand**) Moulins ☎ 85-53-47-51 Closed Sat afternoon and Sun.

MOLOMPIZE 15500 Cantal **RN 588 Map 17-A3**
♀ ⊗ 🏠 **LE RELAIS DU CENTRE** (N° RR AVR 18 067) (Mme Marie-Louise **Filliat**) ☎ 71-73-61-97 ◄ 12 Closed Sat, Sun; part of Nov. Full-board 130–160F per night. Coaches welcome (rest. seats 30). Evening meals.

MONASTIER (LE) 48100 Lozère known locally as LES AJUSTONS **RN 9 Map 17-B3 and 23-A1**
♀ ⊗ 🏠 **1 star NN LE RELAIS DES AJUSTONS** (N° RR MAR 20 128) (M. Guy **Gibelin**) crossroads of Nationales 9 and 88 ☎ 66-32-70-35 ◄ 27 80-150F Breakfast from 16F. Closed Sat, Sun in winter; 18 Dec–18 Jan. Full-board 130–170F per night. Coaches welcome (rest. seats 80). Fishing local. Sites include Gorges du Par and Aubrac.

M

MONDAVEZAN 31220 Hte-Garonne **RN 117 Map 21-B3**
♀ ⊗ ⌂ **LA FERMIERE** (N° RR MARS 26 488) (Mme Alexine **Ferrage**) rte Nle 117 ☎ 61-97-01-52 ⇥ 16 Closed Sun.

MONDOUBLEAU 41170 Loir-et-Cher **Map 8-B3**
♀ ⊗ ⌂ **HOTEL DE LA GARE** (N° RR MAI 23 297) (M. Gérard **Lucas**) 6, rue de la Gare ☎ 54-80-90-59 ⇥ 6 Closed Sat; Aug. Evening meals. Full board 140F. Coaches welcome (rest. seats 90).

MONESTIER DE CLERMONT 38650 Isère **RN 75 situé à 30 km South of Grenoble Map 19-A3 et 24-B1**
♀ ⊗ **REST DU NORD** (N° RR JUN 26 905) (M. Michel **Capogna**) 44, Gran du-Rue ☎ 76-34-03-75 Closed Sun.

MONETAY-SUR-ALLIER 03500 Allier **RN 9 Map 16-A3**
♀ ⊗ **GRIL DE L'ETANG BAZIN** Mme Jeanine **Dumez**) ☎ 70-42-09-45 Closed Tues. Evening meals served until midnight.

MONETEAU 89470 Yonne **RD 84 Map 13-A2/3**
♀ ⊗ ⌂ **AU RENDEZ-VOUS DES PECHEURS** (N° RR AVR 22 751) (M. R. **Gaufillet**) 14 Rue D'Auxerre ☎ 86-40-63-32 ⇥ 6 Closed Aug. Coaches welcome (rest. seats 128). Evening meals. Spanish spoken.

MONLET près d'ALLEGRE 43270 Haute-Loire **RD 13 Map 17-A3**
♀ ⊗ ⌂ **1 Star NN LE ROULIS** (N° RR FEV 20 650) (M. Pierre **Marec**) ☎ 71-00-73-54 ⇥ 10 from 60–98F, breakfast 17,50F. Full-board 160F per night. Coaches welcome (rest. seats 50). Closed Mon. Car park; bar; dogs allowed; recreations (*pétanque*). Places to visit: Richard's Windmill (Ambert), Châteaux, Lakes, Forests. English spoken.

MONNAI 61470 Orne **RN 138 Map 8-A2**
♀ ⊗ ⌂ **LE RELAIS DU CHEVAL BAI** (N° RR JAN 7 428) (M. Gilbert **Roussel**) Nationale 138 ☎ 33-39-42-00 ⇥ 6 Closed Sun; 15 Nov–15 Feb. Coaches welcome (rest. seats 110). Evening meals until 11pm.

MONNAIE 37380 Indre-et-Loire **RN 10 Map 12-A3**
♀ ⊗ **LA BONNE ÉTAPE** (N° RR NOV 26 722) (M. Marc **Rouxel**) 67, rue Nle ☎ 47-56-10-64 ⇥ 6 Closed Sun. Coaches welcome. Evening meals served until 9pm.
♀ ⊗ **L'ARCHE DE TOURAINE** (M. Pascal **Humblet**) Autoroute A10 ☎ 47-56-15-49 Open 24 hours. Self-service restaurant.

MONT-A-LA-QUESNE par BRIX 50820 Manche **RN 13 Map 4-A1**
♀ ⊗ **LE CLOS NORMAND** (N° RR SEPT 26 028) (Mme **Germain**) ☎ 33-41-94-35 Evening meals.

MONTAIGUT-EN-COMBRAILLE 63700 Puy de Dôme **Map 16-B2**
♀ ⊗ **CHEZ CLAUDINE (Mme Claudine Legrand)** Rue de la Chapelle ☎ 73-85-15-32 Closed Wed afternoon, 17th July–12th Aug. Evening meals served until 10pm.

M

MONTANDON 25190 Doubs **Map 10-A3**
♈ ⊗ ⌂ **LE GRAND CLOS** (N° RR DEC 26 418) (Mme Martine **Lepeme**) Saint-Hippolyte ☎ 81-96-51-12 ⊷ 5 German spoken.

MONTAREN 30800 Gard **RN 981 Map 24-A2**
♈ ⊗ ⌂ **LES ROUTIERS CHEZ RÉGINE** (N° RR NOV 26 101) (Mme Régine **Hangard**) Rte d'Alès ☎ 66-22-25-26 ⊷ 9 Closed Sun. Evening meals served to residents.

MONTARGIS see FONTENAY-SUR-LOING

MONTAUBAN 82000 T.-et-G. **RN 20 Map 22-A1**
♈ ⊗ **LE RELAIS DE FONNEUVE** (N° RR DEC 23 585) (Mme Agnès **Salles**) Fonneuve ☎ 63-03-14-68 Closed Sat evening, Sun.

MONTAUBAN-DE-BRETAGNE 35360 Ille-et-Vilaine **RN 12 and 164 bis Map 7-B3**
♈ ⊗ ⌂ **2 Star NN HOTEL DE FRANCE** (N° RR AOU 7 884) (M. Gabriel **Le Métayer**) 34, rue du Gl-de-Gaulle ☎ 99-06-40-19 ⊷ 13 Closed Mon low season; 20 Dec to 20 Jan. Full-board 200–280F per night. Coaches welcome (rest. seats 70). Evening meals until 10.00pm. English, Spanish, some German spoken. Menus 62–120F. Specialities: Seafood, *coq au muscadet far breton*.
♈ ⊗ ⌂ **2 star NN LE RELAIS DE LA HUCHERAIS** (N° RR SEPT 27 032) (M. Alain **Meheust**) ☎ 99-06-40-29 ⊷ 14 100–170F Breakfast 16.50–20F. Closed Sun. English spoken. Evening meals served until 10pm. Dogs allowed, TV, bar and lounge. Coaches welcome (rest. seats 110).

MONTAUDIN 53220 Mayenne **RN 799 Map 8-B1**
♈ ⊗ ⌂ **HÔTEL DE PARIS** (N° RR MAI 21 111) (M. Daniel **Doudard**) ☎ 43-05-30-79 ⊷ 5 Closed Mon. Full board 155F. Evening meals served until 9pm. English spoken. Coaches welcome (rest. seats 470).

MONTAUROUX 83440 Var **RN 562 Map 25-B2**
♈ ⊗ ⌂ **2 Stars NN RELAIS DU LAC** (N° RR NOV 26 110) (M. **Hernandez**) RN 562 ☎ 94-76-43-65 ⊷ 37 Full-board 220–350F per night. Coaches welcome (rest. seats 400). Evening meals. English, Spanish spoken.

MONTBARD 21500 Côte-d'Or **RN 5 Map 13-A3**
♈ ⊗ ⌂ **LE VOLTAIRE** (N° RR JUL 21 574) (M. Louis **Piquet**) 5, rue François-Debussy ☎ 80-89-42-21 ⊷ 10 Closed Sun; 15 Jul–15 Aug. Evening meals.

MONTBAZON 37250 Indre et Loire **RN 10**
♈ ⊗ ⌂ **LA GRANGE BARBIER** (N° RR DEC 27 472) (M. William **Laborde**) La Grange Barbier ☎ 47-26-01-60 ⊷ 5 Closed Sunday evening. Evening meals. Nearby service station open 24 hours.

MONTBENOIT 25650 Doubs **Map 14-B3**
♈ ⊗ ⌂ **RELAIS DES VOYAGEURS** (N° RR JANV 26 152) (M. Pierre **Magnin-Feysot**) Place de l'Abbaye ☎ 81-38-10-85 ⊷ 6 Closed

Tue evening. Full-board 110–145F. Coaches welcome (rest. seats 110). Evening meals.

MONTBOUCHER 23400 Creuse **CD 941 Map 16-A2**
Y ⊗ **LA BERGERIE** (N° RR DEC 26 760) (Mme Brigitte **Belz**) Bourganeuf ☎ 55-64-20-18 Closed Mon in winter and 15 days in Feb. Coaches welcome (rest. seats 60). Evening meals.

MONTBRISON 42600 Loire **RN 496 Map 18-A2**
Y ⊗ 🏠 **LE RELAIS DE LA GARE** (N° RR JAN 20 369) (M. Jean-Pierre **Gacon**) 2, place de la Gare ☎ 77-58-30-33 ⊷ 8 Closed Sun; Aug. Evening meals.
see also ST-ROMAIN-LE-PUY.

MONT CRESSON 45700 Loiret **Map 13-A2**
Y ⊗ 🏠 **BAR DE L'ETOILE** (Mme Gisèle **Dicicco**) 16 Rue de Verdun ☎ 39-90-00-50. Evening meals.

MONT-DAUPHIN 05600 Hautes-Alpes **RN 94 Maps 19-B3 and 25-A1**
Y ⊗ 🏠 **1 Star NN LE RELAIS DE LA GARE** (N° RR JUN 10 820) (Mme Francine **Lacour**) ☎ 92-45-03-08 ⊷ 24 105–200F Breakfast 22–25F. Closed Sat 1 May to 30 June, 1 Sept to 25 Dec. Full-board 195–260F per night. Coaches welcome. Evening meals served until 9.15pm. English spoken. Menus 54–140F. Specialities Truite aux Morilles, Filet de Boeuf, Côte d'Agneau.

MONT-DE-MARSAN 40000 Landes **RN 132 Map 20-B2 & 21-A2**
Y ⊗ 🏠 **BAR DES SPORTS** (N° RR FEV 24 508) (Mme Josiane **Ledoux**) Place des Arènes (Stanislas Baron) ☎ 58-75-05-08 ⊷ 20 Spanish spoken. Coaches welcome (rest. seats 60).
Y ⊗ **CHEZ CLAUDE ET ROSE** (M. Clotaire **Garestier**) 1791 Av. du Maréchal Juin. ☎ 58-06-15-65 Closed Sun. Spanish spoken. Evening meals served until 1am.

MONTDIDIER 80500 Somme **RN 30 and 35 Maps 3-A3 and 5-B3**
Y ⊗ 🏠 **LE RELAIS DU MOUTON D'OR** (N° RR AVR 19 734) (M. Christian **Parmentier**) 10, boulevard Debeney ☎ 22-78-03-43 ⊷ 5 Closed Sun; 1–21 Aug; 24–31 Dec. Coaches welcome (rest. seats 70). Evening meals.

MONT-DORE (LE) 63240 P.-de-D. **RN 496 Map 17-A2**
Y ⊗ 🏠 **CHEZ ROLANDE** (N° RR JUN 25 009) (Mme Rolande **Gravière**) 78, avenue de La Bourboule ☎ 73-65-03-60 ⊷ 15.

MONTEBOURG 50310 Manche **RN 13 Map 4-B1**
Y ⊗ **AUBERGE DES ROUTIERS – CHEZ LE CHAROLAIS** (N° RR SEP 26 640) (M. Serge **Charenton**) 19, place Albert Pélerin ☎ 33-41-14-67 **Minitel** ⊷ 4.

MONTECH 82700 T.-et-G. **RN 128 Map 22-A1**
Y ⊗ **LE RELAIS DE L'AVENUE** (N° RR AVR 21 515) (M. Georges **Taupiac**) 7, boulevard Lagal ☎ 63-64-72-26 Closed Sun; public holidays; 20 Dec to 5 Jan; 15 days in Aug. Coaches welcome (rest. seats 60). Evening meals from May to September inclusive.

M

MONTÉLIMAR 26200 Drôme **Autoroute A7 Map 24-A2**
♈ ⊗ **SODEXAS RELAIS P.L.M.** (M. **Arletti**) Aire de Service de
Montélimar ☎ 75-46-60-00 Open 24 hours. Self-service café and
restaurant. Showers, TV, shop.

MONTEREAU 77130 Seine-et-Marne **RN 1 Map 9-B2**
♈ ⊗ **LES ROUTIERS** (N° RR SEP 25 644) (M. Claude **Spinato**) RN 105
☎ 64-32-44-93 Closed Sun; Jul.

MONTFAVET 84140 Vauclse **RN 100 and A7 Map 24-A2**
♈ ⊗ 🏠 **1 Star NN LE RELAIS DE BONPAS** (N° RR JUN 21 138) (M.
Alain **Laugier**) locally Pont de Bonpas RN 7 ☎ 90-23-07-01 ⊷ 13
155–175F Breakfast from 15F. Coaches welcome (rest. seats 110).
Evening meals. English spoken.

MONTFIQUET 14490 Calvados **RD 572 Map 4-B1**
♈ ⊗ **RELAIS DE LA FORET – Chez Nicole** (N° RR MAI 25 427) (M.
Bernard **Tallendier**) locally L'Embranchement ☎ 31-21-68-74
English, Spanish spoken.

MONTFORT 04600 Alpes de Hte-Provence **RN 96 Map 25-A1**
♈ ⊗ **LE RELAIS DE MONTFORT** (N° RR JANV 26 131) (M. Bernard
Florent) RN 96, St-Aubant ☎ 92-64-11-91 Coaches welcome (rest.
seats 120). English spoken. Meals until 10.00pm.

MONTGENÈVRE 05100 Htes-Alpes **RN 94 Map 19-B3**
♈ ⊗ **LE TRANSALPIN** (N° RR JUN 22 385) (Mme Yvette **Silvestre**) ☎
92-21-92-87 Closed Sat afternoon, Sun; 15 Aug to 15 Sept.
Coaches welcome (rest. seats 60). Evening meals.

MONTILS (LES) 41120 Loir-et-Cher **RN 764 Map 12-A3**
♈ ⊗ **LES DEUX ROUES** (N° RR MAI 23 299) (M. Jean-Pierre **Levaux**)
28, rue du Bel-Air ☎ 54-44-02-40 Closed Sun. Coaches welcome
(rest. seats 110). Evening meals.

MONT LHÉRY 91300 Essonne **RN 20 Map 1-B2**
♈ ⊗ 🏠 **1 Star NN LE SOLOGNE** (M. Jacques **Cheron**) 65 Route
d'Orléans ☎ 89-01-00-98 ⊷ 8 Closed Sun and Jul. Coaches
welcome (rest. seats 40). Evening meals served until 9pm.

MONTLUÇON 03380 Allier **RN 145 Map 16-A2**
♈ ⊗ **LE RELAIS DES MARRONNIERS** (N° RR AVR 20 440)
(M. **Coulon**) Lamaids ☎ 70-51-81-50 Closed 2nd and 3rd weeks
of Sept.

MONTMARAULT 03390 Allier **RN 145 Map 16-A2**
♈ ⊗ **LE RELAIS DE L'UNION** (N° RR AVR 24 932) (Mme Monique
Desbordes) 2, Rte de Montluçon ☎ 70-07-60-05 Closed 1 to 15
Sept. Coaches welcome (rest. seats 120). Evening meals.
♈ ⊗ **LE CHALET** (N° RR FEV 26 815) (M. Alain **Vassort**) 18,
boulevard Tourret ☎ 70-07-60-23 Closed Sun in winter, Aug.
English spoken. Coaches welcome (rest. seats 300). Evening
meals.

M

♀ ⊗ **RELAIS DE L'ÉTAPE** (M. Robert **Legal**) Route de Mauline ☎ 70-07-36-03 Closed Sat evening, Sun. Evening meals.

MONTMARTIN-SUR-MER 50590 Manche **RD 20 Maps 4-B1 and 8-A1**
♀ ⊗ ⌂ **2 Stars NN HOTELLERIE DU BON VIEUX TEMPS** (N° RR JUIN 26 257) (M. Érick **Bourbonnais**) ☎ 33-47-54-44 **Minitel** ← 21 from 94–170F, breakfast 17F, telephone in room. Full-board 210–300F. Coaches welcome (rest. seats 120). Evening meals. English spoken. Car park; dogs allowed; bar.

MONTMAURIN 31350 Hte-Garonne **Map 21-B3**
♀ ⊗ **LE RELAIS COUPE-GORGE** (N° RR MAI 19 336) (M. Pierre **Favre**) Rte de Montréjeau ☎ 61-88-16-63 Closed Tue. Spanish spoken.

MONTMELIAN 73800 Savoie **RN 6 Map 19-A2**
♀ ⊗ **LE GRAND SCHLEM** (N° RR JANV 27 158) (SARL Le Grand **Schlem**) RN6 ☎ 79-65-23-63 ou 84-30-82 English, Spanish and Italian spoken. Open 24 hours.

MONTMIRAT 30260 Gard **RN 110 Map 23-B2**
♀ ⊗ ⌂ **LE CASTELAS** (N° RR JUL 25 500) (Mme Josiane **Gatel**) Rte Nationale 10 ☎ 66-77-81-33 Closed Sat, Sun.

MONTMOREAU 16190 Charente **RN 674 Map 15-B2/3**
♀ ⊗ **LE RELAIS DES ROUTIERS** (N° RR AVR 12 793) (Mme Ernestine **Ferrier**) Route d'Angoulême 3 ☎ 45-60-21-17 ← 5.

MONTOIRE-SUR-LE-LOIR 41800 L.-&-C. **Map 21-A3**
♀ ⊗ **À LA DESCENTE DU PERCHE** (N° RR MAI 27 281) (M. François **Detalle**) 2, rue du Docteur Schweitzer ☎ 54-85-21-39 Closed Sun pm. Evening meals served until 8.30pm.

MONTPELLIER-FABRÈGUES 34690 Hérault **LA LANGUEDOCIENNE A9 Map 23-B2**
♀ ⊗ **L'ARCHE** Aire de Service de Fabrègues 2 sens Passerelle ☎ 67-85-15-06 Open 24 hours. Self-service restaurant. Shop selling cigarettes, newspapers.

MONTPEYROUX see LA VITARELLE 12210 Aveyron

MONTPEZAT-de-QUERCY 82270 T.-et-G. **RN 20 Map 22-A1**
♀ ⊗ ⌂ **1 Star NN LE RELAIS DE L'ETAPE QUERCY** (N° RR JUN 21 121) (Mme Sylviane **Molinie**) La Madeleine Route Nationale 20 ☎ 63-02-07-58 ← 8 + annexe 6 rooms. Closed Sat low season; Sept.

MONTPINCHON 50210 Manche **RD 73 Map 8-A1**
♀ ⊗ **BAR DES AMIS** (N° RR AOU 25 080) (M. Gérard **Marie**) Tobacconist. **Cerisy la Salle** ☎ 33-46-94-00.

M

MONTPON 24700 Dordogne **RN 89 Map 15-B3**
Y ⊗ **LAS DAVALDAS DE MÉNESPLET** (N° RR MAR 23 717) (M. René **Duvillard**) ☎ 53-81-83-67 ⊷ 12 Coaches welcome (rest. seats 50). Evening meals.
Y ⊗ ⌂ **CHEZ MARTINE** (N° RR SEPT 26 992) (Mme Martine **Bouchet**) 27, rue Jean-Moulin ☎ 53-80-32-45 ⊷ 11 Filling stations near.

MONTREAL 11290 Aude **see CARCASSONNE**

MONTREAL 11290 Aude **RD 119 Map 22-B2**
Y ⊗ **LE MALEPERE** (N° RR OCT 25 696) (M. Gabriel **François**) Les Giscarels ☎ 68-76-29-43 ⊷ 3 Closed Sat, Sun. Full-board 220-320F per night. Evening meals until 10pm in winter. Spanish, English spoken.

MONTREDON-CORBIÈRES 11100 Aude **RN 113 Map 23-A2/3**
Y ⊗ **LE STÉPHANOIS** (N° RR MAI 26 246) (M. et Mme **Chalut**) RN 113 ☎ 68-42-08-41 ⊷ 7 Closed Sun. Coaches welcome (rest. seats 100). Evening meals. English, some Spanish, Italian spoken.
Y ⊗ ⌂ **LA CAILLE QUI CHANTE** (N° RR MAI 27 272) (M. Jacques **Gillet**) La Plaine ☎ 68-42-04-36 ⊷ 20 Closed Sun low season. German, English, Spanish and Italian spoken.

MONTREUIL-LE-CHÉTIF 72130 Sarthe **Map 8-B2**
Y ⊗ **AU RENDEZ-VOUS DES CHASSEURS** (Mme Françoise **Bordeau**) Le Grand Gué. Evening meals.

MONTREUIL-SOUS-BOIS 93100 Seine-St-Denis **Map 1-A3**
Y ⊗ **LE RELAIS DES ROUTIERS** (N° RR NOV 11 914; (Mmes **Sol** and **Puech**) 70, rue de Lagny ☎ 48-51-54-41. Closed Sun, Aug.

MONTRIEUX-NAVEIL 41100 L.-et-C. **RD 5 Map 12-A3**
Y ⊗ **RELAIS ROUTIERS** (N° RR JUL 22 429) (M. René **Houdouin**) 17, rue de Montrieux ☎ 54-77-13-98 Closed Sun.

MONT-SAINT-MICHEL 50116 Manche **RN 776 Maps 7-A3 and 8-A1**
Y ⊗ ⌂ **LES CAMPINGS DU MONT-SAINT-MICHEL S.A.R.L. Hôtel Vert Restaurant La Rôtisserie Campsite 2 Stars NN** (N° RR AVR 15 191) (M. Philippe **François**) La Caserne ☎ 33-60-09-33 ⊷ 83 Closed 1 Nov to 9 Feb. Coaches welcome, 2 large restaurants seat 480. Evening meals until 9pm. English, German spoken.

MONT-SOUS-VAUDREY 39380 Jura **RD 471 Map 14-A3**
Y ⊗ ⌂ **CHEZ COLETTE – RESTAURANT DU CENTRE** (N° RR JUN 24 259) (M. Maurice **Creusot**) Rue Jules-Grévy ☎ 84-71-71-94 ⊷ 5 Closed Sun evening, Mon all day; 15 May to 30 May; 20 October to 11 Nov. Half-board 120F, Full-board 160F per night. Coaches welcome (rest. seats 50). Evening meals until 10pm.

MORAINVILLIERS par ORGEVAL 78630 Yvelines **A 13 Map 1-A2**
Y ⊗ **RESTOP DE MORAINVILLIERS** (M. Jean-Paul **Delarme**) ☎ 39-75-92-25 Self-service open 11.00am to 10.00pm. Showers, television, shop.

M

MORANCE 69480 Rhône **Map 2-A1**
Ⓨ Ⓧ ⌂ **REST DE LA MAIRIE** (N° RR JUL 26 274) (Mme Ginette **Roy**)
Le Bourg ☎ 78-43-60-82 ⇌ 5 Closed Sat; Sun evening, 15 days in
May. Coaches welcome (rest. seats 140). Evening meals until
9pm.

MORDELLES 35310 Ille-et-Vilaile **Map 7-B3**
Ⓨ Ⓧ **L'ISATIS** (M. Michel **Edet**) La Croix Ignon ☎ 99-60-41-33 Closed
Sun & Aug. Evening meals.

MOREAC 56500 Morbihan **RN 24 Map 7-B2**
Ⓨ Ⓧ **LE RELAIS DU BARDERFF** (N° RR FEV 26 453) (M. Jean
Lamour) Z.I. Le Barderff ☎ 97-60-18-60 Open 5am – midnight.
Closed Sun. Evening meals served.

MOREILLES 85450 Vendée **Map 11-A1**
Ⓨ Ⓧ ⌂ **AU CHEVAL BLANC** (N° RR JUL 26 288) (M. Claude
Balitrand) Le Bourg ☎ 51-56-11-02 ⇌ 5 Closed Sundays and end
of December. Full-board 125-160F per night. Coaches welcome
(rest. seats 70). Evening meals until 11pm.

MOREUIL 80110 Somme **Map 5-A/B3**
Ⓨ Ⓧ **LE CENDRIER** (N° RR SEPT 26 037) (M. Erik **Deraeve**) 79, rue
du Cardinal-Mercier ☎ 22-09-70-64.

MORIÈRES-LES-AVIGNON 84310 Vaucluse **A 7 Map 24-A3**
Ⓨ Ⓧ **RESTOP MORIÈRES** (M. Eric **Muller**) Autoroute A7 ☎ 90-22-59-
68 Self-service restaurant open 6.00am to 10.00pm. Television.

MORLINCOURT 60400 Oise **Map 6-A1**
Ⓨ Ⓧ **LE RELAIS DU PORT** (N° RR AVR 24 553) (M. Francis **Collinet**)
201), rue d'Orroire ☎ 44-44-01-88 Closed Sun.

MORNAS 84420 Vaucluse **Autoroute A-7 Map 24-A2**
Ⓨ Ⓧ **Cafè-Route** (N° RR RA-8) (M. Pierre **Mess**) ☎ 90-37-03-09
Direction Paris/Provence Open 24 hours. Self-service restaurant.
English, German, Spanish, Italian spoken. Shop.
⚑ **Antar Service Station RELAIS DE L'ATOME** (N° RR JUl 25 061)
(M. Jean-Pierre **Flanquart**) Autoroute A-7 ☎ 90-37-02-07 English,
German, Spanish spoken. Open 24 hours.
Ⓨ Ⓧ **LE RELAIS DE LA CASCADE** (N° RR NOV 25 183) (M. Jean
Bretagnolle) RN 7 ☎ 90-37-02-67 Closed Sat, Sun, 15 days in Aug
and 15 days at Christmas. German spoken. Evening meals
served until midnight.

MORNAY-SUR-ALLIER 18600 Cher **RN 76 Map 13-B2**
Ⓨ Ⓧ ⌂ **LE RELAIS DE LA ROUTE** (N° RR DEC 15 044) (Mlle
Jacqueline **Chevrot**) ☎ 48-74-53-54 ⇌ 5 Open 24 hours. Closed
Sat (3pm), Sun. Evening meals. German, English spoken.

MORTAGNE-AU-PERCHE 61400 Orne **RN 12 Map 8-A2/3**
Ⓨ Ⓧ ⌂ **1 Star HOTEL DES VOYAGEURS** (N° RR FEV 25 798) (Mme
Cassimira **Blochel**) 60, fbg St-Éloi ☎ 33 25 25-46 ⇌ 10 Closed
Sun evening, Mon evening; 20 Dec to 20 Jan. Full-board 170–

M

Mortagne-Au-Perche continued
280F. Coaches welcome (rest. seats 110). Evening meals served until 10pm.

MORTAGNE-SUR-SÈVRE 85290 Vendée **RN 160 Maps 11-B3 and 12-B1**
♈ ⊗ **LE RELAIS DE LA GARE** (N° RR AOU 26 299) (M. Jean-Luc **Arrouet**) 52, route de Cholet ☎ 51-65-11-56 Closed Sat evening, Sun; Aug.

MORTRÉE 61500 Orne **RN 158 Map 8-A2**
♈ ⊗ **LE POINT DU JOUR** (N° RR JUIN 25 948) (M. Jacques **Montier**) 139 Grande-Rue ☎ 33-35-35-22 Closed Sat, Sun. Coaches welcome (rest. seats 220). Evening meals.

MOSLES 14400 Calvados **RN 13 Map 4-B2**
♈ ⊗ **RELAIS DE LA POSTE** (N° RR AVR 26 518) (M. Martial **Becker**) RN 13 ☎ 31-92-40-05 Closed Sat, Sun. English spoken.

MOUCHARD 39330 Jura **RN 72 Map 14-B3**
♈ ⊗ ⌂ **SARL LA TONNELLE** (N° RR AOUT 26 303) (M. Bernard **Miller**) **Pagnoz** ☎ 84-37-81-17 **Minitel** ⌐ 11 Closed Sat evening; Aug. Coaches welcome (rest. seats 70). Evening meals served until 10pm.

MOUEN 14790 Calvados **RN 175 Map 4-B2**
♈ ⊗ ⌂ **LA BRUYÈRE** (N° RR JAN 20 973) (Mme Aunick **Lafosse**) 1546 Route de Bretaque ☎ 31-80-96-77 ⌐ 5. Closed Sat, Sun & Aug.

MOULEYDIER 24520 Dordogne **Map 21-B2**
♈ ⊗ **RELAIS DU BARRAGE** (N° RR JUIN 27 309) (M. Patrick **Delmas**) Tuilières ☎ 53-23-20-55 Closed Sun. English, German and Spanish spoken. Evening meals served until 11pm.

MOULINEAUX 76530 Seine-Maritime **RD 3 Map 3-A1**
♈ ⊗ ⌂ **HOTEL ROBERT LE DIABLE** Tobacconist, magazines (N° RR MAR 22 718) (M. Gilbert **Duroy**) Grand Couronne ☎ 35-23-81-17 ⌐ 10 Closed Sun; 20 Dec to 17 Jan. Coaches welcome (rest. seats 60). Evening meals.

MOULINS 03000 Allier **RN 7 Map 16-A3**
♈ ⊗ **LE RELAIS DES TROIS RUBANS** (N° RR AOU 7 841) (M. Pierre **Molinie**) 1, route de Paris ☎ 70-44-08-51 Closed Sat, Sun & Aug. Evening meals served until 8pm.

MOULINS-DES-MALADES par ORCHAMPS 39700 Jura **RN 73 Map 14-A5/B3**
♈ ⊗ **AU RENDEZ-VOUS DE LA MARINE** (N° RR MAI 6 142) (Mlle **Bullet**) 73, route Nationale ☎ 84-71-32-10 Closed Sat 4.00pm to Sun 11.00am; & Aug.

MOULISME 86500 Vienne **RN 147 Map 15-B1**
♈ ⊗ ⌂ **1 Star NN LA TABLE OUVERTE** (N° RR AVR 22 752)

M

(**S.A.R.L. Gransagne-Baudet**) Route Nationale Montmorillon ☎ 49-91-90-68 ⊷ 7 from 64–125F, breakfast 17F. Access for disabled. Closed Sat afternoon, Sun afternoon (except Aug). Car park 5,500m². Coaches welcome (rest. seats 75). Evening meals; bar; dogs allowed.

MOUSTIOR REMUNGOL 56500 Morbihan **Map 7-B2**
♀ ⊗ **LE POMDI-LOCH** (Mme Marie Madeleine **Lemarsle**) Kerroux ☎ 97-39-86-65 Evening meals.

MOUZEUIL 85370 Vendée **RN 148 Map 11-A1**
♀ ⊗ ⌂ **CENTRAL ROUTIER** (N° RR JUN 21 961) (M. Jean-Marie **Guilbaud**) Le Bourg Place de l'Église ☎ 51-30-72-44 ⊷ 8 Fullboard 130–150F per night. Coaches welcome (rest. seats 300). Evening meals served until 10pm.

MOUZON 08210 Ardennes **RN 964 Map 6-A3**
♀ ⊗ **LA MARINE** (N° RR JUL 26 612) (Mme Danielle **Hisette**) 6, rue du Château ☎ 24-26-19-90 Closed Wed; beginning Sept. Coaches welcome (rest. seats 45). Evening meals.

MOYON 50860 Manche **CD 999 Map 8-A1**
♀ ⊗ **CARREFOUR PARIS SUPER ROUTIERS** (N° RR NOV 27 091) (M. Pierre **Borau**) Carrefour Paris Moyon ☎ 33-05-59-74 Closed Sun & Dec. Portuguese, English and Spanish spoken. Coaches welcome (rest. seats 65). Evening meals served until 11pm.

MUR-DE-SOLOGNE 41230 L.-et-C. **RD 765 Map 12-A3**
♀ ⊗ ⌂ **LA CROIX BLANCHE** (N° RR OCT 26 683) (M. Philippe **Gaugry**) rue de Blois ☎ 54-83-81-11 ⊷ 24 English spoken. Full board 167–220F. Coaches welcome (rest. seats 150). Evening meals served until 10pm.

MUREAUX (LES) 78130 Yvelines **RD 14 Maps 1-A1 and 3-B2**
♀ ⊗ ⌂ **LE RELAIS ICI ON COUPE LA SOIF** (N° RR JUL 12 328) (Mme **Compagnon**) 102, avenue du Maréchal Foch ☎ 34-74-05-04 ⊷ 7 Closed Sun; Aug.
♀ ⊗ **CAFÉ D'ARMOR** (N° RR OCT 26 700) (Mme Germaine **Dolais**) 29, rue J.-Jaurès ☎ 34-74-04-95 Closed Wed. English spoken.

MURON 17630 Charente-Maritime **Map 11-B1**
♀ ⊗ ⌂ **LE RELAIS** (N° RR SEPT 26 632) (M. Albert **Arnaud**) rue de la Libération ☎ 46-27-78-41 ⊷ 5.

MUY (LE) 83490 Var **RN 7 Map 25-A2**
♀ ⊗ **LA CHAUMIÈRE** (N° RR AOUT 26 625) (M. Louis **Fogola**) 7, quartier de la Gare ☎ 94-45-10-81 ⊷ 7. Closed Sun. Coaches welcome (rest. seats 80). Evening meals served until 11pm.

MYENNES 58440 Nievre **RN 7 Map 13-A2**
♀ ⊗ **LE RANCH** (N° RR JAN 22 151) (Mme Marie-Marcelle **Barres**) ☎ 86-28-00-98.

N

NAINTRÉ Lieu-dit LES BARRES 86530 Vienne **RN 10 Map 15-B1**
♇ ⊗ **LA HALTE** (N° RR NOV 20 892) (M. and Mme **Henni-Houas**) Nationale 10 ☎ 49-90-09-69 **Minitel** Situated on exit Sud de Châtellerault from Autoroute Aquitaine. Closed Sat, Sun. Coaches welcome (rest. seats 150). Evening meals. English, Arabic, Spanish, German spoken.

NANCY 54000 M.-et-M. **RN 4 Maps 10-A2 and 14-B1**
♇ ⊗ ⌂ **LE RELAIS DU PORT** (N° RR FEV 18 314) (M. Claude **Dopp**) 5, rue Henri-Bazin ☎ 83-35-49-85 ⊷ 9 Closed Fri evening, Sat, Sun; Aug. English, German spoken. Evening meals.
♇ ⊗ **RELAIS VICTOR** (N° RR SEPT 29 641) (M. Jean-Marie **Hecht**) 7, rue Victor ☎ 83-36-53-27 ⊷ 9 Closed Sat, Sun. Evening meals served until 10pm. Coaches welcome (rest. seats 46).

NANTERRE 92000 Hauts-de-Seine **Porte Maillot Map 1-A2**
♇ ⊗ **AU PETIT ROSE** (N° RR MAI 25 931) (Mme Jasmina **Houguenague**) 108, av. Jules-Quentin ☎ 47-21-13-99 Closed Sat, Sun. English spoken. Coaches welcome (rest. seats 50).

NANTES 44000 L.-Atl. **RN 43 Maps 11-A/B2 and 12-B1**
♇ ⊗ **LA BOUGRIÈRE** (N° RR OCT 23 491) (M. Pierre **Pertue**) rue du Pavillon-Ste-Luce ☎ 40-25-60-84 Closed Fri evening, Sat, Sun (except for coaches, banquets). Aug; Christmas to New Year. Coaches welcome (rest. seats 280). English, Spanish spoken. Evening meals served until 11.30pm.
♇ ⊗ ⌂ **L'ANCRE D'OR** (N° RR AOUT 26 295) (M. Serge **Desmortiers**) 55, boulevard Gustave Roch ☎ 40-35-39-30 ⊷ 5 Closed Sat afternoon, Sun; 1 Aug to 25 Aug. Evening meals served until 9.30pm. Coaches welcome (rest. seats 110).
♇ ⊗ **CAFÉ DE L'AVENIR** (N° RR SEPT 26 043) (Mme Vivaine **Baron**) 1, rue de la Pompe ☎ 40-43-46-03 Closed Sat lunch; Sun. Coaches welcome (rest. seats 54). Evening meals until 9.30pm.
⛽ **Total Service Station LE RELAIS DE LA DIVATTE** (N° RR MAR 24 143) (S.A.R.L. Joseph **Guichet**) 226, Bd de la Loire ☎ 40-06-01-44 Basse-Goulaine. Closed alternate Sun.
⛽ **BP Service Station RELAIS DE LA MAISON BLANCHE** (N° RR MAR 24 144) (Mme Anne **Bouloux**) RN 23 Le Cellier ☎ 40-25-54-07.
♇ ⊗ **CAFÉ DU HAVRE** (N° RR MARS 26 850) (Mme Betty **Guichard**) 4, rue d L'Hermitage ☎ 40-73-29-19 Closed Sat evening, Sun; 15 days Aug. HGV parking (15 vehicles).
♇ ⊗ **LES TILLEULS** (N° RR JANV 26 784) (Mme Marie-Thérèse **Poirier**) 9, rue de la Petite Baratte ☎ 40-49-68-29 ⊷ 13 Closed Sat, Sun; Aug.
♇ ⊗ **AU RENDEZ-VOUS DES SPORTIFS** (M. Bernard **Oubert**) 40 Quai Malackoff ☎ 40-47-75-39. Closed Sat, Sun & July. Evening meals served until 9pm.

NANTHIAT see CHAMBORET 87140 Hte-Vienne

NARBONNE 11100 Aude **RN 9 Map 23-A3**
♇ ⊗ ⌂ **LE NOVELTY** (N° RR JAN 10 223) (MM. Claude and Louis

Strazzera) 33, avenue des Pyrénées ☎ 68-42-24-28 ⊷ 18 Full-board 166F. Coaches welcome (rest. seats 250). Evening meals until 10pm. English, Arabic, Spanish, Italian spoken.

♿ ⊗ ⌂ **1 Star NN LE RELAIS DES 2 MERS** (N° RR JAN 23 601) (M. **Mattei**) ☎ 68-41-00-21 ⊷ 39 Italian spoken.

♿ ⊗ **LA TOUPINE** (N° RR NOV 27 112) (M. Yannick **Canessa**) 3, route de Coursan ☎ 68-65-11-01 ⊷ 4 English and Spanish spoken. Closed Sat evening, Sun evening. Full-board 180–200F. Coaches welcome (rest. seats 90). Evening meals served until midnight.

NASSANDRES 27550 Eure **RN 13 Map 4-B3**
♿ ⊗ **LE PARIS CAEN/CHERBOURG INTERNATIONAL** (N° RR OCT 26 686) (M. Patrice **Boutel**) SARL Le Paris Caen/Cherbourg 11, Route Nationale 13 ☎ 32-45-00-26 Closed Sat afternoon, Sun. Evening meals.

NAUCELLE 12800 Aveyron **RN 88**
♿ ⊗ **RELAIS DE LA MOTHE** (N° RR JAN 27 513) (M. Michel **Cousin**) La Mothe ☎ 65-90-03-00 Closed Monday. Evening meals until 9pm.

NAVILLY 71650 S.-et-L. **RN 83 Bis Map 14-A3**
♿ ⊗ ⌂ **AU BOIS DE BOULOGNE** (N° RR FEV 10 347) (M. **Grapinet**) ☎ 85-49-10-40 ⊷ 3 Closed Wed; 21 Dec to 21 Jan. Coaches welcome (rest. seats 100). Evening meals.

NÉGRONDES 24460 Dordogne **Map 15-B3**
♿ ⊗ **RESTO-ROUTE LA FRINGALE** (N° RR SEPT 26 332) (Mme **Mouret**, M. **Leriche**) Les Riviers ☎ 53-55-24-11 English, Italian spoken.

NEMOURS 77140 S.-et-M. **Autoroute A6 Map 9-B2**
♿ ⊗ **RESTOP DE NEMOURS** (M. **Claude Poirier**) Aire de Darvault ☎ 64-28-11-97 Open 24 hours. Self-service restaurant. Showers, TV, shop.

NERE 17510 Charente-Mar **RD 133 Map 15-A2**
♿ ⊗ **LES ROUTIERS** (N° RR JUN 23 828) (Mme Monique **Metois**) route d'Aulnay-les-Égaux ☎ 46-33-00-30.

NERONDES 18350 Cher **CD 976 Map 13-B2**
♿ ⊗ ⌂ **1 Star NN LE RELAIS DU LION D'OR** (N° RR MAR 9 436) (M. René **Boutillon**) place de la Mairie ☎ 48-74-87-81 ⊷ 14 from 90–140F, breakfast 17F, telephone in room. Closed Sun afternoon; public holiday afternoons; 15 Dec to 13 Jan; third week in Sept Evening meals. Car park; bar.

NEUFBOURG (LE) 50140 Manche **RN 177 Map 8-A1**
♿ ⊗ **LES ROUTIERS** (N° RR AOUT 26 025) (Mme Françoise **Hamel**) 13, rue de Vire ☎ 33-59-00-59 ⊷ 4.

N

NEUFCHATEL-EN-SAOSNOIS 72600 Sarthe **RN 155 Map 8-B2**
♀ ⊗ **Tobacconist CHEZ CHRISTIANE** (N° RR AOU 18 500) (Mme Christiane **Chapellier**) ☎ 43-97-74-10 ⊸ 15 Closed Aug. Full-board 200–220F per night. Evening meals until 10pm. Coaches welcome (rest. seats 55).

NEUILLY-LES-DIJON 21800 Côte-d'Or **RN 5 Map 14-A3**
♀ ⊗ 🏠 **LE RELAIS DES ROUTIERS** (N° RR OCT 15 395) (M. **Manzoni**) 5, Route Nationale ☎ 80-23-01-93 ⊸ 8.

NEUSSARGUES 15170 Cantal **RN 122 Map 17-A2**
♀ ⊗ **LE SPORTING BAR** (N° RR AVR 25 875) (Mme Joelle **Allanche**) rue des Écoles ☎ 71-20-56-89 Closed Sun; 15 days Jul, Aug. Evening meals served until 10pm.

NEUVE-LYRE (LA) Hameau de CHAGNY 27330 Eure **RN 830 Map 8-A3**
♀ ⊗ **LE RELAIS DES AMIS** (N° RR AVR 21 047) (M. Jean-Claude **Guyot**) Hameau de Chagny ☎ 32-08-67-23 Closed Tue; 15 to 30 Aug.

NEUVIC 24190 Dordogne **Map 15-B3**
♀ ⊗ **RELAIS LE REPAIRE** (N° RR AVR 27 265) (M. Jacky **Blanchard**) le But ☎ 53-81-63-05.

NEUVILLE-AU-PLAIN 50480 Manche **RN 13 Map 4-B1**
♀ ⊗ **LA RENCONTRE** (N° RR AOU 25 079) (M. Jean-Pierre **Alix**) Ste Mère Eglise ☎ 33-41-31-46 Closed Sat/Sun; Aug. English spoken. Coaches welcome (rest. seats 52). Evening meals served until 9pm.

NEUVY 41250 Loir-et-Cher **RD 18 and 923**
♀ ⊗ 🏠 **LA CHEMINÉE** (N° RR JUL 26 613) (M. Philippe **Masclet**) Bracieux ☎ 54-46-42-70 ⊸ 9. Closed Wed in winter; 15 to 30 Sept; 1 to 15 Mar. Full-board 180–200F. Coaches welcome (rest. seats 115). Evening meals served until 10pm.

NEUVY-EN-BEAUCE 28310 E.-et-L. **A10 Map 9-B1**
⛽ **BP Service Station RELAIS VAL NEUVY** (N° RR JUL 550000088) (M. Lucien **Blanchard**) A10 ☎ 37-99-91-75 Open 24 hours. English spoken.

NEUVY-SAINT-SÉPULCRE 36230 Indre **RD 927 Map 16-A1**
♀ ⊗ 🏠 **LA CHARRETTE** (N° RR FEV 26 454) (M. Nicholas **Pavlicevic**) 21, place du Champ-de-Foire ☎ 54-30-84-77 ⊸ 7 Italian, Yugoslavian, Polish, Czechoslavakian, Russian, English spoken.

NEUVY-SAUTOUR 89570 Yonne **RN 77 Map 9-B2**
♀ ⊗ **AU BON COIN Chez Gérard et Annie** (N° RR JUL 26 292) (M. Gérard **Charpignon**) route de Troyes ☎ 86-56-35-52 **Minitel** Closed Sat afternoon, Sun. Coaches welcome (rest. seats 40). Evening meals until 9.30pm.

N

NEVERS 58000 Nievre **RN 7 Map 13-B2**
Ⓨ ⓧ 🏠 **HOTEL NIVERNAIS** (N° RR SEP 23 481) (M. Marcel **George**)
106, route de Lyon-Plagny ☎ 86-37-58-32 ⊷ 6 Closed Sun
evening and first fortnight Sept. English, Spanish, Italian spoken.
Full-board 190–250F. Coaches welcome (rest. seats 80). Evening
meals served until 10pm.
Ⓨ ⓧ 🏠 **HOTEL DU LION D'OR** (N° RR OCT 26 682) (M. Thierry
Petillot) 13, faubourg de Lyon ☎ 86-37-55-48 ⊷ 4 Closed Wed,
Sept. Some English spoken. Coaches welcome (rest. seats 120).
Evening meals served until 9.30pm.

NEVERS 58000 Nievre **see PLAGNY**

NICE 06000 Alpes-Marit. **RN 7 Map 25-B2**
Ⓨ ⓧ **VENGA VENGA** (N° RR MAR 24 883) (M. Philippe **Acoca**) 11,
Bld Pierre Sémard ☎ 93-89-58-56 Closed Sun. Coaches welcome
(rest. seats 50). Evening meals served until 10pm. Italian spoken.

NICOLE 47190 L.-et-G. **RN 113 Map 21-A/B1**
Ⓨ ⓧ 🏠 **LE PLAISANCE** (N° RR JUN 24 615) (M. Bernard **Lambert**)
Rte Nle 113 Aiguillon ☎ 53-79-64-07 ⊷ 7 Closed Sat; last Sun of
month and Aug. Full-board 135F. Coaches welcome (rest. seats
100). Evening meals until 10.00pm.

NIEPPE 59850 Nord **RN 42 Map 5-A1**
Ⓨ ⓧ **LE RELAIS DE L'HARMONIE** (N° RR JUL 23 379) (Mme
Christiane **Boulet**) 127, rue d'Armentières ☎ 20-48-74-29 Closed
Mon; Aug.

NIEUL-LE-DOLENT 85430 Vendée **RD 36 Map 11-B3**
Ⓨ ⓧ **CHEZ JACQUES** (N° RR MAR 23 210) (M. Jacques **Pinel**) 8, rue
de Lattre-de-Tassigny between la Roche-sur-Yon and les
Sables-d'Olonne ☎ 51-07-93-71 Closed Sun. Coaches welcome
(rest. seats 40). HGV parking (2000m^2). Evening meals.

NIMES 30000 Gard **Map 23-B2 & 24-A3**
ⓧ **Sté L'AVONAGE** (N° RR NOV 26 099) (Mme Martine **Finiels**)
Rte de Generac, Domaine de la Bastide ☎ 66-38-06-99 Closed
Sun low season. Coaches welcome (rest. seats 70). Evening
meals served until 9.30pm. English, Spanish spoken.

NIORT 79000 Deux-Sèvres **RN 150 Map 15-A1**
Ⓨ ⓧ **LE BON ACCUEIL** (N° RR OCT 24 743) (Mme Thérèse **De-
nibaud**) 424, av. St-Jean-d'Angély ☎ 49-79-27-60 Closed Sat, Sun;
from 1 Nov to Easter; 15 Jul–15 Aug. Coaches welcome (rest.
seats 160. Evening meals until 10.30pm.

NOAILLES 19600 Corrèze **RN 20 Map 17-A1**
Ⓨ ⓧ 🏠 **RELAIS D'ATAN** (N° RR JUL 26 606) (Mme Josiane **Berthelot**)
Fontrouvée ☎ 55-85-85-76 Italian, Spanish, Portuguese spoken.

NOCLE-MAULAIX (LA) 58250 Nièvre **RD 3 Map 16-A3**
Ⓨ ⓧ **LE RELAIS DE LA POSTE** (N° RR JAN 17 715) (M. Marcel
Senotier) ☎ 86-30-80-32 Closed Mon; 1 to 21 Sept.

N

LA NOË POULAIN 27560 Eure **CD 810 Map 4-B3**
Ⓨ Ⓧ **CHEZ MANU ET JOJO** (N° RR NOV 27 088) (Mme Josiane **Langin**) Lieurey ☎ 35-57-90-35 Closed Sat and July/August.

NOGENT-LE-PHAYE 28630 Eure-et-Loire **RN 10 Map 8-B3**
Ⓨ Ⓧ **RELAIS DU MOULIN ROUGE** (N° RR NOV 26 716) (M. Christian **Bru**) Le Moulin Rouge ☎ 37-31-62-68 Closed Sat, Sun; Aug. Evening meals served until 9.45pm.

NOGENT-LE-ROTROU 28400 E.-et-L. **RN 23 Map 8-B3**
⚱ **Total Service Station LE RELAIS DE SULLY** (N° RR SEP 25 629) (M. Claude **Lepretre**) RN 23 ☎ 37-52-45-27.

NOHANT-EN-GOUT 18390 Cher **Map 13-B2**
Ⓨ Ⓧ **RELAIS DU BERRY** (N° RR AVR 27 251) (SARL Ligot) ☎ 48-30-42-90 German, English, Spanish and Italian spoken.
Ⓨ Ⓧ **LA GRANDE HALTE** (N° RR AVR 27 250) (M. Gérard **Lesimple**) ☎ 48-30-42-07 Closed Feb. English and Spanish spoken.

NOISY-LE-SEC 93130 Seine-St-Denis **Map 1-A3**
Ⓨ Ⓧ **LE CAPITOL** (N° RR OCT 25 711) (M. Claude **Magre**) 2, rue Jean-Jaurès ☎ 48-44-59-03 Closed Sun; Aug. Spanish, Portuguese spoken.

NOLAY 21340 Côte-d'Or **RD 73 Map 13-B3**
Ⓨ Ⓧ 🏠 **2 Star NN LE RELAIS DU CHEVREUIL** (N° RR AOU 20 799) (Mme Rachelle **Suissa**) place de l'Hôtel de Ville ☎ 80-21-71-89 ⇥ 14 11 En suite, 150–270F. Breakfast 27–30F.Closed Wed in low season; Dec. English, Spanish spoken. Full board 260–280F. Coaches welcome (rest. seats 100). Evening meals served until 10pm. Local sites. Burgundy vineyard and cellars.

NONANT-LE-PIN 61240 Orne **RN 26 Map 8-A2**
Ⓨ Ⓧ **LE RELAIS DES HARAS** (N° RR MAR 25 345) (M. Jacques **Lampin**) Grand-Rue ☎ 33-39-93-35 **Minitel** Closed Sun. Coaches ⚲ welcome (rest. seats 35). Evening meals until 10pm.

NOTRE-DAME-DE-GRAVENCHON 76330 Seine-Marit. **RD 428 Map 4-B3**
Ⓨ Ⓧ **LE COUP D'FREIN** (N° RR AVR 21 897) (Mme Marie-Josée **David**) rue Claude-Bernard ☎ 35-94-61-35.

NOUZONVILLE 08700 Ardennes **RD 1 Map 6-A2**
Ⓨ Ⓧ 🏠 **LE RELAIS DE LA PLACE** (N° RR SEP 21 243) (Mme Annie **Boquillon**) 15, place Gambetta ☎ 24-53-80-43 ⇥ 6 Closed Sun. Full-board 130F. Evening meals served until 8.30pm. Coaches welcome (rest. seats 32).

NOVES 13550 B.-du-R. **RN 7 Map 24-A3**
Ⓧ **RELAIS DE LA BASSAQUE** (N° RR SEPT 26 325) (M. Joseph **Masi**) Route Nationale 7 ☎ 90-94-26-84 Closed Sun. Italian spoken.

N

NOVION-PORCIEN 08270 Ardennes **RN 985 Map 6-A2**
Y ⊗ **LE FRANCO-BELGE – LE RELAIS DES ROUTIERS** (N° RR
AVR 17 499) (Mme Simone **Boniface**) place de la Gare ☎ 24-23-
20-06 ◄ 2 Evening meals.

NOYAL-SUR-VILAINE 35530 I.-et-V. **Map 8-B1**
Y ⊗ ⌂ **LE RELAIS 35** (N° RR JUL 26 290) (M. Jean **Monnerais**) 20,
rue du Gal-de-Gaulle ☎ 99-00-51-20 ◄ 12 Closed Sat 4.00pm to
Sun evening. Coaches welcome (rest. seats 80). Evening meals
until 1am. English spoken.

NOYANT-LA-PLAINE 49700 M.-et-L. **Map 12-B2**
Y ⊗ ⌂ **L'ÉTAPE** (N° RR FEVR 25 821) (M. Michel **Eono**) RD 761 ☎
41-59-30-40 ◄ 7. Closed Sun. Coaches welcome (rest. seats 80).
Evening meals.

NOYARET 38360 Isère **RN 532 Maps 19-A3 and 24-B1**
Y ⊗ ⌂ **AU BON ACCUEIL DES ROUTIERS** (N° RR FEVR 25 815))M.
Jean-Claude **Compe**) rue de la Gare Le Maupas ☎ 76-53-95-61 ◄
11 Closed Sat evening, Sun. Coaches welcome (rest. seats 100).
Evening meals. Italian, German, Spanish spoken.

NOYERS SUR CHER 41140 Loir et Cher
Y ⊗ **LES NOUETTES** (N° RR JAN 27 510) (MME Beatrice **Lacou**) 110
Rue Nationale ☎ 54-32-76-66 Evening meals. Service station
nearby.

NUITS-SAINT-GEORGES 21700 Côte-d'Or **RN 74 Map 14-A3**
Y ⊗ ⌂ **2 Stars NN HOTEL DES CULTIVATEURS** (N° RR JUN 1 894)
(MM. **Villemagne Père et Fils**) 12, rue du Gl-de-Gaulle ☎ 80-61-
10-41 ◄ 15 39 en suite 95–187F. Breakfast 10–19F. Closed Sun; 15
Dec to 15 Jan. Coaches welcome (rest. seats 60). Evening meals.
English spoken. Visit Hospice de Beaule, the cellars of Beaule
and Dijon.

O

OBJAT 19130 Coprèze
Y ⊗ ⌂ **RELAIS DU PARC** (N° RR JAN 27 492) (Mme Monique
Richard) 1, Avenue Poimcaré ☎ 55-84-11-11 ◄ 14 Evening
meals.

OCTEVILLE 50130 Manche **RD 3 and 900 Map 4-A1**
Y ⊗ **LE VENT D'AMONT** (N° RR MAI 26 885) (M. Jacky **Travers**) 1,
rue Jules Ferry ☎ 33-52-16-16 Closed Mon after lunch. Private car
park (2,200m^2). English spoken. Filling station near. Evening
meals.

O

OGEVILLER 54450 M.-et-M. **RN 4 Map 10-A2**
🍷 ⊗ **RELAIS DE LA VERDURETTE** (N° RR MAI 26 537) (Mme Lydie **Martin**) 22, route de Strasbourg ☎ 83-72-24-65 Closed Sat, Sun and first 2 weeks Aug. Evening meals served until midnight.

OISSEAU-LE-PETIT 72830 Sarthe **N 138 Map 8-B2**
🍷 ⊗ **HOTEL DE L'ESPERANCE** (N° RR SEP 21 653) (Mme **Besnard**) ☎ 33-26-81-97 🛏 4 Closed Sat from Oct–Apr. Coaches welcome (rest. seats 60). Evening meals.

OLEMPS 12510 Aveyron **Map 22-B1**
🍷 ⊗ 🏠 **1 star NN RELAIS DU PAS** (N° RR JUIN 27 300) (M. Jean-Marc **Mayrand**) RD 994 Le Pas Druelle ☎ 65-69-39-11 🛏 8 80 to 100F. English and Spanish spoken. Evening meals.

OLLIERES-SUR-EYRIEUX (LES) 07360 Ardèche **RN 103 Map 24-A1**
🍷 ⊗ **LES ROUTIERS** (N° RR JUN 21 114) (Mme Jacqueline **Loulier**) ☎ 75-65-20-42 🛏 4 Closed Sun. Full-board 190F per night. Evening meals. Coaches welcome (rest. seats 48).

OLORON-SAINTE-MARIE 64400 Pyrénées-Atl. **RN 134 Map 20-B3**
🍷 ⊗ 🏠 **LE TERMINUS** (N° RR JUL 26 603) (Mme Jeanne **Debonne**) place de la gare ☎ 59-39-01-72 🛏 14, 5 en suite 60 to 85F. Breakfast 11F. Full-board 120–130F. Coaches welcome (rest. seats 150). Evening meals until midnight. Lourdes only 40km away.

OMONVILLE par BACQUEVILLE-EN-CAUX 76730 Seine-Maritime **RN 27 Map 4-A3**
🍷 ⊗ **A L'ARRET DES TOURISTES** (N° RR MAR 15 566) (Mme Colette **Devingt**) ☎ 35-83-20-78 Closed Sat, Sun and end of Aug, beginning Sept.

ORANGE 84100 Vaucluse **RN 7 Map 24-A2**
🍷 ⊗ **LE MOULIN A VENT** (N° RR JUN 25 031) (M. Henri **Garcia**) Pont de l'Aigue ☎ 90-34-02-41 Spanish, Italian spoken.

ORBEC 14290 Calvados **RD 31 Map 8-A2**
🍷 ⊗ **LE RELAIS DES ROUTIERS** (N° RR JUN 20 760) (Mme Marie-Claude **Morel**) 37, rue de Bernay ☎ 31-32-70-70 Closed Sun; Aug. Evening meals.

ORGENOY par PONTHIERRY 77310 Seine-et-Marne **RN 7 Map 9-B1**
🍷 ⊗ 🏠 **LE RELAIS DU KM43** (N° RR OCT 14 982) (M. **Saint-Jean**) ☎ 60-65-71-01 🛏 8 Closed Sat evening, Sun; Aug; Christmas to New Year. Evening meals served until 11.30pm.

ORGEVAL see MORAINVILLIERS

ORGON 13660 B.-du-R. **RN 7 Maps 24-A3 and B3**
🍷 ⊗ **LE BELLEVUE** (N° RR MARS 26 201) (M. Eugène **Giraud**) Quartier Paradou ☎ 90-73-00-24 Evening meals. English, German, Dutch spoken.

O

Y ⊗ **AU BEC FIN** (N° RR JUIL 26 948) (M. Michel **Toesca**) RN 7 ☎ 90-73-00-49 Closed Sun. Private car park (6000m²). English, Italian, Spanish spoken. Filling station open 24 hours.

Y ⊗ 🏠 **RELAIS DES FUMADES** (N° RR AVR 27 256) (M. Jean **Etcheverry**) ☎ 90-73-00-81 ⊷ 11 100 to 150F. German and English spoken. Evening meals served until 11pm.

ORLEANS 45100 Loiret **RN 20 and D 951 Map 13-A1**
Y ⊗ 🏠 **RELAIS DU PARC** (N° RR JUN 24 994) (M. Claude **Gibert**) 45, rue du Parc ☎ 38-53-34-13 ⊷ 9 Closed Sat, Sun. Coaches welcome (3 dining rooms = 106 seats). Evening meals.

Y ⊗ 🏠 **LE RELAIS DES QUATRE MARCHES** (N° RR DEC 16 327) (M. Pierre **Guyot**) 163, route de Saint-Mesmin ☎ 38-66-31-12 ⊷ 9 Closed Sat evening, Sun; Aug. Evening meals.

🖳 **Total Service Station LE RELAIS DE LA RETREVE** (N° RR MAI 25 433) Autoroute A10 Gidy Fleury-les-Aubrais ☎ 38-91-30-20 Open 24 hours.

ORLEANS-SARAN 45400 Loiret **Autoroute Aquitaine A10 Map 13-A1**
Y ⊗ **RELAIS DU VAL DE LOIRE** (N° RR RA-10) (M. Loïc **Brasseur**) Aire de Service de Gidy Saran ☎ 38-73-30-20 Self-service restaurant open 6.00am to midnight. English, German, Spanish spoken. Telex 780959.

ORNANS 25290 Doubs **RD 67 Map 14-B3**
Y ⊗ 🏠 **1 Star NN HÔTEL LE PROGRES** (N° RR AOU 20 800) (M. **Perriot-Comte**) 11, rue Jacques-Gervais ☎ 81-62-16-79 ⊷ 15 from 135–150F, breakfast 20F, telephone, WC in room. Closed Sun evening in winter. Bar; dogs allowed; recreations (fishing, shooting, canoeing, swimming, tennis). Places to visit: Loue Valley, Museums. Menus 50–160F. Specialities: Trout, *Terrine maison, Escargot maison*.

OSNY 95520 Val-d'Oise **RN 15 Maps 1-A2 and 3-B2**
Y ⊗ 🏠 **LE RELAIS DE LA DEMI-LIEUE** (N° RR FEV 18 012) (Mme **Massari**) route de Gisors ☎ 30-30-15-12 Closed Sat, Sun; Aug. Coaches welcome (rest. seats 90).

OUISTREHAM 14150 Calvados **RD 514 Map 4-B2**
Y ⊗ **AU COIN DU PORT** (N° RR AVR 26 237) (M. Claude **Morin**) 90, avenue Michel-Cableu ☎ 31-97-15-22 Closed Sun; Coaches welcome (rest. seats 60). Evening meals served until midnight.

OURVILLE-EN-CAUX 76450 Seine-Maritime **Map 4-A3**
Y ⊗ 🏠 **BAR DE LA PLACE** (N° RR MAI 25 924) (M. Jean-Pierre **Pouchet**) Place Jean-Picard ☎ 35-27-60-01 ⊷ 10 Closed Aug. Full-board 120–140F per night. Coaches welcome (rest. seats 45). Evening meals.

OUZOUER-LE-MARCHE 41240 L.-et-C. **RN 157 Maps 8-B3 and 12-A3**
Y ⊗ 🏠 **LA HALTE BEAUCERONNE** (N° RR NOV 11 912) (M. Marcel **Malaquin**) 18, place de l'Eglise RN 157 ☎ 54-82-41-26 ⊷ 5 from

O

Ouzouer-Le-Marche continued
62–105F, breakfast 18,50–19,50F Closed Tue; 15 to 30 Jan; 15 to 29 Jul. Coaches welcome (rest. seats 60 breakfast only). Evening meals served to hotel guests only. Car park; amusements (pin ball etc). Places to visit: Châteaux, Chambord, Orleans.

OZON 65190 Htes-Pyr **RN 117 Map 21-A3**
♟ ⊗ **AUBERGE DU PETIT ROBINSON** (N° RR FEV 25 810) (M. Jean-Roger **Labarde**) Rte de Toulouse ☎ 62-35-70-01 Open 24 hrs. Coaches welcome (rest. seats 120). Evening meals. English, Italian, Spanish spoken.

OZOURT par MONTFORT 40380 Landes **RD 32 Map 20-B2**
♟ ⊗ **AUBERGE DU ROUTIER** (N° RR JUL 23 859) (M. Alain **Deschamps**) ☎ 58-98-65-98 Closd Tue 2.00pm to 6.30pm.

P

PACADIÈRE (LA) 42310 Loire **Map 16-B3**
♟ ⊗ **LE RELAIS DU LAC** (N° RR MARS 27 210) (M. Marcel **Vernay**) RN 7 ☎ 77-64-36-08 ⊸ 4.

PACÉ par ALENÇON 61000 Orne **RN 12 Map 8-B2**
♟ ⊗ **LE RELAIS DES ROUTIERS Tobacconist** (N° RR SEPT 12 434) (M. Marcel **Bruneau**) 12, route de Bretagne (7 km from Alençon) ☎ 33-27-70-69 Closed Sat afternoon, Sun afternoon; Sun during winter. Coaches welcome (rest. seats 70). Evening meals.

PAIMPOL 22500 Côte-du-Nord **Map 7-A2**
♟ ⊗ **LE TRISKEL** (N° RR SEPT 26 649) (M. Daniel **Hello**) 15, av. Chateaubriand ☎ 96-20-82-72 Closed Sun and Aug. English spoken. Evening meals served until 9.30pm.

PAJAY 38260 Isère **RD 73 Map 18-B3**
♟ ⊗ 🏠 **LE RELAIS DE MA PETITE AUBERGE** (N° RR JUL 19 435) (Mme Huguette **Vivier**) La Côte-Saint-André ☎ 74-54-26-06 ⊸ 7 Closed Sept. Full-board 130–160F per night. Coaches welcome (rest. seats 58). English, some German spoken. Evening meals served until 9pm. Menus 50–120F. Specialities: *Grenouilles, Lotte a l'Américiane, Gratin Dauphilois.*

PALLICE (LA) Charente-Marit. **RN 22 Map 11-B1 see ROCHELLE (LA)**

PANTIN 93500 Seine-St-Denis Porte de Pantin **RN 3 Map 1-A/2-3**
♟ ⊗ **RESTODERM** SARL (N° RR JUN 25 026) (M. **Demougin**) 110, bis avenue du Général Lecierc ☎ 48-44-75-84 Closed Sat, Sun; public holidays. Coaches welcome (rest. seats 280 + 40).

P

♈ ⊗ **EUROPE TABAC SABRIE** (N° RR AVR 23 220) (M. Georges **Sabrie**) 203, avenue Jean-Lolive ☎ 48-45-03-17 Closed Sun. German, English, Spanish, Italian spoken. Evening meals.

♈ ⊗ **LE RELAIS DU PONT** (N° RR DEC 27 472) (SARL) 25, avenue Edouard Vailant ☎ 48-45-80-73. Closed Saturday, Sunday and August. Evening meals. English, German, Spanish, Italian, Portuguese spoken.

PARAY-SOUS-BRIAILLES see CHAZEUIL 03500 Allier

PARIGNÉ 35133 Ille-et-Vilaine **CD 19 ET 108 Map 8-A/B1**
♈ ⊗ **FRANK'ELLE** (N° RR OCT 27 066) (M. Franck **Rousset**) 12, rue de la Mairie ☎ 99-97-22-90 Closed Mon pm.

PARIGNE-LE-POLLIN 72330 Sarthe **RN 23 Map 12-A2**
♈ ⊗ **LE RELAIS FLEURI** (N° RR JAN 26 145) (Mme Jacqueline **Bouchevereau SARL NB RESTAURATION**) La Chesnay RN 23 ☎ 43-87-81-41 Closed Sat afternoon, Sun. English spoken.

PARIS 75008
♈ ⊗ **LE RELAIS CHEZ LEON** (N° RR JAN 23 789) (Mme **Grange**) 5, rue de l'Isly ☎ 43-87-42-77 Closed Sun, Aug.

PARIS 75012
♈ ⊗ **CHEZ MADJID** (N° RR JANV 27 146) (M. Madjid **Blaidi**) 8, rue du Charolais ☎ 43-43-63-86 Closed Sat and July. Friday's Special couscous.

PARIS 75013
♈ ⊗ ⌂ **AU RENDEZ-VOUS DES ROUTIERS Chez Smail** (N° RR JUL 22 881) (M. Naït **Mohand**) 117, quai de la Care ☎ 45-84-57-06 ⊣ 24 Arabic spoken. Evening meals.

♈ ⊗ **LE RELAIS CHEZ MOMO** (N° RR OCT 25 062) (Mme Ghylaine **Varin**) 127, quai de la Gare ☎ 45-85-23-42 Closed Sun. Evening meals until midnight.

PARIS 75016
♈ ⊗ **A LA RENOMMEE D'AUTEUIL** (N° RR AVR 23 219) (M. Francis **Zanoletti**) 21, rue Gros ☎ 45-27-49-33 Closed Sat, Sun; Jul.

PARIS 75018
♈ ⊗ **LE RELAIS DES ROUTIERS** (N° RR OCT 15 413) (M. Bernard **Dubreuil**) 50 bis, rue Marx-Dormoy ☎ 46-07-93-80 Closed Sun and Aug. Evening meals served until 10pm. Coaches welcome (rest. seats 50).

PARIS 75019
♈ ⊗ **CHEZ MICHELE** (N° RR MAI 22 354) (M. Guy **Garnier**) 243, rue de Crimée ☎ 46-07-56-23 Closed Sun.

PARIS 75020
♈ ⊗ **ETOILE DE LISBONNE** (N° RR AOU 25 522) (M. Manuel

P

Paris continued

Duarte) 139, bld. Davout ☎ 43-61-04-80 Closed Aug. Spanish, Portuguese spoken.

PARON 89100 Yonne **RN 60 Map 9-B2**
⚲ ⊗ **LE RELAIS DE ST-BOND** (N° RR MARS 25 835) (M. Daniel **Millard**) 32, avenue Jean-Jaurès ☎ 86-95-41-41 Closed Sun. Evening meals.

PAU 64000 Pyr.-Atl. **RN 117/134 Maps 20-B3 and 21-A3**
⚲ ⊗ **RELAIS BELLEVUE** (N° RR MAR 23 204) (Mme **Lorry**) Belair par Buziet ☎ 59-21-76-03 ⊷ 6 Closed Sat, Christmas. Some Spanish spoken.
⚲ ⊗ 🏠 **1 Star NN HOTEL DU BOIS LOUIS** (N° RR SEPT 23 482) (M. **Bareille**) 18, avenue Gaston-Lacoste ☎ 59-27-34-98 ⊷ 8 Closed Sun and first 2 weeks Aug. Coaches welcome (rest. seats 65). Evening meals served until 10pm.
⚲ ⊗ **LE RELAIS DE L'INDUSTRIE** (N° RR MAI 23 801) (Mme Yveline **Sala**) avenue Larregain quartier Montauba Lons ☎ 59-32-07-57 Closed Sat, Sun. Coaches welcome (2 dining rooms = 230 seats). Italian, German, some English spoken.

PAUILLAC 33250 Gironde **RD 2 Maps 15-A3 and 20-A1**
⚲ ⊗ 🏠 **LE YACHTING** (N° RR JAN 26 136) (Mme Louisette **Puyfour-cat**) 12, Port de Plaisance ☎ 56-59-06-43 ⊷ 16 (single rooms use of shower, for bearers of 'Les Routiers card, 100F). Closed Sat in winter. Coaches welcome (rest. seats 100). Evening meals.
⚲ ⊗ 🏠 **LA TORCHE** (N° RR NOV 27 099) (Mme Maryse **Tisinger**) 2, quai A. Depichon ☎ 56-59-19-20 ⊷ 5 Closed Sun pm low season and Jan. English spoken. Full-board 185F. Coaches welcome (rest. seats 40). Evening meals served until 10.30pm.

PAULHAGUET 43230 Haute-Loire **RN 102 Map 17-A3**
⚲ ⊗ 🏠 **LE COQ HARDI** (N° RR MAR 22 715) (Mme Marie-Louise **Meyronneine**) La Chomette ☎ 71-76-62-29. Closed Sat and Oct. Coaches welcome (rest. seats 60).
⚲ ⊗ 🏠 **LES TILLEULS** (N° RR DEC 23 560) (M. Gilbert **Vigouroux**) Saint-Georges-d'Aurac ☎ 71-77-50-75 ⊷ 6 Closed Sat evening; Sun, 2 weeks in Aug. Evening meals until 11.30pm. Coaches welcome (rest. seats 50).

PAULHAN 34230 Hérault **Map 23-A2**
⚲ ⊗ **LE CASTEL FLEURI** (N° RR JUL 25 057) (M. Bernard **Belan**) 11, avenue de la Gare ☎ 67-25-01-23 Public car park; filling station (8am–8.30pm) near. English, Italian spoken.

PAVILLONS-SOUS-BOIS (LES) 93320 Seine-St-Denis **RN 3 Map 1-A3**
⚲ ⊗ **CAFÉ DU STADE** (N° RR JUL 23 368) (M. Marc **Muller**) 31, rue A.-France ☎ 48-48-10-98. Closed Sun, Aug. Evening meals.

PEAGE (LE) (Commune de SERAZEREUX par CHATEAUNEUF-EN-THYMERAIS) 28210 Eure-et-Loir **RN 154 Map 8-A3**
⚲ ⊗ **AU BON ACCUEIL** (N° RR FEV 16 440) (Mme Élaine **Herisson**) Le Péage ☎ 37-65-22-49 Closed Sat, Sun. Evening meals served.

P

PEDERNEC 22540 C. du N. **Map 7-A2**
♈ ⊗ **RELAIS DE MAUDEZ** (N° RR JUL 26 614) (M. Denis **Dutillet**) ☎ 96-45-31-28 Closed Sun.

PELLEVOISIN 36500 Indre **RD 11 Map 12-B3**
♈ ⊗ ⌂ **LES ROUTIERS DE LA POSTE CHEZ BABETTE** (N° RR MARS 28 837) (Mme Elisabeth **Petit**) 30, rue Jean-Giraudoux ☎ 54-39-03-78 ⊸ 4 Closed Mon evening and October. Full board from 150 to 175F. Coaches welcome (rest. seats 70). Evening meals. English spoken.

PELUSSIN 42410 Loire **Map 2-B1**
♈ ⊗ ⌂ **LE CLUB** (M. Alan **Daveau**) Rue Antoine Eyraud ☎ 74-87-61-69 ⊸ 6 English and German spoken. Evening meals served until 9pm.

PERCY 50410 Manche **RD 999 Map 8-A1**
♈ ⊗ **LE RELAIS DE LA GARE** (N° RR OCT 24 704) (M. Bernard **Guillotte**) ☎ 33-61-20-96 **Minitel** ⊸ 4 Closed Sun; 1 to 13 Aug inl. Full-board 130F per night. Evening meals until 10pm.

PERIGNY 03120 Allier **RN 7 Map 16-A/B3**
♈ ⊗ **AUBERGE FLEURIE** (N° RR JUN 26 926) (Mme Patricia **Milius**) Lapalisse ☎ 70-99-81-23 Closed Mon. German, English, Spanish, Italian spoken. Filling station (24 hrs) 5km distant. Coaches welcome (rest. seats 30). Evening meals served until midnight.

PERIGUEUX 24000 Dordogne **RN 89 Map 15-B3**
♈ ⊗ **RELAIS BIBY** (N° RR MAR 21 821) (M. Jean-Piene **Mazarguil**) 202 bis, route d'Angoulême ☎ 53-53-47-46 Closed Sun, Mon.
♈ ⊗ **LES ROUTIERS CHEZ ODETTE** (N° RR SEPT 27 025) (Mme Marie Odile **Lacombe**) 129, avenue du Maréchal Juin ☎ 53-08-64-11 Closed Sun. English spoken. Evening meals.

PERONNE 80200 Somme **RN 17 Maps 5-B3 and 6-A1**
♈ ⊗ ⌂ **CHEZ BÉATRICE** (N° RR SEPT 26 320) (M. Serge **Seilier**) 61, route de Paris ☎ 22-84-10-82 ⊸ 6 Closed Sun; 2nd fortnight Aug; Easter week. Full-board 155F per night. Coaches welcome (rest. seats 25). Meals served until 9.30pm. German, English spoken.

PERONNE-ASSEVILLERS 80200 Somme **Autoroute A1 Maps 5-A3 and 6-A1**
♈ ⊗ **ACCOR L'ARCHE** (M. Aimé **Henry**) Aire de Service d'Asservilliers Province/Paris direction ☎ 22-85-20-35 Telex 140828 Open 24 hours. Self-service restaurant. Shop, TV, Showers. English, German spoken.

PERPIGNAN 66000 Pyrénées-Orientales **Map 23-A3**
⌂   **LA CHAUMIÈRE** (N° RR FEV 26807) (M. Michel **Mallet**) ZL St. Charles ☎ 68-56-57-69 Closed Sat evening, Sun; Aug.
⊗   **POLYGONE NORD** (N° RR MAI 27 290) (M. Claude **Lacaze**) 10, rue Beau de Rochas ☎ 68-61-35-15 Closed Sat and Sun.

P

PERIGNY 03120 Allier **RN 7 Map 16-A/B3**
♀ ⊗ ⌂ **LE RELAIS DE PERIGNY** (N° RR DEC 27 483) (M. Patrice **Cardinaud**) Rue de Perigny ☎ 70-99-84-57 ⊷ 6 Closed Saturday, Sunday. German spoken. Evening meals.

PERRUSSON 37600 I.-et-L. **RN 143 Map 12-B3**
♀ ⊗ ⌂ **LE RELAIS DES ROUTIERS** (N° RR JUN 16 590) (M. Kleber **Lanchais**) 3, rue de l'Indre ☎ 47-59-39-76 ⊷ 8 Closed Sun evening; 15 days in Aug. Holds the Relais Diplôme D'Honneur. Full-board 140F per night. Coaches welcome (rest. seats 120). Evening meals.

PERTHES 521400 Haute-Marne **RN 4 Map 9-A3**
♀ ⊗ ⌂ **LE COMMERCE** (N° RR JAN 26 141) (Mme Gilberte **Douard**) Rte Nle 4 ☎ 25-56-41-79 ⊷ 18 Closed Sat, Sun open 24 hrs. Evening meals.

PERTUIS (LE) 43200 Haute-Loire **RN 88 Map 18-A3**
♀ ⊗ ⌂ **LE RELAIS DU COL** (N° RR SEP 17 888) (M. Simon **Vercher**) ☎ 71-57-60-06 ⊷ 12. Spanish spoken.

PERTUIS 84120 Vaucluse **Map 24-B3**
♀ ⊗ **LE VICTOR HUGO** (N° RR AVR 26 233) (Mme Ghislaine **Pelisson**) 143 Bld Victor Hugo ☎ 90-79-12-29 Closed Sun; 20 days Aug. Coaches welcome (rest. seats 50). Evening meals served until midnight. Italian, Spanish, English spoken.

PERUSE (LA) 16270 Charente **RN 141**
♀ ⊗ **LES ROUTIERS** (N° RR JAN 27 493) (M. André **Troussieux**) ☎ 45-71-11-73 Evening meals. Service station open 8.30am to 7pm 30 metres away.

PETIT-FOSSARD (LE) 77130 S.-et-M. **RN 5 Map 9-B2**
♀ ⊗ ⌂ **LE RELAIS DU PETIT-FOSSARD** (N° RR OCT 20 572) (M. Jean **Guillard**) ☎ 64-32-03-28 and 64-32-17-47 ⊷ 6 Closed Sat afternoon, Sun; Aug; holidays. Evening meals until 11pm.

PETIT-REDERCHING 57410 Moselle **RN 410 Map 10-B1**
♀ ⊗ **REST DE LA GARE** (N° RR OCT 8 908) (M. Bernard **Vogel**) 6, rue de Strasbourg ☎ 87-09-81-09 **Minitel** Closed Sat; 15 Jul–15 Aug. Evening meals.

PETITE-BOISSIERE (LA) 79700 Deux-Sèvres **RN 148 bis Maps 11-B3 and 12-B1**
♀ ⊗ Tobacconist **LE RELAIS DES ROUTIERS** (N° RR JUL 23 858) (M. Jean-Michel **Charrier**) Grande Rue ☎ 49-81-42-72 Closed Mon afternoon and several days in Aug. Coaches welcome (rest. seats 70). Evening meals served until 11pm.

PETITES (LES) LOGES see REIMS

PETIVILLE 14390 Calvados **RD 513 Map 4-B2**
♀ ⊗ **LE COLOMBIER** (N° RR NOV 26 103) (M. Gèrard **Baudel**) Cabourg ☎ 31-78-00-67 Closed Sun; Sept.

P

PEYRIAC-DE-MER 11440 Aude **RN 9 Map 23-A3**
Y ⊗ **RELAIS PORTE DES CORBIÈRES** (N° RR NOV 27 109) (Mme Béatrice **Vincent**) ☎ 68-48-30-88 Closed Sun. English and German spoken. Coaches welcome (rest. seats 85). Evening meals served until 1am.

PEZOU FONTAINE 41100 L.-et-C. **RN 10 Map 12-A3**
Y ⊗ ⌂ **RELAIS D'ARGENTEUIL** (N° RR JAN 26 142) (M. Pierre **Hauville**) RN 10 ☎ 54-23-42-47 ⊷ 5 Closed Sun and Aug. Evening meals. Coaches welcome (rest. seats 60).
Y ⊗ **L'ÉTAPE** (N° RR MARS 27 214) (M. Claude **Chève**) RN 10 ☎ 54-23-42-85 Closed Sat pm and Sun.

PHILIPPSBOURG 57230 Moselle **RN 62 Map 10-B1 see BITCHE**

PIA 6380 Pyr. Orientales **Map 23-A3**
Y ⊗ **AU P'TIT NICE** (N° RR OCT 26 398) (M. Jean Louis **Leone**) Km5 RN 9 ☎ 68-61-05-70 Closed Sun. Spanish, Italian, Arabic spoken. Evening meals served until 11pm. Coaches welcome (rest. seats 50).

PIACE 72170 Sarthe **RN 138 Map 8-B2**
Y ⊗ **LES DEUX RENARDS** (N° RR SEPT 27 004) (M. Jérôme **Brilliet**) Le Bourg ☎ 43-97-02-16. Closed Sat afternoon, Sun. Coaches welcome (rest. seats 60). Evening meals served until 11pm. Filling station at 4km.

PIAN MEDOC (LE) 33290 Gironde **RD 1 Map 15-A3**
Y ⊗ **LE CHAMPETRE** (N° RR FEV 26 176) (Mme Arlette **Decons**) Chabanau ☎ 56-72-04-72 Closed Sat, Sun. English, Yugoslavian, Spanish spoken.

PICAUVILLE 56360 Manche **see PONT-L'ABBE**

PIERREFITTE 93380 Seine-St-Denis **Map 1-A3**
Y ⊗ **LE NORMANDIE** (N° RR JUN 24 982) (Mme **Vidal**) 105 av. Galliéni ☎ 48-26-55-62 Closed Sun; 2nd fortnight Sept. Evening meals served until 10pm. Some English, Spanish spoken.
Y ⊗ **AU RENDEZ-VOUS DES ROUTIERS** (N° RR JUN 26 571) (Mme Aicha **Habj**) 71, ave Lénine ☎ 48-26-53-59 Closed Sun; Aug. Coaches welcome (rest. seats 80). Evening meals. Arabic spoken.
Y ⊗ **AU RENDEZVOUS DES ROUTIERS** (N° RR JAN 27 498) (M. Hammoutz et M. **Glozrane**) 71, avenue Lenine. ☎ 48-26-53-59. Evening meals. Closed Sunday.

PIERREFITTE-NESTALAS 65260 Hautes Pyr. **RN 21 Map 21-A3**
Y ⊗ ⌂ **LE RELAIS DE BEL-AIR** (N° RR JUN 21 131) (M. Raymond **Bellocq**) 5, rue Lavoisier ☎ 62-97-75-22 ⊷ 11 Closed 15 Sep–15 Oct. Full-board 152F per night. Evening meals served until 11pm. Spanish spoken. Coaches welcome (rest seats 25).

P

PIERREFITTE-RONAI 61160 Orne **RN 158 Map 8-A2**
♀ ⊗ **LE PIERREFITTE** (N° RR JANV 27 143) (M. Yves **Delaunay**)
Trun ☎ 33-35-95-06 Closed Mon and Jan. Evening meals served
until 11pm.

PIERREFITTE-SUR-LOIRE 03470 Allier **Map 16-A3**
♀ ⊗ **AU CAFÉ DE LA MAIRIE** (N° RR JUIL 27 322) (M. Daniel
Monnier) Place de l'Église ☎ 70-47-00-87 Closed Wed pm low
season and Jan. Evening meals served until 11pm.

PIERRELATTE 26700 Drôme **RN 7 Map 24-A2**
⊗ **RESTAURANT DU TRICASTIN** (N° RR OCT 25 722) (M.
François **Spagna**) RN 7 ☎ 75-96-34-11 Italian, Portuguese,
German, Spanish spoken.

PIEUX (LES) 50340 Manche **RD 904 and 265 Map 4-A/B1**
♀ ⊗ **T'CHEU P'TIT LOUIS** (N° RR MAR 23 687) (M. Louis **Mabire**) 17,
rue Centrale ☎ 33-52-43-18.

PIN MORIES-LE-MONASTIER Lieu-dit LES AJUSTONS 48100 Lozère **RN 9 Map 17-B3 et 23-A1**
♀ ⊗ ⌂ **1 star NN LES AJUSTONS** (N° RR MAR 20 128) (M. Guy
Gibelin) Marvejols ☎ 66-32-70-35 Closed Sat/Sun and 15/12 to 15/
1. Evening meals served until 9pm.

PINOLS 43200 Haute-Loire **RN 590 Map 17-A3**
♀ ⊗ ⌂ **HÔTEL DES VOYAGEURS** (N° RR JUL 19 853) (Mme **Cornet**)
71-74-11-42 ⊷ 9 Full-board 150–160F per night. Coaches welcome (rest. seats 50). Meals until 10pm.

PIOLENC 84420 Vaucluse **Autoroute A7 Map 24-A2**
♀ ⊗ **LE COMMERCE** (N° RR NOV 25 182) (M. Roger **Sambucini**)
🏧 place Cours Corsin ☎ 90-37-60-14 Closed Wed; Nov. Coaches
welcome (rest. seats 60). English spoken. Evening meals served
until 9pm.

PIPRIAC 35550 I.-et-V. **RD 777 Map 7-B3**
♀ ⊗ ⌂ **1 Star NN LE RELAIS DE LA TOUR D'AUVERGNE** (N° RR
NOV 22 093) (M. Michel **Gérard**) 7, rue de l'Avenir ☎ 99-34-41-34
⊷ 10 80–130F. Breakfast 15–25F. Closed Mon (except lunchtime);
Feb. Full-board 180–250F per night. Coaches welcome (rest.
seats 105). Evening meals served until 9pm. Local points of
interest – castle, glass blowing and craft shops.

PISSOS 40410 Landes **RD 43 and 20 Map 20-B1**
♀ ⊗ **HÔTEL DU COMMERCE** (N° RR MAR 24 533) (M. Jean-Jacques
Mondat) **Au Bourg** ☎ 58-07-70-16 ⊷ 10 Closed Fri; Jan; end Oct.
Full-board 145F per night. Coaches welcome (rest. seats
60).Evening meals. English spoken.

PITHIVIERS 45300 Loiret **RN 51 Map 9-B1**
♀ ⊗ **LA PORTE DE BEAUCE** (M. Christian **Collard**) 6 Mail Ouest ☎
38-30-02-52 Closed Mon and Sept. English spoken.
♀ ⊗ **RELAIS D'INTVILLE LA GUÉTARD/CHEZ LULU** (Mme

Lucienne **Loeillet**) Route de Puttuiviers – Intville la Guétard ☎ 38-39-71-70. Closed Sat, Sun. Evening meals served unil 9pm.

PLAGNY 58000 Nièvre **Map 13-B2**
⊗   **LE RELAIS DE PLAGNY** (N° RR JAN 25 267) (M. Maurice **Chet**) 108, route de Lyon **Nevers** ☎ 86-57-51-51 ⊢ 3 Closed Sun; 1 week at Christmas; 15 days in Aug.

PLAINE-SAINT-DENIS 93210 Seine-Saint-Denis **RN 1 Porte de la Chapelle Map 1-A2**
♈ ⊗ **LE RELAIS DE LA PLAINE** (N° RR OCT 25 127) (M. Amar **Kejat**) 138, avenue du Président-Wilson ☎ 48-20-02-31 Closed Sun. Arabic, Spanish spoken.
♈ ⊗ **LE CRISTAL** (N° RR AVR 25 366) (M. André **Leconte**) 101, av. du Président-Wilson ☎ 42-03-77-78 Closed Sun. English spoken.

LA PLAINE see SAINT-DENIS

PLAISANCE-DU-GERS 32160 Gers **RN 646 Map 12-A2**
♈ ⊗ 🏠 **LA PERGOLA** (N° RR OCT 14 040) (Mme Christiane **Lagisquet**) 11, allée des Ormeaux ☎ 62-69-30-22 ⊢ 10 Closed Sat in low season, 24 Dec–3 Jan. Full-board 125–150F per night. Coaches welcome (rest. seats 50). Evening meals until 11pm.

PLAINTEL 22940 C.-du-N. **Map 7-A2**
♈ ⊗ 🏠 **A LA DESCENTE DES CHAOS** (N° RR AOU 25 616) (M. Jean-Claude **Bonenfant**) gare de Plaintel ☎ 96-32-16-05 ⊢ 8 Closed Tue afternoon, Sun afternoon; Aug. English spoken.
♈ ⊗ **LE SÉBASTOPOL** (N° RR MARS 26 474) (Mme Colette **Helary**) route de Sébastopol ☎ 96-32-15-74 Closed Sun; Aug. Coaches welcome (rest. seats c.100). Evening meals. English, German spoken.

PLENÉE JUGON 22640 Côtes-du-Nord **RN 12 Map 7-A3**
♈ ⊗ **LES GARENNES** (N° RR SEPT 27 007) (M. Jean **Elings**) **Liet dit Les Garennes** ☎ 96-34-52-11 English, Spanish and Dutch spoken. Evening meals.

PLEUMEUR-GAUTIER 22740 Côtes-du-Nord **CD 33 Map 7-A2**
♈ ⊗ **CHEZ CINDY** (M. Herré **Le Foll**) Route de Tréquier, La Croiz Neuve ☎ 96-92-42-19 Closed Sat and 15/8 to 15/9. Evening meals served until 9pm.

PLEYBEN 29190 Finistère **RN 787 and Dle 787 Map 7-A2**
♈ ⊗ **HÔTEL DES VOYAGEURS** (N° RR SEPT 26 648) (M. Jean-Yves **Marzin**) 17, Grande Place, Charles de Gaulle ☎ 98-26-61-06 ⊢ 7 Closed Fri evening, Sun; 2nd/3rd week Aug. Coaches welcome (rest. seats 64). Evening meals until 9pm.

PLIVOT 51150 Marne **RD 3 Map 9-A3**
♈ ⊗ **LE JARD** (N° RR JAN 26 156) (M. **Garcia**) 2, rue Maréchal Leclerc ☎ 26-57-68-15 Closed Sun; public holidays; 15 days in Jul; 15 days Feb. Coaches welcome (rest. seats 60). Special menu available. Evening meals except Mon. English spoken.

P

PLOERMEL 56800 Morbihan **RN 24 Map 7-B3**
Y ⊗ 🏠 **LES ROUTIERS** (N° RR DEC 20 052) (Mme Solange **Rio**) route de Rennes ☎ 97-74-00-48 **Minitel** ⇥ 11 Closed Sat; Sept; 1 week at Christmas to New Year. Coaches welcome (rest. seats 150). Evening meals served until 10pm.

PLOMBIERES-LES-BAINS 88370 Vosges **RN 57 Maps 14-B2 and 10-A3**
Y ⊗ 🏠 **1 Star NN LE RELAIS STRASBOURGEOIS** (N° RR AVR 6 049) (M. Alain **Robert**) 3, place Beaumarchais ☎ 29-66-00-70 ⇥ 13 57 to 150F. Breakfast 20F. Closed Sun 1 Oct to 1 April; Nov. Full-board 158–200F per night. Coaches welcome (rest. seats 80). Evening meals. **Total Service Station** opposite hotel. Thermal resort nearby.

PLOMELIN 29000 Finistère **RN 785 Map 7-B1**
Y ⊗ 🍷 **LE RELAIS DE L'AVANTAGE** (N° RR JUN 10 737) (M. Alain **Le Vergos**) ☎ 98-94-22-06.

PLOUAGAT 22170 C. du N. **RN 12 Quintin exit CD7**
Y ⊗ **CHEZ PIERRETTE** (N° RR AOUT 26 296) (**SARL Drouin**) ZA de Fournello Sortie Quintin ☎ 96-74-28-13 Closed Sat midday, Sun. Coaches welcome (rest. seats 124), reservations necessary. Evening meals until 1am.

PLOUEDERN 29220 Finistère **RN 12 Map 7-A1**
Y ⊗ **LE RELAIS KERIEL** (N° RR JUN 24 264) (Mme Marie **Gac**) Keriel - Landerneau ☎ 98-20-82-53 **Minitel** Closed end Sept to beginning Oct for 2 weeks. Coaches welcome (rest. seats 50). Evening meals served until 9pm. English spoken.

PLOUER-SUR-RANCE 22490 Côtes-du-Nord **RD 366 Map 7-A3**
Y ⊗ **LE BON ACCUEIL CHEZ THEO** (N° RR MARS 26 483) (M. Théo **Yris**) La Gourbanière ☎ 96-86-91-67 Closed Mon afternoon, Aug.

PLOUGOUMELEN 56400 Morbihan **RN 165 Map 11-A1**
Y ⊗ **LE KENYAH** (N° RR MAI 26 893) (M. Joël **Boriller**), Zone Commerciale du Kenyah ☎ 97-56-25-37 Closed Sun. Public car park. English spoken. Filling station near. Coaches welcome (rest. seats 120). Evening meals.

PLOUGUENAST 22150 C.-du-N. **RN 168 Map 7-A2**
Y ⊗ **LE RELAIS DU SQUARE** (N° RR JUL 20 257) (Mme Sylviane **Lafon-Sagory**) route de Moncontour ☎ 96-28-70-47 ⇥ 2.

PLOUHINEC 29780 Finistere
⊗ **RESTO GRILL AN DOAL MEN** (N° RR DEC 27 470) (M. Daniel **Ogor**) 3, Rue du General-Leclerc ☎ 98-70-76-20 Closed Sunday. Evening meals until 9pm. English spoken.

PLOUIGNEAU 29234 Finistère **Map 7-A2**
Y ⊗ **LE RELAIS DES SPORTS** (N° RR JAN 26 151) (M. Paul **Talguen**) 18, rue du 9 Août ☎ 98-67-71-37 Closed Sun (except for banquets); Aug. Coaches welcome (rest. seats 65). Evening meals.

P

PLOUNEVEZ-MOEDEC 22810 C.-du-N. **RN 12 main road exit D 11 Map 7-A2**
♀ ⊗ ⌂ **AUX ROUTIERS – LE RELAIS DU BEG-AR-C'HRA** (N° RR JAN 3 717) (M. Jean- Marie **Rubeus**) N12 Begarchra exit (D11) ☎ 96-38-61-08 ↤ 11 (6 deluxe) Closed Sat, Sun; 10 days between 20 Aug–20 Sep. Coaches welcome (rest. seats 160). Evening meals served until 10pm. English spoken.

PLOUVENEZ-QUINTIN 22110 C.-du-N. **RN 790 Map 7-A/B2**
♀ ⊗ **LE RELAIS DES ROUTIERS** (N° RR MAR 14 273) (Mme **Martin**) place de'Eglise ☎ 96-24-54-05 Closed Sat; 15 Aug to 1 Sept. Coaches welcome (rest. seats 180).

PLOURAY 56770 Morbihan **Map 7-B2**
♀ ⊗ **LE RELAIS DES SPORTS** (N° RR JUL 24 642) (M. Léandre **Le Lain**) 2, rue de l'Ellé ☎ 97-23-90-18 Closed Sun. Evening meals.

POITIERS 86000 Vienne **RN 10 Map 15-B1**
♀ ⊗ **LE RELAIS DES DOUVES** (N° RR OCT 20 854) (Mme **Gremillon**) 2, avenue de la Libération ☎ 49-37-80-04 ↤ 5 Coaches welcome (rest. seats 90). Evening meals served until 1am. English, German spoken.

POIX TERRON 08430 Ardennes **Map 6-A2**
♀ ⊗ **LE GODILLOT** (N° RR OCT 26 080) (M. José **Michel**) 26, Place de la Gare ☎ 24-35-61-46 ↤ 3 (1 double room) Closed Sat, Sun. Coaches welcome. Evening meals.

POMMEVIC 82400 T.-et-G. **RN 113 Map 21-B2**
♀ ⊗ ⌂ ⛺ **A LA BONNE AUBERGE** (N° RR OCT 12 514) (M. Pierre **Hume**) Route Nationale ☎ 63-39-56-69 ↤ 7 Closed Sat evening and 2 weeks in Nov. Full-board 150–180F per night. Coaches welcome (rest. seats 120). Evening meals served until 9.30pm. Menus from 49.50–130F. Specialities Maigret de Canard, Pitard au Porto, Foie Gras.

PONS 17800 Charente-Maritime **Map 15-A2**
♀ ⊗ **RESTO-GRILL CHARENTOTEL** Autoroute A10 Aire de Saint-Léger ☎ 46-91-95-30. Coaches welcome (rest. seats 200). Evening meals served until 10.15pm.

PONT-A-LA-QUESNE see CHERBOURG 50820 Manche.

PONT-A-MOUSSON see LOISY 54700 M.-et-M. **Autoroute A31 Map 14-B1**
⛽ **Les Routiers Total Service Station LE RELAIS DE L'OBRION** (N° RR AVR 22 779) Loisy ☎ 83-81-03-85 Open 24 hours. English, German, Italian spoken.
⛽ **Les Routiers Elf Service Station LE RELAIS DE LOISY** (N° RR JUL 22 883) (M. **Bouilhac**) Aire de service de Loisy ↤ 83-81-17-00 Open 24 hours. English, German spoken.
⊗ **TOURNEBRIDE** (MM **Joël** Frères) Autoroute A31 ☎ 83-81-18-89 Self-service restaurant with TV.

P

PONT-L'ABBE PICAUVILLE 50360 Manche **Map 4-B1**
♀ ⊗ 🏠 **HOTEL DES VOYAGEURS** (N° RR MAR 24 886) (Mme Fabienne **Françoise**) 43, rue de Périer ☎ 33-41-00-59 ⊢ 9 Closed Sun 1st Sep–Easter. Evening meals. English spoken.

PONT-D'AIN 01160 AIN **Map 18-B2**
♀ ⊗ **CRISNO** (N° RR NOV 26 731) (M. Christian **Sanchez**) 56, rue St-Exupéry ☎ 74-39-01-22. Coaches welcome (rest. seats 50). Evening meals.

PONTANEVAUX 71570 Saône-et-Loire **RN 6 Map 18-B1**
♀ ⊗ **Station-service CHEZ ALAMO** (N° RR MAI 27 279) (Mme Lydia **Paris**) ☎ 85-36-71-18 Closed Sat and Sun. Italian spoken. Evening meals.

PONTARLIER 25300 Doubs **Map 14-B3**
♀ ⊗ **CAFÉ DE LA LIBERTÉ** (N° RR SEPT 27 029) (Mmes Michèle **Besand** et Martine **Petit**) 36, rue de Salins ☎ 81-39-01-68 Closed Sun and 15/8 to 5/9. Coaches welcome (rest. seats 60). Evening meals.

PONT-D'ASPACH 68520 Haut-Rhin **Map 10-B3**
⚑ **Total Service Station LE RELAIS DE DIEFMATTEN** (N° RR SEP 24 688) Autoroute A36 Burnhaupt-le-Bas ☎ 89-48-74-00 German, English spoken.

PONT-AUDEMER 27500 Eure **RN 180 Map 4-B3**
♀ ⊗ **RELAIS DE ST-PAUL** (N° RR JUL 26 286) (M. Claude **Virfollet**) Les Saulniers Route de St-Paul ☎ 32-41-16-17 Closed Sun; 1st fortnight Aug. Evening meals.
♀ ⊗ **AU RENDEZ-VOUS DES CHAUFFEURS** (N° RR JUN 25 439) (M. Renaud **Pierrel**) 4, rue Notre-Dame-du-Pré ☎ 32-41-04-36 Closed Sun.
♀ ⊗ **RELAIS DU BOULANGARD** (N° RR AVR 23 0230 (M. Francis **Égret**) Corveville-sur-Riscle ☎ 32-57-01-27.

PONTAULT-COMBAULT 77340 S.-et-M. **RN 304 Map 1-B3**
♀ ⊗ 🏠 **SARL LE RELAIS DU PAVÉ** (N° RR DEC 27 115) (M. José **Da Silva**) 9, route de Paris ☎ 60-28-00-21 Closed Sun and Aug.

PONT-AVEN 29123 Finistère **RN 783 Map 7-B1**
♀ ⊗ 🏠 **CHEZ MELANIE ET MONIQUE** (N° RR OCT 17 916) (M. Bertrand **Le Goc**) Croissant-Kergoz ☎ 98-06-03-09 ⊢ 7 Closed Mon in Summer, Sept. Evening meals only Jun to Aug.

PONTCHARRA 38530 Isère **RN 90 Map 19-A2**
♀ ⊗ **LE RELAIS DU PONT DE LA GACHE** (N° RR AVR 25 357) (M. Jean-Pierre **Rubatat**) RN 90 **La GACHE** ☎ 76-97-30-08 Closed Sat; 15–30 Aug; 15 days at Christmas. Coaches welcome. Evening meals. English, Italian spoken. HGV parking.

PONTCHATEAU 44160 Loire-Atl. **RN 165 Map 11-A2**
♀ ⊗ 🏠 **LE RELAIS DE BEAULIEU** (N° RR AOU 7 869) (SARL Louisette **Praud**) ☎ 40-01-60-58 ⊢ 15 Coaches welcome (rest.

seats 70 + café, annexe). Evening meals until midnight. Menus from 42,30–140F. Specialities: Eels in cider, grilled salmon with butter, prawns à la Beaulieu. English spoken.

♟ ⊗ 🏠 **1 Star NN L'AUBERGE DU CALVAIRE** (N° RR NOV 20 885) (Mme **Couvrand**) 6, route de la Brière 4km from centre of Pontchâteau on Herbignac road. Le Calvaire ☎ 40-01-61-65 ⌐ 12 Full-board 160–188F per night. Coaches welcome (rest. seats 60). Evening meals served until 10pm.

PONTET (LE) 84130 Vaucluse **RN 7 Map 24-A3**
♟ ⊗ **LA CROIX VERTE** (N° RR DEC 24 439) (M. Guy **Prat**) route de Lyon ☎ 90-86-39-56 Closed Sun. Coaches welcome (rest. seats 120). Evening meals.

PONT-CHRETIEN-CHABENET 36800 Indre **RN 727 Map 16-A1**
♟ ⊗ **LE RELAIS DE BOUZANNE** (N° RR OCT 24 000) (M. Gilbert **Boileau**) 15, rue Principale ☎ 54-25-81-54 Closed Wed afternoon; 10 to 25 Aug. Evening meals.
♟ ⊗ **AUBERGE DU PONT** (N° RR JUIN 27 302) (Mme Yvelisé **Lardeau**) 46, rue Nationale ☎ 54-25-81-03 Closed Thurs and 15th to 30th Sept. Evening meals.

PONT GLENIC 23380 Creuse **see GLENIC**

PONT-DE-CHERUY 38230 Isere **RD 517 and 18 Map 2-A2**
♟ ⊗ **RELAIS CHEZ ZEPI** (N° RR AVR 26 490) (SARL **Delaur**) 30, rue Giffard ☎ 78-32-20-02 ⌐ 30 Closed Sun. Coaches welcome at weekend. Meals served until 10pm. English spoken.

PONT-DE-MENAT 63500 Puy-de-Dôme **RN 144 Map 16-B2**
♟ ⊗ 🏠 **LE RELAIS CHEZ ROGER** (N° RR JUN 13 786) (Mme Marie **Pinel**) ☎ 73-85-50-17 ⌐ 8 Closed Wed evening, Jan. Full-board 155–160F. Coaches welcome (rest. seats 80). Menus 55–70F and more. Specialities *Jambon d'Auvergne, potée auvergnate,* trout.

PONT-DE-NERS 30190 Gard **RN 106 Map 23-B1**
♟ ⊗ **LE TAHURE** (N° RR OCT 26 713) (M. Georges **Apostolakis**) Boucoiran **St-Chaptes** ☎ 66-83-65-93 Closed Sun off season. English spoken.

PONT DE POITTE 39130 Jura **RN 78 and 83 Map 19-A1**
♟ ⊗ 🏠 **1 star NN HOTEL DE L'HORLOGE** (M. André **Chiron**) 15 Grande Rue ☎ 84-48-30-09 ⌐ 10 Closed Tuesday (season), Wednesday (low season). English spoken. Heated swimming pool. Local points of interest: Lakes and caves.

PONT-EN-ROYAN
Voir SAINT-JUST-DE-CLAIX 38680 Isère

PONT-DES-SABLES 47200 Lot-et-Garonne **Map 21-A1**
♟ ⊗ **LE MARINIER** (N° RR JUN 24 991) (M. **Flores**) **Coussan-Marmande** Toll exit ☎ 53-93-60-37 Closed Sat, Sun. Evening meals served to 10pm. English, Italian, German, Spanish spoken.

P

PONT-DES-BEIGNERS 45530 Loiret **RN 60 Map 13-A1**
🍷 ⊗ **LE RELAIS DU PONT DES BEIGNERS** (N° RR JUL 17 581) (M. Jean-Pierre **Gueru**) ☎ 38-59-47-72 **Minitel** Closed Sat evening, Sun; mid Aug to mid Sept. Evening meals served to 10.30pm. Coaches welcome (rest. seats 80).

PONTGIBAUD 63230 Puy-de-Dôme **RN 141 Map 16-B2**
🍷 ⊗ ⌂ **LE RELAIS DES VOYAGEURS** (N° RR NOV 15 448) (M. **Sardier**) avenue de Verdun ☎ 73-88-70-35 ⊸ 16 Closed Nov. Full-board 135–140F per night. Coaches welcome (rest. seats 60). Evening meals.

PONT-HÉBERT 50880 Manche **RN 174 Map 4-A1**
🍷 ⊗ ⌂ **LE MADRILÉNE** (N° RR FEV 27 185) (Mme Marie-Thérèse **Hamlet**) Quartier du Pont-la-Meauffe ☎ 33-56-44-18 ⊸ 6

PONTHIERRY 77310 S.-et-M. **RN 7 Map 8-B1**
🍷 ⊗ **LE RELAIS DES TROIS MARCHES** (N° RR DEC 24 054) (Mme Odette **Pothier**) 7, rue de la Saussale ☎ 60-65-77-67 Closed Sun, Aug. Evening meals served to 9pm.

PONTIGNY 89230 Yonne **RN 77 Map 13-A2**
🍷 ⊗ ⌂ **RELAIS DE PONTIGNY** (N° RR AOUT 26 619) (Mme Carole **Leducq**) 9, rue Paul-Desjardins ☎ 86-47-42-83 ⊸ 8 Closed Sun. English, German, Italian spoken.

PONT-L'EVEQUE 71400 S.-et-L. **see AUTUN**

PONTOISE 95300 Val-d'Oise **RN 14 Maps 1-A2 and 9-A1**
🍷 ⊗ **RESTAURANT DE LA POSTE** (N° RR JAN 24 810) (M. Alain **Louat**) 68, rue Pierre-Butin ☎ 30-32-47-72 Closed Sat evening and Sunday. English spoken. Evening meal served to 9pm.

PONTORSON 50170 Manche **RN 176 Map 8-A1**
🍷 ⊗ ⌂ **LE FAMILY** (N° RR OCT 25 157) (Mme Antoinette **Hardel**) 4, rue de Rennes ☎ 33-60-00-21 **Minitel** ⊸ 12 Full-board 120F per night. Coaches welcome (rest. seats 60). Evening meals.

PONTORSON see SACEY

PONT-REMY 80580 Somme **Map 5-A3**
🍷 ⊗ **LE CONTINENTAL** (N° RR JUL 25 480) (Mme Ginette **Therasse**) SARL 9, rue Robert-Bordeux ☎ 22-27-12-89 Closed Aug. Coaches welcome (rest. seats 100).

PONT-ROYAL 08300 Ardennes **Map 6-B2**
🍷 ⊗ **LE RELAIS PONT-ROYAL** (N° RR AVR 24 561) (M. Yves **Detruiseux**) **Chatelet-sur-Retourne** ☎ 24-23-13-27 Closed Mon evening. Evening meals.

PONT-ROYAL 13370 B.-du-R. **RN 7 Map 24-B3**
🍷 ⊗ ⌂ **1 Star NN LE RELAIS PROVENÇAL** (N° RR AVR 15 614) (Mmes **Audibert and Arnadi**) ☎ 90-57-40-64 ⊸ 10 Closed Wed; Jan.

P

PONTS-ET-MARAIS 76260 S.-Marit **RD 1015 Bis Map 4-A2**
 Ⓨ ⊗ **LA FERME NIÇOISE** (N° RR JAN 26 777) (M. Patrick **Nalais**)
route de Gamache ☎ 35-86-50-37 Closed Sun.

PORCHERIE (LA) 87380 Haute-Vienne **RN 20 Map 17-A1**
 Ⓨ ⊗ 🏠 **RELAIS DE LA BORNE 40** (M. Michel **Reyrolle**) Beasoleil ☎
55-71-90-30 ◄ 7 Closed Sat evening and Sunday. Evening meals
served to 11.30pm.

PORT-A-BINSON 51700 Marne **Map 9-A2**
 Ⓨ ⊗ 🏠 **LE RELAIS DE LA GARE** (N° RR OCT 26 363) (Mme Nadine
Negri) 22, rue du Gl-Leclerc ☎ 26-58-30-41 ◄ 4 Closed Sun. Full-
board 135F per night. Coaches welcome (rest. seats 60).

POULIGNY-NOTRE-DAME 36160 Indre **RD 940 Map 16-A2**
 Ⓨ ⊗ 🏠 **LA CHAUME BLANCHE** (N° RR JUN 23 308) (M. René
Pilorget) ☎ 54-30-21-43 ◄ 7 Full-board from 190F per night.
Coaches welcome (rest. seats 45). English spoken.

POURIERRES 83470 Var **RN 7 Map 24-B3**
 Ⓨ ⊗ **LE LORRAINE PROVENCE** (Mme Mireille **Mohr**) ☎ 94-78-41-
28 English and Italian spoken. Evening meals served up to 10pm.

POUSSAN 34140 Herault **RN 113 Map 23-B2**
 Ⓨ ⊗ **LE LANDRY** (N° RR DEC 25 236) (Mme Ginette **Pasquettez**) ☎
67-78-24-74 Shops. Closed Sat afternoon, Sun. Spanish spoken.
 Ⓨ ⊗ **LE CHALET CHEZ CASTOR 05** (N° RR JUL 26 280) (M. Jean
Plawczyk) La Moulière ☎67-78-83-29 **Minitel** Closed Sat even-
⚓ ing, Sun from midday; Christmas to New Years Day. Coaches
welcome (rest. seats 120). Evening meals until 10pm. Polish
spoken. Menus from 55–98F. Specialities *Rouille de Sèche,*
Moules Monières maison.

POUSSAY 88500 Vosges **RN 413 Map 10-A2 and 14-B1**
 Ⓨ ⊗ 🏠 **AUBERGE DES PECHEURS** (N° RR NOV 2 282) (M. **Hingray**)
☎ 29-37-07-73 ◄ 7 Closed Tue; mid Dec – mid January. Evening
meals until 9pm.

POUZIN (LE) 07250 Ardèche **RN 86 Map 24-A1**
 Ⓨ ⊗ 🏠 **1 star NN ROUTIERS** (N° RR AVR 21 048) (Mme Juliette
Vialatte) 64, rue Olivier-de-Serres ☎ 75-63-83-45 ◄ 5 from 55–
85F. Closed Sun; 15 days Aug; 15 days Sept. Evening meals.

POZIERES 80300 Somme **RN 29 Map 5-B3**
 Ⓨ ⊗ **LE RELAIS DES ROUTIERS** (N° RR SEP 24 345) (Mme Josiane
Brihier) Route Nationale ☎ 22-75-23-05.

PRESSAC 86460 Vienne **RN 148 Map 15-B2**
 Ⓨ ⊗ **LE RELAIS** (N° RR MAI 25 409) (Mme Francine **Bouyer**) Place
de l'Église Mauprevoir ☎ 49-48-56-99 Closed Sat; Aug. Coaches
welcome (rest. seats 50). Evening meals.

P

PREZ-SOUS-LAFAUCHE 52700 Hte-Marne **Map 14-A1**
♀ ⊗ **LES 3 VALLEES** (N° RR AVR 24 550) (Mme Eliane **Trommens-chlager**) ☎ 25-31-57-84 Closed Aug. Coaches welcome (rest. seats 140). Evening meals. Open 24 hrs.

PRIMAUBE (LA) 12450 Aveyron **RN 88 Map 22-B1**
♀ ⊗ **LES ROUTIERS** (N° RR MAI 26 534) (**Castanie Frères**) 3, avenue de Rodez ☎ 65-71-40-31 Closed Sun.

PRIVAS 07000 Ardèche **RN 104 Map 24-A1**
♀ ⊗ **LA RENAISSANCE** (N° RR MAR 21 437) (M. **Monteil**) 4, place du Champ-de Mars ☎ 75-64-21-60 Closed Sun, Aug.

PROSNES 51400 Marne **RD 31 Map 6-B2**
♀ ⊗ **LE RELAIS CONSTANTINE** (N° RR NOV 14 593) (M. René **Roselet**) Constantine Route Nationale ☎ 26-61-70-70 **Minitel** Closed Sat, Sun; 15 to 31 Aug. Coaches welcome (rest. seats 150). Evening meals until 11pm.

PROVILLE-LEZ-CAMBRAI see CAMBRAI 59400 Nord **RN 17 Map 6-A1 and 5-B3**

PROVINS 77160 S.-et-M. **RN 19 Map 9-A/B2**
♀ ⊗ ⌂ **LE RELAIS DE LA CURE D'AIR** (N° RR NOV 3 083) (M. **Amroun**) 54, avenue du Général-de-Gaulle ☎ 64-00-03-21 ⊷ 8 Closed Fri; Jul; Aug.

PROYART 80121 Somme **RN 29 Map 5-B3**
♀ ⊗ ⌂ **LA RAPERIE** (N° RR MAI 19 350) (Mme Odete **Mourier**) Route Nationale La Raperie ☎ 22-85-37-30 ⊷ 8 Closed Sat and Sun evening; 23 Dec to 10 Jan. German, Italian, Spanish spoken.

PRUNAY-LE-GILLON see FRAINVILLE 28360 Eure-et-Loir **RN 154 and RD 28 Maps 8-B3 and 9-B3**
♀ ⊗ **LE RELAIS DE LA GERBE D'OR** (N° RR MAI 14 347) (M. Charles **Miklos**) 10, rue du Pavillion ☎ 37-25-72-38 Closed Sun in winter; Feb. Coaches welcome (rest. seats 40). Evening meals. English spoken.

PUCH D'AGENAIS 47160 Lot-et-Garonne **A62 Map 21-A1**
⛽ **Mobil Oil Service Station AIRE DU QUEYRAN** (N° RR MAI 24 949) (M. René **Garcia**) Autoroute A62 (Nord) ☎ 53-79-48-92 **Damazan** Open 24 hours. Spanish, English spoken.

PUGET-THENIERS 06260 Alpes-Maritime **Map 25-B2**
♀ ⊗ **LE RELAIS PUGETOIS EUROPA 202** (N° RR JUL 24 648) (M. Jean-Claude **Daviot**) SARL Route Nationale 202 ☎ 93-05-01-42/ 05-01-67 German spoken.

PUGNAC 33710 Gironde **RN 137 Map 15-A3**
♀ ⊗ **LE RELAIS DU FASSIER - LE GRILLON** (N° RR DEC 22 117) (M. Rémi **Pitois**) ☎ 56-68-80-76 Lafosse. Closed Mon; Sept. Coaches welcome (rest. seats 100).

P

PUISSERGUIER 34620 Hérault **Map 23-A2**
Y ⊗ ⌂ **CAFÉ DE LA BOURSE** (N° RR NOV 27 108) (M. Joseph **Maya**) Place de la République ☎ 67-93-74-31 ⊷ 20.

PUJAUT 30131 Gard **RN 580 Map 24-A2**
Y ⊗ **CHEZ ODETTE** (N° RR DEC 25 765) (Mme Odette **Quinquemelle**) Les Gravières ☎ 90-25-19-70 Closed Sun. Evening meals until midnight.

PUTOT-EN-AUGE 14430 Calvados **RN 175 Map 4-B2**
Y ⊗ ⌂ **LE DAUPHIN** (N° RR NOV 25 733) (M. Jacques **Ribourg**) ☎ 31-79-20-29 **Minitel** ⊷ 6 Closed Sun low season; 15 Dec to 15 Jan. Full-board 155–195F per night. Evening meals until 11.00pm. German spoken.

PUY (LE) 43000 Haute-Loire **Maps 17-A3 and 18-A3**
Y ⊗ **LA TAVERNE** (N° RR JUN 10 835) (M. René **Rolland**) 50, boulevard Carnot ☎ 71-09-35-16 ⊷ 10 furnished. Coaches welcome (rest. seats 50). Evening meals.
Y ⊗ ⌂ **1 star NN LA VERVEINE** (N° RR FEV 24 844) (M. Gaston **Malthieu**) 6, place Cadelade ☎ 71-02-00-77 et 02-14-66 **Minitel** ⊷ 30 Closed 15/12 to 15/1. Full board 230–260F per night. Coaches welcome (1 room, 100 covers). Evening meals.

PUYDROUARD par FORGES 17290 Charente- Maritime **Map 11-B1**
Y ⊗ **CHEZ NÉNE** (N° RR SEPT 26 630) (M. **Bourieau**) ☎ 46-35-07-83 **Minitel** Closed Sun. Coaches welcome (rest. seats 80), weekends only. Evening meals until 9.30pm. English spoken.

PUY-MAURY Commune de CONDAT-EN-COMBRAILLES 63380 P.-de-D. **RN 141 and RD 108 Map 16-B2**
Y ⊗ **LE RELAIS CHEZ LUCETTE** (N° RR JAN 19631) (Mme Lucette **Condon**) ☎ 73-79-00-40 Closed 2nd fortnight Aug. Coaches welcome (rest. seats 40). Evening meals until 10.30pm.

PUYRICARD 'LA PETITE-CALADE' 13540 B.-du-R. **RN7 Map 24-B3**
Y ⊗ ⌂ **LE TOURANGEAU** (N° RR MAI 21 533) (Mme Danielle **Roccia**) Nationale 7 ☎ 42-21-60-65 ⊷ 13 Closed Sun; Aug. Italian spoken.

Q

QUAEDYPRE 59380 Nord **CD 9 16 Map 5-A/B2**
Y ⊗ **AUBERGE DU BON COIN - CHEZ L'GITAN** (N° RR JAN 21 368) (M. Pierre **Lammin**) CD 916 ☎ 28-68-76-94 Closed Mon; Aug. Coaches welcome (rest. seats 550). English spoken.

Q

QUEVEN 56330 Morbihan **RD 6 Map 7-B2**
♈ ⊗ ⌂ **LE RELAIS DE LA MAIRIE** (N° RR JUL 17 317) (Mme Yvonne **Le Gallic**) rue Principale ☎ 97-05-07-50 ◄ 8 Evening meals.

QUIMPER 29000 Finistère **RN 165 Map 7-B1**
♈ ⊗ **LE TRUCK** (N° RR JANV 27 165) (M. Jacques **Le Grand**) 96, avenue de la Libération ☎ 98-90-32-14 Closed Sun. English spoken.

QUIMPERLÉ 29130 Finistere **Map 7-B1**
♈ ⊗ **LA FOURCHE** (Mme Solarge **Le ball**) Route de Loriert ☎ 98-39-11-45. Closed Sundays. Evening meals until 10pm.

QUINCY-SOUS-SEMART 91480 Essonnes
♈ ⊗ **A LA BONNE TABLE** (N° RR JANV 27 170) (M. Pierre **Walter**) 3, av. Henri-Chasles ☎ 69-00-93-81 Closed Sun.

QUINTIN 22800 C.-du-N. **St-Brieux/Quimper Map 7-A2**
♈ ⊗ **RELAIS JACOB** (N° RR SEPT 26 032) (M. Pierre **Jacob**) Zl St Brandan ☎ 96-74-88-19 Closed Sat afternoon, Sun. Coaches welcome (rest. seats 30). Evening meals until 10pm.

R

RACHECOURT-SUR-MARNE 52170 Haute-Marne **RN 67 Map 14-A1**
♈ ⊗ **L'AURORE** (N° RR DEC 26 413) (M. **Narat**) avenue de Belgique ☎ 25-04-41-58 ◄ 4 Closed Mon; Aug. Coaches welcome (rest. seats 36).

RANES 61150 Orne **RN 916 Map 8-A2**
♈ ⊗ ⌂ **HOTEL DU PARC** (N° RR JUL 17 316) (M. Rogé **Cantin**) 9 Rue du Parc ☎ 33-39-73-85 ◄ 5 Closed Sun (in winter); Sept. Full-board 160–200F per night. Coaches welcome (rest. seats 290). Evening meals until 8.30pm.

RASSATS (LES) par BRIE 16590 Charente **RN 141 Map 15-B2**
♈ ⊗ **L'AUBERGE DES ROUTIERS** (N° RR NOV 19 204) (SARL **Doré and Son**) ☎ 45-65-90-24 Closed Sun; Aug. Evening meals until 11pm. Coaches welcome – 5000m^2 (rest. seats 64).

RAVOIRE (LA) 73490 Savoie **RN 6 and CD 21 Map 19-A2**
♈ ⊗ **LA PETITE TARENTAISE** (N° RR DEC 27 476) (M. Hervé **Bray**) ☎ 79-72-94-27 Closed Sunday. Evening meals until 10pm. Service station nearby.
♈ ⊗ **CHEZ COLETTE** (N° RR MARS 26 470) (Mme Colette **Michaud**) route d'Apremont VRU Chambéry exit 1 ☎ 79-33-35-07 **Minitel** Closed Sun. Showers. Full-board 160–250F per night. (2 star

R

restaurant 100m from hotel). Coaches welcome (rest. seats 120). Evening meals until midnight. English, German, Italian, Spanish, Portuguese spoken.

RAZAC SUR L'ISLE 24430 Dordogne **Map 15-B3**
𝟤 ⊗ **RELAIS DE L'ISLE** (N° RR NOV 27 459) (M. Marcel **Dubus**) ☎ 53-54-62-34 Closed Sunday. Evening meals. English spoken.

REALMONT 81120 Tarn **RN 112 Map 22-B2**
𝟤 ⊗ **BAR RESTAURANT DES ALLEES** (N° RR JUN 26 913) (M. Didier **Amalvy**) 27, boulevard Armengaud ☎ 63-55-52-72 Closed Sun. Filling station near.

REBENACQ 64260 Pyrénées-Atlantiques **Map 20-B3**
𝟤 ⊗ **CHEZ PALU** (N° RR DEC 24 776) (M. Alain **Palu**) RD 134 ☎ 59-05-54-11 Closed Monday night. Coaches welcome (rest. seats 80). Evening meals until 10pm.

REDESSAN 30129 Gard **RD 999 Map 24-A3**
𝟤 ⊗ **LE RELAIS DU CANARD** (N° RR JUN 26 577) (M. Thierry **Lafont**) ☎ 66-20-22-02 Closed Sun. Spanish spoken.

REDON 35600 I.-et-V. **Map 11-A2**
𝟤 ⊗ ⌂ **1 Star NN LE RELAIS** (N° RR FEV 26 172) (M. Noël **François** SARL) Rte de Rennes ☎ 99-71-46-54 **Minitel** ⇀ 18 Full-board 98–160F per night. Coaches welcome (rest. seats 120). Evening meals. English spoken. Bar, dogs admitted. 'Casserole' menus 38–145F.

REFFANNES 79420 Deux-Sèvres **RD 938 Map 15-A1**
𝟤 ⊗ **LE CHEVAL BLANC** (N° RR SEPT 26 033 (M. **Chevaller**) ☎ 49-70-25-18 Evening meals until 9pm. Closed Saturday.
𝟤 ⊗ ⌂ **HÔTEL DU COMMERCE** (N° RR JUL 26 005) (M. René **Chiron**) ☎ 49-70-22-08 ⇀ 10.

REGUISHEIM 68890 Haut-Rhin **RN 422 Map 10-B3**
𝟤 ⊗ ⌂ **SARL A L'ANGE** (N° RR JUN 19 085) (M. Raymond **Bertrand**) 90, Grande-Rue ☎ 89-81-12-66 ⇀ 5 Closed Sun; Aug. German spoken. Evening meals.

REIMS see also BEAUMONT-SUR-VESLE 51100 Marne **RN 31-51 and CD 75 Map 6-B1/2**

REIMS 51400 Marne **Autoroute A4 Maps 6-B1 and 2**
𝟤 ⊗ **RESTOP DE REIMS** (M. Patrice **Jezequel**) Aire de Service de Reims Champagne Les Petites Loges par Mourmelon-le-Grand ☎ 26-03-93-57 Self-service restaurant open 6.00am to 10.00pm. Showers, TV, Shop.

RELLECQ-KERHUON 29219 Finistère **RN 165 and D 205 Map 7-A1**
𝟤 ⊗ ⌂ **LE LONGCHAMPS** (N° RR MARS 26 203) (M. Jacky **Alinc**) 2, rue Jules-Ferry ☎ 98-28-26-55 ⇀ 9 Closed Sat, Sun. Evening meals. Weekdays only.

R

REMIREMONT 88200 Vosges **Voir SAINT-NABORD**

REMOULINS 30210 Gard **RN 86 Map 24-A3**
Ⓨ ⊗ ⌂ **2 stars NN AUBERGE DES PLATANES** (N° RR NOV 24 421)
⛨ (M. Gérard **Reynaud**) Castillon-du-Gard-les-Croisées ☎ 66-37-
10-69 ⇥ 35 Full-board 230–265F. Coaches welcome (rest. seats
300). Evening meals until 10pm. English, Spanish spoken. Menus ·
55–110F. Specialities: *Rouille d'encornets carmagueuse, potée
du pêcheur aux fruits der mer* (made to order).

RENAC 35660 I.-et V. **RD 177 Map 7-B3**
Ⓨ ⊗ **BEAUREGARD** (N° RR FEV 27 192) (Mme Marie-Annick **Bonno**)
☎ 99-72-07-83 Closed Mon and 10 days in Feb. Filling station
nearby.

RENESCURE 59173 Nord **RN 42 Map 5-A1**
Ⓨ ⊗ **LA CLEF DES CHAMPS** (N° RR JAN 15 505) (Mme Marlène
Lamiaux) Route Nationale 42 ☎ 28-49-81-12 Coaches welcome
(rest. seats 60).

REVIN 08500 Ardennes **RN 388 Map 6-A2**
Ⓨ ⊗ **LE RELAIS DES ROUTIERS** (N° RR JAN 17 985) (M. **Mahut**) 6,
rue Voltaire ☎ 24-40-12-91 ⇥ 4.

REYERSVILLER 57230 Moselle **Map 10-B1**
Ⓨ ⊗ **LE RELAIS DE LA SCHWANGERBACH** (N° RR AVR 24 924)
(Mme Marie-Christine **Huet**) 63, route de Lemberg ☎ 87-96-10-
72 Closed Wed; Oct. German spoken.

REYRIEUX 01600 Ain **Map 2-A2**
Ⓨ ⊗ **BAR RESTAURANT DE LA GARE** (N° RR MAI 27 271) (Mme
Yvonne **Oritz**) ☎ 74-00-12-00 Closed last week of August. English
and Spanish spoken.

RHODES 36170 Indre **RN 20 Map 16-A1**
Ⓨ ⊗ **LE RELAIS ROUTIERS DE RHODES** (N° RR AVR 25 375) (M.
Jean-Pierre **Perez**) Mouhet-Rhodes ☎ 54-47-65-26 **Minitel** Clo-
sed Sat afternoon, Sun; Aug. Evening meals until 10.30pm.

RIAILLE 44440 Loire-Atlantique **Map 11-A3**
Ⓨ ⊗ **AU RENDEZ-VOUS DES PECHEURS** (N° RR AVR 26 528) (M.
Joël **Aspot**) 7, rue de Bretagne ☎ 40-97-80-95 Closed Wed
afternoon. October to April; 1st, 15th August. Coaches welcome
(rest. seats 60). Evening meals until 10pm.

RIBAUTE-LES-TAVERNES 30720 Gard **RN 110 Map 23-B1**
Ⓨ ⊗ ⌂ **LE VIEUX MOULIN** (N° RR JUN 26920) (Mmes **Coste** and
Riminucci ☎ 66-83-07-94 ⇥ 5 Closed Tue. English, Spanish,
Italian spoken. Filling station near. Coaches welcome. Evening
meals (rest. seats 40, 50 on a terrace).

RIBAY (LE) 53240 Mayenne **RN 12 Map 8-B1**
Ⓨ ⊗ ⌂ **LE LION D'OR** (N° RR JUN 23 351) (Mme Simone **Reboux**) Le
Bourg ☎ 43-03-90-27 ⇥ 7 Closed 20 Dec–2 Jan. Full-board 150–

R

180F per night. Coaches welcome (rest. seats 80). Evening meals until pm. English spoken.

RIBERAC 24600 Dordogne **RN 708/710 Map 15-B3**
Y ⊗ **LAKANAL** (N° RR MARS 27 202) (Mme Jean-Marie **Lagarde**) 1, avenue Lakanal ☎ 53-90-04-77 Closed Sunday out of season. Evening meals. Full-board 150F.

Y ⊗ ⌂ **CAFE DU COMMERCE** (N° RR MAR 23 172) (M. Paul **Ratineau**) **La Borie** Villetoureix ☎ 53-90-05-24 ⇥ 9 Closed Sun except high season. Full-board 150F per night. Evening meals.

RICAMARIE (LA) 42150 Loire **RN 88 Map 2-B1**
Y ⊗ **AU RELAIS SYMPA RICAMONDOIS** (N° RR SEPT 27 008) (M. Franck **Bonnaire**) 5 bis, rue de la Libération ☎ 77-57-89-31 Closed Mon pm. Open 7.30am to midnight. English and German spoken. Filling station open 7.30am to 9.00pm.

RICHEVILLE 27420 Eure **RN 14 Map 3-B1**
Y ⊗ **LE RELAIS DES GLYCINES** (N° RR AOU 21 192) (M. Serge **Gaultier**) Route Nationale 14 ☎ 32-55-61-05 ⇥ 1 Closed Sun afternoon.

Y ⊗ **LE RESTOROUTE LE BALTO** (N° RR FEV 27 173) (M. Pierre **Sadok**) RN 14 ☎ 32-27-10-55 Closed Sun. English spoken.

RIEUMES 31370 Haute-Garonne **Map 22-A2**
Y ⊗ ⌂ **LES PALMIERS** (N° RR AVR 26 524) (M. Jean-Claude **Gilibert**) 13, place du Foirail ☎ 61-91-81-01 ⇥ 7 Closed Sun evening; Feb. Half-board 98F, full-board 140–160F per night. Coaches welcome (2 dining rooms = 105 seats). Evening meals until 9pm. German, English, Italian spoken.

RIEUPEYROUX 12240 Aveyron **RD 905 Map 22-B1**
Y ⊗ ⌂ **1 Star NN CHEZ PASCAL Tobacconist** (N° RR OCT 23 965) (M. Claude **Bou**) rue de l'Hom ☎ 65-65-51-13 ⇥ 15 Closed Sun evening low season; 1 to 15 Oct. Full-board 140–160F per night. Coaches welcome (rest. seats 60). Evening meals until 9pm.

RIEUTORT- DE RANDON 48700 Lozère **CD 1 Map 17-B3**
Y ⊗ **RELAIS DE LA POSTE** (N° RR JUL 26 611) (Mme Simone **Magne**) Place de la Poste ☎ 66-47-34-67. Closed weekends.

RILLIEUX-LA-PAPE 69140 Rhône **Map 2-A2**
Y ⊗ **RELAIS DU BUGEY** (N° RR FEV 26 455) (M. Alain **Rebout**) 1270, avenue Victor Hugo ☎ 78-88-09-60 **Minitel** Closed Sat, Sun; Aug. Evening meals.

RIOM 63200 P.-de-D. **RN 9 Map 16-B3**
Y ⊗ **LE CANTALOU** (N° RR MAI 24 939) (M. Jean-Louis **Tholonias**) 12, avenue de Clermont ☎ 73-38-03-68 Closed Sun; 15 days Aug; 1 week Christmas. Coaches welcome (3 dining rooms = 60 seats). English spoken.

Y ⊗ **AU STAND** (N° RR OCT 25 680) (Mme **Dassaud-Riquier**) 24, avenue de Clermont ☎ 73-38-04-06. Closed Sunday; Aug.

R

RIOTORD 43200 Haute-Loire **RD 503 Map 18-A3**
Ⓨ ⓧ **BAR RESTAURANT DES CHASSEURS** (N° RR MARS 26 824)
(Mme Dominique **Arnaud**) route de Dunières ☎ 71-75-31-40
Closed Mon afternoon; 17/7–31/7. Filling station at 3 kms.
Coaches welcome (rest. seats 40).

RIS/PUY GUILLAUME 63290 Puy-de-Dôme **Map 16-B3**
Ⓨ ⓧ 🛏 **HOTEL DE LA GARE** (N° RR JUN 25 008) (M. Robert
Nicholas) Gare De Ris ☎ 73-94-68-68 ⇥ 10 Closed Sunday and
mid Sept/mid Oct. Filling station open from 6.00am to 9pm.

RISCLE 32400 Gers **RD 135 Map 21-A2**
Ⓨ ⓧ 🏠 **1 Star NN LE RELAIS DE L'AUBERGE** (N° RR DEC 21 307)
(Mme **Portes**) place de la Mairie ☎ 62-69-70-49 ⇥ 10 (with WC)
from 65–80F, breakfast 15–18F. Closed Sun; Oct. Full-board 140F
per night. Coaches welcome (rest. seats 100). Car park; bar;
dogs allowed. Places to visit: Cave de Saint-Mont, Tour de
Termes d'Armagnec, Foie gras cannery.

RIVE-DE-GIER 42800 Loire **Map 2-A1**
Ⓨ ⓧ **RESTAURANT DE LA GARE** (N° RR JUL 27 335) (Mme Paulette
Perrier) 6, Vallée de Couzon ☎ 77-75-45-52 Closed last week of
August. Evening meals until 11pm. Nearby service station open
7am to 9pm.

RIVES-SUR-FURE 38140 Isère **RN 85 Map 24-B1**
Ⓨ ⓧ **BAR DES SPORTS** (N° RR JUL 26 019) (M. Michel **Le Guyader**)
315, rue du Plan ☎ 76-91-04-37 **Minitel** Closed Sun; 15 to 31 Dec.
Evening meals.

RIVIÈRE SAINT SAUVEUR (LA) 14560 Calvados
Ⓨ ⓧ **LES OISEAUX DE MER** (N° RR JAN 27 505) (M. Pascal
Quesney) 28, route des 4-Francs ☎ 31-89-11-62 Closed Saturday
afternoon, Sunday. Evening meals.

RIVIERE-DE-CORPS (LA) 10300 Aube **RN 60 Map 9-B3**
Ⓨ ⓧ **LA QUEUE DE LA POELE** (N° RR MAI 25 404) (M. Gaby
Barbier) RN 60 Sens road, Troyes exit ☎ 25-74-47-94 Closed Sun
evening.

RIVIERE-SAINT-SAUVEUR (LA) 14560 Calvados **RN 180 Map 4-B2**
Ⓨ ⓧ **AUX OISEAUX DE MER** (N° RR AVR 21 501) (M. Daniel
Frabois) Lieu-dit Le Poudreux ☎ 31-89-11-62 Closed Sun; Aug.

ROANNE 42120 Loire **RN 7 Map 18-A2**
Ⓨ ⓧ 🏠 **LE PARIGNY** (N° RR OCT 24 897) SARL (Mme Jeanine
Pamure) LesBas de Rhins Le Coteau sortie sud de Roanne ☎ 77-
62-06-18 Closed Sun and 10th to 20th August.
Ⓨ **LE JOCKEY BAR** (N° RR NOV 27 455) (M. Joseph **Vera**) 1, place
du Champ-de-Foire ☎ 77-71-43-09 Closed Wednesday pm.

ROCHE-CHALAIS (LA) 24490 Dordogne **RD 730 Map 15-A3**
Ⓨ ⓧ **CAFE DU MIDI** (N° RR AVR 21 884) (Mme Violette **Rawyler**)
⚓

32, avenue du Stade ☎ 53-91-43-65 English, German spoken.
Closed Mon, Tues afternoons.

ROCHECORBON 37210 I.-&-L. **RN 152 Map 12-B3**
♈ ⊗ **RELAIS DES PATYS** (N° RR FEV 27 198) (M. Jean-Marc **Nourry**)
1, rue des Patys ☎ 47-52-61-75 ⊸ 4 Closed Sun and Dec. English
and Spanish spoken.

ROCHE-LA-MOLIERE 42290 Loire **Map 18-A2**
♈ ⊗ **LE FLORENCE** (N° RR SEPT 26 659) (M. Michel **Bruyas**) 3 rue
des Carrières ☎ 77-90-58-41 Closed Aug. Evening meals Fri, Sat,
Sun.

ROCHEFORT/NENON 39700 Jura **RN 73 Map 14-A3**
♙ **Total Service Station RELAIS DES POIRIERS** (N° RR OCT
55000005) (M. Daniel **Chaney**) RN 73 ☎ 84-72-40-35 Closed Sun;
9–21 Aug.

ROCHEFORT-SUR-MER 17300 Charent.-Marit **RN 137 Map 11-B1**
♈ ⊗ **LE REPOS DES ROUTIERS Tobacconist** (N° RR SEPT 26 650)
(M. Paul **Guillon**) Le Grand Vergeroux Nationale 137 ☎ 46-84-41-
48 Closed Sat afternoon, Sun. Evening meals until 10pm.
♈ ⊗ **LE DAUPHIN** (N° RR SEPT 26 633) (M. J.-C. **Philibert**) 24, rue
Denfert-Rochereau ☎ 46-99-21-43 Closed Sun afternoon and
evening. English spoken.

ROCHELLE (LA) 17010 Charente-Maritime **Map 11-B1**
♈ **DELMAS BAR** (N° RR JAN 24 479) (Mme Jeanine **Francson**) 32,
bd Emile-Delmas ☎ 46-42-60-23 Snacks. Closed Sat lunch, Sun;
2nd fortnight Sept.
♈ ⊗ 🏠 **LES EMBRUNS** (N° RR JUIL 935) (M. René **Poultier**) 413,
avenue Guiton ☎ 46-42-61-88 or 46-43-69-73 ⊸ 7 Closed Sun; 1
week Christmas. Filling station near.
♈ ⊗ **LE TOUT VA MIEUX** (N° RR NOV 27 110) (Mme Josianne
Verdier-Muon) 1, avenue de Colmae ☎ 46-41-10-69. 24 Hr
service station nearby.

ROCHELLE-AIGEFEUILLE (LA) 17290 Chte-Mme **RD 939 Map 11-B1**
♈ ⊗ 🏠 **LA CLEF DES CHAMPS** (N° RR AOU 22 911) SO-DI-HO-CP
(M. **Maurel**) Z.I. des Grands-Champs près de La Rochelle –
Camp de Croix Chapeau ☎ 46-35-64-43 ⊸ 12. German and
English spoken. Free camping. Coaches welcome (rest. seats
90). Evening meals.

ROCHELLE-PALLICE (LA) 17000 Chte-Mme **Map 11-B1**
♈ ⊗ 🏠 **RELAIS OCÉANIC** (N° RR JUL 25 494 (M. Claude **Chauvin**)
Place du Marché ☎ 46-42-62-37 ⊸ 5 Closed Sat; Aug. Evening
meals until 9.30pm. Full board 150F. Coaches welcome (rest.
seats 220).
♈ ⊗ **CHEZ ANNIE** (N° RR AVR 27 262) (Mme Annie **Bernelas**)
Ancien Embarcadère de l'Ile de Ré ☎ 46-42-53-61 Closed Sun.
Evening meals served until 11pm. Nearby service station open
6am – 9pm.

R

ROCHEMAURE 07400 Ardèche **RN 86 Map 24-A2**
Ⓨ ⊗ **LE RELAIS DE LA CONDAMINE** (N° RR NOV 14 069) (Mme Josiane **Sicoit**) ☎ 75-52-96-26 Closed Sun; 20/12–31. Coaches welcome (rest. seats 40). Evening meals.

ROCHE-SUR-YON 85000 Vendée **RN 137 Maps 11-B2/3 and 12-B1**
Ⓨ ⊗ 🏠 **2 Stars NN LE SULLY** (N° RR OCT 22 072 (Mme Natalie **Bohy**) boulevard Sully ☎ 51-37-18-21 and 51-37-54-02 **Minitel** ⌐ 34 from 120–160F, breakfast 18F. Full-board 180–250F per night. Coaches welcome (rest. seats 150). Evening meals until midnight. English, Spanish spoken. Car park; bar; dogs allowed, recreations (skating, swimming). Places to visit: Haras, museum, dam at Papon.
Ⓨ ⊗ **LE MOULIN DE LA BERGERIE** (N° RR JUN 22 375) (S.N.C. **Mothais**) Aizenay Carrefour de la Grolle Nationale 60 Rte La Roche/Les Sables - Rte de Landeronde - Venansault ☎ 51-40-36-94 Closed 1 to 20 Jan.

ROCHETAILLÉE par LE BOURG-D'OISANS 38520 Isère **RN 91 and RD 526 Map 19-A3**
Ⓨ ⊗ 🏠 **1 Star NN HOTEL BELLEDONNE** (N° RR OCT 22 965) (Mme Mireille **Esposito**) ☎ 76-80-07-04 ⌐ 25 Closed weekends lowseason. Full-board 160F per night. Coaches welcome (rest. seats 100). Evening meals. Some English spoken.

ROCHE-VINEUSE 71960 S.-et-L. **RN 79 Map 18-B1**
Ⓨ ⊗ **RELAIS ROUTIERS** (N° RR SEP 25 115) (Mme France **Brouillon**) Place du Chaucher ☎ 85-37-71-51 **Minitel** Closed Sat afternoon, Sun; Aug. Coaches welcome (rest. seats 50). Evening meals until 11pm.

ROCROI 08230 Ardennes **RN 51 and 377 Map 6-A2**
Ⓨ 🏠 **HÔTEL DE LA GARE** (N° RR JAN 23 633) (SARL **Minucci**) 1, Ave du Gl-Moreau ☎ 24-54-10-32 ⌐ 11. Full-board 200–300F. Evening meals.
Ⓨ ⊗ **REST DE LA JEUNESSE** (N° RR FEV 27 177) (M. Jean-Luc **Lecomte**) Rue Royale ☎ 24-54-25-12 Closed Tues after lunch. Filling station nearby.

RODEZ 12000 Aveyron **RN 88 and 595 Map 22-B1 see also BERTH-OLENE**
Ⓨ ⊗ 🏠 **LE RELAIS MON BAR** (N° RR NOV 12 569) (M. Henri **Cristol**) 19, avenue Victor-Hugo ☎ 65-68-14-59 **Minitel** ⌐ 10 Closed Sat, Sun. Full-board 140–150F per night. Coaches welcome (rest. seats 50). Evening meals until 10.30pm.
Ⓨ ⊗ 🏠 **1 Star NN LA ROCADE** (N° RR AOU 18 491) (M. **Gayraud**) La Roquette RN 88 ☎ 65-67-10-44 and 67-17-12 **Minitel** ⌐ 17 from 65–115F, breakfast 17F, telephone. Open 7.00am to 10.00pm. Closed Fri evening, Sat; 1 to 14 July; 24 December 1988 to 12 Jan 1989. Full-board 156–171F per night. Coaches welcome (rest. seats 120). Evening meals until 10pm. Car park; bar; dogs allowed (only in restaurant); garden. Menu 43–100F. Specialities *Confit de Canard, Civet d'oie.*

R

ROFFIAC 15100 Cantal **RD 926 Map 17-A2/A3**
♈ ⊗ **AUBERGE DE LA VALLÉE** (N° RR MAR 23 193) (M. Pierre **Farges**) St. Flour ☎ 71-60-04-50 Closed Sat, Sun; 15–30 Aug.

ROGNAC 13340 B.-du-R. **RN 113 Map 24-B3**
♈ ⊗ ⌂ **2 Stars NN CADET ROUSSEL** (N° RR AVR 25 353) (M. Jack **Schiele**) Autoroute exit-Berre ☎ 42-87-00-33 ⊷ 13 from 160–220F, breakfast 18–20F. Closed Sun. Full-board 170–230F per night. Evening meals until 10pm. Some German spoken. Car park; bar; dogs allowed. (Rest. seats 90).

ROHRBACH-LES-BITCHE 57410 Moselle **RN 140 Map 10-B1**
♈ ⊗ ⌂ **1 star NN AUBERGE DE LA CROIX D'OR** (N° RR JAN 22 611) (M. Jean-Louis **Lauer**) 6, Rue de la Liberation ☎ 87-09-73-01 ⊷ 10 60–130F. Breakfast 14–20F. Closed Monday, Friday evening, Aug. Full-board 90–125F. Evening meals. Parking, bar. German spoken. Sites to visit: Fort, wildlife park.

ROMAGNY 50140 Manche **Map 8-A1**
♈ ⊗ **AUBERGE DES CLOSEAUX** (N° RR OCT 24 717) (M. Bernard **Clouard**) Les Closeaux ☎ 33-59-01-86 Closed Sat; 3 weeks in Aug. Coaches welcome (rest. seats 60). Evening meals. Full-board 90–125F. German spoken. Sites to visit: Fort, wildlife park.

ROMAZY 35490 Manche **Map 8-A1**
♈ ⊗ **AUBERGE DES CLOSEAUX** (N° RR OCT 24 717) (M. Bertrand **Clouard**) Les Closeaux ☎ 33-59-01-86 Closed Saturday and 3 weeks in August. Evening meals until 8.30pm. Rest seats 80. Coaches welcome.

ROMILLY-SUR-SEINE 10100 Aube **RN 19 Map 9-B2**
♈ ⊗ **LA BONNE ÉTAPE** (N° RR MAI 26 249) (M. William **Faroy**) RN 19, St-Hilaire ☎ 25-24-78-04 Closed Sun; Aug. Evening meals until 9pm.

ROMORANTIN-LANTHENAY 41200 L.-et-C. **RN 722/765 Map 13-B1**
♈ ⊗ **RELAIS DE L'AVENIR** (N° RR AOU 25 075) (M. Jean-Luc **François**) 44, Avenue de Villefranche ☎ 54-76-14-28 **Minitel** Closed Sat, Sun; Aug. Coaches welcome (rest. seats 60). Evening meals only.
♈ ⊗ ⌂ **1 Star NN LES AUBIERS** (N° RR MAR 23 703) (M. Guy **Boivin**) 1, avenue de Blois ☎ 54-76-05-59 ⊷ 20 (2 with bathroom) from 60–120F, breakfast 16F. Coaches welcome (rest. seats 120). Evening meals. Closed Sunday evening. Full-board 170–200F. Parking. Bar.

RONCHAMP 70250 Haute-Saône **RN 19 Map 10-A3**
♈ ⊗ ⌂ **1 Star NN LE RELAIS DE LA POMME D'OR** (N° RR FEV 18 622) (MM. **Cenci Frères**) Rue Le Corbusier ☎ 84-20-62-12 ⊷ 25 German spoken. Evening meals. Full-board 125–170F. Coaches welcome (rest. seats 90).

R

ROQUE-D'ANTHÉRON (LA) 13640 Bouches-du-Rhône **CD 561 et 543 Map 24-B3**

♀ ⊗ ⌂ **AU RELAIS FLEURI** (N° RR OCT 27 058) (M. Guy **Auguste**) **Hameau de St. Christophe** ☎ 12-50-20-24 ➞ 9 English, Italian, German and Spanish spoken. Full-board 250–370F. Coaches welcome (rest. seats 60). Evening meals until 10pm.

ROQUEFORT 40120 Landes **Map 21-A2**

♀ ⊗ **AUBERGE DE LA DILIGENCE** (N° RR MAI 26 881) (M. Antoine **Cardoso**) Rte de Bordeaux ☎ 58-45-57-31 Open 24 hrs. Portuguese, Spanish, English spoken. Filling station near.

ROQUEFORT-DES-CORBIÈRES 11540 Aude **RN 9 Map 23-A3**

♀ ⊗ **LE RELAIS D'EL ROC** (N° RR AVR 22 785) (Mme Anne-Marie **Rigaud**) Motorway exit between Sigean/Leucate. Côtes Roquefort region. ☎ 68-48-20-88 Closed Sunday. English, German, Spanish, Italian spoken.

♀ ⊗ **RELAIS CÔTES DE ROQUEFORT** (N° RR NOV 27 461) (Mme Anne-Marie **Rigaud**) ☎ 68-42-20-09 ➞ 5 English, Spanish, spoken. Evening meals. Filling station open 5am–2pm.

ROQUETTE see RODEZ 12000 Aveyron **RN 595 Map 22-B1**

ROSIÈRES 07260 Ardèche **RD 104 Map 23-B1**

♀ ⊗ ⌂ **1 Star NN LES CÉVENNES** (N° RR AVR 22 783) (Mme Colette **Reynouard**) Joyeuse ☎ 75-39-52-07 ➞ 14 at 90–110F per night. Breakfast 15–17F. Full-board 160–170F. Coaches welcome (rest. seats 150). Parking, bar, dogs allowed. Recreations: baths. Sites: Gorges de l'Ardèche. Evening meals until 10pm.

ROSOY 89100 Yonne **RN 6 Map 9-B2**

♀ ⊗ ⌂ **LA MAISON BLANCHE** (N° RR JUL 10 864) (M. **Reinhold**) ⌂ Rte d'Auxerre ☎ 86-97-13-01 ➞ 14 Open 24 hours. Full-board 150F per night. Coaches welcome (rest. seats 145). Evening meals. Menus 50–110F.

ROSPORDEN 29140 Finistère **RN 165 Map 7-B1**

♀ ⊗ ⌂ **LES ROUTIERS** (N° RR OCT 26 703) (Mme Maryvonne **Michal**) 9 Pont Biais ☎ 98-59-20-40 ➞ 17 Closed Sat, Sun, Aug. Evening meals until 9pm.

ROSTRENEN 22110 Côtes-du-Nord **Map 7-B2**

♀ ⊗ **LE RELAIS DES ROUTIERS** (N° RR MAI 14 345) (M. Corentin **Cerno**) 32, rue Olivier Perrin ☎ 96-29-01-30 **Minitel**.

ROTS 14980 Calvados **RN 13 Map 4-B2**

♀ ⊗ ⌂ **LE RELAIS DU COUP DE POMPE** (N° RR JAN 27 163) (M. Valentine **Castander**) Route de Caen ☎ 31-26-53-29 ➞ 5 Closed Sun. English, Spanish spoken.

ROUANS 44640 Loire-Atlantique **Map 11-A2**

♀ ⊗ ⌂ **LA CHAUSSÉE LE RETZ** (N° RR JUN 26 911) (Mme Claudette **Biton**) La Chaussée le Retz ☎ 40-64-22-23 ➞ 6 Closed Sats Oct to Whitsun. Filling station 2 km distant. Evening meals.

R

ROUBAIX 59100 Nord **Map 5-B1**
Ⓨ ⊗ **LE CALAIS** (N° RR OCT 27 073) (Mme Josette **Vaze**) 2, quai Calais ☎ 20-26-14-01 Closed Sat pm, Sun and August. German, Dutch and English spoken.

ROUEN 76100 Seine-Marit **RN 13 Bis and RN 14 Map 3-A1**
Ⓨ ⊗ ⌂ **LES PLATANES** (N° RR MARS 26 468) (M. Roger **Sannier**) 57, avenue du Mont-Riboudet ☎ 35-71-01-52 ⊷ 20 Closed Sun; 24 Dec–2 Jan. Evening meals.
Ⓨ ⊗ **LE RELAIS 207 Chez Joële et Patrick** (N° RR JAN 25 277) (M. Patrick **Clivaz**) 46, quai Cavelier-de-la-Salle ☎ 35-73-18-55 Closed Sat, Sun.
Ⓨ ⊗ **LONDON BAR** (N° RR JAN 25 278) (M. Dominique **Merchi**) 55, quai Cavelier-de-la-Salle ☎ 35-73-03-01 Closed Sat, Sun. Evening meals until 11pm. English, Arabic spoken.
Ⓨ ⊗ ⌂ **HÔTEL D'ORLÉANS** (N° RR OCT 26 715) (M. Guy **Soligny**) 32, quai Cavelier-de-la-Salle ☎ 35-73-36-99 ⊷ 10 Closed Sat, Sun.

ROUFFIGNAC-DE-SIGOULES 24240 Dordogne **15-B3**
Ⓨ ⊗ **RELAIS LA TAVERNE ALSACIENNE** (N° RR AVR 27 245) (Mme Francine **Thomann**) La Tabaline ☎ 53-58-84-13 Evening meals. German spoken.

ROUFFILLAC-DE-CARLUX 24370 Dordogne **RD 703 Map 17-A1**
Ⓨ ⊗ ⌂ **2 Stars NN AUX POISSONS FRAIS** (N° RR MAR 12 788) (**Cayre and Son**) ☎ 53-29-70-24 ⊷ 20 Closed 1 to 31 Oct. Full-board 210–225F per night. Coaches welcome (rest. seats 150). Evening meals. Bar. Parking, dogs allowed. Recreation: swimming, tennis, canoeing, fishing. Tourism recommended. English spoken.

ROUGE (LA) see LE THEIL 61260 Orne **RD 11 Map 8-B3**

ROUGEMONTIERS 27350 Eure **RN 180 Map 4-B3**
Ⓨ ⊗ **LE LUDO** (N° RR FEV 24 871) (M. Jean-Claude **Duboc**) ☎ 32-56-85-22 Closed Sat afternoon, Sun; public holidays, August. Evening meals until 9.30pm.
AU RENOUVEAU (N° RR OCT 27 437) (Mlle Nathalie **Dumege**) ☎ 32-42-07-89 Closed Monday. Evening meals. English spoken.

ROUILLAC 16170 Charente **RN 139 Map 15-A2**
Ⓨ ⊗ ⌂ **LA BOULE D'OR SARL** (N° RR AOUT 26 304) (M. Franck **Chiron**) 56, rue Gal-de-Gaulle ☎ 45-96-50-45 ⊷ 9 Closed Fri evening, Saturday. Full-board 145–155F per night. Coaches welcome (rest. seats 80). Evening meals until 9.30pm. English spoken.

ROULANS 25640 Doubs **RN 73 Map 10-A3 and 14-B3**
Ⓨ ⊗ **LE RELAIS DES ROUTIERS** (N° RR AVR 19 331) (M. Émile **Triponney**) ☎ 81-87-51-72 Open 24 hours. Closed Sun.

ROUMAZIÈRES-LOUBERT 16270 Charente **RN 141 Map 15-B2**
Ⓨ ⊗ ⌂ **LE RELAIS DU CENTRE** (N° RR OCT 24 725) (Mme Marcelle

R

Roumazières-Loubert continued
Chaussonnaud) 25, rue Nationale Place du Marché ☎ 45-71-10-24 ⊸ 8 Closed 26 Dec to 8 Jan.

⍦ ⊗ **LES ROUTIERS** (N° RR MAI 25 394) (M. Charly **Rondeau**) 122, route Nationale ☎ 45-71-10-88 Closed Sun after 3.00pm. English, German, Spanish spoken.

ROUSSET 13790 Bouches-du-Rhône **Map 24-B3**
⍦ ⊗ **LA CENGLE** (N° RR JUN 24 609) (M. **Hoffmann**) 110 Route Nationale 7 ☎ 42-29-00-40 Closed Fri evening, Sat, Sun. Full-board 150F per night. Coaches welcome (rest. seats 110). Evening meals. Italian spoken.

⛽ **Total Service Station RELAIS DE ROUSSET** A8 ☎ 42-29-01-95.

ROUSSON 30340 Gard **RD 904 Map 23-B1**
⍦ ⊗ **RELAIS DU CHÊNE** (N° RR JUN 26 576) (Mme Georgina **Quet**) Pont d'Avène-Salindre ☎ 66-85-65-83 Closed Sun evening. Coaches welcome (rest. seats 55). English spoken.

ROUXIÈRE (LA) 44370 Loire-Atlantique **D28, D29 Map 11-A3**
⍦ ⊗ **CAFÉ DES SPORTS** (N° RR MAI 26 898) (M. Raoul **Mahé**) 123, rue de la Croix Bouvier ☎ 40-96-98-12. English spoken. Filling station near. Coaches welcome (rest. seats 60).

ROYAN 17600 Chte-Mme **Map 11-B1**
⍦ ⊗ **L'ESPÉRANCE** (N° RR FEV 26 169) (Mme Bernadette **Baisson**) 72, boulevard d'Aquitaine ☎ 46-05-01-02 Coaches welcome (rest. seats 45). Evening meals.

⍦ ⊗ 🏠 **LE SYMPATIC** (N° RR SEPT 26 672) (M. Yves **Boinard**) 30 av de la Libération ☎ 46-05-67-21 ⊸ 12 Closed Sat. Christmas–New Year. Full-board 175–185F per night. Coaches welcome (rest. seats 30).

ROYE 70200 Haute-Saône **RN 19 Map 10-A3**
⍦ ⊗ **LE RELAIS DES ROUTIERS** (N° RR AOU 15 771) (Mme Huguette **Kuhn**) 50, rue de la Verrerie ☎ 84-30-06-48 Closed Sun. Car Park. Coaches welcome (rest. seats 25). Evening meals until 9pm.

RUFFEC 16700 Charente **RN 10 Map 15-B2**
⍦ ⊗ **LE LANDAIS LES ROUTIERS** (N° RR JAN 26 799) (M. Jean-Michel **Lapegue**) 34, avenue Célestin-Sieur ☎ 45-31-04-16 Closed Sun and Dec. Coaches welcome (rest. seats 50). Evening meals until 9.00pm.

RUFFEC-LE-CHATEAU 36300 Indre **Map 16-A1**
⍦ ⊗ **CHEZ P'TIT JEAN** (N° RR NOV 26 728) (Mme Micheline **Merandon**) Le Bourg ☎ 54-37-70-05 **Minitel** ⊸ 6 Closed Sept. Full board 130 to 140F. Coaches welcome (2 restaurants seating 30). Evening meals served until 9pm.

RUNGIS 94150 Val-de-Marne **RN 7 Map 1-B2/3**
⍦ ⊗ **LE GRAND COMPTOIR DE RUNGIS** (N° RR OCT 25 698 (SARL **Sogere**) Place St-Hubert Halles de Rungis ☎ 46-86-29-30 Res-

taurant with take-away. Closed Sat, Sun. Coaches welcome (rest. seats 300).

RUPT-SUR-MOSELLE 88360 Vosges **Map 10-A3**
♀ ⊗ **LE P'TIT RESTO** (N° RR NOV 27 086) (M. René **Antoine**) 89 A, rue de Lorraine ☎ 29-24-38-11 Closed Wed low season.

RYE 39230 Jura **Map 14-A3**
♀ ⊗ **Chez Lucette** (N° RR JUL 24 641) (Mme Lucette **Cambazard**) ☎ 84-48-61-60 Closed Thurs afternoon; 1 to 15 Aug.

SAALES 67420 Bas-Rhin **voir COLROY-LA-GRANDE**

SABLES-D'OLONNE (LES) 85100 Vendée **RN 160/149 Map 11-A1**
♀ ⊗ ⌂ **AU COQ HARDI** (N° RR MAI 20 453) (Mlle Françoise **Pajot**) 7, avenue Alcide-Gabaret ☎ 51-32-04-62 ⊸ 8 Closed Sat/Sun low season; end of Sept/beginning of Oct. Full-board 155–190F per night. Coaches welcome (rest. seats 90). Evening meals in July/August.
♀ ⊗ ⌂ **LES VOYAGEURS** (N° RR AOU 26 307) (M. Clément **Pacory**) 17, rue de la Bauduère ☎ 51-95-11-49 ⊸ 11 Closed Fri pm, Sat; end of Dec/beginning of Jan. Evening meals until 9pm.

SABLONNIERES 38460 Isère **RD 522 and 517 Crossroads Map 2-B2**
♀ ⊗ **LE RELAIS DE LA PLACE** (N° RR OCT 24 366) (M. Maurice **Mailler**) Crémieu ☎ 74-92-80-19. Evening meals.

SACEY 50170 Manche **RD 80/D 169 Map 8-A1**
♀ ⊗ ⌂ **LES VOYAGEURS** (N° RR NOV 25 168) (Mme Marcelle **Belan**) Le Bourg ☎ 33-60-15-11 ⊸ 8 Full-board 150–180F per night. Coaches welcome (rest. seats 90). Evening meals until 9pm.

SACLAS 91690 Essone **RN 20 Map 9-B1**
♀ ⊗ **RELAIS DE MONDÉSIR** (N° RR SEPT 27 386) (M. Jean **Picq**) Guillerval ☎ 64-95-60-76 Closed Saturday, Sunday, August. Evening meals until 10.30pm. Spanish, Portuguese spoken.

SAGY 71580 Saône-et-Loire **Map 18-B1**
♀ ⊗ **LE BLUES GIN'S** (N° RR OCT 27 040) (M. Guy **Moreau**) **Les Bulets** ☎ 85-74-07-03 English spoken.

SAHUNE 26510 Drôme **RN 94 Map 24-B2**
♀ ⊗ ⌂ **1 Star NN LE RELAIS DAUPHINE-PROVENCE** (N° RR MAI 16 059) (M. **Aumage**) Route Nationale 94 ☎ 75-27-40-99 **Minitel** ⊸ 10 Closed Wed, last week of Aug; Christmas/New Year

S

Sahune continued
holiday. Full-board 160–190F per night. Coaches welcome (rest. seats 60). Evening meals.

SAILLANS 26340 Drôme **RN 93 Map 24-B1**
♀ ⊗ 🏠 **LE NATIONAL** (N° RR SEP 18 179) (Mme Jeannine **Chauvet**) place du Prieuré - Grand-Rue ☎ 75-21-51-33 ⊶ 6 Closed Wed; Sept. Full-board 160–170F per night. Coaches welcome (rest. seats 35). Evening meals until 9pm.

SAINT, SAINTE: for compound names beginning with Saint or Sainte, see the end of this section.

SAINTENY 50500 Manche **CD 971 Map 4-B1**
♀ ⊗ **LE RELAIS DES FORGES** (N° RR NOV 27 092 (Mme Francine **Cousin**) Les Forges Carentan ☎ 33-42-39-36 Closed Tues and last two weeks of August. Evening meals. Coaches welcome (rest. seats 70).

SAINTES 17100 Char.-Marit. **RN 137 Map 15-A2**
♀ ⊗ **LE RELAIS DE L'OASIS** (N° RR MAI 14 348) (M. Guy **Fumoleau**) Route de Rochefort ☎ 46-93-07-20 Closed Sat, Sun off season; 6–24 Aug. Coaches welcome (rest. seats 50). Evening meals until 9.30pm. German spoken.

SALAISE-SUR-SANNE 38150 Isère **Map 18-B3**
♀ ⊗ **LE RELAIS DE LA SANNE** (N° RR MAR 24 522) (M. Marc **Giraud**) Route Nationale ☎ 74-86-37-91 English, German spoken.

SALAVRE 01270 Ain **RN 83 Map 18-B1**
♀ ⊗ **LE SALAVRE** (N° RR DEC 26 717) (Mme Anick **Grudet**) Coligny ☎ 74-30-15-75 Closed Wed 2.30pm.

SALINS-LES-BAINS 39110 Jura **Map 14-B3**
♀ ⊗ **RESTAURANT DES SPORTS** (N° RR JUL 27 344) (Mme Denise **Reverchon**) 107 Rue de la Republique ☎ 84-73-11-18 Closed Wednesday afternoon; September. Evening meals until 11pm.

SALLE (LA) 71260 Saône-et-Loire **RN 6 Map 18-B1**
♀ ⊗ **RELAIS DU MACONNAIS** (N° RR JUL 26 590) (Mme Valérie **Zorzi**) Lugny ☎ 85-37-51-34 Closed Sat afternoon,. Sun. Italian spoken. Evening meals until 11pm.

SALOUEL 80480 Somme **RN 29 Map 5-A3**
♀ ⊗ **LE TROU NORMAND** (N° RR MAI 25 938) (M. Jean-Michel **Picard**) 75, route de Rouen ☎ 22-95-53-90 Closed Sun. Coaches welcome (rest. seats 130). English and German spoken.

SAMADET 40340 Landes **Map 20 B2**
♀ ⊗ 🏠 **AU PELLE** (N° RR OCT 26 346) (Mme **Darolles-Cassou**) Rte d'Hagetmau ☎ 58-79-19-81 ⊶ 6 Full-board 100–200F per night. Coaches welcome. Evening meals. English, Spanish spoken.

SAMMERON 77260 S.-et-M **RN 3 Map 9-A2**
♀ ⊗ **LES CICOGNES** (N° RR OCT 13 153) (Mme **Meteyer**) 73, rue de
Metz ☎ 60-22-14-06 Closed Sun, Oct.

SANCERGUES 18140 Cher **RN 151 Map 13-B2**
♀ ⊗ ⌂ **LE RELAIS AU BON LABOUREUR** (N° RR JAN 22 148) (Mme
Martine **Dubois**) 54, Grande-Rue ☎ 48-72-76-13 ⊷ 5 Full-board
140–150F per night. Closed Tue afternoon; 15 Jun–5 Jul. Coaches
welcome (rest. seats 90). German, Italian spoken. Evening meals.
♀ ⊗ **LE RELAIS DU CHEVAL BLANC** (N° RR MAR 16 916) (M.
Daniel **Gitton**) 44, Grand-Rue ☎ 48-72-70-38 ⊷ 6 Closed Mon.
Full-board 130–160F. Coaches welcome (rest. seats 35). Evening
meals cooked to order.

SANCY-LES-PROVINS 77320 S.-et-M. **Map 9-A2**
♀ ⊗ **LE RELAIS DE SANCY** (N° RR JUL 26 955) (M. Michel **Tonne-
lier**) RN 4 ☎ 64-01-92-07 Closed Sun. English spoken. Coaches
welcome. Evening meals until 2am.

SARAN see ORLEANS 45400 Loiret **Autoroute A10 Map 13-A1**

SARCEY 69490 Rhône **2 km from RN 7 Map 2-A1**
♀ ⊗ **LE RELAIS DES MARRONIERS** (N° RR AVR 26 223) (M. Patrick
Parisi) Place de l'Église ☎ 74-26-86-65 Closed Wed afternoon.
Sunday lunch. Evening meals. English spoken. Rest seats 75.

SARGE-SUR-BRAYE 41170 Loir-et-Cher **Map 12-A3**
♀ ⊗ **LE RELAIS DE MONPLAISIR Tobacconist** (N° RR FEV 25 827)
(M. Roger **Monchatre**) Mondoubleau ☎ 54-72-72-21 Closed Sat,
Sun; Aug. Evening meals Mon–Thurs. HGV parking.

SARLAT 24200 Dordogne **CD 46/57 Map 17-B1**
♀ ⊗ **RELAIS DE CORDY** (N° RR AOUT 26 982) (Mme Marika
Treillou) Pré de Cordy ☎ 53-31-19-65 English, Spanish spoken.
Filling station near.

SARREGUEMINES 57200 Moselle **RN 74 Map 10-A/B1**
♀ ⊗ ⌂ **AU RELAIS DES ROUTIERS - CHEZ EDMOND** (N° RR SEPT
18 829) (M. Camille **Fasel**) 19, rue du Bac ☎ 87-98-15-39 ⊷ 11
Closed Sun during Jul, Aug. Full-board 160–180F per night.
Coaches welcome (rest. seats 60). Evening meals until midnight.
German spoken.

SARTILLY 50300 Marche **Map 8-A1**
♀ ⊗ **LE VIEUX LOGIS** (N° RR OCT 27 394) (M. Gerard **Cadiot**)
Grand Rue ☎ 33-48-80-31 Closed Sunday afternoon and 1 week
in Feb. English spoken.

SAUCATS 33650 Gironde **RN 651 Map 20-B1**
♀ ⊗ **L'AUBERGE QUI CHANTE** (N° RR SEPT 26 988) (Mme Claire
Dupuis) Le Bourg ☎ 56-72-23-11 ⊷ 3 Closed Sat from 1 Oct–30
Apr; Nov; Feb. English spoken. Filling station 7 km.

S

SAUJON 17600 Chte-Marit **Map 11-B1**
♀ ⊗ 🏠 **1 Star NN HÔTEL DE LA GARE** (N° RR OCT 24 404) (M.
Michel **Mellot**) 2, rue Clémenceau ☎ 46-02-80-33 ⊷ 12 from 95–
140F, breakfast 18–22F, access for disabled. Closed Sun; Christmas to New Year. Full-board 200–250F per night. Coaches
welcome (2 rooms; 110 seats). Evening meals until 10pm. Car
park; bar; dogs allowed; sports (table tennis, *petanque*, swings).
Indoor terrace.

SAULCE 26630 Drôme **RN 7 and RD 26 motorway exit Loriol,
Montélimar Nord Map 24-A1**
♀ ⊗ 🏠 **LE DISQUE BLEU** (N° RR OCT 25 134) (M. Jacques **Brillo**)
quartier des Blaches à **Cliouscat** ☎ 75-63-00-08 ⊷ 8 Closed Sat
afternoon, Sun. Full-board 130–160F per night. Coaches welcome
(rest. seats 60). Evening meals at all hours.

SAULCE-LES-ALPES (LA) 05110 Hautes-Alpes **RN 85 Map 25-A1**
♀ ⊗ 🏠 **1 Star NN LE RELAIS DE FRANCE** (N° RR SEPT 20 281)
(Mme **Ubaud**) ☎ 92-54-25-35 ⊷ 10.

SAULIEU 21210 Cote-d'Or **RN 6 Map 13-B3**
♀ ⊗ 🏠 **LE RELAIS AUX POIDS LOURDS** (N° RR FEV 12 693) (M.
Godet) 30, rue Courte-Epée ☎ 80-64-19-83 ⊷ 8 Closed Sat, Sun.
Evening meals.

SAULNIÈRES 35320 I.-et-V. **RD 777 Map 7-B3**
♀ ⊗ **LA TAVERNE BRETONNE** (N° RR MAI 26 540) (Mme Nicole
Clipet) Bourg de Saulnières, Bel de Bretagne ☎ 99-44-70-61
Coaches welcome (rest. seats 100). Casserole menus 43–99F.
⊷ Specialities: *Fruits des Mers. Escargots, Aiguiltette du canard.*

SAULT BRENAZ 01790 Ain **Map 2-A2**
♀ ⊗ 🏠 **RESTAURANT DUPONT** (N° RR OCT 27 403) (M. Vailery
Archiret) ☎ 74-36-62-88 ⊷ 6 Evening meals until 9pm. Nearby
service station open 7am to 8pm.

SAUMUR 49400 Maine-et-Loire **RN 152 Map 12-B2**
♀ ⊗ 🏠 **2 Stars NN HÔTEL DE LA GARE** (N° RR FEV 17 188) (M.
⊷ Jacques **Gaudicheau**) 16, avenue David-d'Angers ☎ 41-67-34-24
⊷ 16 from 80–220F, breakfast 18–27F, telephone, access for
disabled. Closed 1 Oct to 1 April. View of Loire and castle. Full
board 230–345F per night. Coaches welcome (rest. seats 200).
Evening meals until 10pm. English, German spoken. Proprietor-
ship passed from father to son since 1919. Member of 'Courtoisie
Française'. Car park patrons only, secure; bar; dogs allowed.
Menus 28–80F. Specialities: *Cuisse de poulet bonne femme; Rôti
à la saumuroise; omelette arc-en-ciel.* Places to visit: Stone
circles, châteaux, museums, churches, wine cellars.

SAUQUEVILLE 76550 Seine-Maritime **RN 27 Map 4-A3**
♀ ⊗ 🏠 **LA FALAISE** (N° RR NOV 25 214) (Mme **Levasseur**) **Bas de
Tourvilles/Arques** ☎ 35-85-44-77 ⊷ 11 Closed Sun evening.
English, Italian, Spanish spoken.

S

SAUVIAT-SUR-VIGE 87560 Haute-Vienne **RN 141 Map 16-B1**
𝖸 ⊗ 🏠 **1 Star NN HÔTEL 400 DE LA POSTE** (N° RR AOU 10 941) (M. Pierre **Chassagne**) ☎ 55-75-30-12 ⊷ 12 (10 with WC) from 75–145F, breakfast 18–30F. Closed Wed; Sept. Full-board 150–180F per night. Coaches welcome (rest. seats 120). Evening meals. Car park; bar; dogs allowed; recreations (fishing, hunting); countryside to explore.

SAUZE-VAUSSAIS 79190 Deux-Sèvres **RN 148 Map 15-A1/2 LES ALLEUDS (Chaignepain)**
𝖸 ⊗ **LE RELAIS DES ROUTIERS** (N° RR JAN 20 089) (M. Joël **Quintard**) ☎ 49-29-34-61 Closed Sat. Coaches welcome (rest. seats 180). Evening meals until 10pm.

SAUZET 26740 Drôme **RN 7 Map 24-A2**
𝖸 ⊗ **CHTIMI LE LOGI NEUF** (N° RR AUG 27 369) (SARL Les Tourrettes – Michel **Chareyon**) Les Tourrettes ☎ 75-90-06-02 ⊷ 7 Evening meals until midnight. German, English, Spanish spoken.

SAVENAY 44260 L.-Atl. **RN 165 Map 11-A2**
𝖸 ⊗ **RELAIS 165** (N° RR FEV 27 193) (M. Claude **BOURGINE**) Le Pas de l'Auline Prinquiau ☎ 40-56-64-99 Closed Sat/Sun.

SAVERDUN 09700 Ariège **RN 20 Map 22-A2**
𝖸 ⊗ 🏠 **A LA BONNE AUBERGE** (N° RR AVR 21 880) (Mme **Boutet**) Route Nationale 20 or 73 - rue du Lion-d'Or ☎ 61-69-30-33 ⊷ 6 Closed Mon; Sept. Spanish spoken.

SAVIGNAC 33190 Gironde **Map 21-A1**
⛽ **Total Service Station LE RELAIS DE SAVIGNAC** (N° RR MAI 24 948) (M. Patrick **de Smet**) Aire du Bazadais Autoroute A62 ☎ 56-25-40-93. Open 24 hours. French, Spanish, English, Portuguese, Italian spoken.

SAZILLY 37220 l.-et-L. **RD 760 Map 12-B2**
𝖸 ⊗ **LE RELAIS DE LA PROMENADE** (N° RR MARS 25 862) (Mme Jocelyne **Bigot**) Le Bourg ☎ 47-58-55-50 Closed Sun. Coaches welcome (rest. seats 80). Evening meals.

SCHWANGERBACH par REYERSVILLER 57230 Moselle **RD 37 Map 10-B1**
𝖸 ⊗ **LE RELAIS DES ROUTIERS** (N° RR MAR 19 693) (Mme Joséphine **Volb**) ☎ 87-06-00-64 Closed Thurs; 1 Sep–1 Oct.

SCIEZ 74140 Hte-Savoie **RN Map 19-A1**
𝖸 ⊗ 🏠 **1 star NN LE LEMAN** (N° RR AVR 25 358) (M. Roger **Berthet** Bonnatrait ☎ 50-72-60-04 ⊷ 12 (60–110F; breakfast 16F). Closed Sat in winter; Oct. Full-board 160–180F per night; breakfast 16F. Coaches welcome (rest. seats 70). Evening meals. Parking, bar. Sites to visit: Evian, Genève, mountain walks. English, German spoken.

S

SCOURY 36300 Indre **RN 151 Map 16-A1**
⟨glasses⟩ ⊗ ⌂ **LE RELAIS DES ROUTIERS** (N° RR JANV 26 791) (Mme Roselyne **Pilet**) Nationale 151 ☎ 54-37-98-09 ⊸ 5 Closed Sun evening; 24/12–9/1. Coaches welcome (rest. seats 40). Evening meals until 10pm.

SEAUVE-SUR-SEMENE (LA) 43470 Haute-Loire **RD 500 Map 18-A3**
⟨glasses⟩ ⊗ **LE RELAIS DE LA GARE** (N° RR DEC 24 448) (Mme Denise **Teissèdre**) 105, avenue de la Semène ☎ 71-61-04-86 Closed Mon; Aug.

SÉBAZAC 12850 Aveyron **CD 904 Map 22-A1**
⟨glasses⟩ ⊗ **LE LONGCHAMP** (N° RR SEPT 27 033) (Mme Monique **Guilpin**) 56, avenue Tabardelle ☎ 65-74-93-62 Coaches welcome (rest. seats 50). Evening meals until 100pm.

SECONDIGNY 79130 Deux-Sèvres **RN 148 Map 15-A1**
⟨glasses⟩ ⊗ ⌂ **LE RELAIS DES ROUTIERS** (N° RR JAN 19 615) (M. Noël **Duranceau**) 43, rue de la Vendée ☎ 49-95-61-35 ⊸ 5 Closed Mon; 1st week Sep. Coaches welcome (rest. seats 165). Evening meals.

SEGLIEN 56160 Morbihan **RN 782 Map 7-B2**
⟨glasses⟩ **LE CAFE DE LA PAIX** (N° RR MAR 20 134) (M. Armand **Bigouin**) ☎ 97-28-02-48 Lann-Blomen.

SEGRE 49500 M.-et-L. **RN 775 Maps 11-A3 and 12 A1**
⟨glasses⟩ ⊗ ⌂ **LE RELAIS DU COMMERCE** (N° RR DEC 18 576) (M. Emile **Georget**) 1, place de la Gare ☎ 41-92-22-27 ⊸ 10.

SELLES-SAINT-DENIS-SALBRIS 41300 Loir-et-Cher **RN 724 Map 13-A/B1**
⟨glasses⟩ ⊗ **BAR DES SPORTS** (N° RR MAI 23 813) (M. Robert **Billet**) 2, place du Mail ☎ 54-96-21-38 Closed Sundays; Feb (15 days).

SEMUR-EN-AUXOIS 21140 Côte d'Or **CD 980 Map 13-A3**
⟨glasses⟩ ⊗ **AUBERGE DES QUINCONCES** (N° RR SEPT 26 985) (M. Daniel **Vilatte**) 58, rue de Paris ☎ 80-97-02-00 English spoken (by 1 staffer). Filling station near.

SENAN 89710 Yonne **RD 955 Map 13-A2**
⟨glasses⟩ ⊗ ⌂ **HOTEL DE LA CROIX BLANCHE** (N° RR NOV 26 104) (M. Jean-Claude **Lecourt**) 16, rue d'Aillant ☎ 86-63-41-31 ⊸ Closed Sun after lunch.

SENAS 13560 B.-du-R. **RN 7 Map 24-B3**
⟨glasses⟩ ⊗ **L'ETAPE** (N° RR MARS 21 043) (SNC Veyrier Frères) RN 7 ☎ 90-59-22-81 Closed Sat, Sun; 25 Dec–5 Jan. Evening meals.
⟨glasses⟩ ⊗ **LE RESTO GRILL** (N° RR SEPT 26 326) (M. **Degoul**) RN 7 ☎ 90-57-27-82 Closed Sat afternoon, Sun. Evening meals.

SENE 56000 Morbihan **RN 165 Map 11-A1/2**
⟨glasses⟩ ⊗ ⌂ **1 Star NN LE POULFANC** (N° RR FEV 16 886) (S.A. **Penru**)

route de Vannes ☎ 97-47-47-97 ⇥ 45 Closed 23 Dec to 5 Jan. Evening meals until 10pm.

SENNECEY-LE-GRAND 71240 S.-et-L. **RN 6 Map 18-B1**
♈ ⊗ **L'ARCHE** (Mme Marie-Claude **Debrune**) Autoroute A6 St Ambreuil ☎ 85-44-20-64 Open 24 hours.
♈ ⊗ **CAFÉ ROUTE** Autoroute A6 ☎ 85-44-21-79 Open 24 hours.

SENS 89100 Yonne **RN 5 Map 9-B2**
♈ ⊗ ⌂ **RELAIS DES TROIS GARES** (N° RR JUL 26 288) (M. Jean **Bouju**) 29 bis, avenue Vauban ☎ 86-65-12-76 ⇥ 10 Closed Sat afternoon, Sun.

SEREILHAC 87620 Haute-Vienne **Map 16-B1**
♈ ⊗ **AUBERGE DES ROUTIERS** (N° RR FEV 24 846) (Mme Denis **Vignaud**) Route Nationale 21 ☎ 55-39-10-46 ⇥ 6 Coaches welcome (rest. seats 260). English spoken.

SERIFONTAINE 60590 Oise **Map 3-A/B2**
♈ ⊗ **CAFÉ DES SPORTS** (N° RR SEPT 27 002) (M. Michel **Decaux**) 20, rue Hacque ☎ 44-84-80-33 Closed Sun. Filling station (7am–9pm) near. English spoken. Evening meals.

SÉRIGNY 17230 Charente-Maritime **Map 11-A1**
♈ ⊗ **CHEZ JOHAN** (N° RR MAI 27 288) (M. Johan **Mercier**) ☎ 46-01-40-03 Closed Sun. Evening meals.

SERQUIGNY 27470 Eure **Map 4-B3**
♈ ⊗ **LE RELAIS DE LA GARE** (N° RR JAN 24 480) (Mme Huguette **Lebas**) route de Beaumont ☎ 32-44-08-74 Closed Sat, Sun; Aug. English spoken.

SERRES-CASTET 64160 Pyr.-Atl **Maps 20-B3 and 21-A3**
♈ ⊗ ⌂ **LES ROUTIERS** (N° RR MAR 23 199) (M. Léon **Salis**) ☎ 59-33-91-06 ⇥ 4 Closed Sat, Sun; Aug. Evening meals. Spanish spoken. Full-board 150–170F. (Rest seats 60).

SERVAS 01240 Ain **RN 83 Map 18-B2**
♈ ⊗ ⌂ **LE RELAIS DU POSTILLON** (N° RR AVR 25 364) (**Lastab-Champier**) ☎ 74-52-79-10 ⇥ 7 Closed Saturday; 1–21 Aug. Evening meals. Full board 150F. (Rest seats 80).

SETE 34200 Hérault **RN 108 Map 23-B2**
♈ ⊗ **LE PAVILLON** (N° RR MARS 26 471) (Mme Marie-France **Petitfils**) 23, route de Montpellier ☎ 67-48-62-53 Closed Sat afternoon, Sun. Coaches (rest. seats 64). English spoken. Evening meals.
♈ ⊗ **RESTO ROUTIER LA PENICHE** (N° RR AVR 23 758) (Mme Paquerette **Dupuy**) 1, quai des Moulins ☎ 67-48-64-13 Evening meals. Coaches welcome (rest. seats 100).
♈ ⊗ **LA REGENCE** (N° RR DEC 27 116) (M. Noël **Barthe**) 1, quai de la République Place Delille ☎ 67-74-32-92 English. Spanish and Italian spoken.

S

SEURRE 21250 Côte-d'Or **Map 14-A3**
♀ ⊗ **RELAIS DU CHAMP DE FOIRE** (N° RR JUL 26 580) (M. Jacky **Madesclaire**) 13, place du Champ de Foire ☎ 80-21-03-43 Closed Sun. Coaches welcome (rest. seats 50). Evening meals until 9.00pm.

SEXCLES 19430 Corrèze **RN 120 Map 17-A2**
♀ ⊗ 🏠 **AUBERGE DES ROUTIERS** (N° RR JUL 26 597) (M. Claude **Gubert**) Le Mas ☎ 55-28-70-70 ⊸ 10.

SEYCHES 47350 L.-et-G. **RN 133 Map 21-B1**
♀ ⊗ **AU BON ACCUEIL** (N° RR NOV 14 086) (Mme Laliette **Madec**) ☎ 58-83-60-10 ⊸ 4 Closed Sat. Evening meals until 11.30pm.

SEYNOD 74600 Haute-Savoie **RN 201 Map 19-A2**
♀ ⊗ 🏠 **1 Star NN LE RELAIS SAINTE-CATHERINE** (N° RR MARS 9 372) (M. Lucien **Zerbola**) 181, route d'Aix ☎ 50-69-00-86 ⊸ 10 from 90–130F, breakfast 18–20F. Closed Sat/Sun except August. Full-board 90–130F per night. Coaches welcome (rest. seats 120). Evening meals. English spoken. Car park; bar; large dogs not allowed. Places to visit: Annecy.
♀ ⊗ **L'AUBERGE** (N° RR JAN 27 514) (SARL Carroz) 1152 route d'Aix les Bains. ☎ 50-46-71-02 ⊸ 10 Closed Sunday. Evening meals until 10pm. English, Italian spoken. Service station nearby.

SIDEVILLE 50690 Manche **RD 904 Map 4-A1**
♀ ⊗ **LES ROCHES** (N° RR FEV 27 184) (M. Louis **Galopin**) Hameau Colette ☎ 33-52-02-03 English spoken.

SIDIALLES 18270 Cher **Map 16-A2**
♀ ⊗ **CHEZ MIMI** (N° RR MAI 27 268) (M. Lucien **Le Bellego**) Le Bouquet ☎ 48-56-63-02 Evening meals.

SIGOTTIER 05700 Htes-Alpes **RN 5 Map 24-B2**
♀ ⊗ **PONT LA BARQUE** (N° RR MARS 25 841) (M. and Mme Claude **Faizende**) Serres ☎ 92-67-04-15 Coaches welcome (rest. seats 100). Evening meals until 11pm. Italian spoken.

SILLE-LE-GUILLAUME 72140 Sarthe **CD 37 Map 8-B2**
♀ ⊗ **HÔTEL DE L'OUEST** (N° RR OCT 26 676) (M. Jean-Jacques **Aubert**) RD 304, 8, place de la Gare ☎ 43-20-10-58 ⊸ 14 Closed Sun evening, August. Full-board 100–136F. (Rest seats 35). Evening meals until 9pm.
♀ ⊗ **LA COQUE** (N° RR SEPT 27 005) (M. Claude **Rouzier**) 11 Gis, route de Mans, St. Rémy de Sillé ☎ 43-20-11-84 Closed Sun; 15–30 Aug. Filling station (7am–10pm) near. Evening meals all hours. (Rest seats 50).

SISTERON 04200 Alpes-de-Haute-Provence **RN 85 Map 25-A1 24-B2**
♀ **LE CAFE DES ARCADES** (N° RR MAI 16 570) (SARL – **Bar des Arcades**) place de la République ☎ 92-61-02-52.

S

SIZUN 29237 Finistère **RD 167 Map 7-A1**
🍷 ⊗ 🏠 **1 Star NN HÔTEL DES VOYAGEURS** (N° RR MAR 14
263) (M. Joseph **Corre**) 2, rue de l'Argoat ☎ 98-68-80-35 ⊸ 28
from 70–135F, breakfast 20F. Closed Sat evening (off season); 3
last weeks of Sept. Full-board 150–190F per night. Coaches
welcome (rest. seats 250). Evening meals. English spoken.
Menus 40–65F. Specialities: *Terrine de lapin, Mousseline de
truite, Fruits de mer.*

SOLAIZE 69360 Rhône **Autoroute A7 Map 2-B1**
🍷 ⊗ **RESTOP DE SOLAIZE** (M. Jean-Paul **Goupy**) ☎ 78-02-82-63 Self-
service restaurant open 11.00am to 10.00pm. Showers.

SOLESMES 59730 Nord **Map 5-B3**
🍷 ⊗ 🏠 **HÔTEL DE LA HURE** (N° RR NOV 26 726) (M. **Zurawski**) 2,
rue Georges-Clémenceau ☎ 27-37-32-49 ⊸ 16 Closed Mon
evening. Full-board 152F. Evening meals until midnight.

SOMMERY 76440 Seine-Maritime **Map 3-A1**
🍷 ⊗ **AU BON CIDRE** (N° RR JUN 24 605) (Mme Raymonde **Guillou**)
La Cavée **Forges-les-Eaux** ☎ 35-90-57-11 Closed Wed. Yugosla-
vian spoken.
🍷 ⊗ **LE MONTESTRUC** (N° RR MARS 27 208) (M. Jean-Luc **Édet**) La
Cavée ☎ 35-90-56-16 Closed Wed pm.

SOMMIERES-DU-CLAIN 86160 Vienne **RD 1 Map 15-B1**
🍷 ⊗ 🏠 **LES TROIS PILIERS** (N° RR JUIL 26 937) (M. Martial **Richard**)
place de l'Église ☎ 49-87-70-09 ⊸ 5. Closed Monday. Full board
135–150F. Evening meals until 11pm. (rest. seats 80). Coaches
welcome.

SORGUES 84700 Vaucluse **Autoroute A7 and RN 7 Map 24-A2**
🍷 ⊗ **RESTOP DE SORGUES** (M. Jean-Jacques **Hurey**) ☎ 90-39-10-72
Self-service restaurant open 11.00am to 10.00pm. TV, Shop.

SORINIERES (LES) 44400 L.-Atl. **RN 137 and 178 Maps 11-A/B2 and
12-B1**
🍷 ⊗ 🏠 **LE RELAIS – CHEZ PIERRETTE ET JEAN-LOUIS** (N° RR
SEP 24 673) (M. Jean-Louis **Benoît**) 16, rue du Général-de-Gaulle
☎ 40-31-22-91 ⊸ 7 Closed Sat evening, Sun; 15 Dec to 5 Jan. Full-
board 150–180F per night. Coaches welcome. (3 rooms: 50 seats).
Evening meals.

SOUAL 81580 Tarn **RN 126 Map 22-B2**
🍷 ⊗ 🏠 **LE MAÏZOU** (N° RR JUN 26 912) (M. Jean-Marie **Lemaire**) 12–
14 Grand-Rue ☎ 63-75-52-24 ⊸ 5 Closed Tue evening. Filling
station 100m. Full-board 15F. Coaches welcome (rest. seats 190).

SOUBERAC 16130 Charente **RN 141 Map 15-A2**
🍷 ⊗ **AUX CHASSEURS** (N° RR MAI 26 254) (M. Raymond **Joffrion**)
Gensacla-Pallue ☎ 45-32-13-80 Closed Sat; Aug. Coaches wel-
come (rest. seats 90).

S

SOUCHEZ 62153 P.-de-C. **RN 37 Map 5-A1**
♀ ⊗ **AU RENDEZ-VOUS DES ROUTIERS** (N° RR DEC 20 352) (Mme **Louf**) 5, rue Carnot ☎ 21-45-15-01.

SOUDAN-CHATEAUBRIAND 44110 Loire-Atl. **RN 775 Maps 11-A3 and 12-A1**
♀ ⊗ **CAFE DE LA POSTE** (N° RR SEP 24 321) (M. Claude **Fruchard**) place Tolhouët - place de la Poste ☎ 40-28-62-36 Coaches welcome (2 rooms = 70 seats). Breakfasts.

SOUDE 51320 Marne **Map 9-A3**
♀ ⊗ **CHEZ PHILLIPE** (N° RR SEPT 27 385) (SNC Menis Peral **Fils**) ☎ 26-69-71-10

SOUILLAC 46200 Lot **RN 20 Map 17-B1**
♀ ⊗ ⌂ **1 Star NN LE RELAIS DE L'ESCALE** (N° RR JAN 21 758) (M. Jean **Regnères**) 41, avenue Louis-Jean Malvy ☎ 65-37-82-65 ⊷ 18 Closed Mon.

SOULAINES-DHUYS 10200 Aube **RD 960 Map 9-B3**
♀ ⊗ **LE RELAIS DES ROUTIERS** (N° RR 20 866) (M. Guy **Demongeot**) Route Nationale 60 ☎ 25-26-51-10 Evening meals.

SOULGE-SUR-OUETTE 53210 Mayenne **RN 157 Map 8-B1**
♀ ⊗ ⌂ **LA BELLE ÉTOILE** (N° RR OCT 26 710) (M. Gérard **Couillebault**) Le Point du Jour ☎ 43-02-30-18 ⊷ 10. Full-board 99–145F. (rest. seats 40). Evening meals until 11.30pm. Coaches welcome.

SOULIGNY par BOUILLY 10320 Aube **RN 77 Map 9-B3**
♀ ⊗ ⌂ **1 Star NN AU RELAIS DE MONTAIGU** (N° RR AVR 18 374) (M. René **Braux**) 300, rue du Martel ☎ 25-40-20-20 ⊷ 13 Coaches welcome (rest. seats 70). Evening meals. Full-board 150–200F. Rooms 85–110F. Breakfasts 18–20F. Parking, bar, tourist sites.

SOUMOULOU 64420 Pyr.-Atl. **RN 117 Map 20-B3 21-A3**
♀ ⊗ ⌂ **LE RELAIS BEARNAIS** (N° RR FEV 18 644) (Mme Jeanne **Suberbielle**) 5, rue de Platanes ☎ 59-04-60-45 ⊷ 6 Closed Sun afternoon and Aug. Full-board 160–200F. Coaches welcome (rest. seats 80). Evening meals.

SOURDEVAL-LA-BARRE 50150 Manche **Map 8-A1**
♀ ⊗ **AU BON ACCUEIL** (N° RR SEP 26 635) (Mme Micheline **Petitpas**) 1, place du Champ-de-Foire ☎ 35-59-62-91 ⊷ 2 Closed Sat afternoon, Sun, 1st 2 weeks Aug. Full-board 160–170F per night. Coaches welcome (3 rooms = 60 seats).

SOURDEVAL-LES-BOIS 50650 Manche **RN 799 Map 8-A1**
♀ ⊗ **LE RELAIS DES ROUTIERS** (N° RR FEV 20 659) (Mme Colette **Dufour**) Near La Crois ☎ 33-61-77-99.

STEENVOORDE 59114 Nord **AUTOROUTE 25 Map 5-A1**
♀ ⊗ **ACCOR** (M. Michel **Jaminion**) Air de Service de Saint-Laurent Paris/Province and Province/Paris directions ☎ 28-42-04-67 ⊷

Self-service restaurant open 6.30am to 10.00pm. English, German spoken. Shop.

STENAY 55700 Meure **D 947 Map 6-B3**
Y ⊗ **LA MANGEOIRE** (N° RR MARS 26 841) (M. Daniel **Demaçon**) 1, rue Carnot ☎ 29-80-60-06/29-80-37-64 ⊷ 7 (4 single) Closed Fri afternoon; 15–31 Aug. German, English (some) spoken. Filling station 300m. Evening meals.

STRASBOURG 67000 Bas-Rhin **RN 4 Map 10-B2**
Y ⊗ **AU PETIT RHIN** (N° RR AVR 14 331) (M. Albert **Kupferchlaeger**) 4, rue du Port-du-Rhin ☎ 88-61-35-00 Closed Sun; public holidays; Aug. Evening meals.
Y ⊗ ⌂ **AU RHIN FRANÇAIS** (N° RR DEC 25 227) (M. Marcel **Wendling**) 83, route du Rhin ☎ 88-61-29-00 and 61-40-93 ⊷ 7 Closed Sat afternoon, Sun. Evening meals. German, English, Italian, Spanish, Dutch spoken. Coaches welcome (rest. seats 200). Meals served until 11pm.
Y ⊗ **AU COIN DU PECHEUR** (N° RR MAI 24 584) (Mme Catherine **Lopez**) 1, rue Migneret ☎ 88-60-33-16 **Port du Rhin** German, Spanish spoken.
Y ⊗ **BRASSERIE DES BATELIERS** (N° RR JUIN 27 306) (M. et Mme Jean-Calude **Pccinelli**) rue de la Plaine des Bouchers ☎ 88-39-19-50 Closed Sat from 3pm, Sun and 24/12 to 21/1, Easter and three weeks in September. German spoken. Evening meals served until 10pm.

SUEVRES 41500 L.-et-C. **RN 152 Map 12-A3**
Y ⊗ ⌂ ⊷ **LA PROVIDENCE – Chez Jacques** (N° RR MAI 17 283) (M. Jacques **Bouchet**) 1, place de la Mairie ☎ 54-87-80-88 ⊷ 7 Closed Sat evening, Sun evening; mid Aug to mid Sept. Coaches welcome (rest. seats 140). Evening meals. Spanish spoken. Specialities: *Poularde à la crème, Gras double lyonnaise, choucroute maison.*

SUIPPES 51600 Marne **RN 77 and 31 Maps 6-B2 and 9-A3**
Y ⊗ **AU BON COIN** (N° RR JUL 24 623) (SDF **Tiloca**) 39, rue de la Libération ☎ 26-67-04-84 Coaches welcome (rest. seats 100). Evening meals. Italian spoken.

SULLY-SUR-LOIRE 45600 Loiret **RN 152 Map 13-A1**
Y ⊗ ⌂ **LE ST GERMAIN** (N° RR FEV 21 807) (M. and Mme **Schwartz**) 2, place Saint-Germain ☎ 38-36-27-02 ⊷ 6 Closed Fri evening, Sun evening; Christmas to New Year. Full-board 145–165F per night. Coaches welcome (rest. seats 150). Evening meals.
Y ⊗ ⌂ **CHEZ LIONEL – CAFÉ DE LA GARE** (N° RR OCT 26 077) (M. Lionel **Funten**) 47, rue de la Gare ☎ 38-36-26-11 ⊷ 6 Closed Sat afternoon, Sun; 8 to 23 Aug. Full-board 145–160F per night. Coaches welcome (rest. seats 85). after 1.30pm. Evening meals until 10pm.

SURESNES 92150 Hauts-de-Seine **Porte de St-Cloud Map 1-A/B2**
Y ⊗ **LE RELAIS DES ÉCLUSES** (N° RR JUN 19 083) (M. Henri **Bodin**)

S

Suresnes continued
30, quai Gallieni ☎ 45-06-11-48 Closed Sun, public holidays; Aug. Evening meals served.

SURY-AUX-BOIS see PONT-DES-BEIGNIERS 45530 Loiret **RN 60**

SURY-LE-COMTAL 42450 Loire **RD 8 Map 18-A2**
♀ ⊗ **LE PARILLY P.M.U.** (N° RR OCT 25 131) (M. Simon **Volle**) 13, rue du 11-Novembre ☎ 77-30-80-14. Closed Sat, 3 weeks in May. (Rest. seats 40). Evening meals until 8pm.

SUZAY 27420 Eure **RN 14 Map 3-B1**
♀ ⊗ **LE RELAIS MODERNE** (N° RR AOU 26 977) (M. Jean-Claude **Laurent**) ☎ 32-55-65-01 Filling station near.

SAINT-AFRIQUE 12400 Aveyron
♀ ⊗ ⌂ **LE MAJESTIC** (N° RR JUIL 27 315) (M. Alain **Espinos**) 720, avenue du Docteur Galtier ☎ 65-99-00-0-7 ◄ 12 English and Spanish spoken. Evening meals served until 10pm.

SAINT-AGATHON 22200 C.-du-N. **RN 12 Map 7-A2**
♀ ⊗ ⌂ **1 Star NN HÔTEL BELLE VUE** (N° RR OCT 20 294) (M. **Février**) Bel-Orme ☎ 96-43-80-53 ◄ 20 from 120–195F, breakfast 15F, telephone. Closed Sun; 20 Dec to 3 Jan. Car park; bar; dogs allowed; fishing.

SAINT-AGNANT-LES-MARAIS 17620 Chte-Mme **Map 11-B1**
♀ ⊗ **RENDEZ-VOUS DES AMIS** (N° RR JUN 26 266) (M. Alain **Neveur**) Le Pont ☎ 46-83-30-36 Closed Sat off season. Coaches welcome (rest. seats 100). Evening meals in Jul, Aug. German spoken.

SAINT-AIGNANT-LE-JAILLARD 45600 Loiret **RD 951 Map 13-A1**
♀ ⊗ **LE SAINT-AIGNAN** (N° RR FEV 26 464) (Mme Claudine **Gasnier**) 78, rue Nationale ☎ 38-36-38-21 Closed Wed; End of Feb and Aug. Coaches welcome. Evening meals until 9pm.

SAINT-ALBAIN par MACON 71260 S.-et-L. **Autoroute A6 Map 18-B1**
♀ ⊗ **ACCOR - RELAIS BOURGOGNE** (M. Blaise **Surlet**) Aire de Service de Saint-Albain ☎ 85-33-19-00 Self-service restaurant open 24 hours. TV, shop. English, Italian, Spanish spoken.

SAINT-AMAND-LE-PETIT 81720 Haute-Vienne **Map 16-B1**
♀ ⊗ **LE PROMENADE** (N° RR AVR 25 236) (M. Fernand **Rouby**) Eymoutier ☎ 55-69-15-38 ◄ 4 Evening meals.

SAINT-AMANS-SOULT 81240 Tarn **RN 112 Map 22-B2**
♀ ⊗ ⌂ **LE RELAIS DE LA CROIX BLANCHE** (N° RR JAN 22 637) (M. Antoine **Cuadrado**) 46, route Nationale ☎ 63-98-30-33 ◄ 10 Full-board 120–130F per night. Coaches welcome (rest. seats 50). Evening meals. Closed Mon evening.

SAINT-AME 88120 Vosges **RD 417 Map 10-A2/3**
♈ ⊗ **COUP' FAIM** (N° RR JUN 25 006) (Mme Réfine **Frugier**) Grande-Rue ☎ 29-61-23-26 **Minitel** Closed Feb. ⌐ 2 with showers. Closed Sun and 15–28 Aug. Coaches welcome (rest. seats 66). Evening meals until 11pm.

SAINT-ANDRÉ-DE-LÉPINE 50680 Manche **RD 85 2km from D 972 St-Là/Caen Map 4-B1**
♈ ⊗ **SAINT-ANDRÉ BAR** (N° RR DEC 25 751) (Mme Marie-Claire **Harel**) Bourg, St. Cerisy-lapForêt ☎ 33-57-24-00 Closed Wednesday afternoon, August. Coaches welcome (rest. seats 100). Evening meals until 10.30pm.

SAINT-ANTOINE DE BREUILH 24230 Dordogne **Map 17-A/B3 21-A1**
♈ ⊗ **RELAIS DE FRANCE** (N° RR NOV 27 077) (M. Christian **Noble**) Sarl ☎ 53-24-78-97 Closed Sun. Evening meals until 9pm.

SAINT-ANTOINE-DE-FICALBA 47340 L.-et-G. **RN 21 Map 21-B1**
♈ ⊗ ⌂ **LE RELAIS DES ROUTIERS** (N° RR DEC 17 153) (Mme Rosette **Crozes**) ☎ 58-70-36-08 ⌐ 5 Closed Sat, Sun; public holidays.

SAINT ARNOLT DES BOIS 28190 Eure et Loir
♈ ⊗ **AU REGAL** (N° RR DEC 27 480) (Mme Françoise **Cornucan**) 26, Grand Rue ☎ 37-22-51-77 Closed Monday afternoon. Evening meals.

SAINT-AUBIN-DE-BAUBIGNÉ 79700 Deux-Sèvres Mauléon **RN 159 Map 11-B3**
♈ ⊗ **LE RELAIS DES ROUTIERS** (N° RR AVR 20 438) (M. Raymond **Charrier**) ☎ 49-81-45-06 Closed Aug.

SAINT-AUBIN-DE-BLAYE 33820 Gironde **RN 137 Map 15-A3**
♈ ⊗ **SARL LES GLYCINES** (N° RR MAI 26 889) (M. Joël **Loizeau**) ☎ 57-32-62-11 ⌐ 4 English spoken. Filling station near. Full-board 110–150F. Coaches welcome (rest. seats 50). Evening meals.

SAINT-AUBIN-DES-BOIS 28300 E.-et-L. **RN 23 Map 8-B3**
♈ ⊗ **LA MORICERIE** (N° RR FEV 26 184) (M. Dominique **Libératore**) RN 23 ☎ 37-32-99-25 Coaches welcome (rest. seats 163). Evening meals. Open 24 hrs.

SAINT-AUBIN-DU-CORMIER 35140 Ille-et-Vilaine **Map 8-B1**
♈ ⊗ **LES VOYAGEURS** (N° RR OCT 27 397) (M. Max **Tizon**) 13 route de Rennes ☎ 99-39-17-80 Closed Sunday; August. Evening meals. 24 hour service station. Cards accepted.

SAINT-AUBIN-EN-BRAY 60650 Oize **RN 31 Map 3-A2**
♈ ⊗ ⌂ **RELAIS DES FONTAINETTES** (N° RR SEPT 26 384) (M. Jose **Albert**) Les Fontainettes ☎ 44-80-50-26 ⌐ 5 Closed Sunday and 1st two weeks of May. Evening meals until 9pm. English spoken.

SAINT-AUBIN-SUR-SCIE 76550 Seine-Mme **Map 4-A3**
♈ ⊗ **CHEZ FRANÇOISE** (N° RR FEV 24 513) (Mme Françoise

S

Saint-Aubin-Sur-Scie continued
Soichet) Rue du Gouffre ☎ 35-85-44-60 Closed Sun; 1 Aug to 1 Sept.

SAINT-AUBIN-SUR-LOIRE 71140 S.-et-L. **RD 979 Map 16-A3**
♈ ⊗ **BAR DE L'AMITE** (N° RR OCT 27 063) (M. Didler **Gaumard-Maison**) SNC **Le Bourg** 85-53-91-09 Closed Mon pm. English, German and Spanish spoken. Evening meals until 9.30pm. Coaches welcome (rest. seats 30).

SAINT-AVOLD 57740 Moselle **Autoroute A 32 Map 10-A1**
♈ ⊗ **RESTOP St-Avold** Aire de Service de Saint-Avold ☎ 87-92-23-89 Self-service restuarant open 11.00am to 10.00pm. Bar open 24 hours. TV, Shop, Showers. English, German spoken.

SAINT-BENOIT-DU-SAULT see RHODES 36170 Indre **RN 20 Map 16-A1**

SAINT-BERTHEVIN-LES-LAVAL 53000 Mayenne **RN 157 Map 8-B1**
♈ ⊗ ⌂ **2 Star NN LE RESTAURANT DE L'AULNE – L'International** (N° RR JUN 20 761) (M. Henri **Garnier**) L'Aulne ☎ 43-69-31-74 ⇥ 22 from 100–130F, breakfast 16–18F, telephone, access for disabled. Closed Sun. Full-board 155–175F per night. Coaches welcome (rest. seats 200 + 105). Evening meals. Car park; bar; dogs allowed.

SAINT-BOMER-LES-FORGES 61700 Orne **RD 962 Map 8-A1**
♈ ⊗ **LE SAINT BOMER** (N° RR MARS 26 845) (M. Pierre **Janniard**) Le Bourg ☎ 33-37-61-66 Closed Mon evening. Filling station near.

SAINT BONNET-DU-FOUR 03390 Allier **RN 145**
♈ ⊗ **TRANS EUROPEEN** (N° RR DEC 27 484) (Mme Ivane **Pignot**) ☎ 70-07-72-62 Closed Sunday. Evening meals. English, Italian spoken.

SAINT-BONNET près RIOM 63200 P.-de-D. **RN 143 Map 16-B3**
♈ ⊗ ⌂ **AU BON COIN** (N° RR OCT 16 729) (M. **Levadoux**) 2, rue de la République ☎ 73-63-31-14 ⇥ 10 Closed 15 Sept to 10 Oct. Full-board 110–120F per night. Coaches welcome (rest. seats 90). Evening meals.

SAINT-BRÉVIN-LES-PINS 44250 L.-Atl. **RD 77 Map 11-A2**
♈ ⊗ ⌂ **1 Star NN LE RELAIS DU MARCHÉ** (N° RR AVR 16 002) (M. and Mme **Taraud**) Place Henri-Basle ☎ 40-27-22-21 ⇥ 16 Closed Mon from Oct–Mar. Evening meals. German spoken.

SAINT-BRICE-EN-COGLES 35460 I.-et-V. **RN 155 Map 8-B1**
♈ ⊗ ⌂ **CHEZ VOUS LES ROUTIERS** (N° RR DEC 8 111) (M. Francis **Tizon**) 18, rue Chateaubriand ☎ 99-98-61-45 ⇥ 6 Full-board 150F per night. Coaches welcome (rest. seats 30). Evening meals.

SAINT-BRIEUC 22000 C.-du-N. **RN 12 Map 7-A2**
♈ ⊗ ⌂ **1 Star NN AU BEAUFEUILLAGE** (N° RR JUL 6 292) (M. Claude **Andrieux**) 2, rue de Paris ☎ 96-33-09-16 ⇥ 29 Closed

Sun afternoon; 8 Aug to 1 Sept. Coaches welcome (rest. seats 60). Evening meals.

SAINT-CAPRAISE-DE-LALINDE 24150 Dordogne CD 660 Map 21-B1
⚲ ⊗ **LES GABARIERS** (N° RR DEC 27 128) (Mme Jacqueline **Stève**) ☎ 53-23-26-74 Closed Sun.

SAINT-CERE 46400 Lot RD 677 Map 17-B1
⚲ ⊗ ⌂ **HOTEL DU QUERCY** (N° RR AVR 25 909) (Mme Claudie **Fau**) av. Anatole-de-Monzie ☎ 65-38-04-83 ⊷ 10 Closed Fri evening. Full-board 150–200F. Coaches welcome (rest. seats 100). English, Spanish spoken.

SAINT-CHÉLY-D'APCHER 48200 Lozére RN 9 Map 17-B3
⚲ ⊗ ⌂ **LE BARCELONNE** (N° RR MAR 27 228) (Mme Monique **Vitre**) 33 av. de la Gare ☎ 66-31-01-22 ⊷ 5. Nearby service station open 7.30am to 8pm.

SAINT-CHRISTOPHE-DU-LIGNERON 85670 Vendée Map 11-B2
⚲ ⊗ ⌂ **L'ETAPE** (N° RR NOV 24 423) (M. Claude **Hervé**) Bourg ☎ 51-68-12-11 ⊷ 5 Restaurant closed Wed evening, Sat.

SAINT-CLAIR-DE-LA-TOUR see LA TOUR DU PIN 38110 Isère RN 516 Map 2-B3

SAINT-CLAIR-DU-RHONE 38370 Isère CD 4 Map 2-B1
⚲ ⊗ **LE RELAIS FLEURI** (N° RR DEC 22 602) (M. **Tognoloni**) 3, rue du Commandant L'Herminier ☎ 74-56-43-12 ⊷ 7 Open 24 hours. Closed 1 week in August. Italian spoken. Full-board 160–165F. (rest. seats 110) Coaches welcome.

SAINT-COSME-EN-VAIRAIS 72580 Sarthe Map 8-B2
⚲ ⊗ **LE RELAIS DE LA POSTE** (N° RR AVR 25 381) (Mme Colette **Gueranger**) 66, rue Nationale ☎ 43-97-55-11 Closed Sun afternoon. English spoken.

SAINT-CYR-EN-PAIL 53140 Mayenne RN 12
⚲ ⊗ **LES ROUTIERS** (N° RR FEV 27 182) (Mme Antoinette **Dupont**) Le Bourg Pré-en-Pail ☎ 43-03-03-21 Closed Sun pm. English spoken.

SAINT-CYR-SUR-MENTHON 01380 Ain RN 79 Map 18-B1
⚲ ⊗ **LE RELAIS DES ROUTIERS – Chez Raymond** (N° RR MAR 18 033) (M. Raymond **Ducote**) Le Logis ☎ 85-36-30-69 Closed Sun 4.00pm to Mon; 15 to 31 May; 3 weeks in Aug. Coaches welcome (rest. seats 50). Evening meals until 10pm.

SAINT-CYR-SUR-MER 83270 Var Map 24-B3
⊗ **MICKEY RESTO** (N° RR MARS 25 852) (M. Christian **Reverberi**) 20, rue d'Arquier ☎ 94-26-49-98 Closed Sun low season; 1 week at Christmas and New Year. Coaches welcome (rest. seats 42). Evening meals.

S

SAINT-DENIS 93200 Seine-St-Denis **Portes de la Chapelle et de Clignancourt Map 1-A2**
Y ⊗ **LE RELAIS DU FRET Chez Daniel** (N° RR JUN 26 272) (M. **Dahan**) 53, avenue du Président Wilson ☎ 48-09-41-22 Closed Sun. Coaches welcome (rest. seats 60). Evening meals. Spanish, English spoken.

Y ⊗ **A L'ARRET DES TRANSPORTS** (N° RR FEV 7 482) (Mme **Sahut**) 47, bd de la Libération Génovési ☎ 48-20-13-81 Closed Sat, Sun; Aug. Evening meals.

Y ⊗ **LA CHEMINÉE** (N° RR SEPT 26 665) (Mme Edwige **Brizot**) 56, rue Ambroise Croizat ☎ 48-09-92-92 Closed Sat, Sun; Aug. Evening meals until midnight.

Y ⊗ **LAS VEGAS** (N° RR SEPT 26 666) (Mme Éliane **Duqesnoy**) 4, rue Beau ☎ 20-61-83-10 Closed Sun. Evening meals served until 10pm.

Y ⊗ **LE MORETTI** (N° RR FEV 27 176) (Mme Jeanne **Cervantes**) 72, av. Paul-Vaillant-Couturier ☎ 48-27-35-02 Spanish spoken.

SAINT-DENIS-DE-MAILLOC 14100 Calvados **RD 579 Map 4-B2**
Y ⊗ **LA FORGE** (N° RR AVR 26 871) (M. Yvan **Leroy**) Lisieux ☎ 31-63-73-19 Closed Sun. Filling station near. (rest. seats 44). Evening meals. Coaches welcome.

SAINT-DENIS-DE-MÈRE 14110 Calvados **RD 562 Map 8-A2**
Y ⊗ **LE RELAIS DES LANDES** (N° RR JAN 25 271) (M. Jean-Hugues **Neveu**) Condé-sur-Noireau ☎ 31-69-01-06 ⊷ 7 Coaches welcome (rest. seats 80). Evening meals.

SAINT-DENIS-DES-MONTS 27520 Eure **RN 138 Map 4-B3**
Y ⊗ **Tabac LE LAMA** (N° RR OCT 27 068) (M. Christian **Chuette**) ☎ 32-42-60-10 Closed on Sunday. Evening meals until 9pm.

SAINT-DENIS-LES-SENS 89100 Yonne **RN 5 Map 9-B2**
Y ⊗ **LES CERISIERS** (N° RR SEP 24 670) (M. Michel **Ferrière**) 1, rue de Paris ☎ 86-65-28-52 Closed Sat, Sun; Aug. Coaches welcome (rest. seats 44). Evening meals until 9pm. English spoken.

SAINT-DENIS-SUR-SARTHON 61420 Orne **RN 12 Map 8-A/B2**
Y ⊗ ⌂ **LE RELAIS DE LA GARE - LES AMIS DES ROUTIERS** (N° RR NOV 20 585) (M. and Mle Marcel **Tessier**) Mélivier ☎ 33-27-30-03 ⊷ 8 Closed Sun. Evening meals all hours.

SAINT-DIDIER-DE-BEAUJEU 69430 Rhône **C 37 Map 18-A2**
Y ⊗ **LE CLÉ BEAUJOLAIS** (N° RR JUN 24 249) (M. Georges **Bass**) Les Dépôts ☎ 74-04-87-53 ⊷ 4 Closed Mon. Full-board 160–180F per night. Coaches welcome (rest. seats 100). Evening meals.

SAINT-DIÉ see SAINTE-MARGUERITE

SAINT DIÉ 88100 Vosges **RN 59 Map 10-A/B2**
Y ⊗ ⌂ **LA CROISETTE** (N° RR AVR 25 884) (M. Bernard **Roumier**) 41, av. de Verdun ☎ 29-56-14-37 ⊷ 14 Closed Sat, Sun; end of year. Full-board 135-150F per night. Coaches welcome by reservation at weekends (rest. seats 180). Evening meals.

S

SAINT-DIZIER 52100 Haute-Marne **RN 401 and 4 Map 14-A1/9-A3**
♈ ⊗ **LE MOLIERE** (N° RR JUL 25 978) (M. René **Castello**) 10, rue Le Moliere ☎ 26-56-63-05 Closed Sat, Sun; Aug. Coaches welcome (rest. seats 43). Evening meals until 12.30am. English, German spoken.

SAINT-ÉLOY-LES-MINES 63700 P.-de-D. **RN 144 Map 16-B2**
♈ ⊗ **LE CAFE DU COMMERCE** (N° RR SEPT 26 316) (M. Daniel **Stecher**) 174, rue Jean-Jaurès ☎ 73-85-05-66. Evening meals. Portuguese and Spanish spoken.
♈ ⊗ **CAFE DU COMMERCE** (N° RR OCT 27 062) (M. Manual **Castanleira**) 174, rue Jean-Jaures ☎ 73-85-05-66 Spanish, Portuguese spoken.

SAINT-EPAIN 37800 Indre-et-Loire **Autoroute A 10 Map 12-B2**
♒ **LE RELAIS SAINT-MAURE** (N° RR JUN 22 826) (M. Dominique **Clément**) ☎ 47-65-65-59 Open 24 hours. English, Spanish spoken.

SAINT-ERBLON 35230 Ille-et-Vilaine **RD 82 Map 7-B3**
♈ ⊗ 🏠 **CHEZ MICHEL ET SYLVIE** (N° RR FEV 26 819) (M. Michel **Martin**) Place de l'Eglise ☎ 99-52-28-40 English spoken. Closed Sun; March. Coaches welcome (rest. seats 300).

SAINT-ETIENNE 42000 Loire **RN 82 Maps 2-B1 and 18-A2/3**
♈ ⊗ **LE MISTRAL** (N° RR AVR 26 873) (Mme Martine **Gant**) 4, rue Jean-Neyret ☎ 77-32-95-39 Closed Sat; Sun; Aug. English, Spanish, Arabic spoken. Filling station near. Evening meals.
♈ ⊗ **LE RELAIS DE L'OCTROI** (N° RR FEV 25 816) (Mme Viviane **Merieux**) 5, rue du Cros ☎ 77-21-11-98 Near ring road and market. Car park, HGV also. Closed Sun. German, English spoken. Evening meals.

SAINT-ETIENNE-DU-ROUVRAY 768000 Seine-Maritime **RN 13 Bis and RD 18 Map 3-A1**
♈ ⊗ 🏠 **AU RENDEZ-VOUS DES ROUTIERS** (N° RR AOU 9 847) (Mme **Defosse**) 13, avenue des Canadiens ☎ 35-65-35-23 ⊷ 8 Closed Sat, Sun; Aug. Restaurant closed Sat evening, Sun. Coaches welcome (rest. seats 48). Evening meals until 9.30pm.

SAINT-ETIENNE-EN-BRESSE 71130 S.-et-L. **Map 18-B1**
♈ ⊗ **LE RELAIS DE L'OASIS** (N° RR MARS 25 859) (M. Alain **Sarim**) ☎ 85-96-40-26 Evening meals.

SAINT-EUGÈNE 17520 Chte-Mme **Map 15-A2**
♈ ⊗ **LES DEUX CHARENTES** (N° RR JUN 26 556) (Mme Marcelle **Blanchard**) Fontenelle Archiac ☎ 46-49-13-28 Closed Wed (off season); 15 days Feb. Coaches welcome (rest. seats 210). Some German spoken.

SAINT-ÉVARZEC 29170 Fouesnant - Finistère **RD 783 Map 7-B1**
♈ ⊗ 🏠 **1 Star NN AU BON REPOS** (N° RR JUN 25 005) (M. Roger **Guillou**) **Poullogoden** ☎ 98-56-20-09 ⊷ 30 Closed Sat in winter. 15 Dec to 10 Jan. Full-board 140-180F per night. Coaches welcome (rest. seats 150). Evening meals. English spoken.

S

SAINT-ÉVROULT-DE-MONTFORT 61230 Orne **RN 138 Map 8-A2**
Ⓨ ⊗ ⌂ **HOTEL DU RELAIS** (N° RR SEP 26 050) (M. Daniel **Conan**) Le
Bourg ☎ 33-35-60-58 ⊷ 5 Closed Sun. Full-board 120F per night.
Coaches welcome (rest. seats 120). Evening meals until 10pm.

SAINT-FÉLIX-DE-LAURAGAIS 31540 Haute-Garonne **RN 622 Map
22-A/B2**
Ⓨ ⊗ **LE GRILLON** (N° RR DEC 23 582) (Mme Aliette **Bonnes**) Route
de Castelnaudary ☎ 61-27-65-27 Closed Sun; 15–31 Aug. Evening
meals.

SAINT-FIRMIN 05800 Hautes-Alpes **RN 85 Map 19-A3**
Ⓨ ⊗ ⌂ **1 Star NN RELAIS DE LA TRINITÉ** (N° RR NOV 19 998) (M.
Pascal **Poncet**) Route Nationale ☎ 92-55-21-64 ⊷ 12 from 80 to
160F. Breakfast at 20F. Closed Jan. Full-board 170–240F per
night. Evening meals from 7.00 to 9pm. Parking, bar. Dogs
welcome. Games (children's swings, ping-pong).

SAINT-FLORENT-SUR-CHER 18400 Cher **RN 151 Map 13-B1**
Ⓨ ⊗ **L'IMPREVU** (N° RR AVR 27 252) (M. Bernard **Ruellan**) 60, rue
Jean-Jaurès ☎ 48-55-12-00 Closed Sun pm and 15 days in August.
Evening meals. Filling station near. Open 6.30am to 9.00pm.

SAINT-FLOUR 15100 Cantal **RN 9 Map 17-A/B3**
Ⓨ ⊗ ⌂ **LE RELAIS DU VIEUX PONT** (N° RR AOU 22 015) (Mme
Liliane **Teissèdre**) 49, place de la Liberté ☎ 71-60-23-00 **Minitel**
⊷ 7 Closed Sun, Monday; Jan, Feb. Full-board 150–170F per
night. Coaches welcome (rest. seats 45). Evening meals to
10.00pm. English, Spanish spoken.
Ⓨ ⊗ ⌂ **HÔTEL LE PROGRÈS** (N° RR AVR 23 757) (M. Alain
Mourgues) 61, rue des Lacs ☎ 71-60-03-06 ⊷ 16 Full-board 110-
150F per night. Coaches welcome (rest. seats 50). Evening
meals.

SAINT-GAULTIER 36800 Indre **RN 151 Map 16-A1**
Ⓨ ⊗ **CHEZ PAQUERETTE** (N° RR OCT 22 979) (Mme Marie-Louise
Malpiece) Lespez Commune de Chasseneuil ☎ 54-47-07-20
Closed Sat, Sun; Aug. Coaches welcome.
Ⓨ ⊗ **LE COMMERCE** (N° RR JAN 25 266) (Mme Marie **Pilorget**) ☎
54-47-14-81 ⊷ 4 Closed Thur.

SAINT-GAUX 33340 Gironde **RN 215 Map 20-A1**
Ⓨ ⊗ **LE RELAIS Chez Monique** (N° RR AOU 26 974) (Mme Monique
Buscail) Saint Germain-d'Esteuil, Lesparre Médoc ☎ 56-41-25-15
Closed Sun; 1st fortnight Oct. Evening meals to 10.00pm. Filling
station 4km distant.

SAINT-GENCE 87510 Hte Vienne **RD 20 Map 16-B1**
Ⓨ ⊗ **LE CAMPANELLE** (N° RR FEV 26 445) (M. Albert **Denardou**)
rte de St-Gence ☎ 55-48-02-83 Closed Sat (except for banquets
or wedding receptions); Aug. Coaches welcome (rest. seats 100).
Evening meals.

S

SAINT-GENIX-SUR-GUIERS 73240 Savoie **Map 2-B3**
Ⓨ ⊗ **AUBERGE CAMPANARDE** (N° RR JUIL 27 351) (M. Louis
Ailloud) Joudin ☎ 76-31-80-19 Closed Sat; Sep, Oct. Evening
meals to 9.00pm. Filling station nearby. Parking 500m².

SAINT-GEORGES-D'OLÉRON 17190 Chte-Mme **Map 11-B1**
Ⓨ ⊗ ⌂ **1 star NN RELAIS DE LA PETITE PLAGE** (N° RR OCT 26
688) (M. Jacky **Pasdelou**) Rte de l'Océan-Domino ☎ 46-76-52-28
⊶ 9 Closed 15 Dec–15 Jan. Italian spoken. Full-board 180–220F.
Coaches welcome (rest. seats 170). Evening meals to 23:00pm.
⊗ **AUBERGE D'ALIÉNOR** (N° RR DEC 26 751) (M. Patrick
Audouim) 5, Place de Verdun ☎ 46-76-76-33. Closed Wed (in off-
season) and 15 to 31 Oct. Evening meals to midnight.

SAINT-GEORGES-DE-MONTCLARD 24140 Dordogne) **RD 21 Map
15-B3**
Ⓨ ⊗ ⌂ **LE BON COIN** (N° RR JUIN 27 310) (M. Jean-Louis **Matasse**)
☎ 53-82-98-47 ⊶ 7 Evening meals to 11.00pm. Full-board 110–
140F per night. English, German spoken. Filling station 100m
open from 8am to 8pm.

SAINT-GEORGES-DES-GARDES 49120 M.-et-L. **RN 161 Map 11-B3
and 12-B1**
Ⓨ ⊗ ⌂ **LE RELAIS DES ROUTIERS** (N° RR DEC 19 223) (M. Louis
Jolivet) Chemille ☎ 41-62-79-38 ⊶ 5. (Two twins). Evening meals
to 11pm.

SAINT-GEORGES-SUR-EURE 28190 E.-et-L. **RD 610 Map 8-B3**
Ⓨ ⊗ ⌂ **AU RENDEZ-VOUS DES PECHEURS** (N° RR NOV 26 718) (M.
Amokrane **Mezair**) 9, Raymonde Bataille ☎ 37-26-75-30 ⊶ 9
Closed Mon afternoon; Aug.

SAINT-GEOIRE-EN-VALDAINE 38620 Isère **Map 2-B3**
Ⓨ ⊗ 🍷 **LE MÉNUPHARD** (N° RR JUIL 27 352) (M. Raymond **Brigard**)
La Combe ☎ 76-07-58-70 **Minitel** Evening meals to 9pm.
Parking 3000m².

SAINT-GÉRAND 56920 Morbihan **Map 7-B2**
Ⓨ ⊗ **LA ROSE DES VENTS** (N° RR OCT 27 392) (Mme Nadège
Pellelier) Place de L'Église ☎ 97-51-44-28 **Minitel** Closed Wed
pm. Filling station 100m.

SAINT-GÉRAND-LE-PUY 03150 Allier
Ⓨ ⊗ ⌂ **HÔTEL DE LA PAIX** (N° RR MAI 22 798) (Mme Étiennette
Knoche) Ne 7 ☎ 70-99-80-15.

SAINT-GERMAIN-DES-PRÉS 45230 Loiret **RN 443 Map 13-A1/2**
Ⓨ ⊗ ⌂ **AU BON ACCUEIL** (N° RR NOV 22 087) (Mme Catherine
Lapeyrade) Moulin Plateau ☎ 38-85-78-87 ⊶ 10 Closed Sat, Sun;
Aug.

SAINT-GERMAIN-DU-BEL-AIR 46310 Lot **RD 23 Map 17-B1**
Ⓨ ⊗ **CAFÉ DE FRANCE** (N° RR JANV 27 168) (Mme Mélina **Fran-**

S

Saint-Germain-Du-Bel-Air continued
coual) Le Bourg ☎ 65-31-06-99 Closed Sun. Filling station nearby open 8am–7.30pm.

SAINT-GERMAIN-DU-PLAIN 71370 S-et-L. **RD 978 Map 18-B1**
♀ ⊗ **RELAIS DES SPORTS** (N° RR AVR 26 508) (M. Gilles **Tenedor**) rte de Louhans ☎ 85-47-37-27.

SAINT-GERMAIN-LA-GATINE 28300 E.-et-L. **RN 154 Map 8-A3**
♀ ⊗ **LE RELAIS DE SAINT-GERMAIN** (N° RR AVR 26 869) (Mme Madeleine **Tarrou**) 1, ave de Chartres ☎ 37-22-80-31. Closed Sun. Coaches welcome (rest. seats 60). Evening meals.

SAINT-GERMAIN-LES-ARPAJON 91290 Essonne **RN 20 Map 1-B2**
♀ ⊗ **L'AS DE TRÈFLE** (N° RR NOV 26 084) (Mme Gisèle **Belin**) 7 RN 20 La Petite-Folie ☎ 64-90-02-24 ⊷ 5 Closed Sun. Coaches welcome (rest. seats 140). English spoken. Evening meals to 8pm.

SAINT-GERMAIN-LES-BELLES 87380 Hte-Vienne **RN 20 Map 16-B1**
♀ ⊗ ⌂ **RELAIS BORNE 40** (N° RR JAN 26 139) (M. Jacques **Larue**) **Beausoleil-la-Porcherie** ☎ 55-71-87-12 ⊷.

SAINT-GERMAIN-DE-TALLEVENDE 14500 Calvados **RD 577 Map 8-A1**
♀ ⊗ **SARL LA MASURE** (N° RR OCT 24 718) (Mme Maria **Baclet**) La Lande Vaumont ☎ 31-68-24-02 Closed Sun. Spanish, English spoken.

SAINT-GERMAIN-SUR-MORIN 77740 S.-et-M. **RN 34 Map 9-A2**
♀ ⊗ **LE RELAIS DE LA MAIRIE** (N° RR AVR 5 988) (Maldin **de Letter**) 29, rue de Paris ☎ 60-04-00-63 Closed Sun. Coaches welcome (rest. seats 40). Evening meals.

SAINT-GERVAIS 85230 Vendée **Map 11-B2**
♀ ⊗ ⌂ **LE BOIRAT** (N° RR MARS 27 231) (M. Rémi **Verdeau**) 13, rue du Haras ☎ 51-49-23-40 or 51-49-23-93 ⊷ 4 English and Spanish spoken. Filling station near open 7.30am to 9.30pm.

SAINT-GERVAIS-DE-VIC 72120 Sarthe **RD 303 Map 12-A3**
♀ ⊗ **CHEZ ODETTE-LE SAINT ELOI** (N° RR AVR 26 872) (Mme Odette **Hervé**) ☎ 43-35-09-00 Closed Sun; public holidays. Italian spoken. Filling station 3km distant. Evening meals. Coaches welcome (rest. seats 120).

SAINT-GILDAS-DES-BOIS 44530 L. Atl. **RN 773 Map 11-A2**
♀ ⊗ ⌂ **LE RELAIS DES ROUTIERS** (N° RR NOV 19 193) (M. Michel **Gaidano**) 27, rue du Pont ☎ 40-01-42-15 and 01-44-70 ⊷ 10 Coaches welcome (rest. seats 430). Evening meals to 11pm. Parking 1500m^2. Menus 48 to 280F. Specialities *Seafood Platter. Grilled Lobsters.*

SAINT-GILLES 30800 Gard **RN 572 Map 24-A3**
♀ ⊗ **LE MIRADOR** (N° RR JUL 25 502) (M. Michel **Bosq**) Route de

Montpellier ☎ 66-87-31-20 Closed Mon low season. Coaches welcome (rest. seats 60). English, Spanish, Italian spoken.

SAINT-GILLES 35590 Ille-et-Vilaine **RN 12 Map 7-B3**
🍸 ⊗ **LES RELAIS** (N° RR MAI 26 895) (Mme Jeanine **Abiven**) 23, rue de Rennes ☎ 99-64-63-04 English, German spoken. Filling station near.

SAINT-GILLES 50180 Manche **RD 972 RD 77 Map 4-B1**
🍸 ⊗ **CARREFOUR SAINT-GILLES** (N° RR MAI 26 884) (M. Jean-Jacques **Billy**) Le Bourg-Agneaux ☎ 33-05-24-50. Closed Sun. English, German spoken. Filling station 3km. Coaches welcome (rest. seats 24). Evening meals.

SAINT-GRÉGORIE 35760 Ille-et-Vilaine **Map 7-B3**
🍸 ⊗ **RESTAURANT DE L'ÉTANG** (N° RR JUIN 27 303) (M. Michel **Hubert**) rue de l'Étang au Diable ☎ 99-38-49-43 Closed Sat and Sun. Evening meals served until 9pm. Filling station 100m.

SAINT-GYROMARD 56460 Morbihan
🍸 ⊗ ⌂ **1 star NN LES RELAIS DES DOLMENS DE LANVAUX** (N° RR DEC 27 469) (M. Pierre **Legrand**) Le Passoir ☎ 97-93-81-05 🛏 7 from 110–140F. Breakfast 20–30F. Closed Sunday. Evening meals until 10.30pm.

SAINT-HELEN 22100 Côte-du-Nord **Map 7-A3**
🍸 ⊗ **RELAIS DE LA CROIX DU FRESNE** (N° RR AVR 27 260) (M. Guy **Gabillard**) La Croix du Fresne ☎ 96-83-25-02 Evening meals. Filling station 3km.

SAINT-HILAIRE-DE-LA-CÔTE 38260 Isère **RD 73 Map 18-B3**
🍸 ⊗ **AUBERGE DE LA FONTAINE** (N° RR MARS 27 218) (Mme Raymonde **Glandut**) La Côte St-André ☎ 74-54-60-17 Closed Mon. English and Italian spoken. Filling station 3km, open 7am to 11pm.

SAINT-HILAIRE-DE-LOULAY 85600 Vendée **RN 137 Map 12-B1**
🍸 ⊗ ⌂ **LE RELAX** (N° RR JUL 23 361) (M. Luc **Van Wanghe**) **Les Landes de Roussais** ☎ 51-94-02-44 or 51-06-39-41 **Minitel** Closed Sat; 1 to 21 Aug; Christmas week. (rest. seats 138). Evening meals to 2am. Coaches welcome. German, some English spoken.

SAINT-HILAIRE-DU-HARCOUET 50600 Manche **RN 977 Map 8-A1**
🍸 ⊗ ⌂ **1 Star NN LES ROUTIERS Chez Jacques** Relais du Chemin de Fer (N° RR MAI 20 183) (M. Jacques **Guillochon**) Route de Caen-Rennes - La Gare ☎ 33-49-10-55 🛏 5 82–140F. Breakfast 18F. Closed Sun; 24 Dec to 1 Jan. Full-board 150F per night. Coaches welcome (rest. seats 90). Evening meals. Parking. Bar. Fishing. Places to visit: Mont Sant Michel, The 4 contons Lake. Old Trains Sat, Sun and Holiday, during season.

S

SAINT-HILAIRE-DU-ROSIER VILLAGE 38840 Isère **RN 92 Map 18-B3**
ⓨ ⊗ 🏠 **LE RELAIS DOMENECH** (N° RR OCT 17 652) (Mme Domenech **Lopez**) Route Nationale 92 ☎ 76-36-53-84 **Minitel** ━ 5 Closed Sat, Oct. Coaches welcome (rest. seats 65). Evening meals until 11pm. Spanish spoken.

SAINT-HILAIRE-LA-GRAVELLE 41160 Loir-et-Cher **RN 19 Map 12-A3 and 8-B3**
ⓨ ⊗ **AUBERGE DU LOIR** (N° RR OCT 22 066) (M. **Pierdos**) 10, rue Léon Cibié ☎ 54-82-65-00 ━ 2 Closed Wed evening. Aug. Evening meals. English spoken. Full board 145F. Coaches welcome (rest. seats 120).

SAINT-IGNEUC 22270 C.-du-N. **RN 176 Map 7-A3**
ⓨ ⊗ **LE RELAIS DES 4 ROUTES** (N° RR MARS 26 849) (Mme Annie **Bal**) Jugon-les-Lacq ☎ 96-31-61-77 Open 24 hrs. English spoken.

SAINT-INGLEVERT 62250 Pas-de-Calais **RN 1 Map 5-A2**
ⓨ ⊗ **LA MURAILLE** (N° RR JAN 26 422) (Mme Jocelyne **Salmon**) RN 1 ☎ 21-33-75-44 Closed Sat, Sun and 3 weeks in July. English spoken. Coaches welcome (rest. seats 44). Evening meals.

SAINT-JACQUES-DE-LA-LANDE 35136 Ille-et-Vilaine **Map 7-B3**
ⓨ ⊗ **LA GAITÉ** (N° RR OCT 27 396) (M. Yannide **Echelard**) 26, boulevard Roger Rodin, Route de Redon ☎ 99-31-27-56 Closed Sat, Sun, 15 days in Aug and one week between Christmas and New Year. English spoken. Evening meals to 9.45pm. Filling station nearby open 7am to 9.30pm.

SAINT JACQUES-SUR-DORNETAL 76160 Seine-Maritime **Map 3-A1**
ⓨ ⊗ **LE RELAIS DES ROUTIERS** (N° RR JUIL 27 329) (M. Gérard **Peudeiun**) Route de Gournay ☎ 35-02-10-76 Closed Sun. Filling station across road.

SAINT-JEAN-DE-BEUGNE 85210 Vendée **RN 137 Map 11-B2**
ⓨ ⊗ **L'OASIS** (N° RR JUN 25 953) (M. Guy **Teillet**) Ste-Hermine ☎ 51-30-62-80 Closed Sat pm, Sun; end of Dec. Evening meals.

SAINT-JEAN-DE-BOURNAY 38440 Isère **Map 2-B2**
ⓨ ⊗ 🏠 **RELAIS DE LA GARE** (N° RR AVR 26 496) (Mme Viviane **Laurent** and Josiane **Hingant**) 10 av. de la Libération ☎ 74-58-70-33 ━ 5.

SAINT-JEAN-DE-CHEVELU 73170 Savoie **RN 504 A Map 19-A2**
ⓨ ⊗ 🏠 **LE RELAIS DES QUATRE CHEMINS** (N° RR NOV 26 388) (M. Jean **Rubad**) ☎ 79-36-80-06 ━ 10 Closed Sat evening, Sun and end Dec to Jan. Full-board 270–350F. Coaches welcome (rest. seats 140). Evening meals to 12pm.

SAINT-JEAN-DE-LA-RUELLE 45140 Loiret **RN 155 Map 13-A1**
ⓨ ⊗ **LE RELAIS DE LA MAIRIE** (N° RR OCT 24 389) (M. André **Finet**) 142, rue Nationale ☎ 38-88-44-98 Closed Sat, Sun; 24 Dec 2.00pm to 3 Jan; 3 weeks in Jul or Sept.

S

SAINT-JEAN-DE-MAURIENNE 73300 Savoie **RN 6 Map 19-B3**
Y ⊗ **RESTAURANT RELAIS R** (N° RR JUN 21 971) (Mme Angèle **Dompnier**) Place du Champs du Foire, 66, rue Louis-Sibuè ☎ 79-64-12-03 Closed Sun. Italian spoken. Meals served to 11pm. Coaches welcome (rest. seats 80).

SAINT-JEAN-DE-MOIRANS 38430 Isère **RN 92 Map 19-A3**
Y ⊗ **LE RIO BRAVO** (N° RR JUIL 27 321) (M. M. **Speranza**) Rue Gaston-Bouardel ☎ 76-05-28-65; Evening meals to 10pm. English and Italian spoken. Filling station nearby open 7am to 8.30pm.

SAINT-JEAN-LA-POTERIE 56350 Morbihan **RD 775 Map 11-A2**
Y ⊗ **RESTAURANT DES CARRIÈRES** (N° RR MAR 26 830) (Mme Andrée **Delhaye**) 1, rue de la Butte, Aucfer ☎ 99-72-13-64 Closed Mon afternoon and from 24 Dec–1 Jan. Filling station near.

SAINT-JEAN-SUR-COUESNON 35140 Ille-et-Vilaine **RN 12 and D 23 Map 8-B1**
Y ⊗ **LA JUELLERIE** (N° RR NOV 27 449) (M. **Garel**) La juellerie ☎ 99-55-11-85 **Minitel** Closed Sat. Evening meals to 10pm. Filling station nearby.

SAINT-JEAN-SUR-VILAINE 35220 I.-et-V. **RN 157 Map 8-B1**
Y ⊗ ⌂ **RELAIS DU CHEVAL BLANC** (N° RR DEC 26 118) (M. Alain **Bellevin**) 4, rue de Rennes ☎ 99-00-32-67 ⊷ 10. **Minitel**

SAINT-JOSEPH-DE-RIVIÈRE 38134 Isère **CD 520 A Map 19-A2**
Y ⊗ ⌂ **LE RELAIS CHAMPÊTRE** (N° RR OCT 27 051) (Mme Adeline **Mandrillon**) **Le Pont Demay** ☎ 76-55-49-08 ⊷ 7 Closed Fri pm, Sat (low season) and 15/10 to 15/11. Italian spoken. Full-board 200F. Coaches welcome (rest. seats 60). Filling station 2km.

SAINT-JULIEN-EN-BEAUCHENE 05140 Hautes-Alpes **RN 75 Map 19-A3 and 24-B1**
Y ⊗ ⌂ **AU REFUGE DES AMIS** (N° RR JUN 23 839) (M. **Pizzichelli Certano**) ☎ 92-58-03-59 ⊷ 8 Closed Sat, Sun; (Low season) 15 days in Christmas/New Year. Coaches welcome (rest. seats 40). Evening meals to 9.30pm. Italian spoken. Full-board 220–240F.

SAINT-JULIEN-DE-CHAPTEUIL see **BOUSSOULET** 43260 Haute-Loire

SAINT-JULIEN-DE-CIVRY 71610 Saône-et-Loire **RD 985 Map 18-A1**
Y ⊗ **RESTAURANT DES VOYAGEURS** (N° RR MAR 26 855) (M. Hubert **Dumoulin**) The Station ☎ 85-70-62-10 Closed Tue afternoon, Aug. English, German spoken. Evening meals. Filling station 3km distant.

SAINT-JULIEN-DE-LA-NEF 30440 Gard **Map 23-B1**
Y ⊗ ⌂ **2 stars NN AUBERGE DE LA CASCADE D'AIGUES FOLLES** (N° RR JUN 26 915) (M. Alain **Danis**) Sarl 6 ☎ 67-82-42-78 ⊷ 17 from 180–200F, breakfast 15–25F. Closed Mon (off season).

S

Saint-Julien-De-La-Nef continued
Filling station 3km. Car park; bar; dogs allowed; recreation (bathing, walking, riding, canoeing). Places to visit. Grotte des Demoiselles, Tarn gorges, Bambouseraie d'Anduze.

SAINT-JULIEN-DE-PIGANIOL 12300 Aveyron **RD 963 Map 17-B2**
Ⓨ ⊗ **A L'AUBERGE DE ST.-JULIEN** (N° RR SEPT 26 657) (Mme Yvette **Carrière**) Rte Dle 963 ☎ 65-64-05-92 Closed Mon afternoon. Coaches welcome (rest. seats 190). Evening meals to 8pm.

SAINT-JULIEN-LE-FAUCON 14140 Calv. **RN 511 Map 4-B2**
Ⓨ ⊗ **LES ROUTIERS** (N° RR JUN 26 261) (Mme Gisèle **Goupil**) Livarot ☎ 31-63-80-96 Closed Sat pm, Sun. English spoken. Evening meals until 8pm.

SAINT-JULIEN-LA-VÊTRE 42440 Loire **RN 89 Map 18-A2 16-B3**
Ⓨ ⊗ **L'ESCALE 89** (N° RR OCT 27 065) (M. René **Pasinetti**) ☎ 77-97-85-30 German, Italian and English spoken. Evening meals until 11pm. Filling station nearby.

SAINT-JULIEN-LES-ROSIERS 30340 Gard **RD 904 Map 23-B1**
Ⓨ ⊗ 🏠 **LE MISTRAL** (N° RR OCT 27 424) (M. José **Garcia**) ☎ 66-86-15-29 ⊷ 15 Closed Wed (off season) Spanish spoken. Evening meals until 9pm. Filling station 500m.

SAINT-JUNIEN 87200 Haute-Vienne **RN 141 Map 16-B1**
Ⓨ ⊗ 🏠 **L'ETOILE** (N° RR AVR 25 872) (M. Alain **Noble**) 8, av. Barbusse ☎ 55-02-15-19 ⊷ 7 Closed Fri evening in winter, summer open every day. 20 Dec to 6 Jan. Full-board 130F per night. Coaches welcome (rest. seats 120). Evening meals. English spoken.
Ⓨ ⊗ **L'ESCALE** (N° RR JUN 26 565) (M. Jean-Louis **Gaudioz**) 5, Ave Henri-Barbusse ☎ 55-02-03-11.

SAINT-JUST-LE-MARTEL 87590 Haute-Vienne **RN 141 Map 16-B1**
Ⓨ ⊗ **LE PETIT SALÉ** (N° RR FEV 25 310) (M. Jean-Pierre **Teyti**) Les Chabanes ☎ 55-09-21-14 Coaches welcome (rest. seats 80). Evening meals until 12pm.

SAINT-LANGIS-LES-MORTAGNES 61400 Orne **RD 938 after 138 bis, 1km from Nle Map 8-A2**
Ⓨ ⊗ 🏠 **HÔTEL DE LA GARE** (N° RR JUL 24 278) (M. Jean **Lonak**) Rue de la Gare ☎ 33-25-16-10 ⊷ 7 Closed Sun. Evening meals to 11pm. Filling station 200m.

SAINT-LAURENT-DU-VAR 06700 Alpes-Mmes **Map 25-B2**
⊗ **LE RELAIS** (N° RR JAN 26 730) (Mme Odette **Touert**) allée des Cableurs Secteur BZ1 ☎ 93-31-26-47 Closed Sun. English, Spanish spoken.
Ⓨ ⊗ **AU COUP DE FUSIL** SARL Floreje (N° RR JANV 27 159) (M. Eugène **Bagi**) bd Pierre-Marie Curie ZI Secteur B ☎ 93-31-60-55 Closed Sun. Italian spoken. Filling station 150m. Open 7am to 8pm.

SAINT LÉGER 17800 Chte Mme **RN 137 Map 15-A2**
♀ ⊗ **LES TROIS MOULINS** (N° RR FEV 27 188) (M. Robert **Decker**)
RN 137 Pons ☎ 46-96-91-38 ➡ 6 Closed Sun. German spoken.
Filling station 3km open 7am – 10pm.

SAINT-LÉGER-CARCAGNY 14740 Calvados **RN 13 Map 4-B2**
♀ ⊗ **AUX JOYEUX ROUTIERS** (N° RR SEP 24 683) (M. Charles
Candavoine) **Hameau de St-Léger** ☎ 31-80-22-01 Closed Sun in
winter.

SAINT-LÉGER-SUR-DHEUNE 71510 S.-et-L. **RD 978 Map 18-A1 13-
B3**
♀ ⊗ 🏠 **AU BON ACCUEIL** PMU (N° RR JAN 22 147) (Mme Nelly
Roland) ☎ 85-45-30-65 ➡ 5 Evening meals.

SAINT-LON-LES-MINES 40300 Landes **CD6 Map 20-A2**
♀ ⊗ 🏠 **1 star NN HOTEL DU FRONTON** (N° RR MAI 26 880) (M.
Daniel **Laffitte**) Au Bourg ☎ 58-57-80-45 ➡ 10 (8 with priv. lav. 2
with shower) 130–160F. Closed Feb. Spanish spoken. Filling
station 2km distant. Telephone. Bar. Dogs admt. Games (baby
foot). Places to visit: Château de Peyrehorade (7km). Bayonne
(35km). Coaches welcome (rest. seats 80) Evening meals to 1am.
Parking 1500mk^2.

SAINT-LOUIS 68300 Ht-Rhin
♀ ⊗ **LE PARADIS** (N° RR JAN 26 146) (M. Robert **Metzger**) 57, rue
Gl-de-Gaulle ☎ 89-67-73-59 Closed Tue; Aug. Evening meals.

SAINT-LOUP-DE-VARENNES 71240 S.-et-L. **RN 6 Map 18-B1**
♀ ⊗ **LA PETITE AUBERGE** (N° RR AOU 26 980) (M. Jacques
Demeuzoy) ☎ 85-44-21-87 Closed Sun. Filling station near.

SAINT-LOUP-SUR-SEMOUSE 70800 Haute-Saône **RN 64 Map 10-A3
and 14-B2**
♀ ⊗ **LE RELAIS DE LA TERRASSE** (N° RR MAI 6 059) (Mme Jean
Ballot) Rue de la Gare ☎ 84-49-02-20 **Minitel** ➡ 4 Closed Sun; 1
to 15 Aug.

SAINT-MALO 35400 I.-et-V. **RN 157 Map 7-A3**
♀ ⊗ 🏠 **HOTEL DE L'ARRIVÉE** (N° RR FEV 27 191) (Mme Edith
Eveillard) 83, rue Ville-Pépin, Saint-Servan-sur-Mer ☎ 99-81-99-
57 ➡ 16 Closed Sun in low season; Oct. English spoken. Filling
station nearby.

SAINT-MARC-SUR-SEINE 21450 Côte-d'Or **RN 71 Map 13-A3**
♀ ⊗ 🏠 **LE SOLEIL D'OR** (N° RR DEC 22 133) (Mme Geneviève
Girard) ☎ 80-93-21-42 ➡ 7 Closed Sat. Christmas. English
spoken. Full-board 130–140F. Coaches welcome (rest. seats 50).
Evening meals.

SAINT-MARCEL 27950 Eure **Map 3-B1**
♀ ⊗ 🏠 **LE TERMINUS** (N° RR DEC 26 123) (Mme Louise **Ragazzini**)
3N RN 15 **Le Goulet** ☎ 32-52-50-07 ➡ 18 Closed Sat afternoon,
Sun. Aug. Evening meals.

S

Saint-Marcel continued

♀ ⊗ ⌂ **LE TERMINUS** (N° RR JAN 27 506) (M. Claude **Hard**) 30, Route Nationale ☎ 32-52-50-07 ⊷ 16 Closed August. Evening meals.

SAINT-MARCEL see ARGENTON 36200 Indre **RN 20 Map 16-A1**

SAINT-MARCEL-LÈS-VALENCE 26320 Drôme **RN 532 à 100m Map 21-A2**

♀ ⊗ **LA PRAIRIE** (N° RR SEPT 27 021) (M. Michel **Montusciat**) 8, rue de la Liberté ☎ 75-88-70-38 Closed Mon pm. August. Italian and English spoken. Coaches welcome (rest. seats 100). Evening meals to 10pm. Filling station nearby. Open 7am – 9pm and in 4km open 24 hrs.

SAINT-MARCELLIN 38160 Isère **RN 92 Map 24-B1**

♀ ⊗ **LE RELAIS LE SIROCCO** (N° RR OCT 24 394) (Mme Martine **Glé**) Gare de la Sône, Chatte ☎ 76-38-03-73 Closed Sat 3.00pm, Sun.

SAINT-MARD 17700 Chte-Mme **RN 139 Map 11-B1**

♀ ⊗ **AUBERGE DE SAINT MARD** (N° RR OCT 26 694) (M. J. **Madeux**) Surgères ☎ 46-07-04-26 Closed Mon. English, some Spanish spoken.

SAINT-MARS-LA-BRIÈRE 72680 Sarthe **RN 157 Map 8-B2**

♀ ⊗ **AUBERGE DU NARAIS** (N° RR OCT 27 067) (M. Rémy **Tressy**) ☎ 43-89-87-30 Closed Sun. Aug. Evening meals to 11pm.

SAINT-MARTIAL-D'ARTENSET 24700 Dordogne **RN 89 Map 15-B3**

♀ ⊗ **AUBERGE DE SAINT-MARTIAL** (N° RR OCT 20 840) (Mme **Rolland**) ☎ 53-80-35-74 ⊷ 4 Closed Sat; Sept. English, German spoken.

SAINT-MARTIN-D'AUBIGNY 50190 Manche **RD 900 Map 4-B1**

♀ ⊗ **LES RUETTES** (N° RR JANV 27 166) (Mme Mireille **Burnel**) Periers ☎ 33-46-71-45. Closed Sun am. English spoken. Filling station 3km.

SAINT-MARTIN-DES-BESACES 14350 Calvados **RN 175 Map 4-B2 and 8-A1 see CAEN**

SAINT-MARTIN-DE-CRAU 13310 B.-du-R. **RN 113 Map 24-B3**

♀ ⊗ ⌂ **LA CABANE BAMBOU** (N° RR AVR 13 594) (M. Jacques and Georgette **Giraud**) Route Nationale 113 between Salon and Aries ☎ 90-58-17-25 and 90-58-02-52 **Minitel** ⊷ 10 Closed Sun (except summer time). Open 24 hrs. Coaches welcome (rest. seats 100). Evening meals all night. English, Italian, Spanish spoken.

♀ ⊗ ⌂ **HÔTEL DE LA GARE** (N° RR AVR 26 511) (Mme Andrée **Sicard**) rte de la Dynamite ☎ 90-47-05-18 ⊷ 8 Closed Sat. Full-board 150F per night. Coaches welcome (rest. seats 60). Evening meals.

S

SAINT-MARTIN OSMONVILLE 76680 S.-Mme **RN 28 Map 4-A3**
🍷 ⊗ **LA GRANGE** (N° RR JAN 25 784) (Mme Denise **De La Bois-sière**) ☎ 35-34-14-34.

SAINT-MAUR 36250 Indre **RN 20 Map 12-B3**
🍷 ⊗ **LES TERRES NOIRES** (N° RR NOV 26 096) (Mme Nathalie **Bourdin-Favereau**) Les Terres Noires ☎ 54-92-03-29 Closed Sun. English spoken.

SAINT-MAUR-DES-FOSSÉS 94100 Val de Marne **Map 1-B3**
🍷 ⊗ **LA PASSERELLE** (N° RR OCT 26 699) (M. Jean **Dias**) 45, Bld Gl Ferrier ☎ 42-83-21-71 Portuguese, Spanish spoken. Closed Christmas and New Year. Evening meals served to 10pm.

SAINT-MAURICE-SUR-ADOUR 40270 Landes **Map 20-B2**
🍷 ⊗ **RELAIS DE LA MARIANNE** (N° RR AVR 26 876) (Mme Maria **Toribio**) ☎ 58-45-97-36. Closed Sat. Spanish spoken. Filling station 2km.

SAINT-MAURICE-LA-SOUTERRAINE 23300 Creuse **RN 142 RN 20 Map 16-B1 SEE LA CROISIÈRE**

SAINT-MAURICE-SUR-DARGOIRE 69440 Rhône **RD42 Map 2-B1**
🍷 ⊗ **CHEZ ROSE** (N° RR JUL 26 604) (Mme Rosiane **Blé**) Le Grand Buisson ☎ 78-81-20-10 Coaches welcome (rest. seats 40). Evening meals.

SAINT-MAURICE-SUR-FESSARD 45700 Loiret **Map 9-B1**
🍷 ⊗ **RESTAURANT DE LA GARE** (N° RR JANV 26 800) (Mme Colette **Jehl**) Villemandeur ☎ 38-97-81-00 Closed Sat pm and Sun pm. Evening meals. English, Spanish spoken.
🍷 ⊗ **LE RELAIS DE SAINT-MAURICE** (N° RR MARS 26 840) (M. Pascal **Crouvisier**) Villemandeur ☎ 38-97-80-59 Closed Wed. Coaches welcome (rest. seats 50). 'Total' filling station near.

SAINT-MAXIMIN-LA-SAINTE-BAUME 83470 Var **Maps 24-B3 and 25-A2**
🍷 ⊗ 🏠 **LE RELAIS DU CARILLON** (N° RR OCT 23 989) (M. Robert **Berton**) 5, rue de la République ☎ 94-78-00-38 ⊷ 9 Closed Thur. Coaches welcome (rest. seats 115). Evening meals.

SAINT-MEEN-LE-GRAND 35290 I.-et-V. **RN 164 Bis and 166 Map 7-B3**
🍷 ⊗ **LE RELAIS DU MIDI** (N° RR OCT 26 732) (M. Christian **Posnic**) SARL 25, place Patton ☎ 99-09-60-02 ⊷ 3 Closed Sat after lunch; 15–31 Aug. Coaches welcome (rest. seats 30). Evening meals.

SAINT-MIHIEL 55300 Meuse **RD 964 Map 14-A1**
🍷 ⊗ 🏠 **LES ROUTIERS** (N° RR AOU 22 460) (M. Claude **Rousselot**) 19, rue de Verdun ☎ 29-89-00-44 ⊷ 8 Closed Sat, Sun. Aug. Evening meals served until 9pm. English spoken.

S

SAINT-NAUPHARY 82370 T.-et-G. **RD 999 Map 22-A1**
Y ⊗ 🏠 **LES AYÈRES** (N° RR FEV 22 645) (M. **Monruffet**) ☎ 63-67-85-09 ◄ 6 Closed Sat; 8–31 Aug; 1 week Christmas/New Year. Full-board 115–145F per night. Coaches welcome (rest. seats 150). Evening meals.

SAINT-NAZAIRE 30970 Gard **RN 86 Map 24-A2**
Y ⊗ 🏠 **1 star NN LES TE RAILLES** (N° RR NOV 19 219) (Mme **Menu**) RN 86 ☎ 66-89-66-14 ◄ 12 Closed Sat pm. Sept.

SAINT-NAZAIRE 44600 Loire-Atl. **RN 771 Map 11-A2**
Y   **LE LAFAYETTE** (N° RR SEP 24 671) (M. Gilbert **Renou**) avenue de Penhoët ☎ 40-22-53-82 **Minitel** Closed Sat afternoon, Sun; Jul. Coaches welcome (terrace of 40 seats).
Y ⊗ 🏠 **LA MARINE** (N° RR AVR 26 866) (M. Patrick **Feildel**) 15, avenue de Penhoët. ☎ 40-66-42-40 ◄ 8 Closed Sun. Filling station near.

SAINT-NICOLAS-DE-BOURGUEIL 37140 Indre-et-Loire **CD 035 Map 12-B2**
Y ⊗ **LE RELAIS** (N° RR OCT 25 717) (M. Joël **Joulin**) Le Bourg - Place de Église ☎ 47-97-75-39 ◄ 3 Closed Sun; 15 to 31 Aug. Evening meals to 9pm – *Routiers only*.

SAINT-NICOLAS-DE-LA-GRAVE 82210 T.-et-G. **Aut. A 61 Map 22-A1**
⚙ **Service Station ELF GARONNE** (N° RR JAN 24 812) (M. Christian **Roux**) Le Montet ☎ 63-94-80-30 Open 24 hours. Spanish, French, English spoken.

SAINT-NICOLAS-DE-REDON 44460 Loire-Atl. **Map 11-A2**
Y ⊗ **LE RELAIS DES ROUTIERS** (N° RR JAN 23 081) (Mme Marie-Annick **Hemery**) 84, avenue Jean-Burel ☎ 99-71-01-96 **Minitel** Closed Sun; Aug. Coaches welcome (rest. seats 72). Evening meals until 11pm.

SAINT-NIZIER-SUR-ARROUX 71190 Saône-et-Loire **Map 18-A1**
Y ⊗ 🏠 **L'AUBERGE FLEURIE** (N° RR AOÛT 27 360) (M. Jean-Claude **Biot**) Le Bourg ☎ 85-54-29-33 **Minitel** ◄ 7 Closed Wed pm. from Jan to April. Parking 2000m^2.

SAINT-NOLF 56250 Morbihan **RN 166 Map 11-A2**
Y ⊗ **LE RELAIS BELLEVUE** (N° RR JUN 22 374) (M. Joël **Guegan**) Bellevue ☎ 97-45-44-04 Closed 1 to 30 Aug. Evening meals.

SAINT-OMER 62500 P.-de-C. **RN 43 Map 5-A2**
Y ⊗ 🏠 **LE RELAIS DE LA RENAISSANCE** (N° RR AVR 10 573) (SARL **Vanyper Fils**) 10, place du 11-Novembre ☎ 21-38-26-55 ◄ 18 Closed Sun. Coaches welcome (rest. seats 120). Evening meals until 9.15pm. English spoken.

SAINT-OUEN 93400 Seine-St-Denis **Pont de St-Ouen Map 1-A2**
Y ⊗ 🏠 **AU ROUTIER SYMPA** (N° RR SEP 22 466) (M. Bernard **Delouvrier**) 93, boulevard Victor-Hugo and 1, place du Capi-

taine Glaner ☎ 40-11-00-31 ⊷ 10 Closed Sun; Aug. Evening
meals to 8.30pm. Coaches welcome (rest. seats 70).

♀ ⊗ **LE RELAIS DU PAVILLON BLEU** (N° RR JUN 23 830) (M.
Ramdane **Kerdous**) 7, quai de Seine ☎ 40-11-03-67 Closed Sat
pm, Sun; half-July. Coaches welcome (rest. seats 60). Evening
meals.

SAINT-PANDELON 40180 Landes **Map 20-A2**
♀ ⊗ **HÔSTELLERIE DU PONT** (N° RR MAI 27 286) (M. Jean-Yves
Lasserre) ☎ 58-98-71-17 Closed Mon and Tues pm. Spanish and
English spoken. Filling stations 4km.

SAINT-PAUL 60650 Oise **RN 31 Map 3-A2**
♀ ⊗ **AU RELAIS SAINT-PAUL** (N° RR SEPT 27 035) (Mme Marie-
France **Mouligneaux**) ☎ 44-82-20-19 Closed Sun and Dec.
English spoken. Coaches welcome (rest. seats 42). Evening
meals to 10pm. Filling station nearby – open 7am to 9pm.

SAINT-PAUL-DU-BOIS LA REVEILLERE 49310 M.-et-L. **RN 748
Map 12-B1**
♀ ⊗ **CHEZ MAÏTÉ** (N° RR FEV 20 394) (Mme **Bonnin**) ☎ 41-75-81-44
Closed Sun. Evening meals. Coaches welcome (rest. seats 90).
Parking 1500m².

SAINT-PAUL-CAP-DE-JOUX 81220 Tarn **RD 112 Map 22-B2**
♀ ⊗ **LES GLYCINES** (N° RR SEPT 23 452) (M. Claude **Peyrard**) rue
Philippe Pinel ☎ 63-70-61-37. Closed Mon (midday meal assur-
ed). Coaches welcome (rest. seats 180). Evening meals to 8pm.

SAINT-PAUL-LES-DAX 40990 Landes **RN 124 Map 20-A/B2**
♀ ⊗ **RELAIS PLAISANCE** (N° RR MAI 23 784) (M. Alain **Escos**) route
de Bayonne ☎ 58-74-04-70 English, Spanish spoken.

SAINT-PAUL-DE-LOUBRESSAC 46170 Lot **RN 20 Map 22-A1**
♀ ⊗ 🏠 **1 Star NN LE RELAIS DE LA MADELEINE** SARL (N° RR
JUL 9 786) (M. Bernard **Devianne**) 100 m from Route National, 20
km from Cahors, 35 km from Mautauban ☎ 65-21-98-08 ⊷ 16 from
95–170F, breakfast 18.50F, access for disabled. Closed Sat; 1 Nov
for 8 days; 1 Dec to 10 Jan. Full-board 160–180F per night.
Coaches welcome (rest. seats 85 plus terrace). Evening meals.
English spoken (Spanish in Summer). Car park; bar; dogs
allowed; recreations (*pétanque*, childrens games). Menus 55–
98F. Specialities: *Médaillon de ris de veau maison, foie gras,
cèpes. Confit Magret.*

SAINT-PAUL-LE-JEUNE 07460 Ardèche **RD 104 Map 23-B1**
♀ ⊗ **LE RELAIS ROUTIERS DE CHEYRÈS** (N° RR JUN 23 309) (Mme
Marie-Thérèse **Vernède**) Cheyres-Banne ☎ 75-39-30-09 **Minitel**
Closed Sun. Coaches welcome (rest. seats 70). Evening meals.
Car park 5,000m².

SAINT-PAUL-TROIS CHATEAUX 26130 Drôme **RN 59 near Autoroute A7 Map 24-A2**
♀ ⊗ 🏠 **LE RELAIS DE PROVENCE** (N° RR MAI 21 109) (Mme

S

Saint-Paul-Trois Chateaux continued
Hélène **Entringer**) 11, avenue du Général-de-Gaulle ☎ 75-04-72-48 ⚊ 7 Closed Feb. Evening meals to 9pm.

SAINT-PELLERIN 50500 Manche **RN 13 Map 4-B1**
Ⓨ ⊗ **AUBERGE DE LA FOURCHETTE** (N° RR DEC 25 752) (Mme Henriette **Letourneur**) Carantan ☎ 33-42-16-56 English spoken. Closed Sun, Feb. Filling station 2km distant.

SAINT-PHAL 10130 Aube **Map 9-B3**
Ⓨ ⊗ **RESTAURANT DU COMMERCE** (N° RR FEV 26 821) (M. Daniel **Godefroy**) Evry-le-Châtel ☎ 25-42-16-39 Closed Mon; Aug. Coaches welcome (rest. seats 100).

SAINT-PHILBERT-DE-GRAND'LIEU 44310 Loire-Atl. **RD 18 Bis Map 11-B2**
Ⓨ ⊗ 🏠 **LA BOULOGNE** (N° RR MAR 24 162) (M. Bernard **André**) 11, place de l'Abbatiale ☎ 40-78-70-55 ⚊ 6 Closed Sat, Sun. Full-board 125F per night. Coaches welcome (rest. seats 80). Evening meals.

SAINT-PIERRE DE CHANDIEU 69780 Rhône **RD 149 Map 2-B2**
Ⓨ ⊗ **LE BLE D'OR** (N° RR NOV 27 451) (Mme Marthe **Jacquenool**) avenue Amédée-Ronin ☎ 78-40-32-41 Closed Sun pm. English spoken. Evening meals to 11pm. Filling station 600m open 7am – 8pm. Parking 300m^2.

SAINT-PIERRE-DU-CHEMIN 85120 Vendée **Map 11-B3**
Ⓨ ⊗ 🏠 **LE SAINT-PIERRE** (N° RR FEV 25 307) (M. Patrick **Lamarre**) ☎ 51-69-60-35 – 51-51-71-35 ⚊ 10 English spoken.

SAINT-PIERRE-DES-CORPS 37700 I.-et-L. **RN 751 Map 12-A3**
Ⓨ ⊗ **LE GRILLON** (N° RR DEC 21 721) (Mme and M. **Latour**) 9, quai de la Loire ☎ 47-44-74-90 Closed Sat, Sun; Jul or Aug. Evening meals served to midnight (weekends only). Coaches welcome (rest. seats 60).

SAINTE-PIERRE-DU-FRESNE 14260 Calv **RN 175 Map 4-B1/2**
Ⓨ ⊗ **AU VERT BOCAGE** (N° RR NOV 27 442) (Mme Marie-José **Margueritte**) SARL Les Haïes Tigards ☎ 31-77-80-89 Closed Sat pm and Sun from 11am. Evening meals. Parking 3000m^2.

SAINT-PIERRE-LANGERS 50530 Manche **RN 173 Map 8-A1**
Ⓨ ⊗ 🏠 **A LA GRILLADE** (N° RR AVR 24 197) (M. Philippe **Ledoux**) La Havaudière (5 km from Sartilly) ☎ 33-48-83-71 ⚊ 8 Closed Sat, Sun. Full-board 145–155F per night.

SAINT-PIERRE-LE-MOUTIER 58240 Nièvre **RN 7 Map 16-A3**
Ⓨ ⊗ 🏠 **HÔTEL DU CHEVAL BLANC** (N° RR JAN 6 961) (M. Jacques **Beaudoin**) 1, rue du Commandant-Leiffeit ☎ 86-37-42-45 ⚊ 5 Closed Tues. Full board 180F. Coaches welcome (rest. seats 60). Menus from 50 to 110F. Specialities: Coq au Vin, Picardie Tripe and Escalope. Saint-Pierre.

S

SAINT-PIERRE-LES-ELBEUF 76320 S.-Mme **Map 3-B1**
♈ ⊗ **LA SAUVAGINE** (N° RR OCT 27 418) (M. Patrick **Clivaz**) 611, chemin du Halage ☎ 35-78-37-70 Closed Sun, 15 days in Jan or Feb. 3 weeks in Aug. English spoken. Evening meals to 11pm. Filling station 500m.

SAINT-PIERRE-DE-QUIBERON 56510 Morbihan **RD 768 Map 11-A1**
♈ ⊗ **LA CHALOUPE DE KERHOSTIN** (N° RR MAI 21 916) (Mme **Le Bellour**) place du Marché **Kerhostin** ☎ 97-30-91-54 Closed Sun in winter; 15 Oct–15 Nov. Coaches welcome (rest. seats 80).

SAINT-PIERREMONT 88700 Vosges **RD 414 Map 14-B1**
♈ ⊗ ⌂ **2 Stars LE RELAIS VOSGIEN** (N° RR NOV 14 581) (Mme **Prevost**) Rambervilliers ☎ 29-65-02-46 **Minitel** ⊶ 9 Closed Mon afternoon. Full-board 180–230F per night. Coaches welcome (rest. seats 100). Evening meals to 9pm. Car park; bar; dogs allowed; amusement park. Places to visit: Petit Versailles, Luneville.

SAINT-PIERRE-SUR-DIVES 14170 Calvados **D 511 Map 8-A2**
♈ ⊗ **AU RENDEZ-VOUS DES NORMANDS Chez Liliane** (N° RR DEC 26 764) (Mme Liliane **Desoleau**) 134, rue Falaise ☎ 21-20-53-66 Closed Tue afternoon.
♈ ⊗ **LE PRESSOIR** (N° RR OCT 27 416) (Mme Florence **Villain**) 17, route de Caen ☎ 31-20-56-03 Closed Sun. Evening meals to 11pm. Filling station 300m.

SAINT-POL-DE-LÉON 29250 Finistère
♈ ⊗ **LES ROUTIERS** (N° RR JUN 26 267) (M. Jean-Louis and Marie-Pierre **Floc'h**) 28, rue Pen Ar Pont ☎ 98-69-00-52 Closed Sun; Aug. Coaches welcome (rest. seats 120). English, German spoken. Evening meals. Full-board 100–130F.

SAINT-PONS 34220 Hérault **RN 112 Map 23-A2**
♈ ⊗ ⌂ **1 Star NN LE SOMAIL** (N° RR FEV 22 681) (M. André **Cros**) 2, avenue de Castres ☎ 67-97-00-12 ⊶ 18 Restaurant closed in Feb. Full-board 165–230F per night. Coaches welcome (rest. seats 80). Evening meals.

SAINT-PRIEST-DE-GIMEL 19800 Corrèze **RN 89 Map 17-A1**
♈ ⊗ **LE RELAIS CHEZ MOUSTACHE** (N° RR JUL 20 791 bis) (M. Jean-Claude **Laval**) Gare de Corrèze ☎ 55-27-32-58 ⊶ 3 Closed Sun; Aug.

SAINT-PRIVAT-DES-VIEUX 30340 Gard **RD 216 Map 23-B1**
♈ ⊗ ⌂ **Tobacconist L'ESCALE** (N° RR JAN 18 303) (Mme Ginette **Calcat**) 59, rte de Bagnois ☎ 66-30-09-40 **Minitel** ⊶ 8 English spoken. Evening meals. Full-board 155–185F. Coaches welcome (160 rest. seats). Parking 6000m^2.

SAINT-PROUANT 85110 Vendée **RD 760 Map 11-B3**
♈ ⊗ ⌂ **LE ZODIAC** (N° RR MAR 24 159) (M. Daniel **Arru**) 2, rue G. Clemenceau Le Bourg ☎ 51-66-40-55 ⊶ 5 Closed Mon; 23 Jul to 7

S

Saint-Prouant continued
Aug. Full-board 110–130F per night. Coaches welcome (rest. seats 80). Evening meals. English, Spanish spoken.

SAINT-QUAY-PORTRIEUX 22410 C.-du-N. **RN 786 Map 7-A2**
♀ ⊗ ⌂ **LE RELAIS DU MOULIN** (N° RR DEC 23 049) (M. **Guitton**) 42, rue des 3 Frères Salün ☎ 96-70-40-19 ⚊ 13 Closed Sun in winter. Full-board 165F.

SAINT-QUENTIN 02100 Aisne **RN 44 Maps 5-B3 and 6-A1**
♀ ⊗ **LES ROUTIERS** (N° RR SEPT 26 322) (M. **Balique**) 134, route de la Fère, Pont de Guise ☎ 23-68-26-79 ⚊ 13 Closed Sat afternoon, Sun afternoon; Aug. Evening meals to 9pm.
♀ ⊗ **BRASSERIE DE LA VALLÉE** (N° RR MAI 27 291) (M. Jean **Boyard**) 28 bis, Chaussée Romaine ☎ 23-62-43-67 Closed Sun and August. German, English and a little Dutch spoken. Filling station nearby open 24 hours.

SAINT-QUENTIN-LES-ANGES 53400 Mayenne **RD 26 Map 12-A1**
♀ ⊗ **LE RELAIS** (N° RR NOV 24 419) (Mme Marie-Annick **Trottier**) Craon ☎ 43-06-10-62 ⚊ 9 Closed Aug. Full-board 135–140F per person. Coaches welcome (145 res. seats). Evening meals to 11pm.

SAINT-QUENTIN-SUR-ISÈRE 38210 Isère **RN 532 Map 19-A3**
♀ ⊗ **LA CABANE BAMBOU** (N° RR JUL 24 631) (M. **Ruggiero**) **Le Replat** ☎ 76-93-80-05.
♀ ⊗ **LE GIBRALTAR** (N° RR JUN 26 907) (Mme Isabelle **Brisquet)** ☎ 76-93-65-28 Closed Sun; 15 days in Aug. Filling station nearby. Evening meals to 11pm.

SAINT-RAPHAEL 83700 Var **RN 98 Map 25-B2**
♀ ⊗ ⌂ **1 Star NN LE RELAIS BEL AZUR** (N° RR FEV 19 663) (Mme Marguerite **Magnani**) 247, boulevard de Provence ☎ 94-95-14-08 ⚊ 20 Closed Sat, Sun pm; Breakfast: Restaurant closed 15 Sept. 1st June. Coaches welcome (rest. seats 115). Evening meals until 9.00pm. Italian spoken. Coaches welcome (100 rest. seats). Parking, bar. Dogs allowed. Places to visit: Gorges du Verdun et du Lup. Roman Ruins. Menus 49,50–110F. Specialities: BoualebaisseAli-Oli, Paëlla.
♀ ⊗ ⌂ **2 stars NN HÔTEL MODERNE** (N° RR JUIN 26 568) (M. Michel **Hortal**) 329, avenue de Général-Leclerc ☎ 94-51-22-16 ⚊ 25 Closed Sun evening in winter; 24–27 Dec. Full-board 160–220F per night. Coaches welcome (2 dining rooms: 25/130 seats). Evening meals. Parking. Bar.

SAINT-REMY-SUR-AVRE 28380 E-et-L. **RN 12 Map 8-A3**
♀ ⊗ **LE RELAIS DU PLESSIS – Chez Liliane et Pierrot** (N° RR MAI 24 962) (M. Pierre **Cottereau**) 71 RN 12 ☎ 37-48-92-16 Closed Sun; Feb. English spoken.

SAINT-RIQUIER 80135 Somme **Map 5-A3**
♀ ⊗ **LE CENTULOIS** (N° RR JUIL 26 970) (Mme Lili **Colinet**) 70, rue

du Général de Gaulle ☎ 22-28-88-15 Closed Wed afternoon. Filling station near.

SAINT-ROMAIN-DE-COLBOSC 76430 Seine-Mme **Map 4-A3**
Y ⊗ **LE RELAIS DU FRESCOT** (N° RR JAN 25 257) (M. Jacques **Chapelet**) 18, Nationale ☎ 35-20-15-09 ◄ 6 Closed Sun; Aug. Coaches welcome (high-speed breakfast only, for 40–60). Evening meals.

SAINT-ROMAIN-LA-MOTTE near ROANNE 42640 Loire **RN 7 Map 16-B3**
Y ⊗ **AU BON ACCUEIL** (N° RR JUN 25 463) (Mme Lucienne **Galichon**) Les Baraques ☎ 77-72-00-07 ◄ 3 Coaches welcome (rest. seats 50). Evening meals.

SAINT-ROMAIN-LE-PUY 42610 Loire **Map 18-A2**
Y ⊗ **LE PETIT VINCENNES** (N° RR JANV 26 774) (M. Alain **Bouchet**), 16, rue Léon Portier ☎ 77-76-63-54 English spoken.

SAINT-ROME-DE-CERNON 12490 Aveyron **Map 23-A1**
Y ⊗ ⌂ **RELAIS CHEZ JEANNOT** (N° RR FEV 18 334) (M. Jean **Fabry**) avenue de Millau ☎ 65-62-33-56 ◄ 7 Closed Sat, 15 Sept to 15 Oct. Coaches welcome (rest. seats 70). Evening meals.

SAINT-SAMSON-DE-BONFOSSE 50750 Manche **RD 999 Map 4-B1**
Y ⊗ **CHEZ PIERRE ET MICHELE** (N° RR AVR 25 379) (M. Pierre **Petit**) Canisy ☎ 33-55-73-71 Closed Wed.

SAINT-SAMSON-DE-LA-ROQUE 27680 Eure **RN 815 A Map 4-B3**
Y ⊗ **LE RELAIS NORD BRETAGNE** (N° RR OCT 27 417) (M. Marcel **Poiraud**) route du Pont-de-Tancarville ☎ 32-57-67-30 Closed Sat, Sun. Evening meals until 11.00pm.

SAINT-SAUVEUR 70370 Haute-Saône **RN 57 Map 10-A3 and 14-B2**
Y ⊗ ⌂ **LE RELAIS CHEZ MAXIM** (N° RR AVR 21 055) (Mme Colette **Lack**) 10, avenue Georges-Clémenceau ☎ 84-40-02-91 ◄ 8 Closed Sun evening; Feb. Full-board 125–175F per night. Coaches welcome (rest. seats 150). Evening meals. German, English spoken.

SAINT-SAUVEUR-D'AUNIS 17540 Chte-Mme **Map 11-B1**
Y ⊗ ⌂ **HÔTEL DU CENTRE** (N° RR JUIL 26 972) (M. Alain **Quellard**) rue de Ligoure ☎ 46-01-80-31 ◄ 6 English spoken. Garage, filling station nearby.

SAINT-SAUVIER D'EMALLEVILLE 76110 Seine-Maritime **CD 925 Map 4-A2/3**
Y ⊗ **RELAIS DE SAINT SAUVEUR** (N° RR SEPT 27 017) (M. Phillippe **Guèrin**) Route Nationale ☎ 35-27-21-56. Closed Wed. pm. Evening meals to 10.30pm. Filling station 5km.

SAINT-SÉBASTIEN-DE-MORSENT 27180 Eure **RN 830 Map 8-A3**
Y ⊗ **LE C'Y DOUBLE** (N° RR JUL 26 615) (M. Jacques **Sivroy**) 15, rte de Conches ☎ 32-33-11-52. Closed Wed.

S

SAINT-SORNIN 16220 Charente TD 6 Map 15-B2
♀ ⊗ **LES ROUTIERS Tobacconist** (N° RR AVR 25 914) (M. Jean-Michel **Dubois**) Le Bourg Montbron ☎ 45-23-12-83 Closed Mon 2pm. Evening meals served.

SAINT-SULPICE-DE-GRAINBOUVILLE 27210 Eure **RD 312 Map 4-B3**
♀ ⊗ **LE RELAIS DE ST. SULPICE** (N° RR MAI 27 277) (M. Pierre **Dulong**) **La Place** ☎ 32-41-50-99 Closed Sun. English spoken. Evening meals.

SAINT-SULPICE-LES-FEUILLES 87160 Haute-Vienne **Map 16-A1**
♀ ⊗ ⌂ **HOTEL DU COMMERCE** (N° RR JAN 23 626) (M. Robert **Dionnet**) 1, rue du Commerce ☎ 55-76-70-72 ⊸ 6 Evening meals.

SAINT-SYMPHORIEN-DES-MONTS par LAPENTY-DU-HARCOUET 50600 Manche **RN 176 Map 8-A1**
♀ ⊗ ⌂ **1 Star NN LE RELAIS DU BOIS LEGER** (N° RR JUL 10 872) ⇌ (M. and Mme Raymond **Pinet**) Lapenty ☎ 33-49-01-43 **Minitel** point phone 33-49-36-08 ⊸ 10 Closed Sun evening; 3 weeks in Sept; 1 week Feb. Full-board 160–190F per night. Coaches welcome (rest. seats 50). Evening meals until 9pm. English spoken.

SAINT-THEGONNEC 29223 Finistère **RN 12 Map 7-A1**
♀ ⊗ **REST DU COMMERCE** (N° RR NOV 25 198) (M. Alain **Mevel**) 1, rue de Paris ☎ 98-79-61-07 Closed Sat and Sun. Coaches welcome (rest. seats 92).

SAINT-VALLIER see **MONTCEAU-LES-MINES** 71230 Saône-et-Loire

SAINT-VICTURNIEN 87420 Haute-Vienne **RN 141**
♀ ⊗ **LE RELAIS DE LA MALAISE** (N° RR JUL 26 293) (M. Jean-Marie **Faure**) **La Malaise** ☎ 55-03-87-03 ⊸ 4 Coaches welcome (rest. seats 60). Evening meals. English spoken. Closed Sat pm, Sun and beginning Sept.

SAINT-VIGOR-LE-GRAND see **BAYEUX** 14400 Calvados **RN 13 Map 4-B2**

SAINT-VINCENT-DE-CONNEZAC 24190 Dordogne **CD 709 Map 15-B3**
♀ ⊗ **AU BON ACCUEIL** (N° RR JANV 27 142) (M. Jacques **Magne**) Route de Mussidan ☎ 53-91-82-17 Closed Mon and 15 days in Oct. English and Italian spoken. Filling station on site open 7am to 10pm.

SAINT-VINCENT-DE-PAUL 33440 Gironde **RN 10 Map 20-A1 15-A3**
♀ ⊗ **1 Star NN CHEZ ANATOLE** (N° RR MAR 23 718) (M. Michel **Denechaud**) Ambarès ☎ 56-38-95-11 ⊸ 8 from 72–110F, breakfast 14F Closed Sat. Car park; dogs allowed; sports and recreations (pool table, *pétanque*, swings, shaded garden). Places to visit: Citadelle de Blaye Grot 'Pair non Pair', Bec d'Ambes.

S

SAINT-VINCENT-DE-PAUL 40990 Landes **RN 124 Map 20-B2**
♈ ⊗ **AUX PLATANES** (N° RR OCT 20 315) (M. **Vicente**) ☎ 58-73-90-13 Closed Sun. Spanish spoken.

SAINT-YAN 71600 S.-et-L. **RN 982 (via Flèche Bison Fûté) Map 18-A2 16-A3**
♈ ⊗ ⌂ **LA CHAUMIÈRE** (N° RR FEV 26 463) (M. Pascal **Germain**) 12, rue de la Gare ☎ 85-84-97-20 ◄ 6 Closed Tue; Sept. Full-board 130F per night. Coaches welcome (rest. seats 45). Evening meals until 11pm.

SAINT-YORRE 03270 Allier **RN 106 Map 16-B3**
♈ ⊗ ⌂ **NOUVEL HOTEL** (N° RR JUN 26 559) (Mme Pascale **Rouge-lin**) 17, rte de Vichy ☎ 70-59-41-97 ◄ 11 Closed Sat midday; Feb. Full-board 175–205F per night. Coaches welcome (2 rooms: 120/30 seats). English, some German spoken. Evening meals.

SAINTE-CATHERINE 62223 P.-de-C. **RN 25 Map 5-B3**
♈ ⊗ ⌂ **L'AUBERGE DU MOULIN** (N° RR MAR 27 227) (M. Eric **Gagno**) 135, Route de Lenz ☎ 21-23-41-56 ◄ 7 Closed Sun. Filling station nearby.

SAINTE-CECILE 50800 Manche **RN 24 Bis Map 8-A1**
♈ ⊗ ⌂ **LE CÉCILIA** (N° RR MAI 26 883) (M. Daniel **Le Huby**) Le Bourg ☎ 33-61-07-81 **Minitel** ◄ 5 Closed Sat and Sun. Full-board 165–170F. Filling station 2km. English, German spoken.

SAINTE-CROIX-HAGUE 50440 Manche **RD 901**
♈ ⊗ ⌂ **LE PETIT BACCHUS** (N° RR MARS 27 233) (M. Michel **Oury**) ☎ 33-52-77-53 ◄ 11 Closed Sat, Sun. Filling station nearby.

SAINTE-FORTUNADE 19490 Correze **Map 17-A1**
♈ ⊗ **CHEZ JEAN-PIERRE ET BRIGITTE** (N° RR MARS 25 333) (Mme Brigitte **Cariou**) Taxi ☎ 55-27-14-84 Closed Sun during winter. English spoken.

SAINTE-FOY-L'ARGENTIERE 69610 Rhône **Map 2-A1**
♈ ⊗ **AUBERGE DE LA PLACE** (N° RR AVR 24 915) (Mme Yvonne **Goubier**) ☎ 74-70-00-51 Closed Sat; Aug.
♈ ⊗ ⌂ **HOTEL DE LA POSTE** (N° RR NOV 25 736) (M. Michel **Jenestier**) ☎ 74-70-02-75 **Minitel** ◄ 6 Closed Mon; 8 days end of Aug; 8 days end of Feb.

SAINTE-FOY-LES-LYON see **ACQUEDUCS-DE-BEAUNANT** 69110 Rhône

SAINTE-FOY-LA-GRANDE 33220 Gironde **Maps 15-B3 and 21-A1**
♈ ⊗ ⌂ **CAFE DE L'ORIENT** (N° RR JUIL 26 941) (M. Michel **Thomas**) 2, avenue Paul Bert ☎ 57-46-13-94 ◄ 9 Closed Sun. English, German spoken a little. Filling station near.

SAINTE-FOY-DE-MONTGOMERY 14140 Calv. **RN 179 Map 8-A2**
♈ ⊗ **LE RELAIS DE MONTGOMERY** (N° RR AOU 14 917) (Mme **Planckeel**) ☎ 31-63-53-02 ◄ 4 Closed Sun.

S

SAINTE-GENEVIEVE 60730 Oise **RN 1 Map 3-B2**

⚠ ⊗ **CHEZ L'AUVERGNAT** (N° RR OCT 26 362) (M. Joël **Deroq**), 153, Route Nationale 1 ☎ 44-08-64-38 **Minitel** Closed Sat, Sun, Aug. Coaches welcome (rest. seats 60). Evening meals to 9pm.

SAINTE-LIVRADE 47110 L.-et-G. **RN 111 Map 21-B1**

⚠ ⊗ ⌂ **1 Star NN AU BON ACCUEIL** (N° RR JUL 19 426) (M. **Cougouille**) route de Villeneuve ☎ 58-01-02-34 **Minitel** ─ 10 Closed Sun evening; 24 Dec to 2 Jan. Full-board 145–155F per night. Coaches welcome (rest. seats 140). Evening meals.

SAINTE-LIZAIGNE 36260 Indre **RN 718 Map 13-B1**

⚠ ⊗ **RELAIS DE CHAMPAGNE** (N° RR JAN 25 775) (Mme Jeannine **Samour**) 10, Grande-Rue ☎ 54-04-06-07 Closed Sun; Aug. Coaches welcome (rest. seats 50). Evening meals until 8pm.

SAINTE-LUCE see NANTES 44470 L.-Atl.

SAINTE-MARGUERITE 88100 Vosges **RN 59 Map 10-B2**

⚠ ⊗ ⌂ **1 Star NN LE RELAIS DES AMIS** (N° RR JUN 16 108) (M. François **Bernat**) rue d'Alsace ☎ 29-56-17-23 ─ 16 from 75–120F, breakfast 15–20F. Closed Sun in winter. Full-board 165–175F per night. Coaches welcome (rest. seats 60). Evening meals. Car park; bar; dogs allowed. Opportunities to walk in woods, on hills.

⚠ ⊗ **LE RELAIS DU CENTRE** (N° RR JUN 22 839) (M. Emile **Mathieu**) 183, rue d'Alsace ☎ 29-56-28-74 Closed Sat, Aug. Coaches welcome (rest. seats 40).

SAINTE-MARIE-DE-GOSSE 40390 Landes **RN 117 Map 20-A2**

⚠ ⊗ ⌂ ⌂ **1 Star NN LE RELAIS ROUTIER, ON MANGE ON BOIT, ON DORT** (N° RR AVR 12 815) (M. Marc **Deloube**) RN 117 ☎ 59-56-32-02 **Minitel** Point phone 59-56-34-17 ─ 15 Closed Fri evening, Sat low season; Oct. Full-board 130–150F per night. Coaches welcome (rest. seats 190). Spanish spoken. Evening meals to 10pm. Menus from 45F. Specialities: confits, Foie gras, Fish (in season).

SAINTE-MAURE-DE-TOURAINE 37800 I.-et-L. **RN 10 Map 12-B3**

⚠ ⊗ **LA PIERRE PERCEE** (N° RR MAI 25 937) (MM. **Malin Bouquet**) Route Nationale 10 ☎ 47-65-08-64 **Minitel** Closed Sat, Sun; Aug. Evening meals until 11.30pm. English, some Portuguese, Italian spoken.

⚠ ⊗ ⌂ **LE BELLEVUE** (N° RR MARS 26 489) (M. Christophe **Bardeau**) RN 10 ☎ 47-65-40-61. Closed Mon midday. English, German, Spanish spoken.

SAINTE SCOLASSES/SARTHE 61170 Orne **CD 8 and CD 6 Map 8-A2**

⚠ ⊗ ⌂ **HOTEL DU CHEVAL BLANC** (N° RR SEPT 26 995) (M. Daniel **Millière**) Place de L'Église ☎ 33-27-66-30 ─ 3 Closed Feb. Full-board 150–180F. Coaches welcome (rest. seats 110). Evening meals served to 11pm. Filling station nearby.

SAINTE-SIGOLENE 43600 Haute-Loire **RD 43 Map 18-A3**

⚠ ⊗ ⌂ **LE RELAIS DE LA POSTE** (N° RR NOV 18 246) (M. **Mounier**)

2, place Leclerc ☎ 71-61-61-33 ⊸ 20 Closed Aug and Sun. Coaches welcome (rest. seats 60). Evening meals to 9pm.

SAINTE-SEVERE-SUR-INDRE 36160 Indre RN 117 Map 16-A2

♀ ⊗ ⌂ **LE RELAIS DU COMMERCE** (N° RR FEV 21 783) (Mme Denise **Duplaix**) rue de Verdun ☎ 54-30-50-46 ⊸ 11.

SAINTE-TERRE 33350 Gironde Map 15-A3

♀ ⊗ ⌂ **CHEZ RÉGIS** (N° RR JANV 25 783) (M. Jacques **Astarie**)
⊸ Avenue du Gal-de-Gaulle ☎ 57-47-16-21 Closed Mon and Jan.

TALANGE 57300 Moselle Map 10-A1

♀ ⊗ **RELAIS DE LA LIBERTÉ** (N° RR JANV 26 785) (M. René **Zeuli**) 131, rue de Metz ☎ 87-72-27-29.

TALMONT-ST-HILAIRE 85440 Vendée Map 11-A1

♀ ⊗ ⌂ **HOTEL DU CENTRE** (N° RR OCT 26 698) (M. Michel **Leblond**) 1, rue du Centre ☎ 51-90-60-35 ⊸ 12.

TARARE 69170 Rhône RN 7 Map 2-A1

♀ ⊗ **BAR PROVENÇAL** (N° RR MAI 23 294) (M. Georges **Bidot**) 8, av. Edouard-Herriot ☎ 74-63-33-64 Closed Sun; public holidays; 1 week in Aug. Evening meals until 8.30pm.

♀ ⊗ **HOTEL SAINT-PIERRE** (N° RR NOV 27 458) (M. Jean **Goutlemoire**) Les Sauvages ☎ 74-89-10-49 ⊸ 7 Closed Wed and last week in Aug. One week Christmas and one week in March. English spoken. Evening meals to 8.30pm.

TARBES 65000 Hautes-Pyr RN 21 Map 21-A3

♀ ⊗ ⌂ **1 Star NN LE VICTOR HUGO** (N° RR FEV 26 438) (Mme Patricia **Jouanlong**) 52, rue Victor-Hugo ☎ 62-93-36-71 ⊸ 8 (with WC) from 45–60F, breakfast 12F. Closed Sun. Full-board 120 per night. Evening meals. English, Spanish spoken. Car park; bar; dogs allowed, TV. Places to visit: Donjon des Aigles, Pyrenees National Park (ski-runs), grottes de Bétharron.

♀ ⊗ **LE CLAUZIER** (N° RR OCT 25 665) (M. Didier **Chaussalet**) 2, place Germain Claverie ☎ 62-93-18-57 Closed Sun.

TARTAS 40400 Landes RN 124 Map 20-B2

♀ ⊗ ⌂ **LA CAHUTE** (N° RR AVR 26 517) (Mme Martine **Thomas**), RN 124 Moulin ☎ 58-73-43-17 ⊸ 7 Closed Sat pm; Sun afternoon. Full-board 165F per night. Coaches welcome (rest. seats 60). Evening meals to midnight. English, German spoken.

TASSIN-ECULLY see ECULLY 69130 Rhône RN 7 Map 2-A1

T

TATRE (LE) par BAIGNES 16360 Charente **RN 10 Map 15-A2/3**
Ⓧ ⌂ **LA CAMBROUSSE** (N° RR FEV 26 436) (M. Jean-Claude **Pichon**) Le Pont du Noble Reignac ☎ 45-78-52-83 ⊸ 10 Closed Sat afternoon, Sun. Evening meals.

TAUVES 63690 P.-de-D. **RN 122 Map 17-A2**
Ⓧ **HOSTELLERIE DE LA POSTE** (N° RR JUN 15 262) (M. Robert **Agay**) ☎ 73-21-11-09.

TAUXIGNY 37320 Indre et Loire
Ⓧ ⌂ **AUBERGE DE LA CHAUMIERE** (N° RR DEC 27 490) (M. Dominique **Garon**) 1, avenue de la Gare ☎ 47-43-40-26 ⊸ 2 Closed Friday afternoon and Saturday morning. Evening meals until 9pm. Service station 1km.

TAVAUX 39500 Jura **RN 73 Map 14-A3**
Ⓧ **Les Routiers BP Service Station STATION DES CHARMES** (N° RR NOV 23 534) (M. Marc **Joffroy**) ☎ 82-71-41-57 German spoken.
⌨ **Elf Service Station DECOSNE AUTOMOBILE** (N° RR JUL 550000089) (Mme Nicole **Greco**) RN 73 6, rte de Dôle ☎ 84-81-12-79 Open 6.00am to 10.00pm German, Spanish, Yugoslavian spoken.

TAVEL 30126 Gard **Autoroute A 9 Map 24-A2**
Ⓧ **RESTOP de TAVEL** (M. Sylvain **Guariento**) ☎ 66-50-04-19 Self-service restaurant open 11.00am to 10.00pm. TV, Shop.German, English spoken.

TAVERS 45190 Loiret **RN 152 Map 12-A3**
Ⓧ **LA PIERRE TOURNANTE** (N° RR OCT 27 057) (Daniel **Lecoq**) 36 RN 152 ☎ 38-44-92-25 Closed Sun. Filling station near open 7.30. One to 7.30pm and closed on Mondays.

TEIL (LE) 07400 Ardèche **RN 86 Map 24-A2**
Ⓧ **AU BON COIN** (N° RR DEC 20 616) (Mme Marie **Gineste**) 11, rue Henri-Barbusse ☎ 75-49-02-61 Closed Aug.

LE TEMPLE-SUR-LOT 47110 L.-et-G. **RN 911 Map 21-B1**
Ⓧ ⌂ **LE VAL DU LOT "GOUNOT"** (N° RR MAR 21 817) (MM. Lionel and Christian **Hutrel**) ☎ 58-84-90-26 ⊸ 5 Closed Sat except in summer and in Sept. Full-board (winter) 150–180F per night. Coaches welcome (rest. seats 60). Evening meals. English spoken.

TENCE 43190 Haute-Loire **Map 18-A3**
Ⓧ **RESTAURANT DES CARS** (N° RR AOU 25 623) (Mme Marie-Françoise **Souvignet**) 13, Grande-Rue ☎ 71-59-84-01 Closed Wed afternoon. Evening meals until 9pm.

TENDU 36200 Indre **RN 20 Map 16-A1**
Ⓧ ⌂ **LE RELAIS DES ROUTIERS** (N° RR DEC 11 179) (M. André **Luneau**) Nle 20 ☎ 54-24-14-10 ⊸ 10 Closed Wed low season; 1

week Oct, 1 week Feb. Full-board 150–160F per night. Coaches welcome (rest. seats 70). Evening meals to 8.30pm.

TERCIS-LES-BAINS
Y ⊗ 🏠 **L'ÉTOILE** (N° RR MAI 27 284) (M. Thierry **Mortelette**) Route de Payrehorade ☎ 58-57-68-49 ⊷ 5 English and Spanish spoken. Evening meals served until 11pm. Filling station 50m open 7am to 8pm.

TERNUAY 70510 Haute-Saône RN 486 Map 10-A3 14-B2
Y ⊗ **CHEZ MARTINE** (N° RR JUL 13 854) (Mlle Martine **Géhant**) ☎ 84-20-42-98 ⊷ 2 Closed Sat; 24 Aug to 7 Sept. Full-board 130F per night. Coaches welcome (rest. seats 48). Evening meals.

TERRASSON-LA-VILLEDIEU 24120 Dordogne RN 89 Map 17-A1
Y ⊗ **AU RELAIS DES ROUTIERS** (N° RR JUN 21 142) (M. Jacques **Lasfargeas**) 42, avenue Victor-Hugo ☎ 53-50-00-89 Closed Sat; 20 Jun to 14 Jul. Coaches (rest. seats 100). Evening meals.
Y ⊗ 🏠 **LE RELAIS DES ROUTIERS** (N° RR MAR 9 404) (M. Charles **Leyrie**) 62, avenue Émile-Zola ☎ 53-50-00-75 ⊷ 12 Full-board 180–250F per night. Evening meals.

TERRENOIRE 42100 Loire Map 2-B1 and 18-A2
Y ⊗ **RELAIS DE L'AUTOROUTE** (N° RR DEC 26 771) (Mme Régine **Roux**) 57 Les Marandes ☎ 77-95-70-92 Closed Sat, Sun. Evening meals to midnight.

TESSY-SUR-VIRE 50420 Manche Map 4-B1
Y ⊗ **LES ROUTIERS** (N° RR MAR 26 854) (M. Maurice **Robert**) place du Marché ☎ 33-56-35-25 Closed Thur afternoon; Sun afternoon. Filling station 150m. Coaches welcome (35 rest. seats). Evening meals.

THAON-LES-VOSGES 88150 Vosges RN 57 Map 14-B1
Y ⊗ 🏠 **RELAIS ROUTIER 6010** (N° RR JAN 26 148) (M. Robert **Gehin**) 200, rue de Lorraine ☎ 29-39-21-67 **Minitel** ⊷ 4 Closed Fri afternoon to Mon am. Evening meals.

THAURON see COMBEAUVERT 23250 Creuse RN 940 Map 16-B1

THEIL (LE) 61260 Orne Map 8-B3
Y ⊗ **LE RELAIS DE L'ARCHE** (N° RR AOU 24 665) (M. Gérard **Leroux**) La Rouge ☎ 37-49-62-92. Coaches welcome (55 rest. seats). Evening meals to 1am.

THENEZAY see LA FERRIERE 79390 Deux-Sevres RN 148 Bis Map 15-A1

THENON 24210 Dordogne RN 89 Maps 15-B3 and 17-A1
Y ⊗ 🏠 **LES TOURNISSOUS - CHEZ SERGE** (N° RR MAR 23 159) (M. Serge **Leymarie**) ☎ 53-05-20-31 ⊷ 10 Closed Christmas, New Year. Full-board 120–140F per night. Coaches welcome (rest. seats 80 + 100 on terrace). English, Spanish spoken. Evening meals to 11pm.

T

THIEL-SUR-ACOLIN 03230 Allier **RD 12 Map 16-A3**
♀ ⊗ **LE RELAIS DE LA TERRASSE** (N° RR OCT 19 511) (M. **Tregouboff**) Route de Dompière ☎ 70-92-50-89 → 4 Coaches welcome (rest. seats 60).

THIMERT 28170 E.-et-L. **RN 839 Map 8-A3**
♀ ⊗ **LA CRÉMAILLÈRE** (N° RR MAR 21 829) (Mme Madeleine **Breton**) 1, rue de Chartres ☎ 37-51-60-90 Closed Sat afternoon. Coaches welcome (rest. seats 60). Evening meals.

THIVARS 28630 E.-et-L. **RN 10 Map 8-B3**
♀ ⊗ ⌂ **CHEZ BARBICHE** (N° RR NOV 26 717 (M. Serge **Noel**) 15, rue Nationale ☎ 37-26-40-05 → 9. Closed Sun. Full-board 130–170F. Coaches welcome (rest. seats 50). Evening meals to 10pm.

THOISSEY 01140 Ain **RD 933/17 Map 18-A2**
♀ ⊗ **LA CROISÉE** (N° RR MAI 23 798) (M. Jean **Servigne**) Guereins ☎ 74-66-14-93 Closed Sun; Aug.

THONES 74230 Hte-Savoie **RN 509 Map 19-A2**
♀ ⊗ ⌂ **1 Star NN L'HERMITAGE** (N° RR AVR 26 523) (M. Pierre **Bonnet**) avenue du Vieux-Pont ☎ 50-02-00-31 **Minitel** → 40 Closed Fri afternoon; 25 Oct to 15 Nov. Full-board 150–175F. Coaches welcome (rest. seats 160).

THORÉE-LES-PINS 72800 Sarthe **CD 306 Map 12-A2**
♀ ⊗ **CAFÉ RESTAURANT DES PÊCHEURS** (N° RR DEC 27 135) (M. Marcel **Guillaume**) Le Bourg ☎ 43-45-03-79 Closed Wed pm. English and German spoken.

THORENS-LES-GLIÈRES 74570 Hte-Savoie **RN 203 Map 19-A2**
♀ ⊗ ⌂ **SARL LA HAUTE BISE** (N° RR FEB 26 460) (M. Babacar **Seck**) RN 203 ☎ 50-22-47-61 → 6 Closed Sun. Filling station nearby.

THOU 45420 Loiret **RN 65 Map 13-A2**
♀ ⊗ **AU LIT ON DORT** (N° RR MAI 18 413) (M. Bernard **Bertrand**) ☎ 38-31-62-07 Closed Mon pm and August. Evening meals.
♀ ⊗ **LE CHEVAL BLANC** (N° RR JUL 26 952) (Mme Luigina **Zen**) Le Bourg ☎ 38-31-62-39 Italian spoken. Filling station near. Closed Wed. Full-board 140–180F. Coaches welcome (rest. seats 170). Evening meals to 10pm.

THOUARS 79100 Deux-Sèvres **RN 1 Map 12-B2**
♀ ⊗ **LE MILLE PATTES** (N° RR MAI 24 957) (Mme Martine **Valleau**) 17, rue de Launay ☎ **Minitel** English and German spoken. Evening meals.

THOURIE 34134 Ille-et-Vilaine **CD 163 et 53 Map 7-B3 8–B1**
♀ ⊗ **LES ROUTIERS** (N° RR OCT 27 046) (M. Patrick **Gilouppe**) **Le Bourg** ☎ 99-44-33-67 Closed Sat and Sun. English spoken. Filling station nearby.

THUET-PONTCHY 74130 Haute-Savoie **RN 506 Map 19-B2**
Ⴘ ⊗ **LE RELAIS DES CYCLAMENS** (N° RR AVR 13 654) (Mme **Delavenay**) ☎ 50-97-02-39.

THUILES (LES) 04400 Alpes de Haute-Provence **Map 25-A1**
Ⴘ ⊗ ⌂ **LES SEOLANES** (N° RR JUL 24 620) (M. Hubert **Maure**) Barcelonnette ☎ 92-81-07-37 ⊷ 6 Closed one day a week; Jan. English, Italian spoken.

TIGNIEU 38230 Isère **RD 18 Map 2-A2**
Ⴘ ⊗ **AUBERGE DES CHARMILLES** (N° RR DEC 24 444) (Mme Josiane **Renon**) 71, route de Bourgoin ☎ 78-32-23-57 Closed Aug. Evening meals.

TILLOY-LES-MOFLAINES 62000 Pas-de-Calais **Map 5-B3**
Ⴘ   **Bar Brasserie LE TILLOY** (N° RR MAI 24 973) (M. Denis **Hiolet**) Rte Nle 39 Arras ☎ 21-73-44-15 Closed Sun.

TOLLEVAST 50820 Manche **RN 13 Map 4-A1**
Ⴘ ⊗ **LES CHEVRES** (N° RR OCT 26 705) (M. André **Maleuvre**) Brix ☎ 33-43-77-92 Closed Sat, Sun; Aug. English spoken. Evening meals to midnight.

TONNAY-CHARENTE 17430 Charente-Maritime **RN 137 Map 11-B1**
Ⴘ ⊗ **L'OASIS CHEZ VACHON** (N° RR JAN 23 093) (M. **Vachon**) 27, rue de Lattre-de-Tassigny ☎ 46-88-70-84 Closed Mon; 1–15 Aug. Coaches welcome (rest. seats 60).
Ⴘ ⊗ **LES FONTAINES** (N° RR DEC 27 122) (M. Jean Paul **Revelaud**) 110, av. d'Aunis ☎ 46-83-79-11 Closed Sun. Filling station near. Open 6am to 10pm.

TORCY 71210 S -et-L. **RN 80 Map 18-A1**
Ⴘ ⊗ **LA SPIAGGIA** (N° RR DEC 26 114) (M. Salvatore **Lotito**) Rte Express Montchanin ☎ 85-55-35-45 Italian, English, German spoken. Coaches welcome (100 rest. seats). Evening meals to 11pm.

TORTERON 18320 Cher **Gc 26 Map 13-B2**
Ⴘ ⊗ ⌂ **LE RELAIS DU LABOUREUR** (N° RR JAN 10 216) (M. Céleste **Gosselin**) Grande-Rue ☎ 36-74-48-77 ⊷ 6.

TOTES 76890 Seine-Marit **RN 27 Map 3-A1 Map 4-A3**
Ⴘ ⊗ **LES AMIS RÉUNIS** (N° RR FEV 19 282) (M. Michel **Guilbert**) Route de Dieppe ☎ 35-79-91-27.
Ⴘ ⊗ **LE NORMANDY** (N° RR MARS 26 187) (Sté de Fait M. **Perrero-Morel**) Rte d'Yvetôt ☎ 35-32-91-35 Closed Sat evening, Sun.

TOTES see VAL-DE-SAANE 76960 Seine-Maritime

TOULON 83100 Var **RN 8 Map 25-A3**
Ⴘ ⊗ **LE RELAIS DE L'ESCAILLON** (N° RR MAI 24 967) (M. Bernard **Lemaire**) 1, rue Chateaubriand ☎ 94-24-21-02 Closed 13 Aug – 3 Sep. Evening meals.

T

Toulon continued

♀ ⊗ **LE SPORTING BAR** (N° RR JUN 24 606) (**SNC Calmus & C°** M. René **Calmus**) 676, Bld du Maréchal Joffre ☎ 94-36-27-13 Coaches welcome (rest. seats 55). Evening meals.

♀ ⊗ **LA FRINGALE – Chez Jo** (N° RR JUL 25 059) (SARL **Prim and Gonzalez**) 522, avenue de la République ☎ 94-36-00-47 Closed Wed in winter; 1 week Oct, 1 week Feb. Coaches welcome (rest. seats 25). Meals throughout the night. English, Italian spoken.

TOULON-SUR-ALLIER 03400 Allier **RN 7 Map 16-A3**

♀ ⊗ **LE RELAIS FLEURI** (N° RR NOV 22 088) (M. **Belain**) Route Nationale 7 ☎ 70-44-47-16 Closed Sun; Aug.

TOULOUSE 31000 Haute-Garonne **RN 20 Map 22-A2**

♀ ⊗ **LE NOUVEAU CORTIJO** (N° RR OCT 25 659) (M. René **Andrieu**) 181, avenue des États-Unis ☎ 61-47-68-64 **Minitel** Closed Sat, Sun; 1 to 15 Aug. Evening meals to 11.30pm. Spanish spoken.

TOULOUSE-SAINT-MARTIN-DU-TOUCH 31300 Haute-Garonne **RN 124 Map 22-A2**

♀ ⊗ 🏠 **LE RELAIS DU PROGRÈS** (N° RR DEC 20 037) (M. Félix **Ober**) 185, route de Bayonne ☎ 61-49-22-75 ⊷ 6 Closed Sun; Aug. Coaches welcome (rest. seats 100). Evening meals until 11 pm.

TOUQUES-DEAUVILLE 14800 Calvados **Dles 74 and 52 Map 4-B2**

♀ ⊗ **AUBERGE LA CROIX SONNET** (N° RR OCT 26 344) (Mme **Pedrazzi**) La Croix-Sonnet ☎ 31-88-19-62 ⊷ 4 Full-board 300–350F per night. Coaches welcome summer only (rest. seats 40 + terrace 100). Evening meals to 9pm. English, Spanish, Italian spoken.

TOUQUIN 77131 Seine-et-Marne **RD 231 Map 9-A2**

♀ ⊗ **LE TOUQUINOIS** (N° RR JAN 26 160) (M. Marcel **Breuil**) 8, rue du Commerce ☎ 64-04-18-37 Closed Sun. Evening meals.

TOURCOING 59200 Nord **RN Sortie Tourcoing ouest 17 Map 5-B1**

♀ ⊗ 🏠 **AU SIGNAL D'ARRET** (N° RR DEC 24 452) (M. Michel **Guilbert**) 28, rue des Francs ☎ 20-26-56-74 **Minitel** ⊷ 5 Closed Sat, Sun; 16 to 31 Aug; 24 Dec–1 Jan. Evening meals to 11pm. Full-board 135–175F. Coaches welcome (rest. seats 50).

♀ ⊗ **LE SAPHIR** (N° RR NOV 26 723) (M. Jacques **Mareel**) 11 bis, Chaussée Berthelot ☎ 20-01-88-03 Closed Sun.

TOUR-DU-MEIX (LA) 39270 Jura **RN 470 Map 19-B1**

♀ ⊗ **AUBERGE DU PONT DE LA PYLE** (N° RR MAR 23 698) (M. Jacques **Berger**) ☎ 84-25-41-92 Closed Wed; Oct. Coaches welcome (2 rooms: 90/60 seats). Meals served until 9.30pm.

TOUR-DU-PIN (LA) 38110 Isère **RN 516 RN 6 Map 2-B3**

♀ ⊗ 🏠 **LE RELAIS DES ROUTIERS** (N° RR SEP 24 332) (M. Roger **Cantel**) Le Passeron-St-Clair de la Tour ☎ 74-97-14-88 ⊷ 11 Closed Sun afternoon.

TOUR-DU-PIN (LA) 38110 Isère **RN 6**
♀ ⊗ **CHEZ BABETH** (N° RR NOV 25 744) (Mme Elisabeth **Rostaing**)
St-Didier-de-la-Tour ☎ 74-97-15-87 Coaches welcome (rest.
seats 60). Evening meals to 10pm.

TOURETTES (LES) 26740 Drôme **RN 7 Map 24-B1**
♀ ⊗ ⌂ **MA CAMPAGNE** (N° RR MAI 26 897) (M. Achour **Ait
Aoudia**) ☎ 75-90-06-46 ⇥ 6 English, Spanish, Arabic spoken.
Filling station near.

TOURNES 08540 Ardennes **RN 51 Map 6-A2**
♀ ⊗ **LE GASTRO DES MILLE PATTES** (N° RR SEPT 26 643) (M.
René **Filiatre**) 17, route Nationale ☎ 24-52-94-35 Coaches welco-
me (rest. seats 70). Evening meals until 11pm.

TOURNON-D'AGENAIS 47370 L.-et-G. **RN 656 Map 21-B1**
♀ ⊗ ⌂ **1 Star NN LE RELAIS DES VOYAGEURS** (N° RR AOU 14 918)
(M. **Gary**) rue de Cahors ☎ 58-71-70-28 ⇥ 8 Closed Fri evening;
Sat midday; 15 days in Oct. Swimming pool open 30 Jun to 15
Sept.

TOURNUS 71700 S.-et-L. **RN 6 Map 18-B1**
⛽ **Les Routiers Antar Service Station PARIS-SAVOIE** (N° RR JAN
23 117) (M. Paul **Lucet**) ☎ 85-51-17-76 Open 24 hours, except Sat–
8.00pm to 7.00am. Italian spoken.

TOURS 37000 I.-et-L. **RN 10 CD 152 Map 12-A2/3**
♀ ⊗ ⌂ **L'AVIATION** (N° RR JUN 26 554) (Mme Michelle **Mary**) 295,
avenue Maginot ☎ 47-51-19-50 **Minitel** ⇥ 8 (17 beds) Closed Sat,
Sun; Full-board 145F, half-board 105F per night. Coaches welcome (3 rooms: 45/26/26 seats). Evening meals to 11pm. Parking
5500m².
♀ ⊗ **1 star NN LE RELAIS DE SAINTE-RADEGONDE** (N° RR NOV
27 095) (Mme Annie **Fuster**) 178, quai Paul-Bert ☎ 47-51-28-45 ⇥
14 Closed Sun pm low season. Filling station near.
♀ ⊗ **LE STRASBOURG** (N° RR NOV 26 368) (M. **Bottin**) 76, bd Thiers
☎ 47-38-66-06. Closed Sat pm and Sun; Aug. Coaches welcome
(70 rest. seats). Evening meals to 9pm. Parking 1200m².

TOURS-MONNAIE 37380 I.-et-L. **Autoroute A 10**
♀ ⊗ **Accor L'ARCHE** Autoroute A 10 - 2 sens Passerelle ☎ 47-56-15-
49 Self-Service restaurant open 24 hours. Shop. English, Spanish
spoken.

TOURY 28390 E.-et-L. **RN 20 Map 9-B1**
♀ ⊗ **LE RELAIS DE LA CHAPELLE** (N° RR FEV 25 797) (Mme
Claudine **Comarlot**) 60, av. de la Chapelle ☎ 37-90-64-96 Closed
Sat; Sun. Midday and Christmas week. Coaches welcome (rest.
seats 150). Evening meals until 11pm.

TOUT-Y-FAUT see LOULAY 17330 Charente-Maritime

TRAIT (LE) 76580 Seine-Maritime **RD 982 Map 3-A1**
♀ ⊗ **LE JEAN BART** (N° RR AOU 23 902) (M. **Mahier**) 488, rue Jean-

T

Le Trait continued
Bart ☎ 35-37-22-47 **Minitel** ⊸ 3 furnished. Closed Sun; 10 to 30 Aug. Coaches welcome (rest. seats 110). Evening meals to 22h.

TRAMAIN 22640 Côtes-du-Nord **RN 12 Map 7-A3**
♀ ⊗ **AU RELAIS DE TRAMAIN** (N° RR MAI 26 894) (M. Jack **Hutteau**) rue du Bourg ☎ 96-31-82-28. Closed Sat, Sun; Jul–Aug. Filling station 4km. Coaches welcome (rest. seats 70/35).

TRANSLAY (LE) 80140 Somme **Map 5-A3**
♀ ⊗ **AU RELAIS FLEURI** (N° RR MARS 27 220) (Mme Gladys **Duboille**), 5, rue de Oisemont ☎ 22-28-48-98 Closed Wed pm. Filling station near.

TREBES 11800 Aude **RN 113 Map 22-B2**
♀ ⊗ ⌂ **LE RELAIS DES CAPUCINS** (N° RR JUL 25 041) (M. Gilbert **Laffont**) 34, route de Narbonne ☎ 68-78-70-07 ⊸ 14 Closed Sat, Sun; 1 week in Jul; 3 weeks at Christmas. Coaches welcome (rest. seats 112). Evening meals.

TREBEURDEN 22560 Côtes-du-Nord **Map 7-A2**
♀ ⊗ **RESTAURANT DES SPORTS** (N° RR NOV 27 447) (M. Andre **Courageaux**) 24, rue des Plages ☎ 96-23-50-12 Closed Tues pm. 15 – 30 Aug. English spoken. Filling station 300m. Open 7.30am – 8pm. Parking 6000m².

TREFFENDEL 35580 Ille-et-Vilaine
♀ ⊗ **RELAIS RN24** (N° RR DEC 24 477) (Mme **Guillemot**) SARL RN24 La Gare ☎ 99-61-00-62 Closed Sunday. Evening meals.

TREGUIDEL 22290 Côtes-du-Nord **RD 51/CD 6 Map 7-A2**
♀ ⊗ **LE BOUTOU** (N° RR JUN 25 003) (M. Bernard **Glaudel**) Bourg de Tréguidel ☎ 96-70-02-42 Coaches welcome (rest. seats 110). Evening meals until 9pm. English spoken. Closed Monday pm.

TREILLIÈRES 44119 L.-Atl. **RN 137 Map 11-A2**
♀ ⊗ **LE PIGEON BLANC** (N° RR AVR 26 527) (Mme Règine **Plat**) Le Pigeon Blanc ☎ 40-94-67-72 or 40-94-51-26 **Minitel** Closed Sun low season. Evening meals.

TRELISSAC 24000 Dordogne **Map 15-B3**
♀ ⊗ **BAR DE LA STATION** (N° RR AVR 24 912) (M. Jean-Philippe **Burgarella**) Rte Nle 21 ☎ 53-54-40-24 Closed Feb. English spoken.

TREMOREL 22230 Côtes-du-Nord **N 164 bis Map 7-B3**
♀ ⊗ **LE RELAIS DE LA FORÊT** (N° RR FEV 26 820) (M. Yvon **Sohier**) Bourg ☎ 96-25-21-70. Closed Mon pm. Evening meals.

TREON 28100 E.-et-L. **RN 828 Map 8-A3**
♀ ⊗ **LE RELAIS DE TREON** (N° RR JUL 26 583) (Mme **Cuvellier**) 20, rue de Chateauneuf ☎ 37-82-62-35 ⊸ 7 Closed Sun evening. Evening meals until 9.30pm. Full-board 160F. Coaches welcome (72 rest. seats).

TRESNAY 58240 Nièvre **RN 7 Map 16-A3**
Y ⊗ **LA SCIERIE** (N° RR FEV 27 180) (M. Martial **Pettinger**) Rte Nle 7
St-Pierre-le-Moutier ☎ 86-38-62-14 Closed Sat evening and Sun.
English spoken. Filling station 3km open 24 hrs.

TRESSÈRE 66300 Pyrénées-Orientales **RN 9 Map 23-A3 Voir LE
BOULOU**

TRETS 13530 Bouches-du-Rhône **RN 7 Map 24-B3**
Y ⊗ **BAR DE L'AÉRODROME** (N° RR MAR 26 853) (M. Christian
Daumas) ☎ 42-61-49-45 English spoken. Filling station near.

TRIGAVOU 22490 Côte-du-Nord **Map A3**
Y ⊗ **LE MILL PATT** (N° RR OCT 27 395) (M. Loïc **Renault**) Le Bourg
☎ 96-27-84-14 Closed Monday pm. Evening meals. Filling station
500m.

TRIMOUILLE (LA) 86290 Vienne **RN 675 Map 16-A1**
Y ⊗ 🏠 **L'AUBERGE FLEURIE** (N° RR FEV 15 533) (M. Monique
🔥 **Dufour**) rue Octave-Bernard ☎ 49-91-60-64 ⇥ 5 Closed Sun,
public holidays after lunch. Evening meals (May to Sept). Menus
43–60F. Specialities: *Moules au vert, Medaillon de ris de veau à
la Trimouillaise, Langouste Thermidor.*

TRINITÉ SURZUR (LA) 56190 Morbihan **RN 165 Map 11-A2**
Y ⊗ **AUBERGE LA VIEILLE FONTAINE/SARL** (N° RR SEPT 26 994)
(M. Daniel **Malherbe**) Le Bourg Muzillac ☎ 97-42-16-45 ⇥ 12
Closed Sun. English spoken.

TRONQUAY (LE) 14490 Calvados **RD 572 Map 4-B1**
Y ⊗ **AU ROUTIER SYMPA** (N° RR MAI 26 531) (M. Jacques **Lero-
sier**) ☎ 31-92-38-68.

TRONSANGES par BARBELOUP 58400 Nièvre **RN 7 Map 13-B2**
Y ⊗ **L'AUBERGE DU SOLEIL LEVANT** (N° RR AVR 18 065) (M. Jean
Reichhard) ☎ 86-37-84-02 Closed Sun; Sept. Coaches welcome.

Y ⊗ **LE RELAIS DE LA CROIX DU PAPE** (N° RR DEC 24 770) (Mme
Marinette **Beunardeau**) Nationale ☎ 86-70-01-04 **Minitel** Closed
Sat, Sun; 3 weeks Aug. One week Christmas. English spoken.
Coaches welcome (120 rest. seats). Parking 3000m^2.
Y ⊗ **SARL DE LA CROIX DU PAPE** (N° RR JAN 27 497) (Mme Agnes
Dumaine) Barbecoup ☎ 86-37-84-03 Evening meals. Service
station nearby open 5am to midnight. Parking.

TRONVILLE-EN-BARROIS 55310 Meuse **Map 14-A1**
Y ⊗ **L'ESPÉRANCE** (N° RR OCT 27 036) (M. Michel **Walbin**) 64,
route nationale ☎ 29-78-88-15/78-11-03 ⇥ 4 Closed Sun. Filling
station 3km.

TROUVILLE ALLIQUERVILLE 76210 S-Mme **RN 15 Map 4-A3**
Y ⊗ **L'AUBERGE NORMANDE** (N° RR JUN 25 562) (M. Philippe
Malhouitre) ☎ 35-31-15-21 ⇥ 5 Closed Fri evening; Sun.
Coaches welcome (50 rest. seats). Evening meals.

T

TULLINS 38140 Isère **RN 92 Maps 18-B3, 19-A3 and 24-B1**
♀ ⊗ ⌂ **LE RELAIS DES NÉGOCIANTS** (N° RR MAI 16 078) (M. René **Bracco**) 1, rue du Général-de-Gaulle ☎ 76-07-00-67 **Minitel** ⊸ 6 Closed Mon pm; Aug. Coaches welcome (rest. seats 70). Taxi – Ambulance.

U

UCKANGE 57270 Moselle **RD 952 Maps 6-B3 and 10-A1**
♀ ⊗ **LE PRESSOIR** (N° RR JAN 21 339) (M. Silvio **Piccin**) 22, rue Jeanne-d'Arc ☎ 82-58-20-38 Closed Sat, Sun; Aug and 15 days at New Year.

ULMES (LES) 49700 M.-et-L. **RD 960 Map 12-B2**
♀ ⊗ **LA GRAPPE D'OR** (N° RR AVR 26 498) (Mme Monique **Forestier**) Restau Gril Le Moulin Cassé ☎ 41-67-00-06 Closed Sun evening at 7pm. English, German spoken. Evening meals. Coaches welcome.

UNIENVILLE 10140 Aube **RD 46 Map 9-B3**
♀ ⊗ **CHEZ MARCEL ET CHRISTIANE** (N° RR JANV 21 760) (M. Marcel **Saget**) ☎ 25-26-30-80.

UPAIX 05300 Hautes-Alpes **Voir ROUREBEAU**

UROU 61200 Orne **RN 26 Map 8-A2**
♀ ⊗ ⌂ **LE CLOS FLEURI** (N° RR FEV 26 181) (M. Gilbert **Estelle**) Argentan ☎ 33-67-08-25 English, German spoken. Closed Sundays (except Banquets). Coaches welcome (rest. seats 120). Evening meals until 11pm. Full-board 110–150F. Coaches welcome.

V

VAILLY-SUR-SAULDRE 18260 Cher **RD 926 Map 13-A1**
♀ ⊗ **REST DU MARCHÉ** (N° RR FEV 25 313) (M. Gérard **Coste**) ☎ 48-73-72-25 ⊸ 5 Closed Wed afternoon; Jan. Full-board 140–160F per night. Coaches welcome (rest. seats 50). Evening meals until 10pm.

VALENÇAY 36600 Indre **RN 156 Map 12-B3**
♀ ⊗ **LE RELAIS DES ROUTIERS** (N° RR FEV 15 128) (M. Pierre

Bougault) ☎ 54-00-02-94 ⇌ 4 Closed Sun low season; 3 weeks in Sept and 15 days in May. Evening meals.

VALENCE NORD 26300 Drôme **RN 7 Map 18-B3 24-A1**
♞ **Les Routiers Total Service Station RELAIS DU 45ᵉ PARALLE-
`LE** (N° RR OCT 23 519 (M. Daniel **Bianco**) Châteauneuf-sur-Isère
☎ 75-58-60-22 English, German, Italian spoken.

VALENCE-SUR-BAÏSE 32310 Gers **Map 21-B2**
♀ ⊗ **LADOUCH** (N° RR AOU 25 615) (Mme Ginette **Ladouch**) Place
de l'Hôtel-de-Ville ☎ 62-28-50-45 Closed Sun. Spanish, Italian
spoken.

VALENCIENNES 59300 Nord **RN 29 Maps 6-A3 and 5-B1**
♀ ⊗ ⌂ **AUBERGE DU RELAIS DE LA POTERNE** – Les Routiers (N°
RR DEC 17 689) (M. **Demolle**) 9, boulevard Eisen (Place Poterne) bd extérieur Itinéraire P.L. Exit from autoroute. A2 - Valenciennes Sud ☎ 27-46-44-98 **Minitel** ⇌ 13 Coaches welcome
(weekends only – rest. seats 50 bookable). Evening meals until
9.30pm.

VALENTON-VAL-POMPADOUR 94460 Val-de-Marne **RN 5 Map 1-
B3**
♀ ⊗ **AU BON ACCUEIL** (N° RR OCT 25 165) (M. Marco **Roméro**) 46,
rue Henri-Barbusse ☎ 43-89-06-70 Closed Sun; Aug. Spanish
spoken. Evening meals until 10.30pm.

VALENTY-VENTAVON 05300 Htes-Alpes **RN 85 Map 25-A1**
♀ ⊗ **LA GALERE Tobacconist** (N° RR OCT 24 327) (M. Michel **Da
Silva**) Laragne ☎ 92-66-40-31.

VALERGUES 34130 Hérault **RN 113 Map 23-B2**
♀ ⊗ ⌂ **RELAIS DE VALERGUES** (N° RR JUL 25 495) (M. Claude
Bernabé) RN 113 ☎ 67-86-75-27 ⇌ 8 Closed Sun. Spanish
spoken.

VALEUIL 24210 Dordogne
♀ ⊗ **LA GRÉGOIRE – RELAIS DE SARRAZEGNAC** (N° RR JAN 27
502) (M. Claude **Distingin**) ☎ 53-05-80-24 Evening meals. English, Spanish spoken.

VALLET 44330 Loire-Atl. **RD 756 and 763 Maps 11-A1/B3 and 12-B1**
♀ ⊗ ⌂ **LE RELAIS DE LA GARE** (N° RR AVR 20 151) (Mme **Jouy**) ☎
40-33-92-55 **Minitel** ⇌ 25 Closed Sun. Full-board 140–155F per
night. Coaches welcome (rest. seats 160). Evening meals. English
spoken.

VALLON-EN-SULLY 3190 Allier
♀ ⊗ **ALLÉE DES SOUPIRS** (N° RR DEC 27 474) (M. Cecile **Collard**)
☎ 70-06-50-66 Evening meals. English and Spanish spoken.

VALLON-PONT-D'ARC 07150 Ardèche **RN 579 Map 24-A2**
♀ ⊗ **BAR DE LA POSTE** (N° RR OCT 22 952) (M. Bernard **Garrido**)
rue Jean-Jaurès ☎ 75-88-02-11 Closed Sun low season; Dec. Open

V

Vallon-Pont-D'ark continued
7am–9pm; Spanish spoken. Coaches welcome (rest. seats 40).
Evening meals May – Sept until 9.30pm.

VAILLY SUR SAULDRE 18260 Cher
♀ ⊗ ⌂ **HOTEL DU MARCHÉ** Place du Marché ☎ 48-73-72-25
Evening meals. Spanish spoken.

VALOGNES 50700 Manche **RN 13 Map 4-B1**
♀ ⊗ **AU PETIT MONTROUGE** (N° RR DEC 12 588) (M. and Mme
François **Leblond**) 104, rue des Religieuses.

VALS-LE-BAINS 07600 Ardèche **Map 24-A1**
♀ ⊗ **LE TONNEAU** (N° RR MAI 23 255) (M. Patrick **Guériot**) 89, rue
Jean-Jaurès ☎ 75-37-45-36. Closed Mon evening; 15 days Oct.
Evening meals.

VANNES 56000 Morbihan **RN 165 Map 11-A1/2**
♀ ⊗ ⌂ **1 star NN LE RELAIS DE LUSCANEN** (N° RR NOV 27 104)
(M. Jean-Marc **Giteau**) Route d'auvay ☎ 97-63-45-92 ⊷ 22 Closed
Sun. English spoken. Coaches welcome (rest. seats 60). Evening
meals until midnight.

VANVES 92170 Hauts-de-Seine **Porte de Vanves Map 1-B2**
♀ ⊗ **LE RELAIS DES ROUTIERS** (N° RR DEC 26 395) (M. Émile
Bourget) 38, avenue Pasteur ☎ 46-42-36-08 Closed Sun; 20 Jul to 2
Aug. Coaches welcome (rest. seats 100). Evening meals until
9pm.

VARANGES 21110 Côte d'Or **RN 5 Map à 1km**
♀ ⊗ **L'AUBERGE** (N° RR MARS 27 223) (M. Jean-Pierre **Huí**) Rue
Nouvelle ☎ 80-31-30-17

VARENNES-LE-GRAND 71240 S.-et-L. **RN 6 Map 18-B1**
♀ ⊗ ⌂ **RELAIS DE LA GARE** (N° RR NOV 26 384) (Mme **Meyer**) ☎
85-44-22-76 ⊷ 9 Closed Sun. Coaches welcome (rest. seats 160).
Evening meals until 1am. English spoken.
♀ ⊗ ⌂ **LE MISTRAL** (N° RR OCT 27 042) (M. Mohand **Aitaoudia**) ☎
85-44-12-70 ⊷ 10 English spoken.
♀ ⊗ ⌂ **LE COMMERCE** (N° RR SEPT 27 375) SARLYves-Marie
Goalabre) ☎ 85-44-22-34 ⊷ 14 Closed Saturday, Sunday, 3
weeks in August and 24 – 31/12. English spoken.
☕ **RELAIS DE VARENNES** (N° RR JUL 27 325) (M. Bernard
Guinchard) Axe Chalon/Tournus ☎ 85-44-20-43 Open 7 days
7am–10pm.

VARENNES-SUR-ALLIER 03150 Allier **RN 7 Map 16-A3**
♀ ⊗ ⌂ **LE RELAIS DES TOURISTES – REST. DE FRANCE** (N° RR
⛓ MAI 14 802) (M. Andŕe **Juniet**) 1, rue des Halles ☎ 70-45-00-51 ⊷
9 Closed Sat from Oct to May. Evening meals until 9pm.
♀ ⊗ **LA RENAISSANCE** (N° RR MAR 24 887) (Mme **Gardel**) Route
Nle 7 ☎ 70-45-62-86 Closed Sat, Sun. Evening meals until 9pm.
Portuguese spoken.

V

VARENNES-SUR-SEINE see LE PETIT-FOSSARD

VARIZE 28140 E.-et-L. **Voir ORGÈRES-EN-BEAUCE**

VATAN 36150 Indre **RN 20 Map 13-B1**
🍷 ⊗ 🏠 **LE RELAIS DU CHÊNE VERT** (N° RR JAN 3 823) (Mme
Lahaye) 13, avenue de Paris, sur la Nle 20 ☎ 54-49-76-56 ← 6
Closed Sat evening, Sun; 1 Sep–29 Sep. Evening meals until
9.30pm.

VATRY 51320 Marne **RN 77 Map 9-A3**
🍷 ⊗ 🏠 **L'ETAPE** (N° RR JANV 27 149) (Mme Éliane **Fouquet**) RN 77
☎ 26-67-41-06 ← 7 Closed Sat pm and Sun in winter.

VAUCIENNES Voir Chaussée-de-Damery

VAUDIOUX (LE) 38300 Jura **RN 5 Map 19-A1**
🍷 ⊗ **LES ROUTIERS LA BILLAUDE** (N° RR AVR 25 873) (M.
Georges **Chagre**) La Billaude Champagne ☎ 84-52-07-95 Closed
Sun. HGV parking.

VAUNANEYS-LA-ROCHETTE 26400 Drôme **RD 538 Map 24-A1**
🍷 ⊗ **AUBERGE CHEZ MIJO** (N° RR JANV 27 172) (M. Joël **Piaud
SARL**) La Gare ☎ 75-25-01-57 Closed Wed pm.

VAUVERT 30600 Gard **RD 56 Map 23-A2**
🍷 ⊗ 🏠 **LE CRISTAL** (N° RR JUL 24 647) (Mme Roselyne **Guyon**) 13,
rue de la République ☎ 66-88-21-77 ← 11 Closed Sat afternoon,
Sun; 23 Dec to 2 Jan. Full-board 115–155F per night. Coaches
welcome (rest. seats 70). Evening meals until 9.30pm.

VAUX-EN-BUGEY 01860 Ain **RN 75 Map 2-A2**
🍷 ⊗ **LE RAMEQUIN** (N° RR NOV 27 094) (Mme Michelle **Gallon**) ☎
74-35-95-09 Closed Sat pm and Sun.

VAUX-SUR-SEINE 21510 Côte d'Or **RD 32 Map 1-A1**
🍷 ⊗ **LA TAVERNE DES ROUTIERS** (N° RR JUN 26 567) (M. Paul
Thomassin) Aignay-le-Duc ☎ 80-93-88-04.

VEMARS 95470 Val-d'Oise **Autoroute A 1 Map 3-B3**
🍷 ⊗ **RELAIS ILE-DE-FRANCE** (SERA Vemars) (M. **Fossey**) Autoroute A1-A5 de Vemars - Fosses - Survilliers ☎ 34-68-39-20 Telex
699538 Self-service restaurant open 6.00am to 11.00pm. Showers,
TV, Shop. English, German spoken.

VENANSAULT 85190 Vendée **RN 160 Map 11-B3**
🍷 ⊗ 🏠 **1 Star NN LE MOULIN DE LA BERGERIE** (N° RR JUN 22
375) (**EURL Le Moulin de la Bergerie**) la Grolle crossroad, on
road to Landeronde (9 km from La Roche-sur-Yon, going towards Les Sables-d'Olonne) ☎ 51-40-36-94 ← 12 Closed Fri
evenings from 25/9–9/10; 1 Jan–20 Jan; 15 Sep–1 Oct. Full-board 1
pers 200F, 2 pers 310F per night. Coaches welcome (4 rooms:
120 seats). Dogs allowed, TV, Bar, Billiards.

V

VENDENHEIM 67500 Bas-Rhin **RN 63 Map 10-B2**
Y ⊗ **LE RELAIS DE LA MAISON ROUGE Tobacconists** (N° RR AOU 16 194) (Mme Germaine **Michielin**) 2, route de Brumath ☎ 88-69-51-79 Closed Tues pm and Wed. Evening meals until 10pm. German spoken.

VENDEUVRE 14170 Calvados **RD 511 Map 8-A2**
Y ⊗ ⌂ **LE RELAIS DU VENDEUVRE** (N° RR JUN 23 836) (M. André **Denis**) Saint-Pierre-sur-Dives ☎ 31-40-92-77 or 32-77 ⊷ 11 Closed Sat, 23/12–8/1 and 15 days of August. Full-board 160–190F per night. Coaches welcome (rest. seats 120). Evening meals until 9.30pm.

VENDOEVRES 36500 Indre
Y ⊗ ⌂ **LE GAVFRIER** (N° RR JAN 27 500) (M. Joel **Picouays**) Place Saint Jeane. Closed Monday afternoon. Evening meals. English spoken. Nearby service station open 7am–8pm.

VENDINE 31460 Hte-Gar **RN 126 Map 22-A2**
Y ⊗ **AUBERGE DE VENDINE** (N° RR FEV 26 466) (Mme Yvette **Bertocchi**) Nle 126 ☎ 61-83-12-05 Closed Mon.

VENDOME 41100 L.-et-C. **RN 10 and 817 Map 12-A3**
Y ⊗ ⌂ **CHEZ MEMÈRE** (N° RR AOU 19 132) (Mlle Andrée **Touchard**) 127, faubourg Chartrain ☎ 54-77-00-32 ⊷ 14 Closed Mon; 15 Dec to 10 Mar. Full-board 120F per night. Coaches welcome (3 rooms: 130 seats). Meals served until 11pm.

VENISSIEUX 69200 Rhône **Map 2-A2**
Y ⊗ **LES ROUTIERS** (N° RR FEV 26 458) (M. Hervé **Ligier**), 66, bd Irène-Joliot-Curie ☎ 78-76-49-94 Closed Sat, Sun. 14 Jul to 15 Aug. Spanish spoken. Rest seats 42. Evening meals.

VENOY par AUXERRE 89290 Yonne **Autoroute A6 Map 13-A2**
Y ⊗ **ACCOR – Relais de Venoy** (N° RR RA-21) ☎ 86-52-35-52 Champs-sur-Yonne Sens Province-Paris Self-service restaurant open 10.30am to 3.00pm, 6.30pm to 11.00pm. Telex: 800921.
Y ⊗ **ACCOR L'ARCHE** (M. Gérard **Gain**) Autoroute A6 Paris-Province direction ☎ 86-52-31-71 Télex: 800921 Self-service restaurant open 24 hours.
⛽ **Total Service Station DE VENOY** Autoroute A6 ☎ 86-52-33-72 Open 24 hours. Accepts Carte Bleue, Diners club, Eurocard, DKV.

VENSAC 33590 Gironde **Map 20-A1**
Y ⊗ ⌂ **CHEZ NICOLE** (N° RR JUN 25 466) (Mme Nicole **Figerou**) St-Vivien ☎ 56-09-44-05 ⊷ 6 Full-board 160F per night. Coaches welcome (rest. seats 72). Evening meals until 10pm.

VERCHENY 26340 Drôme **RD 93 Map 24-B1**
Y ⊗ **LA GRAPPE D'OR** (N° RR SEPT 26 653) (M. **Manas**) ☎ 75-21-70-44.

V

VERDUN 55100 Meuse **RN 3 Map 6-B3**
Y ⊗ ⌂ **LE RELAIS CHEZ MARIA** (N° RR FEV 12 050) (Mme **Maffioletti**) 68, avenue Miribel ☎ 29-86-07-28 ⊷ 7 Closed Sun; Christmas to New year. Full-board 150F per night. Coaches welcome (rest. seats 50). Evening meals.
Y ⊗ **A LA BONNE AUBERGE** (N° RR SEP 3 102) (Mme **Gaiotti-Morano**) 11, rue Garibaldi. ☎ 29-86-05-16 ⊷ 10 Full-board 160F. Evening meals until midnight. Rest. seats 140.
Y ⊗ **ROAD BAR** (N° RR NOV 23 547) (M. Christian **Antoine**) 5, rue St-Victor ☎ 29-86-05-08 Coaches welcome (rest. seats 55). Evening meals until midnight. English, German spoken.

VERDUN see BELLEVILLE 55100 Meuse

VERDUN 55100 Meuse **Autoroute A4 Map 6-B3**
Y ⊗ **ACCOR L'ARCHE** (N° RR RA-22) (M. Serge **Monceau**) Aire de Service de Saint-Nicolas ☎ 29-86-41-18 Self-service restaurant open 6.30am to 11.00pm winter, 5.00am to midnight summer. Showers, TV, Shop. German, English spoken.

VERGEZE 30310 Gard **RN 113 Map 24-A3, 23-B2**
Y ⊗ ⌂ **RELAIS DE LA SOURCE** (N° RR JUL 26 279) (M. Richard **Erquera**) RN 113 ☎ 66-35-05-51 ⊷ 9 English, Spanish spoken.

VERGT 24380 Dordogne **RD 21 Map 15-B3**
Y ⊗ **LE PHENIX** (N° RR JUN 26 929) (Mme Raymonde **Legeard**) place Jean-Jaurès ☎ 53-54-91-89 Closed Mon pm; 15–28 Feb; 15–30 Nov. German, Italian understood. Filling station nearby.

VERMENTON 89270 Yonne **RN 6 Map 13-A2**
Y ⊗ ⌂ **AU NOUVEAU RELAIS** (N° RR MAI 6 826) (M. Pierre **Jean**) 74, Route Nationale 6 ☎ 86-53-51-51 ⊷ 12 Closed Sun; Dec. Open 5am to midnight. Coaches welcome (2 rests. seats 80). Evening meals.

VERN-D'ANJOU 49220 M.-et-L. **RD 770 Maps 11-A3 and 12-A1**
Y ⊗ **LE RELAIS DES SPORTS** (N° RR DEC 24 067) (Mme Marie-Thérèse **Chevallier**) 21, rue du Commerce ☎ 41-61-41-32. Closed Fri afternoon; 15–31 Aug. Evening meals until 9pm.

VERN-SUR-SEICHE 35770 Ille-et-Villaine **Map 7-B2**
Y ⊗ **WELCOME-BAR** (N° RR MAI 27 280) (M. Phillippe **Brossault**) Le Clos Berquet ☎ 99-62-83-18 Closed Sun and winter. Evening meals.

VERNEGUES see CAZAN 13116 B.-du-R. **RN 7 Map 24-B3**

VERNEUIL-SUR-AVRE 27130 Eure **Map 8-A3**
Y ⊗ **RELAIS DE L'ESPÉRANCE** (N° RR MARS 26 192) (M. **Agullo**), 65, Porte de Breteuil.

VERNON 27200 Eure **RN 181 and 13 Map 3-B1**
Y ⊗ **LA CHOPE** (N° RR SEPT 26 638) (Mme Josiane **Plantain**) 9, route de Rouen ☎ 32-51-57-94 Closed Sun.

V

Vernon continued

♀ ⊗ 🏠 **HOTEL DE FRANCE** (N° RR MARS 26 193) (M. Thierry **Bonté**) 70, route de Rouen ☎ 32-51-53-55 **Minitel** ⊸ 8 Closed Sat afternoon, Sun. Coaches welcome (rest. seats 150). Evening meals.

♀ ⊗ **CAFÉ NORMAND Chez GEGE** (N° RR JUL 24 282) (M. Michel **Schibiness**) 39–31, avenue de l'lle-de-France Le Petit Val ☎ 32-51-08-41 Closed Sun pm. German and English spoken. Evening meals.

VERRERIE-DE-ROYE par LURE see ROYE 70200 Haute-Saône

VERRUE 86420 Vienne **RN 147 Map 12-B2**

♀ ⊗ 🏠 **CHEZ RÉMY ET PAULETTE** (N° RR SEPT 27 011) (Mme Paulette **Nativelle**) Monts-sur-Guesnes ☎ 49-22-84-01 ⊸ 8. Closed Sun pm and Monday; May – October. Coaches welcome (rest. seats 120). Evening meals.

VESLY 27870 Eure **RD 181 Map 3-B2**

♀ ⊗ **LE RELAIS DE L'AGRICULTURE** (N° RR MAI 24 225) (M. Claude **Benteyn**) ☎ 32-55-62-37 Closed Sat. Coaches welcome (rest. seats 44).

VEUREY-VOROIZE 38113 Isère **RN 532 Map 19-A3**

♀ ⊗ 🏠 **AUBERGE DU VAL ROSE** (N° RR JUIN 26 904) (M. Jean-Louis **Quercia**) chemin de la Rive ☎ 76-53-95-04 ⊸ 8 Closed Sun. English, Italian spoken. Filling station nearby.

VEYRINS THUELLIN 38115 Isère **RN 75 Map 2-B3**

♀ ⊗ 🏠 **1 Star NN LA BONNE AUBERGE** (N° RR AVR 25 874) (M. Raymond **Belingherl**) ☎ 74-33-94-27 Closed Tue. Italian, English spoken.

VEZENOBRES 30360 Gard **RD 106 Map 23-B1**

⊗ **LE GRES** (N° RR SEP 25 108) (Mme Hélène **Pillot**) Route Nationale 106 de Nimes ☎ 66-83-52-89 Coaches welcome (2 rest. seats 80 and 35). Evening meals until 9pm. German spoken.

VIAS 34450 Hérault **RN 112 Map 23-A2**

♀ ⊗ 🏠 **LE PETIT VATEL** (N° RR MARS 26 476) (M. Albert **Matagotte**) avenue de la Gare ☎ 67-21-63-06 Closed Mon; Nov. English, Spanish spoken.

VIC-EN-BIGORRE 65500 Htes-Pyr. **Map 21-A3**

♀ ⊗ **LE RANCH** (N° RR JAN 25 788) (M. Bernard **Griffon**) Rte de Rabastens ☎ 62-96-72-32 Closed Sat; Sep. Evening meals until 11pm.

VICHY 03200 Allier **RN 9A Map 16-B3**

♀ ⊗ **LE RELAIS DE LA PASSERELLE** (N° RR MAI 14 797) (M. **Pesce**) 1, rue de Bordeaux ☎ 70-98-57-70 ⊸ 4 Closed Sun; 2 weeks in Aug. Evening meals.

V

VIEILLE-BRIOUDE 43100 Hte-Loire **RN 102 Map 17-A3**
♈ ⊗ ⌂ **2 Stars NN LES GLYCINES** (N° RR NOV 25 748) (Mme Viviane **Chardonnal**) ☎ 71-50-91-80 Coaches welcome (rest. seats 100). Evening meals. English spoken. ⇥ 17 90–270F. Breakfast 17–20F. Closed Fri afternoon, Sat am; Jan. Full-board 140–210F. Parking, bar, dogs allowed.

VIELLEVIGNE 4416 Loures-Atlantique **Map 11-B3**
♈ ⊗ ⌂ **LE COMMERCE** (N° RR OCT 27 399) (SARL Le Commerce) 7, place de Verdun ☎ 40-26-51-81 ⇥ 7 Evening meals until 11pm. English and German spoken.

VIERZON 18100 Cher **RN 20 and 76 Map 13-B1**
♈ ⊗ ⌂ **MODER'N SPORT** (N° RR MAI 26 247) (M. Anik **Augy**) 141, av. E.-Vaillant ☎ 48-75-13-63 ⇥ 4 Closed Sat. Coaches welcome (rest. seats 60). Evening meals.
♈ ⊗ **AUX MILLE PATTES** (N° RR JUL 26 600) (M. Ludwig **Jakubik**) 85, route de Tours ☎ 48-75-46-38 Closed Sun. Coaches welcome (rest. seats 35). Evening meals until 12.30pm.

VIEUX-CONDE 59690 Nord **Maps 5-B1 and 6-A3**
♈ ⊗ **TORRE DEL SALTO** (N° RR FEV 23 677) (M. **Manti**) 49, place de la République ☎ 27-40-31-74 ⇥ 3 Closed Aug. Italian, English, Portuguese, Polish spoken.

VIGNOLLES 16300 Charente **RN 10 Map 15-A2**
♈ ⊗ **L'IMPRÉVU** (N° RR JUL 26 936) (Mme Monique **Blanchard**) Barbezieux ☎ 45-78-38-54 Closed Sat afternoon; Sun. Filling station 6 km away.

VIJON 36160 Indre **RD 917 Map 16-A2**
♈ ⊗ **L'ESTAMINET** (N° RR OCT 26 684) (M. Dominique **Hayo**) Le Marembert ☎ 54-30-60-95 German spoken.

VILDE-GUINGALAN 22270 C.-du-N. **RN 176 Map 7-A3**
♈ ⊗ ⌂ **SNACK LES ROUTIERS** (N° RR MAR 22 725) (M. Jean-Claude **Certenais**) La Borgnette ☎ 96-27-61-00 **Minitel** ⇥ 10 English spoken.

VILLABE see also LISSES 91100 Essonne **Autoroute A6 Map 1-B3**

VILLARD SALLET 73110 Savoie **RD 925 Map 19-A2**
♈ ⊗ ⌂ **AUBERGE DE LA ROUTE** (N° RR JUL 26 947) (Mme Francine **Loy**) ☎ 79-25-52-20 ⇥ 9 Filling station nearby.

VILLE-AUX-BOIS (LA) par les PONTAVERT 02160 Aisne **RN 44 Map 6-B1**
♈ ⊗ **LE RELAIS SAINT-MARIE** (N° RR SEP 23 921) (SARL **Le Relais Sainte-Marie**) Les Pontavert ☎ 23-20-74-34 Open 24 hours (except Sat night to Sun). English, German, Polish, Spanish spoken.

V

VILLEBAUDON 50410 Manche **RD 999 and 13 Map 8-A1/4-B1**
☿ ⊗ **LE SPORTIF** (N° RR JUN 26 918) (Mme Agnès **Osouf**) Le Bourg
☎ 33-61-20-52 ↦ 3 Filling station nearby.

VILLEDIEU-LES-POELES 50800 Manche **RN 175 and Dle 799 Map 8-A1**
☿ ⊗ **HOTEL DES VOYAGEURS** (N° RR SEPT 26 626) (SNC.
Louaintier-Lecannellier) 37, avenue du Mal-Leclerc ☎ 33-61-
00-76 ↦ 5. Coaches welcome (rest. seats 105). Evening meals
until 10pm.

VILLEDIEU-SUR-INDRE 36320 Indre **RN 143 Map 12-B3**
☿ ⊗ **CAFE DES SPORTS** (N° RR MARS 26 828) (Mme Joëlle **Gatefin**)
69. rue de Général de Gaulle ☎ 54-26-56-18 Closed Mon. Filling
station nearby. Coaches welcome (rest. seats 60).

VILLEDOMER 37110 I.-et-L. **RN 10 Map 12-A3**
☿ ⊗ **LE RELAIS DES GRANDS VINS DE TOURAINE** (N° RR JUN 12
910) (M. Claude **Romain**) La Grand'Vallée ☎ 47-55-01-05 ↦ 4
Closed Wed; 17 to 27 Jul. Coaches welcome (rest. seats 100).
Evening meals until 10pm; menus 44–68F. Specialities: rabbit leg
sausage with Vouvray and kidney sauce; frogs legs.

VILLEFRANCHE-DE-ROUERGUE 12200 Aveyron **RD 926 Map 22-B1**
☿ ⊗ **RELAIS DES CABRIÈRES** (N° RR JUL 26 592) (M. Alain
Toulouse) route de Montauban ☎ 65-81-16-99 Closed Sun.
Coaches welcome (2 rest. seats 130). Evening meals only in July/
August.

VILLEFRANCHE-SUR-SAONE 69400 Rhône **Déviation Nle 6 Map 2-A1 Motorway exit Macon Paris.**
☿ ⊗ **RELAIS CALADOIS** (N° RR AVR 26 513) (M. Denis **Gimaret**)
511, avenue de l'Europe ☎ 74-60-69-88 **Minitel** Closed Sat; Sun, 2
weeks in Aug. Coaches welcome. English, Spanish spoken. Rest.
seats 150.

VILLE FRANCŒUR 41330 Loir-et-Cher **RD 957 Map 12-A3**
☿ ⊗ **LE CONCORDE** (N° RR AOU 26 976) (Mme Andrée **Gehanno**)
Le Breuil ☎ 54-20-12-04 Closed Sat; Aug. Italian spoken. Filling
station nearby. Rest. seats 100.

VILLEGENON 18260 Cher **D 926 Map 13-A1**
☿ ⊗ **LA CROIX BLANCHE** (N° RR DEC 26 752) (Mme Joëlle
Beauvois) Le Bourg ☎ 48-73-86-63 English spoken. Evening
meals until 11pm.

VILLENEUVE 04130 Alpes-de-haute-Provence **RN 96 Map 24-B2/25-A2**
☿ ⊗ 🏠 **LE RELAIS CHEZ ROGER** (N° RR OCT 15 814) (SARL Pierre
Curri) route de Marseille-Gap ☎ 92-78-42-47 ↦ 7 Closed Sat
night; 15 to 31 Aug; 21 Dec to 5 Jan. Coaches welcome (rest. seats
60). Evening meals until 11pm.

V

VILLENEUVE-AU-CHEMIN 10130 Aube **RN 77 Map 9-B3**
Ⴢ ⊗ **LE PETIT SAINT-JEAN** (N° RR MARS 26 859) (M. Mohammed **Nait-Mohand**) 19, route Nationale ☎ 25-42-10-51 Closed Sun, Aug. Coaches welcome (rest. seats 70).

VILLENEUVE-D'ASCQ 59650 Nord **Map 5-B1**
Ⴢ ⊗ **CHEZ GUY** (N° RR MARS 25 853) (M. Guy **Way**) 221, rue Jean-Jaurès ☎ 20-89-25-23 **Minitel** Closed Sat, Sun; Aug.

VILLENEUVE-D'AVEYRON 12260 Aveyron **RD 922 Map 22-B1**
Ⴢ ⊗ **L'ORÉE DU BOIS** (N° RR NOV 26 727) (M. Michel **Boulesque**) Dle 922 ☎ 65-81-65-77 Closed Sat. Spanish spoken. Evening meals until 10pm. Coaches welcome (rest. seats 120).

VILLENEUVE-L'ARCHEVEQUE 89190 Yonne **RN 60 Map 9-B2**
Ⴢ ⊗ ⌂ **L'ESCALE 60** (N° RR MARS 26 188) (M. Dominique **Boire**) 10, route de Sens ☎ 86-86-74-42 ⊷ 4 Closed Sat eve; Sun. Coaches welcome (rest. seats 70). Evening meals; full-board 130F per night. English spoken.

VILLENEUVE-SAINT-MARTIN (LA) 95450 Val-d'Oise **déviation RN 14 and D28 Map 1-A2**
Ⴢ ⊗ **AU VEAU QUI TETE** (N° RR MAR 25 314) (SARL **Saint-Martin**) 12, rue François-Vaudin ☎ 30-39-24-82 Closed Sun.

VILLENEUVE-SUR-LOT 47300 L.-et-G. **RN 21 Map 21-B1**
Ⴢ ⊗ ⌂ **RELAIS DE GASCOGNE** (N° RR AVR 26 519) (M. Alain **Guiraud**) 31, avenue due Gal-Laclerc ☎ 53-70-06-48 ⊷ 8 Closed Sun from 1 Oct–15 May. Coaches welcome (rest. seats 120). Full board 150–180F per night. Evening meals. Spanish spoken.

VILLEROMAIN 41100 Loire et Cher **RD 957 Map 12-A3**
Ⴢ ⊗ **AU BON COIN** (N° RR JUL 27 333) (Mme Isabelle **Renouf**) Grand Rue ☎ 54-23-81-17 Closed Saturday, Sunday. Evening meals. English, Spanish spoken. Cards accepted.

VILLERS-BOCAGE 14310 Calvados **Map 4-B2**
Ⴢ ⊗ ⌂ **HOTEL DE LA GARE** (N° RR JUL 26 287) (Mme Paulette **Golasse-Marie**) 6, rue du Mal-Foch ☎ 31-77-00-23 ⊷ 10 Closed Sun. Full-board 140-170F per night. Evening meals.

VILLERS-SUR-MER 14640 Calvados **RN 813 Map 4-B2**
Ⴢ ⊗ ⌂ **1 Star NN LE NORMAND – Les Routiers** (N° RR MAI 20 735) (Mme Suzanne **Dujardin**) 44, rue du Maréchal-Foch ☎ 31-87-04-23 ⊷ 8 (158–220F) Closed Sun from 1 Oct; Dec. Coaches welcome (rest. seats 50). Full-board 199F per night, breakfast 18F. Evening meals until 9pm. Parking; bar; beach; horse-riding; tennis nearby. Sites to visit: Lisieux and Bayeux.

VILLETOUREIX see RIBERAC 24600 Dordogne **See RIBERAC**

VILLEURBANNE 69100 Rhône **Map 2-A2**
Ⴢ ⊗ **CHEZ NICOLE** (N° RR AVR 27 244) (Mme Nicole **Grass**) 165, rue Jean Voillot ☎ 72-37-52-00. Closed Sat pm and Sun.

V

VILLEVALLIER 89127 Yonne **RN 6 Map 9-B2**

Ⓨ Ⓧ ⌂ **RELAIS 89** (N° RR JUIL 26 956) (Mme Yvette **Petit**) 9, rue de la République ☎ 86-91-11-17 ⊷ 6 Closed Sat afternoons; Sun. Full-board 150F. Coaches welcome (rest. seats 52). Evening meals until 10.30pm.

VILLIERS-AU-BOUIN 37330 I.-et-L. **RN 159 and CD 959 Map 12-A2**

Ⓨ Ⓧ ⌂ **2 Stars NN LE GRAND CERF** (N° RR SEP 23 450) (M. Jean **Meunier**) La Porerie ☎ 47-24-11-06 ⊷ 24 Closed Sat in winter; 20 Oct–14 Nov. Full-board 200F per night. Coaches welcome (rest. seats 140, 130 and 50). Evening meals. Parking, bar, dogs allowed. Sites: Chateau of the Loire.

Ⓨ Ⓧ **L'ETAPE** (N° RR JAN 26 778) (Mme Chantal **Hais**) 15, rue de la Libération CD 135 ☎ 47-24-03-76 Closed Sun (unless booked); 20 Dec to 3 Jan. Evening meals. Coaches welcome (rest. seats 100).

VILLIERS-SAINT-GEORGES 77560 Seine-et-Marne **Map 9-A2**

Ⓨ Ⓧ **L'ESCALE** (N° RR MAI 24 959) (Mme Arlette **Oreste**) 64, route de Provins ☎ 64-01-90-16 Closed Tues.

VIMOUTIERS 61120 Orne **RN 179 Map 8-A2**

Ⓨ Ⓧ ⌂ **LE RELAIS DE LISIEUX** (N° RR FEV 23 635) (Mme Yvette **Larivière**) 37, avenue Lyautey ☎ 33-39-02-62 ⊷ 5 Closed Sun; 2 weeks Aug. Coaches welcome.

VINEZAC 07110 Ardèche **RN 104 Maps 23-B1 and 24-A2**

Ⓨ Ⓧ **L'AUBERGE DES COTES** (N° RR MAI 15 217) (M. Serge **Zagar**) Les Côtes ☎ 75-36-80-10 Closed Sat; 1 to 30 Sept. Evening meals. ⊷ 3.

VIRAZEIL 47200 L.-et-G. **RD 933 Map 21-A1**

Ⓨ Ⓧ **LE RALLYE** (N° RR FEV 24 126) (M. Claude **Marchet**) ☎ 58-64-18-77 Closed Sat.

VIRAZEIL 47200 Lot et Garonne

Ⓨ Ⓧ **Service Station BAR RESTAURANT LE RALLYE** (N° RR JAN 27 499) (M. Jean Pierre **Leglise**) Route de Perigueue – Jabarlan ☎ 53-20-18-77 Evening meals until 11pm. German spoken.

VIRE 14500 Calvados **RN 177 and 24 Bis Map 8-A1**

Ⓨ Ⓧ **L'AVENIR** (N° RR MAI 26 533) (M. Hervé **Gautherot**) 30, rue Émile-Chenel ☎ 31-67-76-94 Closed Sun. Coaches welcome (rest. seats 40). Evening meals until 9pm. English, Spanish, Portuguese spoken.

Ⓨ Ⓧ ⌂ **2 Stars NN HOTEL DE FRANCE** (N° RR OCT 24 705) (M. Roger **Carnet**) 4, rue d'Aignaux ☎ 31-68-00-35 **Minitel** ⊷ 50 (with bath or shower, WC, telephone). Closed 20 Dec–10 Jan. Full-board 180–250F per night. Coaches welcome (rest. seats 200). Evening meals until 11pm. English spoken. Menus 45–150F. Specialities: Tarthe aux pommes flante au calvados.

VIRONVAY 27400 Eure **Autoroute A 13 Map 3-B1**

Ⓨ Ⓧ **L'ARCHE** (N° RR RA-23) Aire de Vironvay (Dominique **Cordier**)

☎ 32-40-21-51 Self-service restaurant open 7.00am to 11.00 pm. Shop. English spoken.

VIRY-CHATILLON 91170 Essonne **RN 7 and RD 91 Map 1-B2**
♀ ⊗ **AU BON ACCUEIL** (N° RR SEP 12 440) (M. Fernand **Gadreau**) 100, route de Fleury ☎ 69-05-28-46 Closed Sun; public holidays. Evening meals.

VITARELLE (LA) 12210 Aveyron **RN 121 Map 17-B2**
♀ ⊗ ⌂ **LE RELAIS DE LA VITARELLE** (N° RR AVR 20 696) (Mme Francine **Falguier**) Montpeyroux ☎ 65-44-36-01 → 6 Closed Sat low season. Coaches welcome (rest. seats 80). Full-board 140–160F per night. Evening meals.

VITROLLES 13127 B.-du-R. **RN 113 Map 24-B3**
♀ ⊗ ⌂ **O'ROUTIERS-ANJOLY** (N° RR MAI 27 274) (M. William **Lequem**) Centre Routier Z.A. d'Anjoly ☎ 42-75-19-60 **Minitel** → 47. With showers. English, Spanish and Italian spoken. Evening meals served until midnight.

VITRY-EN-CHAROLAIS 71600 S.-et-L. **RN 79 Map 16-A3**
♀ ⊗ **TOM BAR** (N° RR AVR 26 232) (M. André **Borrego**) RN 79 ☎ 85-81-02-85 Closed Sat midday; Aug. Evening meals until midnight. Spanish spoken.

VITRY-EN-ARTOIS 62490 P.-de-C. **Map 5-B3**
⚒ **Service Station RELAIS DU PETIT VITRY** (N° RR 550000100) (M. **Deponchaux** SARL) 5, Rte Nle ☎ 21-50-13-63 Closed Sun.

VITTEAUX 21350 Côte-d'Or **RN 5 and 70 Map 13-A/B3**
♀ ⊗ ⌂ **LES ROUTIERS** (N° RR FEV 9 286) (M. **Le Gall**) route de Dijon ☎ 80-49-60-13 → 5 Closed Sun ; Sept or Oct. Evening meals until 9.30pm.

VIVIERS-SUR-RHONE 07220 Ardéche **RN 86 Map 24-A2**
♀ ⊗ ⌂ **1 Star NN CHEZ ESPERANDIEU - LE RELAIS DU VIVAR-AIS** (N° RR FEV 7 485) (M. André **Esperandieu**) Route Nationale
⌂ 86 Lieu-dit-Les Sautelles ☎ 75-52-60-41 → 10 (65–160F) Closed 20 Dec–20 Jan. Full-board 120–150F per night; breakfast 15F. Coaches welcome (rest. seats 60). Evening meals. English spoken. Parking; bar; dogs permitted; fishing and tennis nearby. Note: this hotel is 2 km north of the town, towards Lyons.

VIVONNE 86370 Vienne **RN 10 Map 15-B1**
♀ ⊗ **LE RELAIS ROUTIERS DE VIVONNE** (N° RR JAN 26 143) (M. Fernand **Judes** SARL) RN 10 ☎ 49-43-41-03 Open 24 hours. Coaches welcome (rest. seats 220). Evening meals.

VIVY 49680 M.-et-L. **RN 147 Map 12-A2**
♀ ⊗ ⌂ **1 Star NN LE RELAIS SAINT-PAUL** (N° RR OCT 16 736)
⌂ (Mme Marie-Louise **Bidet**) 30, rue Nationale ☎ 41-52-50-13 and 52-51-65 → 25 Full-board 160–260F per night. Coaches welcome (rest. seats 150 and 250). Evening meals until 10pm. Some English spoken. Specialities: Brochette de loire au beurre blanc.

V

VOINSLES-ROZAY-EN-BRIE 77540 S.-et-M. **Map 9-A2**

Y ⊗ **RELAIS DE VOINSLES** (N° RR OCT 26 354) RN 4 ☎ 64-07-75-20 Closed Sat–Mon morning. Coaches welcome (2 rest. seats 40). Evening meals.

VOISINS par MOUROUX 77120 S.-et-M. **RN 34 Map 9-A2**

Y ⊗ **LE RELAIS DU SOMMET** (N° RR AOU 16 173) (M. Jacques **Santerre**) 968, rue du Général de Gaulle ☎ 64-03-05-47 ⊷ 7 Closed Sun; Aug.

Y ⊗ **AUBERGE DE BISHA** (N° RR OCT 26 681) (M. Moutiha **Duvoisin**) 1072, avenue de Général de Gaulle ☎ 64-03-50-52 ⊷ 11 Closed Thurs; 15 Aug–15 Sept. English, Italian, Arabic spoken.

VOIVRES 72210 Sarthe **RD 23 Map 10-A3**

Y ⊗ 🏠 **LE TAMARIS** (N° RR MAI 26 252) (M. Patrick **Le Guy**) Rte de la Suze ☎ 43-88-52-60 ⊷ 5 Closed Sun evening. Coaches welcome (rest. seats 200). Full-board 148,50F per night.

VOREY-SUR-ARZON 43800 Haute-Loire **RN 103 Maps 18-A3 and 17-A3**

Y ⊗ **LE RELAIS DE LA BASCULE** (N° RR MAR 16 920) (Mme **Tirtaine**) place des Moulettes ☎ 71-03-41-67.

VOULTE (LA) 07800 Ardèche **Map 24-A1**

Y ⊗ **LE PROVENÇAL** (N° RR AVR 26 507) (M. Bernard **Bonneau**) 15, rue Boissy-d'Ánglas ☎ 75-85-35-66. Full-board 145F. Coaches welcome (rest. seats 50). Evening meals until 11pm.

VOULX 77940 S.-et-M. **RD 219 Map 9-B2**

⊗ **LA BRUYÈRE** (N° RR AOU 22 914) (M. Alban **Baldran**) 72, Grande-Rue ☎ 64-31-92-41 Bar. Closed Sun evening; 15–28 Feb; 16 Aug–6 Sept. Coaches welcome (rest. seats 160). Evening meals until 9.30pm.

VOUVRAY 37210 Indre-et-Loire **Map 12-A3**

Y ⊗ 🏠 **RELAIS DE VOUVRILLON** (N° RR SEPT 27 076) (M. Marcel **Le Dortz**) 14, avenue Brûlé ☎ 47-52-78-80 ⊷ 5 Closed Sun and ten days in August. English spoken.

W

WAILLY BEAUCAMP 62170 Pas-de-Calais **RN 1 Map 5-A3**

Y ⊗ **LA CHAILLOTE** (N° RR SEPT 27 389) (M. Jean-Luc **Sieradzke**) Evening meals until midnight. German, English, Italian, Polish spoken.

WANCOURT 62128 Pas-de-Calais **Map 5-B3**
Ⓨ ⊗ **RELAIS DE L'ARTOIS** Autoroute A1 Aire de Wancourt ☎ 21-55-97-83 Telex 133-924 Open 24 hours. Self-service restaurant, panoramic views, rest and games room, electronic surveillance of vehicles, showers, TV, shop.

WANEL 80490 Somme **Map 5-A3**
Ⓨ ⊗ **LA CLÉ DES CHAMPS** (N° RR JUIL 27 318) (M. Mohammed **Lamine**) Hallencourt ☎ 22-28-60-54 Closed Mon, English and Tunisian spoken. Evening meals.

WARGNIES-LE-PETIT 59144 Nord **RN 49 Map 6-A3**
Ⓨ ⊗ **LE PETIT QUÉBEC** (N° RR OCT 25 670) (M. Bruno **Leclercq**) 10, route de Bry ☎ 27-49-97-93.

WASSELONNE 67310 Bas-Rhin **RN 4 Map 10-B2**
Ⓨ ⊗ ⌂ **AU ROCHER** (N° RR SEP 19 489) (Mme **Leippi**) 18, route de Strasbourg ☎ 88-87-06-72 ◄ 8 Closed Sun. German, English spoken. Evening meals until 9pm.

WINGLES 62410 Pas-de-Calais **RD 165 Map 5-A1**
Ⓨ ⊗ ⌂ **LE RELAIS CHEZ JULES** (N° RR FEV 17 205) (M. Jules **Hennache**) 37, rue Jules Guesde ☎ 21-69-52-88 ◄ 9 Closed Sun; Aug. Evening meals until 10pm.

WITRY-LES-REIMS 51420 Marne **RN 51 Map 6-B2**
Ⓨ ⊗ **RELAIS LE 51-08** (N° RR JAN 26 144) (Mme Gisèle **Pierront**) 62, rue de Reims ☎ 26-97-08-30 ◄ 4 Closed Sun. Full-board 110–150F per night. Coaches welcome (rest. seats 60). Evening meals until 10.30pm.

WITTELSHEIM-GRAFFENWALD 68310 Haut-Rhin **RN 83 Map 10-B3**
Ⓨ ⊗ ⌂ **HOTEL DES VOSGES** (N° RR OCT 26 351) (M. **Riedle**) 137, rue de Reiningue ☎ 89-55-10-20 ◄ 11 Closed Sun. Evening meals. Full-board 140F per night. Coaches welcome (rest. seats 60). German spoken.

WOIPPY 57140 Moselle **RN 412 Maps 6-B3 and 10-A1**
Ⓨ ⊗ **LE CHARDON LORRAIN** (N° RR JUN 23 333) (Mme Françoise **de Cecco**) 58, rue de Metz ☎ 87-30-46-61 **Minitel** ◄ 3 Closed Sun; 20 Dec to 15 Jan. Full-board 128–170F per night. Coaches welcome (rest. seats 70). Evening meals until 8pm. German spoken.

WOLFGANTZEN 68600 Haut-Rhin **Map 10-B2**
Ⓨ ⊗ **A L'AGNEAU D'OR** (N° RR JAN 25 217) (M. Etienne **Heimburger**) 37, rue Principale ☎ 89-72-86-66 Closed Wed; Feb. German, Alsatian spoken.

WORMHOUDT 59470 Nord **RN 16 Map 5-A2**
Ⓨ ⊗ **CAFE DE LA FORGE** (N° RR JUN 14 406) (M. Guy **Depriester**) 84, Grand'Place ☎ 28-65-62-33 Closed 15–31 Aug. Evening meals.

Y

YEBLES 77390 S.et-M. **RN 19 Map 1-B3**
♀ ⊗ ⌂ **RELAIS DE L'EST** (N° RR OCT 26 680) (Mme Maria **Nunes**) ☎ 64-06-00-40 ⊷ 11 Closed Sun. Portuguese, Spanish spoken.

YERVILLE 76760 S.-Mme **RN 29 Maps 4-A3**
♀ ⊗ **L'ESCALE ROUTIERE** (N° RR DEC 25 771) (M. Christian **Delahaye**) Rte d'Yvetot ☎ 35-96-80-45 Closed 6pm Fri–12am Sat; Aug and week in Feb. Coaches welcome (rest. seats 140). Evening meals.

YMONVILLE 28150 E.-et-L. **RN 154 Map 9-B1**
♀ ⊗ ⌂ **LE RELAIS DE L'ÉTOILE** (N° RR OCT 21 259) (Mme Thérèse **Brulé**) 31, rue du Haut-Chemin ☎ 37-32-25-67 ⊷ 10 attached to Hôtel de Tourisme. Closed Mon; 2 weeks in Feb and 2 weeks in Nov. Full-board 165–200F per night. Coaches welcome (rest. seats 80). Evening meals until 10pm.

YSSINGEAUX LA GUILDE 43200 Haute-Loire **RN 88 - RD 105 Map 18-A3**
♀ ⊗ ⌂ **LA PETITE AUBERGE** (N° RR JUN 16 996) (Mme **Delabre**) ☎ 71-59-05-32 ⊷ 4 Closed Sun low season; and July. Full-board 150–180F per night. Coaches welcome (rest. seats 70). Evening meals until 11pm. English spoken.

YUTZ 57110 Moselle **RN 53 Bis Map 10-A1**
♀ ⊗ ⌂ **RELAIS ROUTIERS** (N° RR DEC 26 754) (M. Noël **Rubeillon**) 140, rue Nationale ☎ 82-56-00-28 ⊷ 9 Closed Sat, Sun; Aug. Full-board 122–172F. Coaches welcome (rest. seats 130). Evening meals until 11pm.

YVRE-L'ÉVEQUE 72530 Sarthe **RN 23 Map 8-B2**
♀ ⊗ **LE RELAIS DU BON CAFÉ Grocery** (N° RR JUN 25 007) (Mme Annick **Simon**) 25, route du Mans ☎ 43-84-54-63 Closed Wed 2.00pm; Aug. Coaches welcome (rest. seats 80). Evening meals (no meals on Sun).

GERMANY

IMMERT (RFA)
♀ ⊗ ⌂ **ZUR BARRIÈRE** (N° RR JUIN 27 297) (M. Patrice **Le Guillou**) Ortsstrasse 31 ☎ 0 6504/1779 Closed Tues and German and French spoken. Evening meals.

BELGIUM

ANTWERPEN (2040)
♀ ⚑ **Total Service Station DELWAIDEDOK ANTWERPSEBAAN –
HOEK LAAGEIND STABROEK DELWAIDEDOK KAAI 730**
(N° RR 550000109) ☎ 03/568-88-08 – 03/568-88-09 – 03/568-88-10
Minitel Closed Sat evening, Sun evening 8.00pm–6.00am. Free
showers and coffee. Shop, credit cards accepted. French, Dutch,
English, German spoken.

BANDE 6951 **Maquel**
⚑ **LES ROUTIERS SERVICE STATION** (N° RR 550000114) Nle 4,47
Nationale 4 (direction Luxembourg) ☎ 084/34-44-24 **Minitel**
Closed Mon. Credit cards accepted. Shop open 7am–10pm, free
coffee. French, Dutch spoken.

BARCHON 4511
♀ ⚑ **SERVICE STATION RESTAURANT LES ROUTIERS** (N° RR
550000115) rue Lieutenant Jungling, 1 Autoroute E 40 Barchon
exit (No 36) ☎ 041/87-47-27 Shop open 24 hours, credit cards
accepted, free showers and coffee. French, Dutch, German
spoken.

BRULY DE COUVIN 6402 Prov. Namur
♀ ⊗ **CHEZ PIERRE** (N° RR AVR 22 759) (M. Pierre **Libens**) 65, rue
Grande ☎ 060/37-72-02 Closed Mon. English, German, Dutch
spoken.

BRUXELLES 1210
⊗ ⚑ **Total Service Station**, (N° RR 550000104) Port de Bruxelles,
avenue du Port 132, Porte de Bruxelles TIR, ☎ 02/426-0-54,
Closed Sat 1.00pm to Sun. Free showers and coffee. Shop, credit
cards accepted. Dutch, French spoken.

GENT 9020
⚑ **Total Service Station**, (N° RR 550000107) Port Arthurlaan Gent/
Zeehaven ☎ 091/51-61-44 Shop open 7.00am to 9.00pm. Closed
Sun. Free coffee. Credit cards accepted. Dutch, French spoken.

GERPINNES 6280 Prov. Hainaut **RN 5**
♀ ⊗ **LE RELAIS ROUTIERS COMME CHEZ SOI** (N° RR MAR 23
🛏 690) (M. François **Le Pauw**) 251, chaussée de Philippeville ☎
071/21-65-22 German, Italian, English spoken.

GOETSENHOVEN 3311
⊗ ⚑ **Total Service Station AE 40**, (N° RR 550000102) Direction
Bruxelles/Liège ☎ 016/76-72-45 Open 24 hours. Free coffee.
Credit cards accepted. Shop. Dutch, French spoken.

HAVAY 7091
♀ ⊗ **RELAIS ROUTIERS** (N° RR MARS 26 852) (M. Philippe **Nef**) 35,
Chausée de Maubeuge.

BELGIUM

HORION-HOZEMONT 4230

♀ ⊗ **AU PETIT PARADIS** (N° RR JUIN 27307) (M. Joseph **Paquay**) 11, rue Bihet ☎ 041/501614 Closed Sun morning and Sept. Italian and Dutch spoken. Evening meals.

KALKEN 9288 Anvers-Grand

⊗ **ACCOR** (Belgique) Autoroute E3 ☎ (32) 09/167-64-08 and (32) 09/167-64-09 Self-service restaurant, rest room, showers, TV, telephone. **Fina Service Station** (DKV-VTA) Tobacconist, shop.

LAAKDAL/EINDHOUT 3999

⊗ ♔ **Total Service Station LES ROUTIERS** (N° RR 550000111) Hezemeer 1 Autoroute A13 sortie nr 24 ☎ 014/30-19-35 Shop open 7am–10pm. Free showers and coffee, credit cards accepted. Closed Sun. French, Dutch, English, German spoken.

MARCHE EN FAMENNE 5400 **DURUISSEAU**

♔ **Total Service Station LES ROUTIERS** (N° RR 550000113) Rte de Namur 73 Nationale 4 (direction Bruxelles) ☎ 084/31-17-25 Shop open 7am–10pm, credit cards accepted, free coffee. French, Dutch spoken.

MEER HOOGSTRATEN 2321

⊗ ♔ **Total Service Station GRENSEWEG** (N° RR 550000106) E 19 D2 Grenszone, Industriezone ☎ 03/315-88-98 Closed Sat, Sun. Free showers, and coffee. Shop open 6.00am to 10.00pm. Credit cards accepted. Dutch, French spoken.

MENEN-REKKEM 8530

♀ ♔ **Total Service Station KORTRIJK/LAR**, (N° RR 550000108) Riijksweg 746 Pecq/Geluwe N 746, Transportzone LAR ☎ 056/40-00-02 **Minitel** Open 24 hours. Closed Sat midday to Mon 6.00am. Rest room, free showers, shop, open 24 hours, credit cards accepted. French, Dutch spoken.

NOIREFONTAINE 6831 **RN 26, 28 and 47**

⊗ **LE RELAIS DES ROUTIERS** (N° RR MAI 19 777) (M. **Marqua**) 5, route de Bouillon ☎ 061/46-63-74 Closed Sun (except Jul/Aug).

ROTSELAAR 3110

⊗ ♔ **Total Service Station ROTSELAAR**, (N° RR 550000105) AUT A2 ☎ 016/44-82-70 Open 24 hours. Shop, credit cards accepted. Free coffee. Dutch, French spoken.

RUISBROEK 1610

♔ **Ruisbroek Total Service Station** (N° RR 550000110) Autoroute Bruxelles-Paris Autoroute Paris-Bruxelles ☎ 02/378-34-00 (Brussels); 02/876-73-63 (Paris). Free coffee and showers, shop, open 24 hours, credit cards accepted. French, Dutch, English, German spoken.

SENEFFE 6198 Prov. Hainaut

♀ ⊗ **RELAIS DE LA MARLETTE** (N° RR SEPT 26 314) (Mme Clémentine **Le Burn**) 4, rue du Rivage ☎ 064/54-87-72 ◄ 4

BELGIUM

Closed Mon; Aug. French, Dutch, English spoken. Evening meals until 11pm.

VILVOORDE 1800

Y ⊗ **MONICO** (N° RR JANV 25 253) (M. **Pollet**) Schaarbeeck Lei 548 ☎ 02/252-06-85 Closed weekend. Evening meals.

ZEEBRUGGE 8380

⊗   **Total Service Station Baron** (N° RR 550000103) N 31 de Maerelaan 74 ☎ 050/54-54-61 **Minitel** Open 24 hours. Free showers, shop, free coffee, credit cards accepted. Dutch, French, English, German spoken.